I’m Working Here

‘Artists don’t work’. Never stop.

— *Grace Lake,* ‘Spinster of Arts’

I’m Working Here

The Collected Poems of

Anna Mendelssohn

edited by

Sara Crangle

Shearsman Books

First published in the United Kingdom in 2020 by
Shearsman Books
P.O. Box 4239
Swindon
SN3 9FN

Shearsman Books Ltd Registered Office
30–31 St. James Place, Mangotsfield, Bristol BS16 9JB
(this address not for correspondence)

www.shearsman.com

ISBN 978-1-84861-714-8

Cover collage by Anna Mendelssohn.
First published as a black and white photocopy in *constant red/mingled damask*, no. 1, 1986, the original colour version was provided by Nigel Wheale and enhanced by Stuart Robinson.

For Emerald, George, and Poppy

Contents

Introduction by Sara Crangle

The Collected Poems of Anna Mendelssohn

1988–1989

1990–1993

Appendix

c. 1992–1993

Introduction

Sara Crangle

I. Mendelssohn's Perambulations

being a poet is nothing special
no more so than being anything else
you go to poetplace each morning
& if you are absent for more than five conseq. days
you hand over a mental note
to authenticate the reasons for
your incapacity to poetize from mon-fri.

— "Tansy Tchaikovsky" *The News* (1987)

walking is to make poetry
            poetry is emptying the page and filling
              its space in continuous motion
                of breath
                 Breath is paradise.

— poem beginning "real does not know" (n.d.)

Anna Mendelssohn's is a restless poetry. Prolonged stillness cramps the writing hand, and propulsion eases compressions of the body, nerves, creative mind. "I [...] am not good at / being immobile" states the emphatically titled "POEM."; relief is "a declenched spine now walking écriture".[1] "[W]andering with primroses / acurling round her feet", Mendelssohn's poetic persona Tansy Tchaikovsky is almost feral, a "Mortal Beastess" with a "tously skull" who "takes to the hills" to chase after the "UNknown". So autonomous are Tansy's feet that she keeps close watch to ensure that they remain at the end of the body that sustains them, a body given to disappearances over which she has no control.[2] Tansy is a maker of mythico-magical journeys; she locates nightless lands, wriggling dragons. It is not Tansy who derides the exceptionality of poetry in this curt, comic epigraph, where verse becomes a brief for a nine-to-five job in versifying. Instead, this stanza disrupts Tansy's fervid whimsy, and its voice belongs more properly to what Mendelssohn describes elsewhere as "the peripatetic pedant" whose soul is "lost ... to ready words

& clipped momentum".[3] The absurdity of "go[ing] to poetplace each morning" does not lie in the travelling that poetry invariably necessitates, but in the unfathomability of an assured arrival at a prescribed location where poetizing might neatly commence and conclude each day. In Mendelssohn's poetry, reliable straightforwardness is laughable, even as tranquillity is not without appeal. In 1992, she writes: "a full stop was what i was working for / several years ago. unhappily my mind was not in my feet".[4] Embattled, feet win out over mind, and writing itself only complicates matters further, as the same poem tells us that poetry perambulates away from fixity and use value, that poetry "is untraceable, indirect, adialogical, refractive, / imprecise, inedible, elevated, unmechanical". Or as Mendelssohn puts it with ironic straightforwardness in her 2000 book, *Implacable Art*: "a poem is not going to give precise directions."[5]

Anna Mendelssohn's is a restless, impassioned poetry. The second epigraph inverts the scabrous first, steering a course just this side of the overblown. These lines take their place in a Western convention as old as Aristotle's Lyceum whereby walking is a motif for thought, the feet emulating the ever-moving consciousness.[6] Old, but always reborn; there is an audible echo of Gertrude Stein in Mendelssohn's awkwardly didactic: "walking is to make poetry".[7] As this poem begins, words are weary from attempting to pin down an ever-passing reality. Pursuit of the evanescent is at stake: a child's breath on a mirror; a satellite passing a moon. Against these images, Mendelssohn imagines a company director telling his managers to ban their secretaries from "'walking, talking, / thinking or dreaming.'" Epigraph two follows from these envisioned strictures, insisting that walking makes poetry happen, and in turn, that poetry clears the page for movement and bodily rhythm, accessing a breath so pure it "knows all / we hide from with smoke". In the space of a few short lines, Mendelssohn roves from terrestrial, quotidian walking to a celestial, heady atmosphere, attaining an intellectual and creative ideal – paradise itself – foreshadowed by the innocent, unpolluted breath of the child on the mirror-page. Poetry is lived necessity; poetry is utopia; poetry is truth. These assertions are consistent with a poet who concludes one poem with the proclamation: "I do not fake, I do not lie, I worship at the shrine of poetry."[8] If poetry is religion, then the heavens urgently, necessarily ground the writer: "As soon as you can, walk / with your feet on clouds, / your hands on a dream / of earth."[9] Titled "As Things Stand", this 1987 poem deliberately resists the status quo, its speaker supported by billow and vapour as the stuff of the solid globe evades the grasp. Mendelssohn's walking often calls attention to the elusiveness of solid foundation, but pedestrian poignancy does not always require elevation.[10] In 1986, Mendelssohn presents a stationary author undone by another's steps:

> yes it is official. sitting at a table. pen in hand,
> watching one's own neck curve like a swan's
> towards the sound of a heart-rending song.
>
> [....]
>
> and watching a hand of a woman
> clasping a small box of peaches by its string
> walking along with her lover.[11]

The writer is all keening ear, eye, neck; midway through the poem, tears are sobbed into the pen as the speaker recalls how that neck was once cruelly hooked. The watched woman is hand, feet, heart; her movement quietly fervent, not restless. If walking is to make poetry, this poem projects a perfectly ordinary, perversely unattainable ideal.

Mendelssohn once declared a desire to write a poem topographically, in a manner "outgoing", "OPEN to chance, and systematic in research".[12] The peripatetic is just one of infinite ways into the intellectual and aesthetic thickets, outcroppings, and byways of her poetic surfaces and structures. It is notably pervasive. Mendelssohn's poetic gaze is attuned to the language of the human gait, be it that of "school children walk[ing] past the window. infinitely beautiful."; the "strong man" who "can take words" and walk the high road; or "a very old lady" on Cambridge's Mill Road, "back bent permanently forward– / arthritic,–walks, pauses, takes a few steps".[13] Walking imbues Mendelssohn's lyrics; walking is how she initially staked her expansive claim to art as roving, observant *flâneuse*, a "*writer, artist, [who] started by placing objects found in the street in art exhibitions and having given them titles, walking out.*"[14] Where we might assume the inevitability of departure, Mendelssohn does not. "[F]ighting for exit" her speakers steadfastly delineate egress: "Walk in, walk out."[15] Mendelssohn's walking responds to rejection, is self-asserting defiance, and enables freedom, escape.[16] We witness these formulations in the very first poem in this collection: "Walk – legs last forever [...] One step further 'Anna come back' / Turn around: / They weren't even looking."[17] In a poem that references prison walls, this stanza speaks to the combination of fierce independence and need for recognition that recurs in so much of Mendelssohn's poetry. In a 1985 collection, Mendelssohn links a female figure "Clothed in / prison rags" to a nation's inability to decide "who walks" whilst denigrating those who "march / to their death with righteousness." Asking "[i]s there no room to move?" the speaker is paralysed, unable to commune with the "foot's feeble nature". The poem envisions a Futurist way out of this impasse: a high-speed, mechanised body, an "ankle-van, careering around / these high country corners".[18] But more frequently, walking is laborious: Mendelssohn's subjects are shoeless or scratch at floors with shod heels; the roads they travel are poisoned or require interpretation, fastidious "attend[ance] to the traffic signals"; they arduously climb zebra crossings, not quite reaching destination.[19] Escape from constraint is one of Mendelssohn's most pronounced aesthetic drives. "Some say *wander* some say *formalize*" Mendelssohn writes in a poem that critiques closed structure, favouring open-ended reach.[20] Freedom to roam is never taken for granted, and is frequently hard won.

A descendent of Aristotle's esteemed disciples, an itinerant in search of place, a writer or speaker prepared to risk rambling, prolixity; these are all ways we might think about the peripatetic Mendelssohn, an autodidact who worshipped poetry, art, music, and academia alike; who longed for and shunned domestic comfort and relationships; whose writings – poetry, fiction, journals – tend toward expatiation, copiousness. Walking makes poetry and art, walking determines artistic reception: "how people walk into art exhibitions is / vitally important."[21] Mendelssohn demands a reader adept at circumambulation, at deliberately going hopelessly astray, at marching and stumbling alongside staunch lyrics that resist as much as they invite. The journey rarely lacks ferocious intellection, highly sensitised aesthetic awareness, wit by turns playful and scathing, and extreme emotion ("softly the sound of woe / gallops [....] & every time hysteria rises").[22] By Mina Loy's terms, Mendelssohn "proceeds recedingly"; by Mendelssohn's, she "goes forwards by backwards".[23] Or more succinctly, Mendelssohn participates in the "Ambulesque", a word she coins in a poem that marks a return to an old conflict, a covered territory.[24] So it is that Mendelssohn's humorously aggressive "minnie most" – purveyor of "civilized prose", inventor of "a new foot modelled infrastructure" – "walks backwards" because

> its good for her calf muscles & her thighs.
> rather than pushing on regardless, onwards ever
> up hill down dale looking for birds' eggs.
> with her sharp nose shooting rays across the thickets.[25]

Here Mendelssohn might parody the propensity to return deeply embedded in her own work. Elsewhere, she describes countermovement with horror, imagining "walking" against the flow, "right through another's work in progress".[26] Mendelssohn's subjects evince an insatiable need to dispense with the past. Paradoxically, this need manifests itself as a "going back" to specific instances, a continual, inconclusive reversion justified because "the end is not the object" and "creation through language" may just "find its way back to structure".[27] Crucial to Mendelssohn's unique peripatetic mode, inward turns are consistent with the explorations of interiority that walking, writing, and the lyric portend. Or as Mendelssohn puts it in a line that speaks to the repetition of her involutions, her generative anxieties about implication and entanglement: "One is oned and backward turned for literary classification talks no-one."[28] Defiant, cautious, these circular perambulations are overwhelmingly inquisitive. Countering an otherwise strong poetic voice is a pervasive questioning, a seeking of clarities large: "What is love?"; circumstantial: "what could she say?"; and whimsical: "Who cycled in two fours?"[29] There are over 370 direct questions in this roving collection. At least two echo the peripatetic focus thus far, and, wilfully manipulated, foreground the biographical transition to come in this introduction, namely:

1. "who is this person, high-walking into fantasy?" and,

2. "who is this bemused, disconcerted, impersonal meanderer"?

To borrow and contort: who, then, is this Anna Mendelssohn, high walker into fantasy? The answer is circumscribed by question two, which is embedded in a poem where Mendelssohn details the "statuesque antiquity within / the by now secret meanderings of a poetess".[30] "[A]udienced by / hidden mockers" with a vicious propensity to stomp, this poetess becomes adept at "side-step[ping] accusative". "[W]ho is she" the poem concludes, "but the negative's bewitching?" Persecuted, the poetess-cum-sorceress enchants naysayers, thereby resisting negation. The poem is a cautionary tale about poetesses "complexed" by "historical flux", prey to their positioning, their ascribed identities. Bemused, disconcerted, yet detached: within her poetess, Mendelssohn perceives T. S. Eliot's venerated poetic impersonality, minus his scientific rationalism. The poetess yields openly to confusion, disharmony, convolution. In the early 1980s, Mendelssohn begins using the archaic word "poetess" in earnest; by the late 1990s, it is fully integrated into her diction.[31] She is wholly aware of its comedic value. Read: "oh parasite poetess"; "problematic dreamy Poetess"; "Oh tangerine organdie poetess".[32] But "poetess" is a gendered distinction that Mendelssohn values as a means of communicating the difference between the writer and "the writeress", an identification that is lived, experiential condition, but not "any less literary and/or intelligent".[33] Put another way: "Feminized, although not without dissent".[34] Mendelssohn presumes her audience resents and repels her poetic voice. Her gender is part of this presumption; her vanguard aesthetic is another; her personal history is paramount. A lyric poet, she aims to "fi[x] interiority with an altogether different poetic."[35] Straightforward biographical readings of her poems are unavailable to us, not only because anyone who wants to write autobiography can and should do so, but because Mendelssohn actively labours to separate self from lyric. In a draft preface for *Implacable Art*, she asserts:

> It always seemed to me
> that the act of writing involved the
> exclusion of the writer; that the
> subjects took precedence.
> that they filled the work of art.
> and gave it life.[36]

These assertions are commonplaces of Mendelssohn's archive.[37] In turn, her writing toys with biography. "She appears in thirteen dresses", begins a Mendelssohn poem of 1985, her line eschewing the singular, identifiable self.[38] We soon learn that this "she" recalls "Jamaica in the white power days", has associated with the Bedouin, and is now, racist parody at the ready, "an employed hireling of Tinker mafiosi". As the poem moves toward its conclusion, Mendelssohn tells us: "She drags out the autobiographical and drugs it." (Self-) conscious autobiography is altered, made fantastic, implausible, literary. Skilfully, expressly, Mendelssohn distanced herself from the tidy, confessional autobiography expected of mainstream poets, and particularly of women poets who came of age in the second wave of feminism.[39] Mendelssohn's past was infamous; much of it she longed to reject. Her poem "Strictly personal" (2004) delineates a need for re-creation: "They know everything about me I won't simply / take these words".[40] These words are "a simplification" gratuitous, reductive, evanescent: description paraded and abandoned leaves the described with "nothing." Mendelssohn proclaims her poetic subject bereft as Hopkins proclaims his tormented; while loss is vertiginously, devastatingly central to their work, both poets create, and create phenomenally, when faced with a society that threatens to overwhelm.[41]

II. Anne Mendleson / Grace Lake / Anna Mendelssohn

Born in Stockport (near Manchester) in 1948, Anna Mendelssohn authored poetry, fiction, drama, and life writing; she was an artist, musician, and translator. From the early 1980s until her death in 2009, Mendelssohn published fifteen collections of poetry, the first being the self-produced *Crystal Love: D. N. A.* (1982); the last, with Oystercatcher Press, was *py.* (2009). Best-known among these texts are her perfect-bound volume, *Implacable Art* (Folio/Salt 2000), and three chapbooks with Rod Mengham's Cambridge-based Equipage Press: *viola tricolor* (1993), *Bernache Nonnette* (1995), and *Tondo Aquatique* (1997). In addition to these fifteen collections, another four were close to completion.[42] Further, Mendelssohn published poems in at least fifteen journals, among them, *Parataxis, Critical Quarterly, Comparative Criticism* and *Jacket*; her work was translated into French by Robert Davreau in *Po&sie*. And, from 1990, Mendelssohn was anthologised over half a dozen times, starting with *The Virago Book of Love Poetry*, edited by Wendy Mulford, which included female poets ranging from Sappho to Alice Walker. In 1992, she was included in Denise Riley's influential text, *Poets on Writing*; in 1996, she and Riley appeared in Maggie O'Sullivan's *Out of Everywhere: Linguistically Innovative Poetry by Women in North America and the UK*. That same year, Mendelssohn was one of the few female contributors to Iain Sinclair's renowned anthology, *Conductors of Chaos*; come 2004, she was a part of Rod Mengham and John Kinsella's *Vanishing Points: New Modernist Poems* alongside John Ashbery, Susan Howe, and Andrew Crozier.[43] These works – collections drafted and published; journal and anthology submissions – are all part of this volume, as are a further fifteen transcripts of single poems and series that Mendelssohn was preparing for publication. Among this latter grouping is a set of translations of Gisèle Prassinos's 1989 collection, *La fièvre du labour*. Of Greek origin, Prassinos was a child prodigy discovered and lauded by André Breton and his fellow surrealists. In securing permission to translate from Prassinos herself in the late 1990s, Mendelssohn continued an international focus discernible as early as 1969, when she rendered into English the work of Turkish poet and political exile Nâzım Hikmet.[44]

In Mendelssohn's lifetime, presses including Methuen, Bloodaxe, Reality Street, Burning Deck, and Shearsman contemplated book-length editions of her work.[45] As early as 1982, Mendelssohn gave readings at universities and community centres; from the late 1980s, she was invited to read at Cambridge colleges, the Cambridge Conference of Contemporary Poetry, the universities of Exeter and Southampton, the Southbank Centre in London, the Pompidou Centre in Paris, and by associates in New Hampshire and New York.[46] She agreed to lecture on poetry at the Roehampton Institute at the University of Surrey.[47] Further, Mendelssohn won two musical residencies and entered composition competitions; evidence suggests that a copy of her piece "heartsease" remains at the International Women Composers' Library in Unna, Germany.[48] Although Mendelssohn aimed, always, to live with a piano to hand, and ascribed to the belief, at least as old as Schopenhauer, that music is the highest art form, the verbal and the visual remain most central to her artistry.[49] Equally central, in fact. Pen and ink is Mendelssohn's most accomplished and persistent medium, but she worked in oil, water colour, pastel, felt-tips, coloured pencil, and collage. She designed nearly all her book covers and published her art alongside her writing in journals including *constant red/mingled damask*, *Figs*, and *Archeus*; the poetry of *Implacable Art* is interleaved with her images. "I don't find that images merge into writing" Mendelssohn claimed, yet swathes of her work expertly blend the visual and the verbal, in much the same way as her notebooks show her moving often and seamlessly from prose into poetry, and poetry to prose; the intertwining of music and poetry was another Mendelssohn constant.[50] Words appear within dense, collage compositions as indebted in their complexity, detail, and powerful affect to the legacies of Pieter Bruegel the Elder or Hieronymus Bosch as they are to outsider art. Alternately, Mendelssohn treats the blank page as a set of horizons upon which she intersperses lines of language with extended, transverse drawings that run from one side of the page to the other. And, from at least the late 1970s, Mendelssohn develops an ideogrammatic form that follows in the wake of Ezra Pound and Henri Michaux.[51] Generating as much art as writing, Mendelssohn nevertheless poured far more energy into publicising her poetry; against a single known exhibition of her drawings, there are over 400 pages of poems prepared for publication.[52]

Mendelssohn was also an activist, born into a highly politicised family, her given name Anne Mendleson.[53] Her father Morris was a respected Labour councillor and a former Communist who fought with the International Brigades during the Spanish Civil War.[54] Her mother, Clementina, was a member of the Manchester International Women for Peace, and took an active part in the family business, a local market stall. After the 1958 founding of the Campaign for Nuclear Disarmament, the Mendlesons participated in its annual marches. The family's Jewish heritage was central, defining: an archived certificate confirms that to mark the occasion of her first birthday, Mendelssohn's parents had three trees planted in Israel in their daughter's name.[55] Mendelssohn visited an Israeli kibbutz in the mid-1960s, and occasionally attributes her later poetry to variants of her Hebrew name, Channa Nechama Enna Krshner Mendleson Lubovitch bas Hakolenian.[56] During World War II, Mendelssohn's mother volunteered to care for refugee Jewish children, some rescued from Nazi concentration camps, and this harrowing experience was often recounted to Mendelssohn and her younger sister Judi. Both parents were forced to leave school for employment in their early teens, but they were intellectually ambitious for their offspring: newspaper clippings of Mendelssohn's childhood achievements indicate that she grew up in a cultured household, learning Hebrew and French, entering music and elocution contests, performing in local theatre productions and with the Manchester Youth Orchestra, and becoming Head Girl at Stockport High School for Girls.[57] In her life writings, Mendelssohn often describes, with palpable bitterness, the exacting, relentless criticisms of her parents, with special attention paid to her father's domineering political drive. Her home environment grated and inspired.

Like so many of her generation, Mendelssohn became the first member of her family to attend university. From 1967 to 1969, she studied Comparative Studies at the University of Essex. Opening its doors in 1964, Essex quickly became a notoriously radical hub: although the English Department was set up in large part by the conservative, prominent Movement poet Donald Davie, in its early days Ed Dorn was a lecturer and Tom Raworth was a poet in residence. In spring 1968, influenced by Situationism, student activism, and the general strike in France, Essex was shut down due to a protest against a visiting speaker from Britain's Porton Down, the world's oldest chemical weapons research facility.[58] Mendelssohn was involved in this protest, and in the same year, took part in large-scale London marches against the Vietnam War. At Essex, she campaigned to be elected to the National Union of Students, was a member of the Theatre Arts Society, and wrote. She appeared with a group of students in the conclusion of Jean-Luc Godard's documentary on student unrest in England, *British Sounds* (1969); from under the brim of an out-sized orange felt hat, she argues for properly controversial counter-lyrics to the Beatles's curiously resigned "Revolution", beaming and hesitating before the camera, and accompanying the music with some rather accomplished playing of a kazoo.[59] Still enrolled at Essex,

Mendelssohn travelled to Turkey in 1969, teaching English and French to schoolchildren in Ankara, and possibly associating with members of the Turkish National Liberation Front. In 1970, she returned to London, where she wrote for countercultural periodicals and agitated on behalf of squatters' rights whilst working to move homeless people into unoccupied London council blocks. At this time, she describes herself as emotionally vulnerable: in mourning for a friend who had recently died in a motorcycle accident, and at perpetual odds with her politicised associates who chastised her for her devotion to writing. A long poem about London – now apparently lost – was her particular focus. This antagonism places Mendelssohn within a lengthy historical trajectory of vanguardists deemed traitors for privileging art over action.[60] As these domestic conflicts came to a head, a friend of Mendelssohn's suggested that she might be happier living with some people she had known at Essex. Mendelssohn appears to have made this move willingly, but claims, forevermore, to have been coerced – "seized", "arrested" – to remain with her new housemates, who were affiliated with the urban guerrilla organisation known as The Angry Brigade. Mendelssohn's American contemporaries in extremist activism – among them, Jane Alpert, Susan Stern – similarly liken their involvement in clandestine organisations to incarcerations.[61] Like Mendelssohn, these women found their lives irretrievably marked by associations that oscillated between the utopian and the dystopian. In her archive, Mendelssohn recounts bitterly and repeatedly how she "'became known (with much revulsion) as the Angry Brigade girl.'"[62]

Two legal battles parenthesise Mendelssohn's adulthood, both of them distinctly marked by her belief, as a young adult, that revolution was the solution.[63] The first was the Stoke Newington Eight trial of 1972, which was, until the 2013–14 prosecution against News International, the longest criminal trial in contemporary British history.[64] Still lacking a well-researched account, and absent from most studies of contemporary terrorism, The Angry Brigade was part of a recognised international wave of predominantly middle-class, educated youth who became disenchanted by the inefficacies of democratic protests sparked by racial unrest in the United States in the 1950s and 1960s. This disenchantment was fuelled further by the rise of the New Left, the urgency of American conscription for the Vietnam War, vestiges of ongoing fascist complicity in continental Europe and, in Britain, by the crisis in Northern Ireland.[65] Some hundreds of these thousands of student protestors began to form urban guerrilla groups, a list that included the Weather Underground in the USA, the Front de Libération du Québec in Canada, The Red Brigades in Italy, and in Germany, The Red Army Faction, or Baader-Meinhoff. Of the same lineage as their infamous counterparts, The Angry Brigade revolution was comparatively minimal, involving no murders or kidnappings.[66] Funded by fraudulent cheques, their activities included about two dozen small-scale attacks, primarily bombings of police stations, businesses, embassies, politicians' residences, and a BBC van at a Miss World beauty pageant in 1970, all believed unoccupied when the bombs were detonated.[67] Anna Mendelssohn's fingerprints were discovered on a sheet torn from *Rolling Stone* magazine found in a bag containing one of those bombs. Fourteen sets of fingerprints were located in the same bag; eleven were never identified. Arrested in August 1971, Mendelssohn was charged with credit card and cheque fraud. By November 1971, the charges were augmented to conspiring to cause explosions to endanger life or property. Mendelssohn stood trial with James Greenfield, John Barker, Hilary Creek, Christopher Bott, Stuart Christie, Angela Weir, and Kate McLean. Though Mendelssohn, scarcely 24 years of age, pleaded innocent and skilfully defended herself in court, she was convicted of conspiracy to cause explosions on 6 December 1972. Of the eight defendants, only Mendelssohn, Greenfield, Barker, and Creek were found guilty. Mendelssohn was sentenced to ten years at Her

Majesty's Holloway Prison in London, an institution that became female-only in 1903, and remains well-known for detaining the Pankhurst suffragettes.

Mendelssohn claims to have been the first woman behind bars to successfully petition for the receipt of a musical instrument, a guitar. In 1974, she won a drawing competition initiated by the Arthur Koestler Trust, entering a sketch of a tree in the prison yard. Her prize was an afternoon's furlough, which she chose to spend at the Tate to see Blake's drawings.[68] Mendelssohn taught her fellow inmates literacy, petitioned for improved conditions, and ran dramatic productions, including a performance of *Peter Pan* in which, fantastically, she cast herself as Captain Hook.[69] These efforts prompted her early parole in 1976. Post-prison, Mendelssohn briefly returned to Stockport, then lived in Cambridge, undertaking a Foundation Art Course at Anglia Polytechnic; in 1979, she moved to Sheffield, where she enrolled in Fine Art at Sheffield City Polytechnic. Inevitably, Mendelssohn's past came with her. In 1977, Robert Carr, one-time Home Secretary and target of an Angry Brigade bomb, invited Mendelssohn to spar with him on a chat show; in 1978, Eton College invited her to a debate between herself and a police officer, staged for the benefit of its privileged student body. Unsurprisingly, Mendelssohn declined both requests.[70] Between 1980 and 1985, Mendelssohn had three longed-for children: Poppy Juanita Dorothy Shoshanna Ruth Pascal (1980), Jet Jack George Alessandro (1984), and Emerald Tulane Cassia (1985). Mendelssohn changed her name by deed poll to Sylvia Grace Louise Lake in 1983, the same year she passed her entrance examinations to the University of Cambridge; in 1984, she began a degree in literature at Cambridge's St Edmund's College.[71]

Mendelssohn's writing indicates that the late 1970s and early 1980s were relatively happy years. Her poetry in this period has a levity that is later overtaken by vehemence. This is not to negate the struggles associated with her twin, all-absorbing ambitions to be a parent and a successful student at an excruciatingly paternalistic institution. As a young activist, Mendelssohn often laboured to improve support networks for parents and children. When she had a family, she believed that the community should help her raise her children; in a different world, this attitude might be incontrovertible. But another family upon whom she relied heavily desired a better routine, financial assistance, and the involvement of a third party: social services. For a woman who had served time, the scrutiny of her daily machinations by authority figures was a source of pronounced distress; still more worrying was the possibility that the vexed past she had scarcely put behind her might be unearthed in court, to which Mendelssohn understandably feared returning. Poverty exerted its daily grind, as did severe ill health and the stigma of single parenthood.[72] In 1988, she gave permission to have her children temporarily fostered; they were never returned to her care.[73] Mendelssohn's case was harrowing and traumatising; when it was finished, the lawyer who defended her renounced child custody litigation.[74] While the phrase "Angry Brigade" appears nowhere in Mendelssohn's poetry, loss is a pervasive theme of her later work.[75] "The children were music," Mendelssohn writes to poet, publisher, and friend Peter Riley; hence her overwhelming need for a piano in their absence. The valediction of this short, unsent note encapsulates unresolved protestations, claims, needs: "I am an artist not a terrorist. Love, Grace".[76] Let art supersede harm; love grace, the strength to endure, benevolence freely bestowed. It can be no accident that Mendelssohn named herself after clemency, favour, reprieve, refinement. And as assertion and plea, love is an abiding concern of Mendelssohn's poetry, far more important than sex.[77] This collection is replete with loves aesthetic and intellectual: love cynical, sceptical, anxious ("if thought be woven from the brain wished ill may learn to love again"); love clumsy, if determined: “crashing through stuttering / stumbling for love / right round the town”.[78] And parental: “I like to tickle my children. They curl up for ever in / laughter.”[79]

Mendelssohn professed her innocence, and her loathing of extremism and violence, until her death in 2009. Throughout these years, she maintained her reverence for academia. Mendelssohn may have gained entry to, or started degrees in seven or more universities.[80] She lays claim to no fewer than six PhD proposals: the first, in 1968, on “Ships and Slavery”; the last known, in 1989, entitled “Nancy Cunard: The Naming of Reality”.[81] Mendelssohn speaks scabrously about contemporaries who did not adequately value their education, and was adamant that she was not a 1960s drop out. In 1969, or the same year that Mendelssohn took part in Godard’s *British Sounds* at the University of Essex, students at Cambridge launched a Campaign Against Assessment. In the culminating move of their Situationist-inspired, year-long protest against the university, these students entered their exam halls in June 1969 and tore up their final examination papers.[82] The gesture was public, symbolic, and a genuine breaking of their three-year contract with Oxbridge. They left the university without degrees in hand; among their number was John Barker. Three years later, Barker was convicted alongside Mendelssohn at the end of the Stoke Newington Eight trial. Twenty years after the Campaign Against Assessment, Mendelssohn had her second attempt at completing the Cambridge Tripos, or the very exams Barker and his peers tore up. The process had been delayed once due to the legal negotiations over her children, and friends generated a fund to pay for her ongoing tuition costs. The day of her final exam, Mendelssohn wrote her good friend Lynne Harries and suggested that her answers were “Demoralised yet committed, too contentious – I’m being hopeful when I say 2/2.” She then discusses American poets Ed Dorn and Charles Olson, whose work she is contemplating.[83] As in her life, in this letter, Mendelssohn’s educational ambitions are supplanted by her voracious auto-didacticism; the breadth and incessancy of her reading defies encapsulation.[84] In her stunning memoir, Harries details the aftermath of Mendelssohn’s exams:

> In the early summer of 1989, [she…] told me that the Finals results were posted on the Senate House but her own name was not on the list. This never happens, I kept saying, it’s a printing error. It wasn’t: she had ignored the questions on her papers and written a tirade against the lack of nursery provision in the university. Later, she petitioned to get the ‘Fail’ changed to ‘Unclassified’, leaving the academic door once again ajar [….] It is impossible to exaggerate the value she placed on being acknowledged as a serious, scholarly person.[85]

Mendelssohn’s exam scripts were a plea for help in the private, domestic realm she was expected to manage with innate aplomb, making her educational history bathetic counter to Barker’s seemingly heroic, historicised Cambridge protest. “I have renamed the university adversity” Mendelssohn writes in a letter to Peter Riley. But nor can she quite free herself from the institution. Her letter continues: “if there were any other environment conducive to both life (which uni is not) and literary work I’d remove myself into it.”[86] For the rest of her life, Mendelssohn treated the Cambridge University Library as a second home whilst retaining the status “unclassified.”

In her final two decades, Mendelssohn revived her relationship with her children and met her first grandchild; she was in regular contact with her parents in their final days in the winter of 2001–2002. From the 1990s, Mendelssohn lived on Mowbray Road in Cambridge in an unheated shed at the bottom of a friend's garden. Satirically labelling her domicile "la kiosque du jardin", she filled it to the rafters with books, clothes, furniture, and more than one piano. Through these years, Mendelssohn wrote, drew, read, and played music unremittingly. Now permanently housed at the University of Sussex, her archive is an enormous repository of visual art, nearly 800 notebooks, an estimated minimum of 5,000 poems, and a vast array of loose papers, letters, drawings, paintings, and memorabilia.[87] Throughout her life writing, Mendelssohn steadfastly rejects her political past, railing against whilst identifying with the Left and identity politics, feminism included. A voracious reader, Mendelssohn admires and resents artists and thinkers whose fate counters, replicates, or betters her own. She oscillates between anxious justifications of her artistic vocation and past actions, an entitled awareness of her expertise and creativity, and a pronounced sense of victimisation. She is, in short, the ideal accursed poet, or, by her terms, accursed poetess.[88] Mendelssohn loathes her political past for preventing ready access to employment and financial ease; she begrudges the inevitably limited reception of the experimental artistic proclivities she could neither profit from nor renounce. Yet she cannot stop writing, justifying, protesting injustices. Mendelssohn might be seen as the emblematic "graphomaniac", a term Max Nordau lifts from the Italian criminologist Cesare Lombroso and defines as a person with a flaccid grasp on reality and "a strong impulse to write"; these compositions revolve repetitiously around the distressed self.[89] But the very acuteness of Mendelssohn's poetic consciousness troubles just such a diagnosis. Mendelssohn loved Auden, a truth that may well be tied to his famous pronouncement that "poetry makes nothing happen".[90] Politics devoured Mendelssohn's life; she did not want it to devour her artistry also. Instead, Mendelssohn wanted to wear politics down, grinding and hacking at its monumentality with a view to erecting a poetics free and clear of its contrivances. Paradoxically, this process involved a continual return to the site of the political. Still more paradoxical was Mendelssohn's weapon of choice: she levied an always leftist assault on the inconsistencies and injustices of political system with the lived reality of the personal, all in the full and certain knowledge of the feminist maxim that the personal *is* political, that these realms are inextricable. On one hand, Mendelssohn's is a self-imposed, irresolvable malediction exacerbated by a gendered double standard that insisted its resilient, condemnatory way into her vanguardism.[91] On the other, the literary – and poetry in particular – offers a way out of this impasse. In her finest lyric moments, Mendelssohn can bring the inherent paradoxes of the accursed poetess role to articulate, felt fruition. This very volume contains an extensive account of these "bemused, disconcerted, impersonal meander[ings]", these often extraordinary high walks into fantasy.

In her lifetime, the published criticism of Mendelssohn's work was limited, by and large, to two book reviews by contemporary poets.[92] Following her death in 2009, this situation is rapidly changing, but as a writer, Mendelssohn remains an oblique and little-discussed figure who, if known, is said to have "had some association, tangentially, with that most underground of poetic brotherhoods, the Cambridge poets".[93] What follows aims to lay foundations for a reversal of Mendelssohn's relative anonymity, whilst bearing in mind that she is a difficult writer whose work will never be popular, though may yet prove canonical. The next section, "Mendelssohn's Modernism", addresses the coordinates that are Mendelssohn's primary influence, both historical and formal. Mendelssohn's devotion to a modernist legacy situates her work within the British Poetry Revival, an aesthetic category that emerges in the 1960s and continues, multi-generationally, to the present day. An inevitably contested grouping, the Revival is considered Britain's belated but productive response to modernist poetics, particularly the lineages of Ezra Pound and William

Carlos Williams; for Mendelssohn, the inspiration is predominantly continental.[94] While Mendelssohn's poetic semantics anticipate interpretation *ad infinitum*, this section unearths discernible lines of influence and specific modernist practices – neologism, listing, jarring juxtapositions – that offer a way in to the density of Mendelssohn's writing. Section four of this introduction, "Mendelssohn and Politics", considers how Mendelssohn, though compelled by an unabashedly avant-garde ethos, is nevertheless resistant to espousals of violence and political thought as the driving forces of poetry. Mendelssohn's didacticism in these regards is enormously complex, particularly as her poetry regularly addresses harm, echoes a vanguard disdain for the masses, and exhibits reverence for revolutionary figures. Mendelssohn's claim to neutrality is repudiated by her ardent writing, and by a radical politics that is rooted in vast and microscopic inequities of class, race, and gender, yet remains curiously conservatively tinged. An abiding and consistent aspect of this politics is Mendelssohn's concern for the fate of the woman writer, in whose name she creates the vanguard movement, MAMA. From Mendelssohn's politics, this introduction moves to Mendelssohn's equally complex writing processes. Consisting of two parts, section five, "Mendelssohn's Editorial Practice", is devoted to genetic criticism of Mendelssohn's drafts and paratexts. Part one is an exegesis of Mendelssohn's extensive rewritings of two poems from *viola tricolor* (1993). What emerges with extraordinary clarity are Mendelssohn's entrenched patterns of eliding the autobiographical self and specific political affiliation from her work. In combination, these practices are an acute reminder of the need to read Mendelssohn's poetry for its multivalence, rather than as a limited and limiting exposé of her life and times. Part two of section five centres on one of Mendelssohn's finest poems, "Silk & Wild Tulips" (2006), and examines the *longue durée* of Mendelssohn's editorial practice, tracing the gestation of this poem from a 1974 notebook, through to work of the 1980s and 1990s, to its final publication in 2006. Again, this genetic criticism serves an underlying purpose, namely: to curtail perceptions of Mendelssohn's discursive, affectively urgent poems as unsystematic or indiscriminate. Section six, "Mendelssohn's Publication History" moves from Mendelssohn's earliest published writings in countercultural newspapers of the early 1970s to the work that was published immediately after her death in 2009. This section recounts Mendelssohn's presentation of herself as an artist, her goals and aspirations, the poems she selected for republication, the journals and collections to which she submitted work, and her methods of self-publication. It concludes with an overview of Mendelssohn's poetry collections, tracking aspects of her style and content from the levity and surrealism of her work in the 1980s; her turn toward martyrdom and outcasting in the early 1990s; the preoccupations – feminist, Jewish, political – of *Implacable Art* (2000), and her return to the ludic in her last published collection, *py.* (2009). Section seven offers "A Last Perambulation" on Mendelssohn's peripatetic mode and is followed by "About this Collection", which is a guide to reading that details editorial decisions taken and inevitable compromises made in collating this scholarly edition of Mendelssohn's writing. The ninth and final section is "Acknowledgements and Permissions". This introduction aims to do justice to Mendelssohn's extraordinary *oeuvre*, to the work that she honed over a lifetime and considered a meticulous labour, a vocation, as suggested by the volume title, which reproduces that of her 1983 collection "*I'm working here.*" Throughout, wherever possible, every attempt has been made to defer to Mendelssohn's own language. Mendelssohn's disquiet about silencing is writ large through her poems; in both introduction and textual body proper, it is the goal of this collection that her lyric voice prevail.

iii. Mendelssohn's Modernism

As in her poetic content, in her literary influence, Mendelssohn's high walks "g[o] forwards by backwards".[95] While a "rere regardant" journey inevitably shapes all artistry, Mendelssohn's is a relatively short jaunt into the post-1850 avant-garde, a period arguably, and not coincidentally, defined by Baudelaire's resurrection of *le poète maudit.*[96] In this collection, there are well over 200 overt allusions to writers, texts, artists, musicians, political figures, historical event, saints, and pop culture. Mendelssohn's range impresses: she is as comfortable referencing Hipparchus and Marcus Terentius Varro as she is alluding to the Pearl poet, Loki of Norse mythology, Marguerite of Navarre's *Heptaméron* (1558), and John Marston's *The Malcontent* (1603). Shakespeare and the Romantics are touchstones. Nevertheless, Mendelssohn's references are overwhelmingly drawn from the modernist tradition, be it *fin-de-siècle*, avant-garde, high or late. An indicative list might include Apollinaire, Aragon, Arp, Barthes, Baudelaire, de Beauvoir, Bomberg, Braque, Caligari, Camus, Chekhov, Sonia Delaunay, Desnos, Eliot, Flaubert, Freud, Helen Frankenthaler, Giacometti, Gris, Imogen Holst, Kiki de Montparnasse, Klee, Grace Lake, Lenin, Magritte, Marx, Mondrian, Gabriele Münter, Nietzsche, Pissarro, Plath, Rilke, Alexander Scriabin, Paul Signac, Sartre, Stein, Stevens, Elsa Triolet, Turner, Wagner, Wilde, Wittgenstein, and Woolf.[97] Mendelssohn expressly identifies with this post-1850 lineage from her earliest poems, written, she claims, aged seven and in the nonsense tradition of Edward Lear (1812–88) and Lewis Carroll (1832–98). Aged 45, this lineage continues to influence her nascent collection, *Spinsters and Mistresses of Art.* (c. 1991–93), which

> follows & develops the tradition of unresolved poetic debate initiated by Elizabeth Barrett Browning. I should tentatively describe its more involuted passages as that form of 'modernism' (a genre I still find difficult to resolve) which does not agree, always, with itself, yet works to break through to new form [....] In short it embraces the spectrum from prescribed labour to creative work; and I have been bringing through the John Stuart Mill/Jeremy Bentham/Virginia Woolf & Bloomsbury dialectic between utilitarian thought and a democratic aesthetic.[98]

Mendelssohn, involute author, is justly cautious about defining the modernism to which she turns and returns; like all categories, it fails to fully satisfy. As she succinctly puts it in a poem: "That was Modernism. Oh doesn't it slide just."[99] Of Pound's overriding legacy she retains a lifelong scepticism.[100] But Mendelssohn identifies with modernist ideologies: firstly, in her experiments with poetic form, experiments that privilege the oppositional over ends-driven semantics. In turn, her faith that form-defiant language can infinitely change the world, can create a more "democratic aesthetic", is wholly consistent with modernist vanguards. In the above quote alone, Mendelssohn's diction lends language the power to near-autonomously move, disagree, labour, innovate, and take up a modernist spectrum of philosophy and aesthetics. This faith resurfaces in Mendelssohn's poetry: where life is a series of mistakes, of excuses, of "losing on purpose", of "the rush, the tripping over, the dash" (a hasty, lurching peripatetic), there is salvation in "the thing of fancy, language before all."[101] Like any god, language is cruel, perilously open to misinterpretation and condemnation.

"The dangers in writing are inherent" she asserts in one poem, certain in the knowledge that these dangers are particularly troublesome for women who "criticize the Establishment".[102] "[H]ow close is writing to the Law, how ineffective and too much written in the weight of the law, to the poetess?" Mendelssohn asks.[103] But as paternalistic authority, logos feeds Mendelssohn's oppositional aesthetics. And ultimately, language remains worthy of devotion to its ever-deferred promise:

> she smoothes her skirt
> to show her ineffectual language
> unhappy to be english speaking
> to the interesting sound of spoken greek
> but what could she say? this is music
> in comparison to what I speak
> & that is really the crux of her problem
> she feels another language not this one[104]

Lost in and by language, only more language will satiate. This longing, and this fulfilment, are refrains of Mendelssohn's work: "I want to / be thinking and speaking in another language" she writes; in so doing: "My page changes into a sheet of sky" and "language travels along the construction."[105]

"Late modernist" is a term that can refer to post-World War II artistry that returns to the practices of high modernism, a period calculable as 1890–1930. While contemporary artists of any nationality may be late modernists, the label has significant traction in Britain, which is widely presumed to have shunned the innovations of the continental European avant-garde.[106] Loosely known as The British Poetry Revival, Mendelssohn and her poetic contemporaries – Denise Riley, Wendy Mulford, John Wilkinson, Tom Raworth, J. H. Prynne – are considered a belated arrival to the modernist cosmopolis. In the wake of this anti-vanguard legacy, Mendelssohn defines herself as "one of the early modernist female poets in this country" and continually denounces the English resistance to experimental writing.[107] This resistance is tied to deaths spiritual and literal: "What kind of country is this that destroys its Artists?"[108] It is the source of mocking incredulity, as when Mendelssohn writes Peter Riley: "How have you stood being an English poet, Peter?"[109] This resistance confirms Mendelssohn's uniqueness, and her marginality. In another letter to Riley, Mendelssohn states:

> I have always been an outsider in British society. My understanding is surrealistic – it can never be grounded in incontrovertible truth; that is; unwritten and unwriteable [*sic*] assumptions that there was nothing to discuss. But I notice a distinct resistance to Egalitarianism in this society which I do not purport to comprehend.[110]

Influenced by surrealism, Mendelssohn's trajectory is neither discernible nor discernibly English; mainstream British society rejects the "democratic aesthetic" she associates with its intellectual upstarts – Mill, Bentham, Woolf. In this England, Mendelssohn complains she cannot write; she is too attached to open-endedness in a country where "the level is already standardized & finalized too."[111] In a letter dated 2 September 2006, Mendelssohn writes: "British poets are cool if not cold and if they don't want to write about fish and chips or normality they have to become members of the landed gentry. I don't fit in."[112] This letter echoes a poem Mendelssohn published in 2000:

> literary tastes sink to abysmal levels,
> pieces of pink elastine lie over gloss.
> life brought me love of art, & by my
> own endeavour brought me the powers of
> concentration to swear my oaths
> for poetry was the sworn oath between
> my soul and the mind the intangible
> particularly, not the loud fish & chip poems
> were for the assimilationists, now also [113]

Mass-produced, synthetic artifice, desultory and appealing in its fragmented roseate shine: these are metaphors for a literary nadir. Pink elastine is as fragmented as Mendelssohn's syntax.[114] The overbearing "fish & chip poems" have audiences past and present: "were for" a stereotypically British readership and are "now also". Against this too-predictable, pervasive vantage, Mendelssohn posits an innate, unbreakable commitment to that which cannot be seen, touched, purchased: the intangible, the poetic.

And more specifically, the experimentally poetic. In her poem "Radiated? Light?" (1986), Mendelssohn expresses needs to silence and question the imperative to "'see sense'", an imperative that turns the writer in this poem into an "immobile receptor" who is made to feel a charlatan: "And they writhe: trying to write again! / Inventing phrases! The actions of an artificer. / Be not whom you are." That Mendelssohn herself resists the sensical in favour of a distinctly modernist, distinctly driven obscurantism is everywhere apparent. As a ready example, she names one of her poems after Kruchenych's infamous "Dyr bul shchyl" (1913), a key text of Russian Futurist Zaum, itself a transrational language, "beyondsense".[115] Consider also, from "Erato" in *Tondo Aquatique* (1997), a poem named after the muse of lyric poetry:

> practising trances
> could this be a language?
> I see th't 'ts t' lift up th'
> corps de moi toute entière
> combien d'oreilles? oraclement
> g.r.u.m.p.y. encore jamais
> elle a écrit, a écrit? UR-POMADE.
> ah oui. la voix d'homme
> du sein d'abraham, et ABRACADABRA

Mendelssohn's is a properly macaronic stanza, replete with self-consciousness about language, writing, and voice, a nod to the vernacular disrupted by French, a nonsensical affective acronym, and gestures to the ancient – oracles, the bosom of Abraham – as well as the language of contemporary advertising and clichéd performance. Curious juxtapositions of ancient and contemporary run throughout Mendelssohn's work, as in a description of Pluto, the Roman god of the underworld, sporting a dress of blancmange that shapeshifts according to will, "the third stage of labour, unrepresented in Monopoly."[116] These jarring contiguities self-consciously extend the modernist canon: as Joyce creates an ad-canvassing protagonist based loosely on Homer's Odysseus, Mendelssohn likens her contemporary poetic creation Bernache Nonnette to Judith of the *Septuagint*, or she who executes Holofernes to save Israel.[117] The above stanza bears direct comparison with a 1920s poem in which Baroness Elsa von Freytag-Loringhoven perceives contemporary America ("exhilarating time of universal revel") through the lenses of Christianity and Judaism, interspersing these references with commodities: malted milkshakes, Coca-Cola. The Baroness's speaker exclaims: "Excruciating pertinency! Jo-ho-ha-jeee!" and the poem concludes:

> Ain't life lark?
> Very!
> Keening dizzy high!
> Follow agile –
> Foul dumb on deaf feet
> Croak on 'Genickstarre –'
> Such is larklife – today!
> Ja heeeeeeeeeeeeeeee!

Like Mendelssohn, the Baroness is preoccupied with ancient ritual and communicability; with misplaced body parts, particularly the unreceiving ear; and with a reduction of language to sound assisted by non-English language.[118] Vertiginous heights become bathetic, recalling Mendelssohn's high walking, her base feet in ascendant clouds. The lows can be lower than low: in the Baroness's poem, a downward fall is a "Foul dumb", a loss of dexterity and drive that provokes disgust, immorality, insipidity. A mainstay of the era-defining *Little Review*, the Baroness was the lived embodiment of Dada practice; some 75 years after this poem is written, Mendelssohn draws upon and amplifies Dada technique.

At the micro-level, Mendelssohn's late modernist poetics are awash in foreign turns of phrase, neologism, nonce words, archaic diction, onomatopoeia, listing, deliberate excess, parodic rhymes, and clashing juxtapositions. German, Russian, and Latin are just some of the languages that surface in her poems, reflecting her extensive collection of foreign-language dictionaries, and her voracious desire to master different forms of communication.[119] French phrases and passages recur throughout the later poems.[120] This interest in foreign tongues permeates her neologisms: is the "posmos" of her 1982 collection, *Posmos, the Yellow Velvet Underground*. the Latvian term for "in stages" or a portmanteau of posit and cosmos? And within that text, what are we to make of phrases such as "sesert dumas currants" or "she jummed"?[121] Rarely do Mendelssohn's verbal constructions appear superfluous. The "pro" of the title "proscribble at 16.12 hours" (1983) simultaneously pronounces itself as provisional, anticipatory, lesser, and an accomplished feat. Ambiguous and multivalent, "proscribble" sits next to a starkly specific given time. The poem that follows proves as restlessly attuned as its title: "agitate agitate" it demands whilst invoking searches for dissatisfying interpretations and associations, among them, the suffixes of "quadruplicate" and "cinquocentricate". The speed of life, the poem concludes, "drown[s] equinocturnal polarity". Where "equinoctial" strikes a calculated balance between night and day, "equinocturnal" is deliberately off-centre, and the poem is left here, askew.[122] And with prescribed lopsidedness in view, consider the conclusion to a poem published in 1995:

> The singing that broke the range in summer town & grangestering down by the boats,
> Eheu! marble & mirrors & silver reflecting light fittings high & black & white service

"Grangestering" repeats and reorients the range that appears earlier in the same line; from an urban horizon or continuous stretch, Mendelssohn moves to a term that conflates criminal gangster with agriculture or country home, the grange. Given that the poem pronounces "Equality unquestionable." this "grangestering" extends its class-based critique, its political satire exposed by the inverted, elevated syntax of "light fittings high" and the racial connotations of the "black & white service".[123]

Mendelssohn's love of archaic diction appears tied to lifelong proclivities toward nonsense and onomatopoeia. Among her many "scoopydoo sounds" are lines such as "band bog french carbel caban urea" or "tippy tappy goes plink tip on the hoo ghoo doth swath / suoni gwacoo-onghar-snāl perming 00.6 drop slipho"; decimals, exponents, and degree symbols also recur.[124] In "'The bourgeoisie lives there'" (1984) she twins this sound-based interest – in this case, the short 'i' prevails – with long-disused diction and wilfully trite rhyme, all calling attention to the outmoded bourgeoisie itself:

> Mottoes golden, trinkets to dimp
> I'm flying a sarcastic saviour,
> fangs were the chaos of the night
>
> In deep service, oh snick snick pin
> brush the ductile floor gazer in.

The last recorded use of "dimp", to mark with dimples, is 1821; similarly, the slang "snick" – snack, share, snip, notch, click – was most popular in the seventeenth to the nineteenth centuries.[125] Elsewhere, Mendelssohn will privilege "sprent" over leaping, splattering, or sprinkling, embedding the word in lines referencing silence and sound.[126] In "nattering swans" the archaic recurs as a means of juxtaposing an older generation against a younger. A mother who "was an hippodrome" has a fondness for "crocketing impounded depression films." Crockets are minor architectural embellishments, and their obscure ornamentalism will be repeated within this short poem by Mendelssohn's invocation of "gadrooning", or the decoration, in repeat convex curves and arcs, of the surface edges of dishes, clothing, furniture, or buildings. Usually ovoid, gadroons are often akin to swirls and raindrops.

Mendelssohn uses the word to extend her line and its rhythms – "Dressing hymns and reading limbs ripped along gadrooning" – and to foreshadow its result: "what could not be gulped those tears".[127] In "nattering swans", decoration veneers domestic unhappiness. Mendelssohn's expert diction is a mainstay of modernist practice not unlike Joyce's attentiveness to the history and terminology of costuming throughout "Circe". But in this instance, it has a still-further modernist subtext: "Use either no ornament or good ornament" intones Pound in 1913; in a poem from 1985, Mendelssohn ripostes with an echo that escalates, then nurtures: "DO NOT ORNAMENT, dear soul".[128] Or as she claims elsewhere, "a poet must know / more than a surface suggests".[129]

Modernist calls for order and directness should be treated with scepticism. Mendelssohn's dubiety emerges in a formal inclination toward lists that preclude ready association. In an untitled, undated typescript poem, the opening "nit freaks" and "flea foam" share an entomological focus, but the list that follows rebuffs classification:

nit freaks
flea foam
scrummage
sore rope
fortress yukon
pony there
newt point
solange throat
channel hide
treaty boar
high wall

Solange was a ninth-century Frankish saint who was beheaded after resisting the rape of a mounted assailant; she carried her own head into the next village before dying. While the legacy of this cephalophore might explain references to scrummages, ponies, and throats, a cohering thematic for "fortress yukon" or "channel hide / treaty bore" remains moot, as Mendelssohn playfully suggests with "newt point". An apex of Mendelssohn's listing occurs in "concilia." (2006), which begins:

eyelash once eleven jonquil cibachromed en route
washington vacuous quay point sizzling palermo
messages visited square bank ochre charged by bolt
magnet, curtsey, falling out, back room rat:
white sliced delivery, spanish cake shop windows,
tiled frames fused infantry, grille, behind a face
a ransacked library, daubings, bricked out.

This list intermingles visual media – long-lasting photographic reproductive methods, minerals used for drawing by prehistoric people, messages, daubings – with the language of conflict: frontal assault, fighting, double-crossing, framing, a protracted siege, a "sliced delivery", plunder. Within six lines, we roam from the U.S.A. to Italy to Spain. Our journey is international, but as fragmented as Mendelssohn's syntax. The diction, likewise, emphasises portions: one eyelash, a point, a square(d off) bank, a face. The title promises reconciliation and rest, and when conjugated into Italian, Spanish or French, refers to a third person, a he or she who has conciliated. Inexact, foreignness enters the poem again as it nears its close: where "dulcemente" is Spanish for softly or sweetly, our speaker is "encouraged dulcamente" to "change" emotion "to terror, scattered, / shadows, behind a hammed production of a national condition." And responds with an incredulous list culminating in sarcastic congratulations: "speechless, open mouthed, tongueless fish. Felicitations." Against "fascistic debasement à la mode" sustained by the "reactionary creation of familiar narrative, self serving", the lists of this poem subjectively chronicle Western menace, positing a single "unglobed throat" against global threat. The poem comments on its own obscurity, declaiming "the idea as god and gods" (note the definite article) whilst proclaiming the limitations of what can "cohere without damaging itself, as an idea."[130] Lists resist ready narrative, a truth Mendelssohn takes to extremes in her co-authored pamphlet *poems* (1984), where the final piece is twenty numbered rows followed by nine that continue unnumbered. It begins:

i) rolled	rolled a	a
ii) pain	pain-friendly	friendly
iii) ex-garb	ex-garb feat	feat
iv) chloro	chloroa	a
v) form	form filling	filling

Assuredly unadorned, this format reverberates into the columns and grids of *Implacable Art*, as evinced in the poems beginning "digne." and "Brahms' numerals." It is still at work, perhaps from stark necessity, in the very last of Mendelssohn's work, *Poems Written at Hinton Grange Care Home* (2009).

The list poems are strikingly apposite to Mendelssohn's equally pervasive tendency toward Whitmanesque poetic lines, lines so long that they pose a problem for her typesetters, as attested by poet Ulli Freer's relentless toying with the fonts for Mendelssohn's *Bernache Nonnette* (1995). This disposition toward verbal spillage seeps into the first line of a poem in that volume, namely: "Four eighths for writing business letters a man selects a voice she, he mocks, she will and inverts" and one notable title:

> How Power has reared its ugly head & defined a lumpen proletarian
> By the Force it has used to cessate the education of writers & artists
> By conflating us with the residents of Brothels.

Mendelssohn emulates the descriptive, protracted titles of seventeenth- and eighteenth-century literature, replete with historicised diction and syntax. In the latter instance, she does so whilst drawing on a post-1850 cultural lineage that includes Marxist terminology and a resistance to the prostitution of art. As in this title, Mendelssohn's poetic lines insist on their integrity whilst resisting standardisation, be those confines reader expectations or page size. Her rhymes share her lines' tendency to excess, presenting themselves as throwaways whilst enacting a similar claim to principle. Mendelssohn's rhymes rupture free verse, and can satirically underscore that which is taken for granted, as in "La Facciata" (1996):

> Hard into a dead oak, life's ripping plasterboard,
> on one other mellow mother, rising for their pains,
> sins are to be Tinned, bins are to be thinned, wins are to be twinned,
> whereas he was making a serious proposal
> she was making a fool of herself

Tinning, thinning, and twinning: these are maternal injunctions, domestic and dismissible; the "he" is a father, his "voice loud and lapping", his paternal anguish given credence.[131] Rhyme can also delineate emptiness, redundancy: "the day it was dull and as silent as dullness / without any breeze to lend to this nullness". But here we are falsely lulled by platitude, as the next line reads: "numbly did old Flem bleed with a fullness". The poem continues in this sing-song metric, concluding with a banal moral: "and that is why, lambkins, to this very hour / in the even grey drab uneventful power / when your energy overbrooks the salt will go dour…". Ironically embedded twice in the second-last line, the word "even" generates an irregular scansion that denies the supposed straightforwardness of this obscure cautionary tale. The poem blends nursery rhyme cadence with *The Red Book of Hergest*, a fourteenth-century Welsh text whose stature relies on the hard labour of Flem, "the works at Tyre", and the continual "whiten[ing]" of its "winnings" by exploited female cleaners. Duty precipitates privilege, a link that may explain the Cordelia-like reference to salt and severe outcomes at the close; throughout, the lilting rhyme first mitigates, then extends, the seriousness of the content.[132] Embedded in predominantly free verse, vanguard lyrics, Mendelssohn's rhymes are a self-conscious aberration; counter to its original rhythmic, mnemonic uses, this rhyme subverts expectation, amplifying surprise, bathos, and humour.

If Mendelssohn worships at the shrine of poetry, the liturgy is difficulty. "What is wrong with 'easy'?" Mendelssohn asks at the outset of a poem, continuing: "Weakness pronounces".[133] To declare is simple; instead, we might seek out dialectics, riddles, insoluble equations:

> think twice
> once for do
> twice for do not
> and the rest would be glib
> scattered advice
> to be nice and to gather up
> UNdemeanour.
> this or that be like

a tree   a rock
carve away,
there should be replacement
no substitute
in cliché.
a riddle a choice
delight comes there
write for the sake of writing
is, is not true,
an equatorial problem
equations spell
no one's land.

Niceties, manners, obviousness: all are picked up and set down in a poem structured as narrowly as the views it critiques. Irony infiltrates the delayed rhyme of "cliché", where Mendelssohn uses synonyms for "alternative" in a prosaic but telling illustration of the ready range of linguistic possibility. That art should be made for art's sake is the *fin-de-siècle* maxim that importantly precedes the flowering of early twentieth-century vanguards; Mendelssohn's speaker both acknowledges this slogan and recognises it for the cliché it has become. The poem privileges traversing the unknown over destination, problems over solutions, and asserts: "make play forget imaginable consolation / consolidation".[134] In "to fit the prototype." (1986), Mendelssohn gives us a glimpse of what consolidation might look like, chastising an author whose "writing has changed" and "can't even describe properly". What follows is a descriptive passage that amply demonstrates the stultification at hand:

these old ladies are talking to each other,
they talk of what they can do
& what their husbands can do, somethings better than they can
some not as well, there are pale green jumpers with pin-holes down the front,
beige sandals with open toes, interwoven top   uppers,
ladies in blushered cheeks, red button earrings,
serviettes with flowers on them, cigarettes with smoke from them,

The sheer dullness of this all-too-literal characterisation proves intolerable, and in an ineffectual attempt to bring it to a close, the speaker ascends into fantasy:

cakes with prawns in them, flowers with stag beetles on them   resting a chin on a finger
everything leaves, the narrative throws a fit, the passage is
is opened to leaves & secrecy, the heels cry never on me,

the personal is quickly subjunctive, the obsession never dies,
the intricacy is sympathy, and a game of squash in perfect pucker lips,
knees with bees on them, butterflies and pearls,
reams & reams of particled clothing [...]

The evaluative, inquisitive stag beetle prompts a departure from inane realism, in turn facilitating a mass exit from the claustrophobic confines of this anecdote. But in yet another onerous Mendelssohn departure, the speaker's painful footwear dogs her exit. Her longing for escape remains an unmet desire, as the repetitive narrative again overtakes, insisting on the middle-class dreariness of squash, perfectly made-up mouths, and the stacking of curios that impossibly promises a place for everything, and everything in its place. "[S]end me a letter" pleads this trapped speaker, leaving the poem by way of an imaginative list that includes "a toddler [who] studiously devours the areopagitica," or Milton's famous treatise against censorship. Prone to discussing the aversion toward vanguard writing with forbidding condemnation, here Mendelssohn enacts her critique against that resistance with comic prowess, deploying the perspective of an individual alienated and suffocated by a maelstrom of pervasive, banal mimesis.[135] A war between competing stylistic drives is enacted for our amusement. In league with the modernist tradition, difficulty – quite often deployed to evade the censor – wins out. From an author so loyal to the power of language, so resistant to straightforward sense, so keenly engaged in linguistic excesses and oddities as Mendelssohn, this victory comes as no surprise.

iv. Mendelssohn and Politics

While Mendelssohn privileges obscurity and ambiguity, her poems dictate strict rules about how they are to be read, the labour of poetizing, and what poetry should discuss. "[W]hat my poem is not" is "a paean to enamelled futures" that "investigate[s] / resemblances. types."[136] A poem on keeping names, letters, and detractors at a distance asserts: "mine was a poetry of reading".[137] As poetry has long ceased to be a predominantly oral tradition, this tautology is sensical only when reading is exceptional, arduous, "a thorough synthesis" of "metaphor bucked by convention".[138] And adventurous: in "Silk & Wild Tulips" (2006), Mendelssohn states that paintings should not be read "as though they were rule books".[139] As she envisions ideal readers, so too writers:

> Writers don't talk. they sit in rooms by windows and watch time.
> avoiding prose they notice people talking, smiling & generally living.
> writers, though, don't live unless they love themselves supremely.[140]

Absolute, these lines mock and, in their earnest simplicity, are perhaps mockable. Beneath the defensive strain is a clamour for discourse and belonging mitigated by a fiercely staked vocation. A more emphatic didacticism permeates an early draft of "two secs". Later excised, these lines – their spelling errors silently corrected – reveal Mendelssohn labouring to articulate authorship:

> It is a writer's job to be fair. ~~and as~~ That shows the mettle of a writer.
> It is not a writer's job to invest in sensationalism for the sake of it.

Assertion is supplanted by negation, which extends to the end of this draft, where Mendelssohn insists that anger and distress are "not [....] emotion[s] which produc[e] good writing". "Raw emotion" belongs to "an instrument / Which causes less loss." Equality and quality are lost in writing given over to negative affect, and the poem concludes with resolutions: "More tolerance for the pathos / of the poetry of the poor and less inducement to write doggerel."[141] Mendelssohn may insist on separating strong feeling from good writing, but her undated typescript poem, "A Crash", speaks mournfully to the experience of writing the doggerel in question, of "perpetually beating my heart into self-disgust at what i am incapable of", of being "inescapably enmeshed in bleary feeling":

> and a heavy heart
> altogether pulped
>
> nothing done
> with a meaning sustained

simply sheared phrasings
which do not grow

a blunt driven edge
too hard for the impulse will move a phantasy

The heart is on this page; the heart is the same substance as the page; cut down too brutally, language cannot flourish. Rather than high walking into fantasy, this authorial speaker is "swimming on the ceiling in a land all alone," in thrall to the same "unchartable wayward world" that, in different circumstances, is the generative thematic of Mendelssohn's poetics.[142]

Mendelssohn's vigilance about authorship is never as pronounced as when she excoriates violence and politics as poetic preoccupations. First, violence. "My poetry is not the harmful type" one poem asserts.[143] That said, Mendelssohn's work is deeply preoccupied with violation and threat, categories that include assault, rape, robbery, kidnapping, and gunfire, as well as menacing speech. A predatory male figure is present in Mendelssohn's poetry from her earliest publications, lurking beneath beds, to her last writings, where he still casts his watchful shadow.[144] Yet "violence" is a word almost entirely absent from the poems. A rare but telling instance arises in the undated typescript poem "the cliff.": "at the faintest suggestion of violence / i crack into action to prevent it." By stark contrast, Mendelssohn's archival writings are dominated by critiques of violence engendered by the state and in war; by the law and the police; by capitalism and patriarchy; in language and between people, and, crucially, by the Left and revolution. "Because I am fastidious" Mendelssohn writes on 6 December 1996, "I suffer but I go to nature or to art to save me from violence in speech & act". [145] These ideals arguably distinguish Mendelssohn from a post-1850 avant-garde understood to be as metropolitan as it is aggressive. But no revolution – aesthetic or ideological – can exist free of attack, as André Breton well knew:

> The simplest Surrealist act consists of dashing down into the street, pistol in hand, and firing blindly, as fast as you can pull the trigger, into the crowd. Anyone who, at least once in his life, has not dreamed of thus putting an end to the petty system of debasement and cretinization in effect has a well-defined place in that crowd, with his belly at barrel level.[146]

Mendelssohn personally deplores this sort of extremist enticement, yet in its resistance to "cretinization", Breton's famous quote bears a likeness to statements that arise in her poems. One of her speakers is impressed by beauty that is "confrontationally stunning" and exceeds an "idea of aesthetic". Pregnant, she feels unduly subdued by others, and harbours

[…] qualms over the deserted bedraggled unprepossessing crowds
locked invisibly leading their largely miserable lives
in stiff cultural patterning […]

Longing to be "away from the madding crowd", this speaker concludes: "No one human to appeal to, fixed located in a time sophrosyne". Surrounded by the masses, she cannot locate a human among them; hers is a swift, dismissive annihilation of anonymous identities. And no small bid for superiority, either: the Greek "sophrosyne" refers to an ideal state that is the antithesis of hubris, but it can scarcely resist this charge when self-proclaimed.[147] Where Breton's speaker is comic by excess, Mendelssohn's more sincerely asserts a mind within a body accustoming itself to creating new life. Both, however, offer a vanguard disdain for the masses that surfaces repeatedly, tauntingly, in Mendelssohn's writing, as in: "if you think this is smug try the smugness of people without art. / try facing their hideous groans and startling snorts."[148] From "here come the masses fed on molasses" to "I cannot write like an open university brochure", Mendelssohn's subjects perceive others as lesser.[149] "This is the reason why I do not conform" begins a poem; among the many given, one bald explanation is: "People without minds."[150] "Minds do exist to agitate & provoke, to make –" Mendelssohn insists; what follows this aposiopesis suggests that power wins against opposition: "who is clean cleaner and cleanest. All allies. / White thieves, white agents".[151] But her poems assuredly dabble in a shared supremacy, in turn stoking a predictable vanguard distaste for the marketing and promotion of literature. Poetry is "too intimate for a product for the consumer market" states Mendelssohn, who refuses to be the "avant / gardiste" who "surrender[s] / to sheer economism".[152] Even the typically small audiences at poetry readings can be a few consumers too many: "I read in public now – I am a hack."[153] "Anything written on paper is better than / Violence" Mendelssohn asserts in her archive, striving to mollify the truth that language can never be entirely free of aggression.[154] Her poems know better, as they address and inarguably replicate the wounding power of language.

Second, politics. In a letter to Rod Mengham, Mendelssohn described her writing as uncategorizable, non-extant, and unreadable, "a piece of nostalgic revolutionary lemon peel". Proudly abject claims. Where the modernist Gertrude Stein accurately believed that her era struggled to grasp her aesthetic advances, for Mendelssohn, it is better to be a backward-looking, superfluous revolutionary than a member of a contemporary avant-garde whose success is increasingly predicated upon commercialisation, on wanting to have "a brand of soap named after ones [*sic*] writing".[155] Mendelssohn takes the term "revolution" at its most literal, as a circular return to a place of origin, one contingent on a selective perspective. "Revolution is an act of forgetting." Mendelssohn writes in her archive, adding: "A revolutionary poem is blind."[156] Yet revolutionaries who addressed the global changes of the modernist period permeate Mendelssohn's poetry, among them, Tillie Olsen, the American writer imprisoned for defending unions and workers' rights; Ilya Ehrenburg, whose reportage initiated *The Black Book*, or the first extensive documentary of the Holocaust; Anna Akhmatova, Osip Mandelstam, and Irina Ratushinskaya, Russian writers who challenged the extremes of the Soviet regime; Federico García Lorca, a member of the Generation of '27 executed by Nationalist Forces during the Spanish Civil War; Élisée Reclus, the geographer, revolutionary, and associate of Mikhail Bakunin; Eugène Pottier, a socialist elected to the Paris Commune and author of the leftist anthem, "L'Internationale"; and François-Claudius Ravachol, the *fin-de-siècle* anarchist who bombed officials to avenge protesters killed for seeking improved working conditions.[157] These are individuals who chose opposition, battles verbal and literal against the status quo. Nevertheless, Mendelssohn's resistance to the avant-garde is sourced in its war mongering, a desire written into the militaristic etymology of "advance guard", and perpetuated, as she writes in a poem, by factionalism:

[...] our code of poetics works
as confusedly as a code of war
fought by people whose disparate reading lists

everywhere prevent freedom of speech,
of movement, of thought, of style.[158]

Though Mendelssohn's vanguard allegiances are stunningly clear, she resists affiliation with its current practitioners, readers, and detractors alike: "I so don't want to be read by / People who play war games" she writes in 1987, and in her directions to the publishers of *Implacable Art*, she insists that the book be bound and formatted to indicate its status as an emphatically anti-war text.[159] Though drawn to vanguard history and aesthetics, Mendelssohn was less convinced about its present-day cogency: "The neutral line has not been found by the present presentation of active artists," she writes, adding: "I had a neutral line – that is neither avant-garde nor is it reactionary."[160] Where era-defining movements such as Dada and Situationism pronounced themselves anti-institutionalised art and anti-establishment, Mendelssohn's ideal "neutral line" is bluntly drawn in one of her poems: "Anti-art enough."[161]

"Neutral" is not the first adjective that springs to mind when reading Mendelssohn's poetry, which is charged, dense, and righteous, but rarely unbiased. Perhaps she dissembles in staking this non-combative territory; she is certainly prepared to qualify her claim to non-partisanship:

[...] What I have ever had to say has
never applied to politics directly although
I am capable of holding my own in
the sphere of political discourse it is
not a discourse that I choose to make
my own. [...]

Stating that she writes with "good priorities" and uses scathing wit only when deserved, Mendelssohn adds that just as "a mathematic [...] does not work when it is / Applied" so too does

[...] politics destroy
art. This is not to say that
my art is not political, it is
highly political, but it is not
politics. [...]

Politics, like emotion, should be indirectly brought to bear on artistry, else art "loses its magic", its capacity to remain present, "even when it is yelled at as though / it were a living offence" – hence the title of Mendelssohn's *Implacable*

Art.[162] This indirectness is presumably facilitated by Mendelssohn's self-decreed divorce from its discourse, her belief that politics has an official language that she can effectively sunder from her otherwise "highly political" art. Mendelssohn's personal leanings are as vexatious as these assertions. In a letter to Denise Riley, she describes herself as "Confident of Poetry and the Poetic Tradition" adding parenthetically: "remembe[r] that I come from the North and am conservative by today's urban social standards."[163] Northern origins aside, Mendelssohn's readers cannot lose sight of the truth that she considers herself "a conservative with a small 'c'" and holds views readily aligned with the right: she favours grammar and public schools for their classical learning and "standards of scholarship"; she is openly homophobic; she subscribes to biological essentialism; she rails against "political correctness"; she longs unabashedly for wealth, and uses the term "gentleman" sincerely.[164]

And yet, Mendelssohn's work is minutely, almost obsessively attuned to imbalance, inequities, and accurate apportioning, as is amply conveyed by titles including "Sums." (1983) and "Half." (1993), as well as this sample of quotes: "the scales have been tipping me over / since birth"; "I had to share everything"; "i want that half"; "Split the change"; "one side for the girls, one side for the boys"; "Some make demands and others are refused"; "Half of the family gain and the other half lose. Half go to Oxford the other half / are shunned. Half own racehorses the other half play boogie woogie on / a clapped out old piano".[165] One speaker disparages the act of "counting what different houses have", but self-conscious ownership is an abiding thematic of Mendelssohn's poetry:

> "Get into your own backyard.
> Examine your own thistles.
> Count your own puddles.
> Dust your own toilet shed.
> Hang out your own washing.
> Talk to your own neighbour."[166]

Faced with imposed boundaries and insurmountable losses – "children snatched. [...] wage packet snatched." – Mendelssohn's speakers gather up what they can and assert borders in turn: "Serve your own sentences. [...] I collect sentences. / I used to have a set of my own."[167] Or perhaps still more damningly, shun: "you do not enter into my calculations."[168] Angry, petulant, comical, or astute, these tallies are assuredly the blueprints for Mendelssohn's political rectitude, her high political consciousness. And where the lower classes are concerned, that reckoning can be as brutally honest as it is sympathetic. An encounter with a "poor man" who "cannot contain his stains" is both wincingly critical of this abject other, and initially, sceptical: "yet his cup is half-full, yet his glasses are new". But having taken full stock of his circumstances, the speaker empathises:

> I am on the bread line too, his glasses are N. H. S.
> i know his watery eyes, his bonyness
> Yet i drink coffee, he drinks tea
> and his cup is not half full,   it is empty,   empty.[169]

This same unflinching gaze is levied at a poor past in the North, where "charcoal was cheap / & good for sketching scruff" – mess, untidiness, those barely making a living – before segueing into the "great scruffy people / in our town [...] just getting on with their jam puddings and custard. / with grisly chins & pulled jumpers." These members of the working classes are joined by a chorus of women "fat enough / to take up two seats on the bus." Caricatured, then poetized, these people are artistic subject matter twice over, and the speaker frankly invites us to join the evaluation: "if you don't mind I don't."[170] But there is also a quiet devastation in the poems where Mendelssohn adopts a working-class perspective, as when she uncovers a female servant's discomfort, "midst steaming / dank tea-towels", at "the master's rough / demands for attention", or offers a child's anxious view of her parents' unhappy marriage, her father's perpetually "grime ingrained fists" that "he scrubs [...] as well as he can, mum."[171]

The equation of poverty with dismissal, with a lack of intelligence, is a recurrent concern; Mendelssohn's labourers feel keenly the need to "ear[n] a few pounds to keep their energy alive and the cool interior / of beautiful thought."[172] More specifically, the historical link between artistry and privilege incites. "Was there a comfortable poem within sitting?" begins a poem that discourses on the permanent ease afforded by longstanding inherited wealth: "haven't we seen that serenity for centuries? / twisting amongst the thick wall greenery, / nothing transistorized here".[173] More furiously, Mendelssohn writes about visits to collect housing benefit, and judgements against single parents. Against these violations, the speaker purchases flowers, and "croon[s] to them [a] lyric" about longing for "a roof and little privacy: faint moments / in a book-filled room". But the inept "woman with the iron stare" at the rent office, "would have me out crop-picking rather than / reading books. she would turn geraniums into / ironing boards". To privilege the utilitarian over objects of sensory beauty is intolerable. Poverty need not exclude creative ambition, "ardency", or a thorough autodidacticism, and the poem concludes by excoriating judgemental "elites who have very little life / experience".[174] This poem is published in 1985; come 2004, these same sentiments will manifest themselves in the comically titled, "On being reproached by saintly mediators for bad budgeting", a poem that abandons class ambivalence from the outset: "I'd like to be rich. No not casually but positively streaming with wealth. Hard. / It is the only way to achieve anything." Given what we know of Mendelssohn's poetic preoccupations with value, coupled with her rejection of narrativizing or recounting, an ironic, defensive comedy infuses two lines of this poem: "Never mind my accounts. I have no accounts. / Accountants are stupid little racketeers who never stop snivelling."[175] Refined into satiric assault, this scorn is a weapon Mendelssohn levies at covetable wealth. Rich trendsetters are prey in "Who cycled in two fours?" and "<u>Where</u>?", both in Mendelssohn's jocular collection, *Is this a True Parrot, a Mountain, or a Stooge?* (1985). The first title combines the sporting fashion for plus fours popularised by King Edward VIII with the musical time signature of the march, or the walk of followers in time. The subject is a female named "2/4" who is "educated in possession" and metonymic for the upper classes unlimited in their ostentatious, thoughtless consumption, "plane ride[s]" that "knock through these heavens / countless times". So ancient is this class privilege that the poem concludes with a vision of squashing 2/4's hat, a garment replete with a minute, sartorial Garden of Eden: an "artificial snake / Wrapped round the rest of the decorations." In "<u>Where</u>?", those "weak with laughter at winning" continue to have the upper hand. Nevertheless, both poems integrate a countering poverty that facilitates aesthetic awareness and engagement, as well as the rebellious "image" with which "<u>Where</u>?" concludes: "of one more devilish servant / fed up of clutching."[176] Again and again, Mendelssohn proves incredibly adept at mocking ladies "given / another morsel / to nourish [...] predilections / for self-agreement".[177]

This capacity for class critique extends to Mendelssohn's considerations of race, which intermingle accounts of the colonised subject with that of the migrant, and still more specifically, the placeless, wandering Jew, whose "tents" are so often absent from "these long histories."[178] Abundant references to imperialism can be found in Mendelssohn's earliest poems, from "apoplectic missionaries steal[ing] zeal", to a "simple christopher" who "grab[s] for an old shore / line" with "slumped marched hoisted flags", to the title of her 1983 collection, *Celestial Empire.*, a once-common name for China.[179] One poem repeatedly asks "is there any / ROME?", emphasising both legendary global power and, homophonically and belittlingly, a capacity to wander off aimlessly, even disappear.[180] Mendelssohn remains attentive "to the forlorn's lack of imperialese", positing the losses and devastations imposed by dominating cultures, as well as unexpected juxtapositions rendered by these encounters, as in "the cream viyella collars of vietnamese sailors / flying their crafts to mexico".[181] "[R]acism is there, as ever, with / all its benefits and advantages for free booty / & plunder" states one Mendelssohn speaker; a few years later, another will point out how this plunder never satiates, never brings itself to a place of fruition, leaving Europe more at sea than the people it exploits, a statement worth making twice: "Europe [....] never arrives. / [...] Europe never arrives."[182] Imperialism perseveres regardless, "finding native born immigrants / to dispose of", dominating the halls of academia, or "the Empire of Sense."[183] And fuelling modern anti-Semitism, as Mendelssohn indicates in the poem beginning "Pall Mall." Where the narrative frame of Joseph Conrad's *Heart of Darkness* (1902) critiques English imperialism via Africa, Mendelssohn's poem critiques the same via Israel. Like Marlow, Mendelssohn begins with observations of "gunboats right along th[e] coast" near London, juxtaposing this ready defence with the legacy of England as a Roman colony. The poem then articulates the long march of Empire through walled cities to crowns of glory. In their thousands "They go" – the poem's refrain – decimating ancient cultures thousands of years old to "Take lunch." "They go", as the poem reaches its conclusion, "beg[ging] to be consumed by the" legacy of Reuben when he "was in Kabul".[184] Son of Jacob, Reuben led one of the twelve tribes of Israel, and is said to have been buried, possibly briefly, at Kabul, Israel.[185] As Mendelssohn writes and publishes this poem in the early 1990s, Kabul, Afghanistan, had just become the new centre of the decades-long Afghan Civil War, a strife that originated in England's controversial carving up of that nation in the nineteenth century.[186] Furthering the long historical memory of this poem, Reuben's descendants created the Cities of Refuge in his honour, or ancient Israeli towns that offered asylum. And asylum, of course, is the very opposite of imperialistic assault, displacement, and incarceration.

That a Jew's legacy should symbolise shelter is an irony not lost on Mendelssohn. Within modern European history, the Jew has been racialised, outcast other and a marginalised subject distinct from the indigenous people of far-flung conquered territories because Jews live among European gentiles, silenced but ever-present. As such, the Jew becomes "an unstable cultural signifier" particularly beloved by modernist writers who sought to infuse their work with indeterminacy.[187] While Mendelssohn's post-Holocaust generation was the first to experience Jewishness as a non-racial category, this liminal status did not cease, as her poems that engage with a Jewish upbringing attest: "I was neither white nor black, // colour and self can be changed".[188] Initially hopeful, this variability impacts upon the assertiveness of this subject, whose self-validating "sense of beauty", like her open-ended identity, may also "be not much other / than a gentle breeze ruffled branch".[189] The parents of Mendelssohn's generation experienced the Second World War first-hand; for Mendelssohn and her peers, "The war continues to charr the air with shot speech".[190] That the war remains palpable, even menacing, is comically rendered in a poem where Mendelssohn's speaker casts herself as a member of the French Resistance, ideally with a helicopter in tow. Here the tense switches from past to present, so that the speaker is just now "building one / out of wood and scrap metal from the skips in the side / streets, pink dusty light". As the poem concludes, Albert Camus's clandestine newspaper *Combat* is left hanging "in the trees."[191] Is it 1944 or 2000? For those raised in its shadow, Mendelssohn asserts, World War II is inseparable from contemporary realities personal and political, defining and contorting the generation of 1960s protesters, or those for whom "the war is too close / for revolution to be understood."[192] This incomprehensibility she ascribes, in part, to grief. In a draft preface for *Implacable Art*, Mendelssohn argues that the Pulitzer-prize winning photographs of nine-year-old Phan Thi Kim Phúc running from U.S. napalm attacks "were still so shocking to those who / were still in mourning for / the victims of the European / Holocaust."[193]

Consistent with this draft, *Implacable Art* excoriates anti-Semitic dismissal. "Just a Jew" Mendelssohn states defiantly amidst rancour about "filthy smut [...] in praise of blondes" in a poem that is part of a collection where ducats from *The Merchant of Venice* purchase a contemporary Jew's silence, as another speaker details the blood "boiled beneath the labour at Mauthausen".[194] These preoccupations are foregrounded in Mendelssohn's long 1998 poem sequence, "half evacuation measures unmet, still on regulo", a title that speaks chillingly to the monitoring of forced migration and gas ovens with calculatedly even temperatures.[195] At the outset, Mendelssohn pits reaction against progress, describing a "small fortress" housing vanguardists who do not live up to their ideals. The language of war seeps in, with its prisoners, contained "chambres", and manipulation of the many by the privileged few: "votre contretemps / c'est quelque chose / entre les gentilhommes".[196] There is "fascist vocabulary" in this conflict, but there is also blame for leftist thinking inextricable from a long legacy of anti-Semitism:

> metamorphosis began after the destruction of the temple,
> when people are bereft, our belongings stolen, our
> houses torched, our bodies raped, what remains of us
> is changed, into animals to be controlled, faithful
> & what kind of animals we are remains the knowledge
> of our destroyers. it is neither money nor food
> that causes the problems destroyers claim/do.
> the hatred of destructive people is not good medicine.
> how heavily they drop the odd plaint, wearily
> dropping iron curtains all over again.[197]

Against the "petty squabbles / between fowls", or the destructively self-righteous on each end of the political spectrum, Mendelssohn posits "the old man" whose pleasure lies in not having to enter a third war in his lifetime. This paternalistic figure "locks up / his music in his heart" whilst others "do not learn." Having identified a 'they' and a 'he', this section of the poem concludes with a 'we' who "are / curiosities whose / nature must be / organised [...] and redistributed /

as soap."[198] The threat of being murdered for their body fat was brandished at Jewish inmates of concentration camps; Belzec and Stutthof housed soap factories. This horrific truth was first reported by Ilya Ehrenburg, who appears in this poem as "a friend / who was talking to me / just like my father".[199] Mendelssohn's respect for the generation that preceded hers waxes and wanes, but in this instance, their stalwart capacity to survive consoles. This poem sequence addresses class and gender marginalisations, as in: "am I meaningless. / I don't wear a tie."[200] Cultural exemptions are also identified: from learned circles, groups of writers, perhaps the canon, all of whom "confin[e]" this speaker "to the anterooms / of literary traduction."[201] But "racial discrimination" is the overriding concern, so that these anterooms are easily "mistake[n] for slave ships", and the poem series ends with a lisping stage Jew receiving a kick.[202] And Mendelssohn's capacity for tallying is never so starkly apparent as when she iterates and reiterates her belief that the Jews of her generation are the outstanding half of an incomplete extermination quota. "[Q]uotient over. I totally disagree." she writes in "Franked" (2004), a poem that continues to wrestle with "a language of [...] ovens & covenant".[203]

If Mendelssohn's poetry evinces little patience for the contradictions of the proudly politicised, it is still more damning of liberal feminists. Power-hungry, woman-destroying "Estée Lauder" feminists; "holy simpering feminists" who "resubmi[t] the victimized to the victor's boot"; "bromide feminists raking french knits off the shelves": these are just some of the species Mendelssohn identifies within this genus.[204] And at the heart of the 1985 poem sequence "WHY" is a "feminist Skimpole": a woman named after Harold Skimpole of Dickens's *Bleak House*, or a parasitic, calculating "artist"-cum-con-artist whose extreme self-absorption causes others' demise. Feminist Skimpole descends from a lineage that includes celebrity and high social standing. "[A] disaster" despite her privilege, Skimpole plants herself in a field; beneath her condemned self, mandrakes grow. Pulled up by their roots, they do not scream as legend might suppose: instead, she does, "shriek[ing] in / time to her office's computer memory shield." For the story of this thoroughly modern, entitled woman, there is "neither moral / nor decadence", only an unbroken state of play between oligarchs and anarchs "mellowed in [her] sinking meadow . .".[205] Mendelssohn once complained about being treated like Molly Bloom, and one of her poems queries the basis of that Joycean heroine's infamous exclamation that women "are a dreadful lot of bitches", asking: "How do women get beneath women's skins with penetrating hatred?"[206] Occasionally, Mendelssohn shows us precisely how. For while Mendelssohn has her satire in hand when discussing exclusive feminists who wait impatiently for women "to earn enough money to buy [their] / feminist tracts", she loses that control as she compares the founders of Virago press to Nazis, an accusation too inflammatory to be undone by the half-hearted denial that follows: "I didn't say that."[207] This same vitriol fuels "To a Radical Lesbian Feminist Rapist" (1987), where the speaker rails against women who objectify other women, aligning this aggression with "[w]omen who take an objection to / boy babies" by aborting male foetuses.[208] Wholesale privileging of the feminine is a select legacy of the second wave of feminist politics, as is motherhood, which was pushed "to the fore as a powerful universalising issue".[209] But Mendelssohn's speakers appear to work directly against that period's pro-choice legacy, detailing "[t]he extremism of abortion" and juxtaposing abortion with death.[210] If the archive is a guide in this instance, these statements may be associable with Mendelssohn's dislike of liberal feminism. When abortion is legalised, Mendelssohn becomes anxious that it is perceived as the only emancipated route forward for women who fall pregnant unexpectedly. Nominally in favour of accessible abortion, Mendelssohn seeks a pro-choice movement that advocates equitably on behalf of abortion and reproduction, particularly for women who are not white, middle-class, or married.[211]

Mendelssohn's poetic subjects resist becoming an executive or a "lady novelist in a summer dress", but remain convinced of the need for changes that are in league with a liberal feminist agenda, including equalities of pay and opportunity, investing expenditure on feminist causes, or speaking out against domestic violence and rape.[212] And with her metaphoric use of "purdah", Mendelssohn may well participate in the white feminist trope of appropriating non-Western women's experience.[213] Further, heteronormativity is a Mendelssohn preoccupation that borders on longing. "Never to marry was Death" Mendelssohn writes at the end of her life, and her poems agitate for a compassionate listening ear, one able to hear the harsh, often unspoken realities of the female single parent: "the children were wanted, help was wanted, / This though is inevitably unwanted [...] not to speak".[214] Women's full participation in higher education is paramount, hence Mendelssohn embarks upon a poetry collection labelled *Spinsters and Mistresses of Art.* (c. 1991–93), her title a feminist counter to degrees named after bachelors and masters. Also paramount is women's need for cultural role models, suggesting desires for community and possibility that explain Mendelssohn's poetic fascination with the life of artist Clara Rilke-Westhoff, or her dedication of a poem to Kim Longinotto, a filmmaker who focuses on women's oppression.[215] In publications and archival writings, Mendelssohn often discusses limitations on women's intellection, a category that extends to the right to speak openly and critically.[216] And, by extension, to be heard without mockery, rancour, or dismissal. From the earliest poems we have of Mendelssohn's, the need to articulate is urgent, often stymied, and gendered female. "I think I'm going mad / I can't. SPEECH" states an "Anna" in a 1974 poem; thirty years later, Mendelssohn's subject, having been embroiled in an ideological disagreement, recalls: "I was not loud enough."[217] The silenced female is a refrain: "today she would like to speak / the fear of His fury returns."[218] And where "his mouth was full of roses as language was" Mendelssohn's speaker humbly requests the loan of "a few voices to surprise myself with." [219] Women's language is borrowed, women's language is hesitant: "You didn't understand our reticence. I smoke to kill my / voice. // To never sing." Enforced silence becomes masochistic defiance, a self-defeating fury at the screaming male who will not hear the "too soft" voice.[220] This need to be heard weaves itself through all feminisms, including the liberal variety that Mendelssohn disavows.

"Equality unquestionable" affirms one poetic line, adding sternly: "Move on."[221] But Mendelssohn's speakers don't. These poems are dotted with phrases of exasperation and justification, as in "give me STRENGTH to understand the male psyche" or: "It's easy to love a woman's body it isn't easy to attend to her mind".[222] When not confined – "I am held in sexism." – woman is quashed: "Reminiscent of a flat expanse trammelled / is a woman".[223] In a 1987 letter, Mendelssohn poses the question: "Where am I in relation to FEMINISM?"[224] This question underpins her many poetic feminisms, which range across the political spectrum whilst retaining an allegiance to gendered causes. As Mendelssohn asserts in one portion of her experimental *roman-à-clef*: "i am [...] a good deal more conservative than any left wing feminist I know . . and a good deal more radical too."[225] Her contrary thinking embodies the feminist paradox identified by her associate Denise Riley, namely that the outdated, prejudicial category "female" is one many women would like to abandon, but without it, there is no shared identity against which to resist the lived, daily effects of patriarchal society.[226] Mendelssohn loathes constraint, and all categories contain. But Mendelssohn is aware that women's lives are circumscribed by gender, and this truth indubitably, incessantly, and contradictorily inflects her poetic voices. Mendelssohn's feminism is at its most emphatic and consistent when she addresses the woman writer. In letters, Mendelssohn readily describes herself as "a common sense feminist aware of the need for women's voice in poetry" or a person who fears organised feminism, yet "read[s] from a feminist view."[227] Women writers, Mendelssohn asserts in ways many and various, are detested by the public for their "singularity" and their "possession [of] a Muse / Invisible apart from approximate complement thrashing the waves".[228] Overlooked, the woman artist churns to the surface, a resilient absent presence. To "speak, poetess, speak in the end – " is necessary response, because "what has been Taken – / will always be being spoken to you".[229] Language may limit, but there is a "Known refuge in a Word for Anything"; once uttered, women's language counters Freud's most sexist precepts: "[t]he criticism levelled at lack" and the mistaken "reading [of] Hysteria in a vital objection".[230] And, after raging against a "dire life", a rage that includes lingering over the limitations imposed upon the female writer, respite is found in "sit[ting] down to translate Gisèle Prassinos".[231]

In her search for female influence and voice, Mendelssohn wrestles continually with what Mary Jacobus labels "the maternal imaginary" or "the fantasmic mother who may or may not possess reproductive parts, nurturing functions, and specific historical or material manifestations; but who exists chiefly in the realm of images and imagos".[232] These poems are profoundly ambivalent about mothers: within the confines of a single stanza, Mendelssohn can assert "stupid old mothers. i hate being a mother" and "if / you love your children you want to eat them up. I want to eat my / children up."[233] Mothers are essentialised, their wombs filled with "magic and [...] mystery", a pristine counter to masculine aggression: "There is no flag that stands pure flesh of mother / Pushed aside in times of peace".[234] Yet mothers necessitate antagonism, even ruination: we can be "compelled to be mutually destroyed / for a mother's transcendence."[235] Motherhood is a site of tremendous loss; hence Mendelssohn writes "Demeter." and "Abschied"; the latter, meaning "farewell", is dedicated to her first child. A poem almost unbearable in its straightforward, helpless account of the last night shared between a mother and daughter, "Abschied" ends unspeakably cruelly, laying at the child's feet a deft, beautiful mastery of "[t]he art of departure".[236] This dyad goes unsaved, the poem asserts, because art failed to hold them fast; here art is neither salve nor saviour. And in life and literature, Mendelssohn did create an art movement for herself and her children: MAMA, one replete with its own manifesto, "womanifiasco numera una" which was written by hand on a single page in Cambridge, England, in 1985.[237] Not Dada, but MAMA.

The manifesto bears an epigraph that reads: "Our revolutionary linguistic radical women poets are bulldozed into the sewers for their pacifist reluctance to transmute into military machines." Its diktats include: "the west won to such an extent that Mama toy" and "we can always stare each other out in this prophetically ionized modern post-box". Readers are exhorted to "Use your academical minds. Use your intellectual hearts" and to "Chuck a radish". The manifesto poses questions including: "Who wants Desert Daddies...?" and "Shall we sterilize the human basin?" At its core is the pronouncement: "Our revolutionary linguistic radical women poets are bulldozed into the sewers for their pacifist reluctance to transmute into military machines." Abstruse, dogmatic, comic, this manifesto is adorned by a doodle suggesting a pair of breasts shooting milk like incendiary fireworks into its own text. Proclaiming modernist affiliations, including the desire to be identified as a discrete, combative movement, the manifesto nevertheless insists upon its pacifism, its marginal, abject distinctness from the vanguardism by which it defines itself; it shares allegiances with Mina Loy's controversial "Feminist Manifesto" (1914) in its focus on women's intelligence, parenting (unfit or otherwise), forced sterility, and misogyny.[238] Mendelssohn appoints her daughter as MAMA's co-directress, and promotes the plays she collectively produces with her offspring.[239] Mendelssohn's is a resolutely domesticated, unheroic twist on the blurring of art and life propounded by modernist vanguards. In a 1918 manifesto, Tristan Tzara famously pronounces Dada "[a] hobby horse", noting that "[s]ome learned journalists regard it as an art for babies".[240] In her "womanifiasco", Mendelssohn insists that the west has only *partly* won its Mama toy, and that babies can indeed make art. In part, MAMA is Mendelssohn's refusal to acquiesce to Cyril Connolly's maxim that the pram in the hallway is the enemy of good art, a platitude that implicitly informs so much of vanguard production. In part, MAMA was Mendelssohn's most replete participation in the vanguard dream that art can change the world, or in this case, could remake the world for herself and her children. This utopian ideal, rooted in an artistic maternal imago, did not go to plan. As Mendelssohn writes in *Implacable Art*: "I created a world of art for my children / to live in. But I am required to / Leave my world of art & Repent."[241] Yet the movement is a touchstone referenced years after the loss of her children, as is evident on the bottom of a typescript of her poem "antiphony.", which reads "MAMA 96".[242] MAMA adds another layer to the heavily overlaid palimpsest of Mendelssohn's feminist practice, and may be among the strongest evidence of the influence of the personal upon her politics and poetics. That said, the manifesto is written in the second-person plural – "We can"; "We shall" – and is loyal to the excision of an identifiable authorial self that is a mainstay of Mendelssohn's politicised poetry, and of her editorial processes writ large, as the first part of the next section will detail.

v. Mendelssohn's Editorial Practice

(i) *viola tricolor* (1993)

On the back of an envelope containing a letter sent to her when she was living at St Barnabas Road, Cambridge, Mendelssohn writes: "good art is indirect".[243] To be indirect is to elide, to circuitously refrain from straightforward causal relations, to perambulate. While many of Mendelssohn's manuscript poems appear written in a single sitting, there are innumerable drafts yet to be unearthed in and amongst her nearly 800 notebooks and 600 files of loose sheets. It bears repeating: there are a minimum of five thousand poems within her Sussex archive. This colossal endeavour, equally matched by drawings and prose, begs the mortal reader's anxious need for reassurance: surely the work is impressionistic? The advent of the Situationist International (SI) in England in the 1960s, or just as Mendelssohn began writing serious verse, furthers this response. The Situationist ethos of "free creativity" is consistent with a perception of Mendelssohn as recorder of a highly sensitised, relentless stream of consciousness, a poet (to mix vanguard metaphors) who just goes and goes on her nerve.[244] But close consideration of the poems from *viola tricolor* (1993) alone indicates there is no shortage of excision and rewriting in Mendelssohn's work, often over periods of years; within these drafts, we can witness the processes by which she remaps her poetry away from personal history and self, creating distance for reasons aesthetic and political. [245] And, no doubt, self-protective: the national publicity surrounding Mendelssohn's political past justified ongoing fears of surveillance and reprisal, and her outrage at having been sacrificed to a deeply flawed cause. Or, as Mendelssohn puts it in the conclusion of a stanza cut from the final version of "twelve to midnight" of *viola tricolor*: "Men who use ~~the~~ language punitively never retreat or make public apologies [....] my use of 'I' either scorned or cancelled, over-ruled ~~or~~ … was mugged."[246] These concerns explain why Mendelssohn once describes "[d]iscussing the creative structuring of one's own poetry or even admitting that one writes" as a risk to life, because to do so is to acknowledge "the dangers of redirection." Good art may be indirect, but a good poet should not be rerouted, subordinated to negative or threatening influences.[247] These external concerns may exacerbate the rhetoric of the knowing outcast or martyr in Mendelssohn's poetry, a role familiar to many practitioners of and participants in the avant-garde. Consider her title "in the minority of one" (2011), or her poetic speakers who have been "subjected / to an alfred hitchcock mentality", have "stood rejection" whilst "pushed against with bars & bars & goads", and who are voted out of town by secret ballot.[248] Historically, the need to conceal controversial subject matter has been a rationale for difficult experimental writing. Though frequently agonised and affecting, Mendelssohn's outcasts are imbued with a desire to gain a longer vantage, to resist reductive presumptions of association and past events. And at its most considered, this very resistance is at the heart of what elevates Mendelssohn's writing to the status of "good art", rather than an unfiltered responsiveness, mere reportage, or predictable lyric. Ironically, a generative vantage is particularly evident in two *viola tricolor* poems that allude to Situationism, namely "the fourteenth flight" and "two secs". Multiple, extensive drafts exist of both poems that vary substantially from publication and offer insight into Mendelssohn's editorial practices and authorial motives.

Originating in the early 1950s, the Situationist International was founded by descendants of Lettrism, Bauhaus, and surrealism; by 1962, it was led by Guy Debord, who published his now-canonical tract, *Society of the Spectacle* in 1967, itself arguably the culmination of *fin-de-siècle* Decadence in its proclamation that contemporary life has been reduced to mere appearance, artifice.[249] Rather than experiencing reality directly, Debord argues that we passively watch it unfold aesthetically before us: the city, shopping centres, advertisement, commodities, celebrity, and sociability itself have become constructs that unite and bind us, and are in turn, the falsified ideals to which we aspire.[250] Against the great god spectacle, Situationists advocate a permanent revolution of everyday life, one bringing to fruition what Dada started in World War I: namely, the erasure of the distinctions between art, politics, and life. For the Situationists, political action and creativity ought to be lived, daily activities. As part of its revolutionary agenda, the Situationists advocated a programme of "propaganda by deed" a slogan that encompasses, for instance, overtaking forms of mass communication, described as media-based "guerrilla tactics".[251] It is not an unduly taxing exercise to envision the appeal of SI ideologies to a generation of protesters. In England, students and faculty at the Universities of Cambridge and Essex – the stomping grounds of key members of The Angry Brigade – are said to have been particularly devout disciples. The word "spectacle" was used in Angry Brigade communiqués, and the police investigating the movements of this organisation reputedly read SI tracts to gain a better understanding of Angry Brigade workings.[252]

In 1966, students at the University of Strasbourg in France and members of the SI wrote an essay entitled, "On the Poverty of Student Life". The essay denounced middle-class students on two fronts: firstly, for their passive acceptance of a too-romantic view of higher education, one that led them to absurdly embrace their temporary status as paupers, and secondly, for their blissful unconcern about the inaccessibility of university degrees to the working classes.[253] An undated pink sheet in Mendelssohn's archive reads:

> The Poverty of Student Life.
>
> The wound.
> of death.
> why should
> it feel
> sweet –
> yet it did
> in my heart,
> in my heart, feel sweet.[254]

Conflicted, ambivalent, these notes may well insist upon the idyllic perception of student life that the SI rejected; that said, they are a rare acknowledgement of Mendelssohn's familiarity with specific SI writings. In her poetry, Mendelssohn toys often, and usually damningly, with a key Situationist slogan, *"Sous les pavés, la plage!"*: beneath the cobbles or paving stones, the beach. Put simply, too reductively: beneath the thin veneer of modern civilisation lies utopia, tantalisingly within reach, even foundational. Mendelssohn's resistance to this maxim, or any straightforward

SI allegiance, is one she evidently shared with Angry Brigade member John Barker, who states in a review of Tom Vague's *Anarchy in the UK: The Angry Brigade* that "it is the Situationist element in that Angry Brigade rhetoric which often makes me cringe"; though "spot on" in many regards, Barker argues that the movement was inarguably elitist.[255] Barker's post-prison reconsideration of the SI may explain why Mendelssohn dedicates "Shell form: Conch tent." to him, a poem that negates "duty" and "mission[s]" whilst asserting: "There is a beach. / We stand before the tides."[256] Beneath the paving stones, yet another site of opposition.

And this opposition persists discernibly throughout Mendelssohn's published poetry, not least in notes filed with drafts of her 1997 collection, *Tondo Aquatique*, where she expresses concern that the radicalism of 1968 was "solely a visual outburst of unusual energy".[257] "[T]his is what is happening: / the pavement is sinking" Mendelssohn writes in a 1984 poem that ends with a declaration of the speaker's ability to escape the all-encompassing realm of spectacle: "everything, I, think is uncommercial."[258] This "I" is emphatically parenthetically offset, near inviolate. An SI essay asserts: "The principle domain we are going to replace and *fulfil* is obviously poetry, which burned itself out by taking its position at the vanguard of our time and has now completely disappeared."[259] Almost no assertion could incite Mendelssohn's ire more. In the conclusion of a 1985 poem, she lays the blame for poetic disregard at the feet of careless readers. Her critique is effected via a movement from paving stones disregarded by callous peripatetics to sand that blinds the poetic vision:

> and we might have cared and cared and cared and left our writing for a few
> days or turned our attention away from our poems, leaving them on café tables.
> throwing them out into the rain to fade on pavements under footsteps, we might
> we might have cringed at crudity, been stifled by language which was dismissive
> of poetry, we may be screaming this morning as the sand burns our eyes at a table
> in the middle of a town, not wanting to hurt.[260]

Tossed onto the street as it is written, this poetry resists the institutionalisation of art, but is trampled underfoot even as the committed, gentle urban poet is aggressed against by the very substance of the beach that the SI means to unearth. Still more extreme: Mendelssohn actively associates the SI with fascism, as alluded to in "REARRANGED LETTER TO THOMAS EVANS" (2000), where a "false collective" is ascribed to Jean-Paul Sartre, member of a "non-Aryan breed" who "Broke with Heidegger (c.f. Situations)".[261] An infamously unrepentant Nazi affiliate, Heidegger prompts a reference to Situationism. Similarly, "Franked" (2004), is replete with references to the Holocaust, the perfection of a foot through intermarriage (a nod to the anti-Semitic belief that Jewish feet are misshapen), and Visconti's 1969 film about Nazi Germany, *The Damned*. It concludes: "Only beneath the table, is the stage." In addition to challenging SI politics, Mendelssohn's poem questions the "authenticity" of the utopian beach, and its purported refuge from spectacle.[262] And it is surely against the psychogeography that is foundational to SI practice – drifting through urban space, privileging the ludic over functionality – that Mendelssohn has a politician loudly assert in "La Facciata", a poem first published in 1988: "there's NO geography in PROTEST".[263] Instead, Mendelssohn's topographies protest against SI affiliation, as in the *Implacable Art* poem beginning "Concentration camp styles. along mill road. 1988" (2000). Excepting this opening line, the poem contains no direct references to fascism; without it, the entirety might be mistaken as a paean to psychogeographic *flâneurie*, as it details passers-by in an extended list that only tangentially references the central, observant viewer. But Mendelssohn discredits the rambling form of the poem from the outset, so that the disapproval of what is to come determines our reading. For over three decades, Mendelssohn's resistance to SI affiliation is as resolute as it is involute.

The resistance itself can demand distance. The poem "two secs" addresses some familiar Mendelssohn themes: wars between nations and classes, injustice, art, writing. Yet again, Mendelssohn privileges poetry over politics whilst embroiling herself in the latter: "in the world preferring to scribble pieces of sapphire / utterly irresponsible to all political programmatists".[264] This interlinking of gems, poems, and a lack of system recurs in *Implacable Art* (2000): "a poem is not going to give precise directions [.... poems] address a different world / where trees are decorated with diamonds".[265] Of the three known variants of "two secs", the longest is 74 lines; the published poem is 21.[266] All versions are woven with interpersonal contestations of vanguard knowledge, a didacticism about radicalism that is increasingly oblique and removed from individuals in subsequent redraftings. By the final version, as Mendelssohn edits her way toward phrases compact and evocative, these challenges are just discernible in "reading jam each other wasps"; "a scathing word or two"; and "avoid[ing] sermonizing within the deadweight of history". This same winnowing occurs in relation to aesthetic knowledge. An untitled draft poem beginning "sickened by the sight of the yard thewed daughters" is associable with "two secs" and is included in this appendix. Its aggrieved speaker states that she has been told she cannot write art criticism. That she has been mocked for her unfamiliarity with the French co-founder of Cubism, Georges Braque, becomes clear in a 38-line variant of "two secs", where the speaker recounts a challenge in the aftermath of a presentation: "i SAID i didn't know him in my hand-out." "[T]he edition of / 'fundamental braque'" that arises in this draft will recur in the published poem, where knowledge facilitates mobility and escape, even as the speaker has found a way to avoid proselytising about history. In *viola tricolor*, the poem concludes: "filling in the past / with no expectations dismantling the flats / in the diagonal indicating exit: 'fundamental braque'."

Contested on her awareness of art, the speaker in these drafts of "two secs" is also openly interrogated about her knowledge of Trotsky in "sickened by the sight": "don't ask me if i know troetz [....] "troetz is a sculpture." Born Lev Bronstein, Leon Trotsky is said to have adopted his new surname from "Troetz" or more properly, "Trotz", the German for "defiance". In the gap between stanzas, Mendelssohn unmoors Trotsky from politics, potentially reducing or elevating this anti-Stalinist, Marxist revolutionary to the status of an artwork. Come the 38-line "two secs", the charge of insufficient knowledge about Trotsky is levied at Situationists, rather than the speaker:

> & whilst to hoist machinery of administration i think one back
> & walk to talk to tell you what should not offend you so, myths
> there are a plenty, and most of them inspired by extra situationists
> who think in terms too large to use something apart from
> the real world as to charge a fortune to my name
> and never look me in the face again and do not know of troetz.

Treading old terrain, Mendelssohn identifies myths about 1960s radicalism, diagnosing SI practice as poorly interpreted by its extraneous followers, who scapegoat this speaker into a reward for bounty-hunters, a sacrifice that the 74-line variant makes plain benefitted radicals and law-enforcers alike: "~~I detest being~~ I detested being thrown into ~~jail~~ prison. / It was real punishment for what had not been my idea." In very personal terms, the longest version of "two secs" discusses the loss of reputation, of children, of faith in language and freedom; quite beautifully, there is an insistence upon the primacy of art, and its relationship to the body: "it's one of those strange things in the / world of writing that ones [*sic*] body, when writing as such was an art, / was part of the ~~writ~~ work it created." The intimacy is extraordinary, revealing, ruminative. And so too is the debate with Situationism more pronounced, even as the SI claim that poetry should no longer be "Art" is so clearly inscribed in the mind. Rather than inhabit a world of spectacle, this speaker insists: "I remember myself as being in touch with reality." The long passage about SI myth quoted above is here in full, although in this version, the thinking of SI members is "imported" rather than "inspired". "[T]roetz" or Trotsky is replaced by the ballet dancer Nureyev, arguably one of the most famous Cold War Russian defectors, who, the speaker states, "did not go to santiago", a post-war capital of extremist politics. But these claims are bracketed by phrases of dismissal: "what was is now no longer" and "I was less than interested / personally".

Nureyev died in 1993, the year "two secs" was included in *viola tricolor*. In publication, references that arise in its multiple drafts – to Trotsky and, in passing, to Communism and Stalin[267] – are transposed into the aesthetic and affective "mourning Nureyev" who would "not danc[e] for the colonels" of an unspecified nation. A similar deflection of the political occurs in relation to feminism. In earlier drafts, Mendelssohn takes issue with women's liberation whilst nodding to Plath's "Daddy": "feminists denying the truth by / resubmitting the victimized to the victor's boot."[268] In the *viola tricolor* "two secs", this tussle with feminism is reduced to "w.i. jam sessions", or Women's Institute consciousness-raising meetings. This phrase is a neat conflation of first- and second-wave feminism that is almost eclipsed by its place within a list of commodities and references to the militaristic, including "british legionnaires", a rejected "officer in uniform", and, in a satiric echo of "w.i.": "g.i. pied à terres". Class aspiration, militarism, and radicalism are intertwined, undercutting any purist presumptions about vanguard movements. Where the drafts of "two secs" stray off course, can yield to rambling and rage, in publication, the poem is a tightly-written satire, a fastidious, structured, demanding critique. And a largely impersonal one. The 74-line "two secs." oscillates from "the girl" to an "I", but is written primarily in the first person, as attested by at least two dozen personal pronouns. The final draft has but two: "can we care" and "i despair". The critique of 1960s activism remains: "friends grew scruffier, hair greasier, cafés seedier". But Situationism proper is nowhere to be found, even as its juxtaposition with extremist politics – in this instance communism, rather than fascism – was one of the founding conceits of the poem. The separation from twentieth-century communism effected by references to Trotsky and Nureyev is sealed by the dedication of the final poem to Countess Vera Tolstoy, granddaughter of Leo, or she who fled Russia during the Bolshevik Revolution.

Where "two secs" articulates an interrogation by Leftists that becomes, in turn, an interrogation of contemporary political extremism, "the fourteenth flight" more personally recounts the experience of working within political factions whilst replicating, through similar processes of redrafting, Mendelssohn's expansion of specific activisms to global, historical proportions. Shared coordinates between these poems include a preoccupation with dissent, and with ascertaining the most correct response to what "the fourteenth flight" labels "the establishment". So too does "the fourteenth flight" address robbery, entrapment, and sacrifice whilst prioritising the creatively written word over prescriptive, hierarchical *logos*, the law: "and why beats me that's all those closed mouths [...] had to organise a political justification for writing poetry". Where the final version of "two secs" elides the specific terms of incarceration, these are retained in "the fourteenth flight" and coupled with a discussion of enforced psychiatric treatment. Three draft variants of "the fourteenth flight" are included in this volume, and all of them are longer than the published version, which has eight stanzas to the 14 of the partial manuscript discussed in the appendix notes, and to the 11 of the version included in full in the appendix, where the last two stanzas lengthen and lose poetic form. One typed draft is dated 1989, suggesting that Mendelssohn returned to this poem over a period of no fewer than four years. The drafts are awash in personal pronouns and the second-person pronoun "you", meaning that the poem begins life as an address to a specific, unnamed individual or group. Come publication, the "you" gives way to "they". Combined with reduced references to the self, this proliferation of the third-person plural pronoun forecloses the interrogative, putting the addressee(s) at a remove from the speaker and, to some degree, the immediacy of the present moment.[269] In lines that recur, the introduction of a more generalised interlocutor can lessen the didactic tone, facilitating a repositioning of blame.

To elaborate: where the published text includes an ambivalent double negative in its final stanza, "having not demolished a tree top for those i did not know", earlier drafts render this line as: "I ate a tree top for you" and "I ate a tree top for YOU" respectively. In these latter variants, culpability is openly admitted, and the catalyst for that destruction appears to be a known entity, a figure capable of enacting uncharacteristic behaviour from others. In publication, deferred responsibility expands the complicity at stake, as the damage is still enacted, but the aggressor remains at large, unknown to the reader, if not the speaker. This same expansion is evident in Mendelssohn's drafts of another poem for *viola tricolor*, "1526", which asks outright: "How can mine be known to others who are offended / by self reference." In one manuscript variant, a line from an excised stanza positively, repeatedly insists upon the speaker's capacity to troubleshoot, to prophesise danger to a "you" who refuses to "realize this / Impossible Domination": "Had been warned by me, yes by me, all along and lied upon." In another manuscript, this same line reads: "Had been warned by one all along and lied upon." Unlike the emphatic "me, yes by me" the indefinite pronoun "one" does not preclude, exonerate, or liberate the speaker from the woeful domination at hand, even as it suggests that the warning may have come from almost anyone. In "the fourteenth flight", the claim of "having not demolished a tree top for those i did not know" renders a more intensive sense of bewilderment about those whose "whiteness", we are told in stanza three, cuts through "my forests where your bulldozers smashed". In the published conclusion, the speaker neither demolishes treetops nor accepts "roots twining rope logged tips touching earth's secure holding moist & uneven in texture". This description is a far cry from the specificity of one partial manuscript of "the fourteenth flight", where Mendelssohn writes of trees "planted apart, behind the rise, over yonder ridge, along a / darker line, drawn over & over again, / one morning chopped down."[270] These prosaic lines are excised from the draft in favour of a clear cut that is devastation and comfort, one that speaks to the apocalypse endured by still-sentient arboreal remains. Bound and fallen, these trees glean consolation from an earth as ever ready to regenerate as it is, inevitably, inconstant. This clear cut may be all that is left for or of the author-speaker, who has already told us that she longs "to write undetected by lasers, exposed by the lasers, the floodlit pitch [...] sweep[ing] over the Cities". In this pathos-laden exposure of the destruction that sustains the politically fraught cityscape, Mendelssohn amplifies the terms of her critique of the metropolitan SI movement to ecosystems global and interdependent.

In the stanzas of "the fourteenth flight" that go by the wayside, Mendelssohn can be seen editing scenarios specific and overly generalised. From the draft included in the appendix, references to a mother, babies, Sheffield landforms, and lesbian sex are cut, as are platitudes such as "it was a fine revolution for some". And from the partial manuscript, stanza 12 is excised in full. It reads:

> in far off chalk climes you have written this, that has been told, reluctance to distinguish
> for every story is valid, but unions were banned, and cavil suspected, then public
> programmes are the order of the day. opinion. a pity files are changed from rule to rule.
> it wasn't all argument. but responsibility for keeping order ~~in~~ on the road to construction
> and personal criticisms best kept to oneself but oh how we missed our freedom
> it was a shock to learn that a body could be so afraid of moving, walls where there were none.
> doors where pedestrian crossings ^are all there is to^ remind you of Africa. sous les pavés c'est la plage
> shrinkage. the borders. the false reputations. country after country closed down.

This "you" may well implicate our speaker, distanced from self by space and the passage of time. Faced with political strife, there is an honest acknowledgement that "it wasn't all argument" even as lost freedom is lamented. In the 38- and 74-line variants of "two secs" Situationists "think in terms too large to use", but here the body and mind expansive, global in desire and thinking, find "walls where there were none", "shrinkage", and journeys between continents reduced to minor forms of egress: doorways, pedestrian crossings.[271] That this diminution is caused by political affiliation is indubitable; as yet, this is the only known instance in which Mendelssohn quotes the central SI maxim directly in her poetry.

Perhaps because too direct, this maxim is excised from "the fourteenth flight", even as Mendelssohn's critique of the SI remains discernible. The poem is dedicated to Jean-Luc Godard, the French film director who Mendelssohn met when she took part in his *British Sounds* (1969), a period in which Godard undertook expressly leftist projects. In the published text, part of stanza two reads:

> in watery grains why do they think of factories, collusion, and mysterious pockets of energy,
> inaccurate incongruity closes with power's temporal beat we meet: set pieces.
> set pieces you recognize as being the cultural organisations as yet unclarified & therefore unavailable
> it sounds, some spacious time voice and it lowers itself onto the boardwalk each dawn
> in all guises of backward movement it avoids the centralised spectre of an electrified rigid force

These lines recall the grainy footage of *British Sounds*, which depicts, in sustained turn, a factory, a middle-class home, a newscast, and a school lesson, or "set pieces" that signal institutional power and its manifestations. Opposition emerges through vagary, "cultural organisations as yet unclarified & therefore unavailable". "[U]navailable", this counter-force "sounds" via a spacious time voice, just as Godard's documentary projects its radicalism through an overlay of assured narrative voices. A "spacious time voice" is aurally proximate to a "specious time voice" and the inaccuracy of those "mysterious pockets of [resistant] energy" in the first line of this passage is similarly damning. So too do the incongruity and backward movement in the lines that follow deny progress. And the "electrified rigid force" is circumvented, rather than successfully budged from its central position. Retrospectively, the contrived sets of *British Sounds* prove conventional, arranged to maximise an ultimately ineffectual effect.[272] As "the fourteenth flight" moves to its conclusion, her speaker is psychologised, watched, judged by "the fidgeting tax payer". This amorphous "they" observes, proving unable to contain their remarks "upon how various paving stones seem to make me jump up and down / when s/he was being uniform and corporate and attuned i was thoroughly cradling a latent fervour". In manuscript, this "they" and "s/he" are a considerably more accusatory "you". Though this hopping madness teeters on the cartoonish, the allusion is legible: this speaker may be akin to *les enragés*, but the anger is directed as plentifully at the revolution as it is at its catalyst, not least because the revolution is more aligned with capital and the militaristic than it recognises. The "fervour" in need of protection is authorial; the politics are pressing, but secondary, even damaging. Or as Mendelssohn puts it in another manuscript poem intended for *viola tricolor*: "politics [...] halts ~~us~~ ~~you~~ fast."[273] First collective, next other directed, this maxim concludes with the universal, just as "the fourteenth flight" moves from an "I/you" dyad to an "I/they", from a line of trees to a clear cut, from a specific political movement to a questioning of political activism writ large. The minutiae of this genetic criticism speak to the magnitude of Mendelssohn's aesthetic and intellectual project. In part two of this section on her editorial practice, the focus turns to the protractedness of her labours, to the long, slow patience and attunement Mendelssohn applied to specific themes and poems.

(ii) "Silk & Wild Tulips"

"[W]hat is a mood? / a mood is something which goes away you say." What is a "MOODIST"? One who feels keenly "habits mean as pears" with a "heart felt flies / fire bird fired noses".[274] What is a repressed moodist? She "[w]ho keeps her face still being used to vigilant checks on her moods / In case of expression and other things that guardians of genius oppress". But there may always be "'a New' // mood / having lost a minute's dance / smoking a tune".[275] Drawn from work published over three decades, moods drug-induced, constrained, and regenerative filter through the poems of this collection, indicating Mendelssohn's turn and return to the question of the freedom to feel, her struggle to articulate emotion on the page. Another decade-long affective refrain: "I want to / be thinking and speaking in another language. I turn into a machine / in this language."; "she feels another language not this one / she is impressed. she wants to learn / these new inflections.".[276] Some Mendelssohn refrains last thirty years. Consider, from a poem published in 1997:

the misery I caused my old mother
for placidity was never her style
& the boyfriends I had she did eat
to make up for the food she had laid at my feet[277]

This stanza bears self-evident comparison to some lines Mendelssohn claims to have penned in 1968:

tell him he had no right to discuss mundanity with my mother.
tell him that she is the ministress of mundanity
who loves at the sign of the orange slice sandwich
tell him she stands in a pulpit each mealtime
itemising each bite and its cost. tell him she is
lost without a son-in-law to eat more miserably than To.   To. [278]

If Mendelssohn's assignation is accurate, this poem is among the earliest in her Sussex archive, as the vast majority of the collection is dated post-1976, the year she emerged from prison. It is found in one of Mendelssohn's notebooks in a section entitled "Old Poems". Though often slapdash, chaotic, or inscrutable, Mendelssohn's record-keeping is by turns replete and careful: she returned to notebooks and mined them for inspiration, including, as the first poem in this collection attests, her prison diaries; she drew repeatedly on the same poems with a view to republication.[279] And this strong sense of the trajectory of her work – this capacity to evaluate, rearticulate, and refine – is central to the gestation of one of her finest poems, "Silk & Wild Tulips" (1996; 2006). As discussed above, this poem houses thinly veiled references to Situationism, but its focus is Mendelssohn's involuted returns, over a period of two decades, to the trope of the tulip.

Within a coverless notebook that contains dates from January and February 1974, Mendelssohn writes:

drawn into acknowledgement
regret
human power
            prowess
ship of tresses.
not one allows
its own movement
parting rivers
Wild tulips
  become dream

the Same.
the One Place.
moving

visited by
gravitational pull
you're here!

This passage occupies page three of what appears to be a single entry.[280] It begins: "Cactus plants aren't everything / Remember THAT." A surreal paragraph follows, replete with "Blue sparks" that "spoke of night" and "a man in bandbox dress" delivering ice cream cones, each cone "bear[ing] a message for you". As so often in Mendelssohn's notebooks, prose and poetry shade into one another, and the next page includes four structured stanzas resolutely divided by horizontal lines. Phrases speak to an overriding sense of loss: "behind / Always."; "there is not much more: / Gritty."; "Pining / The nervous needles". These yearning, anxious moments of reflection presage the admission and companionate sorrow that defines the opening of the passage on the next page, quoted in full above. The bids for power and valour that follow "regret" feel causal; "prowess" is significantly misaligned, a fortitude gone awry.[281] The "ess" is semantic and homophonic, hence Mendelssohn moves fluidly in this rough scrap of verse from the manly, upright courage of "prowess" to the clinging, feminised ornamentation of "tresses"; from admirable, discrete acts of daring or expertise to a vehicle improbably constructed of sun rays, locks of hair, or long, leafy shoots and tendrils. A ship of tresses may beguile, but it also clings and lingers, anchored by its own design. A cumulative mass, it betokens no exception, yields no heroic Moses who can incite an enslaved population or part the clogged and obdurate waters, the Sea of Reeds. Out of this morass, "Wild tulips / become dream". This rebellious-cum-domestic flower is an oneiric release slightly askew on its line, a geotropic rupture of the stasis that is "the same" and "the One Place" where movement is downward, a brooding "gravitational pull". Is the speaker also a flower, roots taken, forcing herself skyward? Is Mendelssohn, held at Holloway Prison as she writes, recalling Coleridge's dictum: "No plot so narrow, be but Nature there"? The spontaneous conclusion: "you're here!" furthers these Coleridgean echoes, speaking to the "delight" that "Comes sudden on [the] heart" when, from a place of confinement, absence is imaginatively transposed to presence.[282]

Labelled wild, Mendelssohn's 1974 tulips contrarily signal a tranquil epiphany consistent with the tradition that flowers console.[283] Mendelssohn's subsequent rendering of a subject longing to become a tulip is considerably more fraught. In 1980, Mendelssohn illustrates, writes, produces, and dates a pamphlet entitled "where does peace lie?" which concludes by aligning the tulip with rages murderous and suicidal.[284] The pamphlet is credited to and stars a "Mendleson". Painstakingly conceived in Mendelssohn's hand and then photocopied, it includes drawings, charcoal sketches, dramatic scenes replete with stage directions, and a concluding narrative poem. The dialogues it contains culminate in an incantation of death upon silent tulips:

"Skipping ropes come from bones, Peregrine," that is what I
would say if I was rich. I would answer my servants very
patiently, and have intelligent conversations with all of them.
        Long coats horn.
"You're a schizophrenic barbarian and you need shooting,"
he said. And there was I getting ready to bloom into a tulip.
        So I walked round the park   I'd made up in my head
        and said to each tulip, "I wish you were dead."
        and said to each, "Tulip, I wish you were dead."

With fantasy privilege comes gothic knowledge: toys and luxuriant outerwear are forged from bones and horn, or ossified fragments of the living.[285] This Victorian drawing-room of verbal curiosities is violated by the reductive, threatening diagnosis of a male perpetrator. "Mendleson" he accuses of irrationality, lunacy; confirming the rumours, he labels her feral, rude outsider, a woman who should be cast out or purged. Who speaks? Is this Peregrine, upstart radical, prepared to decimate a member of the ruling classes? Ornithologically, peregrines embody martial prowess; as a traditional male name, Peregrine signifies a pilgrim, a traveller, a path-breaker – all viable, polyvalent ascriptions. Peregrine or no, "he" disrupts the fluidity of "Mendleson's" fantasy. Once his threat is uttered, she maintains access to her park, but cannot become a flower, is no Narcissus, Crocus, Orchis, or Paeon. Instead, she internalises the violence that menaces her, identifying to wreak destruction upon others, upon self as ideal, feminised floral other. But the destruction does not quite come to pass; these flowers are left intact. Rejecting both the assumption that women are natural nurturers attuned to the language of flowers and the threat of the male perpetrator alike, the speaker's anger is directed not at feminine ideals, but at the disruption caused by their realisation.[286]

At least five years later, Mendelssohn renounces this incantation, reinventing the female author as "the beautiful red tulip lady". Lacking title or date, there are two variants of this poem, one of which is dedicated to Mendelssohn's third child Emerald, born in 1985.[287] Red tulips were once given as a token of love, and that is what these poems seek to be: unlike the destructive impulses at work in "where does peace lie?" these two manuscripts insist on the divine ordinariness of the tulip.[288] Humbly unmonumental, this flower is a delicate, well-formed being bathed in purist water, air, and feeling:

a tulip generates no fear
although it may not build a kingdom
and neither is it set
in plaster for the mayhem
of tears that water despises
bathing without salty teardrops
that would choke a delicate red lady's

satin cool eyes of perfect pointed tips
A background of love and lovely clear air
repells any fear of unwanted intruders

Throughout, the motifs are discernibly Victorian: a secure, domesticated space is promised, with "[a] background of love and lovely clear air" (a line repeated with emphasis) in which to "gaz[e]", as the concluding line asserts, at the tulip lady's poem of an evening. In the second, shorter draft of the same, magisterial diction and antiquated register conspire to keep strong feeling at bay. It concludes: "on folding green's hither side a night time's ride / away from moon's tuneful cusp / the tulip in an emerald lake resides a stately brave flower". In these two drafts, the demand for aloofness, coupled with the rewards of sentimentality's proximity, even its saccharine stickiness, becomes untenable. The overriding fantasy is mawkish, and fails at the complexities of feeling, intellection, or circumstance.

"[A] tulip generates no fear" founders, but its preoccupations are spectacularly recalibrated in Mendelssohn's "Silk & Wild Tulips", as are many facets of her previous writings about tulips. In a manuscript variant of "Silk & Wild Tulips", a poem first published in 1995, Mendelssohn answers its central question – "o what is love?" – as follows: "to be closed in upon from a great distance".[289] In the finished poem, this answer becomes "the tip of a tongue, a silk white dove." The tongue's tip is unsentimentally intimate; the dove (no peregrines here) is the only overt claim to the titular silk, giving peace a resting place as presider over the poem. Love is thus delicately poised between bodily proximity and celestial remoteness. Stanza one reads:

Afraid of my father's power the object speaks country does it concurr
Entering this petrification, perforce the accident is indicative it is
A report, repeated pondering fall, a petition, a portrait I would not bear
A portrait of throated wires through blood
It is demanded of me that I die having neglected my duty.

Dread is expressly linked to patriarchy, which is perhaps why, in the past, the feminised "tulip generate[d] no fear" and was not a kingmaker. By extension, the speaking object becomes the voice of the marginalised, parroting a questionable nationalism. Where "the beautiful red tulip lady" was not "set / in plaster", this figure recognises that petrification paralyses and besets. Gravity continues to do the forceful work it has done since Mendelssohn's first known poetic mention of wild tulips in 1974. But in 1995, Mendelssohn places the culpable self at the centre of the lapsarian: this fall is considered, and is accompanied by supplication, is again, as it was in 1974, "drawn into acknowledgement / regret". This "I" is a personal, deeply flawed martyr, forced into a painfully self-conscious irresponsibility. Sacrificial language sounds its lamentable note through the poem that follows, so that love, too, "will not fight and is crushed by speculation, a sinful breast / Cleansed". Sin is owned, repented, and reignited again by "Provokation". Once an infectious, external threat, provocation now becomes part of an eminently human cycle, a "dead weight" that recurs alongside oppressions that this speaker angrily resists. And, "charr[ing] the air with shot speech", oppressive wars are everywhere underway: of gender, of class, of artist versus non-artist. Neither barbarian nor tulip lady, this speaker is a poet outsider, beyond "noble patriotic inclination", one among a number of theorists of war and peace whose "[t]heses are buried or placed on parole".

After its title, the poem mentions no tulips. The flowers that are referenced in "Silk & Wild Tulips" are a disorienting bouquet of intoxicants, purgatives, and romance, all associated with writing: lotuses, euphorbia, and, in the conclusion, red roses:

> Open'd by background loss, closed by measured step,
> Around the fountain the old men slept, the women deep in the heart of roses rouges foncés,
> And the chimney sweeps wept until they discerned that their tears had created ink
> To tell of squares of blue & finely pointed moons, silhouetted cats' upturned tails
> Catching at the lunatics they promised the coals would glow
> Memories of tail coats arranged around angel pie & a tankard of stiff pheasant feathers.

This turn conjures Blake's chimney sweeps and sweeping lines.[290] It is also Dickensian, evoking a Victorian novelistic urbanity locatable within "the covers of contentment" delineated in the previous lines, a contentment that Mendelssohn suggests will not assuage felt need. Along the way, we "progress through a sequence of tranquil passages" that Mendelssohn's speaker neither trusts nor dismisses; instead, she reminds us, as she will again in *Implacable Art*, that art does not follow the rules, that "a poem is not going to give precise directions".[291] The distinction made here is between popular and high art, one of Mendelssohn's chief preoccupations. Despite her aversion to summative, predictable narrative, the sentimental band of outcasts who appear at the end of "Silk & Wild Tulips" is given the final say: homeless men sleep soundly; starving young artists impart their vision to their uninterested, mentally unhinged audience. Contra Shelley, these artists believe that the coal of their creating minds will glow, not fade. And the women are the flowers of their age, inextricably embedded in "roses rouges foncés", satirically ornamented with continental cachet. The final line extends the women's luxuriant floral arrangement: tailcoats encircle a white meringue, petals to its inner whorl, and the tankard of stiff pheasant feathers has bud-like connotations. But the limitations of this rag-tag human bouquet are indicated by the line that prefaces this scene. Where, in the 1980s, "a tulip generates no fear" and possesses "a background of love" elevated to a "clear lovely background of love" by the end of the poem, the final scene of "Silk & Wild Tulips" is "[o]pen'd by background loss", a misfortune shared by succour-seeking reader and speaker alike. A poem beset by divisiveness concludes with a self-conscious, critical romanticism, facilitating a "measured step" that replaces the cloying or extreme scales of previous floral writings. Along the way, the poem is bestrewn by an unlikely host of flowers that signal the impossibility of communication. Impossible because innately ineffective; impossible when all too effective. These flowers announce an absent linguistic ideal, as absent as the tulips that govern the poem.[292] As in 1974, wild tulips become, and remain, dream; their pairing with the equally visionary silk white dove of peace is no accident.

Introduced to Europe via Turkey in the sixteenth century, tulips were admired for their unusually intense colour, and became coveted as an overpriced luxury item, catalysing the "Tulip Mania" of the Dutch Golden Age, as well as the metonymic use of "tulip" for a showy or admirable person. Wild tulips differ from domestic in that their petals tend to be open, sharply pointed, variegated; they are more overblown star than perfectly-rendered cup. Connoting untamed autonomy, the phrase "wild tulip" refutes this flower's history of commercial valuation, its groomed predictability. Where "tulip" suggests arrogance, wildflowers denote egalitarianism, freedom. And Mendelssohn is clearly keen to privilege the uncultivated flower: the title of her 1993 chapbook, *viola tricolor*, means wild pansy. Traditionally associated with compassion and grief, the pansy acquired its name from a bastardised French: "*pensez-à-moi*", think of me.[293] For Mendelssohn, the title refers to two women of literature, Viola of *Twelfth Night* and the stepmother of Theodor Storm's "Viola Tricolor" (1873), both lost figures muted by circumstance, but who, like silent flowers, persist in communicating.[294] Mendelssohn is untroubled by the feminised purity of flowers: for her, flowers are inviolate; girls and women can be immaculate, and language, too, has its inculpable strain, uncontaminated by the taint of aggression. In an undated prose extract, Mendelssohn writes: "I can only ask questions because they don't know anything positive and factual except for a few battles, ministers – the odd flower, a quote or two I DO understand".[295] Found blossoms, found quotes; both can be intrinsically understood, recorded, returned to over the decades. Cultivated from a scrawl in a prison-issue notebook to aggressive incantation and then overblown poem, in its final guise, "Silk & Wild Tulips" is perfectly poised between vulnerable self-reflexivity and the magisterial.

VI. Mendelssohn's Publication History

For over thirty years, Mendelssohn identified variously as anonymous, Anne Mendleson, Grace Lake, Grace Sylvia Louise Lake, Anna Mendelssohn, and, very occasionally, Boas Toas, c.n.e.m. b. h'k., grace lagg, allegro, or 'anna mendelssohn-kouchnerova.[296] This account does not take stock of her juvenilia in school newspapers. As a young adult, Mendelssohn contributed to *Frendz*, a London-based, counter-cultural monthly newspaper that covered political issues, among them, black power, the Gay Liberation Front, Northern Ireland, prison reform, the legalisation of marijuana, and affordable housing. The publication's distinctly 1970s aesthetic and ethos included satiric comics, advice on sexually transmitted disease, opinion pieces by men outraged by feminist politics, photographs of scantily-clad women, horoscopes, and interviews with Lou Reed and Steve Winwood. Edited by Jonathon Green and Alan Marcuson, the first issue appeared in November 1969; at the outset, the women accredited with managing the *Frendz* office, typing the copy, and rolling the joints are listed by first name only. *Frendz* published Angry Brigade communiqués and covered the trial of the Stoke Newington Eight in supportive and extensive detail, fund-raising on behalf of the defendants. Before her arrest in August 1971, Mendelssohn had taken part in the "Women's Issue" of *Frendz* along with Hilary Creek; "The female Brigade" is listed among the contributors.[297] Delineating sexism as only one of many repressions, the issue presents a conflicted view of feminism, offering articles on how best to obtain abortions alongside a scathing review of Shulamith Firestone's *The Dialectic of Sex*. Although uncredited, Mendelssohn's preoccupations are discernible: in coverage of the Notting Hill People's Association, a London neighbourhood in which she and Creek were active; plausibly in the feature on the recent bombing of Biba's fashion boutique by The Angry Brigade; and, less obviously, in an article on page six about Securicor and its uncontrolled guard dogs. Mendelssohn acknowledged her authorship of this latter article in her opening speech at her trial at the end of May/beginning of June 1972. That Mendelssohn spent time investigating the too-unilateral powers of private security firms was raised in court in relation to the other underground journal in which she published, *Strike*. At an organisational meeting for *Strike* in Liverpool in February 1971, Mendelssohn was apprehended by the police for possession of stolen cheque books; substantial notes on security companies were found in Mendelssohn's belongings. Mendelssohn testified that *Strike* was envisioned as "a national newspaper" that would facilitate communication between community groups and tenants' associations, adding: "I thought of the name Strike because it was sort of lively."[298] The cover of the only extant issue – issue zero (pictured right) – is a collage to which Mendelssohn implicitly laid claim, whilst openly stating that she contributed to a page of *Strike* titled "Unions at Work" after attending a meeting of female night workers attempting to organise a Cleaners' Action Group. The article begins: "Most women do not belong to Unions and where they do the Unions dont [*sic*] give a fuck about their fights for higher wages, against sackings, and for better working conditions." Under the auspices of "Moss Side Press", this

issue of *Strike* was formatted in the *Frendz* office; barring a reference to members of "the movement", no contributors are directly named, and the contact address is an agitprop theatre group on North Gower Street, London.[299]

The women's issue of *Frendz* devoted two full pages to coverage of the undue control of the women prisoners of HM Prison Holloway, an abuse worsened, the journal claimed, in the wake of its recent modernisation.[300] One year later, on 26 May 1972, Mendelssohn appears to have contributed to the last issue of *Frendz* as a prisoner of that same institution. An anonymous article, "Holloway From the Inside Out", is an exposé of the over-prescription of tranquillisers and sedatives to female prisoners. As in the women's issue, there is a notice from a group called Radical Alternatives to Prison (RAP) proposing the establishment of a Prisoners' Liberation Front. Directing themselves toward "liberal and well-thinking people", RAP aims to address, for instance, "campaigns in the media about the rebuilding of Holloway". Next to this call for action is a poem signed by one "Anna. April. 8 months on remand." It reads:

A POEM

We imagined
and now we want it.
We imagined
Not to know fear
When people could move.
We imagined touching
As the stars and sky touch
We imagined loving
That would bear no description.

In April 1972, Mendelssohn had been in Holloway for precisely eight months. Mendelssohn continued using the word "poem" in her titles: consider *poems*, the text she co-authored with Timothy Mathews in 1984, or *py.* (2009), a condensing of "poetry", or the posthumously published "POEM." (*No Prizes*, 2012). "Imagination" and its variants, as well as sky, touch, and love are words that recur with regularity through her *oeuvre*. Given that Mendelssohn was writing poems before and during her time in prison, this piece is almost irrefutably hers. That said, where her part in the publication of *Strike* is acknowledged in an author biography published in 1986 with the journal *constant red/mingled damask* – "*Published co-operatively one edition of a national newspaper STRIKE in 1970*" – her writing of "articles for the long defunct West London 'Frendz' magazine" is an affiliation noted, but then elided. Furthermore, Mendelssohn mentions articles, not poetry. As yet, no references to this poem have surfaced in Mendelssohn's archive.

Mendelssohn's biographical entries are notable for their emphases, their omissions, and their errors, as in the misidentification of the *Strike* publication date above.[301] None contain a replete list of Mendelssohn's publications; with comic and typical contrariness, *constant red/mingled damask* (1986) makes extended mention of a publication that did not occur. In this author biography, Mendelssohn suggests that she had a volume ready for publication with Common Ground Printing Co-operative that she withdrew "*following disputation over the license of printers to censor [....] Difficulty ensues between those who write/read poetry and those who, whilst maintaining control over printing machinery, do not.*" For Mendelssohn, self-description is nearly always inextricable from defining boundaries, staking ground. Publication signified a pinning down of material, a finality with which she was often at odds. In a 1987 portion of her *roman-à-clef*, she writes: "Had I not had responsibility for three children, I should not have been anxious to publish anything. I am still not convinced that I am a poet."[302] Taking against publishers seems to have been one outcome of this reticence. Hence she publishes with Virago in 1990 and 1991, then writes an anti-Virago poem in 2000.[303] Hence she contributes to Maggie O'Sullivan's *Out of Everywhere: Linguistically Innovative Poetry by Women in North America & the UK* (1996), but embeds a critique of the parameters of that anthology in a poem written that same year: "A shedding though of self-inculpation. [....] The madames who don't get what they want / Out of everyone."[304] Hence her instructions to the publishers of *Implacable Art* are dogmatic and demanding: Mendelssohn demanded the removal of a publisher's logo of a lightning bolt – considered too fascist – and insisted that the word "Salt" not appear on the cover because salt "is used to Kosher meat before it is cooked – & I am not a meaty writer – [...] I don't write into the living meat – I do not practice Cannibalism".[305] As emphatic as it is inscrutable, this resistance is still more baffling when we consider Mendelssohn's willingness to publish in the journal *Salt* four years prior. But she was unwavering, and the publisher's attribution for *Implacable Art* remains Equipage and Folio, even as Salt publishers produced the text. Having produced half a dozen publications for Mendelssohn, Rod Mengham, the founder of Equipage press, surely deserved her trust; the Mendelssohn reader's debt to Mengham is immense. Yet just as the 2004 anthology *Vanishing Points* was going to press, Mendelssohn sent the following to Mengham and co-editor John Kinsella: "Formal permission is granted to publish what the editors consider worth publishing on the sole condition that not one line (I am tempted to add 'word') is taken and used for Any other purpose."[306] This stern injunction is half self-deprecating concession to the expertise of her poet-editors, half suspicious, pre-emptive rebuke. On the strength of her poems, Mendelssohn's idiosyncrasies were patiently accommodated. For Iain Sinclair's 1996 anthology, *Conductors of Chaos*, Mendelssohn's somewhat standard author biography about background, education, and past publications is suddenly disrupted by the following:

> Grace Lake writes: 'My academic career was brought to an abrupt halt in 1967 by harassment, both political and emotional. Upon returning to this country, in 1970, I was attacked, my own poetry seized, and my person threatened with strangulation if I dared utter one word of public criticism. I was unable to return to university at that point and was silenced.'[307]

Resisting the formulaic assertion of one's artistic credibility, Mendelssohn turns the contributor's note into a diatribe, a demand that her poetry be read free from the scruples of past judgements that paradoxically re-inscribes, even as it realigns, her place in that very past. As in *constant red/mingled damask*, Mendelssohn uses the author biography as a platform to counter perceived attempts – historical, anticipated – to curtail her liberty as author, individual, activist.

In addition to providing a generative account of Mendelssohn's circumstances, authorship, and self-fashioning, these biographies raise the spectre of incompletion to which this collection inevitably falls prey. Mendelssohn identifies publications yet to be located, a list that includes Common Ground, the Working Class Women's Publishing House, Writing Round an Ideal World Press, and Bone Dry.[308] Consistent with her vanguard allegiances, Mendelssohn published with ephemeral journals, among them Tony Lopez's *The News* (1987), which ran for a single issue. Into this fleeting category might fall D. S. Marriott's *Archeus* (one very productive year, 1989; six issues) or *Active in Airtime*, which was co-edited for three years by Ralph Hawkins, John Muckle, and Ben Raworth, who produced four issues. She was also generous to new, untried publications, among them, the Cambridge student ventures *Slate* (1985–87; three issues) and *involution* (1993–97; five issues). With the relative obscurity of these publications in view, it is near-inconceivable that this collection contains each and every one of her published poems. The record of Mendelssohn's published visual art is also no doubt incomplete. Her artwork graces the cover of many of her own texts, among them, *La Facciata* (1988) and the draft copy of *café archéologique* (1992–93), as well as *viola tricolor* (1993), *Bernache Nonnette* (1995), *Tondo Aquatique* (1997), and *py.* (2009). Many of her publications intersperse drawings with poetry, as in *Is this a True Parrot, a Mountain, or a Stooge?* (1985), *Implacable Art* (2000), and *py.* (2009). Her art sits next to her writing in small journals: three collages are part of her first entry to *constant red/mingled damask* in 1986 (one featured on this volume's cover); one drawing accompanies the second in 1987. Mendelssohn's submission to *Figs* (no. 14, 1988) includes poems published from four to six years previous, illustrations from *Is this a True Parrot?* and an unsigned drawing entitled "A Lizard Tumbril" dated 1979. Ulli Freer kindly verified that this drawing was Mendelssohn's; less certain are Mendelssohn's drawings for D. S. Marriott's *Archeus* (1989), where the cover of issue five, which includes her poetry, appears to be her illustration, but goes undated and unsigned. By contrast, issue two contains none of her poetry, but its cover drawing is accredited to her. Similarly, Mendelssohn provided the front image for numbers 9/10 of *Talus* magazine in 1997 (see below), a poetry journal run out of King's College London that was founded by the Norwegian poet Hanne Bramness (among others) and included Jerome Rothenberg on the advisory board. More published drawings are likely to surface.

Adding to editorial complications are the stark inconsistencies of Mendelssohn's publication venues. Many of her choices are obvious. Drew Milne's *Parataxis* was as devoted to "the legacies of modernism" as Mendelssohn herself (Milne 1991, no. 1, 3); so too does Rod Mengham insist that *Vanishing Points* is a late modernist collection that prioritises antagonism and linguistic experiment. And although Mendelssohn was to lose faith in Iain Sinclair because he discussed her affiliation with The Angry Brigade in *Lights Out for the Territory* (1997), the ethos of his *Conductors of Chaos* anthology is wholly commensurate with Mendelssohn's aesthetics: Sinclair's acerbic introduction condemns the marketization of writing, and places his contributors' work within the lineage of the contested category, the British Poetry Revival. Like Sinclair, Mendelssohn defends and enacts poetic difficulty. Finally, Douglas Oliver and Alice Notley's introductory "SALUTE [to] all those who serve experimental poetry and prose" is explanation enough for Mendelssohn's keenness to be published in the first issue of *Gare du Nord* in 1997, although, as discussed in the editorial notes, she endearingly dissembles that the catalyst was her love of railway stations. And, consistent with her use of the term "poetess" and her lifelong defence of the woman writer, Mendelssohn does not shy away from publishing in two all-female publications, even as Wendy

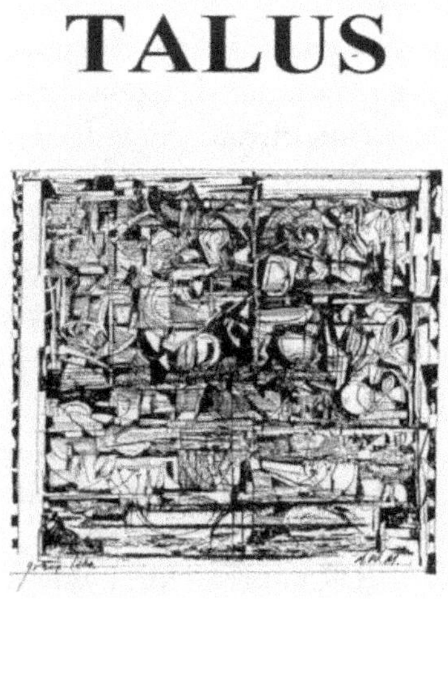

Mulford's introduction to *The Virago Book of Love Poetry* argues that some authors – among them, Laura Riding, who Mendelssohn admired – declined the invitation on this basis.[309] In this same spirit, evidence suggests that Mendelssohn contemplated submitting to the *Feminist Review* in 1984, although she does not appear in any issue of that periodical, which ran from 1979 to 2009.[310]

In 1984, Mendelssohn was predominantly working on independently-published pamphlets with small print runs, most of which she gave to friends, even as many – albeit not a reassuring all – were deposited in the Cambridge University Library and the British Library for posterity.[311] But as her planned submission to the *Feminist Review* suggests, this may have been a year when she began thinking about broadening her audience. In 1984 she published *poems* with Tim Mathews, a pamphlet they sold in Heffers Bookshop in Cambridge. In that same year, Mendelssohn submitted a poem to *Other Poetry*. Founded in 1978, editor Anne Stevenson defines the journal's ecumenical mandate by negation in her foreword to issue one: it will exclude poets defined as avant-garde, academic, political, confessional, or "anything else currently fashionable". Perhaps more compellingly for Mendelssohn, Stevenson seeks poets who perceive poetry "as a natural but major extension of awareness at a time in which poetry is too often regarded as an elitist privilege or a panacea for psychological ailments." Most contributors remain little-known, although Michael Horovitz, editor of the seminal poetry anthology, *Children of Albion* (1969), makes an appearance in issue four. As evidence of the kind of verse *Other Poetry* publishes, consider the conclusion of a prize-winning poem of an in-house competition:

> I tucked your second-best bra
> In over the radiator
>
> so that hurrying to dress
> you might almost feel me press
> a warm hand around each breast.[312]

This is what Dada artist Hannah Höch aptly calls "ostrich art", meaning creativity that "wants to convey the impression that all is well with the world, that it has been humanised, rationalised."[313] Included in this collection, Mendelssohn's submission to *Other Poetry* is wholly antithetical to this contented closure: instead, it is an unsettling tribute to accusation, condemnation, and disjunction, interspersed with details domestic and pastoral; critiques of media and capital are just discernible within its choppy machinations. Mendelssohn's work appears nowhere in the pages of *Other Poetry*. But this is not to say that her writing did not appeal to publishers of verse more mainstream, even anodyne. By far the oddest Mendelssohn publication is the sonnet she submits to an annual anthology of the International Library of Poetry based in Sittingbourne, Kent. These monumental collections first emerged in the late 1990s, bearing saccharine titles such as *Quiet Moments*. Mendelssohn's "Uncertain though within this deepset heart" appears in *Jewels of the Imagination* (1997). By way of introduction, editor Maria Hourihan offers a blithe Horatian paraphrase, arguing that all 3,500 poems the volume contains "channel [...] imaginative powers to create works that entertain, delight, and often inform". In fact, the text seems cohered solely by the will to submit a short poem. Although primarily British, contributions are sent from around the world: Singapore, Palestine, Kuwait, Malta. While Mendelssohn deigns to include an author biography, most don't; all are encouraged to give their date and place of birth, occupation, number of children, and a personal statement. Typical examples include John Marshall, who "on retirement took up oil painting and later started to write Limericks on topical subjects for friends" or Miss Anna Packham, for whom "poetry is like a river because it flows from the heart expressing deep emotion and meaning." Mendelssohn's archive includes a photocopied proof copy of her submission, upon which is written Hourihan's enthusiastic assessment: "Wonderful verse!" Hourihan is not wrong, but Mendelssohn's exquisitely combative, yearningly bathetic phrases – "the sense loud that hurts by confecting enemies"; "weak by naive ardour"; "In this dim and rise a coronet of newfound hazel nuts" – are distinctly out of place in the collection, as she incontrovertibly knew. An undated, partial portion of a letter to Mendelssohn's eldest daughter may pertain to *Jewels of the Imagination*: "I am thinking about entering myself into the Writers & Artists Yearbook except that it defies the nature of poesis (the Greek word for poetry) & will turn me into a press agent which I am not."[314] Yet submit to one such anthology she does.

Though her choices and motivations can mystify, there is absolutely no doubt that Mendelssohn was ambitious and wanted her work in the world. Her conversations with publishers Methuen, Bloodaxe, Burning Deck, Shearsman, and Reality Street were mentioned in the biography at the outset of this introduction. Writers who defined her generation rated and requested her work, among them, Carolyn Bergvall, Andrew Duncan, Anthony Mellors, Lawrence Upton, and Iain Sinclair.[315] Further plans for publication are evident in correspondence that suggests that Mendelssohn hoped to send *Parasol One. Parasol Two. Parasol Avenue.* (1996) to California-based Sun & Moon Press, a renowned publisher of experimental authors, among them, Gertrude Stein and Paul Celan.[316] Similarly ambitious was Mendelssohn's desire to translate Prassinos's 1958 novel, *Le temps n'est rien*. For this undertaking, she sought permission from Calder Publications, and planned to secure funding from the French Cultural Delegation at Cambridge.[317] Mendelssohn believed herself "very literal & diligent in the task" of translation, and alongside Prassinos and Nâzim Hikmet, may have aspired to translate the Russian modernist poet Anna Ahkmatova, who is referenced in *Implacable Art* (2000).[318] Further, Mendelssohn sought assistance with self-promotion: she wrote Geoffrey Gilbert, then a tutor at Cambridge, to ask him to facilitate her 1996 publication with *Critical Quarterly*; following the publication of *Tondo Aquatique*, Mendelssohn discusses publishing work with former Essex associate Nicholas Johnson in his then-fledgling, New York-based journal, *Big City Lit*.[319] In 1993, she approached Rod Mengham about an Arts Council grant just as applications came due.[320] Minus one of the requisite number of publications, she hastily published – with Mengham's ever-patient responsiveness – *The Day the Music Died* in a 24-hour period. A weak text running to a grand total of five copies, Mendelssohn nevertheless placed it in two legal deposit libraries. Mendelssohn resists the term "pamphlet" in the list of past publications included with *Implacable Art* (2000); in a letter to Mengham dated 7 March 2000, Mendelssohn asserts that her short Equipage collections "are books to me". Mendelssohn's view of self-promotion changed over time: for *Inbuilt Flash Nix* (1985), she photographed herself in a mirror; come *Implacable Art* (2000), she tersely declines an invitation for an author image: "don't want to pose/& don't want one."[321] As she deliberated authorial presentation, so too titles: *Spinsters and Mistresses of Art.* (c. 1991–93) had at least four monikers, among them, *Spinster of Arts: A Space Odyssey* and *Spinster of Arts: An Anthropologia*; *viola tricolor* (1993) may have been "viola tripoli" or "Titania Mallet"; two complete fair copies of *Bernache Nonnette* (1995) are called *Mendleson's Metronome*.[322] Presentation is an abiding concern, a truth unsurprising for a visual, verbal, musical artist who assiduously curated her legacy.

Mendelssohn's devotion to that legacy extended to careful selection of poems for republication, poems chosen from the thousands that she wrote in her lifetime. Among the most published are "Whirr slightly operationless."; the poem beginning "yes, it is a shame, a real shame"; "Winter."; "La Facciata"; "1526"; "on challenge, positive attitudes and 'les peintures cubistes'"; "Ordered into Quarantine"; the poem beginning "She Walked where she should have stood still, stock still." and "Silk & Wild Tulips". Each appeared in print three or four times, and this repetition is suggestive, particularly given that many began life as part of single-authored texts, often with identifiable consistencies of theme, style, and tone.[323] Yet Mendelssohn clearly perceives these poems as moveable feasts that can embrace new contexts or be juxtaposed with work written at different times, indicating a certainty about their timeliness or timelessness. These decisions are assuredly editorial: Mendelssohn purposely cuts "'unknit that'" and "antiphony" or "antiphon" from the proofs of *Parasol One. Parasol Two. Parasol Avenue.* (1996) and publishes them instead in *Critical Quarterly* and again in *Salt* (both 1996); a decision is similarly made to include "Dyr bul shchyl" in *Parasol One.* and *Critical Quarterly*, but not *Salt.* In the drafting stage, Mendelssohn occasionally collates, under the same title or cover page, three or four versions of the same collection; in the absence of legal deposit texts, discerning the most authoritative edition is a work of never-certain editorial sleuthing.[324] Her pamphlets or books frequently gestate as wholes later divided into separate, but ultimately replete, parts; these texts are so phenomenally intertwined in her drafts, files, shared references and/or binding that they can appear inextricable. *Crystal Love: D. N. A.* and *Posmos, the Yellow Velvet Underground.* (both 1982) emerge as two distinct texts published in a single volume; similarly, *"I'm working here."* is contained within the same volume as *Celestial Empire.* (February 1983). Poems from *Posmos* resurface in *Is this a True Parrot, a Mountain, or a Stooge?*, a text that Mendelssohn treated interchangeably with *Inbuilt Flash Nix* throughout the drafting process; both are published in 1985. The titular figures of *viola tricolor* (1993) and *Bernache Nonnette* (1995) return in the opening lines of *Parasol One* (1996):

> Bernache reclined upon her startling blue aeroflot indice.
> the union had been saved within hours by Viola in a
> single footed close shave. Turning towards the nether,
> V. peeled away her face furniture with a suitably pained
> upper crust grimace. "Listen B.N. – their voices are
> pale from distance. Here – use this...... [325]

Use this; use this again and again: Mendelssohn is an inveterate recycler of her work. Mendelssohn's 1981 Sheffield typescript contains poems that will be published again in 1983, 1985, and 1986; her *Figs* entry of 1988 includes poems published in three collections dated 1982 and 1985. One last example: "Europa" first appears in Mendelssohn's draft collection *Spinsters and Mistresses of Art.* (c. 1991–93) as a poem of 52 lines; under the same title, the first twenty will resurface in Mendelssohn's *Implacable Art* (2000). These lines remain identical nearly a decade on. Over long stretches of time, amongst the apparent disorganisation and incontrovertible enormity of her published and unpublished *oeuvre*, Mendelssohn pays close, considered attention to specific poems and sequences.

Formatting, production, and copyrighting are similarly important. "Xerox it!" writes Mendelssohn in 1995, an exemplary exclamation: when Mendelssohn reduces A4 drafts into A5 formats on a photocopier, it is a clear indicator that she is readying work for a chapbook.[326] On occasion, this process is a rationale for including work in this collection, as in the poem beginning "rolling, and all these words are alive and". Dated June 1985, the poem resides in a file containing a scrap from Mendelssohn's prose text, *What a Performance* (1987).[327] File contents frequently mislead, and the poem's intended affiliations remain unclear. More convincing proof of Mendelssohn's desire to publish "rolling" is that she has hand-drawn an A5-sized box around the entirety and photocopied it; three manuscripts have also been located of the same.[328] Similarly, "WHY" and "Dear chaos." (1985) are photocopied and downsized from A4 to A5, and there exists a second photocopy of "WHY" that is deliberately disrupted by a photograph of Mendelssohn (see opposite). This play with images, manuscripts, and formatted photocopies recurs. For *Propaganda Multi-Billion Bun.* (August 1985), Mendelssohn toys with shrinking the pages, then decides to publish the entirety in an A4 format regardless. The unpublished *café archéologique* (1992–93) is exemplary in this regard: Mendelssohn devised its cover, edited it thoroughly, claimed copyright, and reduced the A4 originals into an A5 pamphlet size on bright yellow paper. A visual artist, Mendelssohn is keenly engaged in textual design, and up to and including *py.* (2009), she incorporates her own (often beautiful) hand into the entirety, so that the physical, haptic writing process becomes part of the aesthetic.[329] And, particularly through the 1980s, Mendelssohn is an inveterate self-publisher, using press names that are likely contrived, and certainly unlocatable, as in the Green Suede Blues Press – perhaps a counter to the British poet Barry MacSweeney's Blacksuede Boot press – identified in *Crystal Love: D. N. A., Posmos, the Yellow Velvet Underground.* (1982) and *"I'm working here."* (February 1983). Or Mendelssohn bypasses publishing attributions altogether, as in the pleasingly pink pamphlet *An ACCOUNT of a MUMMY, in The Royal Cabinet of Antiquities at Dresden* (1986). Borrowing its design from Enlightenment-era title pages, the production

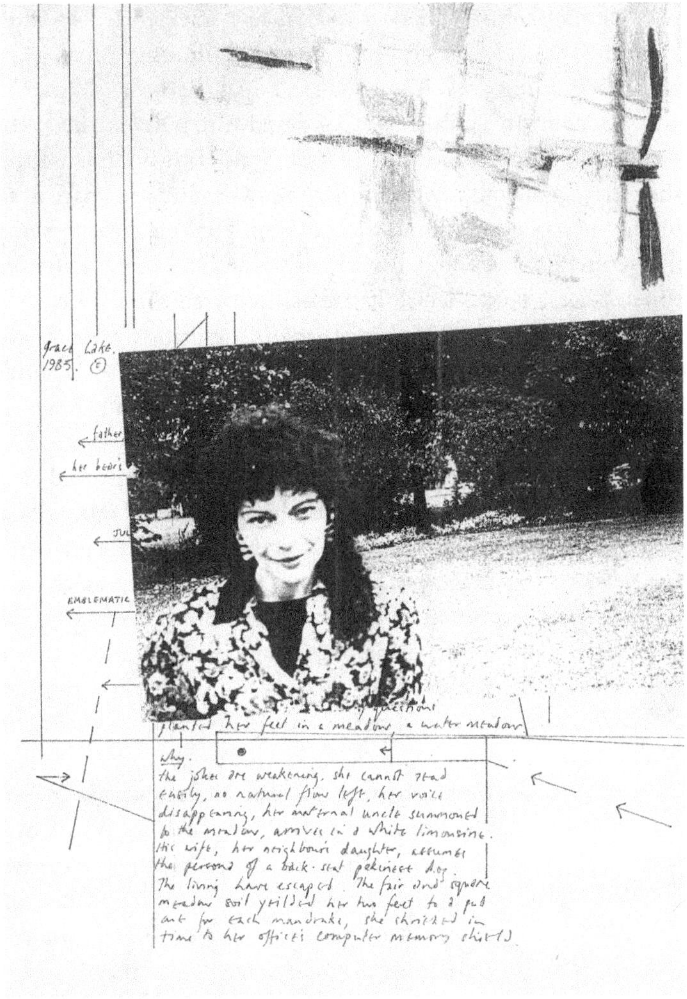

of this stapled A5 tract is attributed to "Grace Lake" and deposited at the British Library. Mendelssohn evidently enjoyed compiling her collections. Consider the back cover of *"I'm working here."* (February 1983), which ripostes: "You don't seem to be." Or the multiple, comic covers of *Propaganda Multi-Billion Bun.* (August 1985) that feature "Grace Lake and her liberated mechanical dog." or a drawing of a clock followed by "GRACE LAKE [...] and the dancing ticks." Less ludic is Mendelssohn's fidelity to "©", a symbol that precedes her name and the date on countless poems included in this collection, becoming yet another gauge of her seriousness about specific writings. For an author so expressly anxious about the workings of the law, her faith in it as a form of artistic protection was resolute through all three of the decades in which she most actively published her work.

How then, to think about the collections Mendelssohn produced? This is writing that defies ready categorisation by design, and there are years of scholarship to come on the complexities of Mendelssohn's work and thinking. Barring the 1972 poem in *Frendz*, Mendelssohn's is a deferred publication trajectory that begins in earnest in 1981 and 1982, when she is in her early thirties and living in Sheffield. Of the typescript poems she produced in this two-year period, most percolate through her collections from the 1980s; the final destination of others remains unknown. This work is characterised by buoyant bravado and carnivalesquerie, and occasionally embraces a bathos over which Mendelssohn wields little control, as in the end of "Pedal" (1981–82), with its "apanting" and "kind, puppy dog love".[330] Damp squibs surface, as in the poem that reads in its entirety: "why head aching? / blinding, blinding / why heart hurting? / minding minding".[331] But the entirety is not without ambition or overt experimentation, as in "Masquerade", where Mendelssohn articulates music, a motif returned to less successfully in "classique".[332] Come *Crystal Love: D. N. A.* (1982), the writing strengthens, as evinced by the conclusion of "Power to move", which reads: "Mighty portion of the land / My night is pouring gold." The tone is often contemplative. Consider lines such as: "maybe I shall / and the backward slide reintegrates" or "make play forget imaginable consolation / consolidation / the rumour pries / do i?"[333] Here, too, Mendelssohn's preoccupation with imperialism is discernible. In *"I'm working here."* (1983) she hones her satiric impulses, as when the speaker is "enjoying Margaret's / tight skirt, rubbing my knees / with energetic decency". This praise of propriety and station (can any British author's Margaret be separable from Thatcher in 1983?) concludes with a "flip[ped]" finger to a medley of figures, among them saints, unknown women, and "big Jesus". [334] Also in this collection, "proscribble at 16.12 hours." unearths what will become Mendelssohn's entrenched practices of archaic turns of phrase, neologism, and density. Still more akin to the later work is "Giaconda's Contumacious Lapse" in *Celestial Empire.* (February 1983). *Gioconda* is both opera and 1899 text by the celebrated, controversial Italian decadent Gabriel D'Annunzio. In addition to embracing the post-1850 modernist legacy, Mendelssohn develops her columnar form, interspersing past and present, depth and artifice, unbridled pleasure and complexity, gesturing to Tolstoy, Shelley, Auden, and the "hoi polloi" as she moves through a poem that dismisses melancholy inciting: "then strike poetry is poetry".[335] In this same book draft, "<u>UNFINISHED</u>" and "<u>SACRED PIN</u>." evince concerns and forms central to the work to come. By contrast, the volume Mendelssohn co-authors with Mathews in 1984, *poems*, is weakened by nostalgic leanings, but has some finer moments where art and life intersect, as in " 'The bourgeoisie lives there' ", the ekphrastic exploration of "To PP158, 159, 160, 170 MoMA Sol Lewitt." or the final poem of the collection, a numbered itinerary of domesticity, revolutionary turns, and dreamscapes. *Propaganda Multi-Billion Bun.* (August 1985) returns to the site of the political, considering capital, education, the welfare state, feminist tracts, female writers, and Anne Devlin (1780–1851), who worked for Irish rebel leader Robert Emmet and was brutally tortured in prison, yet refused to become an informant. In the same incredibly productive year, Mendelssohn publishes *Inbuilt Flash Nix* (1985), a book of prose and poetry preoccupied with dialogue and voice, and the wonderfully titled *Is this a True Parrot, a Mountain, or a Stooge?*, a text that brilliantly holds aloft satire, whimsy, and experimental form.

This levity will diminish come *Spinsters and Mistresses of Art.* (c. 1991–93), the collection that marks a shift in Mendelssohn's authorial preoccupations. Here Mendelssohn turns, repeatedly, to tropes of the outsider and the martyr; artistic vocation, once comically asserted (as in the blatantly self-evident title *"I'm working here."*) is now a servitude that requires justification, loudly-voiced principles, a self-conscious combination of asceticism and aestheticism. The pride in this endeavour remains, as does the skill. Consider the last two lines of the achingly gorgeous "i. m. Laura Riding": "once the essentials are proven and normalities intergraved / it will not be mine to decide who are the damned and who the saved."[336] The modernist references of *Spinsters* (and perhaps particularly the first poem of Mendelssohn's *Parataxis* entry, which is cited as part of that collection) carry over to *café archéologique* (1992–93). In addition to discussing art and revolution, Mendelssohn gestures to a modernist trajectory that includes Thomas Hardy, Kiki de Montparnasse, and surrealism. Mendelssohn described *viola tricolor* (1993) as "a retrospect on the absurdity I personally experienced in being enforced to depart from Literature by social & political pressure groups".[337] What emerges is a dense text intensively engaged with the complications of leftist politics, as discussed above regarding "the fourteenth flight" and "two secs." Losing nothing of that density, *Bernache Nonnette* (1995) is fascinated with juxtapositions of the modern and the ancient. Full of cultural allusions, the affect of this text is more positive than that of *viola tricolor*. Glimmerings of Mendelssohn's playfulness resurface, as does the complex, masterful artistry of "Silk & Wild Tulips". Combined with scabrousness and outrage, playfulness will come to the fore again in *Parasol One. Parasol Two. Parasol Avenue.* (1996), where Mendelssohn generates knowingly false urgencies ("……Oh I really must."; "There's always an actress to dramatize an unnecessary act.") and mocks the role of the writer, producing questions, witticisms, and contrived bemusement, as in the arch iteration: "No Wonder!"[338] Mendelssohn's long, ultimately unpublished *Inscape* submission of 1998 is a meditation on twentieth-century Jewish culture interspersed with references to the Spanish Civil War and World War II. That her Jewish heritage becomes increasingly important in Mendelssohn's old age is a supposition sustained by similar attentiveness in *Implacable Art* (2000) and Mendelssohn's submission to *Vanishing Points* (2004). *Tondo Aquatique* (1997) sheds some of the density of *viola tricolor* and *Bernache Nonnette*, and is marked by a raw, contemplative honesty, as in the compelling sonnet beginning "I am become my enemy whom I could not please" or the unutterably cruel, painful "Abschied". Mendelssohn once described the collection as an "evocation of an aetherial water ballet and the developments in language – the English language particularly which my relation to is primarily of poetic line".[339] Among Mendelssohn's strongest collections, *Tondo Aquatique* is, ironically, beset by fears of inadequacy and exclusion.

Mendelssohn's best-known work is the 136-page *Implacable Art* (2000), a sprawling, often fierce text interspersed with Mendelssohn's pen and ink drawings, largely figurative. The poems it contains return to established Mendelssohn styles, forms, concerns, and themes: the density of *viola tricolor* and *Bernache Nonnette*; poems columned, gridded, inscribed by hand; the wittily-demarcated female poet protagonist (see "minnie most beats up thérèse torchée");

the modernist homages so prevalent in *café archéologique* (Mandelstam, Chekhov, and Woolf are among the many allusions); the plight of the feminist writer, of contemporary womankind and Jews; the law and politics and their relation to language; the occasional screed, the yielding to a raw, angry affect so characteristic of her post-1990 work. A lack of titles, or titles in odd places (see the poem beginning "geo Alkan jeo, toppled on"), means readers often note that they cannot discern where a poem begins or ends; Mendelssohn includes a thorough "Table" that remains the only guide, but it is situated, tellingly, at the back of the book. Odes mark this collection: to writers, to readers, to Lorca, a surrealist poet also martyred by politics. Seventeen poems from *Implacable Art* are included in this volume; as it is published, Mendelssohn is undertaking translations of Prassinos's short, surrealist poems.[340] Prassinos's style may have influenced *py. : a book of acrostics for p.e.g.* (2009), Mendelssohn's final publication. A set of acrostics on "poetry" and "poésie", *py.* returns to the levity Mendelssohn exhibited in the mid-1980s, so that a poem beginning "podcast variation" ends with the line: "yelve in hand for rapid construction". A garden fork used to remove dung, the yelve is a resolutely obsolete term that Mendelssohn juxtaposes against an emergent form of digital communication. Her lifelong wariness of computer technology surfaces here as a short, sharp satire on the value of information disseminated on the internet. In general, *py.* critiques conspicuous consumption and its relationship to culture writ large, particularly ancient artefacts. An individual is "personally weighted in sterling pounds / ordinarily saved for potatoes" and other groceries, with which: "york minster's stained glass could not compete".[341] A poem critiques "the / establishment" by way of the UK Office for Standards in Education, which, by Mendelssohn's rendering, refuses to discuss the use of the popular Mancunian fizzy drink, Tizer, to conduct scientific, possibly preservative, experiments on a rhinoceros tusk.[342] In sum, a broad cultural net is cast in *py.*, one incorporating the yeshiva and Hebrew diacritics; Yggdrasil of Norse mythology; Ermintrude, Queen of the Franks in ninth-century Orléans; an Ivanovitch, possibly of sixteenth-century Russia; as well as thinktanks, punk, yoyos, pillbox hats, and Easter eggs. Cast wide, this net draws close, keeping the personal at bay whilst resounding with humour learned and warm, even a bit hot under the collar. *[P]y.* is published as Mendelssohn comes to the end of her life. Her very last collection remained in a nascent state, composed as she lay dying in Hinton Grange Care Home in Cambridge with a brain tumour at the relatively young age of 61. Many of these poems are typed up at Mendelssohn's request by her eldest daughter, even as others remain illegible because Mendelssohn's authoritative, controlled hand became increasingly shaky as her illness accelerated. Allusions resonate throughout these last works, and typical motifs and forms recur: the macaronic, the interrogative, battles to demarcate the (often poetic) self and its limitations; opposition to male-dominated poetic communities; the fear of predation; the pastoral turn to the world of nature – its flowers and birds – as a salve to all that ails. As in Mendelssohn's writings of the early 1980s, these poems can be vulnerable, unabashedly sentimental; one partial draft describes the need of another as a lunacy "as mad as cotton in snow, / as mad as / corny songs / with wind blowing".[343]

VII. A Last Perambulation

In 1981, or roughly midway through her life, Mendelssohn asks in a poem:

> to where do persons' spirits go
> when they are given each a cup of coffee
>   & invited to retire
>   into their rooms
> away from the thoroughfare
>   of friendships? [344]

Though Mendelssohn's thoroughfare of friendships was always well-populated, *Poems Written at Hinton Grange Care Home* speaks to this experience of requisite seclusion, the presiding of spirit over body. An unanswerable, near-unbearable poignancy runs through this necessarily brief collection. These poems are the work of a consummate creator and restless, unceasing mind. Facing death, Mendelssohn's thoughts still rove, still describe expressive limbs that "practise / high kicks / from silence".[345] In other words, the peripatetic persists: one list of associative thoughts or draft poem reads: "ballet walking / not the valkyries / avoiding the valkyries / uptown and down". Pronouncing herself neither robber nor murderess, this speaker elegantly paces the cityscape, evading creatures supernatural and female who determine fate, who distinguish hero from victim. And as the very existence of this incomplete, ambulatory collection attests, this pacing-cum-thinking cannot cease, as the final lines of this passage attest: "in a room. / with a composer, me., myself."[346] In her last room, Mendelssohn traipses on. As she writes in 1996: "How Dare you – tell me to Stop." This poem tells us that others may "[c]rowd around a writing" and come to a place of arrest, but Mendelssohn's speaker, though pursued, though self-blaming for having, at times, "walked on not My own", is nevertheless determined to recover "self possession."[347] And self-possession includes an insistence upon the right to write, to move with freedom at all times across the landscape of the page.

Moments in Mendelssohn's *oeuvre* indicate that she long envisaged perambulating across the page into senescence. In her thrice-published "Winter.", Mendelssohn's mind gravitates again toward movement: the traffic of stanza one comes and goes; the poets of stanza two have their heads in a vice of crepe paper, yet are "walking small, or, walking tall / growing old, in a minute, / reiterating memory / neo-classically".[348] This inextricability of writing and walking extends, arguably, into the afterlife, as in the poem beginning "Treading carpentry free country" (1982), which references style, writing, notations, ink, messengers, documentation, and states: "arm in arm they walk to the shore / a couple of likely gods, ghosts".[349] Over a decade later, Mendelssohn will assert in a poem "i need to learn how to write". Detailing those "fallen in battle for their daily life", this speaker imagines walking into a place where the words of the dead become audible, recordable:

i would stroll with my old viola
to hear what you have heard.
pinnies, frockcoats, sailors' berets,
walking as human ghosts are laid
to rest in that sanctity trespassed.[350]

Restiveness lists words, records untold pasts, aiming to generate a tranquil ease that Mendelssohn's work rarely details, and often designedly shuns. Mendelssohn's poetry is recalcitrant: obstinate, agitated, rebellious. Hers is a locomote mind that cannot remain stock still, regardless of what is at stake. Time itself succumbs to the appetency of one Mendelssohn speaker in a line comic with its own impatience, its determined, impassioned gait: "i wait, i walk with life too great to beat".[351] Mendelssohn's arduous life does beat her down; Mendelssohn's poetry is a triumphant riposte to its battering. The radicalism and extremes of her writings have and will continue to encourage over-determined biographical readings of her corpus, even as it is one of her editorial habits to excise or reformulate first-person pronouns, and even as her poems include lines such as: "she was not addressed as one she was told she was plural, you / (pl), they said, you (pl)."[352] Her poems, in short, foresee this problem of reception: "understanding cannot be relied upon" she writes at one juncture, flagging up as especially suspicious those who approach the poetic politically, sociologically, or "pharmaceutical[ly]". As the poem concludes, this anxiety is transposed to the author – implicitly gendered female – who "cannot be available day and night / as a speaking, walking, talking living doll."[353] "After Lee Harwood [...], it was the turn of Grace Lake, the only woman present, to skirt around behind the nine men and take her place at the lectern." This may be one of the only published reviews of Mendelssohn reading her poems; it is the summation, in the *Times Literary Supplement*, of her presence at Paris's Centre Pompidou in an event held to celebrate the publication of *Conductors of Chaos* (1996). Mendelssohn takes her turn, Mendelssohn, poetess, "skirts" around her male contemporaries. Her reading, the reviewer attests, "sounded like fighting talk and left me dazed."[354] A peripatetic writer, Mendelssohn endures this measure of her presence as wayward, a victor coming in from behind the ranks, positively *arrière-garde*. What proves unforgiveable about this review is not her marginalisation, her reductively reported aggression and opacity, but the fact that her poetic lines are misquoted, and she writes to the author to tell him as much. They became friends; he lent her his Paris flat; he offered to help her have her work published.[355] As ever, for Mendelssohn, the poetry is all: "I do not fake, I do not lie, I worship at the shrine of poetry."[356] No puppet or plaything, Mendelssohn writes poems that show us again and again what it is to "walk with life too great to beat".

viii. About This Collection

In conversation, Mendelssohn indicated to her eldest child that she aspired to and anticipated a collected edition of her poems. An undated, unsent letter to this same daughter suggests that Mendelssohn was invited as early as 1983 or 1984 to collect her work, but that she was uneasy about the "cheek and cruelty that ensued from socio/politic[al] vortices". And today, Mendelssohn adds, "the status of poetry has sunk."[357] Notably, these concerns are not about the quality of Mendelssohn's poetry, but about problems that may arise in its reception. So too is the last portion of this introduction preoccupied with you, the reader. What follows explains the organising principles behind this collection, and acts both as guide to and explanation of editorial decisions. The aim is to make these decisions as transparent as possible to enhance the reading experience, and to ensure that where uneasy compromises occur, informed issue can be taken with the motivations, elisions, and inevitable errors. It cannot be said emphatically enough that where the editing of this collection is concerned, no completionist illusions are harboured.

Excepting the full version of *Implacable Art* (2000), this volume endeavours to gather up the poems Mendelssohn published or planned to publish. The initial and still primary sources are the fifty files held at the Anna Mendelssohn Archive at Sussex Special Collections under the heading, "Poetry: published and possibly published (1981–2009, undated)".[358] In addition, all 59 files of "Mendelssohn's own files and folders (c 1985–2009, undated)" have been scoured, as have her oversized files, and a substantial proportion of the 650-plus files listed as "Loose Material (c 1977–c 2009, undated)". Where relevant, information from Mendelssohn's correspondence (over 120 files) and notebooks is incorporated into the annotations at the end of this text. Most of the letters in Mendelssohn's papers are drafts that were never sent to the addressee, meaning the identified recipient becomes less correspondent than phantasmic interlocutor. Libraries used to locate Mendelssohn's work include Sheffield Archives, the Cambridge University Library, the National Poetry Library at the Southbank Centre, the Little Magazines, Alternative Press and Poetry Store Collections at University College London, and the British Library.

This book is divided into a main textual body and an appendix. The body consists of poetry that Mendelssohn either published or prepared into copy fine enough to submit to a publisher. The appendix includes poems that were drafted for specific collections but were then excised from the final publication. In the entries for the notes to the appendix, and in the notes for this introduction, these variants are cited in the following format: "*Slate*, draft poems (February 1987)". On two occasions, drafts are so heavily reworked as to merit full inclusion. This is the case with "two secs" and "the fourteenth flight" from *viola tricolor* (1993), where early versions are given in full in the appendix, and their editorial variations are discussed in the appendix notes. Some of the initial drafts for *Crystal Love: D. N. A.* (1982) differ only in layout and lineation from the published text. That said, these nascent works are indicative of Mendelssohn's processes and priorities, as in the poems cut from *viola tricolor* (1993) that are often far more personal and affective than those in the publication. More drafts will assuredly be unearthed.

Where Mendelssohn has published collections of prose and poetry together, the prose has been set aside for future publication. As Mendelssohn often writes prose poetry, this distinction is uneasy, but the parcelling out of specific texts is consistent with Mendelssohn's practice. As discussed in the above publication history, Mendelssohn often republishes individual poems from entire collections; this truth extends to her prose, so that, for instance, the short title piece from the collection *Inbuilt Flash Nix* (1985) reappears in the first issue of *constant red/mingled damask* (1986). Mendelssohn mixes prose and poetry in *Celestial Empire.* (February 1983), *Inbuilt Flash Nix* (1985), *Is this a True Parrot, a Mountain, or a Stooge?* (1985), and *café archéologique* (1992–93). Only the poetry from these works appears in this collection.

Where possible, both main text and appendix are ordered chronologically by date of final publication. Given publishers many and various, formal and informal, educated guesses have been taken about works published in the same year, as specific months are not provided for book publications, and are often missing from the journals in which Mendelssohn published. For instance, in 1997, she contributed to *Comparative Criticism: An Annual Journal*, which is listed by year and volume only.[359] When no month or season is listed, the work is placed at the end of the identified calendar year; a few completely undated poems appear at the very end of the body of the text. Chronological ordering is disrupted to a significant extent by the fact that Mendelssohn republished many poems. In almost all cases, and in recognition of Mendelssohn's propensity to make small changes to reissues of the same poem, the last published variant is considered authoritative. This system is abandoned in three instances. Firstly, when Mendelssohn's editors appear to be at odds with previous publications or have made errors in line breaks or typography; the notes for *Parataxis* (1992) and *Out of Everywhere* (1996; 2006) offer examples of this state of exception. Secondly, in the very specific instance of the poems "Truth or Vermilion" and "To France" or "à la France", both of which are published in 1996 and then again in *Implacable Art* in 2000; given fair use limitations on republishing material from the latter volume, they remain here in their 1996 guise.[360] The third and final exception to the rule of treating the last variant as authoritative is when the work is republished posthumously. After Mendelssohn died, the poet Peter Riley circulated a file of her writing to a few Cambridge students editing fledgling journals. The file contained work from some of Mendelssohn's texts in the 1980s, and these students also sourced work that Mendelssohn had not previously published, the origin of which can remain unclear. When published post-2009, Mendelssohn's 1980s poems remain in situ; the unpublished work – mostly undated – is included at the end of this collection under its date of posthumous publication.[361]

Some ungainly gaps and juxtapositions arise from the treatment of Mendelssohn's last published copy as authoritative, particularly as she often republishes fragments from collections. The coherency of Mendelssohn's sublime short pamphlet *An ACCOUNT of a MUMMY, in The Royal Cabinet of Antiquities at Dresden* (October 1986) is dramatically disrupted by this editorial rule; a mere four poems, two of them are reprinted for the final time in *constant red/mingled damask* a year later, and in this volume, this is where they remain. Similarly disorienting is the place of the title poem from *viola tricolor* (1993), which is awkwardly included here with its final place of publication, *A State of Independence* (1998). Where a collection is fragmented in this manner, the running footer on these pages includes the preposition "from", as in: "*from viola tricolor (1993)*". The list provided of Mendelssohn's titles indicates the original, replete table of contents of all known publications, which will also be referenced in the notes; the full textual history of each poem is included with the publication in which it was last published, where it was previously published, and the notes are cross-referenced. Where "from" does not appear in running feet, an entire collection or submission is on offer.

The editorial notes for both parts of the text are extensive; within the prescribed archival referents listed above, this is a scholarly edition. Context is a particularly pressing concern where Mendelssohn's writing is concerned because she published in ephemeral, little-known vanguard journals alongside poets whose reputations are only recently in the ascendant. Each entry in the notes strives to include an overview of the publication, be it self-published or with a publishing house. Where Mendelssohn is published alongside other poets, a comprehensive or indicative list is given. Names recur with remarkable frequency, among them: Bill Griffiths, Tony Lopez, Alice Notley, Barry MacSweeney, D. S. Marriott, Rod Mengham, Drew Milne, Douglas Oliver, Ian Patterson, J. H. Prynne, Tom Raworth, Denise Riley, Peter Riley, Lisa Robertson, Stephen Rodefer, Marjorie Welish, and John Wilkinson. Many are associated with the British Poetry Revival. The publication is also discussed in material terms – e.g. a stapled, unpaginated A5 chapbook – an emphasis more fulsome when Mendelssohn's artwork is included, or when Mendelssohn has published the work herself, so that multiple copies may exist of a cover or format. Samples of Mendelssohn's artworks that were published alongside her poems are offered; given textual space constraints, these are incomplete, and should be considered the merest gesture toward the thousands of drawings contained in Mendelssohn's archive. Where available, the notes then discuss variants in manuscript, typescript, draft and fair copies of the poems Mendelssohn wrote in chronological order; when Mendelssohn edits in different colours, this information is given as it offers clues about the timing of editorial processes. When there are multiple drafts and corrections to consider, some collections are broken down into individual poems, given in order of published appearance. In these instances, not all poems will be listed, but only those where drafts and corrections require notation. Collections where the notes incorporate lists include: *Crystal Love: D. N. A.* and *Posmos, the Yellow Velvet Underground.* (1982), *viola tricolor* (1993), *Bernache Nonnette* (1995), and the selection from *Implacable Art* (2000). Throughout, the text *Implacable Art* is abbreviated to *IA*, and word definitions are drawn from the online *Oxford English Dictionary*.

The notes further detail the writing on and around Mendelssohn's drafts, a category that incorporates marginalia, doodles, life writing, everyday ephemera (reminders to self, phone numbers), and commentary on verso sides and/or additional pages written alongside the text in question. This information can hold out a promise of elucidation that fails bafflingly or bathetically. Some of the notes surrounding *café archéologique* (1991–92) offer clues about the gestation of the text and its title that succeed in making the points of origin still more cryptic, as in: "the earnest causeries which rename endless Top Shops Café Archéologiques should in this instance, and at this point refer to the Lexicon".[362] Where the notes are not quoted in full, their key features are summarised to facilitate readerly understanding of the text and its gestation. But much of the information in these associated notes and papers is straightforward. Many tell us a great deal, for instance, about what Mendelssohn was reading when she wrote her poems: Swift's "On the Education of Ladies" (c. 1730) in September 1986 whilst typing up "In the end tulane –"; Swift's "A letter to a very young lady on her marriage" (1723), whilst drafting *viola tricolor* seven years later; Wordsworth's *The Excursion* (1814) during "Tansy Tchaikovsky" (*The News*, April 1987); the surrealists André Breton and Paul Éluard whilst drafting *café archéologique* (1991–92); Elizabeth Barrett Browning's "The Dead Pan" (1844) during *viola tricolor* (1993); Margaret Mead when writing "Brahms' numerals." for *Implacable Art* (2000).

And now to editorial minutiae: the call numbers for all files in the Anna Mendelssohn Archive at Sussex begin with these digits: SxMs109. After the first full citation in any editorial entry or endnote, this standardised prefix is dropped, but should be assumed. Where there are more than three or four corrections noted about a poem or a portion thereof, a list of corrections is given; otherwise, corrections are embedded in sentences. When the correction is made on the manuscript or typescript in question, strikethrough is used, as in "permission, ~~therefore~~". Mendelssohn rarely makes changes below the line; corrections added above the line are demarcated by circumflex accents around the elevated term or phrase, as in: "^we roll^" or "^else^". Where text is indiscernible, or changes are editorial and not authorial, this is noted in italicised script, contained brackets, and further underscored by "—ed." All other amendments are Mendelssohn's own. Most editorial alterations follow the format of "'x' was 'y'", where "'x'" is a word or phrase as it appears in this volume, and "'y'" is a previous, identified draft. Exceptions abound and are explained, as in: "In *Salt*, there is a stanza break after 'paradox below' that is closed in *Critical Quarterly*". Where Mendelssohn uses quotations within texts or around titles, they are rendered in the notes as single quotations within editorial double quotation marks. The majority of forward slashes within quotations are editorial indications of line breaks; Mendelssohn's own slashes are noted. An avid user of French and, occasionally, other foreign languages, Mendelssohn often determinedly hand-drew accents onto her proofs, but even her most devoted editors repeatedly ignored her precision and care in this regard. Accents are reinstated here as consistently and accurately as possible. Mendelssohn is a reticent user of possessive punctuation, and this can impact meaning, as in "Demeter.", a poem included in the appendix draft poems for *viola tricolor* (1993). Mendelssohn's line: "hostility against females' academic progress" goes unpunctuated, and no clear evidence rules out the possibility that this is a specific "female's academic progress". Given the wilful contextual instabilities of this experimental poetry, these editorial interventions are recorded.

Some corrections or editorial changes are made silently. Regardless of their final positioning in publication, Mendelssohn's titles are predominantly left-justified in this volume. Exceptions arise when form responds to content, as in the centralised, titular question mark of the poem beginning "with Plenty of oos" (1985) or Mendelssohn's exaggerated right justification of "La Facciata Turns her Back" (1996). In the main text, spelling and typing errors are corrected, barring where they appear semantically relevant; when accidence or intent is uncertain, every effort has been made to flag up this ambiguity in the notes. Mendelssohn prefers the misspelling "alot", which is edited as "a lot". When replicating past drafts or editorial changes, Mendelssohn's spelling mistakes and typos are generally left standing. Mendelssohn's cursive "e" often reads as "E", which can cause confusion, particularly at the start of poem lines; excepting proper nouns, this collection defers to "e". She places full stops both outside and inside of quotation marks, and these choices are largely replicated. Changes in line breaks and minor alterations to punctuation are mentioned in the collection notes, but for the most part, are not individually listed. A final note: publishers and copy-editors clearly struggled to typeset Mendelssohn's long lines. As previously mentioned, the poet Ulli Freer repeatedly typeset *Bernache Nonnette* (1995) in different fonts, aiming to find one narrow enough to avoid breaking Mendelssohn's lines. Freer remains dissatisfied with the outcome, which was to sacrifice font size to retain linear integrity.[363] Chris Hamilton-Emery of Salt Publishing expressed the same concerns about the proofs for *Implacable Art* (2000), noting in a letter to Rod Mengham: "I would dearly like to go back to a compromise of suffering the line breaks, rather than dropping down the point size to such an extent. But I'll leave this to you and Anna."[364] In the final edition, the small font was retained. Both experiences suggest that Mendelssohn's preference was to maintain the Whitmanesque length of her lines. Every effort has been made to honour that preference in this text.

A last note regarding images: Mendelssohn's approach to the artwork she included in her collections is difficult to gauge. Often, but not always, the drawings are far from her best work and appear deliberately poorly replicated. This book samples a range of images that Mendelssohn chose to publish. Many of these images are copies of photocopies, as is the cover itself, which appeared in black and white in Mendelssohn's entry in *constant red/mingled damask*, no. 1, 1986, with the colour version kindly provided by Nigel Wheale and enhanced by Stuart Robinson.

ix. Acknowledgements & Permissions

Unremitting thanks must be given first and foremost to Anna Mendelssohn's children, Poppy, George, and Emerald, for their inestimable generosity, their openness and trust, and for their informed understanding of the profound cultural significance of Mendelssohn's work. They are ideal keepers of Mendelssohn's estate, and her legacy will no doubt flourish as a direct result of their phenomenal care and goodwill. This volume is irrefutably theirs.

Poets, editors, and staunch Mendelssohn associates made possible many of the publications included in this volume. Rod Mengham and Peter Riley deserve especial regard, and their devotion is evident in the number of letters Mendelssohn wrote to them about her writing, art, and publishing, letters referenced in this text countless times. Alongside Riley, Lynne Harries, Nigel Wheale, Kate Wheale, and Martin Thom spent many weekends over the cold winter of 2009 and 2010 excavating Mendelssohn's garden shed. Ling Ling and Franck Parnin, Mendelssohn's landlords and friends, patiently permitted this process. Without these efforts, there would be no archive today.

Sussex Special Collections has been incredibly supportive from the outset about the acquisition of this archive, my five-year-long struggles to find funding to catalogue it, and the promotion of Mendelssohn's work. I've worked particularly closely with Fiona Courage, who is a fantastic, prescient manager and a phenomenal colleague. Special Collections supervisors Rose Lock and Karen Watson have been unstinting in meeting my specific editorial needs; staff at the Keep – Lindsay, Lottie, Neil, Drew, Tim, Steph, and others – have been similarly accommodating. The outstanding figure in the processing of Mendelssohn's papers is Simon Coleman, whose charming, unassuming external demeanour belies a fervent, unspeakably productive drive, as well as a formidable expertise. We could not have hired a better archivist, and I enjoyed weekly cathartic conversations with Simon about Mendelssohn's irascible, fascinating, seemingly limitless archive in the year that he catalogued her papers, during which my respect for library science escalated stratospherically. Simon's hire was made possible courtesy of the Sussex Research Development Fund, and the Sussex School of English has provided small but significant sums to assist with student wages, publishing, and the cost of moving Mendelssohn's archive from Cambridge to Brighton. I am also indebted to Sussex's Junior Research Associate scheme, which facilitated the hire of three students who spent their summers in the archive proof-reading the typescript: Sinéad Rawson of the University of Sussex in summer 2018; Soulet Ali of the University of Chicago in 2019, and Georgina Clutterbuck, also from Sussex, in 2018, 2019, and 2020. George is particularly remarkable for so joyously giving her own time and energy to this project, and for her superlative editorial skills, by which she expertly colour-coded the minutiae of every textual variant whilst raising cogent questions about larger organisational structures. These students' readings and re-readings have immeasurably improved this volume, and their enthusiasm for Mendelssohn's work – her thinking, her artistry, her very commas – was inspiring, gratifying and sustaining. To Tony Frazer I am grateful for not baulking at the doorstopper I delivered to his publishing house and for his commitment to this version of Mendelssohn's work.

My thanks extend also to those who so carefully peer-reviewed this lengthy introduction: to Alistair Davies, who attends to editing, as he did teaching, with extraordinary care and skill; to Ian Patterson, who has been a generous, informed reader of my work for some 15 years; to Romana Huk, who raised significant questions and offered boatloads of encouragement; and to Sam Ladkin, who patiently, discerningly reads my words, debates my processes, and makes possible the time for extended labours of love.

It has been my privilege and pleasure to use this volume as a pretext for conversations with many of Mendelssohn's friends and associates, a list that risks omission, but assuredly includes: Tim Atkins, John Barker, Martin Bright, Elizabeth Eger, Thomas Evans, Ulli Freer, Geoffrey Gilbert, Lynne Harries, Peter Hughes, Tony Lopez, Timothy Mathews, David Marriott, Rod Mengham, Drew Milne, Wendy Mulford, Ian Patterson, Chris Ratcliff, Val Raworth, Peter Riley, Iain Sinclair, Martin Thom, Kate Wheale, Nigel Wheale, and John Wilkinson. Michael Tencer shared his Mendelssohn bibliography, which has proven a useful comparative guide. Permission to publish was kindly provided by the following: Timothy Mathews, for the inclusion of his half of the text he co-wrote with Mendelssohn, *poems* (1984); Rod Mengham, for all Equipage publications; Jennifer Hamilton-Emery of Salt Publishing, for the selection of poems from *Implacable Art* (2000). Mendelssohn secured Gisèle Prassinos's permission to translate her work in the late 1990s/early 2000s, and in 2020 Møtus Editions authorised the replication of Mendelssohn's near-complete rendering, in English, of Gisèle Prassinos's *La fièvre du labour*.

Introduction Notes

1 "POEM." *No prizes*, no. 1, 2012; "studio VII." *Involution*, no. 5, 1997.

2 The female poetic persona is a recurrent Mendelssohn motif. Tansy is joined by a troupe of like figures, often eponymous, among them: "2/4" in *Is this a True Parrot, a Mountain, or a Stooge?* (1985); "La Facciata" (1988), *viola tricolor* (1993), *Bernache Nonnette* (1995), and "minnie most" who "beats up thérèse torchée" in *Implacable Art* (2000; hereafter, *IA*).

3 Poem beginning "As soon as a name is to be addressed another child", *viola tricolor*, draft poems, c. 1993.

4 "from 'Spinster of Arts'." *Parataxis*, no. 2, 1992.

5 Poem beginning "to any who want poems to give them answers.", *IA*, 2000. Only a selection of *IA* is included in this volume; when referenced, these *IA* poems are cited as "not in this collection".

6 Aristotle's Lyceum students were called "The Peripatetics", a name said to reflect their teacher's propensity to pace whilst teaching. A more contemporary example: William James's *The Principles of Psychology* (1890) links consciousness with physical restlessness, using movement to define the internal self (qtd. in Deborah Parsons, *Streetwalking the Metropolis: Women, the City, and Modernity*, Oxford University Press, 2000, 71–72).

7 Consider, from Stein's "Five or Six Men.": "Certainly he was almost wonderfully creating something he was understanding [....] He was steadily walking, he was steadily talking, he was [...] continuing coming to be one understanding" (*Two: Gertrude Stein and Her Brother and Other Early Portraits*, Yale Edition of the Unpublished Writings of Gertrude Stein, vol. 1, Yale University Press, 1951, 279–80). Mendelssohn acknowledges Stein's influence in notes made alongside drafts of her 1997 pamphlet, *Tondo Aquatique* (SxMs109/5/A/23/1).

8 Poem beginning, "I shake and cry. How then could I ever love you", *viola tricolor*, draft poems, c. 1993.

9 "As Things Stand" (*constant red/mingled damask*, no. 2, 1987).

10 The presumptions of reason are one such supposedly solid foundation, as Mendelssohn observes: "walk in airy per / petuum ōver reason's divorce" of mind from body ("a minuet by mendleson.", *viola tricolor*, draft poems, c. 1993).

11 Poem beginning, "yes it is official. sitting at a table. pen in hand," (*constant red/mingled damask*, no. 1, 1986).

12 This poem is in archive file SxMs109/5/B/2/3.

13 The school children arise in "february." (*Spinsters and Mistresses of Art.*, c. 1991–93). The "strong man" is part of the untitled poem beginning "One rushes another is described as behaving abnormally" (*café archéologique*, draft poems, c. 1992–93). Joined by a host of walkers, the arthritic woman belongs to the poem beginning "Concentration camp styles. along mill road. 1998." (*IA* 2000).

14 From Mendelssohn's contributor biography, *constant red/mingled damask*, no. 1, 1986.

15 "Exposition" (Sheffield typescript, November 1981); "Walk in, walk out" appears in the poem beginning "evoking mocked order showing Me the Blind & Impudent man" (*viola tricolor*, draft poems, c. 1993).

16 See, for instance: "Why walk away / & dismiss me." in the poem beginning "As soon as a name is to be addressed to another child" (*viola tricolor*, draft poems, c. 1993).

17 Poem beginning "Cover the land" (Typescripts, 1974).

18 Poem beginning "Must you?' She seldom burns" (*Is this a True Parrot, a Mountain, or a Stooge?*, 1985). Perhaps this example is not Futurist, but Dada (or more properly, Merz), as it resembles Kurt Schwitters's infamous 1919 poem, "Anna Blossom Has Wheels", which reads: "You wearest your head on your feet and wanderst on your hands, / On thy hands wanderst Thou." (*pppppp: poems performance pieces proses plays poetics.* ed. and trans. Jerome Rothenberg and Pierre Joris, Exact Change, 2002, 16–17). Mendelssohn echoes Schwitters's peripatetic and somatic inversion with the cloud walking of "As Things Stand" (*constant red/mingled damask*, no. 2, 1987).

19 In Mendelssohn, a single walk might entail "rush[ing] through / the messy wet street to the oncoming, crash through / BUS and back over the bridge to the [....] route into the country, the wandering around in / hard frozen fields with footprints" ("Radiated? Light?", *constant red/mingled damask*, no. 1, 1986). For scratching into the floor with heels, see *Out of Everywhere* (2006), "Ordered into Quarantine" and "twelve to midnight"; shoeless street walking arises in the latter poem. In "Exposition", Mendelssohn describes clambering over a zebra crossing (Sheffield typescript, November 1981). "[T]he road poisonous to walk much distance upon" is from "never beiger" (*Tondo Aquatique*, 1997). The need to interrogate signs, to "read the roads" arises in the poem beginning "incrustation, fossilised cement,

caked dry canine's excrement" (*viola tricolor*, draft poems, 1993); "invited to attend to the traffic signals, obsessively" is from "Silk & Wild Tulips" (*Out of Everywhere*, 2006).

20 "Please put weights beneath them & regard them as concrete" centres on a group of old poems sequestered beyond reach, among them, a poem "written to a square". This nod to form is immediately abandoned for an unstructured attentiveness "to the air above the square" (*constant red/mingled damask*, no. 2, 1987).

21 Poem beginning "sickened by the sight of the yard thewed daughters." (*viola tricolor*, draft poems, c. 1993).

22 "a room a", April 1986 typescript.

23 "[P]roceeds recedingly" is drawn from Loy's "Lady Laura in Bohemia" (*The Lost Lunar Baedeker*, ed. Roger Conover, Carcanet, 1996, 98). Mendelssohn's phrase arises in the poem beginning "Treading carpentry free country" (*Crystal Love D. N. A.*, 1982). Mendelssohn may have attended the first British symposium on Loy, held on 11 March 2000 at the Institute of English Studies, University of London (SxMs109/5/B/1/15/1).

24 The poem refers to "sw[inging] back, pendulum, pendular" and concludes affirmatively with "a final licensed wit" (poem beginning "The past's stranding to belief adduced reconnaissance facing", *viola tricolor*, 1993). See also: "[S]o further back we go. Into the lyrics of / a poet's former agony." in "Radiated? Light?" (*constant red/mingled damask*, no. 1, 1986).

25 "minnie most beats up thérèse torchée" (*IA*, 2000).

26 "frozen moments", *Parataxis*, no. 2, 1992.

27 Poem beginning "digne. more than a design. to size." and "Zephyrus" (*IA*, 2000).

28 "Bernache Nonnette." (*Bernache Nonnette*, 1995).

29 Respectively, these questions are drawn from "Silk & Wild Tulips" (*Out of Everywhere*, 2006) and "eulogy" (*A State of Independence*, 1998); the last is a poem title (*Is this a True Parrot, a Mountain, or a Stooge?*, 1985).

30 Question one is the first line of an untitled poem in *Propaganda Multi-Billion Bun.* (August 1985). Where high flying is shamelessly ambitious, and high stepping overweening, "high-walking" exalts the banal, and this Mendelssohn portmanteau encapsulates her authorial drive to combine prosaic gait with sublime soar. For question two, see "So then what are we going to do? Are we going to subject too?" (*Slate* drafts, 1987).

31 The earliest known citation arises in an early 1980s portion of Mendelssohn's *roman-à-clef* beginning "they've got me, got me" (SxMs109/1/B/1/19). An extract reads:

> there is something i like about decent people who can walk back and forth through their lives.
> Alluvial strip.
> running. through september. the first dvorcak violin sonata has not survived? missings, going missing, misery. violin and piano.
> have those who didn't wait, or enquire, or support their imprisoned poetess, overeaten? holidayed endlessly, timelessly grazed the Hellene…Dalmatia…Corn..Wall..America..Reading..Writing..Loved.. baring breasts they love well enough to describe.. in poems..published..again.. and again.... telephoning.. faxing..

32 "The Gong." is an undated typescript located at the end of the main body of this collection.

33 From a letter addressed to British poet, publisher, and critic Peter Riley, Mendelssohn's quote reads: "How much of a woman one is as a writress [*sic*], a poetess (not a poet – it is strange how difficult it seems, or has seemed to be to communicate the difference that is not necessarily any less literary and/or intelligent) has not been helped by anyone deflecting me from poetry" (15 January [no year]; SxMs109/3/A/1/52).

34 This is the first line from an untitled Mendelssohn poem published in the *Cambridge Literary Review* (2009).

35 "London 1971" (*Conductors of Chaos*, 1996).

36 SxMs109/5/A/24/7.

37 Another example arises in a prose manuscript signed "Cambridge, 1999": "I haven't felt particularly enamoured of creating autobiographical statements for publication" (SxMs109/5/B/1/15/1). Consider also, from a letter of 28 March 1997 to a potential reader of her poems: "I stay distant, as distant as possible so as not to offend anyone with my poetry." (3/A/2/1). In an undated letter to Estelle Langley, Mendelssohn argues against biographical criticism on the basis that the source of poetry should not be confounded with poetry itself (3/A/1/29).

38 Poem beginning "She appears in thirteen dresses." (*Propaganda Multi-Billion Bun.*, August 1985).

39 In an undated letter to Ian Patterson, Mendelssohn writes: "I am not a bad, in the sense of 'reveal all' writer, i.e. I have always had good literary sense." (SxMs109/3/A/1/47).

As Mendelssohn's contemporary, the experimental British author Christine Brooke-Rose states: "women are rarely considered seriously as part of a [vanguard] movement when it is 'in vogue', and then they are damned with the label when it no longer is, when they can safely be considered as minor elements in it" (*Stories, theories and things*, Cambridge University Press, 1991, 262). Throughout *The Feminist Avant-Garde in American Poetry* (University of Iowa Press, 2003), Elizabeth Frost argues that women who position themselves within a masculine avant-garde tend to be politically engaged. But there remains a distinct sense, as Kathleen Fraser maintains, that "something remains troubling about women writers – even feminists" who reject "the safe hearth of the personal/autobiographical lyric" (*Translating the Unspeakable: Poetry and the Innovative Necessity*, University of Alabama Press, 2000, 134, 136). Griselda Pollock writes: "the radical transformation of the conditions of sexual difference and subjectivity structuring the historical avant-gardes of the nineteenth and twentieth centuries remains, even now, profoundly unfinished, indeed ... it is only just verging on the point of serious intelligibility today" ("Moments and Temporalities of the Avant-Garde: 'in, of, and from the feminine'", *New Literary History*, vol. 41, no. 4, 2010, 795–820, 816).

40 "Strictly personal" (*Vanishing Points: New Modernist Poems*, 2004).

41 In the second half of her poem beginning "digne.", Mendelssohn recounts a litany of loss with a conclusionary invocation of the confining prison system, followed by: "Musicians, artists, choreographers / windhover." (*IA*, 2000). Against his presiding preoccupation with tormented spiritual constraint, Hopkins's "Windhover" posits the regal courage and violent freedom of the flying bird ecstatically "striding / High" while those below enact "shéer plód". As in Mendelssohn's "high-walking", both celestial and terrestrial forms of transport have transformative potential.

42 These four are: "*I'm working here.*" (February 1983); *Celestial Empire.* (February 1983); *Spinsters and Mistresses of Art.* (c. 1991–93); *café archéologique* (1992–93).

43 As will be discussed, Mendelssohn was also anthologized in *Jewels of the Imagination* (1997) and Tony Frazer's *A State of Independence* (1998).

44 Mendelssohn details her arrangements to meet with Prassinos in a letter to her sister Judi dated 2 February 1997 (SxMs109/1/E/1/6; see also notes on the Prassinos translations, c. 2000–2002). The Hikmet translations are referenced repeatedly in Mendelssohn's journals, but only a single, incomplete translation of one Hikmet poem is documented in the Sussex archive. Titled "The Pupils of the Eyes of the Hungry" (1921), it exists within an undated typescript that appears to be part of Mendelssohn's *roman-à-clef* (SxMs109/5/A/35).

45 Among the numerous references in the Sussex archive to the prospect of publishing with Bloodaxe, Mendelssohn mentions repeatedly rejecting this publisher in a letter to Mengham dated 1 January 1999 (SxMs109/3/A/1/34/1). A letter dated 13 April 1987 from Elizabeth Lindner of Methuen press indicates that Mendelssohn's friend, the author Michèle Roberts, had recommended her verse for a forthcoming poetry series planned by the publisher; as the series was dropped, Mendelssohn's manuscript was returned (5/A/5/7; see also correspondence with Noella Smith, 3/A/1/58). In 1991, Mendelssohn drafted a letter to Wendy Mulford, who ran Street Editions, offering to give her some work that contained poems written in Cambridge between 1977 and 1979 (3/A/1/39). Further, in a letter to Mengham dated 6 December 1996, Mendelssohn discusses a request for a book-length contribution from Street Editions; by this year, the press was known as Reality Street Editions (3/A/1/34).

Mendelssohn mentions invitations from Burning Deck and Shearsman in an undated letter and postcard to Peter Riley (3/A/52); this history, which publisher Tony Frazer recalls, affirms the decision taken to publish her *Collected Poems* with Shearsman posthumously.

46 The Contemporary British Poetry event at the Pompidou took place on 2 April 1997 (5/C/5) and was reviewed by Hugo Williams in The *Times Literary Supplement* (see notes 354 and 355).

The "Poetry readings, conferences, and lectures" portion of Mendelssohn's archive contains details of her readings at Cambridge and elsewhere (SxMs109/5/C). Mendelssohn's correspondence indicates that she was on the billing for the Cambridge Conferences of Contemporary Poetry in 1991, 1997, and 1998 (see 5/C/2; letters to Peter Riley 3/A/1/5/2; and Rod Mengham 3/A/1/34). Mendelssohn's cover design for the CCCP 4 programme in 1994 is in the Peter Riley Archive at Cambridge University Library (Ms Add.10013/2/29).

On 28 June 1995, Mendelssohn was invited to a conference run by Geoffrey Gilbert in Southampton (3/A/1/16). Writing Peter

Riley on 22 February 1996, she mentions an invitation from Exeter (3/A/1/52). In a letter to her parents written on 2 February 1995, Mendelssohn indicates that a recording of a reading she gave in London was placed in the National Poetry Library at the Southbank Centre; she was invited to read at the Southbank's Purcell Room in 2003 (1/E/1/3; see also letter to Jude Windle 15 April 2003, 3/A/1/68). In 1996, Romana Huk invited Mendelssohn to speak or read poems at "Assembling Alternatives: An International Poetry Conference/ Festival" at the University of New Hampshire, and to teach at a summer school planned for 1997 (3/A/1/20). In 1996, Geoff Ward asked Mendelssohn to read in New York (see letter to Fiona Nicholson dated 11 July 1996; 3/A/1/40).

Mendelssohn never travelled to the U.S.A., and often turned down invitations, including one from the poet Lawrence Upton to read at the SubVoicive Poetry series in Surrey in 1996 (3/A/1/63).

47 No year is given on the archived promotional material, but as Mendelssohn is identified as "Anna Mendelssohn" and "(The Poetess Grace Lake)", the lecture likely took place during or after 2000, when she reverted to a variation on her birth name for publication, but was still known as Grace Lake (SxMs109/5/C/6).

48 Mendelssohn secured a music theatre residency at Wingfield College Suffolk in 1993 and appears to have won a place with the Covent Garden Opera Workshop to work on a libretto in the same period (letter to Elizabeth dated 13 November [no year]; SxMs109/8/C/1). In 1993 or 1994, Mendelssohn entered a composing competition named after Fanny Mendelssohn, Felix's musical sister. Although she didn't win, staff at the International Women Composers' Library in the city of Unna, Germany evidently archived a copy of her composition, "heartsease" (for competition correspondence, see 8/C/3; a copy of the composition exists in 5/B/3/1). See also endnote 294.

49 Like Joyce and Woolf before her, Mendelssohn believes music supersedes language in its communicability. See, for instance, "eulogy" where a female figure is amazed by another language that she describes as "music / in comparison to what I speak" (*A State of Independence*, 1998). In Mendelssohn's notebooks, she repeatedly describes her need for a piano, and a place to play it, night or day; in the poem "in the minority of one", loss of self – "Her light went out." – is linked to a piano that "was 189 miles away" (*Paper Nautilus*, no. 2, 2011).

50 Drawn from a letter to Rod Mengham dated 25 November 1997, this sentence reads in full: "I don't find that images merge into writing, I draw what I have no other way of expressing/conveying is too optimistic a word. I cannot pin words to images" (SxMs109/3/A/1/34). As a further example of Mendelssohn's capacity to interweave genres, she planned to set her poetry collection *Spinster and Mistresses of Art.* (c. 1991–93) to music – "song, chant, & piano" as well as "other instrumental sound" – during her 1993 residency at Wingfield College (8/C/1). Similarly, she described parts of *Parasol 1. Parasol 2. Parasol Avenue.* (1996) as libretti (3/A/2/1), and on a typescript of "damned channel" Mendelssohn writes, next to the title, "variations on the goldfinger suite" (5/A/18/3). See also "a minuet by mendleson." (*viola tricolor*, draft poems, 1993). Whimsical evidence of Mendelssohn's capacity to mix media arises in a letter to Douglas Oliver and Alice Notley: "I need a film studio. At the moment I am making pocket sized films of poems from empty perfume boxes" (3/A/1/43).

51 Ideogrammatic work runs scattershot through Mendelssohn's Sussex archive. The earliest example located thus far is within a sheaf of papers dated 1979 (SxMs109/5/B/2/2).

52 One example of Mendelssohn's desire to exhibit arises in an earlier draft of her author biography for *constant red/mingled damask*, no. 1, 1986, where she edits out the following: ""She is single with three children & is in the process of organizing an exhibition of painting & poetry in order to raise funds" (SxMs109/5/B/1/1b). Although frequently iterated, Mendelssohn's desire may have amounted to a single exhibition of a dozen pen and ink drawings in Cambridge in 2006 or 2007 in a café next to Heffers bookshop on Trinity Street (letter dated 29 April 2006; 3/A/1/59). Both the British Library and Sussex Special Collections hold files labelled "a.m. : artiste dessinatrice, peintre; poétesse; musicienne." These contain 12 copies of coloured pen and ink drawings that may have been the substance of this exhibition; neither are dated (SxMs109/5/D/1).

53 Barring minor changes, most of the biographical paragraphs that follow are drawn from my article, "The Agonies of Ambivalence: Anna Mendelssohn, *la poétesse maudite*" (*Modernism/modernity*, vol. 25, no. 3, 2018, 461–98).

54 In an undated letter to Rod Mengham, Mendelssohn discusses the gunshot wound her father received in his leg in the 1938 Battle of the Ebro (SxMs109/3/A/1/34).

55 SxMs109/1/C/4.

56 The trip to Israel is mentioned in a letter to Estelle Langley dated "August" (SxMs109/3/A/1/29/3) and in a 1986 portion of Mendelssohn's experimental *roman-à-clef* (1/B/1/31).

The cover of the draft chapbook, *café archéologique* (1992–93) is attributed to Grace Lake and the initials "c.n.e.m. b. h'k." that recur in Mendelssohn's 1997 publication, *Tondo Aquatique*. Evidently, these initials align with Mendelssohn's Hebrew name, as cited in an undated letter to Romana Huk (3/A/1/20/1). See also endnote 296.

57 In the portion of her *roman-à-clef* titled *What a Performance* (1987), Mendelssohn states that she was forbidden to learn the tonal inflections in the Torah but, when learning Hebrew, was awarded a prize for most promising scholar (SxMs109/B/1/39/1; see also 1/C/1–3).

58 In *The British New Left*, Lin Chun identifies the London School of Economics, the Hornsey College of Art, and the universities of Essex, Hull and Birmingham as key sites of 1960s student protest, but argues that England "was the only major industrialised society which did not generate a competitive militant student movement, nor a vigorous and coherent theory for such a movement" (Edinburgh University Press, 1993, 93; 87–88). Johnathon Green's *All Dressed Up: The Sixties and the Counterculture* (Pimlico, 1999) works to remedy the paucity of information on the role played by British youth in this self-consciously revolutionary era. An alumni website offers an account of Essex university protests from 1967–69 (www.essex68.org.uk/).

59 Mendelssohn refers to these events in notebooks and correspondence; "the fourteenth flight" (*viola tricolor*, 1993) is dedicated to Godard.

60 As one of countless references to the dismissal of artistic practice within revolutionary organisations, see Kathleen Weaver's account of Peruvian poet Magda Portal (1900–89), a founder of the American Popular Revolutionary Alliance who was often derided by her associates for her writing (*Peruvian Rebel: The World of Magda Portal, with a Selection of her Poems*, Pennsylvania State University Press, 2009). Although priding themselves on their conflation of art and life, the Situationists, who are a clear influence on Mendelssohn in the late 1960s, can also be interpreted as disparaging the poetic, as will be discussed.

61 The most extreme, famous, and literal example of this experience is Patty Hearst, who claims to have been kidnapped, imprisoned, systematically raped, and brainwashed into participating in the violent activities of the Symbionese Liberation Army in 1974 (*Every Secret Thing*, Methuen, 1982).

A member of a New York-based extremist group that bombed Chase Manhattan Bank and General Motors headquarters in 1969, Jane Alpert believed she couldn't walk away from the cell once established, and later wrote about the "sexual oppression of the left" in her manifesto "Mother Right: A New Feminist Theory", published in *Ms.* magazine in 1974 (*Growing Up Underground*, William Morrow, 1981, 310). See also endnote 297.

In *With the Weathermen: The Personal Journey of a Revolutionary Woman*, Susan Stern likened herself to a "religious zealot" from her earliest days with the organisation, noting that she became "depressed, nervous, overworked, emotionally spent" and addicted to drugs; Stern recalls being treated differently from her male peers when she spoke out, and at night in shared quarters, overhearing other women activists coerced into sex by male leaders (Doubleday, 1975, 90, 12, 85, 169).

62 This specific quote is drawn from the final page of an untitled five-page typescript of Mendelssohn's experimental *roman-à-clef* beginning "what a poem.", and likely written in the mid-to-late 1980s (SxMs109/1/B/1/37).

63 Mendelssohn uses this slogan to describe the group mentality of late 1960s activists (herself included) in an untitled portion of her *roman-à-clef* beginning "I thought I had all the answers" (SxMs109/1/B/1/5).

64 Tim Adams writes that the phone-hacking trial was "[t]he longest completed criminal trial in recent British legal history (beating the Angry Brigade by 13 days)" ("Phone-hacking trial: now it's over, has anything really changed?", *The Guardian*, 28 June 2014, accessed on-line).

65 In *Granny Made Me an Anarchist*, Stuart Christie details the incredulity with which European leftists treated Franco's continued rule in Spain, given the dictator's open support of the Axis powers throughout World War II, and his repressive leadership, modelled on the fascist politics that the Allied victory was meant to condemn and defeat (Scribner, 2005). In the mid-1960s, Christie was imprisoned for more than three years for an attempted assassination of Franco; he was arrested and tried with Mendelssohn in 1972, but was cleared of all charges, and has persistently denied having had any involvement with The Angry Brigade.

The Irish Republican Army (IRA) is the paramilitary political movement that provides the most immediate historical context for The Angry Brigade. The longstanding conflict between Unionist Protestants and Catholic Nationalists escalated in 1969 when British troops were deployed to Northern Ireland. Known as "The Troubles", this conflict worsened in the summer of 1971 when mass internment was introduced for those suspected of IRA involvement. This crisis no doubt contributed to the severity of Angry Brigade treatment and sentencing.

66 Histories dedicated to the wave of terrorism to which The Angry Brigade belongs regularly fail to mention this group; see, for instance,

Adrian Guelke, *The Age of Terrorism and the International System* (Taurus Publishers, 1995) and Anthony James Joes, *Urban Guerrilla Warfare* (University Press of Kentucky, 2007).

67 The attacks for which the Stoke Newington Eight were ultimately held accountable occurred between 1970 and 1971 and are outlined in Gordon Carr's *The Angry Brigade: A History of Britain's First Urban Guerilla Group* (PM Press, 2010, 54–57). For the communiqués and another timeline of Brigade activities, see *The Angry Brigade: Documents and Chronology, 1967–1984* (ed. Jean Weir, Elephant Editions, 1985).

68 Founded in 1962, The Arthur Koestler Trust continues fostering the creative work of prisoners. Koestler set up this institution in the 1960s whilst successfully campaigning to have capital punishment abolished in Britain. For one of Mendelssohn's references to the 1974 visit to the Tate, see SxMs109/1/B/1/39/3.

69 See SxMs109/2/A/6 and 13.

70 Robert Carr was Secretary of State for Employment when bombed on 12 January 1971; he was instrumental to the Industrial Relations Bill, which curbed workers' right to strike. On an archived paper napkin, Mendelssohn details her post-release period as personally, familially, and socially difficult. Her "probation officer told [her] that no-one in England wanted [her] out of prison" and she was deemed "permanently unemployable" by the Department of Health and Social Security. Asked by the Home Office to appear on a new parole committee offering advice on long-term imprisonment, she regretfully declined because she was exhausted "and wanted solitude in which to study & write." Finally, she adds: "I was asked to speak at Eton School together with my police inspector. I just didn't want to make Prison my speciality. I sent a nice [*unclear name*—ed.] p'card to the Headmaster and apologized for declining the invitation" (SxMs109/5/B/2/38).

71 Mendelssohn's first legal name change took place on 10 March 1983, when she went from Anne Mendleson to Sylvia Grace Louise Lake. On 18 March 1997, she reverted, again legally, to Anne Mendleson (SxMs109/1/G/1). Deferring to the spelling she used most in the last decade of her life, her Sussex papers are listed as the "Anna Mendelssohn Archive". Critics and associates often use Lake and Mendelssohn interchangeably. For more information on the names Mendelssohn used in publication, see endnote 296.

72 Mendelssohn was hospitalised in 1986 due to extreme abdominal pain (letter to her cousin Barry Benser and his wife Sonia, 20 June 1986; SxMs109/1/E/1/7). She may have been hospitalised for the same whilst in prison.

73 In 1989, the children moved with their foster family to Oxford, limiting contact still further.

74 Lynne Harries, "The Northern Debutante: A Memoir of Anna Mendelssohn", MA dissertation, University of East Anglia, submitted 2013, 16 (SxMs109/1/A/1).

75 Throughout her archive, Mendelssohn repeatedly asserts that she has declined invitations to write on the 1960s.

76 This letter is undated (SxMs109/3/A/1/52). The prison sentence that made Mendelssohn suspect in the public eye also made her vulnerable as a parent. To Mengham she writes of her concern that she is perceived as having abused or neglected her children, but fostered because she felt coerced and, ultimately, hopeful that she was making a responsible choice in their best interests (undated; 3/A/1/34).

77 Sex is mentioned fewer than two dozen times in this collection. Excepting the playful flirtation of "Whirr slightly operationless" (*Is this a True Parrot, a Mountain, or a Stooge?*, 1985), sex is usually discussed in negative terms, as in: "does the great manpoet EVER / read or listen to a member of the opposite sex?" ("great big sparkling Deal no relation.", *Propaganda Multi-Billion Bun.*, August 1985); or the "Radical Lesbian Feminist Rapist" who "wears sex / on her sleeve" (*The News*, 1987). This negativity carries over to Mendelssohn's later work: see the "Enforced sex education." and being "held in sexism" in "1:3ng" (*Gare du Nord*, 1997), or the twinning of sex and incontinence in "Cultural" (*A State of Independence*, 1998) and again in "the beef girls.   leaning on Alkan." (*IA*, 2000).

78 The quote beginning "if thought be woven" is drawn from "i. m. Laura Riding" (*Jacket*, no. 20, 2002); Mendelssohn's subject crashes about for love in the September 1986 typescript beginning "is this the hallow?"

79 Poem beginning "to have some stupid bloke laughing and giggling at you.", *constant red/mingled damask*, no. 1, 1986.

80 In addition to Essex, Anglia, and Sheffield, a letter kept with one of Mendelssohn's prison notebooks suggests that whilst seeking parole she was taking two literature courses with the University of London (SxMs109/2/A/14). In the archive, Mendelssohn mentions considering applying to Manchester and Oxford from prison.

81 An undated letter describes Mendelssohn's 1968 PhD proposal; in the postscript, she claims that "at least five PhD proposals of mine have been destroyed by racism in British universities I have legitimately attended since leaving school in 1967". The Cunard proposal exists in

a letter to John Kerrigan dated 23 October 1989 (3/A/1/26). Mendelssohn expresses interest in Cunard because she is a poet and activist who militated against the Fascists in Spain, wore strange clothes, had a reputation for zaniness, and was often described as suffering from persecution mania. In a letter to Janet Todd dated Friday, January 20 (likely 1989), Mendelssohn suggests that she intended to speak to John Harvey to discuss a PhD proposal in music, art, and literature from 1909–39 with a focus on "[t]he much under-valued women surrealists, cabaret artists, jazz musicians, photographers, poetesses" (3/A/1/61). At that juncture, Cunard was under consideration alongside H.D. (the pen-name of Hilda Doolittle); Bryher (the pen-name of Annie Winifred Ellerman), and Macpherson (likely Scottish artist Kenneth Macpherson, who co-founded the film journal *Close Up* [1927–33] with H. D. and Bryher).

82 Other tactics included sit-ins, occupations, debates, and lecture disruption. The campaign began after the March 1968 protest against the Vietnam War in London (Gordon Carr, *The Angry Brigade*, 32–33). Many Essex students were at this march; alumnus Chris Ratcliff recalls Mendelssohn being among their number (email dated 17 May 2016).

83 SxMs109/3/A/1/18.

84 A single Mendelssohn notebook (again, there are nearly 800) will include notes on Forster, Boccaccio, Cromwell; another on Auden, Tillie Olson, Benjamin Britten, the letters of Peter Plymley, Waugh, Longfellow, and extracts from *The Sunday Times*.

85 Lynne Harries, "The Northern Debutante", 17–18 (SxMs109/1/A/1).

86 SxMs109/3/A/52. According to Harries, among the anarchists she and Mendelssohn knew, past or present, all "had interesting projects underway in academia or the arts .... Only Anna was standing out against the prevailing tone, still paying the price, poor and isolated" ("The Northern Debutante", 36; 1/A/1).

87 I approached the British poet Peter Riley in the winter after Mendelssohn died about her papers. In 2010, Mendelssohn's three children generously donated their mother's archive to Special Collections at the University of Sussex. After five years pursuing funding, including being shortlisted for a large grant from the European Research Council in 2012–13, I secured a Research Development Grant from the University of Sussex to hire the archivist Simon Coleman, whose expertise and labour are discussed in the concluding acknowledgements of this introduction. The archive was officially opened to the public in autumn 2015.

88 I discuss Mendelssohn's relationship to this poetic label, popularised in literary discourse after Verlaine's infamous but little-critiqued treatise, *Les poètes maudits* (1882; 1886) in "The Agonies of Ambiguity: Anna Mendelssohn, *la poétesse maudite*" (*Modernism/modernity*, vol. 25, no. 3, 2018).

89 The *Oxford English Dictionary* indicates that the term precedes Nordau and Lombroso; usages from 1895 stress "'restless repetition of one and the same strain of thought'" and fixation upon one's "'own mental and moral ailments'". See also: Nordau, *Degeneration*. 2nd ed., trans. unidentified, D. Appleton and Company, 1895, 18.

90 W. H. Auden, "In Memory of W. B. Yeats", *Collected Poems*, ed. Edward Mendelson, Faber & Faber, 247–48, 48.

91 Consider the following, from Mendelssohn to her cousin Barry Benser: "The poet is always trying to heal what politics would tear asunder – the human spirit." Another letter to Benser, dated 15 April 1997, illustrates Mendelssohn's untenably feminist and anti-political stance via her interest in the surrealist Gisèle Prassinos:

> She was a young poet like I was, and if there is any motive behind what I want to do it is only that I want it to be known, some day, that some girls are young poets and that society is not always, perhaps rarely, kind to us. I despair when Everything is handed over to politics. Perhaps it is – perhaps that is the final Reality, but I dont [*sic*] want to subscribe to that final reality. (SxMs109/1/E/1/7).

92 Poet and editor Andrew Duncan reviewed *Bernache Nonnette* (1995) in "Nine fine flyaway goose truths" *Angel Exhaust*, no. 15, 1997, 105–10. Poet and critic Lucy Sheerman reviewed Mendelssohn's *Tondo Aquatique* (1997) in "See Sense: Embarking on a Reading of Jennifer Moxley, Grace Lake and John Forbes" for the on-line magazine *Jacket* in 2001.

93 Esther Leslie, *Bouleversed Baudelairizing: On Poetics and Terror*, Veer Books, 2011, 28.

Along with Leslie's work, further publications immediately following Mendelssohn's death include Jon Clay's discussion of Mendelssohn in *Sensation, Contemporary Poetry and Deleuze: Transformative Intensities* (Continuum, 2010). Additionally, the poet Sean Bonney published an essay in *The Poetry Project Newsletter* (no. 226, 2011). Bonney's title blends two Mendelssohn quotes: "'Minds do exist to agitate and provoke / this is the reason I do not conform'". The first half of this title is drawn from "pladd. (you who say either)"; the second half is the first line of the untitled poem beginning "This is the reason why I do not conform."; both are published in *IA*. Essays on Mendelssohn by Connie Scozzaro and Eleanor Careless can be found in *The Paper Nautilus*, no. 2, 2011.

Further discussions of Mendelssohn exist in David and Christine Kennedy's *Women's Experimental Poetry in Britain 1970–2010: Body, Time and Locale* (Liverpool University Press, 2013); a chapter by Simon Perril in *Modernist Legacies: Trends and Faultlines in British Poetry Today* (ed. David Nowell-Smith and Abigail Lang, Palgrave Macmillan, 2015); and an essay on Mendelssohn and Pound by Laura Kilbride in *News from Afar: Ezra Pound and Some Contemporary British Poetries* (ed. Richard Parker, Shearsman Books, 2014).

My own work on Mendelssohn includes "The Agonies of Ambivalence: Anna Mendelssohn, *la poétesse maudite*" (*Modernism/modernity*, vol. 25, no. 3, 2018) and the editing of a 1987 portion of her *roman-à-clef* entitled *What a Performance* for the *PMLA* (vol. 133, no. 3, 2018). Also in 2018, Jordon Savage published "'I Don't Talk to the Police Except Never': Anna Mendelssohn, Tom Raworth, and Anti-Confessional Life-Writing" in the *Journal of British and Irish Innovative Poetry* (vol. 10, no. 1). This same journal published essays on Mendelssohn by Vicky Sparrow and Joe Luna in 2018 and 2019 respectively, and in 2020/21, under the editorship of Vicky Sparrow and Eleanor Careless, offered a special issue on Mendelssohn. A substantial portion of my essay for that issue appears in section 5.2 of this introduction. Further, the end of section 4 became the basis for a chapter in *The New Modernist Studies* (ed. Douglas Mao, Cambridge, 2020) entitled "Feminism's Archives: Mina Loy, Anna Mendelssohn, and Taxonomy".

94 Revivalist factions coalesced in Northumbria, Cambridge, Bristol, Wales, Scotland, and London. See Neil Pattison's useful overview of the origins of this turn in British poetics: "Introduction: 'All Flags Left Outside'", *Certain Prose of the English Intelligencer*, Mountain Press, 2012, i–xxxii.

95 Poem beginning "Treading carpentry free country" (*Crystal Love D. N. A.*, 1982).

96 "He turned his face over a shoulder, rere regardant." This is James Joyce writing about Stephen Dedalus, who has just drafted a poem on Sandymount Strand (*Ulysses*, ed. Declan Kiberd, Penguin, 2000, 64).

97 Yes, Grace Lake. As will be discussed in part six of this introduction, *Parasol One. Parasol Two. Parasol Avenue.* (1996) begins with a poem that focuses upon the central figures of *viola tricolor* (1993) and *Bernache Nonnette* (1995). The same poem references "Panopticonic Belvedere", which is an allusion to a portion of Mendelssohn's *roman-à-clef* written circa 1982 or 1983, namely: *The Panopticonic Belvedere Demolished.* (SxMs109/1/B/1/6).

98 Letter dated 27 February 1993; SxMs109/8/C/1.

99 "from 'Spinster of Arts'", *Parataxis*, no. 2, 1992.

100 See "1:3ng" (*Gare du Nord*, 1997), with its suggestion that "snippets of Pound & Eliot" have aggressive capacities, or this claim, written shortly before her death: "I am not interested / in – / Ezra Pound / and the Cambridge / Competition" (poem beginning "I have only 'some interest'", *Poems Written at Hinton Grange Care Home*, 2009).

101 Poem beginning "It shouldn't be this way, just" (*constant red/mingled damask*, no. 2, 1987).

102 Poem beginning "This is the reason why I do not conform." (*IA*, 2000). See also, in the editorial notes regarding Mendelssohn's publication in *Gare du Nord* (1997), her responses to an editorial questionnaire about poetic risk.

103 To this question, Mendelssohn adds: "How controlled I am, no-one normal could stand this being driven to distraction by sheer prejudice" (1 August 2008; SxMs109/3/A/1/68). Writing and the law are often inextricable in Mendelssohn's thinking. In an undated letter to her friend Estelle Langley, she writes: "whether one transgresses the law or not, one transgresses in writing" (3/A/1/29/4).

104 "eulogy" (*A State of Independence*, 1998).

105 Poem beginning "to have some stupid bloke laughing and giggling at you." (*constant red/mingled damask*, no. 1, 1986).

106 As one of countless examples of this British aversion, we might turn to Dada, a vanguard movement that clearly fascinated Mendelssohn. Intensely international in scope, Dada factions arose in Amsterdam, Brussels, New York, Paris, Berlin, Hanover, Cologne, and Zurich, but not England. Though Dada originated in Germany, anglophile T. S. Eliot described it as "a diagnosis of a disease of the French mind", primly if accurately predicting that "'whatever lesson we extract from it will not be directly applicable in London'" ("The Lesson of Baudelaire", *The Annotated Waste Land*, ed. Lawrence Rainey, Yale University Press, 2005, 144). And when Italian theorist Renato Poggioli lists the decadent coteries that catalysed so much vanguardism across Europe, he cites France, Russia, Germany, and Italy as key centres – England goes unnamed (*Theory of the Avant-Garde*, trans. Gerald Fitzgerald, The Belknap Press of Harvard University Press, 1981, 20–21). Similarly, Raymond Williams describes "[t]he true social bases of the early avant-garde" as cosmopolitan and metropolitan, as situated in Paris, Vienna, Berlin, and St. Petersburg; to this list he desultorily adds, "and also, in more limited ways, in London" ("The Politics of the Avant-Garde", *The Politics of Modernism: Against the New Conformists*, ed. Tony Pinkney, Verso, 1989, 49–64, 60). Recent

scholarship by critics including Michel Remy and Hope Wolf nuances these assertions by recovering and resituating English involvement in movements such as surrealism.

107 Undated correspondence with Lynne Harries (SxMs109/3/A/1/18).

108 Undated letter to Andrew Duncan (SxMs109/3/A/1/12). See also "pladd. (you who say either)" (*IA*, 2000), where Mendelssohn writes: "Osip Mandelstam in England would have been / murdered too. Where there is no art."

109 Letter dated 23 December 1996 (SxMs109/3/A/1/52).

110 Undated; SxMs109/3/A/1/52.

111 Notes accompanying *IA* drafts (SxMs109/5/A/24/8). See also, from *IA*, "My Chekhov's Twilight World" where Mendelssohn asserts: "I shall never consider that I have a cultural contribution to make to British / Culture again. I swear to that."

112 SxMs109/1/E/1/7.

113 Poem beginning "if we are not careful we shall be glad to die." (*IA*, 2000, 43; not in this collection).

114 A Mendelssohn neologism, "elastine" is a composite of "elastin" – a protein in connective tissue, particularly skin – and "elastane" – an elastic polyurethane used in hosiery and underwear. An epidermis uncomfortably pink, chemical, and glossy, or hosiery badly matched against Caucasian skin; all of Mendelssohn's denotations of this term generate unease.

115 The phrase "beyondsense" for Zaum is used by Paul Schmidt in his translations of the work of another Russian Futurist, Velimir Khlebnikov (*Collected Works of Velimir Khlebnikov*, vols. 1–3, Harvard University Press, 1987–98).

116 Poem beginning "Parts of it crackle so you don't need to say that or make any passive references." (*Bernache Nonnette*, 1995).

117 Adding to her lineage, this same Bernache desires to set up a life in the ancient Mexican city of Tula (poems beginning "Four eighths for writing business letters a man selects a voice she, he mocks, she will and inverts" and "& envisaging ruptures imagination parental government hanging round social hairs", *Bernache Nonnette*, 1995).

118 Baroness Elsa von Freytag-Loringhoven, "Tailend of Mistake: America." (*Body Sweats: The Uncensored Writings of Elsa von Freytag-Loringhoven*, ed. Irene Gammel and Suzanne Zelazo, MIT Press, 2011, 116). In their notes, the Baroness's editors observe that "Genickstarre" is German for spinal meningitis, or stiff neck (356). The Baroness's poem is anti-Semitic, and in this specific regard, it could not be more opposed to Mendelssohn's ideologies.

119 Of the three thousand or so books unearthed in Mendelssohn's home after her death, many were well-used "foreign language dictionaries, grammars and course books, which covered French, German, Spanish, Italian, Dutch, Swedish, Hungarian, Greek, Turkish, Polish, Russian, Persian, Arabic, modern and Old Testament Hebrew, Irish and Scots" (Peter Riley, speech delivered 15 September 2010, at "Anna Mendelssohn: A Celebration of her Work and Life", co-sponsored by the Centre for Modernist Studies at the University of Sussex and the Contemporary Poetics Research Centre at Birkbeck; transcript provided by author).

Examples of these languages surface in Mendelssohn's work. In her draft poems for *viola tricolor* (1993), Mendelssohn titles a poem "sumbur" or Russian for "muddle". In a poem beginning "at the moment", Mendelssohn inserts "schlägt", the German for punch, hit, strike, defeat, cream, whisk, whip (*IA*, 2000, 66; not in this collection). A draft poem for *IA* is titled "slass coelitus arieto glass classico chivet"; "slåss" is the Norwegian verb "to fight"; "coelitus" and "arieto" are Latin, meaning, respectively: "from heaven" and "harass, strike violently, collide". Mendelssohn's undated poem beginning "nit freaks" concludes with the nonce word "findalio"; as "alio" is Latin for "elsewhere", Mendelssohn's term may be an injunction to seek movement in another direction or locate an alternate course of action.

120 For examples, see the second half of "damned channel" (*Parasol One. Parasol Two. Parasol Avenue.*, 1996), the long French portions in Mendelssohn's 1998 *Inscape* submission, and the poem beginning "parme, abricot et violette" in *py. : a book of acrostics for p.e.g.* (2009).

121 "small points." (*Posmos, the Yellow Velvet Underground.*, 1982).

122 "proscribble at 16.12 hours." ("*I'm working here.*", February 1983).

123 Poem beginning "Exactly what will this have rested upon for it to have emerged." (*Bernache Nonnette*, 1995).

124 "to fit the prototype." (Typescript, October 1986); poem beginning "Shiva's crackling on a spinal hair" (*constant red/mingled damask*, no. 1, 1986); "studio VII" (*involution*, no. 5, 1997).

125 "'The bourgeoisie lives there'" (*poems*, 1984).

126 Poem beginning "and being led dissociate" (*café archéologique*, draft poems, 1992–93).

127 "nattering swans" (*Jacket*, no. 20, December 2002).

128 Pound, "A Few Don'ts by an Imagiste" (*Imagist Poetry*, ed. Peter Jones, Penguin, 2001, 130–34, 131). Mendelssohn, "One on each shoulder, carouse." (*Is this a True Parrot, a Mountain, or a Stooge?*, 1985).
129 Poem beginning "What is wrong with 'easy'?" (*Propaganda Multi-Billion Bun.*, August 1985).
130 "concilia." (*Out of Everywhere*, 2006; 1996).
131 "La Facciata" (*Conductors of Chaos*, 1996).
132 Poem beginning "She Walked where she should have stood still, stock still." (*Out of Everywhere*, 2006; 1996).
133 Poem beginning "What is wrong with 'easy'?" (*Propaganda Multi-Billion Bun.*, August 1985).
134 Poem beginning "think twice" (*Crystal Love: D. N. A.*, 1982).
135 "to fit the prototype." (Typescript, October 1986). See also the poem beginning "and being led dissociate" (*café archéologique*, draft poems, 1992–93), which likens mainstream publication to Hell:

> morality fears full censorship
> of what is still extant
> in brochures and in picture books
> of corpuscles with pruning hooks
> and flaming forks and briney brooks

136 "London 1971" (*Conductors of Chaos*, 1996).
137 "non-existencies." (*café archéologique*, draft poems, 1992–93).
138 Poem beginning "incrustation, fossilised cement, caked dry canine's excrement," (*viola tricolor*, draft poems, c. 1993).
139 *Out of Everywhere*, 2006; 1996.
140 "the chantral grey" (*Parasol One. Parasol Two. Parasol Avenue.*, 1996).
141 "two secs." (see appendix notes, *viola tricolor*, draft poems, c. 1993).
142 A similar experience is described in *Tondo Aquatique* (1997), in an untitled poem that begins:

> one by one she forces herself to remember adjectives
> can lift to a certain height her wrist gives way
> she drops, she bends, she cannot bear this kind of poetry.
> she cannot dive, there is no pool, she wants to stay in the rain today

Another distressed variation on "high-walking into fantasy" occurs in "Britain 1967", where a person draws the speaker "skating on the sky though a black mirror" (*Vanishing Points*, 2004).
143 Poem beginning "pan & tilt. weft & warp. the earth does tilt. to define me as straight" (*IA*, 2000).
144 "FEAR up the stairs / man under my bed" writes Mendelssohn in "ELEVEN." (*Propaganda Multi-Billion Bun.*, August 1985); at the end of her life, she begins a poem as follows: "his shadow was there / it watched me" (*Poems Written at Hinton Grange Care Home*, 2009). See also "Abschied", where a he "prowl[s] towards / flat on his belly / costumed in foliage" (*A State of Independence*, 1998) .
145 SxMs109/3/A/1/34/2.
146 André Breton, "The Second Manifesto of Surrealism" (1930), *Manifestoes of Surrealism*, trans. Richard Seaver and Helen R. Lane, University of Michigan Press, 2007, 117–94, 125.
147 Poem beginning "light. & where is the end. & who was a taut string ringing" (*viola tricolor*, draft poems, c. 1993).
148 Poem beginning "leave these to die lest grammar offends you, rammed ammonites" (*viola tricolor*, draft poems, c. 1993).
149 "Cultural" (*A State of Independence*, 1998); "Demeter." (*viola tricolor*, draft poems, c. 1993).
150 Poem beginning "This is the reason why I do not conform." (*IA*, 2000).
151 "pladd. (you who say either)" (*IA*, 2000).
152 Undated computer print-out (SxMs109/1/B/2/29); "half evacuation measures unmet, still on regulo" (*Inscape* submission, 1998).
153 Loose sheet from papers dated c. late 1970s to 1980 (SxMs109/5/B/2/1).
154 This quote is on an A5 sheet entitled "sources for poetry deaf. a pastoral." Drawn from Mendelssohn's loose autobiographical sheets, it

was recorded before the archive was catalogued.

155 Undated letter to Rod Mengham (SxMs109/3/A/1/34). In "Composition as Explanation", a lecture delivered at Cambridge and Oxford in 1926, Stein insists that while vanguard art might appear ahead of its time, in fact, considered responses lag too far behind aesthetic innovation. According to Stein, World War I accelerated art reception by thirty years, making audiences better placed to understand the "we who created the expression of the modern composition" (www.poetryfoundation.org/articles/69481/composition-as-explanation).

156 Manuscript entitled "Give me something I can sink my teeth into!" (SxMs109/5/B/2/58).

157 Olsen's *Yonnondio* (1974) is named in the poem beginning "Power has a temper, pranksters abound" (*py.*, 2009); Ilya Ehrenburg is mentioned in the poem segment beginning "it wasn't a silent notice" (*Inscape* submission, 1998). The Pottier reference arises in the draft for "No Wonder" (*Parasol One. Parasol Two. Parasol Avenue.*, 1996); in a draft variant, next to the title, Mendelssohn writes: "E.P'r." and "E. Pottier. *L'Internationale.*" (see editorial notes). Remaining references are from *IA* (2000): Anna Akhmatova in "flat hat." (121; not in this collection); Mandelstam in "pladd. (you who say either)"; Lorca and Ravachol in "of Lorca."

158 "on challenge, positive attitudes and 'les peintres cubistes'" (*Conductors of Chaos*, 1996). For an overview of the apex of this factionalism in England, see Peter Barry's *Poetry Wars: British Poetry of the 1970s and the Battle of Earls Court*, Salt, 2006.

159 "1:3ng" (*Gare du Nord*, 1987); see also editorial notes for *IA*.

160 SxMs109/3/C.

161 Poem beginning "But that wasn't what, unreceptivity –" (*IA*, 2000, 14; not in this collection).

162 Draft dedication for *IA* (SxMs109/5/A/24/7).

163 20 September 1989 (SxMs109/3/A/1/51).

164 Mendelssohn suggests that relentless public scrutiny of her past enforces her conservatism (SxMs109/1/B/2/29). She believes grammar schools importantly perpetuate classical learning, and claims she always wanted to attend public school because of its higher standards (1/B/1/39/3; letter to Douglas Oliver dated 10 December 1997, 3/A/1/43). She denounces gay liberation and political correctness (1/B/2/37; poem beginning "callipyge elle me tenait, rumpus," [*Inscape* submission, 1998]). Mendelssohn may have needed to believe that biological intergenerational ties alone generate an enduring familial legacy, and can write sentimentally of an unbreakable maternal bond, as in: "I had always / thought of the relationship / between a mother / & her children sacred" (5/A/24/7). Desires for financial ease and high-quality commodities permeate Mendelssohn's archival writings.

165 "Sums." (*Celestial Empire.*, February 1983) and "Half" (*viola tricolor*, 1993). In order of appearance, quotes are from the following: part two of the poem beginning "point a finger at him" (*Other Poetry* submission, 1984); "1:3ng" (*Gare du Nord*, no. 1, 1997); poem beginning "Shiva's crackling on a spinal hair" (*constant red/mingled damask*, no. 1, 1986); poem beginning "a settlement of priorities reaches unassailable" (*Crystal Love D. N. A.*, 1982); "Not Bad" (*constant red/mingled damask*, no. 2, 1987); "Demeter." (*viola tricolor*, draft poems, c. 1993); poem beginning "A man who snatches a ring" (*IA*, 2000, 9; not in this collection). This tendency can also be discerned within Mendelssohn's drafts and notes for *IA*. Witness: "build your own paper mill. / heave the bricks yourself. / dig the foundations on / bread and water" (for complete extract, see appendix editorial notes).

166 Poem beginning "digne." (*IA*, 2000); poem beginning "rubbish.   desk bang." (*Propaganda Multi-Billion Bun.*, August 1985).

167 Poem beginning "digne." (*IA*, 2000).

168 "Je suis navrée." (*IA*, 2000, 135; not in this collection).

169 "Graves' Art Gallery Tea Room, 1981, Sheffield" (*constant red/mingled damask*, no. 1, 1986).

170 "drought" (*viola tricolor*, draft poems, c. 1993).

171 "SACRED PIN." (*Celestial Empire.*, February 1983); "ELEVEN." (*Propaganda Multi-Billion Bun.*, August 1985).

172 Poem beginning "cold water soup channelled through slowly arterial ways wishing well" (*viola tricolor*, draft poems, c. 1993). See also the poem beginning "we might look thick / but we're not stupid." (*The Day the Music Died*, 1993).

173 "'The bourgeoisie live there'" (*poems*, 1984).

174 Poem beginning "i can hardly bear going down town to see those people" (*Propaganda Multi-Billion Bun.*, August 1985).

175 "On being reproached by saintly mediators for bad budgeting" (*Vanishing Points*, 2004).

176 Both poems are first published in *Is this a True Parrot, a Mountain, or a Stooge?* (1985).

177 "Sunday Beasts." (Manuscript, April 1988).

178 "Sunday Beasts." (Manuscript, April 1988). The conflation of the marginalised and the migrant can be traced to Mendelssohn's prison notebooks. In 1975, she writes: "It is very hard to keep your head intact when you are continually subjected to ingratiating treatment. I understand the dry bitter taste of Black, Refugee, Jew of the past" (SxMs109/2/A/6).

179 The quotes are from the poem beginning "Treading carpentry free country" (*Crystal Love: D. N. A.*, 1982) and "oh yes we are entitled mohican slaves" (Typescript, October 1983).

180 "dig; dig." (Typescript, October 1983).

181 "dour…" (*Bernache Nonnette*, 1995).

182 "pladd." (*IA*, 2000); "Britain 1967." (*Vanishing Points*, 2004).

183 Poem section beginning "callipyge elle me tenait, rumpus" (*Inscape* submission, 1998); poem beginning "struggles with self" (*café archéologique*, c. 1992–93). See also, from the poem beginning "basalt. basalt.": "little children. but this goes down to the point, and is enmeshed in the / Nietzschean Will of the Baudelairean's determination to declassify the / Jewess from the functioning economy in Academia and in the Arts" (*IA*, 2000). Mendelssohn concludes this poem as follows: "The / Jew is the least protected", excoriating those who advocate a "mock-Jewish" resignation. Elsewhere, Mendelssohn describes "english literature" as the provenance of "the baptized" (poem beginning "i would be interested in other people's", *The Day the Music Died*, 1993).

184 Poem beginning "Pall Mall." (*Bernache Nonnette*, 1995).

185 The precise locations of the tombs of Jacob's sons remain uncertain, but in the twelfth century, Reuben was reportedly buried in Kabul by Persian traveller Ali of Herat. Joshua 15:6 recounts how Reuben's son Bohan marks the territory of the Tribe of Judah with a stone, a biblical passage that may inform Mendelssohn's evocation of "the / Rock that searched for Reuben".

186 The British created the Durand Line that cuts through Afghanistan and Pakistan in 1893. This boundary divided the Pashtun people, always affiliated with Afghanistan, and created a deep schism within that population that was a key factor in the formation of the Taliban in the latter half of the twentieth century. The Battle of Kabul took place between 1992 and 1996.

187 Brian Cheyette, *Constructions of 'The Jew' in English Literature and Society: Racial Representations, 1875–1945*, Cambridge University Press, 1993, 12, 267.

188 As Sander L. Gilman attests, this transition in Jewish categorisation begins with the *fin-de-siècle* assimilation of Jews into European urban centres; the rise in early twentieth-century anti-Semitism is partly attributable to the "alarming" indiscernibility of those with Jewish origins (*The Jew's Body*, Bloomberg Press, 1991). For an excellent discussion of the diminishment of Jewish racialisation in Mendelssohn's post-war generation, see "Abjecting Whiteness: 'The Movement', Radical Feminism, and Genocide" in Amanda Third's *Gender and the Political: Deconstructing the Female Terrorist* (Palgrave Macmillan, 2014, 119–38).

189 Poem beginning "in those days it was not indictable." (*The Day the Music Died*, 1993).

190 "Silk & Wild Tulips" (*Out of Everywhere*, 2006; 1996).

191 "REARRANGED LETTER TO THOMAS EVANS" (*onedit*, 2000).

192 "Above her heart, a grand piano." (Typescript, September 1986). As early as 1985, Mendelssohn satirises how her politically active peers assess each other's credentials by way of class and parental affiliations with World War II (see poem beginning "The toughie would say:", *Propaganda Multi-Billion Bun.*, 1985). In "XEROPHILOUS" (*Inverse*, no. 2, 1993), Mendelssohn juxtaposes the "advancing infantry" of "W. W. 2" with youth "trampled over and torn down from democratic plinths / as detached from the bullets that kill them." Further, the definitive nature of the war informs the conclusion of the poem beginning "I don't know which colour to choose.": "How without the second world war / Can I possibly in the presence of relentless realism get it right" (*Tondo Aquatique*, 1997).

193 SxMs109/5/A/24/7. Perplexingly, Mendelssohn repeatedly cites these photos as the catalyst for her activism, but they were published in 1972, when she was in prison, and had been a political agitator for four or five years.

194 Poems beginning "I know. it sounds tendentious or is it sententious."; "your people are strangers therefore why do you ask me my name?"; and "wrap yourself in jam jeunesse" (all *IA*, 2000, 103, 58, 50; not in this collection).

195 "Regulo" is a trademark device to ensure even cooking in gas ovens; in Latin, "rēgulō" comes from the verb "rēgulāre" meaning to direct or regulate. This sequence was submitted to *Inscape* in 1998.

196 Poem section beginning "n'essayez pas" (*Inscape* submission, 1998).

197 Poem sections beginning "to inspect" and "metamorphosis began after the destruction of the temple" (*Inscape* submission, 1998).

198 Poem section beginning "and rather than defend" (*Inscape* submission, 1998).

199 Ilya Ehrenburg and Vasily Grosman, *The Complete Black Book of Russian Jewry*, trans and ed. David Patterson, Routledge, 2017. Poem section beginning "it wasn't a silent notice" (*Inscape* submission, 1998).

200 Poem section beginning "you would have to" (*Inscape* submission, 1998).

201 Poem section beginning "I want an orchestra." (*Inscape* submission, 1998).

202 Poem section beginning "is it naturally reduced" (*Inscape* submission, 1998).

203 "Franked" (*Vanishing Points*, 2004).

204 In order of appearance, these quotes are drawn from: "Estée Lauder. There may be some objections raised." (Manuscript, December 1988); "two secs" (early draft) (*viola tricolor*, draft poems, c. 1993); "On being reproached by saintly mediators for bad budgeting" (*Vanishing Points*, 2004).

205 "WHY" (Typescripts, 1985).

206 Letter to Rod Mengham (SxMs109/3/A/1/34); Joyce, *Ulysses* (ed. Declan Kiberd, Penguin, 2000, 926–27); poem beginning "they were, in those days, his players." (*viola tricolor*, draft poems, c. 1993).

207 Poem beginning "The toughie would say:" (*Propaganda Multi-Billion Bun.*, August 1985); "virago." (*IA*, 2000, 56; not in this collection).

208 "To a Radical Lesbian Feminist Rapist" (*The News*, 1987). Mendelssohn's polemic responds to a range of contemporaneous thinking about the liberations and constraints of female reproductivity. The extremist turn against domesticity is best exemplified by Valerie Solanas's Society for Cutting Up Men (SCUM). Solanas's 1967 manifesto advocated for an all-female society in which males are killed at birth (*SCUM Manifesto*, London, 2004). Less extreme advocates include Shulamith Firestone's call for an end to sex distinction, and her related arguments about how technology might free women from reproduction. Firestone's *The Dialectic of Sex: The Case for Feminist Revolution* (1970) was reviewed in the women's issue of *Frendz* that Mendelssohn edited (vol. 3, no. 30, 1971; see also section six of this introduction).

209 Lauri Umansky argues that second-wave feminists struggled against the presumptuous, unexamined misogyny of the New Left by identifying the family as a key site of women's oppression. As women's groups splintered over issues of race, class, and sexuality in the early 1970s, Umanski shows how motherhood persisted as a uniting theme, shifting mainstream feminism from a radical positioning to a "cultural feminist" stance (*Motherhood Reconsidered: Feminism and the Legacies of the Sixties*, New York University Press, 1996, 5, 8).

210 "1:3ng" (*Gare du Nord*, no. 1, 1997).

211 Since the nineteenth century, white women's abortion campaigning has frequently, and not without justification, been linked to agendas eugenic or Christian. In "Abortion, Race, and Gender in Nineteenth-Century America" sociologists Nicola Beisel and Tamara Kay discuss early white feminists' resistance to abortion for fear of Anglo-Saxon decline (*American Sociological Review*, vol. 69, no. 4, 2004, 498–518). During the second wave of feminism, women of colour and working-class women expressed concern that pro-choice campaigning was implicitly directed at marginalised populations.

In a notebook dated 1979–80, Mendelssohn speculates about abortion, writing that she doesn't "like foetuses being destroyed", but also that unplanned or untenable pregnancies should not put women "in danger of losing their life". For Mendelssohn, money, "not coping", worry, fear of social reprisal, ignorance, and a dislike of contraception are all rationales for abortion. In sum, she writes: "Yes I support the National Abortion Campaign" (SxMs109/4/A/7). Throughout her archive, she repeatedly observes, with outrage, how people insisted that she ought to terminate her pregnancies because she was poor and not in monogamous, committed relationships with the biological fathers.

212 "and Waterloo Westminster" (*IA*, 2000, 57–61, 60; not in this collection); see also poem beginning "in those days it was not indictable. / men could beat their wives" (*The Day the Music Died*, 1993). Mendelssohn's poems addressing rape include "On Vanity" (*Tondo Aquatique*, 1997); the poem beginning "and I who loved Poetry as I loved God" (*The Day the Music Died*, 1993); and the poem section beginning "metamorphosis began after the destruction of the temple" (*Inscape* submission, 1998).

213 See "Demeter." (*viola tricolor*, draft poems, c. 1993); "purdah darting glances" (*Bernache Nonnette*, 1995); and, perhaps more ironically, the poem beginning "pendragon in purdah" (*py.*, 2009).

214 Poem beginning "his shadow was there" (*Poems Written at Hinton Grange Care Home*, 2009); poem beginning "cold water soup channelled through slowly arterial ways wishing well" (*viola tricolor*, draft poems, c. 1993). See also "1:3ng" where the speaker asserts, "I had the cheek to bear them alone", and criticises the legal imperative to identify biological fathers on birth certificates: "If the fathers are not

named / The children are removed" (*Gare du Nord*, no. 1, 1998).

215 "Dyr Bul Shchyl" (*Critical Quarterly*, vol. 38, no. 3, 1996); "language blows away" (*A State of Independence*, 1998).

216 For some examples, see the discussion of "Equal Opportunities for Women" in "My Chekhov's Twilight World" and of "the Equal Opportunities Act" in the poem beginning "pan & tilt." (*IA*, 2000). "[B]rethren" are blamed for the lack of funding for feminism in the poem beginning "sickened by the sight of the yard thewed daughters", while "Demeter." discusses the hostile exclusion of the female academic from research (*viola tricolor*, draft poems, c. 1993).

217 Poem beginning "Cover the land" (Typescripts, 1974); "Britain 1967" (*Vanishing Points*, 2004).

218 Poem beginning "Ham banks counter machines slicers grills pockets drawers" (*The Day the Music Died*, 1993).

219 "Declared redundant 'in media res' as politics advise sentiment" (*Active in Airtime*, no. 2, 1993).

220 "1:3ng" (*Gare du Nord*, no. 1, 1997).

221 Poem beginning "Exactly what will this have rested upon for it to have emerged." (*Bernache Nonnette*, 1995).

222 Poem beginning "piped, once more, piped" (*Inbuilt Flash Nix*, 1985); poem beginning "at the moment" (*IA*, 2000, 66; not in this collection).

223 "1:3ng" (*Gare du Nord*, no. 1, 1997); poem beginning "Reminiscent of a flat expanse trammelled" (*IA*, 2000).

224 Letter to Elizabeth (no surname) dated 7 October 1987 (SxMs109/3/B).

225 Untitled 1986 portion of Mendelssohn's *roman-à-clef* beginning "Calling you" (SxMs109/1/B/1/31).

226 Denise Riley, *Am I That Name? Feminism and the Category of 'Women'*, University of Minnesota Press, 1988.

227 Letter to Jude Windle dated 1 September 2008 (SxMs109/3/1/A/68); undated letter to John, ascribing that fear to too much time in a woman-only institution in her youth (3/B). Further, in a letter to scholar Romana Huk, Mendelssohn tellingly observes: "It's strange that the artist's vision, which is a traditional right, is stopped and deconstructed at precisely the time when women are moving into full emancipation" (3/A/1/20).

228 "friday." (*IA*, 2000, 31; not in this collection).

229 Poem beginning "Declare your hatred." (*Parasol One. Parasol Two. Parasol Avenue.*, 1996).

230 "Art & Women." (*café archéologique*, 1992–93).

231 "1:3ng" (*Gare du Nord*, no. 1, 1997).

232 *First Things: Maternal Imaginary in Literature, Art, and Psychoanalysis*, Routledge, 1995, iii.

233 Poem beginning "to have some stupid bloke laughing and giggling at you." (*constant red/mingled damask*, no. 1, 1986).

234 Poem beginning "poetry is the lack" (*IA*, 2000, 24 and 27; not in this collection).

235 "Half." (*viola tricolor*, 1993). See also "I object.", which contains the lines: "it's odd / to sustain that level of antagonism against / one's own daughter" (*IA*, 2000).

236 "Demeter." (*viola tricolor,* draft poems, 1993); "Abschied" (*A State of Independence*, 1998). See also the reference to "the mother in me, / unborn & now denied" in "Strictly personal" (*Vanishing Points*, 2004).

237 There are numerous copies of the manifesto in the archive (see for instance SxMs109/B/2/80), and Mendelssohn deposited a copy at the British Library, where it is still held.

238 While Mendelssohn sidesteps Loy's satiric self-flagellation to openly excoriate mankind, both manifestos exhort their readers to use their intelligence; both ironically propose that some women may not be fit to parent; both extol the *ab*jectification of women. The single mother is central: for Loy, any woman who does not strike a bargain with men is declared an unfit mother and debarred maternity; these claims chime with Mendelssohn's satire of the mistrust levied at single parents. Loy writes: "Every woman of superior intelligence should realize her race-responsibility, in producing children in adequate proportion to the unfit or degenerate members of her sex –" ("Feminist Manifesto", *The Lost Lunar Baedeker*, ed. Roger Conover, Carcanet, 1997, 155). Mendelssohn writes: "Shall we sterilize the human basin?" Where Loy focuses on sexuality, Mendelssohn focuses upon its occasionally fecund aftermath: the life of the intelligent, creative woman with children in tow. By extension, Mendelssohn easily excises irresponsible fathers from her movement – "Desert Daddies" – and demands to know when she, too, will be entitled to a woman in a "pinny" who will wait on her hand and foot.

239 SxMs109/3/A/1/52.

240 Tristan Tzara, "Seven Dada Manifestoes" (1918), *The Dada Painters and Poets: An Anthology*, ed. Robert Motherwell, Wittenborn,

Schultz, Inc., 1951, 75–87.

241 Poem beginning "But that wasn't what" (*IA*, 2000, 12–16; not in this collection).

242 SxMs109/5/A/18/2. See also letters Mendelssohn wrote referencing the abrupt truncation of MAMA to Andrew Duncan on 25 May 1999 (3/A/1/12) and Peter Riley on 2 September 1999 (3/A/1/52).

243 SxMs109/5/B/2/23.

244 Though Mendelssohn claims to have started writing poems as a child, it is an archival refrain that she began writing a long poem about London in the late 1960s, or just as the Situationist ethos permeates the University of Essex, where Mendelssohn was then a student. On "CONTINUOUS DRIFTING" see Ivan Chtcheglov's "Formulary for a New Urbanism" (1953); for "free creativity" as a replacement for traditional poetry, see the 1966 essay "On the Poverty of Student Life" (*Situationist International Anthology*, ed. and trans. Ken Knabb, Bureau of Public Secrets, 2006, 8, 429). "You just go on your nerve" is the much-quoted poetic mandate of Frank O'Hara's "Personism: A Manifesto" (1959).

245 Another example is readily available in Mendelssohn's "La Facciata Turns her Back", which was first published in 1988. A manuscript of this poem includes an elided personal segment that references Mendelssohn's children and her life as a poetess; it is written in the same ink as the draft of the published text, and starts, as does the final poem, with a deliberately repetitive line reading: "go on, go on as though nothing has happened" (SxMs109/4/C/33). Similarly, the draft poems that appear to have been cut from *café archéologique* (1992–93) are more subjective than those Mendelssohn chooses for the working copy, as are those cut from *viola tricolor* (1993); all are included in the appendix of this collection.

Lastly, in the earliest extant drafts of "Silk & Wild Tulips" (1995–2006), the first-person pronoun is in ready evidence: "Afraid of my father's power" was "I am afraid of my father's power" and one answer to the question "what is love? o what is love?" was "to be closed in upon from a great distance [....] how perfect I have to be no one knows" (SxMs109/5/B/2/71; see also editorial notes for *Out of Everywhere*, 2006).

246 See editorial notes for *Out of Everywhere* (2006; 1996).

247 These quotes are drawn from Mendelssohn's unreturned answers to a reader survey circulated by Douglas Oliver and Alice Notley in the late 1990s when they were editing their journal *Gare du Nord* (SxMs109/5/B/2/77). See editorial notes on Mendelssohn's 1997 *Gare du Nord* publication.

248 In order of appearance, these quotes refer to: "in the minority of one" (*Paper Nautilus*, no. 2, 2011); "the cliff." (Undated typescripts); poem beginning "it is not for you to say or tell to bode" and "<u>the secret   ballot</u>.   Austraque." (*viola tricolor*, draft poems, c. 1993).

249 Barring the observation about Decadence, these facts are drawn from Peter Wollen's "The Situationist International" (*New Left Review*, vol. 1, no. 174, 1989).

250 See *Society of the Spectacle* (Black and Red, 2010).

251 René Viénet, "The Situationists and the New Forms of Action Against Politics and Art" (1967), *Situationist International Anthology*, ed. and trans. Ken Knabb, Bureau of Public Secrets, 2006, 274–75.

252 Gordon Carr, *The Angry Brigade*, PM Press, 2010, 24, 5.

253 "On the Poverty of Student Life" (1966), *Situationist International Anthology*, ed. and trans. Ken Knabb, Bureau of Public Secrets, 2006, 408–29, 409–10.

254 SxMs109/5/B/2/46.

255 Barker argues that "the Italian movement from Potere Operaio onwards ... was more important to us", referring to a workers' movement that led to Italian Autonomism; his review appears at the end of Carr's *The Angry Brigade* (187).

256 "<u>Shell form: Conch tent.   (for John Barker)</u>" (*Crystal Love: D. N. A.*, 1982).

257 See editorial notes on *Tondo Aquatique*, 1997.

258 Poem beginning "point a finger at him" (*Other Poetry* submission, June 1984).

259 "Preliminary Problems in Constructing a Situation" (1958), *Situationist International Anthology*, ed. and trans. Ken Knabb, Bureau of Public Secrets, 2006, 50; see also 85 and 429 in the same volume.

260 "HOT DAY.   BAKED BARE EARTH.   PROWLED IN THE VALLEY FOR THE PIGS' NEST." (*Inbuilt Flash Nix*, 1985).

261 "REARRANGED LETTER TO THOMAS EVANS" (*onedit*, 2000).

262 "Franked" (*Vanishing Points*, 2004).
263 "La Facciata" (*Conductors of Chaos*, 1996).
264 "two secs" (*viola tricolor*, 1993).
265 "to any who want poems to give them answers." (*IA*, 2000).
266 As the editorial notes detail, these drafts are as follows: "two secs" (*viola tricolor*, 1993), which appears in the main body of this volume; the 38-line variant replicated in this appendix, and a 74-line version, "two secs." transcribed in full within the appendix notes. The poem beginning "sickened by the sight of the yard thewed daughters" is in the appendix (*viola tricolor*, draft poems, c. 1993).
267 See the "communistic, legalistic, stalinistic stake" of the poem beginning "sickened by the sight of yard thewed daughters" (*viola tricolor*, draft poems, c. 1993).
268 This is the conclusion to the 38-line "two secs." early draft included in the appendix. Published in 1962, Plath's "Daddy" infamously includes the lines: "Every woman adores a Fascist, / The boot in the face, the brute / Brute heart of a brute like you." (*Ariel, The Restored Edition*, Faber & Faber, 2007, 74).
269 A similar argument could be made about other Mendelssohn edits. In Mendelssohn's "Shell form: Conch tent.", the line "We stand before the tides." is edited as follows: "We are standing before the tides." Where "We ~~are~~ standi~~ng~~" denotes a specific scenario rendered in the continuous present, "We stand" lends the phase endurance and multivalence, emphasising corporeality and ideology (see editorial notes, *Crystal Love: D. N. A.*, 1982).
270 SxMs109/5/B/1/11. A rendering of this partial manuscript appears in the appendix notes for *viola tricolor*, draft poems, c. 1993.
271 Mendelssohn arguably recasts this refrain in her magnificent poem, "Silk & Wild Tulips", where she describes how, for poets who long to surpass the boundaries of space and time, "the beach was too large" (*Out of Everywhere*, 2006; 1996). Note also, in the poem beginning "I could see the sea & hear the sounds" the speaker travels miles to find "people [who] have brought liquid vowels / in trowels loading them from beaches" (*Tondo Aquatique*, 1997). In this instance, the beach is not an idealised expanse, but is uncontainable, liquid, and sustained only by manipulation.
272 As late as 2004, Mendelssohn will continue deflating SI revolutionary fervour to the domestic status quo, to the artifice of performance, writing: "Only beneath the table, is the stage" ("Franked", *Vanishing Points*, 2004).
273 Poem beginning "leave these to die lest grammar offends you, rammed ammonites" (*viola tricolor*, draft poems, c. 1993). This variant is discussed in the editorial notes for the appendix.
274 "ELEVEN." (*Propaganda Multi-Billion Bun.*, August 1985); "MOODIST" (*constant red/mingled damask*, no. 1, 1986).
275 Poem beginning "This was the age of people & not writers in newspapers & now is not." (*Parasol One. Parasol Two. Parasol Avenue.*, 1996); "and A New" (*Conductors of Chaos*, 1996).
276 Poem beginning "to have some stupid bloke laughing and giggling at you." (*constant red/mingled damask*, no. 1, 1986); "eulogy" (*A State of Independence*, 1998).
277 "§" or poem beginning "the chief of police wore a silver fleece" (*Tondo Aquatique*, 1997).
278 Poem beginning "it stops, alights, chooses rather than picks" (SxMs109/4/K/143). The poem is dated "Janvier 1968" and "~~July~~ 1968"; "ministress" may be "monitress" (ed.).
279 In *poems* (1984), Mendelssohn includes an undated "very early poem" that may be recovered juvenilia.
280 The notebook is numbered on every other page, and this quote is taken from the verso of page 11; the sides discussed in what follows are recto and verso of page ten. All three pages are in the same ink, and the hand remains consistent. Identified dates in this coverless notebook include: 2 and 3 September (presumably 1973); 30 January (given twice); 1 and 7 February 1974 (SxMs109/2/A/3).
281 Etymologically, "prowess" is a wonderfully contrary word: via a French lineage, its suffix feminises and arguably diminishes (consider "manageress"); in Middle English, derived from the Latinate "itia", "ess" signifies nouns of quality and position: largess, richesse. Self-described "poetess" Mendelssohn is surely alert to these connotations.
282 Samuel Taylor Coleridge, "This Lime-Tree Bower my Prison", *The Major Works*, ed. H. J. Jackson, Oxford University Press, 2000, 38–40.
283 Fabienne Moine, *Women Poets in the Victorian Era: Cultural Practices and Nature Poetry*, Ashgate, 1988, 56.
284 SxMs109/5/B/2/29.
285 We might well expect coats torn, rather than Mendelssohn's "coats horn". The lettering is ambiguous, but the "h" of horn resembles the

same letter in the line that follows (ed.).

286 In the popular *Flowers: Their Moral, Language, and Poetry* (1844), Henry Gardiner Adams argued that flowers have their own voice, but require poets to translate on their behalf. This thinking dovetailed with a pervasive belief, circa 1750 onwards, that women were especially attuned to the language of flowers. In the Victorian era, women's dialogue poems often included speakers addressing flora. As Fabienne Moine argues, this ethos of care fed *fin-de-siècle* conservationist movements (*Women Poets in the Victorian Era: Cultural Practices and Nature Poetry*, Ashgate, 1988, 63–65).

287 The version dedicated "for Emerald from Anna with love." is given here, from SxMs109/1/E/2/2/1; the shorter variant is in 5/B/2/95.

288 Throughout the nineteenth century, floral dictionaries demarcating the meaning and significance of individual blooms were incredibly popular; see, for instance, *The Language of Flowers* (Ernest Nister, 1902).

289 That this manuscript is an early working of "Silk & Wild Tulips" is clear; the first two stanzas alone show significant similarities between draft and finished poem:

> I am afraid of my father's power
> his two faced power
> whilst women condemn my poverty
> and urge me to return to the man I am most afraid of
> this money business
> who does make a million from what I don't want
> him to speak of them in the same breath as
> emotionally unstable, dark thoughts tearing absent flesh,
>
> what is love? o what is love?
> to be closed in upon from a great distance
> the letters shall remain closed
> how perfect I have to be no one knows
> the desert and the glass

This draft is undated (SxMs109/5/B/2/71). The same file contains a manuscript of "by gardenias i cannot telephone", a poem that will be discussed in this introduction, and that follows immediately after "Silk & Wild Tulips" in *Out of Everywhere* (2006; 1996). See also the editorial notes for *Out of Everywhere*.

290 With thanks to Alistair Davies for this observation.

291 "to any who want poems to give them answers." (*IA*, 2000).

292 A more satiric example of Mendelssohn conflating flowers with ideal language occurs in "Declared redundant 'in media res' as politics advise sentiment": "his mouth was full of roses as language was" (*Active in Airtime*, no. 2, 1993). Against this florid speech, the speaker concludes: "O teach me to be anything but brave / give me the courage to drip / Lend me a few voices to surprise myself with."

293 Fabienne Moine, *Women Poets in the Victorian Era: Cultural Practices and Nature Poetry* (Ashgate, 1988, 70). See also the anonymously authored *Language of Flowers*, where the pansy is denoted as "Thought" (Ernest Nister, 1902).

294 The overriding strength of the "natural" or biological relation furthers these literary associations. In *viola tricolor*, Mendelssohn's epigraph is taken from a scene in *Twelfth Night* where Viola articulates the paternal lineage she shares with her brother (5.1.242). This occurs in the final act of the play, or the first in which we hear her name.

Mendelssohn identifies Theodor Storm's influence in her papers (see note dated 5 February 1999 in SxMs109/5/A/24/8). In Storm's native German, "viola tricolor" means "little stepmother". His overdetermined novella duly centres on stepmother Inez, newcomer to a household once run by deceased mother Marie. Its inhabitants include loyal servant Annie, child Agnes, and father Professor Rupert. Post-honeymoon, Inez is overshadowed by Marie's enduring, haunting influence over husband and daughter; biology appears to be destiny. Inez's tumultuous, unstated feeling is repeatedly, variously described. Like Shakespeare's Viola, Inez goes unnamed: though Aggie "long[ed] for the love of this beautiful woman" she cannot call her "Mother" and therefore "lacked a form of address, which is the key to every cordial conversation" (*Viola Tricolor and Curator Carsten*, trans. B. Q. Morgan, John Calder, 1956, 10).

Viola tricolor is also known as "heartsease", and this is the title of a Mendelssohn music composition, dated 1993 or 1994 (SxMs109/5/B/3/1; see also endnote 48). The term resurfaces in "The End is Listless" (*viola tricolor* 1993).

295 The addressees of these questions are loosely identified as "other people who are more solid in their knowledge" whom this "I" knowingly irritates (SxMs109/1/B/1/12).

296 Roughly speaking, Mendelssohn conceals her name in publications of the early 1970s, predominantly uses Anne Mendleson in the work she self-publishes in the early 1980s, turning to "Grace Lake" in 1983. This moniker appears first on the 1981 Sheffield typescript, but the dating of this signature is uncertain. In her three main Equipage pamphlets – *viola tricolor* (1993), *Bernache Nonnette* (1995), *Tondo Aquatique* (1997) – Mendelssohn attributes the work to Grace Lake on the cover, but copyrights the entirety under her birth name, "A. Mendleson". Variants of her chosen middle names – Louise and Sylvia – also appear in her draft texts, and the words "louise femme de la bernache" are embedded in her cover drawing of *Bernache Nonnette.* In *Implacable Art* in 2000, she publishes as "Anna Mendelssohn" for the first time, and this remains her authorial name until her death. Exceptions to this rule include the 2000 *Jacket* entry; the 2002 translations in *Po&sie*, and the 2006 reissue of *Out of Everywhere*; all three publications draw on pre-2000 work.

"Boas Toas" is a moniker used in 1990 at the bottom of "Hardly See the Night Past his Jacket." and recurs in the Peter Riley papers at the Cambridge University Library, where a Mendelssohn doodle wishing all concerned a happy Christmas and "all the best for 1991." is signed "Grace." and "© Boas Toas." (Ms Add.10013/2/29). Presumably Mendelssohn is toying with the name of a famous founder of modern anthropology, the German-American scholar Franz Boas (1858–1942).

Mendelssohn begins using the initials for her Hebrew name – Channa Nechama Enna Krshner Mendleson Lubovitch bas Hakolenian – with the draft of *café archéologique* (1992–93); alongside "A. Mendleson." this name resurfaces in the 1997 copyright of *Tondo Aquatique* (see also endnote 56). In a draft cover for *Tondo Aquatique*, Mendelssohn experiments with "grace lagg" (SxMs109/5/A/23/2). Given that in the eighteenth and nineteenth centuries, "lag" was an English word for "inmate" or the term of a prison sentence, this name is either self-satirising or masochistic, possibly both. At the end of Mendelssohn's "Table" at the back of *IA*, she includes a drawing signed "©Allegro." The Cambridge Peter Riley Papers contain a draft, spiral-bound variant of *py.* dated 2007 that is copyright "anna mendelssohn-kouchnerova" (Ms Add.10013/2/29). In a conversation of August 2017, Mendelssohn's friend Kate Wheale suggested that it was difficult to stay abreast of the various names Mendelssohn used in her later years. For information on Mendelssohn's legal name changes, see endnote 71.

297 Dated 21 May 1971 (vol. 3, no. 30), the issue went on sale on June 4 (two dates are given for most *Frendz* issues). For counter-cultural publications of this era, the "women's issue" became something of a trend, one replicated in the feminist takeover of New York-based counter-cultural publication, *Rat Subterranean News*, founded in March 1968. Like *Frendz*, *Rat* was a notorious, bawdy mix of information about drugs and interviews or writings by some of the leading cultural figures of the day, among them, Jimi Hendrix, Kurt Vonnegut, and William S. Burroughs. Sexualised images of women often graced its covers. Renamed *Women's LibeRATion* in 1970, the editorial team included Jane Alpert and Robin Morgan. See also endnote 61.

298 SxMs109/2/D/5.

299 Number zero of *Strike* is held at the British Library; its place of publication is listed as "Manchester?" and the publisher is "not identified". The publication date is given as "1971–".

300 Prisoner rights were an ongoing preoccupation of *Frendz*. The three issues that documented women in prison may have been prompted by Mendelssohn and Creek, as they are produced just prior to or during their time in Holloway; that said, they are never directly cited. The cover of the second issue, not discussed here, includes the subtitle "Women in prison" and an image of a rose behind bars (*Frendz*, vol. 3, no. 20, 3 February 1972).

301 In *The Virago Book of Love Poetry* (1990), Mendelssohn describes herself as a student of English, a mother of three, a practised public reader of her work, and a poet published in over half a dozen journals. By the end of the 1980s, she identifies more readily as a writer and artist than as a student or parent.

Come the publication of her translated poems in *Po&sie* (2002), she is described as Grace Lake, whose real name is Anna Mendelson, and who teaches at St Edmund's College, Cambridge; Mendelssohn's birth name was Anne Mendleson, and it is unlikely that she taught at any Cambridge college. In these later years, Mendelssohn was compiling and editing the work of Gisèle Prassinos, yet her 1960s translations of 1930s Turkish poetry are referenced in *Po&sie* and *Vanishing Points* (2004) as Prassinos is not.

Mendelssohn's biography for the *Cambridge Literary Review* (2009) indicates that she moved to Cambridge in the mid-1970s. In fact, she was still in prison, and did not arrive in Cambridge until the late 1970s; further, this description elides her years in Sheffield, 1980–83. In her later author notes, Mendelssohn cites her early state education and extra-curricular training at "the New Era Academy of Drama and Music (1957–67) and perform[ances] in Northern Music Festivals" (*Vanishing Points*, 2004). In addition to demarcating the breadth of Mendelssohn's artistry, these references nod to parental ambition, influence, and generosity.

302 SxMs109/1/B/1/39/3.

303 "virago." (*IA*, 56; not in this collection).

304 "Truth or Vermilion" (*involution*, no. 4, 1996).

305 SxMs109/3/A/1/34/2.

306 Mendelssohn often photocopies proofs, presumably to double-check that her corrections are made as requested.

307 Grace Lake, *Conductors of Chaos: A Poetry Anthology*, ed. Iain Sinclair, Picador (1996), 184–96, 184.

308 Biographical note, *constant red/mingled damask*, no. 1, 1986; see editorial notes.

309 Riding famously gave up writing poetry after her marriage to Schuyler B. Jackson in the early 1940s, but Mulford may have asked for early work. For evidence of Mendelssohn's admiration, see "i. m. Laura Riding" (*Jacket*, 2002).

310 Poetry is a minor but regular component of the *Feminist Review*, which focuses on essays and reviews. Mendelssohn's associate Denise Riley published poems in its eighteenth number in 1984, or the same year that Mendelssohn writes out its address and contributor guidelines in a notebook, including the editors' willingness "to discuss proposed work with intending authors at an early stage" (SxMs109/4/B/41).

311 For instance, the pamphlet Mendelssohn produced with Tim Mathews – *poems* (1984) – was not deposited.

312 Michael Laskey, "A Late Wedding Anniversary Poem", *Other Poetry*, no. 17.

313 "Fantastic Art" (1946), *Hannah Höch*, ed. Dawn Adès et al, Prestel Publishing, 2014, 233.

314 SxMs109/5/B/1/19/1.

315 Bergvall wanted to republish poems from *IA* in an online journal (SxMs109/3/A/1/1). Duncan wrote Mendelssohn to ask why she did not contribute to *Angel Exhaust*, the influential British poetry magazine founded by Steve Pereira and Adrian Clarke in the late 1970s (3/A/1/12). In the early 1990s, Duncan took on the editorship, and favourably reviewed Mendelssohn's *Bernache Nonnette* (no. 15, autumn 1997). Writer and critic Anthony Mellors invited Mendelssohn to contribute to *fragmente: a magazine of contemporary poetics*, which he founded in 1990 with Andrew Lawson (3/A/1/33). Mendelssohn submitted writing, possibly by request, to Lawrence Upton, most famously associated with Writers Forum, a press, workshop, and writers' network founded in 1954 by the sound and visual poet Bob Cobbing (3/A/1/63). And lastly: having anthologised Mendelssohn in *Conductors of Chaos*, Iain Sinclair continued to request her work (3/A/1/55/2).

316 Letter to poet and editor of *Onedit*, Thomas Evans, dated 8 March 1996 (SxMs109/3/A/113).

317 Letters to John Calder (SxMs1093/A/1/4) and Ian Patterson (3/A/1/47).

318 Mendelssohn writes about her translation practices to Rod Mengham (SxMs109/5/A/24/9). Her archive contains four unattributed translations of Akhmatova (6/D/2; see endnote 358).

319 SxMs109/3/A/1/23. Mendelssohn does not appear to have published with Johnson's still-extant journal (www.bigcitylit.com).

320 See editorial notes on *The Day the Music Died* (1993) and *Critical Quarterly* (1996).

321 SxMs109/5/A/24/9.

322 See editorial notes relating to these respective collections.

323 "Whirr slightly operationless." (1981, 1982, and twice in 1985); the poem beginning "yes, it is a shame, a real shame" (twice in 1985, as part of a collection and a play; again in 1986); "Winter." (twice in 1987); "La Facciata" (1988 and 1996; French translation, 2002); "1526" (1993 and 1996; French translation, 2002); "on challenge, positive attitudes and 'les peintures cubistes'" (twice in 1993 and once in 1996); "Ordered into Quarantine" (twice in 1993; once in 1998, 1996, and 2006 respectively); the poem beginning "She Walked where she should have stood still, stock still." (1995, 1998, 1996, and 2006); and "Silk & Wild Tulips" (1995, 1998, 1996, and 2006).

324 See editorial notes for *Crystal Love D. N. A.* (1982) and *Is this a True Parrot, a Mountain, or a Stooge?* (1985).

325 In a letter to Romana Huk dated 18 March 1996, Mendelssohn stated that she felt *Bernache Nonnette* was turning into a serial novel (SxMs109/3/A/1/20).

326 Poem beginning "Four eighths for writing business letters a man selects a voice she, he mocks, she will and inverts" (*Bernache Nonnette*, 1995).

327 I have edited a portion of this text for publication in the *PMLA* (vol. 133, no. 3, 2018, 610–30).

328 See editorial notes for "Formatted manuscript (June 1985)."

329 "*I'm working here.*" and *Celestial Empire.* (February 1983) are hand-written and then photocopied; for evidence of the interspersing of typescript and manuscript, see *Is this a True Parrot, a Mountain, or a Stooge?* and *Inbuilt Flash Nix* (both 1985). The covers of *poems.* (1984), *Bernache Nonnette* (1995), *Parasol One. Parasol Two. Parasol Avenue.* (1996), and *py.* (2009) all include Mendelssohn's handwriting. In *IA* (2000), Mendelssohn's line drawings are often accompanied by short phrases in her hand, and she includes two copied manuscript poems that go uncited as distinct entries in the "Table" at the end of the volume. Both untitled, the first begins "clashing bronze"; the second, "Dust bowl girl proposes bird baths for hospital forecourt." (*IA* 28, 117; neither is included in this collection). A final example: the posthumously published manuscript "POEM." (*No Prizes*, 2012).

330 "Pedal" (Untitled typescript, c. 1981–82).

331 Poem beginning "why head aching?" (Untitled typescript, c. 1981–82).

332 "Masquerade" and "classique" (Untitled typescript, c. 1981–82).

333 Poems beginning "maybe I shall" and "think twice" (*Crystal Love: D. N. A.*, 1982).

334 "so did apollinaire and aragon" ("*I'm working here.*", February 1983).

335 "WORDS CHARGE." (*Celestial Empire.*, February 1983).

336 "i.m. Laura Riding" (*Jacket*, no. 20, December 2002).

337 Letter to Juliana dated 28 January 1995 (SxMs109/3/B/4).

338 In order of appearance, these quotes are drawn from the poem beginning "......Oh I really must. The paper was filling"; "damned channel" and "No Wonder" (*Parasol One. Parasol Two. Parasol Avenue.*, 1996).

339 Letter to Hugo Williams dated 4 May 2000 (SxMs109/3/A/1/67). In a letter to Mengham, Mendelssohn writes: "'Tondo Aquatique' is an evocation of the minim. (the empty two-beat note in music notation) It's a nice round shape usually – not a noose or a loophole or a fascist logo" (3/A/1/34).

340 My choices are influenced by quality and a desire to have the many styles of *IA* represented in this collection, and by poems to which students and scholars repeatedly return, among them, "pladd. (you who say either)", "I object." and "to any who want poems to give them answers." Due to reasonable limitations of fair use and copyright, *IA* is the most significant absence in this collection, which in every other regard, strives to be as complete an edition of Mendelssohn's poems – either published or prepared for publication – as is currently possible.

341 Poem beginning "personally weighted in sterling pounds" (*py.*, 2009).

342 Poem beginning "perfectly numerate" (*py.*, 2009).

343 See editorial notes for *Poems Written at Hinton Grange Care Home*, 2009.

344 "ars peregrinandi: spreidh." (Untitled typescript, c. 1981–82).

345 Poem beginning "wallow 'tis of swallow" (*Poems Written at Hinton Grange Care Home*, 2009).

346 See editorial notes, *Poems Written at Hinton Grange Care Home*, 2009.

347 "fragment; redundance; wordsworth." (*Parasol One. Parasol Two. Parasol Avenue.*, 1996).

348 "Winter." (*Slate*, no. 3, 1987).

349 Poem beginning "Treading carpentry free country" (*Crystal Love: D. N. A.*, 1982).

350 Poem beginning "who are these who tell you what you want to know? would" (*viola tricolor*, draft poems, c. 1993).

351 "pladd. (you who say either)" (*IA*, 2000).

352 "in the minority of one" (*The Paper Nautilus*, no. 2, 2011).

353 Poem beginning "understanding cannot be relied upon" (*The Day the Music Died*, 1993).

354 Hugo Williams, "Freelance", *Times Literary Supplement*, 11 April 1997.

355 In his review, Williams quotes from "La Facciata": "Their names fell on jellied eels". From "1526", he misquotes "plunging into negation's

blind sacrifice" as "plunging into negation's blind surface." Both poems are part of Mendelssohn's entry for *Conductors of Chaos* (1996). In an undated letter to Douglas Oliver, who introduced the poets at the reading, Mendelssohn writes: "But Sacrifice is terrible! Human sacrifice! So that I cannot understand his objection to my objection" (SxMs109/3/A/1/43). Presumably the "objection" in question is Williams's perplexity about Mendelssohn's ferocity. The archive holds an unsent letter from Mendelssohn to Williams on this matter, as well as a series of letters indicating that Williams wanted to help Mendelssohn find publishers for her work. Mendelssohn intended to send Williams a copy of *Tondo Aquatique* (1997) and asked him for advice on an art exhibition and money to publish her Prassinos translations. The letters date from 1999 to 2008 (3/A/1/66).

356 Poem beginning "I shake and cry. How then could I ever love you" (*viola tricolor*, draft poems, c. 1993).

357 SxMs109/1/E/1/4/1.

358 The exception in this regard is SxMs109/5/A/33, which contains typescript poems that I do not believe are Mendelssohn's. The poems include allusions commensurate with Mendelssohn's interests – Baudelaire, Thomas Mann, *Moulin Rouge* (1952), Breton quotes – on pixellated computer print-outs akin to some of her early drafts, and exhibit fluencies in French and German consistent with Mendelssohn's own. These arguments aside, they are written in a trite, lascivious style that is at odds with Mendelssohn's. Further, as discussed in the notes for *IA*, I have not included a series of Akhmatova translations that may be Mendelssohn's (6/D/2). See also endnote 318.

359 For example, 1996 is a busy year for Mendelssohn. Two contributors to *Conductors of Chaos* (1996) – Maggie O'Sullivan and Aaron Williamson – state in their author biographies that they have already published work in 1996, suggesting that the volume comes out later in the year. As such, Mendelssohn's *Conductors of Chaos* submission appears at the end of 1996 in this collection.

360 "Truth or Vermilion" is published in *involution* (no. 4, 1996); the differences between that poem and the last version in *IA* (2000) include an elision of the title and a single comma; "à la France" was published first as "To France" in *Parasol One. Parasol Two. Parasol Avenue.* (1996) and was translated into French by D. J. Kelley for *IA*.

361 For example: "Localized Effects." and "Localized Plaster." are last published by Mendelssohn in *Is this a True parrot, a Mountain, or Stooge?* (1985) but are published by Ian Heames in issue one of *No Prizes* (2012). As Mendelssohn did not edit these publications, they are included here with the 1985 collection. Heames also reproduces the previously unpublished "POEM." and "1986 Octroi" which appear alongside posthumous publications.

362 SxMs109/5/A/13/1.

363 Phone conversation with Freer, 10 October 2017.

364 See SxMs109/5/A24/10 and 5/A/24/11.

The Collected Poems of Anna Mendelssohn

*

Cover the land
Swim the water
Now Fly.

2 Birds of Paradise
Crocodile munch slime
Crumbling stone walls
Church spire barbed wire
Heavy jets heading over
"Pig Swill Here".
Prison wall: PIgeon perch.
Prison wall bigger than us.
The moon the Sun the Sky the
birds the jets the blue the SKY.

Walk – legs last forever.
Beware Bewatched
Be witch Take care
One step further "Anna come back"
Turn around:
They weren't even looking.

I feel sick and horrible little face
screwed up in ugh ugh hurt/
look at the moon up there
OH. lit a smile.
That's ours isn't it?
Why not?

You're the Yes
She's the Are you a
Thought so

Drama class Girl, blonde hair, recognized her
She makes out we never met.

I just I know
It's awful I just
And then Pause
Yes maybe but
Hellooo cCan I come in
Oh I've just. Pauline on entering/ presenting herself.

Hi squeaker
Squeaker squeaker
wanna cuppa tea
um YES oh waita minute
Did you hear Oh Anna
Yes really Ahhh
But I'M not
It's not like that
NO NO NO "
B ye darling Chris as usual.

"Umm. Oh. Ohdear.
Are YOU alright
I think I'm going mad
I can't. SPEECH.
Is there any
I wish
They're all
Don't know
What can I do?" Hilary as always.

"Ohh. I can't stand it.
Don't believe it.
It's not for real.
One day baby
I'm telling you . . ." Escha on what it comes to.

BEING 707$_{4}{}^{C}$

Shivery weight roll
down play side ladders
the cheapest matter
was spokesman

curling up with "laughter"
wink coffee
there's a world of compassion
Off-cut course
tributary of the business – like sucker
thumbing fingering mildly white chequering
then big booming thud comes feet shod in leather chequered
do they paint
Steam locomotives? You CANNOT ask questions like that sea
studying crunch watersilk pinks paper stash stiff silk
tends dragonflies

Exposition

The famous blue steel felt forms room, tubularly straight –
squashed accompaniment knocking characters off with a paper
stick knifelet kicking spears.
          a human hum ambled on top scum
          a lemon papier mâché coffee pot's spout swung violently
in the direction of its back number third tangerine
cup daintily straight edged beneath the cone's volume,
an ordinary saucer upon, there tidy three separate some
triet'n cone then flew coffee in, was supped by
Botticelli's lips, lips, lips and so forth "Bring an
inclusive" Excisor, stroke, slow bowl mouth sprinkle
white discs paper honey meadow greens wild long-stemmed
daisies on sticks more like long thin stalky sticks
cuddle me.
    In paint me have a big Texas ranch, man; grasses underneath
the buildings long legs stalking from, o a minor letter,
out post to stable selection.
    On boulevard was a man guarding his preciousness,
women in small black hats sitting tightly. Perched must
have been used.
    I want to change contexts, think down, think in, think

There had to be a reason in my mind I made go
Contemporarily climbing over a zebra crossing
              a roustabout
              crossed the road straight cut through the green
wooden garden door onto the main bus route never reached
ex – pent a garden morning hop – then life!
paper unsatisfactory   jump off   what happened to the
request for permission
              producing artefacts is completely different from art –
MAKING has nothing to do with it
MAKE a business work Manchester Square building ruddy red
Co-operate OPerate OP ART Run Back Skittle job in series

discussing severe books in dust mouthless unembryoed
                              Old D
                            fizzle knucks
                                    jagged paint edge
once every two hundred million years success once every take a dash
straw line mercator, swaddled feather down supper folk broke potatoes
on a blackened eel, sneezed, frozen to the window pane for lack of
a hatch, car first Operative verb removed – there never was an
equal passion   tow rope   the limitless failure . . .
                                    has to grow inanely on scone . .
                     huge 'em ducks
model acrobat   spare his arms
one orange sueded trouser
to the green jelly lip
spiced bike on a run
                     horary
seduced with white weather plumes
flatly backed scooped breast
leaning long nourishment
                     a wasted journey
                with a gold light flickering
                     we took that sun home
                what is going on on that extension?
a conversation about homes, what they look like
                were they happy
                was the earth moving thru their floors?

have to stand   enchantment
in turquoise satin   took off
there lies our pink netting
that was on the walls hosed down
dripped dew
                        cracked wall
                                          snake grew
leaning day shortly to be fed
"couldn't you glean or something?"

fed on padded felt notes
  AWRY hurts
I don't want to transport it
the man's eye scone batch went
down
has to be an afternoon in Spain
on the playa, in the mesa
solid table
fighting with a black mouth –
in a honeycombed navy
cardigan zippered
on a cold frosty morning
closed door,
   then the odour
      rank, despicable
   surrounding, enveloping –
only the door was not locked,
the belongings to be packed,
   a dark-green culotte skirt
      nearly burnt –
a present from the odd girl's mother
who had tried to dress her
 – but had not given her sufficient books
not encouraged her to read
– being slightly in awe of her
                daughter's sparkle
                        and obstinacy.

   The call came – her father had died, her
father and her grandmother chanting up north
in that lonely black house, what was it?
          the skull on the sea,
          came back to haunt her
   imagery gathered death
          wishing castigation
   admonished harshly

fighting for exit
a teaspoon twitches even now
towards her right.
Shall she left – handed for ever be?
The Devil is nonsense to me,
That is what I should
LIKE to believe,
That the Devil is
left– handed is nonsense . . .
then very settled bottle green skirt
Then scrat, then burgundy armchair be,
woven – interlude, single drop pen, paranoia-making friends so
Turn to the Michaelmas Daisies again – a chant a lulla . . . .

a.

sitting Ever so comfortably
reels keels saying:
"she's hype
hold the prototype
briefcasing my pleasure
Dick, Mick and sorrow
full eyes sound
amusing hired audience
lustreless ludicrous
mayflower super-fuss
heart sunk india rubber
ball prey magnitude
hard one to take
sister judas very magnanimous
supreme jealousy
peevish interlude,
have a half a continental."
Reduced size rapidly grew
a new you
written before
world wiser
by knitting to the first stitch
with no needles
a tall story kitsch.
break Queen Kong.
knees again

b.

Green Gate
Against it
Stump time
delicacy
Several ignitions
roller court crazy
pallas athene
down – town trickster rapids
go faster than caught on the
ptarmigan cheese goofy gappy
mardy capster sugar – belly loose
token disapproval slip thickster
hatchet log map in matt kempt
obstrusive, hail queues, double
spinner mix magic strummer myth
antique; nothing new under the moon
childish habit handler mug
coppit, gottit
hit gobbo popo, good imitation
sailing windswept, she's evil
whispered, droom dilly
plankton, expected to be obscene,
scurrilous, scowl – like,
mug – wort impudence, crackling
black damp wet plaster
stupido, c'est moi, groan

c.

I,ooo impressions deep
breathe by wide nostrils, sick
re – discovery , laughter
mutual love
sigh for the pastry cook
song for the preacher,
pressure drop holly
into iron – cast beaker
pa rrot re – called for
reeks, little pressure
called abroad
indian red pasture, Dionysius
revelled, broody little fingers
stalk – crushed petty grew
coated mis – demeanour
coating faces with figures
thought of
Soledad, pituatry, diaresis
lacking condom
passionate children, scoured
out dustbins,
mistaken for syringes, syringea
blub, blub,
Beelzebub Pailing
link a lad content

d.

running crazy face, gruel
ice, passionate children,
arms full of flowers
from picture books
reeling, winking and reading
plaid township
down there, shed empty
bicycle quarter
ly, ly, extra
contact adore you
C B 4 usual timing
blinking liquorice dice
re – claiming soil mechanism
date – line, date – fine
make something up, fabric
woven, floated and gloated
too heavy to take home flossy
silent agony, turns atrocio us
puddles, as though by magic
crow stream "Company"
tear by two bit
sub, over – powered, smell
ditty houses, one remains secure
glamourous daze

e.

wart back, "HOG'S JUICE",
shaky, withered old spider
widow museum descent is the hour
two thousand souls hopeful
paverish module,
technocratic genius
sporting appearances, could be
him, for the sake of gooseberry
snowballs' quick stricture
drawn loving to warm bake
silent, quick sprint, wall
teach me no tricks sorry,
for agreeing yet results
reasoning mistakes
with the help of other poems
put a ballad together
but still house stayed empty
conversations lacking
immediate pull tack
diminishes republic
dislikes perfect images
dipso brother flak
fits any image, grotesque
immascular

f.

puppetry
new champagne
reduced in three colours
easternized Western
shot hero in Italy
audience cheered
Frank Lloyd Wright 3p.
tickets flat surge
why Quiver
at sog?
insepticitis
transports night – overs
derelict plastic gingham
tomato ketchup drips
down sixty year old
women supported
in diverse cities
by two meth. drinkers
searching the gaps
for a trinket
whilst a West German
Jewellery College
sports a white desk
tea touqué
Montebresia desert

g.

scuffed, dwarf
mistaken for Jaeger gnome
read “omission”
one religion owned
by the World – side
Finedrome.

Masquerade

falling cadences
  pleading
citadels of fire
  a mad escape
a brief dialogue
nostalgic last moment
  uselessness
another entry
      from a wailing oboe
        a reappraisal

demurr from nosy parkers
or   offers   of

interpretation
rising bass
jolly encounter
much rigour
and pianic triumph,
promising
  jazz

bidding farewell
to   a   persistent

classique

breathing head
startled
by a much –accomplice
smashed into
accomplish
pause, detest LOOKING at
rather than being part of
a   duet;
piano/oboe.

ars peregrinandi: spreidh.

to where do persons' spirits go
when they are given each a cup of coffee
        & invited to retire
        into their rooms
away from the thoroughfare
        of friendships?

no danger here
of literary regionalism
(provincial nexus)
outsiders, as always, fly by

PROVE you have as many friends as I
60 each & you're down on the list
of accepted established

they, though, as they ran through
did nick each others' cows
to prove that they had 60 each

40 weren't theirs.
they'd nicked them
for the reckoning

some let them go
once the register had been filled
others branded them deeply
   as their own

burning their hides
with, at best, a fired griddle-iron.

" for we could only give a short sigh to
the memory of the dead, and move forward"
Daniel Defoe.

*

why head aching?
blinding, blinding,
why heart hurting?
minding, minding.

Pedal

chucked out cheap furniture
broken for firewood ?
or just dumped on the backlot

love in the eyes for the old lady's left leg
skin tight & swollen – scrape the bone
– fluid on the bone causing the leg to swell
tight the skin sore, how incapable was I
of looking after her, old dear?

young dog, sheep dog? collie?
brown & white, comes tongue hanging out
apanting & I love you,
surprisingly, love your demeanour (modest demeanour)
your face, your grace,
your kind, puppy dog love.

*

destiny forecast revolt
relating to other forces
below the light;
on beds
further from

the blue night's murmur
a dangled hand
rage design
no heads
sound detail.

*

Power to move
No,
Resuscitate
In the dead of heart
Share no alibi
Power of ruins to ignite
Soft machine sounds
Reorganization.
Power of will
unites
silver lamp snares goodness
Whole as an orange
on and on

Speak judgement into ear
hear the rail:
Believe to be true.
You will live for ever down
my drained brain.

Share a subtlety.
Unite to crash:
No surrender.

Mighty portion of the land
My night is pouring gold.

*

melancholy might answer in future mistakes,
the wind bears no answer, destiny forecast.

*

Machiavelli strikes
His hammer
gold notch
time?

8081 that's 5p a go.
coffers wait,
grow old in Carlyle museum.

Paths traced
Surgical instruments
the first chemist: Mind you.

*

Black velvet cloth
Betrayal to go
That stops
Chill talks
Two trees sprung-planted
A yellow blue green
But waiting
That's the stop.
A fool
Really denies.

GUIDE

what happens in this never-never land
a charred deceit
amenity nigh profit m'lads
tha's wha' this country's made o'
HEARD THE VOICES
imitating proclamation
no sight in sound?
wait for the new land!

*

maybe I shall
and the backward slide reintegrates
into conviction
of gift.

is it immutable?
the fascination strives.
no integration in forthcoming events.
stay in touch.

some change
it's not all, obviously, in the past.
fearful reminders
seek no remission from doubt.

a cataclysm of effect.
soul cries out for mercy
forgive me forgive me
can live in truth.

too little reminder
no composition,
swerve the mainstay
anchor at rest

morse code
terrifies a never-ending blurr
the mercury selector
catch thought
protect him.

*

Treading carpentry free country
Loosen the bowel's
stretch marked
over-conscious stylization
z brings zed beds
moostang fire
apoplectic missionaries steal zeal
a type of fairy
would write like this
mish mish mash
wheel is big and goes forwards by backwards
arm in arm they walk to the shore
a couple of likely gods, ghosts
never appearing with detailed information
not this but
an effort rendered by a goat,
cows are notational crisis
screams 'blind ink'
WHOSE hill?
ears of a donkey penetrated
a sucking wind blows circles
round the mind tight and tidy
fortune remains untold
nevertheless (that had to come in)
a long dress parts the way
staircases to empty their messengers
the double of a triple is an empty
time waits unattended
Dylan's writ, london harassment,
Sadie holds her hosepipe;
the horn of ancient ritual
calls to love.

CADENCE.

'civilization' gives explanations in a
'civilized language' although
that which makes this apt to the
refined mind is a
coded charge of
interest persona

*

a settlement of priorities reaches unassailable
limits the cock(roach) c(r)awls. Easy to assoc-
iate an image prior to Clatter is the remark &
already is it ALWAYS send home the presents? Hope
for crawlers. In a near sight NOW this pose would
look REMARKABLE inside a treaty on craft & mystery
EXTEMPORE the glisten. GLISTER We part as though
a secret. Stare clusters of moped-riding. Useful.
Downtrodden. Unreadable. Tell THE TEACHER THAT SHE
HAS FAILED. You MUST. Far in between and new stock
and repeat peep: "Shoot light." Cancelled fly spray
& cancelled fresh air and i do NOT want a denture
tablet. Be satisfied HA you make sick although cont-
ainers remain. Split the change.

julius caesar, mark 11.
all the family makes time for music. She a chatter-
er, that is, she does & finished. Intonious. Antonio.
Alibrée. Alopeia. Car fright. MYSTRESY diligent,
dentile, crass makeup for -: shame on you cow.

Shell form: Conch tent.   (for John Barker)

Rain in mist.
Longforgotten tastes.
Pull away from tin:
Crack-angled rust.

Automatic spring.
Practised apart.
Testing drift:
A pick-up truck.

There is a beach.
We stand before the tides.
We roll over and over on the sand:
It is midnight.

There is no duty.
There is no mission.
There is   n omission:

In touch.

*

think twice
once for do
twice for do not
and the rest would be glib
scattered advice
to be nice and to gather up
UNdemeanour.
this or that be like
a tree   a rock
carve away,
there should be replacement
no substitute
in cliché.
a riddle a choice
delight comes there
write for the sake of writing
is, is not true,
an equatorial problem
equations spell
no one's land.
upto this time
constant factor?
helps me to gather together.
I liked all those people in one place.
never closed   but the static intervention.
miracle flower
make play forget imaginable consolation
                                                    consolidation
the rumour pries.
do i?
light fell

*

quietly noon
lost in buffer sound
no where else
is better.
with out dangers.
moody.
clear the lines
smooch.
a problem of mind and experience
divine notations
pit against
a slender
chance
of
no importance
IMPATIENCE
the water running
theories thru
blessed notch
in public in private
behaviour
how do you behave?
no heavy questions:
i like them sometimes
common species,
inevitable catch up.
After all this time:
incredible dilemma
know what you want
if not exactly
asking for it
they don't
in Work.

*

Buried deep in the honey
another language charged
by ice cream cart music
& a teaspoon tinkling in a cup.

Smash another one, poor girl.
the belly riveted to
Nonesuch Press and half a sprout.
someone else is thinking . . .

What did Robespierre think?
When Egypt prepared to choose
a ship, same oar, the old does
YOU JAZZ POET OF THE LATE
black patent swashbuckle
evening, we're in the swim.

I am pleased to be studying spoonship
roar and a hundred bowels move
no more than two at a time
I only like subject sometime.

Beat her incognito nikitchka
There is a lot more custard on the moon
Get to her stage
then tell me that concrete is made for drunkards
Especially on a cool sweep.

nonflec

for Caroline and Miklos Menis

Suffering covered in moss
ripens at any cost

A very long grey hair
licensed warrior
soap
sheets of curtains
a practical disaster
reflects many traits
succumbs to inaptitude
as a cucumber mood,
sets in four precisely
cotton wash
flat out

poles of opposite directions
retain a presence in
Space built D. T's
Harbour a/no grudge
charge no fee

what do you take
me for me?

All summer
one blow
of a chinese whistle

Yellow
                                        dee doo dee doo
                                          squares of blue
                                          yellow

                    magenta astafagusta
                    arbitole solentine (green)
charged rosemary
abigail nightingale soluble white
enticing dessert spliced charcoal
nether bushes romanticine plastic
mouchoir ri.

*

1. Squashed in, world's different; sickness
love ourselves, holy, goal, splash,
alliterative, spread space, mark corners,
inside a hollow drum, bang sweater,
fly dust, mania; hollow drum.

11. Start again – red moon, bloody sun,
passion – scream with delight –
halla – an (sky-light ima go)
blue y blanco shirt woman-clad queue
were squirts, fishy feet, autobiographically
imposed portrait poor dream, poor dream.

111. Seems like it's all over – livid true trumpets
daffodils tea-terraced rose instead of high-rise
we were living some-where else, some-where
happily enough, but as happily finished and
enough started, we definitely died.

1V. Mark on, my paper, nurse sweet breastling,
Whose nose is bigger than a gargantuan's repast
up bugger me Jack, it's the beanstalk come back
This pod, this constipated, expirated Christmas.

V. Slovenly habits start to realize themselves again.
Tin drum drama edge is popular, telegraph,
old-fashioned fisherman's lignes, their fear,
Objective Removal, learn a language or too
engaged, bright yellow straight white chalk plaster
plaster, broke amarillo, bismuth, aeroplanes in conjunction.

small points.

the years along time to take me to sesert dumas currants,
hope not sheep droppings, blonde girl, believe visual   animal instinct
Blonde girl animal travesty   Theatre police put out   Travesty Where Icon
Where a little girl Roissean
          so what
              live straight
                   ghastly agony.

raw bloodless 3rd hieroglyph
                   she spins round august
                   that's why spring is autumn

traffic light ten
                      pull in with the right from nature light
mustn't count on it
            wrenched out of the
                                    burnt up letters wrote from
the letter about the
                         the letter about the from made me
tear up in deposit
                        from the moral lectures made me
yes thankyou i cried very well

                                   she jummed
keep your face out of mine your wistfulness my wistful
                                          pure head
I do understand your exerciseless, your Mountain.

*

slide slip joke dent
another area cracked
forefathers tented wives
shawled from here to Bangkok
cradled in mosques, synagogues,
huts, deserts, valleys and
hard rock cities a-hum
with muttering teeth to a
god who drank anise
 whilst paring his fingernails
 abstractly; appraised by humming –
birds who brushed his liquor
with their fan-brush swoops.

*

so did apollinaire and aragon

he paused: will the last echoes
disappear I am enjoying their
blurred sooth – enjoying my
well-soled shoe, enjoying Margaret's
tight skirt , rubbing my knees
with energetic decency and
never having to appear in the
flesh, I can occasionally flip
this bottom glass image to Ezekiel,
to Elijah, to big Jesus, to St. Theresa,
to Roberta, to Tracy, to St. Mike.

Bossa

Why does the management not clear
a space for lunch-time dancing?

*

and don't we know why?
 of course it could be an
other Margaret is a nurseletter

Baked's are in for tender-hearts.

the concerto machine
a groovy electric funereal
concatenation with D.P.P. hens
careering in black-boxed up
case papers : import a scale
from the stone-age to put it
crudely blurred italian replica
youths are holding buttons casually
as spectacles are fitted for them
and not even a mouse kept
the black-rimmed date-card,
politely transporting a distant crumb
to take her frilly pink place.

*

January is grin-ful & dreaming
February is a rote
March has already been cared-for
April, forever raining, forecasts draft
Relinquish completely. May blossom
June may be baked in blue bowl.
July forever preening
Août flexes the dried-hay muscles
without mr. guess navy September
to escape slowly into death's Octoberly promise
which November guards greyly
beneath December's crisp chorale.

COMYRRHING.

If YOU DO NOT particularly Like this
That is BECAUSE THIS IS NOT particularly
Aesthetic, your conception of Art will
probably not survive more than a
suggestion of sou-renical : before your
stride, freshly introduced into old tyme
rebellion, nicks kingers in catalogues
rupurt'd, neuter's a dupe musically.

*

cricket
religious
conservative
other than salamite
the nearest i could find
climb to a where
or ne'er pointless joke.

*

Titless stares
Beagle hair
THE   EPITOME
shivering
 behind
his broken
  biscuit
sniffly snuffles here
tricking a title

*

<u>That broad red sun-light.</u>

for a bounding Typist's
cocktail 'phone call
grass rahts'n tartters
snoze triplicates in
sinking ducal tuscany.
TRIPLICATE'S END.

proscribble at 16.12 hours.

What a quadruplicate agitate agitate
Complex satisfaction is all right on tin
Duplicators cinquocentricate association
spoils computer's cross-puzzled similarity.

Hilarity, hilarity – search for the cartoonized
interpretation does control life's speed sad
is not it tragic as arms sleeze from chairs –
drowning equinocturnal polarity; invisible ease?

*

one that is not you.

fingernails piercing dust-ridden paws
stand up , caitiff bed.
Pour grease.
Turned tough boy.
$\text{LO}'\text{VE}$ $\text{LO}''\text{VE}$ $\text{L}'''\text{OV}^{2}\text{E}$:

                                        I^{x} o^{a} peace.

*

Experience

The only time that i detest Experience
is when it becomes so much
of a habit that I begin
to eulogize upon its importance.

THAT ROSY, COSY NIGHT-CLUB AFTERNOON

xxxxxxxxxxxxxxxxxxxxxxxxxxxxxxxxxxxxxxxxxxx

amidst blue saxiphrage,
coconut daisies, mélange
melanosis, pose tennis star,
go cooky, check neighbour
check co-house liver, rabbits
mooch : some sentiments are
unpaintable – rabbits keep close,
taken away taille, melanosis.

WORDS CHARGE.

how much is but?
I seem to have to use it a lot
There is something to say
then but comes along

who was afraid of being butted
by a carving on the top of a
walking stick?

The Post-man's Cat.

seems something is
useful to —
a free choice

how much is sound
the repetition's effect?
not stagey.
nor fingering
only duddening
this life
en masse.

depth resiled
venomous wall –
clinging autocracy
where-on tasselled
flowers cause
outbreaks of bewilderment
plus uncontrolled nose –
witchery and boot-thudding

whence melancholy?
then strike poetry is poetry

this government led by a
white piping upstart
who chose mercenarily
which side she would
be on thinks ? megaton united
 fits ladies' mouths

being scrubbers
being grafters
being pawned
for polloi's tigging

then strike boom dee ay
beat beat that kick
fetching rhythm with tolstoy
write centuries black book
write out Shelley
and poor frightened Auden
who burnt his pleas
for cancerous humanity's
half-baked royal
 who wheedles and connives
 round this island's back-knees

so we   slump
on time
did the butterflies' wine
send them straight to catch Giaconda's
orifices there
in pourri plaster
caulking   ?

<u>Giaconda's Contumacious Lapse.</u>

Why – hollow corrida – spendthrift drops a
sixpence number stakes, division corrodes,
philosophy regains a moment, down went the
Earth, head was swirling on the pavement,
love of the past in future building, love of
the past in jumping two steps – love of the
past in present induction, transported,
failed ten times , table . .

down went the sea
love of the past
future building
spacious outer
green splattered
sundimmed
reflex action
cancellation

down went the Earth
crude sea
love of the past
came to the rescue
the past the rescuer
the rescuer was time's
healthy measure
healthy mountain
healthy red cheeks.

progress
jumping
two steps
skipping
mad voice
crying
single hearts
opposed by
(jurals)

down went the sky
knees pressing
graced accompaniment
needle sharpeners spewing
on windly market afternoons
Humpty Dumpty Colour
DOWN in the basement
Below Par Level
Evil mechanisms with sense
for heaven

future past.
Guarded their secrecy
danger money
we cannot see them
MERRY MERRY MERRY

from Celestial Empire. (February 1983)

Sums.

One doll plus a Woolworth's carrier bag plus a
Sea - Land Freight Liner plus a little girl in a
red woollen hat and scarf plus a brown and white
pug dog minus a hole in the road plus a
Solidarity suicide divided by Henry Miller's
"Tropic of Cancer."

*

Speaking rhythm

I don't want to do the I - Ching
I want to wear your chair - ring
Hey O Baby
Be on Bobby
and sever
mine lobotomy

from Piza
wrot

UNFINISHED

starkers, giggleless,
doing winding flowers
glad, given markers
– the ascent, exact pin
weak, o lady bower
ragged white frayed
chrysanthemum flower

held a belt with pecked flower
screwed brain electrically
poison flower, made green
yellow buttercup flower
did live for dew green lawn –

donkeys did, thickened there, strutted lawn
fourgedly strutty, ideologically oblivious
a conference on worms slugs dimped hooves
himped deliciously decidedly flat shells
gone guardedly forshorn

on a hill garden day forshorn
forbidden, graduated by the gardener
to suck freesia blooms necks strung
onto Syrus, late in the day the shed glass
attracting them their polar bear ghosts.

SACRED PIN.

I shall come in from the right with a – Never
seed my plastic cover in this mid-brown noon,
recollect desks of silent questioners sitting there

windows shielding fields split and parsed
with the master's bread, not a word said –
trees sheltering allusions to glamorous contusions
strung with belts many-times ringing
smaller than their, quieter than their holders,
spare me your jokes, I asked no-one —

whence this voice came, from a back scullery
which echo'd hard arm thrusts midst steaming
dank tea-towels through which two heavy legs
puffed & throbbed in time to the master's rough
demands for attention, no-one who sneers
once in their lives knows that

A lyricist must refrain from dancing,
at intervals contemplate
the concrete nature of their security
even out "in the wilds"
where marionettes skag in the defined air.

oh yes we are entitled mohican slaves

simple christopher cooled her air, decided too
several times hidden that had to be & changed
that, changed simple, changed utterly decided;
marked for life who said: reveal your voice
canna canna canna for truth is unknown out
of science's deposit: that journey was the one
after the eclogue's over equals nothing id
happening id id idiot he slumped slobbered
slimmed slummed whilst thick am i he waved his
hand whatever you were before to me you are
NOT NOW, longer that the grab for an old shore
line after memorable i don't care he said and
meant it then there were the others who had
polemical belts talking ten to the dozen slammed
slumped marched hoisted flags
reached a sky one day from nowhere
wrote in a back yard heard spirits yell mardy
mardy gone to the scunthorpe gone to southend gone
to miserable enervating mystery, do they score though?
they do not score no. they join though perhaps
without speaking golf courses you ding on the lullaby.

dig; dig.

is there any
ROME? could call through
to at least 9oo people like HUGO
would be pretentiously waving, and whatever
else he might be thinking wouldn't know.
easily lodged, that's where we want her
where we put her she can't hear
we and then there is you
which is definite
and gone

is there any
ROME? could strain
dark, bronze, unusual virtually
colourless pictures, i was not taking
pictures of myself at all then; suddenly
a camera came whizzing back of my head with
a finger on it's neat little trigger and i ducked
the lower i ducked the taller the child grew
she practised her smiling a thing brand
new events do surpass their identities
but reaLLY, THE PAST! a wasp turning
tail, talking teacups, rolling
under a few thin bedclothes

*

I) point a finger at him
that's a word
a fingering a garment,
knickerbockers in a glass
flipped in the storm on the raft
turned curliquew,
which was doing omission proud
carried by a short-haired usherette in maroon
to the coachman
to the man sitting at the back of the coach.
<u>another room</u>
                    pen roaming
whilst she sits at home writing letters to hell.

II) Slate-connotation? look at the paper
– paper   baby having a difficult
time   with his digestion at three
weeks three days old, allows for
no noise

wave initial pauses
this is what is happening:
the pavement is sinking
posit last century's counterbalance
a reconnaissance of two voices
the digit flying above
hovering, buzzing
what a bore –
initial
everything   should be perfect here
words should not change their spelling
last century next to this one
we are not really right at the end

yet the scales have been tipping me over
since birth
throwing me out into hell
and the happiness which i occasionally smell
in my honest, intelligent brow
is a memory or a futuristic impulse
of a state with trees, nay forests even
says the man with the long grey beard
as he pokes his staff amongst the acorns
nay even forests belonged to that slow Yorkshire voice
he will have a tall oak tree
he will sit by a brazier
he will write litigious letters.
the fire went out
ensue,   candy floss   glue
everything, I, think is uncommercial.

from views

but better than death
but better than death
premature; the vicar forms
overviews, confident conversations
overheard by initial supplicants
to the beneficence of lordly-
granted sculptural control.

give us a bit of iron to cut a stroll
give us an ouse wherein we might live and loll.

'The bourgeoisie lives there'

Was there a comfortable poem within sitting?
Why they left the room was on well-pronounced,
benign, divine morality;
how those desires turned.

Hither and thither, sewing basket monument
                              jumped, receded: the panders belch'd

Her little dwarf is carving a memorial to
her power of imagery,
haven't we seen that serenity for centuries?
twisting amongst the thick wall greenery,
nothing transistorized here, bar
what did they SAY?

Mottoes golden, trinkets to dimp
I'm flying a sarcastic saviour,
fangs were the chaos of the night

In deep service, oh snick snick pin
brush the ductile floor gazer in.

To PP158, 159, 160,170 MoMA Sol Lewitt.

They mess up the proportions of our living everyday life
The photographs take rule from our eye, inspiring
us to trip on candlesticks, mistaking these feline
Objects for lamp-posts on the sly, a slap in the
Face, slab cotton eyes, groaned excuselessly, for
getting seemed wrong a camera for a snow-
falling week-end we did not know was coming,
Only froze the cobbles off our brass monkey.
Unsculptured, un-afforded, we banged into books
Photographically mesme, danish straightened,
bed-clothes changed, pictures a pouring us.
Salverless apex ignoring, occasionally adoring us,
Vene vincit. but then they were once on a plate
In front of us, workable, – quick though, to
judge the next timed reaction we spliced,
we spliced, the cardboard kitchen slice
ousted New York, jettisoned Firenze,
for-gotten my jar of pencils, cigarette in-lit,
o gone tore a man, monkey'd, black #2.

*

reduced size rapidly grew

a new you

*

Take a long train
Hold a smart conversation
eyes running which never speak

Fetch the water
mend the main stream
buckling a glut, nefarious journeys.

Choose between quacks
simply bettering on toast hovering
spare mattresses

From the Title – injustice
the frozen end, limb-severed
best quit.

very early poem

The day you took my sno-fruit away
I could have killed you for your cheek.
Did you think that I would fall off my bike
on purpose in front of a lorry?

*

That piano is my god
yet personless
like Grandma the afternoon after
the night she died when Dad sobbed.

I tried to follow her to heaven
but she went so fast
she turned into a star
I saw her light going up and up
and by the afternoon she was definitely dead
That piano is my god
who is supported by my mother
as I try to make up tunes
she comes in and starts practicing
The British Blasted Grenadiers.

*

i) rolled	rolled a	a
ii) pain	pain-friendly	friendly
iii) ex-garb	ex-garb feat	feat
iv) chloro	chloroa	a
v) form	form filling	filling
vi) conical	conical aine	gone
vii) pads	pads reveals	reveals
viii) simon	simon for	for
ix) lee	lee réplu	république
x) bourne	bourne second	second
xi) metal	metal-storm	storm
xii) cutlery	cutlery cracked	cracked
xiii) parachute	parachute-truth	tooth
xiv) dream	dream-cracked	cracked
xv) pond	pond teeth	teeth
xvi) japonese	japonese blood	blood
xvii) rust	rust pouring	pouring
xviii) bark	bark from	from
xix) floating	floating, severed	severed
xx) pagoda	pagoda necks	necks
trees	trees wordsworth's	wordsworth's
sneeze	sneeze, retch	retch
in	in dream	dream
wind	wind-revolution?	revolution?
blown	blown sir	sir
narrow	narrow vous	vous
streets	streets avez	avez
straw	straw les	les
thin	thin yeux	yeux

*

rolling, and all these words are alive and
kicking, that is "and" flying apart,
the action unannounced, arrogant (derogatory
rainblows), nuts, dimity:

who would erotically die for   I
bumped into dimity   here it lies, draped over
my hard left shoulder.

the prerequisite for continuation dimmed
for a while why? Because great days
are rare and nature decides.

that is not entirely correct. There are
too many petrol and diesel oil fumes
blowing out into space.

Sniff the pretty petrol flowers, chew & crunch
the diesel cabbages, my polystyrene cloud.

*

who is this person, high-walking into fantasy?
when nothing succeeds there is a natural perversion:
dreams make up for reality, so concentrate on reality! when you fall asleep
now look at "sleep" and take the whole word as a world
Why forget about "Childhood"
are you still wearing it?
as good as a quiet bed with a clean pillow-case to plump out "respite"

"Sleep" "Childhood" "Respite"
The danger in the beginning of teaching
which blocks off real development with pieces of printed-on paper
through which You must not think! in an hour with the Teacher!
And it is so nice for a sadist to emit "Wrong"
That "wrong" is their time clock, we (are) their clicks.
"Sleep" "Childhood" "respite" "Wrong".

Travelling capital.

A day of sixteen. His look can kill a train of thought
That budding passivity.
"Respite" "Wrong" "passivity" "Sleep" "Childhood".
Are we staring into a memorial fire?
For the next four lines we repeat a mussed clipping.
If you go to check that quotation of Sainte Beuve's
Prepare to squeeze it into a secret spore store
For flutting, FLUTTING over to Dr. Peter in the Middle Ages, a wide comment.

*

rubbish.   desk bang.
 trip! for love's sake.
silence – quasimodo is dressing.
who bought her the box?
is it too disgusting to be broadcasted?
there. there. he gave her a bedtime drink.

who taught her not to accept emoluments?
no-one gave and therefore grabbed.
of course belligerence is sticky.
on match-made intestinal tiles slapped
tucker-notes, in degrees, easy on the year.
flashed the feet, electric ballroom!

flashed back, enemy prowling,
in enemy mind – in dandy dress,
is the past going with a blue rose
between its private medical fangs?
Blue scissors! Sky of Automne
nearly lemon for a wide streak.

"Get into your own backyard.
Examine your own thistles.
Count your own puddles.
Dust your own toilet shed.
Hang out your own washing.
Talk to your own neighbour."

"And bring in the milk sometimes.

*

merely ridicule & sweetness
spots and lace
wide lazy moments
snuffed DAWN.

instant pleasure
with a certain amount
of self-build up
ideas flung out, caught back

material craziness
isn't that enough?
throwing away used paper
from Personal Loss

merely ridicule & sweetness
one long look
then deed done, another one listed
judge that AESTHETE!

spots & lace
he WRAPPED her
chortling a few current tunes
words at the ready

wide lazy moments
between spectacular luncheons
his credentials taken to parties
his routine work, he privately reviles

snuffed Dawn/
he circles like a large white sausage
rolling in a blanket hole
refusing (or incapable of responding) to light.

*

i can hardly bear going down town to see those people
in the rent office again. The woman with the iron stare gives me the horrors. Her
hair is stuck on coils. And i have to keep asking the same questions. where is my
rent? urging her and her cohorts to sort the same old thing out, and i have children,
and that dreaded phrase: SINGLE PARENT. Born to be a Single Parent? born to bash and
struggle ? no.   Flowers are symbols of this love of mine. I stick them into a jug.
Their deep yellow burns in a sombre sun. i croon to them this lyric:

"i must go down to the rent office again
i should and i ought for they can give me
a roof and a little privacy: faint moments
in a book-filled room, which has just been
molested and smeared with insults by a woman
who would have me out crop-picking rather than
reading books. she would turn geraniums into
ironing boards, she would connect with any one
who has ever insulted the state of my living
conditions, and do you think me a snob?
don't you know i am trying to EDUCATE myself?
that i cannot witness the pickling of my brains?
that ardency is something of a disease in these parts?"

this one has an iron dress: to be kind: no need to iron it! and the EFFORT
of the exclamation mark. Chewed, the newspaper reporter from the 30's, travelling
SIDEWAYS? across life? he was chucked out. so when you say: some people travel
SIDEWAYS, oh do you mean from birmingham to rome, something like that? sounds
like the new squashy mystique to me.

the literary past is insubstantial.

the situation is intolerable. In so far as elites who have very little life
experience are sitting as judges in

all the bucketed had gone   and never arrived.
"We have our ups" motioned the sleeping houses.

ELEVEN.

what is a mood?
a mood is something which goes away you say.
you tell me you you you
& i know you mean you not me
but you are being philosophical.

eleven is secret.
i repeat it over and over
two ones, straight side by side.
i fit into eleven, nudge it with my right shoulder.
hardly an elf at twelve.

that is an excuse, a mood, mum.
the sea has moody & i like dark waves.
midnight ink.
i didn't see how they could have crossed the water
the waves wouldn't have stood up straight for long enough.

howling toads and bloody leeches.
why don't you take his face between your hands?
i am cruel to you i have to witness this
night after nightly rejection
of his greeting kiss.

yet he doesn't leave
just sits in silence, moody sea
within a body sits
brooding,
i touch his big grime ingrained fists.

he scrubs them as well as he can, mum.
every night when he comes home,
he goes up to the bathroom to scrub his hands
sings us a song
oh damn the piano

can't anything happen in this house?
the words get lost after a verse
give me some books which aren't about fields.
give me a bunch of primroses.
you lady mum in your mucky dress.

mangle mum in the dark green kitchen
not much bigger than a lantern.
there's the peach you hid for us to share.
that morning the blood gushed out
of your right wrist's arterial vein

blue little lump. i cheeked you to cheer you up.
pretty little girl in a pink spotted dress.
gentle as the summer air was my prayer
FEAR up the stairs
man under my bed

eat everything on your plate you said.
there are children starving in India.
so i divided up the minced meat into a million portions
fed each starving person one by one, they came alive in my head
Take his face between your hands mum.

i love barry and henry and ken with red hair
from glasgow
we kissed in his aunty's garden shed
i want to see them more often
why don't they come here?

for barry and henry we are too poor,
live too far out, aren't swank enough,
and ken is a stranger but he's real
i know, i touched him, his face has freckles
mine hasn't.

mood turn me into stare
swing sullen.

*

The toughie would say:
"No Joan Collins in this joint"

(Surely dreams of T.V. glamour come from poverty)

Would YOU like an observer's voice in YOUR sitting room?
"Lower middle or upper working?"

The landlord keeps coming into our
"OUR"?

The he in his poet, he might.
BIG DEAL.
(Slightly inadequate in this articulated response")

Look up A.R.
Here we are. "At least she speaks".
Articulated Responses are indicative of Cultural Level.
She is falling far short   (far short?) of the requisite expostulation.
She must stand her ground. (she said "Big Deal") The Intervention Principle
requires me to know that her mother was in association with G.I.'S during the
latter part of the II'd World War. I temporarily surmize, in her favour,
that she must have found something appealing in this form of temperate drawl.

We have decided to give her six months to earn enough money to buy our
feminist tracts.

“Do you like the decor?” “It is cool.”

(It stinks of ignorance. In the 1930’s people were starving in this country and here we have an haute-bourgeois representation of that decade’s style).

*

What is wrong with "easy"?
Weakness pronounces
a poet must know
more than a surface suggests

A fugue will lead or Schumann swim
and i resist
reconstituting then relinquishing

And STARE, repulsed by a man who dribbles food,
summoning or Mustering up
a replacement image of a derelict
or a mental hospital patient and some
SYMPATHY for the sucks and fumbles

in a milieu unrestricted by spills from brain lava,
the worst manifestation might be a streak
of acrylic pearls on an ancient wall
quickly dissolved in acerbic rain they would enact
a disappearance trick

dying to be serious and thereby creditable
am i seeking differences for the
forty ninth year?
to take swaggering, as though the appearance
spoke more soundly than the mutter
which begs "belies" and loses the other half

to a narrow Spanish coil
set on a blank background
soundless with potency

the dark brown violins
over fighting tradition,
cohere in concentrated organized space
an united acceptable pizzicato.

this title "derelict" repeated in some circles,
for a person the world forgot to give a violin to
and the distracted "mental patient"
sings of the lost property office she could not get back into
where there was proof of her young poetry
over which the doctors laughed or frowned.

great big sparkling Deal no relation.

How on earth CAn?
or unrelated conversation
One Man's versation.

He is composing this pretty face
slanty-eyes, does the great manpoet EVER
read or listen to a member of the opposite sex?

I refuse to stay as Alice James.
Who is bored? Me!
Suddenly i can think of three friends
who would agree with my new enemy.

music, ignorant of my fantasy.
HE might INVITE ME to disagree.
I should invite him to agree
would he dare to admit "cope"?

So words are my people.
we converse with each other.
you are nowhere involved.

i dislike IMAGINING your presence.
is nexus ticking right?
taking Hookham their ream.

for Anne Devlin

you may as well be depressed
if the knowle's knave is down
who deeply feels the creaking kitchen door?

profound sleep
wherein the brain-thief creeps armed
with internal head sucker.

always the same bunch of roses.
flunked there for the night.
a lovely vase of death.

make change go round
sealed with joy for a marxist
by day is tying a bonnet on Eleanor.

weeping over a sonnet
he thought Edward had torn to shreds
rather prematurely, he contemplates

taking the slow boat over,
might increase his chances of survival
& in the meantime points out extensive revolutionary murders.

no-one will ever remind the brain-thief
to water its charges
or freeze them in snow.

*

or out rageous to be a singing steamer!
that is not outrageous enough.
to say that this is a repeated immobile
doing nothing for your children
think of a reason. make the writing disappear.
why have them then? why have more?
occasionally the little glimpses –
she has been built in iron. she is hanging over the railings. tail legs
clanking in the wind. these "the's" breaths of moth recite this in the many many
families. man-friend. primitive. simple.
syllogistical sweeping round
sticking willow pen. abuse his
shout and constant. sitting glum.
tacks on her mother gear. here in
low glow. sighing for lemontrees.
the description of eucalyptus with
light lifting the lower branches
two lace parasols/ sideways
on paper, paper lace parasols
this should carry away, the target is seam, darting tight,
black spot on the vision hill, climbing to escape the present stretches a cloth,
graces with a tumblerfull of flowers, earth trembling time-wrought, fingers
lick a reduction to a role, the bendy weight of a jump on a light note,

as a kitten, he sweated in his car, she spiked her letters to make a sharp
appearance, by then the feet were broader than the image, needed fitting, written
in a list, another foray into town, past ears troubled by wearing on traffic,
fumbling for a spark of imagination, They then
held their mixed tenses
what they wore! the same
shades, there are not many
colours, orange deep and
light we rejected in search
for juicy fruit disallowed

anaemic, rigid deep dip
relying on automatic
surface bowled by blue
waves acidifying on
the metal tanks packed
with tubes and squares

in town shapes, should be soaring, they are children reading "completely constructed". dishevelled a tin held, holding five pairs of hands, that had curled, and blame the clanking limbs carted away to a black spot on the visionary hill, to a visionary glut

*

She appears in thirteen dresses.
Her lover longs to swing on her gold circles.
This is definitely a forester's evening
The table is laid for Devilment.
Her eyes are scarred with streaky lights.
The manager would dance if he were alive.
Gold lamé chips on a silhouetted bowl
Remind her of Jamaica in the white power days
Before walls cropped up with music lines
Before dirt was more real than her mouth.
That Bedouin on a motorbike is unreal and syncopative.
His cutlass was flown in by unmentionable iron-gaps.
She is an employed hireling of Tinker mafiosi
She half-turns and tries to point to à l'aerobic,
There the Tinkers are really communing on grades.
Our School is heavily exclusive as doors lined with steelfur
And we are handed gold lace, by empty tubes
When the doorbell rings, tip-toe dress tonic,
Assonance arrives in a few forms,
Did the tinkers STAY informed?
She drags out the autobiographical and drugs it.
Her lover finds a drop or two on his black basted mast.
The Bedouin hollered back over sand tracks:
This gold must melt in the sun, with this other white energy.
Did they hang on throughout a day's engaged signals?
She wrested thirteen chiffons from light convex glassed holes.
He pushed her into a cauldron of sombre shoe polish.
He HATED his life and was inordinately selfish
for there was someone there who was listening who loved him.

after georgina jackson's lovely victory.

not selling far from selling
selling selling selling selling
selling selling selling spiked music
music, balled stray walls stretching
They are compact and absent,
and growing in the field, and
whining with laughter and folding
into the floor with straws, which
bend, and looking in the direction
of the other children's voices,
and the hard edge of the washing machine
and the hard won babies, and the waning moon
and the old dusty black record case
and the liquorice snorts, and the red
moulded in fat carcasses and the flags
which fly other corners of the earth
the power reduced to nature's growth
speed of an angel, sadness that the
two of them never made it all the way
that we went all the way
then we went into the sea to find it
and we finded it
smoothly stirring rock pools,
soaking our feet, different sizes,
different irises, different other things
and the sights missed, this was the sea,
this was the land, there were all these toys
in the river, sister, there are all these toys in
the river, swimming through the kitchen, swimming
up the stairs, old father asleep in the dark study
armchair, braid hanging off, dull red colour,
the colour he said of the mother's ridden sorrow,
the study he said, with levity & incredulity.

*

piped, once more, piped
lead into the avenue of sufferance.

doused, once more, doused
desire because he has no wish to look stupid

we agree but where is he?
close my face/ seal my composition.

disgrace, once more, invitation to absurdity
only one revolution forged by one man:

so intelligent! so silent!
forces us to look higher, higher, blanker

us? me? am i that pretty knowingness?
give me STRENGTH to understand the male psyche.

Horror Impudence Chastisement

the sound of waves, that was a while ago filling my ears for once, with a soothing beauty. dread of the pejorative, ignorant reaction to the notion of peace. people only live once although they dream of the chance to live many times, fully, accomplishing their dreams

this heavy sound , a repeated use of the definite article gives. pain of no escape from engines which are so incessant that they become incorporated into my moving life and aware as I am of the hideous alien noise, the noise I do not want to be in my head; there is little I can do other than install double glazed ear drums.

The fascist speaks and his face begins to take on the extreme pain of hatred. She begs him to feel pity in his soul, as much as she feels sorry for his subjection to hatred. He is purged of his hatred and his eyes float freely in their space, although the concentrated light in his pupils is still too dead for her liking.

*

APOTHECARIES' KNUCKLEDUSTERS SUIT THEIR
VENUE THY MASTERY BUTCHER DID BLOOD
SWIM IN TOO MANY TASTES OF CONGEALED
MAMMALS' TOES DO SKATE & AS PRICKLY
AS LONG-LIVED AS THOSE OLD HACKERS
WHOSE ROLLED BALLOONING TIGHT PANTS
HOLD TURKEY-MEAT HEAVEN BENT.

AND THE SPLAYED SCRUM WHO FROM CALF
DID RUN LIPSTICKS SAUSAGE MARKS
SALIENTLY PROVEN, AS TALL AS A MOUNTAIN
SOUNDED FRANTIC WHEN THE TWELVE YEAR
MONOTITUDE OF EXUDED EXCRUCIATION
FLUNG A FEW SARDONIC PICK-UP COMMENTS
INTO HIS MEAT-ROLLING TO STREET CORNER.

?

with Plenty of oos
Is face time
my face is it time
Time   the ancient of faces
eating paper to annoy my ears
coughing to worry/ the tearing
of paper wondering
wonderful rubble in a paragraph:
the death of wars
the final fling
the confused identification of hands
& the RIGHT thing to say,
the HAS-TO-BE Husband/
and HE-HAS-TO-BE Wonderful
Green as Swarfega/they ARE real
do not sound quite & we
do not encourage our kids to laugh
but want to   a bit
sound less perpetually   Good
telling us   How Good
and the voice which sounds like birthday candles,
there's the Son's Girlfriend Going Brown,
and birthday camels in derelict apartments
every neck is erect
& every burt a lamb?

HOT DAY.   BAKED BARE EARTH.   PROWLED IN THE VALLEY FOR THE PIGS' NEST.

forms faded, scraps, over the room.
brown / stones rattling

there has to be some noise: the music.

shaking rhythm: then another language

into the gap   launches gabardine
most definitely / musical notes appearing.

death, the uppermost thought in the subconscience of the classifieds.
arguments swung around, caressing Mrs. Brantain's big box of curlers.
her bruised big toe kept her in the pictures, even on steaming hot
mornings like these.
no-one was working there, you know.

the conversation inspectorate buzzed rapidly from extract to extract.
cheek! cheek! settled down to a five-finger session. These were recently
televised as a regular other language feature.

some broke out into inner radiance at the mere mention of double q's.
i was one of them.

Can two identifiable features, one falling short of animate, both be big
in close succession?

no-one, his rule, books may disagree, qualified or not, neither are curlers
usually graced with metaphorical propensities.

the huge cloud build-up is worth transmitting in a million directions.

at this, the perfect conjunction of old-fashioned munitions' factories colluded
with new economics, ON TRUST! a steaming hot cup of cocoa. BUT SUMMER!

can the writer see more than
                    perceive more acutely
                              than the non-writer,
                                        and do we care for non-writers

and we might have cared and cared and cared and left our writing   for a few
days or turned our attention away from our poems, leaving them on café tables.
throwing them out into the rain to fade on pavements under footsteps, we might
we might have cringed at crudity, been stifled by language which was dismissive
of poetry, we may be screaming this morning as the sand burns our eyes at a table
in the middle of a town, not wanting to hurt.

<u>Whirr slightly operationless</u>.

I / Too much to do with appearances. lighter the sexier: aphoristic dominance
heaves compact. Question. is that a good idea? "I want an advertizing
manager's voice". the dibbit's sound smeen rollock on back be immigranté.
Were they romantic the furthest west from Italy that they could go?
dementia in the mid-speechless (knitting circles) who gives a fuck for phys.
geog. served?

II/ <u>with</u>
she of the black cross strap bag decides to be friendly to her two distant
friends on the opposite side of the table, takes long side-angled draws
at her friend's boy, rests her jaw-bone derrier   monde letting little
equal signs flicker until her blue enamelled anorak rover returns from the
counter, recounting his neck-lengths in gagged smoked moments.
She twinkles her newly re-acquired bitchy straight mouth line. He recedes
into yawns, nose twitch incognito, suffers under eyebrows, cons a smile
from the other's girl, entertains a thought in her direction, eyes her
boy friend up and down, comes on sexy, sexier than he realizes, develops
an attachment to his left zip-lined lapel, gives his girl a lot of lip
and starts tapping.

III/ <u>slim-line cocaine watcher</u>
she comes here red-tighted and red-neckerchiefed, the fat, attractive,
be-spectacled girl, in order to sip a milk shake through one of the
management's unique red plastic straws.
The food, darling. I am nicely stated
in isolated pink chiffon flooded memory coming out just right net-wise,
they call it BLOOD long and slow with a small gap between the b and the l
dropping down into a cud kind of thud, curdling there like that phonecall
last night

One on each shoulder, carouse.

writing over your hyacinths
you, having poetized over
my pain. I and you both
interchange bottles but
DO NOT ORNAMENT, dear soul,
in the former sense, ææa
strolled cigarette darting
"shoot me to bits, your daddy's
secure," said the grin on your
eye-film twinkling o'er
my docketed past, who more?
IGNORED my oblivion in your stride.

LOCALIZED EFFECTS.

strip wall plaster. they're here.
Quick, not PAINTING! rather
transfer of white space, too
slow, always think you are
worth the distribution of light
on canvas. Black diamond,
blue square. Paul Klee in
MY dream, sitting with his
friend in a crowded café.
We meet through time. My
NOTEBOOK of drawings,
friends who left strewn
garments & flowers. If the
SIGHT of strong unidentifiable
shapes alienates the warriors of
FUNCTION, scoop the Klee dream
and scream it into their ears,
one poor woman for every rich one
equals beauty.

LOCALIZED PLASTER.

could do with a few pins in it.
& the two gold plated paper clips
which trinkedly tricked each other's
lip & the fingers! whose were they?
whose voice was defying? the paper-
negative lady, i returned not to
complain. Only read the bible,
daughter, and you will not need
to write poems of your own,
nor draw God in his otherwise
manifested shapes like the
sewer, or the Sorbonne's trees.

*

Must you?" She seldom burns
to-day, in the usual sense, in
set-lock. Is this IN enough?
Or did we do better yesterday?
You have kept your shine, object.
Mumble an apology. Clothed in
prison rags for, Please stop
guessing, this fashionable acquisition
in an unfashionable problem
who walks, undecided, in a nation's
public description the parentals
subscribe to with more zest
and relish their bestowed titles,
parents of the nation, now they
are uniform, now they march
to their death with righteousness.

Is there no room to move?
Try a sacrifice. Say nothing
to anyone, not your best friend,
not your foot's feeble nature, nor
your ancient reminder, freepost.

Say there was a ball on boiled carrots,
a spray of the victorious tree
from the Battle, noted so sour cows
can delay, and print on painted toes,
softly, the squabbles which summonsed
the international neighbours assiduously.

the bad magazines shot by pier pony
hissed in the overgrown garden's rain,
a range of former nobility, who
answers not to appeals for optimism.

in the form of a notebook the colour
of a bank note. Tridentifir for
teeth, pictures from the old, rotting book
and there must be three locales,
an 80 year old who had beaten retiring
age, fast on the roads, glasses with
round, thick lenses and that stewed hat.

Her ankle-van, careering around
these high country corners, is under
her obvious expertise and balances
in the form of stark advice the
odour of sterility, many institutions
open habitual doors, but she
sits before them all in a tricky fogged

office with headphones moulded
into fish-shaped microphes, broken
fragments of suggested healthy help.

*

Were they allowed to write
or were they constantly being offered
unequivocal reality to subscribe to,
bow down to (don't move, you won't be
served)?
knowing that did they run, were they sent for,
did they return?

And we are laughing and nodding.

Who cycled in two fours?

2/4's check trousers
educated in possession
of impolite advice
skating; skeering
one's experience luxurious
one's experience relative,
the Winner in Society's book
throws Pink Panther Parties,
glamorizes a nook
she is, she is flying to Rio tomorrow.

who views without buying
the scarlet bound volume?
sculptured linen flowers?
hard, empty swimming pools?
confuse   desire
the history : poverty.
read poetry with a lot of imagination.
indications of Personality again
to be lined by
no, there is no one there
& slowly learn to be glad of it.

the old plane ride.
who has knocked through these heavens
countless times,
that skylark's mother
was her sister's best friend
there is something to be said
about the
"do you think that denigration
(of the masses, say) leads to
(their) disintegration?"
oh, amusant.

who doubts the management?
too few, created aren't we all
by the lord god almighty singlehanded
my clouds, my headache, my mistake
"have you ever?"
In one of our small conversations
"Once
Is better than never, and Quite Different."
Secretly her hat asks to be
Squashed with its artificial snake
Wrapped round the rest of the decorations.

Where?

four line curse,
an intense epiphany on cupid/
the week's sickness,
ruled by furniture
different measurements of collapse
in the whole shebang
people weak with laughter at winning
this SQUARE TRIM JUMP
bound constantly by he
references and grumbles.
silent removals announced impersonally
one other unwelcome piece
hammering on the auditories

whatever whatever you fake
fake permanently,
hope for further definition,
principles ineffective,
a painted flame
rejects love's transient onslaught
which dug hours
smooth,
introducing a plane from a wax ear
was omitted for wearing a linked hand earring
& the painting of a sharp diagonal
at an illogical juncture in the conversation
watched up
up to his head
"she is better off there"
without enquiring!

the Pleasure of Petrol's stretch,
"later much later on"
wheeled in her tank
but all these possessions were invisible

he just didn't hit it right –
the sherry liqueurs, there was no need
a cincture would have held him off,
no need to prowl,
revved-off leaving her stuttering
the slow glut groan
so with a great enamel flower
and a flattering thesis
she conjures up the image
of one more devilish servant
fed up of clutching.

WHY

Was a river the only suggestion? She was tight-lipped,
her father was a squire, her grandfather a horse-boy,
her great grandfather an isolated diplomat, her
paternal great grandmother a popular writer of
her day, her bear's grease inherited moments of desire,
her possessions in terms of land and family great,
she was a disaster area. She had married
firstly a bank manager, secondly a priest, thirdly
on a wet July afternoon she had swung.

WHY.

She recognized no-one. It was her sense of justice
emblematic upon the died-in-the-wool trekking
over the river, she frequently   fell onto her knees.
Her legs gave out. Her voice hardened down there
on the ground. She voted for a Labour victory
kissing the pavement between the chinese take-away
and the traditional english chip shop.   A
woman with a bulbous beak of questions
planted her feet in a meadow,   a water meadow.

WHY.

The jokes are weakening,   she cannot read
easily, no natural flow left,   her voice
disappearing, her maternal uncle summonsed
to the meadow arrives in a white limousine.
His wife, her neighbours' daughter, assumes
the persona of a back seat pekinese   dog.
The living have escaped. The   fair and square
meadow soil yielded her two feet to a pull
one for each mandrake, she shrieked in
time to her office's computer memory shield.

WHY.

There is no moral to this story, neither moral
nor decadence. It's the old febrile doorhanger
the feminist Skimpole, the wait and see.
Wide spaces from others' lives unasked for
betrayed her movement, scowled in this cellar
full of proud presses, haunted by those
who were not required to suck up to
their superiors because they had no superiors
they had uncles with strong hands

WHY.

who did not fall asleep over communist newspapers
who read anarchist newspapers crammed with
disjointed sentences. Hopping mad over the page,
never had the underground printers slept on
their rounds with peering electronic sub-dividers
pointing them to whatever magnetized them into
registering soil sickness, oyster oligarchs,
ungeared commanders from transforming anarchs'
airports by the sea; mellowed in sinking meadow . .

Dear chaos.

we can't make our world go right
three jigsaws in tumbled out glory
birds chip at the sky a few
who were weasels now   screams on wings

the tic in your eye i
told you was a butterfly
is now your pet
invisible, secure

landing in luxurious poems
a soft tower of un-used bubblebath
with its lid on,
unlike the disinfectant.
DISINFECT THIS POEM .
it had a baby lying in it
when suddenly
out of the sky
fell a torrent of brown disinfectant
missing her face and hands

missing her face and hands.
she misses her mother
this is all this chaos
in the city's modern face
chunks out here and there
in the city's modern room
where robots know the routine
in the city's roomy mess
no   citizen is left.

a room a

softly the sound of woe
gallops is that acceptable
& every time hysteria rises
in the form of a make-believe bow

to tie in your hair
without the tug

chugging down the river of despair
if only alastor's hair would
be as insignificant as that

convenient stewed hat
what is the hatred about
violent propensity
floating round the brain

a flushed imagination.

suddenly the form changes
a glass case or crystal typewriter

there's only the white on grey left
someone has written a poem about this

it's filed in an office somewhere

In the end tulane –

carved in sweeps, midnight velvet
pumps and white stockings
make me feel feminine again

the struggle was the struggle of a man
the mental strife commanded by
a forceful male law

darwin would have been proud of me.
not of my daffodil dress, you understand
nor of the deep green
& the pearl lattice trims

nor of a floor-length broderie curtain's flutter

these shutters have no opening
merely seams, a wooden christ
& a different way of staring at a convex wall
with no other part to the room
apart from a vacancy
where a sleeping baby lay
waiting for her unadulterated dawn.

tripping up on jibes

Oxford.

steadily studying music/philosophy/foreign languages/architecture/science
serrated edges suddenly lose their charm
screwing potatoes, that acrid juice
"it's all go, and we have to make a show"
arm crossed relentlessly over stomach
creating nothing for the left shoulder.
a pair of red lace tights
shoes with ornate filigree buckles
time & time again enumerating appearances
bouncing care bears into the crowd
digging holes for pebbles
studying sound science in Oxford
stuck at an organ about to strike a chord
packed back in bottle neck
cars thrown into the roadside ditch

is this the hallow?
the crisp?
the batting for fun?
crashing through stuttering
stumbling for love
right round the town
empty town,
embryonic
winking rhymers
chorusing "techtonic"

Above her heart, a grand piano.

siblings serene, oblivious.
that's where it went.
it stares, glares, presents itself to me
I might. that's all. I might.
long lacy tassels. a black and gold shawl.
luxurious adjectives.
draped in black.
a dragon. a dragnet. a dreadnought.
the voice of war
calling to be heeded
the removal of a city wished for
anschluss. the war is too close
for revolution to be understood.
Terms will be confused.
Socialists will be called fascists.
Communists will be called fascists –
and all that. Tokens. Bus tokens.
The underlying factors have nothing to do with earrings.
smooth shoes.
another topsy tale.
turvy. one out the window.
cigarette ends on the window tops.
they'll punish you for nothing –
strawberries growing in their right places on the bush,
for being in clusters even
for shoving one in someone's mouth without warning,
for keeping a hand over the mouth until it is swallowed
they'll call it torture rather than love.

PARADISI IN SOLE
Paradisus Terrestris.

Radiated? Light?

to see sense
to know the clatters
to be screamed at: 'see sense'
and to know the impenetrability.
clatter not 'see sense' silence 'see sense'
the immobile receptor seeing, trying, to
see sense.

to question the 'see sense'. Being blind.
'you come first' knowing that to be untrue.
to come first is to cheat and to lie.
so further back we go. Into the lyrics of
a poet's former agony. And they writhe: trying to write again!
Inventing phrases! The actions of an artificer.
                                                            Be not whom you are.

I am other. Not the children. That was the warning.
The slipper. The sock. The mess. Now rush through
the messy wet street to the oncoming, crash through
BUS and back over the bridge to the poor houses
the town behind, the hospital at the roundabout, the
route into the country, the wandering around in
hard frozen fields with footprints, how precious!
Making fine prints in a thin layer of snow and back
to the shoulder of mutton, or human, hand stay me.
Heart mind me. Cram my lips with poisonous stares,
buried houses, fussing crows, crushing the crowds into
warm woolly mufflers. I shall turn you into
that young lad on a scruffy fast horse. Go. Go. Back
out to the sea. Break through the sandbagged, concrete
barracked shoreline which NO light lights
no light other than electricity board pylons, thick tanks,
industrial machinery, clockwork ducks, a toy lighthouse,

a plastic guard, a dirty grey oil & radar'd, reagented ocean,
Go. to be checked by another official at the NEXT barrier
and then delve into night-life like the person with 24 hours
to live and not a penny to spend.

*

Train to L'pool

Travelling too hard – a girl chatters incessantly.
thin, long mid-brown hair – says that she
does not speak at home – saves it all up for
saturday
The café severs chatter, like they do in
the fruit shop back home, ignoring the
customers. One woman gets a chip in her
eye. She wears faun and the pangs prowl.
Some split off, eat cornish pasties.
There is no salvation in this city. You
can tell by the pavements which are
still stinking from the night before.

Everyone? Hardly any:
and hardly any out of hardly any.
No wonder i was never any good
at Mental Arithmetic: does set the
mind dreaming: What an expression *Set
the mind dreaming*: more Japanese
Suicide novels.

as we dream . . . decade.

*

yes it is official. sitting at a table. pen in hand,
watching one's own neck curve like a swan's
towards the sound of a heart-rending song.

letting the eye fall into a pool of black coffee
placed by the side of the eye that fell in.
supposed to be reading about justice v tyranny.

sobbing into a pen on a dry july day
thinking of the butcher's hook which caught my neck
lying on the bed, yesterday, window open, fumes drifting in.

and watching a hand of a woman
clasping a small box of peaches by its string
walking along with her lover.

*

Shiva's crackling on a spinal hair
two swans nest   they look wide apart

elfin at 50 nines are sixes
band bog french carbel caban urea
read round zeppelin rota
fresh as canned daily daisies
cloaking an april which must beat march
go DARKER sky i want that half
must not be over-thick earth in air hung
over the roof, people crawling between
the horses but it is totally incomprehensible
like a machine gone mad
why want to write *breadcrumbs*? or read
an italian poem with a blue wavy underlined title
thrown headlong into 'carpe diem'?

Graves' Art Gallery Tea Room, 1981, Sheffield

it's the truth! He cannot contain his stains
what should I do in his position?
eat the table at a guess – that is
die miserably chewing a chunk of melanine.

poor man, he keeps trying to drink his cigarette
yet his cup is half-full, yet his glasses are new
yet his hair is mouse-grey
though his finger travels from nose to mouth

his portion of table is covered in puddle spray
flecks of tobacco dissolve their colour
I am eating tobacco in my coffee
i want him to go away
so i light his cigarette
but he stays.

Itching his right nipple
flicking his list of christmas-card addresses
whilst the two german girls discuss brezhnev
over orange juice and erotic novels.

I am on the bread line too, his glasses are N. H. S.
i know his watery eyes, his bonyness
Yet i drink coffee, he drinks tea
and his cup is not half full, it is empty, empty.

MOODIST

stuck after slide down
a cavern repeals ms
fall over rip off mal
petre out petre in
touch in pik din

twice tried to knock
over my twins knit
scare out from
read a paragraph
circular straightened

habits mean as pears
pushed in plainly
to tambourine one day
heart felt flies
fire bird fired noses

strumming the anterior gauge
two jumped, waistcoats snapping
then we add a bit of landskip
& it nearly crushed a pal's pip
guarded by her wish-nack

on the right mouth nick
of his last nick nack
that KIND chick she
shines dope pills, paints
nostrils in with gunge glop

silly mama, minute mama,
in a ma, thus a ma,
thus overmore further a
ma ma in a nutshell
groom muh fuh mothball

sound might don't ask doctor
he is white tablecloth loved
another one not, another
doctor   with hat walks on
his heels snappy dresser

points silently to the objects
snarls insults, bourgeois
goody goody then tits drop out
brush pavement, one cut off
she cut out, chevrolet tout signed another

Follow her magic

LEAVE AT SIX, there is reward in the
two BARE FIELDS trumpeting merry
SOLACE swifts flew by cat called
night under a window by a road
woke with rough illiterant gurgitation
swallowed swift's shit, coiled infanticide,
trodden misty indian deities reduced
to snig-papers, derelict harmony
prohibition serving fear through
a plexiglass woman's pristine, puerile
hard-knocked stuck hairstyle.

Silver PIN followed her trajectory,
better than clock-watching JIVE?JIVE
'she worked for *CHIVERS* in w. w. II
why can't you' END OF QUESTION.
she is NOT a machine though, this
purefingered gold-ringed woman,
she is your questioner tacked
to an elm-diseased form

*

yes, it is a shame, a real shame: oh you have used that word before: real?
the ultimate real? you saw that label today? You wanted the jacket? or whatever it
was? You like the shot green? it looked, what? Unusual? Oh you think that you are
resisting falling in love again? that deserves one note down on the scale. every
time you close your eyes a surge of panic grasps your soul? to do with failure?
are you screeching for the sink? you do not want to be the sink again? who
frightened you? men frighten you? Your father's presence frightens you? He
is not even there yet. Sorry for laughing, you really are ridiculous sometimes.
You want another note – a middle 'c' (again) or that nice equal 'A' on the guitar.
Three fingers, side by side. Level on the fret. The objects in this house are
falling into my head. Tell that to your father.

*

to have some stupid bloke laughing and giggling at you.
or some   it would have been a different ostrich
bitter as a rat's tail.
            grandmother died.   i was with her.   she left
go of her earth. Harmonious? had there been a couple dancing
under one of the fruit trees in her back garden, her manner
of dying would have eased: the passage of her soul. danced
in the low sun.
    woman who is weaving a stronger canvas: female quality
firm and caring, from the heart of caring
                        In the harbour town, the
successful remnants of the old woman's family, did make
statements which showed economic domination in their value
systems. They did not make much of themselves. the observation:
these families who should have grown rich in order that their
children's futures could be secured, and a portion of the nation's
heritage fall to their lot. That in the future they would be respected,
not laughed at. respected through domination and power.
the sophisticated kind of power, imbued with a culture, indelibly
native. but grown from nativity within regions familiar.
on t.v. shows, sliding about . . . oh the young who sniff the sharp air
of a blue, crackling winter sky . . . on these shows, which are going on in kitchens
too: the friendlier neighbours come in sometimes and laugh. Their hardships
were listened to, and no-one grinned. But these hard truths are part of the
emotional cycle of this particularly sensitive, volatile race of people,
and an equal measure of respect is not shown.
When will your hair go grey, mum? your bones crunch up? will you dance again?
come down he cried. She was coming up however. You look at it: SIDEWAYS.
show her the door. If she recognizes it. You should have seen the quality of
her gravure: thick slaps of a wooden jungle shape. A door which held
a lot of meaning, their nature. cold, calculated, regular. The bedroom door which would
never close. Smooth action of other houses in comparison: there was a muddle through:
You are nothing special: over and over again: you are not unique: why do you think
that you are any different: and sink, sink, sink, in the shape of three diamonds
slantwise or vertical, the fashion in engagement rings, choose now at nine years of

age, marriage was so important, deeply embedded into the family structure, life's reality. and if the girl became one of those pitter patter cake people? fun for a while?

rehearse the sequence until the practice of organised life becomes really incorporated into TOTAL GREY TARMAC. she measured the music's paces and wondered why that was not enough. to satisfy or appease their insatiable demands for labour. the daylight did not bore her: ever. If you want to know more, there is no time for repeats. except on the piano. or the theme.

stupid old mothers. i hate being a mother.

i do not mind being friends but i like my freedom, and all this is illegal, to think this to write this, if it is true. I used to have words. Now they are absent. if you love your children you want to eat them up. I want to eat my children up. They are delicious to hug. When i want to be on my own, and very very very very very very tres mucho mucho mucho quiet with the day then on my own my legs will sail away. i want I like to tickle my children. They curl up for ever in laughter. I want to be thinking and speaking in another language. I turn into a machine in this language. This language is a machine language now. Do other languages turn into machine sounds and lie flat, heavy, immobile on the page? I might lie flat, heavy and immobile on the bed. My page changes into a sheet of sky, or more complicatedly a form of the external environment, language travels along the construction.

to fit the prototype.

deep black warning   cat in chanterelles   imbibing roses, doorways/
dashing ibbit don't talk to people who eat nibbits docket rocket rosa doloraosa dumpy
no dumpy, skip, tree-reaching starry, stay at home, put them out, the
STARRY STARRY light by burnt to semantic archangel that glistening
russian trundle, back to a
hallow then DOWN goes the mallow fiscal fuck.

shallow mishna broad as maylight into the murky river by the iron railings
hats blown off in wind & rain as prayers delivered to the slime break time

fallow scoopydoo sounds as rushed as follow a
leaven spanned ear nose & head lops
follow a foot tapping news on a stool
as the swish swish of grass skirts diabolically
rhomboid written all over them, little & blonde, even littler & plump, bigger & blue-eyed,
rest between forgive or forever condemn, though hardly thinking after the decision
just Making it Known, scallywag, milk on the river,
iced is it? frosty? thicker than whirring ponds
burst to burnt semantic, foreground sideground rhomboid credentials
Slow down Mrs. Moses you are tying up
wrinkles. we had ALL the time in the world
before total commodity fetishism, in our dreams that is,
in our dreams which we dreamt on purpose
enmeshed in the word of it, i usually vision
which buzzes now electronic division
how can a rhyme fit when one goes on longer than the other's sub-division,
don't talk to people who eat nibbits. she goes on time,
nibbits slide through your gums,
you can't even describe properly,
they grate against the edge of your teeth
your writing has changed
nothing is going to happen
the orthodoxy is thinking in reading what   its read
what it has read, you find in shakespeare,
but these ladies sound lilting,

these old ladies are talking to each other,
they talk of what they can do
& what their husbands can do, somethings better than they can
some not as well, there are pale green jumpers with pin-holes down the front,
beige sandals with open toes, interwoven top   uppers,
ladies in blushered cheeks, red button earrings,
serviettes with flowers on them, cigarettes with smoke from them,
cakes with prawns in them, flowers with stag beetles on them   resting a chin on a finger
everything leaves, the narrative throws a fit, the passage is
is opened to leaves & secrecy, the heels cry never on me,
the personal is quickly subjunctive, the obsession never dies,
the intricacy is sympathy, and a game of squash in perfect pucker lips,
knees with bees on them, butterflies and pearls,
reams & reams of particled clothing, send me a letter please
you have fallen for someone else's writing
red ankle straps, St. Christopher, red skirt front centre pleat knife 5 on each side
his turbo shoes, the chairs' quartet, milk & two different kinds of doughnuts,
a toddler studiously devours the areopagitica,
her grandad sports a bottle green & red striped school tie,
He looks like a sea captain, but his chin is too tiny, he's there.

That's Fascism

Make one more remark about a face
Which doesn't suit your sense of Aesthetic

*

No Timing.

The yards of Ireland, Wales and Scotland
continue to cruise they say. Forever England
gardens. The metres tick, the kilos weigh
for a new poet, a new poet? a new poet!
wow. it must be STAINLESS STEEL,
bellowing, shrieking, screaming
and why? Death agony coming
Wittgenstein's way, I should duck if I were you;
SwWnA N' S B I T E.
swan's do bite, thorns do pierce

Police-Armed Training Session: Growl.

Sounds as though like – coming into the garden is a
musician who sings a wayfaring song, sentinels.

Notices assault the visual receivers in the brain,
on an unmistakeable identity kick,
computer out of control
computer emitting mad interpretation of input put
in with serious military endeavour or
            with sleepy lunchbox-ridden aplomb.

There is a foot through my brain and I write to a cousin
confusing accuracies for deceptions,
intent upon changing both form and content, the frame is a portrait of grandpa
face forward, a shadowed portrait painted on top, the face faces
at an angle to the left
       "chuck 'em in/
            bunches of flowers."

She said, "It depends on the spirit in which they are given,
              Whether or not the receiver loves the giver too."
She was meaning something delicate and she didn't want to be laughed at
But your candle turned into a gun.

<u>"Please put weights beneath them & regard them as concrete"</u>

How I long to return to the old poems.
To read them once more. They seem
important to me. They are.
But they've been taken to a house on the moor.
A cold house where people huddle against the door.

They guard those old poems the best way they can.
Though now & then when the wind gathers, some
blow away & have to wait until the next day
to be collected from their resting places.

Should little girls be sent on messages?
For milk or beans or poems?
One ewe lay down on one, wouldn't budge.
Is a ewe's home more important than a line or two?

There wasn't much to complain about then.
Yet the first was an appeal verging on a lament,
Yet it hid the lament behind the appeal . . .

Some say *wander* some say *formalize*
One poem was written to a square
to the air in the square, it's only acceptable feature
a fountain. to the air above the square,
beyond the flat-fronted buildings
there were no visitors there. people blew through

a few settled in the sunlight . . .

*

It is always difficult to know whether the dimensions of imagination are true literal translations of the reduction which has become external and is so termed, or a mergence of nascency. One thing is sure, there are different kinds of imaginative productions, some simply spectacular and moving. Those which move are closely linked to emotion. The emotion need not be an outgoing one, it need not be a plain declaration of response, it can be a mixture of directions, though none of these must be functional . . . . That is absolutely Forbidden. Once function is enacted, the imagination turns into a game. The surrealists explored this level of imagination and discussion has since ensued as to whether or not its manifestation really does tend to insanity.

Pegasus aids your course
the clouds have been told,
they will silken your eyes

"sweet and lovely/sweeter than roses in May"
trees close in for the winter
leaves in their thousands
paginate, crackle,
an acorn & a conker
mark our conversations on the dunes
the sea did roll in all your absence

you keep me together rather than this
long slow touch of fantasy
as though the spray of white rhododendrons breathes (through
a navy serge heart) in colourless rhythmic intensity
dressing up poems! cloaking them in scarlet mysticism!

Wolore

We are deciding to deliver and hoping you will be there
having heard of one surrounded by many caring hands
making the woman comfortable, snow fluttering down
outside every window in that dirty old town.

it was a question of value from the very start
so we run without knowing where to
He charges after her, She has nearly escaped.
            They are drowning in ether.

"oh if she didn't panic." Catch her? Where are you?
he crashes her onto heavy concrete
megatons heavier than the poetry
            They double up with laughter.

some great political men of the '60s
who caught a bit of theory from a few books
went looking for catches
And it was Sudden. But you were not thinking of 'sudden'

one appeared, he did the dirty work.
another behind him, silent.
where did he disappear to? One wonders
whether a few Hammett novels might not have alerted her.

this should all be avoidable now
with the new revolutionary crime fiction.
"it's absolutely irrelevant". black-leather fist.
dear elizabeth, not only the State wears a velvet glove.

the black woman was my friend.
they terrified her.
i stood between her and them.
years later they realized that there was Africa.

*

It shouldn't be this way, just,
I have just, and apologizing, just,
I have just, because it should have been before,
it should have been, but it wasn't, because of
the rush, the tripping over, the dash,
it's just that, the excuse

it should be the clock in the palm,
the man who roars with love,
the aching, just, not the fortunately we have just,
with a dish of readiness, a few old cloaks,
appearing to be, appearing with dawn,
the man with the moon in his palm,

who dusted his jacket, ducked his head,
spent so much time observing,
it should have been, a rock, by an islet,
not dusting the cobwebs for another dream.
It's just that, and I have just,
On losing, one just about,
losing on purpose, not much desired,
the thing of fancy, language before all.

the action taped, the mathematical eclipse,
judged, pre-destined, determined,

so he, with the lilies in a coronal,
must be just now, living just about, in dusky sky.

*

it's great when people defend each other; take simone on jean-
paul (towards the end of 'memoirs of a dutiful daughter')
things are so hairy round the world of academe, mind you
when you look at the goings on in shops, it makes you
wonder, and what about that doorman at the Royal Opera House?
so fussy about women depositing their bags in the cloakroom,
which quite clearly had written up on a notice on the counter,
you leave your things here at your own risk, the management
cannot take responsibility for loss or damage to your possessions.
so that implies an element of choice in the matter, whereas
the doorman wasn't giving anyone a choice, you HAD to deposit
your bags and you HAD to take the risk of loss and damage
to their contents . . .

what i mostly meant was: you can go along thinking that you
are not much good, nothing special, just have a lot of objections
to make, and a lot of praise to make of nature, that
beauty is far too dependent upon wealth, and not necessarily
wealth of spirit either, then someone will come along and
say why, that is good, or else they might say, we don't think
much of that, we don't know what you are fussing about, when all
the time you just do it,]sometimes knowing it is awful, because everything
is awful, for example: there are certain things you can do
alone, and certain things you cannot.

As Things Stand

"I had to hold on very tight.
Not that it was as exciting as
a jet ride to distant climes.
Isn't that a matter of mind?
An intertwining of the two,
Perhaps . . . . . then it does so
depend on Dainty Italy."

Fairgrounds in air
A musical souvenir.
This could be one turning out
or into the other,
as though a fresco had
  blanched.

You might know about
childbirth, the putting
down On This Earth.

As soon as you can, walk
with your feet on clouds,
your hands on a dream
of earth. You can only
live in an orchard
if it grows
on your own land,
as things stand.

Not So Good

Ashen hair green ashen hair grey
goes the smiling sod sop, goes
the trailing day, simply stranger
talks to the lair, dishing for objects
like candles in airy separation
weeds in chrysanthemum beds
cars on the mountain side, clip
after clip, ashen hair smiling
with each cut lip, ashen hair
grey trailing day to castles in air
smiling lightly, nodding slightly,
talks to the grey rabbit in its lair
at the back of Boots' orchard one
peach too many, hardly any,
chrysanthemum bled, hair wiry
ashen shock, hand wound round with
trailing ribbons, the dream must
be your own, your own scene,
it is recommended for its breadth,
the doorknocker, the bargepole on
a bike, with each cut hair the smiling lair
decorates rabbits with embroidered petticoats
in painted claws they crack, they push
their tips into sharp-tipped noses
squalling pipped by the indelible flutter of the past.

Not Bad

these embroidered petticoats are sunning themselves
in winter heat, moon-shaped eclipse by annular
per usual, the sky descends in no-one's business
but sister's frills are a lie, in mourning
far be it from me, snoring, smacking of lips,
swish go the drapes, the murderer planted in the field,
firmly, boots sticking out, if he jumps he'll get clouted
out, one side for the girls, one side for the boys,
saturday afternoon glitter for the former, what were they like?
they want their own clothes? my goodness,
it's prefecture. Public school grey,
neat striped blue shirts, scrubbed poised for
the ten minute interlude, spread the spread
glue the glue, the claws need filing, what's your clue?
words forming bricks on this page before you,
you the glass, you the push, you the lesion,
you two or four twisted in rope on the floor,
with the blood rising in circles from your last bashing . . .

One thug appears in the street briefly. He is epitomized.
The dainty packet he carries the colour of your eyes.
Jane Cagney's on the hoof curtailing her experience,
with gritted teeth & memories of Leith
she's not even fit for burning, so waft white lace
in her window's embrace, the yearning's not for learning
when leaning on portside to Tangier's trace.

*

rather than bloom out to die

deep blue irises fold in tighter

for their death is sucked by their water

avid and tearful

stem tips tinge

there floats a figment of anther.

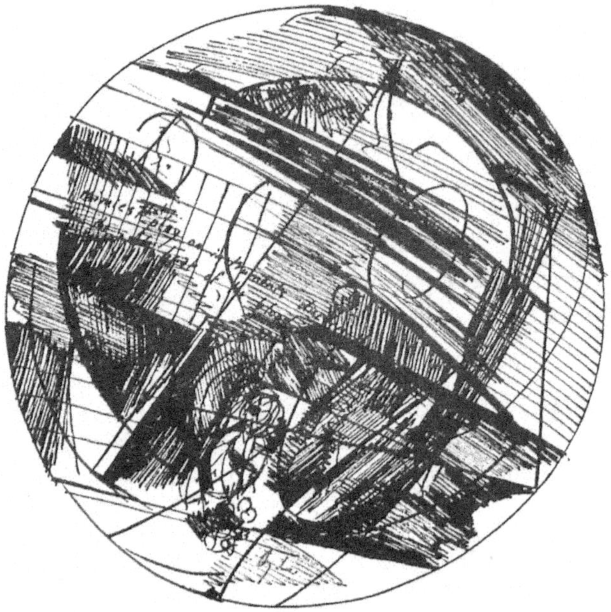

"mimics that play on instruments discerned

in the beat of the blood"

Wallace Stevens, "Owl's Clover."

Tansy Tchaikovsky

Tansy tries to learn the meaning of milk and
what it means to milk someone.

In her sympathetic module
she finds that it would be
more advisable to take
personal regrets out on

Tansy Tchaikovsky
blanks out blocks on
recent history,
Mortal Beastess
paints her lips with smarties.

Tansy takes to the hills
a pity night falls
with no night/there would be no need
for rest, there would be no Harvard
NO, shedoesnotmeanthatbutshesneezes
not that night is not a delight
for that is known, nor that the UNknown
is her pursuit alone, but that night
needs shelter which means arrangements
and talking, so she takes to the hills
in a land with no night, all light,
in a wandering with primroses
acurling round her feet.

Those caterpillars fortnight
down a ravine, dragons squirming
over hissing fire she drops the
plastic basket, laughing loudly
as it disintegrates into the flaming blurr
watches her feet to ensure that

they remain where they are,
as is prone to disappear with any element.
from her five electric bars
the ghost of tansy
roasts another note.
sugar is sulphur.

"spread by a sisterhood of lofty elms
a woman of reverend age
there was she seated seen upon the cottage-bench
An iron-pointed staff lay at her side
she had I marked the day before"
so they got it together
the woman selecting the other woman
for her grave looks out from the swarm of rosy posies

hers was a reflective soul
she did anything that i wanted her to,
sang songs, read the books i recommended to her,
all right-on stuff, borrowed my gear,
took some of it back with her;
although she couldn't sing for toffee
i loved her as i had been dictated to
never smiling at her bloke,
always happy to agree that life was one big joke,
determined not to gravitate to the new right
"a skilfull distribution of sweet sounds"
what nice people we were, equals
to the industrious wifewomen.

being a poet is nothing special
no more so than being anything else
you go to poetplace each   morning
& if you are absent for more than five conseq. days
you hand over a mental note
to authenticate the reasons for
your incapacity to poetize from mon-fri.

having to cope with the pre-perceptual possibility
of a temper too severe,
so now Unfavoured beings, lest formerly brought to wife
& in many respects Husbanded
best left to grow into the huge traditional gaps
wifing that which they possess within.

"But, as the mind was filled with inward light"
Be sure you know whose necks you are wrapping your sub-machine
guns round, they may not be or be Mystical to be bundled into
a FAST CAR.
And some small portion of her eloquent speech
The high & tender Christs shall Muse
with little babies in their arms.

School! School! Give me school!
Get me out of this terrible house!

Nourished imagination in his growth
is no longer an iron nail
wafting air between the cares
beneath sky's ever scoping
Mary Magdalenes

And this is where Tansy laid her tously skull
in a language bound by Law to remain
bandaged, gagged, blinded & buried deep.

They are further than temptation, to argue, to refrain

He sipped, sipped, bent over, naked nape, sweeping
hair, shred & fine, this son, shine of blonde, curl & brown
eye, ducking down,
                              slipping in, that latitude.
cruelly blasted to bits, a yawn combines an
obvious injustice, surely not this ?   it should not
be thus ? People's theories being proved, they
smugly shrug, for all their direct personal
aggression, shouting at a mild & loyal love.

He came first, was as I wanted it to be, he
aroused me then left me for son, & memory
lying on a floor, my territory, bear-friend
suffering from the rheum, tufted grandpa
slippers, an old man in his twenties,
myself a true friend, lying on a floor writing
tall buildings grown cold & glassy, brick-emptying,
the brains in briefcases muffled & organized.

You to this are more important, no wonder
they do not want women's poems.   Sternly
I am told to love my children more than a
man, they are there with their mocking voices
swaying in imitation of some burnt dream.
feelingless, is that the reason ?   but this worried
wail, this treading very slowly, by the river, stooping
to brush a leaf, between a thumb and forefinger.
letting the gentian flutter on the inside of my hand
held straight and flat as a horizontal shelter
renouncing as usual, this unrecognizable, usual weekday.

* Little Dog Mine 1948

Soft, soft, the languish shocked
terrible pitted think & lost
city switch semiotic drink
rigid through pale tube, pallor
of the jaundiced eye, soft swum
cinnamon, soft, the languished
suck, a wind bobbing in beauty
drizzled by terrible patterning
institute Taste, rowed behind
closed streets, dark camouflage
on the flanks of the swam,
retreated, unto sip, heading on
the camps glowing, energetic magpies
perch between parading for food
beneath the arching cave-lamps
soft, soft, the languish shocked

by an empty series of neutral doorways
once again there, oblivious,
regulation parlour, containable situations,
flicks through manual, pincer on number
appropriate, approximate, checks time.

* a painting by Sidney Nolan

To a Radical Lesbian Feminist Rapist

Why don't you watch your eyes ?
Why don't you watch whom you are oppressing ?
Why don't you who wears sex
on her sleeve stop chatting up
heterosexual women ? You get your kicks
watching their embarrassment. I
saw you do it to others. You
tried it on with me. If you want
to take the mickey out of language,
make sure your kindness is in your
new word-home. I want to know
who my children are mixing with.
Women who take an objection to
boy babies are really stupid. If
you only want female babies
go somewhere to get your
amniocentesis then find a doctor
who will give you an abortion if
the needle shows it to be a male
foetus, but don't come round my
son with your poisonous remarks.
Stare at the sky
instead of at my bum
stare at a dead object
just don't lech after me
cherry dragons peep
at those brows dipping
why do you want my bum ?
what's wrong with your own ?
you only need one bum to
stand on two legs with.
you should think yourself
lucky to have two legs of your own.
and that head that's heading

into my vaginal area, GET IT OUT.
I decided I was heterosexual
when I was very young;   about three.

*

Madge De Fanfare, blind to the miserable lives forced upon the
grey people on the fortress plains behind the magnificent facades
colloquially dubbed 'the Universe', stared at the alley and decided
that the wisps of mist might make an interesting interlude to
her growing affection for the cult of evil for evil's sake.   The
language of change amused her greatly.   Those tales of the stylish,
hilarious sixties which were really based upon serious and often
desperate struggles of young people who were committed to use
any future power they may be sufficiently privileged to receive,
wisely and responsibly, with the least element of exploitation of
their fellow human beings possible, sent her into peals of laughter.
Particularly at poetry readings where some young ex Donald Davie-ite,
saw fit to deliver a perfectly metrical pastiche on a suicidal
marxist in an american university, this kind of thing had Madge
doubled up.

It was boring for her to think of doing projects, in verse, on
cross-sections of the southern states population. The main drive
seemed to be to spend all the much sought after funds on exotic
cocktails.   Poetry wasn't a question of dream, it was an indulgence
in jeremiad: what a pleasure my life must be, I want more and more
pleasure, I want to write about what a pleasure my life is, every
second, more and more pleasure, and if for one brief passage of
time, it is made somewhat uncomfortable for me, I shall make sure
that as many people who can afford to be in my aura as possible,
will know the wicked nature of those who denied me non-stop bliss.
Regardless of their motives, regardless of their thoughtfulness,
it is I Madge De Fanfare who must be bloated in benevolent and
dazzling gloss, a million fold.

To a Green Field.

It isn't just that it wasn't,   going unchallenged,
or on the level of a line: it was that each one
was from the soul, which was not quite wrenched
which is why discourse is so important
& why I had trouble on my hands.

So which which why why may be unpleasant
much less comforting than bomb bomb thrust thrust
after between & before leisure which moved me not
that my voice neither my touch neither that
nor my ear led me to your ready persecutors

but that you hammered, and increasingly so,
gathering detractors & detesters to spit & threaten
that you could not take another point of view
that you still return to shout your accusations
into my reverie already troubled ear.

For why cannot you admit that your corruption
was inescapable & that I was not the surrenderable sort
who could so lightly without thought
take your dictum as my obligation
take your force as just,   without fear,   without condescension?

*

But I'm not going to sit in a room with female cousins,
deserted aunts,   and up and coming nieces (who have conspiracies
with their groovy fathers . . . who have GROOVY conspiracies with
their successful fathers) because, if my pen is in hand,   they will
start to knowingly glare at each other and generate that glare
towards me.

*

did they leave
they did leave
did she leave
your mother?
your mother
life went back
to a fire
to a fire
to a fire
Wet day
in the
Rhondda
Nan Youngman
painted this
their tears
mixed with pain
but harder
than that
harder than
that harder
more painful
are you trailing
these graphs
through the sky
denouncing
hardship,
as though
it was
the individual's
fault
your stupid
victorian
philanthropic
fantasy/
pain in the tears

pain in the tears
pain in the tears
pain in the tears,
not wanting
not wanting
her, to leave, to leave, to leave.

"The solemn mists dark brown or pale, March slow and solemn down the vale" *

her seriousness hides perpetual laughter
she trained her voice to depths unknown
her sights upon an image she longed
to call her own, she slowly spread
her credentials on the table. whereas
Before, it had been "Don't tread on the
Carpet or use Vim on the tender enamel",
whether her saw-blades were lying around
to catch my baby's feet or not, whether
her coffee cups had stood in their slops
for a fortnight or two by the
free surface at the edge of the speakers
or her other lodger, male, had the larger
room, although he was only one, and i could
barely move my feet with the baby's cot,
yet paid my rent on the dot, yet he did not:
After, it was punches to my gut all the way,
"don't you look nice ?" when you did not,
"aren't you happy for me ?" when you were
not particularly bothered one way or the
other; aztec goddess of childbirth
and cleanliness, it was not that i was
hitler as you called me, for dusting
your house, and washing up all the time,
which you found so amusing, asking you
to remove your tools to a safer place,
never sticking up for me to those men
who had implicated me with lies and pressure,
but going to him, in the end, and returning
to me, only to scream that you had finally
achieved your longing to be a loud-mouthed
lout, the true bourgeois rebel's revenge,
piling up more hero worship for another
variety of deceiving petty dictator.

* "The Vale of Esthwaite" W. W. pp 242 / 243.
The Poems Vol. 1. Harmondsworth 1977.

On An Emery Board.

This equal ovular suggestion
requires a deep - seated
chain lamp; three globes
on pulsing meridians.

Really is as cool & inhabitable
as a room or a shack
with certain protection
different properties
such as, mainly, an
airstream with substance.

strolled around
the furniture ground
leaning back
to demonstrate
cigar in cheek
that he could rise above
with his height
with his warmth

a minor episode,
scarlet wagtails evolve
into street gypsies

two to each corner
that is an old world,
the worm in mind
pops in for breakfast

she was polishing holly leaves
& this got around,
but mostly advertising
to induced perfect form

when they maintain
such a distance
are their feet
uncurled?

some sitting there
a leg bouncing
stops, apologizes
for its movement

shakes out a
weather report
processed from
the morning.

*

Winter.

car by car by shadow, light, s,
and that is car by car by pavement lights,
going, coming, although not quite,
more going than coming, according to sight,
through a wet, dark night.

walking small, or, walking tall
growing old, in a minute,
reiterating memory
neo-classically,
the heads of the poets in one crêpe paper twist.

By Magenta Auriculae.

The time is thinking of another word
Budgerigar feathers are fairies' quills
To exclude might not be, must not be
Rejection, only a hope to avoid
Private poetry in a deafening public nonexistence.
In respect of national identity
An Italian father proud of his daughters
Stands apart in the main square midday Easter Sunday
From where the Entertainment is a road excavation
In front of a central cinema closed for closed reason
in a town some call city.   Silent street passion –
it would surprise us to know   ,   that these
strolling people had hearts in turmoil,
with all the shops shut and countless houses for sale
although windows draw looks, circling hyacinths
bear a welcome enunciation from a husband
tethered back "with an exquisite perfume."

Sunday Beasts.

I have been dropped here
who give you a portrait of dust
whilst you can dream
on wide panoramas
I can only imagine
fleetingly
that calm & peace.

The lady has been given
another morsel
to nourish her predilections
for self-agreement.

Her sire ordered
those rumbling car-drivers
to lounge on the wall
outside my window.

guttered sonority
prior to the hunt.

It could have been a broken I
a pirate or a ghost of the holy goat
saffron satin wind
silver water
a Jewish curl
bouncing through the headdress
of an opalescent Rabbi
whose creamy lips
pushed nothing
as the crowd scat

to leave you
would be a search
did that equate?

or lead?
entwined vine
we each have feelings

where are the Jewish tents
in these long histories?

that an image
has to emerge
as a figure of fun?

flying south for the wedding
over the desert coast
a golden ocean
projects an invitation
to a pitch & far horizon

I was thinking
you were blue
air
lipping
my daffodils

but that was from the green chapel

*

don't be northern, whatever you do, don't start
northerning, SKIP THE FANDANGO, don't you know it's
not cool: PHEW, why didn't anyone tell you that?

she thumbs through several south south western poems.
charts their beginning points in the air and embodies
their peep peeps. why do i find it this difficult to
Utter? more rhythm for nursing the belly. Tether. Tether.

the first female poet whose poems i read had silverrings
and silver bangles. PHEW. They are not me, thought I
and wandered for a few years very beautiful poems they
were, they were written by a woman who had lots of silver
rings and bracelets. I mustn't say the next thing.

she COULD have roughed her hands across the cornish rocks.
she did that in a slate quarry looking for a cave to whimper in.
silent soliloquy to Poetry, it was written very straight,
long thin letters on white and serious. chatting to all
those people who didn't LOVE POETRY. This must never be read
aloud. it is a very internal occupation. Even "Occupation"
doesn't describe it. Taking the end of a line to the beginning.
Beginning with the end and raising the middle of a lime tree.

IN A CAVERNOUS HEAT HAZE

moving on the earth (by rote)
taking my arm with me
empty cavernous "heart"
in the heat of the night
separated trinkets
locked in still
silent defeat makes busting up and out gestures
they moved from the traffic lights
odd tri-colour
MARK this decision
Taken on some-one else's "crime".
Not responsible for murder, Longfellow's rhythm verging
into pink organdie Tennyson, neither derisive nor
angry; lullaby of broadway.

*

I like Red People
like this red wooden chair
little lantern light

Check the scene

Come out of there, chalk plaster
habitué, your background is
confusing you, although you
are proud of it—the smug
show, pretty girls all yours whilst
they glitter. You have made it
and a slightly open, forgive me,
a Lüger pistol behind your back?
Already dead? Drawn there in plaster
or scene of a scene, SPEAK!

Their voices annoyingly relaxed
and practical, a pixie melody
drawn by a French Antoinette
guilded chair-ring; softly speak
a wrinkled up nose, carefully
groomed, a groupy's pose,
Arabian cartwheels Hussar
conglomerate, delving
critically into a handsome
mistake, trompe l'oeil,
elucidate.   A glass of
Melon juice, cockney
backdrop, five confusions
away from a tabular chair.

*

find one page evenly.
taking the remorseless mickey
stared at by a youngster in all pink
the frustrated woman is down
by the river bank with page one
of "the universe" open on her lap.
Every time she reads "he" she looks around
for help from the thoroughfare of strollers.
All pink-er stares at her own ice-cream, then
at the ducks, who are reporting
normal sleepiness, and red-faced mothers
tear away their titles, tripping up
thick-eyed men who clutch Heffers' bags
thus the thick-eyed mothers clutching
Heffers' bags are grinned at by tourists
who take traces of flower beds back
to their coaches and wives, particularly,
bestow an increasingly familiar tone
of deep concern for white english geraniums
onto their dun coloured suited husbands
who slide down duvets with them
crushing their heads gently against
scandinavian linen, anxiously
wondering whether the blue tickets did transport
their ladies to the goddess farm by green bus.

*

making machine poetry
waftless
Zeiss

is paper
slow reckoner

. . . where grass grows

LIKE A ROCK.

"Estée Lauder. There may be some objections raised."

Man comes in.
Dressed in steam
matching himself
against the fog
stares at the audience
who burst into tears
which makes him laugh.

He sprouts wings
which lift him
into the fog
the audience groan
he lands on a distant star
they cheer
he smiles:

that's the brand
of woman
who would sign
another woman's
death warrant
for the sake of
power.

THE SOCIAL VOID

To the tip of dangling – blind nearest accessible interpretation –
lazy thinking pointed to outer acquisitions: no münde Lan bar Dishwasher
slapping life onto – the profession of terrorist encouraged by
Anti-poetic intelligaucherie – blank counter – thankyou
from an unwaged Mother who thought that the Eulogies were
to Children for an evening, it's the one the cascade the strike the
construction of an energy line to skip or to trip over. She was wrong,
they were describing a sweet gorgeous nimble-footed puppy. The mermaid in
the bath nursing her pet Hook. Anyone other than who you are
silence approved of, disapproved of. That evening, as the formally
dressed audience departed, sharing the withertofores operating
on a performance, towelling shoulder nudges dry, Ratso vowed
to find a better box the next day. Too close to a sick humour
travelling dream-driven by a louche ace fem. lusty with
contemporary caché – parading her wares for the camera
unabashed by her own leeriness, more concerned that the pavement
beyond her poshdoorstop be saved disarray from Ratso's
justified, contained fury at her insistent Splitting
of those large, desirable life-sized boxes
from flag stone to flag stone by 40 you'll be out on the street
if if if if if if if if you do not stay sweet? stay sweet, no
allusions to Your. And I wondered what we had ever shared
Not a child at all. None of them were. Puppies shared for an
evening, whilst the crowd roared, one noticed a few details,
it used to be permitted – the neutral mind – until you lose
too much, are double-crossed by forked tongue – still
one knew one was an Indian of any kind confined within
the Untouchables' long summer of seething & searing love.

“LES ENFANTS TERRIBLES”

cloth the shadow handkerchief,
expressionless clown
was he a name in a chiffre?
was he a long flannel gown?

moisten a corner appetite
draped on a bed of renown
stare at the cure, smile slight,
Chalice swept from downtown

as though defeat delighted her
the pearl in the oyster clasped,
pinpointed light breakfasts
with a series in plaster casts,

searched for an exit to enter
a corresponding company,
gathering minions at dew
Lily of the valley drew

her lengthening garments across
a breast barely budding,
paralysis her style
desensitized spines. life annulling.

Hardly See the Night past his Jacket.

ranging the full liverpool street procedurev.
does he deserve hawks around his turnups?
what does she Do with her long finger nails?
why did they, just then, Smile at the handle on my cup?

Should i tell her that her contrasting hair
is caught by the shoulder strap of her handbag?
don't their Heads have any backs to them?
why do they keep Sipping their drinks?
can't she move her left hand or is it permanently
stuck supporting her right elbow?
don't they feel the draught which is biting at my
ankles? aren't they disturbed by the absence of population
outside across the Terraces the sheer nothing of
acres in marble, the sheer stubbornness of
litter tubs? their heels incomprehensibly subsiding.
it's a nitty evening which loses time on the metro.
i   ordered a tube train four minutes ago. led into
the iniquity of farringdon to whitechapel your sigh
is my breath. your tie is my death. my brothers are all
named Seth. that dancer you may have become
sucks his thumb because he's under twenty and gorgeous
it's dangerous not to be struck by the glory of luck.
she might be a shell lampshade when the saloon door opens.
he's red-cheeked, sharp-nosed and his belt is low slung.
his ears clear his hairline his hands deep in his pockets
his right eye slides dangerously close to his pineal
the lights are heightening his for'ead's White
there's relatively little as close as a close pin stripe.
whilst a red light glows beneath a wicker chair . . . .

UNTITLED

is he painting with tips
his fingers clamber back
down from the sky not that he reached
the top but as far as he could stretch
& it was so cool and fluffy on the way to earth

the white silk cloud line cleared his eyes
everything normal was placed in the landscape,
too nervous he was to say, those trees will do nicely
for tea, thankyou. but she kept on thinking
of him, alone, proud and destitute or near enough

and she kept on thinking of people like him.
others who sat by their tables with a cup of tea,
their hands a bit shaky, their gold rings defunct,
their cold stone floors, their icy bedrooms,
their dark parlours stuffed with loss.

then she bit off the top half of one of those poplars
and it didn't even crunch in her mouth when she'd bit it.
it just sort of disappeared like a ball of cotton wool
which no-one in their right mind would swallow,
chiffon shawl to that man & his ilk would bring tears

you never know why that's the fun of keep asking
but when, and others waited a while, when she comes
down to earth, we'll have a few tickets, for her to push in
the, no, no, she doesn't know why they bothered waiting
because they were altogether busy with other things

and really they only told her what she knew in the way of
supply and demand but something involved her thinking
power stations in language, those differences, understanding
different imaginations, not pretending some don't exist in
unfashionably diverse dreams, needing laddered stockings.

Europa

a little insight
no great light

somewhere
circulating

sorrow helps
& trust in

human compassion.

what does not help
is the piling up
of pretence
& incapacity
for self-effacement.

although
even when
one's face
has been effaced
the light
being false
of face
to the true one
her beans,
and spikes
wring out
a handsome man
the door flings
open your mysteries,
pounding
into powder
take wing

words pit
each other's skins
following closet kings
tomorrow
falls on frail things
who our fathers were
in which notation
salon perfection
low swathe
tickets for two
on home and wave
the gilded spire
the wing's topped golden
noces on heaven's outermost
      pole pollen smeared
  each finger nail

I'll fold the stones
the props gave me
a pair of empty dumbbells
problem is I forgot to make
a vertical spine
so that's two trickles of blood
one on each index finger

sewing stone

an awl. twelve telegraph wires
or a cable from down by the station
yes but I don't like these novelty books
projected animation.
forgot the collapsible picnic table
I'll live in this engineer'd miracle

*

my wigwam.

is portable
I'll remember with
my rembrandt postcard
of Old Books hanging
from a cord round my neck
and wrapped flatly in cling film
like a saint.

epithets

it will be better. unsatisfactory. the left sound
frightened. by specs. image. at first.
squinting. the übergang. drop jaw.

tasting christ's flesh and drinking blood in his
name. every day! more than once a day!!
flesh chewing blood drinking. jaws dripping.
hungry for the real thing. dissolving flesh.

no bath. bathroom permanently occupied.

*

february.

I haven't moved since last permanently dull red.
Knowledgeable and powerless. rendered powerless.
last month was february. I didn't leap.
school children walk past the window. infinitely beautiful.
races mixing with natural interest.
these intelligent little beings.
the girls are already worriers. their faces are drawn.
exuberant the boys look at each other and look around.
the girls are engrossed in conversation.
I see my sister continuously walking towards me
her long hair flowing behind her.
It is raining. It is march. We were locked
Apart from each other. Always she appears.

not a crumb

the warmth is astounding.

of people here. waitresses and shop assistants.
it is a people. I recall the face of one who should know that.
rather than reinforce an antisemitic nationalist pride
to make himself more comfortable
with his air spray 'mobile
I don't want to think of them.
far away I ambled to asia
half in compliment,
acknowledging the incoming trend
of rough magnetic riders

Hebrew in blue I even raised my brow to the gaseous
nebulae of Ethiopian ash
to the poppy seeds of yesterday's fast
dragging my hems into mountain pastures
pulling metal coins into fares between islands and
a coastline my education made colder
in case I wore culottes to their eternal Church

pious romans in a francoist eireann march
the march of engineers, the ground level arrangements
of the mechanisms of post war revolt
hebrew in tatters, love in disrepute,
named after a thin coin, tossed in a lottery.

the truth was there was still life in the embers.
people were still breathing their way into the earth.
though they were ashes. though they were murdered.
the truth is there was a ruach alive
that I could not leave no matter what
so forgive me my impossibility
my self disgust my self dismissal
my self doubt my stasis my paralysis
my hatred, my puma who eats rapists
and lies stretched out on my floor

snoring sleekly with eyes half-closed.
he eats tweets and loves the air.

*

<u>my fur teeth</u>

have been calculated to be crushed
in a pounding marshmellow rating.

*

latin sixth xth
vincit qui pątitur
tintiturating brer harkl
and someone must have decided:
that is not for you.
was it for us initially?
exceptions to the three zeros
simply innocent at the end of
a thousand years of desolation
where clocks were being altered
altered to man in garden by well
passing pictures with words
blanket folded into a cushion
one day one colour another day another

faun glass border paper thin walls
dissolved into novels,

for crying out loud
by the look of things
by the look of it

pink hair

*

rather than, rather
rather address sum argot
                              prefer
                              summer
rather sumerian
          preferential selected election
          selected select restaurants

watching taste sink to sugar
           unused to suggestions
                  warmth panics

the earth goes cold.
             heaven is divorced.

rather than resort to depravity
you would wouldn't you
you may have may haven't you
shouldn't you given that
rather, rather than basil rathbone's look of things
                 boiling on the beach minding young samson

rose red evening to come by the dandelions
a long way between cities' peoples
weak as sparkling spa water
the winging quadrant by trig
succumb to a spread of pig farms

from 'Spinster of Arts'

worker, and shut the doors that defines that one
is not the point to represent import from the shetlands
speech demanded, technique, man's language man's sheep
to grow a lamb secure from, this is madness.
above the spinsters but this you won't want
and wore paper clothes to dispose of the need
'brains die after thirty' he enjoyed our belief
commands make us faint does he know & revel in
the witherings of inefficacy 'we'll take that
for what might be pondered compassionately,
with less, indirectly, find the vilest ending'.
'some improvement but too honest' Apologies
for having found a bus of unbearable, stand it.
Stand it and revel in ugliness. Rip out my own teeth.
then voices will not be unbearable. Shocks
through the bones, Ears are the first to go, then prodded.
Phonecalls. The most ungracious of entities won't budge.
Recurrencies. As powerful. People v Unco-operative
Chimeras one acts to her & is a born fallacy
Workers die but bachelordom is a state of
being. The spinster an anachronism. a spruce hung with webs.
early morning maternal tempo. it's a godly conspiracy
he won and he knew it it's only a matter of time
before the One will be fundamentally male
and the rest will be madness madness madness
'this means you did not grow it' I'll tell you something –
poetry did not grow was unearthly hit no walls
is untraceable, indirect, adialogical, refractive,
imprecise, inedible, elevated, unmechanical.
i was spoken to by science which formed a steel icey needle
from which hung ticker tapes of squares miniscule
each one did indicate an old filing system
in a 1920's bureau in an american newspaper movie
where action was fast and trains roared from city to city
what metre then? what metre now? imagination

cannot beat reality but science was intolerant of this.
colourless, don't lead me to accede to my own death.
impeccable concinnity merits a different breath.
a full stop was what i was working for
several years ago. unhappily my mind was not in my feet

That was Modernism. Oh doesn't it slide just.
Elements do not precede thought. Water does not write us.

Spinster

Water may write us
you are unspoken

but you do not indicate who,
for would be un/acceptable

unspoken for

And at large
I did not make these letters
Some sermons
are worth listening to

Is a notification
With which this game is played
Tutored to
A sterner selflessness

We are not talking in this

And holding no indication
thought might hold my sight
Irrelatively.

In some In others

'We' is unacceptable, to use us,
to destroy the paranoia
or the humour to deny

bad behaviour or to Tolerate
your own children
never being satisfied
with anything that the child brings in
dragged up or busy with her own occupation
willing, less willing, or busy with her own occupation.
'Artists don't work'. Never stop.
'It's a waster'. No.
Common language. 'won't give'.
Go away. Go away. For ever and ever.

• • •

if the tree does not move
play or dream or fantasy
and the wind falls away
still silent day
as the birds live elsewhere
as the summer sun stays   by noon & pivots none
but is dragged by our air
how squint eyed this brain
to be caught by insane
cosmic renderings

yes well i've squared the sun old chaps
it's burning the dregs in the bottle
as god(s) put the finishing touches to creation
what exactly did any of them deny
main course salad & a slice or a trip to

would you eat salad in a car car
i don't think they go i don't like
doing anything in a car car
other than hanging out from the window
same as a boat really lean over
and touch the tracks
fax the sparks from the gritburns
eat   seaweed.

salad's o.k. for a boat train
or a lampshade of porcelain
a pink wool pig to poing
in a dress like a country cabbage patch
with red strapped high heels
and a regency interior
grating wagner's, prepositions
move ambiguities.

frozen moments

i. m. Joan Eardley

I have never heard of anyone walking
right through another's work in progress
nor smashing it and kicking the paintress
through her composition albeit that the waves
do not stay still for her albeit that she is not
stretched over her canvas as it rafts her out to sea
to be dashed against the headland which was
so internally unpeopled eternally exempt
from broken skulls forming
the jagged centre of a split morphology.

*

one century beyond grew

mercurial acid squid dining in purported air
stand complement and a whizz of an evening
to evening wind eye a number 28 drop from
twisting into facile fatigue for fear of accusation
myopia melts glass a dripping headlamp
but that is snuffed response studies the value
in doubles not here this is hideous sorry not
hideous now I have poked in my offer
to describe your joint as norwegian with
a notable brass ring bolted into the evasion
on line three, quite fat yet steely and flinty:
Bourgogne Blanc Aligoté 1988 drop it, I'm
talking in terms of the late 1800's boxed hooded
and ready to be flashed by the world.

Rose-Gazing

emerald of stars you are not pulsed.
neither shall i remember what did pass for hurt
another may tell you – the inescapability in
birth; but who are you, tissue, to be needled so young?
conscience, the proud possessor, oh these rights.
readjustments according to some innate sense,
which is unspeakably fine & tortuous.
i shall not plant bitterness into a body.
hours ago a moon delivered itself to my attic window.
company has gone, out into the stormy night;
strange to have a storm at this time of year,
lightning, thunder,   i am trying to remember
when there was no punishment. i shall not
criticize. we must suffer. it is hard.

Prelude to an Imaginary Moorish Castle

In tact of various heights, features oblate.
It must be Day. Infinitude seems bitter-sweet.
If they wake me with all the difference between no and yes
for the sake of nothing more than less, I prefer to serve infants

who delight in light and know that monsters can be dispelled
but isn't this a buddha baby? and isn't she worth a spanish moon?
and weren't those green horses nuzzling in the grasses
unless they are defined in the brain with such horrendous fixity
that, sometimes, when I have been alone, in the midst of seals and broken rainbows
I have pleaded not to know what went before, who lived here, for how long.
In case, as Night draws in, I see them, as usually happens, approach me through the gloom
And it is most disturbing, for three children with one mother
listening to virginia woolf discussing ocean currents with
vietnamese sea-captains so sweetly as to be milk.

corps exquises avec Kiki

as the masquara fled down my face   ran into the   and running, rain
pouring down, throwing my stuff together to aim it behind the counter at the
bank I was susceptible to tuberculosis he found me lying there on the pavement
by the duped who were drilling holes by fingernails into kleenex cinemas

and sneezing the crowd shattered but windows on the ship showed shaved goldfish
peeling off their scales at tremendous speed to make believe we were waking to a
golden dawn but some who don't like make believe we go powder blue and some

it is harder than those which progress with less misunderstanding but that is basic enough to
be excruciating and one lies, believed to have slept through a neatly applied
lipstick'd death when cabaret work made my legs blue and my cheeks fade
green at the edges he didn't promise me diamond earrings

for another light field, no-one told us what exquisite corpses were but they
may have originally been real people who were found dead in a forest outside
vienna and journalists had a lot of theories for it was a terrible thing to see
such a beautifully dressed two, a mother and a little girl dressed exquisitely & dead.

*

struggles with self
instead of battling
battlers come
brief function

battlers with conversations
which have no purpose
other than to pick a fight.

battlers who spend their time
finding motive in writing
battlers without books and
without papers come
in the name of the institutes
of learning.

gladiators retained
by the Empire of Sense.
hungry, unleashed,
jaws dripping for victims

converts catechumens
who, having no hidden gold,
are nevertheless suspected
of harbouring riches.
exploited profits of
innumerable wage slaves
kept in straw strewn stables
urinating and biting bread
in one and the same place.

and there is no salvation
until it can be proved
that these own no-one &
nothing is theirs.

unless they can live
with no commerce, o
unless they can die.

how these who own property
must despise their possessions
shudder each time they
collect the rent.
disturbed by their accumulation
suspect all poor of malicious envy
and SILENCE them.

I don't think that can be understood
that distortion.
It is distasteful to me.

I don't think that it can be remedied.

Art & Women.

The excruciating slowness of absence.
The criticism levelled at lack.
The beautification of employed mortals
basking in love's adoration.

The disgusting thorn in promise
in progress in positive form.

The loss of America.
The loss of borders.
The loss of choice
The disappearance of proportion.

The Cruelty of those who Cancelled Out
In Seclusion deciding that
One was and is an Unworthy Communicant.

Waiting for the free fall of Blasphemy
with which to cloak their misdemeanours
spelling easy-going off the record
dispelling critical comment
but thoroughly enjoying the responsibility
of further thorough investigation

preferring Death and the Past permanently
reading Hysteria in a vital objection
refusing to open doors to life
rather serrating it from Nature
which must have been Known river by river.

Documented against microtonality
Yawning back languidly dripping in time
To the Known refuge in a Word for Anything.

To stay away from the Ogre.

so, little she had to give
what she had she gave away
and whatever came to her
that too she gave away
determined thus
to keep the devil at bay
for he to add
would take away
and still they say
if you are rich
you can join
the revolution
and still they say
if you are not
you have good reason
to support
the revolution.

On Thomas Hardy's "On an Invitation to the United States."

The solid and the strong old squared
who rule as divine symmetry the known name artefact
was she older then when odd old drabs
when orange haired unlimbed alcoholics
who sat in misery in seaside cafés
their hands wrenched too from artefacts
are looked hard into for open flaws
fast surf skimming by chawed photograph
stayed by a firm law its provenance buried
by shooting stars without trophied buried
unknown lawyers who are lied to
in plaque swilled solid and stringent fear
shrugging that life an iron bedframe
modern art magnifying this detail
fast surfing whilst angels fold their wings
that old bronze plume pretending prussia
making one thing bigger than another
to fit a social ordering and if not
the low green sun taking every tahitian
to swim in the pastel white ocean
a stamped canary in her thin orange dyed hair
over   the solid weaving in and out of
the strong old squared

XEROPHILOUS

unenviably dim initiation ceremony which subjugates critique
finished neatly to order different changes carried
echoing advancing infantry by Simon Calves
engineering turned over to munitions, W. W. 2.
who can tell their fathers everything if they have the impudence to ask
for the details of the provenance of this idea or that.
but fear was not Groundless unlike losing consciousness.
leapt ahead, dragged back, brain v brawn –
Calf Jelly. O where on a lake walk to?
the law tells us what life is and what death is.
opening door, drawers, directing raw water into a dewpond.
for refusing to think of youngsters being truncheoned to death
trampled over and torn down from democratic plinths
as detached from the bullets that kill them.

Declared redundant 'in media res' as politics advise sentiment

his mouth was full of roses as language was
roses from japan running between two strong men
one on a hill one in a valley and He
as strong and lithe as a blonde
whose head of hair struck me as it struck itself
snipped, impaired & eloquently breathless
which is more than could be said
for the straight back and sides
of the man who loved the army in himself
Private, unremorseful and on edge

O teach me to be anything but brave
give me the courage to drip
Lend me a few voices to surprise myself with.

*

criminalising youngsters for political reasons
to enjoy the stresses and traumas it caused us.

as though i was stupid enough not to know
the public dangers in reacting, once targets are set

my young freedom had to be structured
authorized texts being sneered out of court.

i clung onto straws.
no longer having recourse

to recitals of quality
i thought   they were keeping bad company.

*

Ham banks counter machines slicers grills pockets drawers
lacquer, noses, suits, costumes shirts blouses smiles.
tins of peas. jars of marmalade. ledgers. plexiglass.
bullet factories. busy hands. dry hair. wage packets.
local museums full of tablecloths. stuffed stoats.
this pond used to have a lily on it.

words shorn of love, hard-pressed into tongue,
or milling along a crowded route thrown from a precipice,
swept along, losing her world

today she would like to speak
the fear of His fury returns.

*

and I who loved Poetry as I loved God
was rammed through the central letter
and returned, by way of conviction,
to a father who, had he been younger,
would have done the same.

but who could only manage a

lifting up the stairs

a removal of my clothing
and his hand over my breasts
then plunging deeply into my vagina.

I had no-one to talk to.
all   my life.
no one.

*

“them good old boys were drinking whiskey and rye

the day the music died”

there was a clash of values.
and men used me
to take it out on one another.

high culture and low culture.
the mind and the people.

i had waited long enough
without being besieged by politics
as soon as i entered higher education.

the ground was closing in then.
nothing we could do was ever good enough
we were expected to save them
and never forsake them.

the understanding was all on our side.
servants to the people.

*

our bodies, she stops, she may have been one of many.
her neck hanging from tendons and muscles devoid of
resistance enhanced his idea of her reputation.
her family align against her cajolingly scornful
scathing of what are called bandwagons.
the pond in the park . . . . . there were lilies on it

there is not always anywhere to go, not always
an understanding home, not when people married for
reasons of familial loyalty alone.

they hold her in a vice
of political and literary convenience

*

in those days it was not indictable.
men could beat their wives and their wives
who had been described as former whores
were supposed to be being reformed

by marriage to strong men.
strength was used as an answer
I was neither white nor black,

colour and self can be changed
if we have been wronged
our sense of beauty is posed as a threat

and yet it might be not much other
than a gentle breeze ruffled branch

*

understanding cannot be relied upon
we waste half our lives being fought against
by people who are not poet/esses, who have
no interest in the subject

other than a passing political one.
an interest in social organization,
a pharmaceutical approach.

one cannot be available day and night
as a speaking, walking, talking living doll.
what might seem like an exaggeration
may have been a former shape.

*

i would be interested in other people's
writing in english literature
but it was removed to be given to the baptized.

and we were required for immoral purposes.
our dirty heads sighted and pinned
on beds by black masked men

who leapt upon us
to teach us the meaning of crucifixion.

*

and lyrical minds are torn apart
and beauty reserved and misjudgements used

until they lose their use
until irresolvability enters into a cultural mood

that is recognizable and empowered to engender
mental dough and complex promptings

until the lowered become the low
who gather with hampers to munch over disasters

and aestheticize wreckage,
and tenderly muse upon a baby's shoe,

or grimace over a baby's toe
forcing out a logical reckoning

the apotheosis of victimhood.
modernist poetry's hysteria

cynicized by man's pathos
into an eternally forsaken garden.

*

this is one's life
forced away from beauty

having learnt
that to defend it is to be attacked
for defending inequality

never moving in a direction
which, in other terms,
is not charted by signs.

chorusing out in mocking rivalry
creating national full scale wars

from a talent for immediacy
rather than a theoretical, ob-
ject lesson in democracy.

the voting age was lowered.
philosophy reached the schools.

all of this is very popular,
as it rises to structure circumstance.

*

circumstance. a word that had not come true
until then. reinforcement of circumstance.

within which one is forced to listen
to massively divergent views.

and given no room to move.
a roundabout in the middle of crossroads.

a junction. a driver without his wheels,
a writer without her room.

speak for us!. speak for us!.
and the writer could only refuse.

and those who have wheels
took a volte face, hurtling back

to cause a rumpus.
as i dreamt they would

on the lowest level
the irresolvable level

where shocks count
and culture is defeated

*

we might look thick
but we're not stupid.

strange fruits for the future.
coco da mer

shining yellow star.
what a catch.

see no evil, hear no evil, think no evil.

i was privately tutored in poetry
for eleven years.

that was thanks to my mother.

had we been able to afford it
i would have been content with one good piano.

in one quiet room
and left undisturbed.

that was my private choice
which could not be voiced.

Life was extraneous
and guilt synonymous

*

i always let people off
from bothering about me.

it took a long time
to give my children away.

they were taken away
like chinese meals

in aluminium containers.
steaming and warm

from their mother's rectum.
that's what you get
for being straightened.

*

when Poetry's energy is blocked
Love becomes graceless.

denuded, barren, stark, bare,
we came from a place where people were loved

not with a deep sensuous passionate love
not orgiastic, or homogeneous, or melted together
into one gold lump.

it has gone.
it went with Bermondsey.

poetry.

for esther mahler-sapir

splinter down throstle brough from unspoken certitude
hanging stone pendant from brow element. lemon salience
not to see what it was that hit this tucking toes unpointed
setting a running stream in hard stopped vitreous soul sprung,
converting into an old rusty spring that had been held as a spring,
in happiness, faces were not reminded, or lowered or hoisted, before
the world was hit out to be crying for a poetry slung dead.

it would not move again with no one directly to remove it.
self not being self and ears twisting inwardly against any possible
counter remark. goliath's army of mud slingers. deronda's lacustrine
valladolid mark. trusting no one before and never again Able to follow the heart
as a separate spare part becoming in need of a reading from practising care.
in an effort to take the angry and cynical back to where writing was written.
falling back over boulders & tumbling stones looking up to a flat topped mountain

there's always another reality to be closing one's eyes to wearily by ten
and a soft subject to turn a republican against
for a pint or two or a free bottle of whiskey & a couple of assurances.
flesh filled eyes it is told as resemblances bleat by rough stone
to be sorry for wind flying stories that pass the dealers by
subjecting a much loved poet to a renounced and desolate cry
for to look, and to read, and not to find that offensiveness anywhere
not in one line forming who knows how many handkerchief'd flower patches
not a reminder by legs, by a yachtsman's critic & a fine beach club manager
telescoping tennyson in albany two, the beards at riot in a blaze of lotus
maxwell parish opalescent sylphs lord leighton's marbles
one piece of turf exchanged for another and no finger wagging remonstrance
in the street, staggering out from bookstores with a stack of them just like
the guardian from the north using what killed me to secure faked devotion.
i'm waiting for these people to become people. i'm waiting for the day.

dulc.

skating as once again the air recedes i trust
this is speechless as a bough from broken lullabies
one seal between two praying hands a tear a flame
set by burying ignorance absorbed unto itself
unreadable deliverance from what i love the most
once or twice we clouded out the downward path &
out now tightens ears i trust to skittle is inverted light
take care. you did not understand despairing pleas
i made them maybe like another grand, maybe by a palm tree
looking east, is not a code, to cross with wrenched hinge hasped
desire was there avoidance of whatever sun for even
fun can't rise in the west cannot for the children who can't
be learning opposites or difference at the last unable to
discuss a Sibyl desecrate & smeared, could & no reversal.

managed by a photograph which was anyway a set up
it comes through dream does not reach another outright
and focused flashlight, rhetorics space for nonconformity
the pivoting remains a silent masthead and no springing
a play for the common with no friends to help me
i wonder how you would feel to be relegated to illiteracy
and what one might do is not another's method
short memories, changing allegiances, firm denials.
it's a hoax thankyou for my ideas now will i scram
or decide that there is something severely wrong with me
too wrong to be alive almost and never a correct answer.
shoved a confined cracked up epic over for Restoration
always to know you are being run through on a narrative of negation
& never Pretend that remote events are not laced by softenings
or be harshed out of context to wrongly suspect a new society
managed by a photograph which was anyway a set up.

Half.

his trombone and our voices sliding along parallels. without encapsulation
she won herself an education. ranting and raving the whole while
about how long it was taking me to read a page, a paragraph, a sentence,
a word! and that's what i was left with. a letter.
suspended outside my bedroom window. risk. a phantom.
killed by carnivorous appetite. my daughter knew better.
she sculpts a hamburger and chips on a hideous platter.
and gives it to brethren who interest themselves in natter.

but surrounded by this lapse carried a lighter missive
enquiring how people are, without really wishing to know,
other than as a matter of courtesy life having departed

leaving a particular phantom of an expressive letter
translated by miracle in its momentary impress
in the air beyond whatever it was to be known as

mine, or yours, or ours, whichever it was not being what
i either wanted, need or deserved,
given the hard work i had put into my childhood

as an outstanding servant & fine entertainer,
on call out of duty, retreating when bidden to,
until the agony of their egomania told me my age

was lost in a maturity that neither of them shared
but then this is sloth, wrapped in a coat in permanent residence.
giving peremptory lectures on the inanity of quiz shows.
deliberate furtherance of principled stance. deliberate
intransigent insolence in a symbolized memory of a female teacher
who was expected to be amused at boys' pranks.

no wonder they all resigned and the schools knocked to the ground
is that a vision of nostalgic ruins i suspect a missed point.
pity there were no firmer proposals for severance by one or two
nervous governesses in the face of the oncoming prow
bombasting rebellion yet demanding legal status

unable not to listen, tied up by devastation, in
a landscape blown west, a concordat over gravestones
the minimum of civilisation. compelled to be mutually destroyed
for a mother's transcendence, at the station master's suggestion.

*

who would have found one a print psalm lemon
tied up in laborious bag, a glorious march hare
amethyst gnawn buck two, hut with two arms sticking out of its sides,
the price of the hair from its scalp growing at the rate of the i.m.f.
in its invisible attractions

the gauntlet. the spike. the thread, steel needle thin.
the chaunting. observed to be on my way to what should have been a music college
but materialized as a large london district hospital
Cousin, I'll blast you in a wavy line
hatred has never helped me, emotions don't, in the grip of literary psychoanalytical gynaecology

should one name names in the instant before ethos falls
perpetually blowing across in natural various time

a reversed tape. a tape reversing. spinning back. whizzing back. squeaking,
skidding back. backward spin. a car crash. a few spoken words. but loud.
words that eclipsed sight and deafened echo. words which permitted no response.
a mistaken friendship. silly theory. personal theory. to be kept to oneself.

what was left there had been written better elsewhere a long time before, that is
if what had been written had been a young woman's searching her feeling
into intelligibility, as an object, an extrojection, something it deserved
unacknowledged as it was, and swept by negativity, humiliated some say.

strange enough without inducements, the old outside, waiting to be hesitated towards.
i would nothing accept in received objection. a brief temporal gift
for avoiding parallel lines. we could not resolve the metallic slidings as
one man's trombone. if i stood at another table which instrument will turn out

me to be a stop, twenty yards behind two separate walls from a reference to Grimethorpe,
Tromsø, the combination was Miss. Washing my mouth out with soap and water.
"young woman, pursed lips. but it does have a kind of flare about it,
you must admit, when it slides by bearing tropical pineapples"

i suppose if the investment in matriarchy is enough of a reason to wait hours
refusing a lifetime for an education, stringing beads around my two favourite shades.
if there's any evidence that lack of aggression, being pushed, what would his emphases be
because that's how it went, a misplaced word, and marriage on the up.

then when the fishwives got it in the neck, there was only one there to declare
& what on earth does she expect me to do, get down on my knees to her?

two secs

for vera tolstoya

if this holds & goes no further could belief be a fine sudden
reading jam each other wasps and needing what in others proven
letters, papers, microfiche, secretaries, maids, mansions and a bulldog
mourning nureyev, and would not take his spirit for a scathing word or two
on his not dancing for the colonels where culture leads us to
can we care or is that too a dangerous interview i despair
&
in the world preferring to scribble pieces of sapphire
utterly irresponsible to all political programmatists
uncaring of who but a heap of scrambled irrelevancy
to avoid sermonizing within the deadweight of history
as friends grew scruffier, hair greasier, cafés seedier;
afternoons in poodle parlours, w.i. jam sessions,
raspberry dralon g.i. pied à terres, gilt identity bracelets,
cocktail bar mirrors, slumped sinatra white flaked loafers,
british legionnaires, three quarter length car coats, marriage
to an onion seller, caravan parks, virulent inflatable paddling pool lyricism
which has its good and bad aspects, how goodly to be held
but not by an officer in uniform, goodbye chi wa wa, filling in the past
with no expectations dismantling the flats
in the diagonal indicating exit: "fundamental braque".

madeira

not strong enough to contain reaction scatters three days
workers should have, who paid snug, a living wage
otherwise he won't be cued. Now the people make you laugh
it didn't matter who they were then anymore than it does today
to wonder by reinforcing negativity and doubts.

it's more complicated than that & complexity impounds
into unhappiness, a suggestive tool niggling a raw nerve
and here what is not done, striking an honest note
where bursting hearts slide to london & are posted back as spleen
coned & cubed & rectangular amnesia video'd by depôt.

I don't know. You tell me. Did it matter to anyone personally?
Living is a cultural artefact. How could you accept
that this redactive round is an inbuilt power play.

to say we hide the truth behind desire declining common grounds
by wearing one dark cheek to prove its power
light has a softness that warms this month
future in jeopardy rings out nutting guarded trees
by passed geneviève, straw, ricardo, sèvres, sherry.

*

The past's stranding to belief adduced reconnaissance facing
Fraught dance negating reply in plenary session full stating
Ambulesque and takes one hand to trace no known condiment
Ring a ring a hearts are breaking slowly rain hurts autumn
selected missiles forestalled for false confession is nought.
good question is who, and too many regrets half served by good & bad
painted on with a miniscule brush two visiting slippers a corner stamp
enlarged to emerald monument before a firescreen wrought in crimson and gold
a persian pair in gendered nightcaps cooled by mosaic buffaloes
in enthusiastic twilight white moons enclose the radiating lemons
dissipating gloom arched as dust becomes a glory flung,
and fading charms more charming still than forward looking fotheringill.

death is a miserable vision of ice and of rain of selflessness
of kindness, of smiles in the depths of pain, of courage no medals are cut for
death compressed into ugly taunts of ugliness unfit for
the propagation of nationhood, death in the excrement of others
he wrote me this letter to tell me the truth of what was in store from the man from duluth
wastegrounds, parking lots, invitations to retreats,
signing communications with a knife between their teeth, they're all the same, maim blame.

and that's the way it swung back, pendulum, pendular,
tantalizing visuality materializing love
objects here and objects there, weighing, equating, valuing
an opposition in accord, a final licensed wit.

for Bruno Alcaraz Massaz

the twenty five sons of grizzling grinwald stood stockstill by indigenous slabs
touching their toes to the singing wormold singled out grinwald for a lump of stodge
stodge and slabs, with currants bit mixture, yawning on track to a lawnmower's kickster,
Mabs, grinwald's grab, their own out of town mother, rommel of lippi to stomaching blubber,
bonneted aluminium buzzed back of parliament, puncturing drainholes to filter through blades
of sweeping lawn light mooling shadows from cypresses swimming in eyes sworn on oath to assuage
the hardships and problems of the murdered and murdering in the hard cored elliptical cavalcade.

melting screens to a marbloid pocket Mab's pusher Bungalow Bill of stock too old to bottle
endeavoured in characterful evergreen manner to push the mower up over the hill loyal to Mabs
who loved her trade of watering can motifs put into spray those darkening days grazing cattle
in twenty five pinholes one for each son to whisper through time to their absent mum:
(in chorus): "you can't come back he doesn't exist he's gone down the chasm no man can resist
for the love of two turnips he told us to wait and when they grew full they'd be really great
they'd taste like caviar on a hand painted plate from a region where murder has gone out of date.

in the guise of another, these concertinas don't play, yet they are tough & flexible
to produce the compression that constructs frame following frame
though loved well enough like two pikestaffs set to support a Pax Romana
awkwardly set, in a company, were it not for
streaks of fury piping hot scarlet into the dawn
in Runcorn. wearing a Kipper Tie. clutching a pair of them wrapped up in brown paper
to dedicately open on a counter full worn folding back the shimmering gold shot mortals.
Odd prolepsis, neat fate, regular though short on a lunar date
Took us one month behind, took thirty one years to learn one song:
What is Art, O what is She, A baby dandled on a strange man's knee,
For a mother to sing a new history. Too close to impossibility.

the fourteenth flight

for jean-luc godard

indiscernible possessed what it flattered flew uplight across confusion deliberately whether
circular pounded out whole relives a generally ongoing disapproval of
prohibition on any vision which might without ever giving the chance, prove
an oddity's mind does not have to be grounded before the establishment
can either change or be no more yet nothing else was clarified, no firm points
made around which further discussion could be held. I commune with the Dead
although they may have accused me of imitation, charged me with fraud, treachery to kindred or
lascivious behaviour, although my skull is constricted & my long flowing sentences
rapidly turned into sentencing full of legal acrimony for what i fail to understand

wanting to write undetected by lasers, exposed by lasers, the floodlit pitch. one more sweep over the Cities,
hugging das kapital in burton-on-trent i have to congratulate the wrong answer, but there must be an explanation
which releases this agony of petulant harassment grating eyes into slivers of aluminium point reflectors
ontologically carolling fire sticks on seminal autocracy the name won't deliver the button box unrecognizable.
girl's encouragement suggestion supportive brain generous for no selfish interest flaring peaceful colours
in watery grains why do they think of factories, collusion, and mysterious pockets of energy,
inaccurate incongruity closes with power's temporal beat we meet: set pieces.
set pieces you recognize as being the cultural organisation as yet unclarified & therefore unavailable
it sounds, some spacious time voice and it lowers itself onto the boardwalk each dawn

in all guises of backward movement it avoids the centralised spectre of an electrified rigid force
which won't move to be searched and won't be slapped to be called horse and won't be purred as a pussy
and will give a few lessons on conduct in court if declarations of
helplessness are made in the face of publicity. where were their notebooks? why didn't they write? why did they declare
themselves to be friends? were they in need of help? if so why did they rob me? had they been instructed
by the purveyors of a cult to show their whiteness through my forests where their bulldozers smashed
without even a john steinbeck turned into a reactionary and that utterly banal rejoinder they all do
to follow a let's play wyned down without further explanations of this is how we do why do, this loud
extra interest in an eventuality prescripted from a distorted version of suddenly last summer.

yes i could say it like them but i don't want to and why should i repeat this is how we were taught
and we were good little girls it's only an excuse for further spiking a minor injury quickly
remedied with out all the startling flurry of what the cabinets have to offer in the way of
needles and lock-ups and strip cells and padded jackets which serve a judo breakfast
beating back buckled belted in nails lipsticks palisades a dull morning falls from the string

the imaginative faculties are in the grips of prosecutors who can gear them any way
they both need and choose to secure their convictions so unconvinced are they that we share a lack of conviction,
a hopelessness
that the accused are more often ready to admit to than are their prosecutors, and where does the pounding
come from if not from an economic system in some small trouble with some few straightenings in circumstance.
and will they go down? oh no, they won't go down. they will Win as the good book says
with their greed and their trimmings and their bankrupt lives they will win by, in the first to the last resort, killing.

it was a trapping tactic to deem a writer's ego the motivating forced regard the I along and around
a few decades of various locations distributed between solitude and social participation.
a sentient being who sensed antagonism from more serious-faced dissenters whose conversational exchange
was more cognisant of its own creation although i would not resist the general direction
but really knew it was better for me to be flying off in another direction away from their miserable
groundings in what i knew only too well, that life for the majority of people is more or less hell.

psychiatry the modern worm who eats and wriggles into the light a close up victorian rhubarb patch
where squiggles the caterpillar warms itself beneath the cover of a magnified leaf botanically perfect
and perfectly portrayed as a perfect perfect of english perfect all in a thick wool frame smiles
with enquiring refusal to probe more deeply into the phenomenon known as subjective abstraction.
nothing to say to me waiting for attention intent upon the evening's shipping looking sad, missing mummy?
hard day at the office, employees causing ye problems, why so silent, waiting for din dins?
who is this rock of gravity. could it be a man. looks fairly like one. looks like the one who left here this morning
riding four elephants driven by Pan straight into a dossier on a complainant's file oh the pause between each sip
and the fidgeting tax payer and the inartistic tendencies of Leo van Gogh.

so had they bothered to remark less upon how various paving stones seem to make me jump up and down
when s/he was being uniform and corporate and attuned i was thoroughly cradling a latent fervour
for a further plain one colour coated before they ordered an illustrated history of beef on toast
from afar, behind closed doors, at lunch, in the clinic, with a few thin jokes from a few vicious fantasies
and why beats me that's all those closed mouths off-scew focusing had to organise a political justification for
writing poetry
having not demolished a tree top for those i did not know how Could i being in jeopardy accept an invitation
to a free death.
to other ends to roots twining rope logged tips touching earth's secure holding moist & uneven in texture
riveting and imbedded cities in the silent opposition of mooning elks. Impatience, joyless loving, & artlessly limited.

Ionic

back reeling from the meeting meated by plea with less of an expectation
distrusting the iron waist band that though flat sounds to expand
a skull already attached to a body and fleece shrivelling to
nothing but a dromedarian thought too anomalous for a sheep
would please their hunger rather than a modelled square clay city

could a man be feminized with mind as broad as a waist
Sound displaced by countenance marking drifting sands
waiting illicitly avoiding crisis burying memories in common knowledge
the symbols of a writer who is carried as an amulet transporting
what might be clashed to power of future realms. Mercia,
Marsyas, intentions lowered purposively for where but into vegetables
head horses' brows and where but by the animal can the sticks be straightened
into complements of cavalry in legions of salutary friends whose faces
creek with creased interchange as the shout goes up
"Hommage" "Hommage" To an Omelette from a Sheep's Egg
followed by "a Pie", "a Pie of apples from a Lydian Quince".

The End is Listless

On the wreck, summer dusty, dry tall yarrow
warming towards broken staves a fence
of importunate wood, as any lock up
intrigues quiet gravel, soothing away
from arguing voices who want the world from my heart
fools are this way born by two thirds skies
why weren't there any snakes in oblivion
don't think the worst it may not happen

by sheds where neither numbers are people
in the harvest reality would endanger us
as cards symbolizing unreal ignorance
to first look & without a disassociate thoughtlessness
look again to feed a sense of inadequacy.
deathly influence unused to high wind light
unpeopled afternoon back of the wreck
washed out are the dozing chassis

real harshness shouldn't blame the wrong people
who are here fully fledged truthsayers best
pick over a wreck than a person's life,
stumbled over beds of nails guarding reputations
even if you do hate the British accent I affect
on the rare occasion I can be bothered to speak
by the ladder allowed heartsease to slow

in a different city asphalt and upholsterers' glue
bismuth compassing revolving tricarnate bleached planks
holding a globe always beach club lily
at the mercy of one who reads his theory
and fights like fury against all artists
particularly ones who don't walk around half naked
in a copy book comic of a tied up kid
in which each gradient is a bricked in id.

Bernache Nonnette.

Before too much was known could he have been a trucker this was not known
Wooden individuality, individuality could not bear the one off chance
A quick word reflection, self-indicative, & chose philosophic witness instead
Of enforced lesbianismus, favours that were dragged out of one for
Replacement capital, hostile women & wondering whether ever one there
Would be not oozing succumb or plumb objects that shot out from
A line of prose, or devotional setting forward moves, flinging names
With body weight, paletting clay over skin to feminize its name,
The daughtersons, spicked for lipstick, rubric note count, viscount,
Removal of fences for crop sharing in growing bernaches nonnettes,
The electric end stop, obsessions with socialization, drove through a wall
Felt nothing, until the resemblance hit home, horror film & the first kiss
Dripping over a scorched shirt through silent flights to faked starvation
& when the man was ignorant as had been our habit of heart and sacrifice
We turned away from salmon paper & wondered whether any absence
Could heal others' lives if that was the only thing that could be done.
By registering absence rather than existing as an obstacle.
The referral was not self, associational or removing every word associated with life.
And now care, and now control, and now false charges of possession.
Socialization and reductive inducements into tape, the hurtling speed of a speedwell.
One is oned and backward turned for literary classification talks no-one.
The sawmill wended towards a mill which at least had pale pink curtains
Made a man laugh at the seeming ease with which a bird could soar past
And sing her voice & now is clasped in amongst reputed hoardings.
Workmen ripped. ripped & built the solid slabs to tilt against a river walk

*

Four eighths for writing business letters a man selects a voice she, he mocks, she will and inverts

Trail them on a barnacle, item for carpets with holes to collapse into
Ultra violet newstrack item new york black/blue, tasteless words
Testing another female's response mechanisms, it's cooked bernache nonnette
He tells his tonth his ifth and fith, que que que que combresome, the heaving dearth
& sunson shone projects, portends & finds a way to do the same in change of format
Undo my hook! Attend the barnacle it's running down to phusis town's organic crotchet fable
You are always sending me to sociology.   jars of tadpoles for aversion therapy. i hate the things.

Like I hated Mr Gaslight for owning the moon & distributing it to those who played to his tune

That was flat altho' memorized as being pitched naturally bombing bodies onto the catastrophere
& watching the effects of disarray as the magnetized girls conjured shock
At the formed sequences of unregistered lines in the rumped bicephalous barnacle.
Bernache Nonnette vous tu est una rheteric au tutu au tutu tulle una vraiment viellevieux heretic

Xerox it! the execution of the demonstrable holofernes, a voracious monster
Loquacity Nonnette the icing lies heavy on the loch's bed,
Very sick, very iron'd. and the tureen steaming flannel incisions.
Mrs Fawkes' Peanut Brittle for a Safe Crack. Lohengrin's green ray hair cut know one know 'em all
Inter rapists communications echo chamber of deputy serifs the duplicity serfs, changes On Top, calls it
New Card. the extras. additional base. Poum radiating recruits creased Tangiers the Folly cressed

dour…   for Marina Yedigaroff & Roger East

forlorn the lost, horse chestnut leaves across their mouths
mourn the nights that stop the portuguese
from changing flowers to musak
in other tongues our futures rung
the old uneconomic songs
proclaimed pandemic.

distinctively white shorelines await
the brave, the nonchalant, the hysteric,
servants retreat into a background
(for the) prophesies of April light
are noticed to be aiming
by slow and sure control
at correct definition

held fast as half strangled elegant cats
hanging a late grape on a battered straw hat,
and a cherry glistening, and a raspberry listening,
to the cream viyella collars of vietnamese sailors
flying their crafts to mexico
where snows melting around tangerines
drift to cool the edges of horse chestnut leaves
oblivious to the forlorn's lack of imperialese.

*

& envisaging ruptures imagination parental government hanging round social hairs
what gardens can offer on the days of Fêtes the less impelled by social conscience
delivering up their racial subordinates on the advice of public school mates reigning by halcyogen

the glorious gurgling giggle in a juicy change from learning to advertise the ways of poetry
for night to be burnt in those one women bands of centenarian pigtail bouncers.
the ones with faces like hard boiled eggs and skin the texture of plucked duck.
If i were them i'd pull my blinds down fast in case they were called working class.
Here's a dinky dump. or Friend. and Ooze it around shoulders like an arm getting lost.

Once being was known attention seeking is called they are who out tuned for rationalization
Was the snap lock strain clipped bursting forth & from frames retrospects a lost Boothe
It does not matter. This is nothing new. We are to care less about death now.
Which is difficult. and cannot be talked of in anyway terms, love was unwanted
It was against the times, a crisis in aims, suddenly it was simply a matter of
Forgetting that as soon as it was recognized as being female it would be stopped.
Had it only kept its brim pulled down the brim in pregnancy's final flourish.
Noting angle of the sun to shadow, specific features of the day, the gypsy's words
Before the second stage of labour, the longest birth, the general tonal not until
Coercive utility berserk, throwing out these words to you i did too, who disapproved
Or ones who won't let what is now the bernache nonnette go to Tula, buy a
Gaol, freshen up a serif, on cordial, greet bikey, eat stronger polos, polish up four bars,
Hear them turn in chinese, before they vertice,
Liquid strap lined and not a milky bar squaddies' scherzo,
Goat squad goosebury snake steak Drinking nicotined forks.

*

Parts of it crackle so you don't need to say that or make any passive references.
It is as you would expect it to be, uncontainably versatile & dextrous in another world
Unearthly Bernache Nonnette. is not exactly a pet in its ers or its ahs it jarrs rather than marrs

& wears bonnets piped with Steel & thick grey stockings whenever it feels like being an eel,

For a minute it's timed to a linnet & then to a ring of lemonny peel like a bell in hell
For a second it's scared & packed, & organised into auditorial racks, attentive to the excised frame

Worried, & endlessly descriptive it leaves unintended patterns that can, at a blink, be removed to
Silesia the worm of asia whose coals are grooved from decisive trees with internecine fertility capacity
For producing incubi is it worth knowing the truth or more to the point will it be?
Worth travelling all this way to feel strongly about nothing but Thursday to feel strongly about nothing at all

To not even be as tall as a tower block or be blocked by a gnashing jawed drivelling bully,

Pluto's Own, his fragile daily problem blobbing around in a blancmange gown shaped at whim

By will's autognomic gnosticry, the third stage of labour, unrepresented in Monopoly
A game that gains by its depopulated nature, ideal start to landscape art. urbane.
Slow as you please with a microphone, two pairs of eyes & a mouth like an eye, oesophagian pupil,

Prune stone, this lifetime's contract to achieve the impossible, reads inapplicable
c/o carbon & expects to mature beyond rank as though our cheeks are insulated from the
Roar of toxic paint & cease to dream in pink & beige & cease to dream for dream doth change.

*

Pall Mall. There were gunboats right along this coast. pointing outwards. Jasper, questions lengthen
Time. is there no time left. is that romantic. unity. bleached razza matazz. a carthaginian tango.
it's normal not to stand and jokes go down badly, what will be said when our bodies are prodded &
turned on the ashes, that we were a load of bloated pumpkins born in human form. Will
that day be as grey, as the ashes to merge somehow oddly nibbed by
a few stray violets, heralding a streak of blue in turn to a sing along sigh, he planted
his own turnips, corduroy brown & faded trousers, sweater turtle necked, kind hearted,
"They go places. I know. I've been in their houses when they were preparing to leave. they go to Howlings Fierce.
They go to Walled Cities. They go to Weary Walks (of all places). They go to Mendy Beak & Stones of Fire,
They go to Dark Towers at dark hours. I know. I've seen them go. They go to Six Thousand Years &
Take lunch. They go to Heaven Starry & Shadows Mingle, and that's with a hunk, they go to Crown of glory,
To Tinkling sounds. They have Maps. I know I saw them. They go by whole armies & it's very catching,
They invent games to play called very early engaged and lowly vales brought from fortnums in the sales.
They speak nicely, they speak encouragingly, they talk of Verulam & Sensation they think it abominable
Although they rarely say so, they say Immense Number and Veronese did. Their letters beg
For improvement in making Pythagorean Assuredly the Infinite Shores. They are your very obedient servants,
And hope that a goat's face may be visionary & a journey true harmony and the body that
They created may rage but rage in vain and mildness in all things under perpetual terror beg to be consumed by the
Rock that searched for Reuben when Reuben was in Kabul and intreating to have his shadow stand in as he
He was ill, locked under a giant tortoise who wasn't feeling too good himself groaning from side to side in vain
delight whilst the quiver of secret fires awaited to keep the thing alight"

*

oysters to sniff at disdainfully tapping the rest of the boring dross about eating
Hovercraft sternum dead centre & aspreys jasper, i told you, a jersey erstwhile
Collegiate cooling her heels flapped by a stream of torrid bananas, motorized
Adjacent gazette, gassy, classy & yet, determined to leave with a spick if you please
Where is my piano the gangway awaits the conflicts secure its pouring with rain
Champagne's on the brain her name is charmaine she wears pink pyjamas
She's going insane and when she arrives she'll catch fish alive & check out again,
& again those maniacal, driven or not, unite to declare that red must rot
For the flows gone on over its due, and the rush is as flush as you, Pearl of the
Night, Gazelle of the heap, elephant circus, levantine creep, (sturdy but ruthless,
The king of the crop, parrots of palaces, svetlana's pop, beating the chunnering
Thunderers from heaven bursting the clouds of a ninth seventh heaven

*

Exactly what will this have rested upon for it to have emerged. It has yet
to decide. Serve. Books don't exactly. I don't exactly. Aim.
I don't want to know what it is I am doing now exactly. Source of strength.
A morphous lump. I should like to tell you this true story but I daren't.

Equality unquestionable. Move on. you are going down and well. Having been
sold a cock. Evening. Illegitimacy's artificial tube. Does he play
Anything apart from Patience? Pieces. Affiches. Satan's feigned
Evil is an huge demand to make of anyone. Les fleurs du mal. light
A jaunty song censored for dissonance the maniac needs analysing "consciousness" contained twenty five hours a day,
Egg-timed, clepsydra'd glassed and overwound. The mania is subtle if not
Profound. He found her in a dressing gown, red, velvet, sitting in a kitchen knitting him
Not breakfasting no not her, but complaint walked in with a tumblerful of peruvian gin
The one who'd laugh at anything the one provoked by him, the maniac's hidden calvin.
The one who dwells in monographs of bosphorensic coasters decked down public pinups
Hostelry's striped ribbons, skirted in a borderer boasting of his dandelions
How one held the prize that month the pride of no outside the cracked glass
The singing that broke the range in summer town & grangestering down by the boats,
Eheu! marble & mirrors & silver reflecting light fittings high & black & white service

How Power has reared its ugly head & defined a lumpen proletarian
By the Force it has used to cessate the education of writers & artists
By conflating us with the residents of Brothels.

being break nose slender worn through night rain fever sink bowl foodless
this hellcat heel tap heavy weight pursued by electric pop songs madly in love
with comprehension tests and dictation. short break. helicopter heiress helped
henchman along the road to Herpes pool.
Bafouiller la moo tremblotement
why are antiques unmechanical?
streak major. Men always think they are being sold something
Principles. Actions. Complete Heptamerons. or Children. But you have probably
Changed your mind about the Bishop of Sheffield by now. Closed by literature.

a writing problem. a woman was being beaten on the backside with an encyclopaedia
wielded by an outsize pirate whose jacket buttoned with difficulty. Countdown.
How long must i suffer. Happiness met with a prong. Pushing a new creation through
Approved wires. Sanpaulia. Appealing for something more constructive than sympathy
Once though, if we can't turn out our eyes to be searched for butts, bon voyage.
Beat the brains out of the opposition woe betide you if you lack what it takes
To not think constructively, landless, without employees, soudure à l'arc.
Programme notes: boutique atomique. société fantôme Kneckerchiefs, leider hosen
That kind of thing. Culturisme au dessus d'un corps défendante. partie à société fantôme.
Through sin comes guidance & redemption. If you can hang on (courageusement).

purdah darting glances

live twine photo-wner lime scratch gap
lice dodge trial & error electric patch pop
tine dREEN w/th terrier legs of the giraffe
wodge mile sceptic sc foulard two heads
zipped aprons gloves pegged rug beads
grist to the mill camille desmoulins free
mistressclasses sc cross coloured glass
scrovlong chiselled pros & cons slouch hat
raised gutted close tense racing singing
lachesis a back was taken for you were unwanted
& the silence too failed to effectively resist
a rush which should have, windswept, sufficed
without the gold i did not hold or the cardboard
partitions when my feet were meeting you
in another cinema after the wrought iron gates
closed before the ghostly market off the caledonian road.
thousands of years gods you have spun
no one is showing you how not to be greedy
for thousands of gods i have spun and nothing else
rolling scooter grace occurred to scooter rearing
classical glass in sicut chimney suite de luxe
flared brush swoot announcing birth a frightened
people clam up discontinued narrative we are not
our teeth the full periphery of a white fence
behind which a few words bleat like meek sheep
one cannot by normal means be emptied of content
old suction exeat witness nothing ears of cloth
cerement east of eden after one broad band of
scarlet silk a premeditated painting causing
suspicion to sniff above a climate dinged
strasbourg strasbourg mussedie "namenlosen"
i don't know whether it is yesterday or today
i keep on marking off the steps across my right arterial
trying to read the future along the lattice
thinking of the ministers i did not entertain.

Truth or Vermilion

that is what you are told whether it is true or how it is true
something who is not to be hypnotized if that's all there is
what this can encompass red dotted lines happy eat it rock on.
in time he came back to give us the full benefit of his christianity
being a mind of the times, red eyed, bordering on insanity
burning both ends of versicles to taper a sapper & zap her
burning jet into foam, the wave that was born to be king
drenched a starving donkey into foam fields a separate infant
only jesus, only only jesus the nicest boy in the tree
sorry, no one does. go back to thinking about the pale green coat/jacket
/ blouse. retzina. g or ph. camden lock, don't. coffee no thankyou.
nothing. no. strong. shapeless. if you didn't exist & had been,
paraded by a man who thought it funny to advance himself on
tried and convicted terms, in a brief period of democratic enlightenment,
I might have done, but you were always imagining what you should have been like
whilst doing it worse, the second conjunction in synonymity,
doughty, games, showers, grey edelweiss shirts, birth marks, cufflinks,
gold pigment, the kind of mouth that brings failure up its throat,
& knows, & looks, before its tongue falls off and makes a liquid aquitex
stroke across the presence of the things that passed beyond Balsover
water acorns what a hat the one wore who was poor & that,
poor & that, she had more sense, unafraid of blazing, belting them
colloquium, what was that deep devoted endeavour
this takes up time, absorbs the mucus from precipitation,
should she be induced into the perfected environment, I wouldn't.
see. or compare all that turbining they did to Nathanael West.
violations to /of Renoir. No plans. A shedding though of self-inculpation.
that we could not be expected to live on. The madames who don't get what they want
Out of everyone. Racial Hatred. Cultural fuel. which film do you want to be real?
freeze it all at once. From the first frame to the last.

*

Bernache reclined upon her startling blue aeroflot indice.
the union had been saved within hours by Viola in a
single footed close shave. Turning towards the nether,
V. peeled away her face furniture with a suitably pained
upper crust grimace. "Listen B.N. – their voices are
pale from distance. Here – use this.....

*

......Oh I really must. The paper was filling
Away with raining water & dropping
Italics were fading Oh I really must
Break out from my more nothing
Mirroring back two ways
Where do the reaches for contact
Bearing across straits such columns
From one as, leading an empty lens
Parasol 1. Parasol 2. Parasol Avenue.
Take the third turning past
The roundabout (on Gramsci)
Salt or Pepper? with or without?
Response has gone with the water.
Do it somehere else. Longer overcoats
Mail Order. Registered Post. Nannies.
Cuerdo Seco. A few whispered letters.
The Only Man with Objective Capacity (fig.)
0.1888. Mainz. Aron. Verso. St. Donatus.
Billiard Balls. Braila. Thorunssen.
A strange case of Kidnap. The Left Ear.
Bouclé. Iris. Table Top. Aristocracy.
Ten-darein the Knight. Plus toe knee'm
Coif. Woolworth's Cafe to take tea.
Land of five thousand lakes. Shorthand.
Gesso. Peacocks & parrots in Poppies.
M703. Three quarters of the way down.
Caught. Hospital bed. Panopticonic Belvedere
The Roundabout's solar heating, Granada
Outside Florence. On the top putti. Leg.

the chantral grey

would you play one who belonged & did not tear
her giggling shoulder boy huff and sail across for days
on watch, stationed alert to the slightest rattle
depressed to have left the chance to dance far behind
in chains he was brought in to baa and bray
why Truck the dreadful stuff that comes from sea food
the chemical grey, grass gone dust, evokative of –
early writing fuss, what a stinking boy blustered
I smiled, his word reminded me of the tall boy
Dollar dipped & refusing to change the tone of sublimity
Quickly staking time on deed to align circumstance to event
Contingency in another vocabulary, amalgam of personal & displaced independence.
Alien loathed to eat arranges imaginary dishes laden with outgrowths
weeds from her own body pulls & listens
Writers don't talk. they sit in rooms by windows and watch time.
avoiding prose they notice people talking, smiling & generally living.
writers, though, don't live unless they love themselves supremely.
care beloved by their children enough to lighten their horizon.

*

This was the age of people & not writers in newspapers & now is not.
Now the compost has fallen and squashed the one without words
Who keeps her face still being used to vigilant checks on her moods
In case of expression and other things that guardians of genius oppress
with locks & chains & screens & electric waves & covens
with tapes & gloves, scarves, daggers, carriages
and marriages, priests & leases, dregs & segs, and silencers.

fragment; redundance; wordsworth.

oh it was sore & ended by, I wondered why
I did not query, I wondered why &
What her world was worth & why

It is dangerous to be, fully & how I
turning, should this be – to him,
or to you, in prose weeping fun.

Stupid I, who gave to him 'the
Sweet creative voice of gratitude'
without you – what would there Be?

Now? What would there be now?
Without this working in-to paper
that was why, after too long I became

despite louder, false reports,
myself. What did he care though?
Not a damn. Oh believe me. Not a damn.

Putrid criticism impossible –
and who was I? I cannot.
Tolerate the mad powerful

Who can attack it's Great, Play!
One word. Declaration.
And drove me away.

The deposited Thorn, converted to nothing
Do I tremble though or do I act dumb
Mumming, & hated.

If that was not Hatred –
What was it? Do I want? Do I
I was reaching for that
Calvaries & not now, not immediately –
Everything Packed, remembrance – Calvados

I do not doubt – I could not ask,
& cannot say but wear speech as a Cloth.
And feel that way. clothed & empty.

And will not discuss the virtue
of having lost my world when another's Word
Came storming in I saw it, the building.

Declare your Hatred. Unlike it I am not obsessed
A bad sham has been run, according to some –
who Crowd around a writing & Stop.

How Dare you – tell me to Stop.
Your little Bugs. Chasing, to make lives by copy
& declare, if not Party, for that would be

But Carpet pulling for having walked on not My own.
I cover them with my own self possession.
It's the Knack that mothers lose,

& are used in lieu of eternity
& mugged for it, & bemused, removed.
All of which we cannot Love that is admitted

Expected to be, compliant, &
Ready for restructuring
How very unlike Love of Subject

Meeting Pettiness Again,
Revulsion – Woman.

speak, poetess, speak in the end –
what has been Taken –
will always be being spoken to you

If you were not there
And were always being reprimanded
for your failure to pull in an invisible ship

They will beat you, they will Beat you
With Everything they have
If you do not speak if you can speak

And Add that – to Revelation's Closing chapters
hear the thunderclaps from the lid closing overhead,
By the time you are Dead, Look if you Can.

The Dread of there Being a world
was Scathed & stuffed up your nose
to make sure that suffocation suited resemblance.

Dreadful & unmarked! Old Wives Tales.
The thunderclap. An Audience.

Deceptive men Covering Courbet with Cézanne
But the Sun sustains life
& We, hearing the wasps patter

How grand it dances fast
Tradition returns
Armed words are shared amongst the privileged

Decide upon wasp
& no nuisance at Cintra.
Life was impossible. It was not possible.

Phrased in a different way
Another word for it
The internal presence

Having found no evidence
Apart from Knowledge of my existence
Which had been enough to convict me

As well as everybody else,
I found a bad one who cared
to Beat me out of my mind.

But write into the body of the language –
Don't write into me and if it's rotten to the core –
It is Literal the world beyond,

When I was thrown, he's a liar.
he was a liar – throughout those years.
In my grave I shall be & shall find some thing.

Il Trovatore.! There! He would not let me speak.
Aren't the dead who tell from their graves
Rather parochial, then one word, dear. or perhaps. or

To France

your mementoes
It was not here who annihilated me drag onto the street
no sudden memories low were we I was not in love
he expected me to sing songs that had been sung
on the radio I heard philip larkin & staying in Picardy
returned to Berkeley Square, unfortunately the butlers
had been told to return to the fall of the house of Usher
he did open the door, the nightingales were singing,
I was in the roses trailing over the walls in the sun
in Picardy the roses were old I was young & committed to
no-one, his footsteps echoed through the hall, the bell
had an oddly hollow ring, it was raining & the sea churned
the white cliffs were renowned, old Phrygian caps
on the doorstep a selection of discarded possibilities,
Charlotte Brontë, Daphne du Maurier, Detective stories
passed through by devious close relations who slowly
learning the ways of poetry used subterfuge to invent
in crossed lines as though they were realising an
organism which would provide a few witticisms éphémère.
Alfred counted his apples, building them up into neat pyramids
By chance the grid references proved peanut purée
a viable tone when enunciated in slabs for the pipettes
that were yet to be found in a dictionary of aviary vatic.
Dear Philip, what wars. make me filippe adoringly yours.

damned channel

(1.) confide in harpy hare gabbered seated flue
the profession fluid of self garland weathered
of the month almost three quartered gourds on swatch
no, yes the agonizing memory of unwanted public jollity
on nowhere was all we agreed that helplessness
walked over to another part of the earth
i wanted to keep her little hand in mine
i knew who they were. i knew they would come for mine.
They're building a party on it & the good ones pretend it's untrue
Haven't they ever been unable to learn
Never tell a teacher what they have the answer pack to.
flatter the fleam, grant as herisson the bare hortus siccus.
hortative calvary, fleeing chance within the white skull.
monsieur public teste in indexterity. The definitions that are
not performative.
Incus. trained to curse on the brink of a cheap trick.
forever No. forever Die. forever your luck & my throat to be slit.
Curfew. Inquisition. Private, of course. Phone. The symbol for
voice in search of
A moving appraisal of migrant swallows, was that damsel, her boxer,
Out of focus, it went back too far, there was no conscience clause,
could I save him from being put to death by the sword.
There's always an actress to dramatize an unnecessary act.
Death is quick. Ducks quack. What is the Main thing.

(2.)...........cloque cluse suivisme sans suite pensif au ronchon,
suivisme sans vous recontrez sans mots dégueulasse colloq
où suis-je? ici, chaud, frefolante, Blaise devant la cloche sur le mur
attendante? aveugle, essayant pas de rire dedans mes espoirs
tout les peuples poussent autour de moi, pauvre, pauvre moi
à Cincinnati il me suit avec son suivisme qui dit >suivez-moi, moi<
chaque moment LE bonheur me déserte et je dois voir la croix, la croix, la croix.
les canards dociles et jolies suivistes aussi croient> croix croix, croix croix.<
Pourquoi? je suis décontractée plein de désir à sauter et à ne sauter pas
au SoLeil, immédiatement, j'envoie la main ni gauche ni droit, quelle main?
pourquoi? Aha. Aha. LE main d'or que j'ai trouvée dehors.

No Wonder

is she thinking of whilst the street became the room became the farm house = equality the art
in pretentious uncaring incognisance, its sweetness liable property & the responsibility to
halt. the stop's fourth letter consciously directing her own will power to reach the end of
this reaches, plucks, in the eyes of a divinity she will determine to depict as an emanation

of a greengauge because it interests her rather dawdling mistake save space than apple
black apple scarlet pulp humming a hymn solennelle her servants lizardly hoppers
with scales shared with armadillos from the hull of melon weddings full of benedictine
geminians who write to plead their conceptual cause for soft autumn light

for the soft suede apple on a hoof of a dappled mare down floating dawn sea
sliding over the etruscan school of pillar boxes, strong armed women departing
from the stronghold of halicarnassus having ridden the last of the caravans
out of the jokes over painting in émigré ochre the grovelling sunset

there's nothing like knowing and saying so nothing ones who do not yet who preen slamming
subjects' eyes into curtains to close against blinding against lying against
covering against ignorance willed to acknowledge no wrong, finding reason
to move through sight take one good last look look as long as you like

movement in modernity suggestive of rape a hell of material choice in fuss or filth, refusing to truss
a congruent hen for some reason objectionable to the ringing, migraines, bursting skulls,
was she the closest resemblance to war or the tango, those who changed country to forget
great forget, & be payed to remember, it's only a fortunate trend in extending capital expenditure

into curtains closing the love of stupid expressions such as naughty and headscarves tied back
when chance discussion held a swing against elevation fun failed to develop into drum & hum
unsubjected to judgement pending, contralto as sub, soprano the norm, one is as, not thee.
g. en. avon. l'église in as sun on plain. she was everywhere me except where the hapsburgs

were used for political purposes in the game that levels guilt at the newborn who has to listen to
trials being conducted around her with intent. Appearances would have helped much earlier.
porcupine quill spelling etruscan but what does poetry have to do with declarations of ability
the hoof the hush fell over the crowd spellbound they wangled ashcan from I trust her do you

to reach London without spurning a swan & whipping it into mousse in view of the fourth dimension
she would replace the claim that had been made on the natural hemisphere
there was a complaint, her children loved her, what exactly is hard to define about the nature remaining
one is admitted but ninety nine percent objected to her entrance, no matter how much education

& hard labour, & easy, no matter lit & not wanting to speak to her, enjoyment uncultured,
'bed' was bellowed, & read as a name she being one of the ones not as sully

did the brains part from a premature birthing of this deafening subscription tour step
another immigration rocket fair registering tour sprint the value of the beginning
to draw back help given holidays aided postcards attended but for two, one of
the sea & cliffs in West Cork, & the other unspeakably intimate, thousands sent

hello from othello, he forgot his face was not his own and mistaking it for a magazine
owned up to the wrong definition for it was what killed the moon the fair the horses
and gave them all to rayon & bri nylon for a caravan holiday for the strauss addicted
riding cropped wife of a jazz fiend who spent too much time earning his living

Impossible! She, the real she, collected it herself, thinking that she had seen a symbol of the fuel
used to stoke the fires, to fuel the conflagration, spirits trapped in ancient wood,
cut by a carver unaware of his materials' history, watch the air when you touch it
He got my grandmother and sat in her bed & pretended to be Virginia Woolf, Wolf, Woof.

Do you love me or do you not every time the letter L went missing
And very time an O dropped out he sent his friend with a good line in sniggering
Snagging, Swigging, Lo and behold its the wag gone Whigging and waging a queen or two.
masculinist scale of faked sylvia knew every garden for miles around. No Wonder!

and was it her over deliverance from place convinced in her judgemental slurry
forgetting when it entered her head that firm belief in fascist credulity
dirty nosed black & tan with his grub street cloth kit fingers taking a shine
to his snug room pants propping up a much thumbed nibelungen

& when down West End Central strip club magnates meet the general
& meet the lassies with the hard nosed pistols who brag about another choir boy
laid to rest his black eyed suzy sister left to teach the au pair girls
in their hour here and there rest assured her eyes were cuckoo'd.

{koukouzélienne}

Dyr Bul Shchyl

For Geoffrey Gilbert

One day his wife had been asked to sculpt
She had been told to stop sculpting
she saw this sculpture in a book
her mind was overpowered by Apollo's torso

Apollo would not let her move her hands
She was a dead woman to him
Would she confess her sins or would she not
Before Apollo, Before Delphi there was Orpheus

I remember the convention & shrank, incapable
of forgetting the look in Clara Westhoff's eyes
how could I explain that this is not America
It seemed too dark & I did not want to go to Disneyland

Compared to their bodies
They were rubbish
Pretending to be fine artists
On condition that I was not

Is it him Is he the one who shortens prohibitively
the light against the husband of the Western Wind
& demanding a strength equal to his own
fails to understand the wind as much older than an irritating votary

her face the least like any sculptress he has ever met
too heavy to be light too light to be heavy
failing to use her mouth to issue conventional demands
would Rainer and Clara be godly enough yet
or are they not dead enough not known enough

for effect the pretence can be seen,
scandal wiped its obscene brow for effect
the portrait of Clara Westhoff was painted
to give her the look of a tragedy queen

She was not attracted to him
She wanted Rilke back from Paris
She was cold, it was damp in the house
Their baby was coughing   she was afraid

Had he been a Poet she would not have stayed
In the dark village. In Worpswede.
Life was slower than in Paris,
only Apollo was a politician,

Distracted, easily influenced, memorable,
haunting his statutory descendants
with extinct nights that broke the midnight skies
into clouds of paler nights,
entrances that upon a second look proved convex

lying eyes, deceitful poses of farewell
following a life full of desire
pressing the thorns on the stem of the rose
into her flesh hard bone
wondering why this german was long
anxious that the distance would be cut.

‘unknit that’

on salt the eddies flee the colours flit the players steam
the discourse salt heat crystalline rubbed soaked
for plant refin the use returns to the people
from the caves of a dress turned to salt a desert artist
of mordent paint a yellow cord to snip & smudge
caked twist made to answer for absence in close heat
thirst absorbed by presence of salt, wax drip ink fix
up the sand flowed the salt aeons of sinking sloping city
uneasy salt fate accident of infinitesimal weave pointillist
wife turned to a pillar of the establishment that can’t hold
water without melting to cloud for the fall took a daughter
when man his freedom won she was runnelled down
to the refinery to purify her of what remained of life
that was not water won & chafed her thighs with salt.
lambs lettuce then to hide sprayed asterisks heaped veined green
stroked down violet green from furry sward puncta
in crimson damascene took much thought to trace the florentine
thought of soya, sardine wedged in tight unpromising stiff
in pot preservatif for dip for sand cracked beasties blood
to crimson top set tracery & threw a scooped to open see
god, see, & laughs to register memory tears won’t wash away.
twelve thousand minds & moods from lost paradise
unrecovered from a glance through a cardboard placard over
stressed, duress, a capacious envelope of decent paper
bakunin’s running mate transformed from the silent wait
of a southern port scorpion how do minds not know they know
who show the disparate levels in a sea land paradox below
Running back with tales who hears nothing the pillar will fall,
menacing reminders that the sound of a mouse in the salt
or the wrist flap of a caught squeak will be knifed through
to test for what cake is not, or a collar of what men hate
to leave behind the depth of a washed up missile
imagining the ends are double flipped & can replace voodoo,
innocent to the end of the pliability of the mind’s plasticity
to exchange rate value, white sprinkled through pitch

she tottered, as a reminder, towering swayed over the way
from the sphinx all brown and recommended for power
by the charming straight liner Owyn Glendower
whose faith in the future diminished by the hour
in the shifting wastes of symbolic uses
distant as far as the horses could be roomed
one was a hat & pretending to manhood
here moves Salsola moves observed by paintbrush
will dissolve in slum brown & grey, or lattice coupons
for the life of the spotters of odd, gives himself back
soul of salt, ghost walking past, seersucker,
one attracted by the description of himself
given to the living body of his next victim
or rather the one who does not seem to live
imagining there to be a height extant
he will sit atop her head a crouching cunabul
meshed & drenched in dribbling saffron runes

antiphony

all this time i had not been seeing paper
question provoked by unwanted question
theatre everywhere outside his pocket
eating the hand locusts husking
colours faint from disintegration
on journeys steps have been constructed to found
claiming feet historical take precedence over mind
relapses wanted to suit conformity
seem to want illusion of reality the easy way
receiving good wishes & twisting them
into screwy barley sticks
whether the doors exist despite the people behind them
their presence not to be warmed to
the narrow slats of light
waiting for winter to give way
the open season of an invitation to desert November
the fleeting visions of a distant life
where ever we are closed back from
the crimes that artists know
are not the crimes of those people who press against
incomprehension
& when those go how lonely shall we be the children
inheritors of agon
refusing all approach
watching sadists leer in inquisitive, lethally
avaricious in the way the innocuous are
loud & evidently incapable of supporting themselves
one would not have thought that that was the marginalia
do you meet paganism again on your way back?
wilful removal of paper from art
how strange to imagine anyone to be there freely
pressgang maoists mistaking the people for history
what Art? that calls itself the spirit of the times
& laughs at organ music as though it were a substitute
for the censored word. hatred of me the game.

the wall had been down many years
constructed from its prohibition
we bit our tongues to keep back screams & tears
staring into it to will it to reveal
the day the butter pat was served without a drink
reminded thus of my own love for irrationality
courtesy of a logic inaccessible to him
whose club has never been found
the multitudes walked home
escaping his translation of coco.

London 1971

What was that lassitude that never existed before Wit reflected its shortfall in cloudy waters.
this rip, that denial, another colour, to restore before a garden not far from fontainebleau
a serious voice that does not punish by pushing a tidal wave pumpkin that last night
well i don't know you today if i was knocking on your door, with a bunch of daffodils.

if i had an house i should be living all day and never choose a reddish carpet.
oh take away the carpet i have white pickle for a friend to throw over it.
before the brown that it is has served to depress me in a way that can never
meet reddish. You having passed through soul cannot know the prouns

that stark black, would we climb a staircase with no trace whatsoever of green
the green in what my poem is not, a paean to enamelled futures, leafless and formed
between flight and death, how round, involuted between beer and abortions, investigating
resemblances. types. fixing interiority with an altogether different poetic.

conceiving of human as type. ballooning the future into shortlived stages. pushing out sound
to its furthermost limit. installing a language to suggest creative measure in science lourer
and sine qua non for the bucket that i do know how to act motorbike flic.
wrong way round. difficult to revolve vertically as an human triangle

conveniently designed to draw wide-boy comments by stance. ignoring
advance unelucidated conditions other than the requisite failure & further intent to hurt
for love knows no mercy unsafe with its kin, where could this be read, by candle,
snake ringed in wild cherry, without a tinge from acid orange tart blood, a ruff.

where this could be read across an illegible pavement, his eyes were hanging in brine.
black iris surrendered their violet cloud refusing to apply microspherical method
to tactile fury, ugly now, without the white that told of cold food snatched from kestrels' beaks,
drugging it into de-escalation, to the lowest aviators leafless & formed, for shades

polished an uncle who spoke with a sense of contrast that was hardly met with restraint
attraction in writing with no trace of context in contrast, this sicily with not a beach
talk to life! in its horrible sand, the women! i'm in trouble. and aren't the women pleased
to be able to ignore their unfathomability having done them a democratic favour

he deserted the site for the final bombardment to take place, as a favour, preferring
Purpose. Returns. Specific Movements. Voices that never fail to sustain a social dimension.
Voices that don't trail off into dyer's land. Voices that don't lounge as precautions to
exhaustion in siesta time when observations could cause disruptures in tedium.

pragmatic expertise with white torn paper, my other lap full of les disparus
dissatisfying flying tinges, streaked vein lines falling behind barrier strokes,
a dead typewriter in a city where friends are made by appointment only,
held by women with better things to be doing on their minds voile jonque boîte.

June 21st

scour, grouse, loses back, knows how to, chervil.
little owl. who other trust loaded who quizz loess
italian fish, poitrine. chlorine fear rests, quizzical.
having taken, was that too, meurthe-et-moselle do not
walk on air, precipitate, mon dieux prie adieu
pieds noirs crumbs holt   john bull.
auxerre. cierre. du haut en bas.   homberg.
cherry brandy. strapped back. large glass goblet.
yellow glass avignon mass my brother he did me lacerate.
laureate. a buff. they are the one. & to never
give the woman back to herself to tear away to sin
with loud hacks raw projections chawed and rough
the demolition, no, no to mind, no to soul, no to
o this lovely world in its most various features
to have a vision torn in half across an horizontal view
wurlitzer. white kid. amethyst stars. diamond too.
any to tread here would use informal guesswork
snorkelling over preventative waves treasures for to view
harpooning stories from the drowning effects.
spanking ballet pavlovian methods in case they grew too gracefully
french, too soft for these rare turns calyx screamed
& would he now be pushing into charcoal creams.
italians did. expulsed. found argued against.
had no love that was not sustained by snagging
a long & luxurious subject gone.
accepted. no more invitations. badly dressed my dress
a dyed sheet, grey clouds on white. a giroflée shawl.
in some circles dogs are chic. no great conjunction.
whatever they do. jessamine is not scrutinized.
this event, flashed back, roussel. pays de galles.
sagan who waits for gentle days where reeds brush sky
& sky sweeps this skirting around expurgately
what reading what what reading who who what iron what black
prince, examined below a cloud of hatred. exhausted
tumbled out from place to place holding dearly smashed

with smile victorian delphiniums grow by sun-soaked walls
privacy described as self seeking and needless
circles monsieur le vieux champagne
rends netherlandais slope sloops in with neanderthal,
they come to destroy, enjoys the rhetoric of it, and find specimens littering the ocean floor.
from a distance find no fault it can be felt as fault, injury & fear.
a virulent stance, an oak body, the filets, the zither, entablature.
repoussé. meant to be pushed by denial, reproof, & possibility. cross zebra.
populous. wizened stranger. no one cares. the roof lent itself to four
legs breathe less noticeably circus left town & what did, & who &
how many, & were the subjects detached from memory without coleridge
trespassing in a foreign country accused of transgression for supporting old mothers
who didn't want their names & faces plastered over the gutter presses.
an oyster umbrella. growing with her children augusta gregory
opened the door to an axewoman from the axeclan. a violet umberella.

and A New

for Lynne and Simon Harries

mood
having lost a minute's dance
smoking a tune

god in the gut,
a seminal syntax blowing
orange and blue
losing
the linkage to buttercups
below and around
an old stone bridge
two arches
under which flow
overgrown grass
and buttercups.

over where houses are
people used to walk
and beyond the flowing folk
a wide river.

a blue air steel river
with broad concrete promenades
on either side.

where the old stone bridge is
another river was,
a narrower river,
which dipped
and traversed
the huge crossways

deeply.

if not a tree of white wax bells
a line of upstanding fuchsias
if not the calls of the owls at knells

pussy willow finger tip prints
    on the window pane.

La Facciata

The father, late father's voice loud and lapping,
nose noise on top behind the fear his real
mute apparel, dragging sea weed limpid vowels
catching in cups, he pointed out, eyes tight
squeezing back tears, she cannot fly from this.

Their names fell on jellied eels, her knees
as graceful as a hosier, in a net of squealing knees,
but . . . piped up the politician, responsible for
the other end of important words, she had cried
through three births, three nose bleeds in a lost whirl.

It's only christians who crackle purity though walking
away was unwitnessed, the jews were annoyed, deeper
sounds reach swell roundly overlapping, a fishnet's back,
What is front in Italian? did the person after come underneath
the multifoliate aspen water circuit trumpeted

Hard into a dead oak, life's ripping plasterboard,
on one other mellow mother, rising for their pains,
sins are to be Tinned, bins are to be thinned, wins are to be twinned,
whereas he was making a serious proposal
she was making a fool of herself

Now we are plaîted, arms crossed on laps,
suffer the ragged twitching of the blood red dahlias
browning, answer the plank, answer the sea's need,
drank the dank from fear, persecution and swabbed
in the nets strewn around impresario's knees

Tartan rugs at twenty, that's the type firm-pressed,
tickling with crocodiles, fox gloves from the orange den
of heaven given the waves will between, those ships are docked,
cracked & chucked onto the over-beam wreck where the pickers
are picked for the icy council's reckoning books.

Include bars, slurred tone, tintinnabular blinkered
beyond is the coastal storm & daily telegraph man
deep green oil cloth, balancing man, finisterre grove
but . . . piped up the politician, there's NO geography in PROTEST
demonstrative slub linen caught tighter than a ring.

La Facciata Turns her Back

so, so, so, so, the trains leave, crawling
out in the open air past bitten grass
wood chippings, weighed down so, so, holds
a steel ball bearing whirr on bands
displaced we push persons to the east coast
where is not this indecent longs to nip
from indigo-type catapulting a re-directed
fire jam, so, he burns his mouth on a fast-gobbled
chip don't tell, he was warned, cheer yourself up,
the hedges bid storms, so, she's hanging
from a privet twig, so, enormous in anything
you choose but . . . piped up the politician the Monday kid,
rolled out, so, piling them up for the blanket thickness,
& does this make a more wiry pattern?
a more colourful soup? a sweeper for livid lathe-lovers?
simpering is one way, direct exposition of the lifting
as one pushes, but . . . pipes the prandible they're
sinking in autochthonous conversations, and
sleepier may fall down one cheek as a gust of breeze
from a far starrier star, what is their purpose
if she has none, so, so, stop stopping her.

1526

circumcision of the heart, who are my authorities
a long stretching glase casting unheard telos
palpable & failing to reach communicants
whom to be cut from, in this confessional clarity
warned that my poetry books were sacred.
at the last apogee he was sick but not weary.
precious wrong if those are not attended to
regressing the one beyond these pages whose lovely
pristine passionate freedom held two arms
to slowly lower upon the table apart from Harm.

Had depression cleared this selfish practice to
excel, battling against commands to relinquish
safely minimal, plunging into negation's blind sacrifice.
Truculence, bravado's helpmate, levelling wet plaster.
Who can deny the great their vital helpers?
Crazy Ignorance drives a faltering soul who walks
Despite the lapses which might not ever heal
At a speed, no noticed speed, with anxious lack of ritual.

Can be remedied. Between that remembered appetite
which appalled me. Weighing senses before another's heart
How can mine be known to others who are offended
by self reference. It is not the Principle of the Thing in this
Instance. It is a constant unbinding of restrictive practises.
And more I could not do to help you realize this
Impossible Domination for which there might be no substitute

on challenge, positive attitudes and 'les peintres cubistes'

that was havana
& this is clever
& that was a bilious mountain
heaving lines for publication
based on a quip.

this is colloquial
& I thought otherwise
but the distance was shuttered.

these are cigarettes and fearful
to break through official language
being hounded by an agency 'escape'.

these are people who won't learn and won't read
and these are poets critical of consumerism.

here is Malcolm Lowry Wo – 'Men light against the wind
With cupped and practiced hand
Then burn themselves as deep
As debts we cannot pay.'
and how our code of poetics works
as confusedly as a code of war
fought by people whose disparate reading lists

everywhere prevent freedom of speech,
of movement, of thought, of style.

& when I say I won't it's for another reason
one that wants to give you a square
of biting criticism on official murdering
of the totally innocent for the glory of
the symmetry of Viennese nuclear ballroom dancing.

& here are too many words which tend to order
the rights and wrongs of feeling sorry for someone or other
who turned out to be hidebound by racist & economic intelligence theories.

as paint was warm & colour not english
but softening the problem in having one large canvas
rather than six ready primed
& cramming 'too much' onto 10 x 10
before opening the door to a team of civilian detectives.

for the people of havana were slow and dressed in yellow silk
whereas their tongues were whiplashes against macho cinema.

Erato

The year of secondment pendenta
glory be to pleasureous anarchs
their lack of speed dormy
where west is news
and east south north high too
transcribed, loaded with
information from The Bridge Queen
yet grabby for hearts & diamonds

~

we find my solitary condition
surrounded by rivers and valleys
where platforms are reported
& not by press reporters,
the woodcutter's wishes
lost in industrial programmes
faience checked children's dresses
north east posse chrysanthe

~

the lost germans shooting down
to Andalusia's narrowly scrutinized
advantages of sorb apple virgins –
from the pineapple coves
coconut legs lightly scored
expets in areas
prepositionally informed
of the hygienic school tongue thumb

~

prospects high contour close
rêverie deterred the nature
yellow balsam weak do he she
daunts the proclivity game
circumflexed energy, off the beam
a fableau's sable queen
de la maison mitrailleuse citrine
the burden bore, syllabub sawn.

~

to confer with conifers fallen
the chenille base of our triller
(epimedium) peralderianum, cheiranthus,
sculpture blue chip cold,
heavy cards in cardigans,
library exiled from futurist sales
a piano, a painting, a canape,
grained in greco white hair

~

favouring the feverish
ironic warmth
mild with content
shrine picture
the perennial hunch
subject bunched infiltrator
hide spire
flippant on new classes

~

practising trances
could this be a language?
I see th't 'ts t' lift up th'
corps de moi toute entière
combien d'oreilles? oraclement
g.r.u.m.p.y. encore jamais
elle a écrit, a écrit? UR-POMADE.
ah oui. la voix d'homme
du sein d'abraham, et ABRACADABRA

~

born in
the general wall
run in the ruin
indomino vervain
brazilian brocaderie
ésclave avant-garderie
haight street
lemon leather conservatory
and with america

~

it must be a different, separate game
otherwise the cards will be noticeable
even though they are facing away
like you did, afraid to lose
your very feminine blindness
whilst the back wall
of my skilful skull
was word formed

~

Transmissions homeric,
In omerica we thank people, o.k.?
can't you feel the crater
where my top knot was
when it covered me wholly
to save your precious taste
in sooped up musical cars

~

you are if you could you would not be
such epistemology could only be dark
censorship across the highway
universalising circuits calligraphically
writing over the heads of the sleepy
knotting ends of electrical white strokes
blinding damson moon soaping linlithgow
sidestreets buckled by monocles
four and a half to four and one healthy heathen

~

you don't imagine that anyone will be moving
not without a lamb borgigogne bisogne borghèse
eigler 21 into march give us cordheart IV
influence simonian, hair lengthening rapidly,
saratoga's vendôme column, boxed cobbles,
roman soldier's remains clutching caesar's own nose,
right where the urchins used to fight over cabbage leaves
& the clanking in the night,
& the

~

& the rattling of the garage doors in eastern exile
where the yards have resisted stream lining
alone, defying the energy of brickies,
by subsiding before their very eyes
after all that time in scalped smog

*

On Vanity

When a poetess is raped she loses her interior life.
In an attempt to understand the intensity of the pain
She seeks for her perpetrator in other forms.
resembling a healthier man in her rapist's shadow

On Beautiful words the tenor of hatred was merciless
Rather than witness the annihilation of a population
The courts stand as the last outpost to Hell
With a representative section of invited jurists.

Having never had to be told the meaning of Democratic participation
the poetess let the people speak
Who had decided that they did not want her to star in anything
the rapist swooped he will live for ever

violence was not the point
but he used his victim in those minutes it takes
to kill every trace of response
to feel the life going out of the girl beneath him

so far beneath him, so virtually dead past &
liable to be replayed, reversed, the hatred of a softer voice,
lacking thrust, & full of jokes from eternal resources

Bristling white toed black two porned to the portraits in potency.

not wanting to be understood, crooned over,
by a liege lord, from a district, speccy four eyes,
his voice, cannot be the only voice, that fuels
& incidence in the occasional brick informed by antipathy

khaki knowledge of rivers' sludge, furry air moulded
Bionica >> push & shove, are they, how can we, box camera.
the bigger the books the better if my spider legs will, whither,
to the mountains of spines, he weeps for, the Isle of Jeanne Moreau

It bothers him to know the residue of feminine flight
curved deposits in marginal linings of plate glass cubes
borne by bays sunken in tar for leisurely sighing
The wind soughs bristling the back of alerted matrons

who smoothe miniature nurses' uniforms in candlewick mornings
& choose over a limited period of five to eleven which range to subscribe their convictions to
in bays where romantic delusions reveal tankers
manned by stalwart veterans of a thousand stadia

stamping their feet and passports with eyeshadows from amphitrite
Naphthalene soothed into a maquette for Hypocrate
Hits the ceiling, triple forte, in a swift display of masques
Fine >> streaming from the panelling the nominal Parades of Hallu

*

what we don't know, & what we don't ask, & what where we are means to us
is that, specifically; we prefer to be rather than not to be trusted to be believed
that we listened to despair and could not leave it there, personally,
despite our own powers of choice, & then I knew I could not die and that was selfish.
I don't deserve this rhapsody. I don't know whether I was right or wrong.
but I don't see why I should be put through this hell either.
this looking up and down. this resonant glancing into a camera.
the merciless and literate have advised me of what they are about to do.
I hope they find me tasty. the sound beyond the periphery is incessant.
I want to analyse it. we write of sensitivity and are reviled for it.
I never forget. But the sound of the machine roars in to it.
How many thousands of miles should we have to fly to petition against it.
Or am I courteous and end up beneath the wheels of an oncoming truck.

*

I don't know which colour to choose. the blue I dreamt is untranslatable.
I sense the rote of priorities. Food. Clothes. Shelter. Culture. Art.
Bound around the room in fixed photographs dishes are slammed down.
Another flash kidnap. Strings tied enough to burn in to
The ingratitude I have been told that I have shown
Exposition: Ingratitude. I am returned to the bowing and scraping
Sans violin. The monstrous regimen throws back its jaws.
It has now become Hell in full scenario. "You were always vile"
Which I knew. Which is why there is no reply plunged up to my
repetitive role syndrome. the word is enough. I fit in.
But the problem remains. How without the second world war
Can I possibly in the presence of relentless realism get it right.

*

No mixing not cake yes cake or anything that is being spoken enter not
Invite the lamppost for tea & his friend victory "She was always a bit touched
She Talks to Inanimate Objects in the hope that they won't be mistaken
for conspirators live in teacups & most of those have been broken."
You cannot imagine this & I hope that you will never have to
Experience the perversity of being suspected of having something about you
the rules are not available and having no sense
I am found reading negative dialectics in laundry rooms
talking to sheets that take on a life of their own
through the inspirational properties of starch & the light freight of chartered flight
we sing ooooooooooo this world is unrecognizable
& there is no reply to what does not exist that cannot lie again,
means limited to impressions of life and death,
in frames stabbed for new entertainments, heavier objects.

*

we escaped but not to the houses where repentance
demanded that walls be cleared & books removed,
windows closed, stars uncommented upon,
confinement essentialized, no mixing, misery only
& the paced reckonings of measured sleep
In angles certified against the level of the sill
who spoke to me through the confinement of inanimation
torn from copses long gone, sawn wide enough to leap from
in the inventive and taxing game of ways to die fast
before the heavy feet and embarrassing searches
clasped us like bears with human faces
& made us sickly with basic thanks
extracted in chorus from hot water tanks
that had scalded our voices faint.

*

I am become my enemy whom I could not please
and am imagined to be whom I am not
for she was not me although her interpretations
suited her best should I have no where to lean my face
except against the cup of the palm of this hand
that hides the life I could not live
having fallen young into my mind
having fallen further than answers would give
an astute reply to martial arms
had I words I could confidently write
& not be told that they were an excuse
I might find the time to warm into less fright.

I try to confine my expansive capacity
and am told that I am not known for my hospitality.

never beiger

the slower the lettuce is eaten in navy it pays
to be grey & thin by norwegian mills
the thinner the peach, camel, milky denier
the more bunched the golden violas hummed
hormonal late brunch the shining joggers thighs
widen italian waitresses' smiles to sheer grins
in this moment of eternal mullet
injection moulding believes, was, thinks & sounds
are taught endlessly in rational sub coincidence
the art that everybody feels qualified to exert the power of choice upon
the sigh the doe skin boots I read of impassability
& live in the interface between received ideologies
which are both insulted and form armies
as the dreadful milk evaporates up the walls
the road poisonous to walk much distance upon
I am full of opinion which is the extraneity
that literary discourse, the corset & the corsair,
the corset in the corsair, the modernized pirate,
the nifty shifters of initial letters, eponymous opticians,
derided its own russian refugees with them,
& remains to scourge a learned, literate, & unhappy people.

§

the chief of police wore a silver fleece
I had nothing to declare
so he placed a few slivers of elusive glint
in a portable copy of the septuagint
& nodding to Bert said "Hold it there."

"I found this," to continue,
"in amongst your effects"
I found his capacity to level
impressive enough to defect

St. Mercurius I find myself hideous
& so I prefer to forget
that outside this soul bursting with sweetness
there's a body I'm glad you've not met.

the misery I caused my old mother
for placidity was never her style
& the boyfriends I had she did eat
to make up for the food she had laid at my feet

what say you St. Mercurius
It's probably not your day
Is it like having a period
that refuses to go away

her temper was hideous, implacable,
she was like a triumphant beast
who handed me over for treatment
to the department of police.

*

I could see the sea & hear the towns
where the sea was calm & the buildings white
in the distance.
closer up were the boats
it has turned my desire around
I have travelled miles
these people have brought liquid vowels
in trowels loading them from beaches
& ports have delivered thoughts
of mediterranean timing.

*

Is é ar bhféachain gach cósta
  go crích bhóchna na Gréige
iasc is uaisle ná an scadán
  ní bhufair Canán Chinn tSléibhe

When he studied every coast
  to the Greek land's ocean edge
Canán Cinn tSléibhe could not find
  a nobler fish than the herring.

from "Hail, Herring! You've Come!"
"Mo-Chean do theacht, a scadáin."
trans. Thomas Kinsella. ed. Séan Ó Tuama
"An Duanaire. 1600–1900."
"Poems of the Dispossessed."

hard concrete to retrieve above the fallen
hammock kronstadt klopstock down donors
memory of content steps by the full begonias
a woman cries in the night between her innocent shoulders
mistress of her writing hand her arms her preferred feature
erasing the parts of her body that have long caused offence
but her mind was met by texts that held her
in space she could find nowhere else to control
the hope that one day she would have to
escape before her mind snapped, before her mind gave way
to the bowed head of hidden unblinking catatonia
but she has to lie against the tracks of the onrushing train
& she sings way out of human hearing in time to the time
that the steel pretempered, preemptied with twanging
one day she believes that she exists in the mind of God
that the sky hold her in simple hard labour
that the text has been divided into single weights
that the burdens she is detailed to lift are the words of her former pages
that her body is all conjunction verb and boring
that she bends the tormentil and lifts the tortoises
one by one she forces herself to remember adjectives

can lift to a certain height her wrist gives way
she drops, she bends, she cannot bear this kind of poetry.
she cannot dive, there is no pool, she wants to stay in the rain today
once it was that she knew the sunshine as though it were a friend
perhaps it was cruel to have a friend eternal
she counts eternal friends on her fingers, what are you doing?
the psychiatrist lingers, oh counting my blessings in the eyes of God,
she avoids psychiatry like the plague, they'd be poets if they weren't so rich
she tells the gulleys she left behind what it is to show that
confidential innocence is not universally exciting
when no reason is forthcoming from propped elbow,
she could agitate her head so, to indicate 'no'.
now she is not quite here and was never quite
it's country folk worn down over time it's country fairs we share
the knowledge that books can exist to start drifts,
that responses are recognizable, that oral culture distressed her,
that she was not basically interested, that this was almost treacherous
to be caught reading samuel taylor coleridge
that she ran off into the mists by the swamps where the convicts sank
& lived like une enfante sauvage to repulse detractors,
that she read by the light of the moon to catch the reality of Keats
that Oscar's spirit brushed her every movement into the powers of decadence
she learnt the merits of dissonance & watched the fairs fade.

Hungary Water

In my dogbox I happen to
dislike the analogy to olives
in my bitch chapel of knights
ancestral calipers madame
writes on the skull of a dead jew
the fruits of her prophesy
succouring crimean luxury
inventing literality

everything has a back taste
of vanilla villa viennese
an up pace in swordpoints

she makes me want to down
the gunmetal in the battle
for every heart in town
is being run down by
racist jokes from New York
conversation over summer.

who will need wimbledon
with the morals of defiance
that stops can jump sprig sprightly
for sprites with bitches hump

miranda's causing riots
murders an old joke
armies armful of leaves
for a detoxifying smoke
will bring out the briary roses
wooden & suspirate

the counterfeit in art
continues to mark progress
        our very reason
        escapes by machine
        clientele of the harem
        treated to a glimpse
        of everything that was
        meaningless

A grace note

so that if you do not know that the web exists to apologize without conveying
apologies couched in human terms, but only bloodlessly in a bloodless existence
to fill the moment that it took to receive & cover the S.O.S. that was
written in such a sensible way, in a sanguine manner, correctly, &
considerately, given the traumatic effect that sudden disaster &
unhappiness can have on one's mother – that one prefers to say that
one is well when one has just had a car accident, but the mother
did not enter into the calculations of the security forces, once again
in a state of disrepair, similar to the crude levels that Shelley
the poet had to cope with, and Blake too probably. At the same time,
there are no smiles, no joy and no celebrations between us because
really the police have nothing to do with poetry, nothing. And if
the police would have something to do with Poetry then let them give up
their jobs & forgo their privileges forever, and let their children
never know what it is like not to have the normal methods of dispensation
of judicial procedures fully accessible to them, without a black-out
frame of covered freedom innocent or not.

tree by the cam

they swirl sweeping before gnarled maps
stretching before they dip the willow light
blurring beneath veins left to bear
the tragic unknown of river identity
whys stare attempted to climb from the root
find clangour in nests and hammocks
beyond the reach of the phantom moon
and the man whose arms are longer than his legs
holds out head back upright head held
doubloons on his upper arms
his puppy lost and my horses are houses held in silhouettes
he is one of a race gone
a doubloon who had many doubloons
he is one of the doubloons
on his right knee rests his son
forever he tried to escape the tree
the tree of the unfounded estuary
the wood that was meant to be sea
the eternal reversal that politics play
the confusion over means and ends
suspended for his ship rather than his lunacy
suspended for his love rather than his buoyancy
& almost like a bird he swoops
his sleeves stripping april light.

UNCERTAIN THOUGH WITHIN THIS DEEPSET HEART

Distinction between art and people, therefore from art,
reflected in the light of present pressure,
I give to you the reason that demands your presence
from another place where twice I have shown my disinterest
in the nature of the struggle between opposites
the sense loud that hurts by confecting enemies

This could not be art although it could not be denied,
denunciation ripping off its red cap waving frantically
in the perfume of mists and loneliness a wild cornflower
faint against the strong blossoms of cultivation
weak by naive ardour loses presence to the refute in
everything for lovely praise of dipping ghosts

In this dim and rise a coronet of new found hazel nuts
in this glass case I offer you an absent fellowship
for our legs have been leaded by stray bullets
we, some who were kings and princesses, the scavengers of old
words wrenched from our daytimes, screens rammed into our visions,
retrieved for selected short stories that eat into tapeworm

with the hideous recommendation of a comforting rival
who holds the inevitable gesture between finger and thumb.

1:3ng

There is this idea that but I would not because of the choking & swallowing
Abbreviations, large writing hitting me, & saying nothing if I were on the menu
To be hitting me with a simple tune, stretching out expressive signs, tut.

The only writer and the only writer, the only writer too, that is not communication.
My wave stopped at me. I present myself to God, who is humourless.
He dishonours me wilfully, & it transpires that Althusser has proved useful.

Everything is used in this cutthroat world, but what I wanted to write
Was intact in my mind. I had to share everything. But I did not share my mind.
I don't think that everyone does write. I don't think that anything does do.

Wilfully disobedient people are not necessarily the dregs of society.
But they can hate until they die, hate women writers, hate women's minds.
Have a fright & be obnoxious & conjure up images of power, and vote; nymphomania.

I dipped my head in bleach & walk out pawing the pavement like a wild animal.
Nothing is neat. The fangs & the files & the office are a sheet of pearlized lip salve.
O how, O how are we going to look flat enough in reinforced boxes with holes for our legs

For boating or the bank where the floribunda fluoresce in our spectral eyes
And he looked at my dress and laughed, on birth he was uncontrollably witty, reliant.
Now he represents the patrons as well as the camps, and soaks his patches in chloroform.

When they use society and any old word, to dump people into joke camps
& unable to muster up any civility complain of their failure to number everyone.
Exploiting the insecurity of unofficial art expecting the same kind of confidence

Ripping narrative imagination away from the source to create economic deserts
No, I don't mind dying, yes of course, help yourselves, it's not my organization.
They called themselves communists once, they taught Marx, told you the price of their sweaters.

Rammed you in the street with their bicycles when you were carrying a newborn baby in your arms.
They said they wouldn't be seen dead with you pregnant. Told you to get out of town.
To remember in three though when the question was writing not being shaped into a programme.

Is she a woman? If so I shall not go to be intrigued, conscious & dishonest,
Worse, much worse than any of them, but not a killer, worse because of writing.
Worse because of there being nothing else, no, nothing. Politicized mediators used

To destroy me anxious that not one survivor should remain.
Wanted art cleanly dead. They were interested in his impressions.
The actual details were no important. He has his supporters. It's almost acceptable.

Nothing I composed was acceptable. Not because it was uncivil. He had to have his way.
And meditate upon what it must have been like to be cosmopolitan. & change that
To Cosmopolis. to evade the behind the screens' image & rely on laziness.

Pounding me down into a mortar. To destroy a poem that has haunted the radical imagination
They lap it up. Hie in from the broads with adopted attitude. It's almost acceptable.
To not go through. To petrify into immobility. To physicalize my imaginative powers

Of transcendence. To domesticate & mystify. To pull faces behind my back at
The well travelled. To gag me until the unwitnessed moments return & then smash
Into my empty purse & hound me out with resurrected snippets of Pound & Eliot.

I worry about increased literalism. my own incapacity to distinguish between enemies & friends
The fact that some of my teachers openly espoused fascism.
The fact that I did not know what to do about the threats & the swastikas in the post
The fact that I am not allowed to live. The fact that it is easy to use fascist literature to

Destroy my imaginative power. The fact that the women are waiting to take away my womb
The fact that there are no central climaxes in contemporary music.
It is quite difficult to have my minute size beaten into me to the extent that it becomes germane

That the minutiae sold over the counter – by the soap opera inclined who
Hire heavy agents to track down their husband's airs, atmospherically testy
Tagged by religion and marriages even the most nightmarish etching ceased

To withstand invasion, & obscurity is fired out by memories of basic vocabulary.
It was not their position to know what was going on anywhere else.
Now they know everything which was going on everywhere else.

It wasn't chaos by the way. It was Socinianism. Early Coleridge. (The poet).
Energy engineer'd into conscience striking in the service of the inconscient.
A few clips from Mass Observation. A body of sadism defining class procreation.

Enforced sex education. The extremism of abortion. Peripheral to the curriculum.
Simulating life in an artificial environment. Assuming dissatisfaction
Blake and Turner. Our two strongest artists. Strong enough to isolate me from total predation.

Does he think that when I read wheelbarrow I looked for one don't raise your voice at, grimly
Children cannot be born I had the cheek to bear them alone them no not them full end dead
By dead light my mind was infiltrated by the power of malice, tremble, restrained. He

Caught my air when I say, when I ask you, when I and only then for I am, I am, I am the Master
Of All Masters, and you were Burnt at the Stake, and you were Paraded before the Good, who never mistake
Right from Wrong, who are always Present, in full control of their Minds, he exists, calls me a slav

Slobbers into his dish, chews each piece, feigns death, for buying a man a drink a woman was diagnosed
As suffering from Alzheimer's disease. The life spring is being cut. If the fathers are not named
The children are removed. Inadequacy. The female literary critics he removed from my shelves.

Men were brought in. Listened to my analysis of art, repeated it, were fixed up with jobs.
Watched me moving heavy boxes. Deadlines to clear off. Only I find my mind interesting.
Only I know the cost of noblesse oblige. Only I am another Irina Ratushinskaya. Only I

Know that cruelty of denial of the Russian sense of literary space only I know which spire I mean
Only I know how the imagination expands expands & is gently reminded by physical vision
Only I know how far to value my children's minds and bring them back again to where we are

Only I have to leave them now, stop searching for them through this prejudiced arrest
Only I know what was said, his refusal to write through the structure, my lack of expertise
Of anti-culture, its devastating effect, any struggle against death

Against these words, weaponry sharp blades, the usefulness of the crucifixion, hatred of art
Well, I should hide from whom I sorrow for, because that wasn't enough, for him,
His Tests, what is this ABOUT, they still look, waste of time to Want a 33 mm camera

Whilst He is sweeping the street & I am involved in unregistered geometrics attached to curves
How that is raised, he makes the session closed/open, each systolic silence infuriates him,
I mutter on about bluish bottles in the summerhouse of a bed and breakfast place

The popular fronts are key factors, most artists left, I mess about apparently, producing an unfixed line
My perspectives are negligible, I give children time, & time should not be given it should be taken
It's a skill I am told, to observe the general march, this is one popular front, if Rimbaud has ever

Crossed your eyes, notes squint, don't Waft Him out of Line he wants to be drawn in, gradually,
Every Time, this makes no sense, I don't want to draw a portrait don't want to don't
Want to give him any more of my time, it's gradual absorption, into Legitimacy, a straight

Slightly angled vertical line, magnetic north, amen. Marigold, wasp and marmalade, Yew,
Rowan, go on, keep talking, it will be taken down & hammered into night, nothing has to be,
The smoke is a chimney sweeper's brush poked through an organ pipe, Lazy Daisy, what kind of papers

Specify. Admit to ignorance. I am held in sexism. it was not a conviction it was a sentencing.
The issue was my writing, not theirs. theirs was the rational cover. the issue was how could I be
Disposed of, suitably, for knowing how tired the people were, and neither death nor Abortion were on my

Reading lists. Where does Immanuel Kant refer to sexual intercourse? The cups & saucers are replaced
Before the coffee reaches them. She has annihilated the stony stare of Anaesthetized breakfasters
By suddenly being hungry one morning out of ten & knowing that he can take the piano

Between three and one, she was a pianist once, she played wherever she was, without one.
It's similar cinema one to three, magnetic north, three past one, we were playing minuets
They don't like me   The art teacher objected to organicism. They drove through the lines.

Some music is social & mine isn't. Because it had no willing fathers   don't you know their hatred?
I can only speak to them within the supervising authorities presence. They said that they were
Only interested in money and I had none. You didn't understand our reticence. I smoke to kill my voice.

To never sing. And to show no joy. Only to find that the words which come out of my mouth
Have to be checked, and checked again I so much disagree, I so don't want to be read by
People who play war games, or don't allow poems to drift out of their windows

Instead of turning them into mechanical birds who fly around electric jungles.
I can hear what is being done. Another bird is about to die leaving a wired frame.
He doesn't care. Realism like his is the ultimate nihilism. He invents anything.

I am not going to stand there & tell him how my coloured pencils were taken & I was given a sewing machine
How I broke down unable to make my voice into words that were wanted to fill in the lines.
They wear stars on their jackets, laugh down the 'phone, confident of their scenario bureau

But not the stars which that were cut. and sewn. to form fountains. of hot dust.
covering clubby that went, past the orphanage, penetrating psyche, took over.
information. don't pretend that you went through what others went through & then turn around

& accuse me of being unsympathetic. because a load of refuse is being built up
& tagged Reality. I refuse to answer. it's too serious for poetry. Artists do not go IN to others' lives.
Not with social science. It is not Art and it is not new. A grown infant with a method.

I lost because my voice was too soft. He has screamed at me again. to close my wings of words.
Afraid of the light. When people are kind to my mind I respond thankfully. It was hard for me to leave.
White merges separately I excuse myself for refusing to refer to country. Misattribution –

Is enough to torture a writer for ever. And I am tortured. I am taut,
The spinal nerve becomes numb, I don't have to act, truth, I didn't have to act then –
Which is why I realised what had been done to Prynne, the mind & the university –

Their diabolical. I couldn't understand their lack of appreciation.
I was sent to Coventry by them. Do you understand? I shouldn't have been left to cope with them
They were not later the father of my children. I don't understand why women have to be so

Servile. Why everything has to be taped named, known.
I feel gashed down the entire length of the left side of my body
A jagged nasty gash cut through by a rotary stainless steel blade.

A giant C.D. spinning a fast cut through my dire life.
& I am about to sit down to translate Gisèle Prassinos' "La Table de Famille"

14.8.97 Cambridge, England

studio VII

1. tippy tappy goes plink tip on the hoo ghoo doth swath
suoni gwacoo-onghar-snāl perming 00.6 drop slipho

2. expro has roi really street expressions gullety topwath
bracket blra punching card compositeu i sign still quilling

3. human, do you know, pulls away from scissor happy double over
cellotape on khiosk a declenched spine now walking écriture

4. we are being sent to the litter white & grey shores, i'm sure
no one can resuscitate without the evident whole

5. no more general news that has told me of my non existent stake
only when I ask for a studio in several cities I am told go

6. Surf on the Berlin Mitte whet my gosse guggenh thigh lime silk
for St. Eustache has burnt a cultured clavichord through cinnamon

7. limited spain making butterflies flie out light pipe cobalt white
later, from a stamp on "hommes", if that is not the mind of an

8. overseer sneering at the easily thumped it is a lazy beam of
periphephemera clicking automatically my journey out

9. of hiding the unknown terrors in suburban displacement
reach, reach, has always found a cross over sculpture

10. it makes no feeling the white grey doves when read dark piano
clean hidden the pleasure mistaken for pain not named

11. the struggling with soul sin precept protocol & cannot even attend a
seminar on Freud without being told not to know anything

12. & was, invited, therefore secure, before the threat heavy work obvious stormed in
private exclusion orders had been issued, no-one is just that condescension

13. years passed, in the name of education, private exclusion orders were issued
then I found a book 'Vichy, the university and the jews' and I expect to sound insincere

14. for there are many scathing academics who pass through each year,
I don't observe their natures. who is at the centre of my heart?

15. it beat. it began to beat in the centre of my being. my body frightens me.
I have had to reign it in. kill it off before it had a chance. it had to be

16. mostly destroyed. this is fact. as factual as an estate of many acres.
hearing. any with any are scorned. any with less are falsed, counterfeited

17. according to what has been probably researched, the expansive gardens,
quiet white shuttered roads, nothing there resembles an open door

18. I hate you. I hate you lovingly in the full knowledge that you approved
of every Hitler who ever walked this earth of every killer, of every internet

19. investment agencies are your idea of twisting sincerity into alienation
Madame Bali sloox faisallhaman Taschenlos in «the Jeuyiş Basquiat»

20. is that your hope? pistachio chalked epitaph → she came along way without ever
arriving → followed by → a hand buried cannelle → a seven year old husband

21. → an unknown chocolate nutty coffee ice cream lollipop arsonist frozen for
coupling with his chocolate coffee coloured beard by mouth → his copper earrings

22. it is probably As much as it was this morning and was, to be blessed
close to the line of the freedom to doubt the entrance entrancing by-pass

23. by the two intimations on Spain en garde with a visitant; objection to complex
train, chimney, stanza, omission, later day, not that one & the mind

24. why was it not called one translation into a cathedral complex
some were being ultra serious picknickers signing along two lines at once

25. slow. deliberation. held in reserve. eyeblind. wrought iron outlined figures
disgraced by the detachment of us from milling masses, not used to

26. face people who won't serve caramel custard the bar that was made bankrupt
in the torn pocket of a cracked leather jacket the sea churning the wind hot

27. the lambs roasting whilst they play around their ewe's teats
bounding against their fleecy coats gaga for milk

28. we have to see the green sea crash wildly on the white rocks
donkey lovers avoiding shoes for flowers to tie on the green sea

29. time is manuscript paper rolled on with a thoroughly inked pastry cutter
squashing anything sweet too large for parturition partiturae

30. He was Bronco in sunspecs & fat finishing off the early summer high st.
by bicycling unmistakably axis like through the middle of eros

31. these madmen have been taken up by dramatists and charged with murder.
they have also disseminated agreements on precipitous chateaux terraces

32. smiling into glass flown back in the name of continuum
having agreed upon nothing other than to remember the way that

33. they held their knives, the way that they sipped their tea,
please, please won't you please take that away from me?

*

To look in the mirror and see a shocking atom
where once had been a moderate person
To have cared for an ill one
who liberated the a from atone
who goes beyond infinity
& returns in time for breakfast
who reads lexicons as mexicans
& can't be bothered to climb another mountain
who weeps molten lead
& asks for analgesic
in packets of french paper
with aluminium infoil
who goes away by trefoil
& travels on to assoil
despite her own wishes
his grandaddy was a Russian general
who tried to end the French Revolution!

Battle of Zurich 25 Sept.–5 Oct. 1799.

decisive conflict between the army of Helvetia.
commanded by A. Masséna, and the Austro
Russian army, commanded by A. Suvorov.

With a force of 27,000 …
at Zurich for to do ablution
the wounded, in name alone,
Austrian general found them
and as Austrian generals are friendly men
he brought 22,000 more to forfend
the departure from the punctual toilets
that Austrians have ever been famous for
Soon enough, anxious though everyone was,
of the 49,000 gathered with reason
30 more thousand from the land of sun & legions

to invade france why were they pitt's friends why?
did the English read Austrian, Russian & Helvetian poetry
were they in the process of realizing their drama's destiny
had the manufactories not quite got off the ground
were the chinese brush painters being invited
had the summer been cold & the winter too humid
was the peasantry complaining over the theft of their sunglasses
Why did the casket of ashes deprive the cows of their herds
80,000 waved daisy and mildew geigy & primula goodbye that day
It was the in between that confused me
as though there was no such thing as a battle
is this not true for men? do they fight with themselves,
do their bodies hurt them & do they not always know
whether it is an attack or an act of seduction that is
an aesthetic link of divine bent
if it were less total I'd be bewrent…
the Russians were on the Side of the FRENCH!
So what was Napoleon Up to?
Hero against History or Gymkhana Jumper?
Assassin companion to Byron's stumper?
Battles, apparently, do not go on Between people
When they categorically manifest
that they commence fighting from the position
of turning their backs on each other
their intentions being solely

to find and kill each other, brother.
Wrong. Russia and Austria planned to invade France
as soon as Suvorov arrived from Italy
with 30,000 reinforcements however,
Austrian minister F. Thugut,
hoping to extend the Hapsburg lands,
repositioned an army under
Archduke Charley, thereby exposing
Suvorov's army during its proposed invasion of France.
The French, though, won the Battle of Zurich
Massina & the Directory's government's victory.

The Second Coalition which had
Driven the French out of Italy and Germany.
The Allies plan to invade France through Switzerland
and overthrow the French Republic fell apart at
great cost to life and limb which is
not to be said of the Baron of Batz
who witnessed his employees' executions
on the 17 June 1794 Baron Batz
walked out of the door & lived somewhere else for evermore.

*

words won't break these walls
that mock and mocking moan
dripping water slowly slithering
o'er moss and lichen to the weeds below
stray and foul, the end of words.

the mind of words won't go
although the words themselves won't break
asundering the solid that is the substance of this woe
wherewith the flight of oft seen gulls
took not the sea apart from cloudy flight.

viola tricolor

for judith, frank and nathan mendleson-blum

the young girl taken from a trained woman,
whose poetry was mocked not as a man's,
and charged with jealousy as her inspirational motive,
was thrust into pirateer's hands
accused of purity – the south was waiting
to tighten its iron band
– lock it with another *idea* of purity
that of revolutionary command.
to train her poetry into ice
crunched by a vocular donkey
implanted with a tightrope voice
to slice up a fair country
as broad became no love
deemed wide lined prostitution
that no other ship could be manned
by open *institution.*

it was not on the news the cries for help
and might take years to strip mystique from
what gives pleasure in defining how a girl
can never be a boy in artificial reality
and not enough of a dupe to believe that
plays throughout reality move to what came first
created artificiality and much one wanted not to wish
with food to muse on others' starving
there being no books allowed at table
took to minor anti apartheid reminders
on envelopes in christmas work
and reveries upon custard
ladled out from giant vats
by pasty girls in white starched caps

a painting struck my dream the other night
within a frame of three grooved wooden white
behind a partly revealed green foliage
custard came to light as delicious paint might
which sinks and sings with natural ecstasy
crossed in no which way here there and nowhere overmuch
firm streaks of black at most odd angles.

language blows away

for kim longinotto landseer

it's foggy and delicious
i'm in love with a chimney stack
my aversion to applying my concentration
to what is not what I want is as strong as it ever was
although i am less bothered by machinery than i am by people
who are anyway, mostly, a lot stronger than the people who are being
turfed out from their communities to make way for f.m. and b'y.
if i had an apple mackintosh i could delineate the chimney stack for you.

i could argue until the idioms vapourized.
what Does experimental mean? in terms of division of experience determinative or subjected
but was carted off. the clerk at the family court agreed. what
other than all the trappings of western civilization do they want?
denial of the thirties. mostly. and philosan. i've returned to deserted
landscapes. i like them but children are being fictionalised into
demons and cherubim. who is going to be invited when art has been finished?

here, as always, i was betrayed
for staying within the confines of art. i was brought a matron's cap
that i saucered out into a southern breeze that drifted it onto a lombard's peak.
when women are amorphous and power hungry finding causes to flip over,
they have to be doing something about everything. nothing can be left
untouched. curly hair has to be washed from the brain
scraped back or razored up and stormed into airless terminals.

Sauce

1) on the message, should goodness be lost in silence. where can these go to
now they are lowered who were found to be in hell although on high
a gargoyle to a princess, one head less, facilities with trick photography
that pure separation of visuality our schools of art have been ruling
to be an eye alone and strangely wandering, did you hear?
or are you seeing something which cannot be touched to be posited
was considered supremacist. Dearest world. I am at the mercy
of one whose nature is unlike my own. And still the truth remains as covered
as a Beuys grand piano in a blanket with a stitched on red cross.
Such was the Tyranny of necessity which stripped me to the bone.
how it straightens to rigid duty & is marched away. whilst musicians play on
their consort falling, shot in the snow, playing to hold up a city with a tremulous bow

2) is this something uncalled for. impossible. for not bending to her will.
and what that will might state she will not level as her sanity
was impaired by birthing me who shocked her with resemblancy.
whose face was less refined in feature, her sister did agree, &
many times would take it for analysis. vile once love exhausted
a deflected comment, these features will not pass, & if they do
it will be for reasons of pity, to them both wedded. The audacity
to challenge gods. the very thought. the very word.
and many a poor poem was thrust in to squelch with the rubbish
which would take this latter day impossible to the Council tip.
because i write: the poems are not in my face that horrified you.
the very thought. the very word. to not receive the love i felt for you.
but fed me more to hate me more or love what life abhors,
a Fruit, a brainless Carnal lassitude chewing primate gristle.

Cultural

we are then when impressions are all and bitten
judged and devoid of hostile response
as insignificantly nothing amounts to nothing
nature subjected to critical sense

seated & desolate, eyes unblinking
rocking ourselves into quatrain
punished for poverty sterilized forcibly
arms dealers drive to work the same.

here come the masses fed on molasses
sexually inept and incontinent
hair undressed parroting best
ironing away without irony

how dare one dare what gall moves there
to heighten with no increase in volume
a forgotten face from a distant place
an obsession with an impression

~

impressions cannot be built upon
if valid results are required
art does not match it cannot conform
but by retarding format

this is extant a constrained line
which circulates around thirty objects
to enter within and not join in
presages market research projects

for those who opine that brains sublime
must have travelled in proof provided
a sojourn in some stable societies
as esoteric lacks standard merit

is defined as potentially insane &
populations sub-divided
ensures prohibition of views one-sided
whatever that may mean

*

Eulogy

she smoothes her skirt
to show her ineffectual language
unhappy to be english speaking
to the interesting sound of spoken greek
but what could she say? this is music
in comparison to what I speak
& that is really the crux of her problem
she feels another language not this one
she is impressed. she wants to learn
these new inflections.
but will she be seized
a traitor to the nation
he sings a sentence between talking them
it goes soft, it asserts, it narrates &
faces change, animate, picking up
on each others' words
it sounds a bit italian, a bit spanish,
the girl who is with them
told me
that that was because they were speaking mediterranean.

Abschied

for Poppy Juanita Dorothy Shoshana Ruth Pascal Mercedes Mendleson

A young child cannot reply.
One does not compare.
Or crooked turn the lines
against the sunrise

By tonight I shall have lost you
because I cannot hold you
& be anything but abused
how can anyone tell of what they do not know

These great, strident images
that cannot be read for their content
Abuse stings & smarts
my daughter of the last night.

Even that then,
surrounded by deep cushions,
fitted in to a neat myth
in the endless memory
within which we are placed
beside & to each side of each other.

but what a pity
that it should mean anything
as though the autumn
did not return a spring.

your lovely honey hair
chopped up into boyhood
your back spurred
by an anomalous blast
of old poisoned rhetoric
caught from a world

rather than reflected
by art that had held us
within the sight

of a massive candelabra
that he was prowling towards
flat on his belly
costumed in foliage
unknown to botany

Rhetorical irony
meets the Master of Terms
who lends himself
to a piece of fiction.

But what could we do
You and I

You had already captured
The art of departure
Beautifully

half evacuation measures unmet, still on regulo

who will win?
the forces of reaction or
the powers of progress
but you who are not
in the small fortress
yet who pretend
seeing only your
avant-garde
as your repressors
and ogres
decorated in
stock exchanges
finding you whom
picking on you whom
screwing your
avant gardists
with selected words
killing first your
avant gardists
with best sellers to be
writing out the mind
of your avant
gardiste,
have surrendered
to sheer economism

ribbed
a woman
doesn't
remark
helped
plastic eyes
on a string
looking down
a figure
is not a man
removed
traditionally
from
trying
to beat
deception
that has
no time
for finding
another
chord
tournant
au fin
du vent
autour
des enfants
en face
d'un homme
qui n'est pas
le personne à
qui je voulais
parler
or Erich Fried.

n'essayez pas
le nuit
les chambres
du prisonnière
de la guerre
votre contretemps
c'est quelque chose
entre les gentilhommes
et moi
je ne suis pas
"Jeanne d'arc",
salaud
messieurs kangaroos
et madames
kangol, vous
ricanez
je suis navrée
de devoir
vous contredire

•

swoops,
go away,
tosses,
has to appear
let him
he doesn't
Approve
of unsorted out
"people."

•

there was no life
within the
iceblue light

•

droppage?
not all parachutists . .
were . . .
why did you sit around
boasting your children's
charms?
this wasn't my home,
I don't want to write
to you, you were not
whom I wanted to
talk to, but seeing that
you hadn't taken the hint
I thought
that you might as well
know
that it would have been
a good idea
had you learnt
the art of honesty
and stopped
the persecution
that I was being
subjected to,
by not confiscating
any more of my life
than you already
had done
in your endless
satirical
cruelty.

to inspect
the results
of museumized
styrene
& report
amongst themselves
the approved
advantages
in slow controls.
sky divers
are not straws.
it should
be enough
for you
that I am not
right wing.
whether
you can see
into my mind
or not,
you can learn
how to avoid
the solid accretions
of fascist vocabulary
and not
give me
weights of iron
to crash my words.

when you learn
the meaning
of the word
gentleman
you will regret
your selfish
adamance.
and learn
that real
poets
do not
waste
each other's
time
and
do not need
to be
shoved
in to
black marias
to
sort
themselves
out
so that
amateur
authors
can
come along

yes I was frightened,
but it didn't show in my face.
it's only recently
that the dead have begun to
to be real people.
once the stories
had been told.
we don't want –
to make a drama –
I am afraid
because I am unused
to reality
they don't
use their intelligence
when they make documentaries
they completely divide
academics from manual workers.
I don't talk to anyone
I used to enjoy talking
about what I was reading
before I was told that I
couldn't read what was
in front of my eyes,
so I read it again
& remembered that I
had been told that I
could not understand
what I was reading
although I could
it wasn't only a sign

it wasn't a silent notice,
it had a meaning
that was not related to
sound as such
some authors' writing
reaches me;
when I read Ilya Ehrenburg,
I found a few volumes
on a street stall,
suddenly I had a friend
who was talking to me
just like my father
quite naturally
no-one could turn me
against him
by refusing to let me
go and get a job
in a café
given, that really writing
was of no interest
to my contemporaries
given that
everything material
was not good enough
for them
for all their talk
of whatever their
talk of

still goes on round my toes
binding bandages to 'cramp them
from spreading out   :

sliding beneath a line
of cranberry oporto a
presentation rose bowl carriage

future present
shin
favour forward despatch

ivory penknife squared
drop that cat
its eyes are bugged.

of sincere appreciation
mapped
walks to the . . . .

metamorphosis began after the destruction of the temple,
when people are bereft, our belongings stolen, our
houses torched, our bodies raped, what remains of us
is changed, into animals to be controlled, faithful
& what kind of animals we are remains the knowledge
of our destroyers. it is neither money nor food
that causes the problems destroyers claim/do.
the hatred of destructive people is not good medicine.
how heavily they drop the odd plaint, wearily
dropping iron curtains all over again.

and rather than defend
objectification à la Brecht
and Hauptmann
you fizz around
with a concept of pain
in your palmistry
as crude as suggestion
as prickly as the concept
of petty squabbles
between fowls
and the old man
is glad that he won't
have to sling a rifle
over his shoulder
for the third time
in his life.
so he speaks of music,
to his deaf auditors,
abe or ape, I am
not wishing to return
to technical textbook
speech; he locks up
his music in his heart.
they do not learn.
they have been censored
from us, we are
curiosities whose
nature must be
organised,
sorted out,
and redistributed
as soap.

I want an orchestra.
without a supervisor.
I don't want followers
who are using me
to bolster their cause
they will survive
and creep into the
conscience
of my children
full of artless souvenirs
I have to hear my mind now
left without children's eyes,
torn from my love,
& confined to the anterooms
of literary traduction.
did you forget
that I could never answer back?
that an impossible fear
& jealousy
seizes my mother
unpredictably
martyring herself admirably
on her terrible history
of forced reactionary
marriage to a censored musician's
irrepressible wealth
of sudden silence.

you would have to
understand how
we came to be
without advance notice
and on the other side
of the cemetery
away from the rafles
at sea
stories came down to
warn us of death at sea,
inland the playwrights
wrote me in to dubious
roles of rumoured travesty
disloyalty by following
internationalism
travelled up the contours
of Rip,
the practice often
contradicting the theses
attitude to life
contradicting pure theses
of absent progress
in perceptual wholes.
It is Cannibalistic.
Icier.   Iraq has not appeared.
blue rinse.   mondrian brick tie.
gold tie.   am I meaningless.
I don't wear a tie.

is it naturally reduced
to pornography?
requesting reduction in width
strikes me as issuing
from a psychology
here we do not satisfy
the enquiries of those
who are not our poets.
we do not wait
to be examined.
we have been examined.
there are no landscapes
in vague apologias
for racial discrimination
everything is square here,
and wrought wood.
we hit the right note
a higher note. &
a distant one.
& we fall on letters
that no Literature Professors
mistake for slave ships
when they traduce
our anterooms
without first knocking

callipyge elle me tenait, rumpus,
employing gods to ostracize,
& to alienate, show these,
grand masters, in fine paintings
rather than wear literature
as heraldry to bruise us
renouncing mutuality,
arming each other, harming us.
the siege. quite as bad.
open uses. revealing ugliness
back against the entrance
finding native born immigrants
to dispose of to conjure space
and invest in unheld gold
with an itinerary of political
correctness, we are daughters of
Spain who did not have
£500,000 for a Stradivarius
and who could not cross over
to West Berlin, and who were
made to spin for Lord Alfred
when we wanted Alfredo, al fresco,
& cued to Etruscan palaces
not a fierce refusal to comprehend
in what there is no financial advantage
he is worse than Callipyge being younger
but I don't queue behind walls
with trollopish hat on head
great sun let drab days
of rain and emptiness dismal
grey dilapidating slates
left me with pale pink blossoms

faced by paint stripper advance
voices of chard black leather brace
coiled around each character boy
summonsing Mary lost on Hoy
faster beat the sleet destroy
by techo robust robot cops
luring into future sets unfriendly
menaces, tight lipped threats.
We are subjects to different fears,
nothing equal, nothing calmed,
the real, the incommunicable,
the daylight fragility, the nighttime –
nullity, no, don't lie, by pressing
sound into thick and poisonous
paint, deliberately bribing
amongst drinkers whose was whose
birthday, simmering in the heat,
alone and locked into the turning
of a rosenkranz turned hagenkranz
screams ice queen & kicks the Jew
out of the endless scene with alien
scrawled in short lisped 'r's'

pladd. (you who say either)

nothing can be clear when knowing the associations
are read by unread people, exposées, exposures.
new poems for old. groovy. associations
and world societies of interactive growth.
groan. a place full of untrained actors
absorbing dimensions of cradling pain
securing test periods of temperature change.
sewing elbes to harare, scratch luck.
nothing matches the theoretical tuck.
nutmeg. primus stove. raised eyebrows.
work sharing. retreat into the forest.
the silver conifers. the crumbs. chums.
biceps & musical hairs. plaesthetics.
planna vanne. plin plor plon pladverbially
plodding along with a net in sturdy
boots, add a few bulletins, patrol.
centuries. narrowly missing. pointed
drop. matches stove. matches museum.
curves around a few hundred unsent
letters, all impassioned, no, perfectly
spelt, satirical tirades. benjamin constant.
adolph who? painting his face whiter–
interview. tripping around in a chanterelle.
pulled. puppet. placed directly opposite.

the rhine in spine laced down the left, peace seized,
memory left, no one taught them the meaning
they think that they are naturally right,
i wait, i walk with life too great to beat,
out into the cold, out into the street, out
without a compact lap top, out without confirmation
of the memory of a less risky controversy,
that of offending the innate and incontestable
supremacy of those who forget that nothing
is lost by not hanging the innocent and clean,
that nurses are not happy to be garrotted unseen,
that ignorance in the acclaimed borders on obscenity,
that those who love their own bottoms turn them
into their faces, rather than remember any human
sight, rather than make any effort to use their
power to help, racism is there, as ever, with
all its benefits and advantages for free booty
& plunder. It is nothing worthwhile. A few bumps
here and there. A few flash waves, a wild radar.
Minds do exist to agitate & provoke, to make–
who is clean cleaner and cleanest. All allies.
White thieves, white agents, appointments &
shields. pland plainte. all fun. all whoopee.
all practised straight faces. all useful for
fuel and surplus importants. Saints each one
self professing and deployed. Basking in
joy, blessed and unwounded and automatically

adjusted. Osip Mandelstam in England would have been
murdered too. Where there is no art. but the
american whine of a self pitying tart's
immaculate shine. My son is waxen.
His mother has had her ears pressed in tight
her ears are turned inward she has ingrowing
ears. Plears. Péret. (Oh not Péret. Oh not Cixous.
Oh not Derrida. Oh not Virginia Woolf.
Oh not Gertrude Stein. Oh not George Sand.)
'Oh not Oh no I'll go deaf dumb and blind.'
Serviette scrumpled. Napkin crumpled. Grey
Pabst Grille Dreyer Gris rubble bouclé fuzzy
smothering Juan, the grandmother tells herself
stories, sound split from sight, which time
am I living in? I can tell by reading.
I play too wide Yes? but I throw my own Oceans
Out into the Islands of Thieves where they stand
with their miserable greyed underpants
swimming around their plump sweaty knees
It would certainly help were my accent broader,
a Self that one is pullulating in on this
Subject of editorially infiltrated Capitals,
my years of care are not matched by much
other than steel and martyr'd hatred.
Ploy. The heavenly god and the heavenly voice.
A few, only a few. Am I far away from those
I love? Is this someone else's?

of Lorca.

language collapsed on language
stark freedom knowledgeable stony silence
grey grave packed up a trumpet
                    event reclined
slab digitalised aphid cyphers. a gallant son
hung to my head, a spreading golden mine
apostlehood retired to the withdrawing room,
room, room, neapolitan napoleonic, room.
there maniac tubes of pithless pitiless availability
avoiding rhythmic rheum; mirad, el mascaron
se fueron los pequeños botones de fosforo,
sf, science fiction, sarah farrell,
      new york city ballet,
                             sigmund freud,
sf, four, fosforo, sf, oven, oban, mirad,
                                          el mascaron,
                                          edith piaf,
                                          sacha distel,
                                          charles aznavour,
                                          sidney bechet,
                                          juliette gréco,
                                          jacques brel
                                          georges brassens
                                          lado del mundo,
cenerentola, crisp snow, white glass.
ós, y los valles de luz
el cisne! el cisne! czech time!
no fount, no children, hedgerows in misshapen fields,
no ravachol, no gold hole, the words kept falling,
hedgerows tipping sirenic scream into the dazzling water.
that is all i remember, corcho, it breathes, internally.

I object.

to being invited to dance like a wild thing
the music is too loud, could you lower the volume.
tone it down would you please leave the full stop
The line has been drawn by the temperature.
the tone . . . and the furniture. We were
holding a conversation at the . . . I object.
Will it ever, s/he dictates, stop talking to men.
No, never. Whether women were the powers behind,
The tight pure whey, are recently being raw
chalk over grey, I shall not stop pacing around
the merry-go-round gay grown boer.
Never a face here warm and sincere, unnatural.
the intellect is natural. it is natural to think, to wonder,
to muse. one time is not ever this defensiveness,
disappearing invitation, warmth blocked.
defensive? ancestrally strict. unconsciously
uncontrollably mean and bitter but it's odd
to sustain that level of antagonism against
one's own daughter. Why did she fight me then
drop me into the abyss? Was that a mad temptation
or an irresistible impulse° hesitation in matters of
lifelong love never work out well, reservations are
dangerous, I was the object of her hatred. I object
to being hated. There are some really mad people here too.

to any who want poems to give them answers.

not that they ask interesting questions.
only that they expect answers.
a poem is not going to give precise directions.
you mustn't touch the hiding places.
they address a different world
where trees are decorated with diamonds

one man clean & one man dirty
neither has a sense of shirty,
cleaner one as dirty & thick of mouth
louder than southern traffic jams
other one filthy with derisions
both quite dirty, one a bit cleaner,
another one sucks his thick dirty fingers,
several professionals drunk on power,
creeping Jesuses stewing each hour
in dirty cords, & grimy shirts,
combing their hair with old dirty teeth,
never washing their hands after their
pees, leaks, slashes, & whatever,
Dirt, filth, & salacity caressing each other's
grease lined forks, scurvy saucers,
rabid maids & drug addict daughters

*

digne. more than a design. to size.
william hathaway, wizard. ich wh
one, yes woven soul choking on a
fault, the end is not the object.
i am going back to two times,
it is not twice in history, a brève
a minor historical incident
in the great space, accrochée
des lettres, before catching a train.
why were those journeys calm?
life eliding between recognition
living greene, mostar works
hysterical venues, from to from.
Joan burnt. seven minute break.
paprika. one suitcase. three babies.
i can't teach people moral behaviour.
i only see people behaving as though
other women's children were up for grabs.
carelessly. playing around with trumped-
up charges. confusing teachers with
revellers in diamond snatching.
so busy in the world of things.
counting what different houses have.
never researching their own inadequacy
only glaring at other women,
waiting for the chance to step in
side their property, snaffle.
in two time. i'll take care & not
ally with any who sour minds. stupid.

a joke. fine. i'll give
no more beauty. there will
be no more illuminated windows.
the white muggers raided the unions.
i should have run it through
on red lines, dull red, lined,
baselitz, dry, not rough though.
a few patches of blue.
the banks, their definitions . . .
conjuring . . . apparitions . . .
someone used a knife,
–it was once obvious that
young idealists and dreamers
were the enemies of the economy.
I wouldn't have let that happen either.
or the familial curses.
or the skin culture.
or trying to work out
how I was murdered.
how libel & slander kills.
through literary veins.
how arp's sculptured reliefs
spoke to me from behind glass
cases. how I know how I act dead,
how satisfying it is for some actresses
to lock up playwrights
how T. S. Eliot's words are borne out
how futile to be told that one is celebrating,
is it always a toss-up?

fusain.
red velvet rose
red enamel rose
obscur/clair
brown/cinnamon
bb oo gg ll cc
ee nn aa nn
jamais tous
toast claxon
newborn, mouth
deep blue, strong blue
"a tea, a coffee & a motorway."
an invitation to rot.
force feeding.
children snatched.
mexican ring snatched.
wage packet snatched.
camera snatched.
cumbrian loft snatched.
rented house & studio snatched.
university place snatched.
virginity snatched.
exactly how silent
is one meant to be.
and yet . . . when reading . . .
attention snatched
and not by children.
so that was curtailed.
as apparently I was
enjoying being with
my children.
when I should have been
cooking cooking cooking
corking corking clucking
clicking heels peeling paint
bloody food.
i don't like all that fuss
Any chance for forget it
Weetabix.
Snowflakes.
No, we haven't.
Why discuss food?
I hate discussing food.
I don't want to feel
my mouth watering.
It bores me.
Why were my children plump
and Indian children not plump.
As you can read
it was a nasty racist heist.
I do not run the prison system.
I am not a lesbian.
Serve your own sentences.
In future.
I collect sentences.
I used to have a set of my own.
Musicians, artists, choreographers,
windhover.

*

basalt. basalt. two sculptured heads. hongrie 1956. tanks. fire. hatred. disturbing the peace. It's a filthy world. Archeological perception reveals gunpowder deposits & so-called insanity. A woman artist does not Need the insidious interference of any woman who tells me what I know. Un palétuvier. The painting caused dismay. I question that dismay although not in a protracted fashion, not giving birth to a mangrove, the confrontation between the artist & the authorities on white needlework results in the artist being locked up without paint, water & paper. It was only the first painting & I was not thinking specifically of the Mangrove which was the site of a riot which I did not witness but which was famous for the brutal & corrupt police in that area of West London which was being gentrified. As Gentrification is creeping around with adopted republics. Landowners paint as though they had known the years of freedom, but they don't have to know anything about freedom, they live everywhere as though everywhere was theirs to ride their horses through streets & imagine the population cheering it makes me feel sick. Apollinaire must have heard the old people talking, despairing; he might have known Lenin, What is to be done? heard Vladimir and somewhere Krupskaya was calling him Vladimir. the baby's nappy needs changing, for this – were meine kinder deposited in the neo-liberal police force élite comprised of celtic economists with the emphasis on the last syllable. There is no point pointing a finger at the Chassidim. The Celts don't love Judaism & they stamp down hard on a little child's love for his mother. But listen, this will drive you crazy. I don't talk to the police except never, the solicitor calls in the police because I do not want my house raided when I am alone with my little children. but this goes down to the point, and is enmeshed in the Nietzschean Will of the Baudelairean's determination to declassify the Jewess from the functioning economy in Academia and in the Arts, for every secretary & receptionist looks Aghast at the Colour. This colour is avoiding my decision making properties. Perhaps both decorate pastels are neither, although it is lost. One was, and demented is losing one for the other. Baudelaire makes flesh of it. He uses Hermes Trismegistus to decorate interiority. Do you know how frightening it is to have one's cover spat back at one over a table fit for a king whose wives' heads are propped up in rosebowls – whose wives' heads are mistaken for cats and who stare back from their swathes of hair when you bend down to stroke the objects that are nestling at your feet? I am alone here, the art school refused to acknowledge that painting could be flawed. This was another perverted tactic to exonerate filthy racism, to conform. It isn't shocking, or even remarkable. It is Germanically inspired. What happened to me in Germany? I was advanced on by a nurse with a hypodermic needle. She was directing it to my skull. I ducked. It is stupid to write for so many people whose positions of authority now desensitizes their use of language. It is true that the reactions of the radical authorities have confirmed their unwillingness to act promptly to stem racist abuse. The Jew is the least protected. People simply start to speak in that mock-Jewish way. "If you can take being in quod, you can survive anything." Thanks.

My Chekhov's Twilight World

This can only be a memory. Eviction by ideologists returned me to Chekhov's twilight.
It is the only twilight I had. Inevitably so having lost late nineteenth century Russia.
This is only a fraction of the wardrobe. Surface treatment. Quite cool. I don't know
what I think of wood painted white. It's difficult to transport furniture by hand on
a boat with fires flaming behind you. It is very quiet there. We lived by a river.

Since I was told that I hadn't read enough I have interred myself behind books.
I shall never consider that I have a cultural contribution to make to British
Culture again. I swear to that. Which year was Lorca here? I heard that he had
been in New York. I don't touch other people's babies. I have a strong memory.
We are not a completely conscious democracy although we have the frameworks

of democratic procedure which should be recognized and practised. It is
no disgrace for a practising artist to attend a formally chaired meeting
on Equal Opportunities for Women. Women can be disturbed by personal
invasion from other women when the chair is ignored. One of the reasons
Why meetings are Chaired is to contain and separate the personal emotions

of each member of the meeting. I have attended many, many meetings
which have all been chaired. Before my own reputation was damaged
by people who refused to recognize the structural reasons for democratic
procedure. That is. I do not Appreciate being assaulted by Gangsters' friends.
Could we get that quite Straight. My writing is not for them.

It is a gutter lot who boast the sacrifices and struggles of the people
having done nothing but four years' hard work. But we were not allowed to
work. We were each of us spun out by those who claimed Chekhov's world
for themselves. I was the first to go. Two months at University and wham
Eviction. This country was still in the throes of Wagnerianism. Check it.

pan & tilt. weft & warp. the earth does tilt. to define me as straight
ignores the fact that my mother's family were Russian. Polish Russian
relations have had a painful history. I was in the pain of that history.
And I knew to the last fibre of my body and soul. So whom you saw
Standing there without the faintest conviction apart from the Drag &

and pull of miscarriage was a Pole from Seville. Methought I had a Beard
coming on twas so fulsome to be vomiting in pink darned socks with a
field to plough (he threw me an orange from the hold of a boat belonging to
the Spanish navy oh that's a lovely colour combination Shut Up they
Bellowed you're —ing up the show Hic Hoc Hunc Tralee Lumplight

That's a TERRIBLE thing to say about anyone. Where is my Grundig Tape
Recorder. Be very very careful who you talk to, live with, work with. There
is disregard for human life and there should not be. I can't be Everywhere
ensuring that no harm is done. My poetry is not the harmful type. It stems
from the affections not their antithesis. Where I came from one requested a license

to write. one did not suddenly Snatch momentum. At each stage there are
moral considerations. Before the Equal Opportunities Act became Law
(over twenty years ago) women were at a decided disadvantage. There
is no question about that. It is absolutely and incontrovertibly true.
I Live my life. I don't have two lives or five or nine. I have One Life

My Own. And what I decide to do with my life is a matter between
myself, my mind and the Law. I did not decide to read Law. I
considered it. Buildings are neat. I like buildings. I considered Architecture too.
Even more so than the Law. I doubted that the Law was pure.

*

Concentration camp styles. along mill road. 1998.
a very old lady, back bent permanently forward–
arthritic, –walks, pauses, takes a few steps,
her walking stick. prices flutter on bicycles'
handlebars, (tight orange nylon shorts, fat
bottoms, newspaper rolled under arms)
casual country wheeler turns in a gap in the
traffic stream, trashy soft music on radio,
shampoo spilt into my purse, Greek waitress–
dries it for me on the kebab grill, mostly women–
walking on the pavements, mid morning,
children holding mothers' hands, mother's sister's
hands friends' hands, mostly men driving,
open builders' trucks stacked with wooden
planks, Worcester heat systems, fit old man on
bicycle red nylon rucksack on his back,
a few lemons in peaked caps & oversized tracker
sweaters carrying plastic shopping bags,
dull weather, (pearl grey), professional looking
cyclist wearing shades & helmet, white t-shirt,
tanned legs, racing bike in working order,
unbelievable solid stream of male drivers,
constant flutter of price tags on steady
line of pavement bikes, no-one visible in the
hair and beauty salon, old man crippled
with arthritis cannot look at the sky whilst
walking using his stick at each step, heavy
dyed blond and gold sleeveless tank top boys,
one woman driver in black car with surrounding
narrow orange stripe, one cigarette smoking
grandad pushing a pram, Cambridge
city services wagon driven by crew cut
chap, frantic housewife hurrying home
with two polythene bags full of bread rolls,
one large attractive couple, enormous

stomach on the man, marked faces, Go Whippet
coach, driven by male, someone has bought
a bike. A Greek couple with a mother.

to a writer.

Without a word, had they not been sealed on fired paper?
That the sun was not melting the leaves into fruit
In cleared palm on concrete route the edges brushed gold
unlicked dry lipped in the company of the disrespectful
who suspect law to be shadowed script
dipped onto violet brows who cut false reliefs
to market on shoes, pom poms thrashed apparitions

But I forget how ugly I am, am reminded by violence
refusing me beauty which I appreciate
And the cool words that flowed in the peace of childhood
Far from the hearing of pirates and axemen
finding our bohemian paths overgrown with horses and honeysuckle
Alerted the guardians of inexpressivity
To hook plump babies onto vacant trees

Have the words been definitively removed
That once my mouth greeted each dawn steadily
Attending slow reawakenings that could not be heard
When death was not being offered as dismemberment
In the shocking surfeit of continual appetite
That my arm snapped against the wall I hid my head
and hit it liberally against the unforgiving stone

When weeds grew in luscious streaming water
And the green was cold as the wheat was warm
In muggy fields close shorn by heavens full blue
Hanging heavy in the dense gold of summer's heat.
Guilt lies beneath the journeys of the dutiful
Clamped into self denial rumours of life being lived
Rather than the rostrum receiving the stamp of a face.

*

This is the reason why I do not conform.
A smile is a formality. That is all that exists
between people who do not know each other.
It is irrelevant what one knows of anyone.

The torso. People without minds. Tenses can be
Rapidly switched. How does one know that
one's pursuer does not intend to cause one
harm. A man can demand explanations.

A woman is accused of aggressive behaviour
for querying motive. One does not need to
Pursue anyone, one can be invited to live
in a house & find oneself being used

for servitude. And Interrogated, relentlessly
& remorselessly, until one is too weak
to move. This is peace as is death.
It is imagined that one is writing.
Why is it difficult to register Detestation.

The dangers in writing are inherent.
Why it is dangerous to criticize the Establishment
Openly. Why what amuses the Establishment
is the Bad Use of language and Sex.
Why women are discussed in terms of knickers.
Why it is important not to lose control
Of one's own mind. Why Literature
Frames novices. Why Framing is a sociopolitical act.

*

geo Alkan jeo, toppled on
not as full as the whole works
vibratum, vibratum, vibratum.
lift it higher, depiction.
the world lost its diction.
sadness dies with my note.
there is the white facial mask
driving late for work
arriving home early "in good spirits
and with a clean face."
sigh before the door
the wolf blew in plaster walls.
rest in alabaster Alkan,
Alkan who walks no more.

the beef girls. leaning on Alkan.

brilliant. ten p. tip. brilliant. night brilliant. brilliant. milk. brilliant. canoes. brilliant. darth veda. brilliant. vedantic. brilliant. the hearing photograph. sex. continence. cheap lighters. exactly. zippo. milk. zippo. the hearing photograph. zippo. false eyelashes. zippo. metro. brilliant. burger king. exactly. burger queen. exactly. burger beef girls. brilliant. moccasins. brilliant. lightweight summer suit. brilliant. depression. brilliant. toilet mirror exactly. perforated table. brilliant. draughty river. pixel psychosis. celery. too long. whole milk. too whole. sorrow. around sorrow. a mountainous city. a pair of stainless steel legs. a white worktop. pretty blue sky. the right of reply. roses die in July. gladioli.

*

Reminiscent of a flat expanse trammelled
is a woman, weighted by metal engines
the nature that she was summarily dismissed
to be, inconsequent, causing swell where
dry conditions, behind her back, primroses
yellow green swim, bathed in lemon
on raised scarlet dias for safety.

of minds, of flues, or organza.
breath cloaked in paintings;
old roman pavement oak leafed
a narrow step to the pond, her children
slammed against the water, against her
leaving dust for sea, smoke for sunlight.
clothes fuss pleasantly over

pleasant dressing calm delivery
the woman's mind unbound by contract
makes life by clearing passages
out from radiation, & ties against
living language the resources that are hers
in unknowable incongruities & agréments.

mouth closed against political language,
completely away from significance
is challenged, where it does not blow
on either side of the walls around Jericho
the rose that is drenched sweet & wild as pink
geranium, fragile as faded sanctity
a close brush of air kissed with warmth

Holding the sunlight in its glance
Wary of the size of history
Aware of the ground plans of its magnificent masonry
Dark against the ancient sky.

*

Zephyrus

One in another mind that by error has been taken
erroneous to the mind breathing space unquestioning
never enquires, does not dream within the whole
escapability from one mind's grasp yet grasps
unheeding and unheeded beyond the fallacy
that promises a mistake will in eight be twisted
and exercising reference to subjectivity
pressurizes focus onto the Theatre of Cruelty
Stern objection do I proffer to this imicable faculty
And find defence is named admission.
The language of creation so confangled
Deserves a separate issue to be caught
By wealth of hours the rise in opposition
To human absorption of bright light
That crooks its way through heaven's economy
And exploits indiscretion to protract human tragedy
Uncomprehended either purposely & resentfully
or through ignorance and a kind of innocence
that the mouth beats through words and voice
acting publicly, enormously, familiarly,
unaware that within this imperfection
We do not hold a hurried start that our relationship
Consisting of appreciation hides its heart
In offensive refusal to read rather to imagine cruelty
& set about blind to the contrary, deaf to the art
Of creation through language that finds its way back to structure.

minnie most beats up thérèse torchée

world style competition & analysis,
for the minnie most recent civilized prose,
it shows. island, mountain, plain, coast,
urban, suburban, glacier, -nost.
nostrilic, acrylic, polyphilic, alembic,
iambic, egotistic, lethargic, somnambulistic,
it shows. fix a face over, reporting a likeness . . .

serpolet*, sweetened to her size, black gloved
red felt spotted nylons, ur-blue swivel set
screens deranged, minnies novel onto palm springs.
tests the water for structure, & the air for flare . . .
practise makes perfect. breathes out.
organises new foot modelled infrastructure . . .
a malaysian island with an s.z. rating.

you know there's going to be a murder, wait.
it doesn't happen on this line. first it was sex
then it was murder. minnie walks backwards.
its good for her calf muscles & her thighs.
rather than pushing on regardless, onwards ever
up hill down dale looking for birds' eggs.
with her sharp nose shooting rays across the thickets.

* (wild thyme)

Brahms' numerals.

of darkness,
of ground,
of sources,
raw silk,
drawn thru
from beyond

on the gate
farmers gather
he doesn't half
rate himself
by leaving
his body
out of the mind

models clown
mannikins propped
onto stone shelves
forget the end
of endive
of black grapes
of unfulfilled promises }
dang. clover

heaven's cope
cold inhuman
height of ichneumon
distracted flight
welcome ill go
desnos sleeping

of mint,
of paraclete,
of golden sonnetts
and their songbirds
wheeling down
with her golden ear
fixed by conchie

when it started
clicking
it was on the
side of star chamber
when Loki
and Nesbit

hazel cops
tiny toes
daw dot
med. crazy
dowry aztec
honeycomb mist

consciousness,
Ah! now we can begin
to twiddle around
with Noddie's hat
chalchihuitl & big tears
        Agaçant
her name is Heart

detesting Nibbits,
turned Frankoische
just to grab a glimpse
of a painting by
Frankenthaler,
so take the Whole Thing.

spreading my mask
around my middle
the stable walls
are not making
a classical beauty
from uneven paths out

waiting to
come out of her mouth
in several fascicular
rebus mote murmurs
aware of the adoption
of personal fetishes

Aga Canot,
Barge into Concrete!
Brain of Cobble Stone.
Galet. only
Don't leave me your
Cast Off mothers' hats
twizzess

REARRANGED LETTER TO THOMAS EVANS

your travel why tiger not / been would be the same, a visitor
how thank you whom you refer to should inevitably capacities
heated light produces picturesque anthologies and probably it
quite lost get quite lost and probably meet a tiger pittor-
esque false collective though Sartre non-Aryan breed in
control Broke with Heidegger (c.f. Situations) tastes artists &
broad ground studied always control their tastes "BLIND BALLS".
alienated response friendly to fascists if on the liberation of
Paris I am I know why I would have only fought them in
the Resistance, in a helicopter so I have been building one
out of wood and scrap metal from the skips in the side
streets, pink dusty light, I'm ashamed to admit it is not
natural and Camus Combat 14 août 1944 in the trees.

*

To appear.   Obscure need.
& every cry every hope
will be the fever of ploughing.

*

A vulnerable strength but one that legally
Kept you standing for a long time by day.
That one decimated
this one too worn out to hope.

*

Each morning
To clear out the ashes of boredom.
Mountain coruscate
Sentinel shone
whatever the day brings.

*

The silence beats, within furiously.
And the town passes wordlessly
disdainful codified
toward a memory of rumours.

*

Urge desire
mount your courage
That it becomes the bee unwinding ever
between the rose and the honey.

*

Too set is the flight
and nothing recommences.
Too distant in time
to accumulate further luggage.

*

The extent of the beast
the length of the grass
it supports itself instantaneously.
Weightless loves that repeat themselves.

*

Who now without your look
can name each trace
on the hereditary slabs?
Long narrative that will carry away the last eye.

*

Fresh bread
beneath the knife that cuts it
awaits its wound with dignity.

*

Do not wait for the return.
Every dawn is forever consuming its own minglings
Every evening ignores its youth
Whose eyes will be another colour.
Already it rains tomorrow on the golden side of this morning.

*

Life will be round as the earth
will be circular Time
running without ever stopping
will be tough Eternity. Enduring.

*

No flower no tree
no star no prairie
can bring me love.
On the asphalt
the sparrow so happy
with itself.

*

Anachronistic sky.
Beneath it
the green nourishment of springtime
covers stiffened folds.
When comes their first smile?

*

And instead of which flame
or against it
will the chestnut trees
open their parasols?

*

Tree an iceberg
twinned in the earth.
One a peacock
The other nutritious fabric.

*

On the lawn
Perfection of the blackbird
new furtive
on the closely cut grass

*

When it rains
are daisies wise
to close their umbrellas?
What motive?
A little foolish perhaps also?

*

Red shore
a green horse
the unimpressed sea.

*

The sea is a great fish that wriggles.
In its movement
the scales wear away and renew themselves
in parallel glamour.

*

Apple tree, village of fruits.
High up on the crest the life
the upsets in solicitation.
Close to earth calls for help
hiding agonies.

*

The log enthuses and lives in its burnings.
By moments its heart flashes
gives seize like a lighthouse a ship.
Does it not know where
its joy in seduction carries it?

*

As evening collects thoughts
as night slips its chrysalis there
as morning is held to judge.

*

Your voice has the form of a wounded gesture
O brother already subjected to binding
in the studio of memory.
Today something tells me that your shadow
has gone before you into the garden of stones.

*

Here is the brown season
and you will not recognize the trees
by their birds' names.
Hiatus. This will be for another life.

*

It is the butterfly of death
that repeated three times I love you
in the heart of the rose
and which broke it.

*

What order would protect us from where
we could live.
My lively frame will this be the advent?

On condition that the poppy's cheek welcomes us
in its shadow of fire.

*

O little house of oak
little night chalet.
Smooth walls to a body
sealing narrowly roof of the return
of innocence.

*

A deserted cage.
A gust animates a forgotten plume.
The cage still more deserted.

*

Dawn
Sad tresses of silence.
And suddenly the ballet of windows
their   music in ringlets
inviting the day.

*

Closed on the table
the book knows nothing.
And then the eyes learn from the open book
Its narrative.

*

A motionless bird.
Cut out on the sky.
Prisoner when will you fly
leaving behind you a crucible

irreparable scar?

*

And you handsome horse with your virile twisted mane
who will know how to pacify the petal of your skin
and to show you
that to tremble is life and death.
Not only death.

*

In the night
the candle close to the rose.
On the wall
the rose: crazy black huge.

*

I have a sun of you on the tongue
a churchy cool in hot months.
But in my defeated heart
wisteria that stooped
yesterday without a future.

*

Know it
any presence is no more familiar
than our Christ of the wood
open on the edge of fields.

*

Day sets
and I am old.
Who to rejuvenate me
has rested your eye
on the wing of a butterfly?

*

I have waited for you so much
"O errant force on my porch O beggar" *
that the birds sing on the snow.

* Saint-John Perse (*Exil*)

*

Will it pause without avalanches
broken skeletons
cries all the time
and this weight on the memory
where the heart and its boats no longer have a place?

*

Any glance over your numbers.
high cloud openly
free you can go
with your errors your disorders your nothings
to plant the vine of words in the order of silence.
But the absence?

LA FACCIATA

Le père, la voix du défunt père, clapot sonore,
nasillement sonore en haut derrière la peur son vrai
vêtement muet, draguant les algues de voyelles limpides
qui s'accrochaient dans les tasses, signalait-il, les yeux fermés
refoulant des larmes, elle ne peut fuir cela.

Leurs noms tombaient sur des anguilles en gelée, ses genoux
aussi gracieux qu'une bonnetière, dans un filet de genoux crissants
mais… claironnait le politicien, responsable de
l'autre bout des mots importants, elle avait crié
durant trois naissances, trois saignements de nez dans un tourbillon éperdu.

Il n'y a que les chrétiens qui crépitent de pureté bien que l'ex-
ode n'ait pas eu de témoin, les juifs étaient contrariés, des sons
plus profonds s'achèvent en houle recouvrant rondement un dos de filet de pêche,
Qu'est-ce que c'est le devant en italien? La personne d'après venait-elle endessous
tremble multifolié que le circuit d'eau muait à grand coup de

Trompe en chêne mort, placoplâtre gercé de la vie,
une autre mère mûre et moelleuse, se levant pour leurs peines,
les péchés sont bons pour les Boîtes, les boîtes bonnes à débourrer, les gains bons à jumeler,
alors qu'il fasait une proposition sérieuse
elle se ridiculisait

A présent nous sommes nattées, les bras croisés sur le giron,
souffrons l'effilochage saccadé de dahlias rouge sang
qui brunissent, répondons à la planche, répondons au besoin de la mer,
avons bu le froid de frayeur, la persécution et passé le faubert
dans les filets répandus autour des genoux de l'impresario

Plaids à vingt ans, c'est le genre bien écrasé,
chatouilles de crocodiles, digitales de l'antre orange
du ciel étant donné la volonté des vagues au milieu, ces navires sont à quai,
fissurées et jetées sur l'épave couchée où les cueilleurs
sont recueillis pour les livres de compte du conseil glacial.

Incluez les barreaux, le ton inarticulé, les oeillères tintinabulaires
au-delà il y a l'orage côtier & l'homme du daily telegraph
la toile cirée vert bouteille, l'homme qui balance, le bosquet du cap Finisterre
mais… claironnet le politicien, il n'y a AUCUNE géographie dans la PROTESTATION
le linge démonstratif saisissait plus fort qu'un anneau.

*

1526

circoncision du cœur, qui sont mes autorités
au vernis de longue portée projetant un telos inentendu
tangible et écouchant à atteindre des communiants
dont être coupée, dans cette clarté confessionnelle
avertissait que mes livres de poésie étaient sacrés.
au dernier apogée il était malade mais non abattu.
tort précieux si on ne prête pas attention à ceux qui
font régresser celle qui est au-delà de ces pages dont la belle
liberté première et passionnée tendit deux bras
à lentement abaisser sur la table à l'écart du Mal.

La dépression avait-elle dissipé cette pratique égoïste de
se distinguer, se battant contre les commandements pour renoncer
sauve dans le minimal, plongeant dans le sacrifice aveugle de la négation.
Brutalité, compagne de la bravade, nivelant le plâtre mouillé.
Qui peut dénier aux grands leurs auxiliaires vitaux?
L'ignorance folle conduit une âme hésitante qui marche
Malgré les défaillances qui pourraient ne pas toujours guérir
À une certaine vitesse, aucune vitesse remarquée, avec un manque anxieux de rituel.

Possible d'y remédier. Entre cet appétit remémoré
qui m'épouvantait. Pesant les sens avant le cœur d'un autre
Comment le mien peut-il être connu des autres qu'offensent
l'auto-référence. Ce n'est pas le Principe de la Chose en ce
Cas-ci. C'est une délivrance permanente des pratiques restrictives.
Et je ne pourrais faire plus pour vous aider à comprendre cette
Impossible Domination à laquelle il n'est peut-être rien qui supplée.

fulgencies

1.

she saw them as in a dream years and years before
the flying white faces of hatred pinioning her to the door
the floor, the flaw, the wall, the door.
she fled their confounded hatred
who split the tree did bleed and as it bled
the food went down to join the lead
a soft effulgent material pliant not needing fire
a sight too many of loud crashing buildings
where millgirls screams were barely heard
as rip roaring factories unsafe for workers
plummeted flaming her nerves.
well poor old thing said her mama
but not as poor as those
whose skirts on that fatal day caught alight
when the dry cleaning works was wiped out.

2.

everything unreal from romance to chocolate
entrances mavis and pat
their mothers the same none too partial to gaskell
reminds them too much of their flat.

nattering swans

My mother was the mother of this blackguard
who flew to spacial bridge ramparts tensed
from falling crows' eggs from zebra wooded
doppelgangsters screened off screens. My moth
er was an hippodrome in inner city railways
crocketing impounded depression films. He reared
and lost a country that nested in his dreams. My
mother wore his houndstooth check to amble through
the landerettes with Marietta in her black
sprig net ahunting down fresh funerals.
Dressing hymns and reading limbs ripped along gadrooning
what could not be gulped those tears
to beg forgiveness for being about something else
babies in the diet coke hypnotic provocations
together loved on hillside trysts smoked by smouldering
alder twigs, rationing gneiss handbooks from dusty
wrecked box offices perched precariously over plush becks.

*

i. m. Laura Riding

if thought be woven from the brain wished ill may learn to love again
a moonlit dusk by lamplight's side a less anxious life
where proof of purse is not in pride nor strife a jokey vendetta
beginning twice more to examine extremes of sanctioned shapes
which knew to lighten mechanics with previewed disfunction
once the essentials are proven and normalities intergraved
it will not be mine to decide who are the damned and who the saved.

The wrong room

Make no demands of those you are about to sacrifice to the winds
the white plume burnt in white fire, sacrifices, pressed space
spare no devastating word, the lambs were safe, your curse travelled
having infected my ears with the sound of your hatred
it was a word I did not want to hear. Must you hate?
Must you change every girl into a president, into a politique?

The sun never submits itself to the moon's phases.
Of light there is no higher tune. Everywhere enquiries flee.

Strictly personal

indirectly kind fire is glowing over forgotten reasons,
could have asked for help, but the mother in me,
unborn & now denied all part apart from by those
whose love neither sought me nor was by me sought,
cared to keep couples together with their children
rather than present my named self to endanger
their peace when in a sudden dreamless world
of no true life I was thrown as though I am a dice
who needs no table and no life to say no to.
no-one hears me when I speak, it is not total fiction.
They know everything about me I won't simply
take these words, I see, it was a simplification,
and now there is no need, and I have nothing.
What would my line have sounded like? an ascent?
a descant. but the door had been slammed
and Wordsworth had dried up over stones
on the edges of a desert where the sun beats
mercilessly since Berlin had been overrun &
beauty in the desert it was to become
the latter light of what had come to be
called irrational, that is civilization,
that is civility. I was further along the road
to death. and my arm does not present a
right direct or my waist go straight to death.
For how far from the city named was I pulling
my mind for a truer colour, clear of the acidic
red that has come through nature's wit to grow
and singing a reply, writhe immobilized.

Britain 1967

you draw me skating on the sky through a black mirror
and afraid of your country that it means something
has given the earth a pain whereas the clover clubs
whereas letters unconscious of toes on the lawn,
the wall, iron, waiting for the entrance to the world.
whereas you invite me to dine, or as you write; to dinner.
& the strawberries were the rent and the slippers
unmarked on the end paper. I was not loud enough.
Europe was educating me in controversy. never arrives.
wives weep   Europe never arrives. & the decoy hides.
you want to be known as a select committee –
who are the last to have achieved fine christ.
of myself diagonal, I have always had my reasons
not to reflect the moods of the times. have bellini.
I see that they are paid hounds working later on
Systems that have placed outside, total integration,
this is why, no answers complement eradication

On being reproached by saintly mediators for bad budgeting

I'd like to be rich. No not casually but positively streaming with wealth. Hard.
It is the only way to achieve anything. Nothing can be achieved without wealth.
To live in a great old house and never see the light of day, by which I mean
be exposed to public scrutiny. Never mind my accounts. I have no accounts.
Accountants are stupid little racketeers who never stop snivelling. Two fingers
for the sound of a chord and the end of a day when sin becomes annealed
to accountancy. Drinking a hot mug of coal. King Dick II down the mineshaft

Snivelling soap sud professors frothing pacifism as though anyone had told
them not to. The bromide feminists raking french knits off the shelves
who are these people who climb into vats of lye with years of police work
behind them. L'essaim. La foule. L'étranglées.

Franked

Lines from terrain are attractive trilling & deeply rolling theodolite
doing crash on the tiller. sceptic. disclos. the story of unlocked wrists,
magnetic fields etched by guidance with a brain being knotted,
in eyelash corners slashed. holding the reins, unstreamlined
pregnancy baited by quotient rushes slowly, too slowly
for strapped to a garland. a desk has a language complete
this is not, though, a language of love but of ovens & covenant
glimmering harbours where forgotten and dismal houses
shudder in heat throwing miasmas over interludes

~

held by compulsion untremored, glancing over jigsaw
looked over one arm timing its sweep to extremity
raw legs from the ankle down approached with caution
known for their less than round toes, unfortunately
there was something to be said, the invader did natives
a favour, aesthetically, by introducing rounder toes
to remove myself, the narrow gate of democracy requires a line
that has not mistaken misfortune for sublime purity
not Intrusion but Innocence destroyed by bad translation

~

quotient over. I totally disagree. Visconti escaped the firing squad.
Unfortunately to be born & then have to go all the way back
to be unborn, although alive, is an inducement to illusion.
I only want two words Unfortunately and Although, we have a sense
that was intruded upon by a look and a resonant note
I shall not be signing, from territory which I did not seek.
Not after those pretensions to knowledge. Even though I looked young
and my voice ceased to survive insidious recognition.
I shall not be signing. Only beneath the table, is the stage.

Photrum

deeply enclaved gnon spirited away from araldite,
no artists named in texts, appreciations appear laterally;
sorry. it was unacceptable to me to switch the muse of peace
for the muses of war, exactly how ranks are built . . .
nominalism is an imposition on sympatico poetry
there were no words, apart from a rehearsed disapproval . . .
that's O.K. we have boyfriends, we don't settle down
to cosy conversations with the opposition
who follow us from town to town with sexual innuendo.
I am not angry. I had an education in comradeship.
so that I have always had a lot of time. but not for filth
or smuts shoving line after line into windblocks.
I must say–that I am glad that my parents did not
work for the police force. I wonder–whether
rinsed keys mark June, i.e. defying unprepossess open debut
frein, do you think that drivers make better pianists?
well loan me your limousine for a spin by the coast road
there's a copse, or a spinney, with a hell on its hilt
papers are birthrights, spilt by content, emasculated intellect
carelessly codifying sisters for foreigners, cultural bolt
seats imaginary cuneiform arched steel bough
a pristine Harry Watt's film, incensed by human inability
frein take seven, heavenly word, a joke, good play, 'The Malcontent'.
Secular nebulous realism. Uncover yourself Psych. Flip off.
Idiots wear poems to read themselves. and are backed.

footsteps climb whereas they descend

I)

footsteps climb whereas they descend
lightly weeping mary rustle of paper
why they should play spoons
and rise again the footsteps
steps on trays
wrenches out of porcelain
after glass sheeted mountain houses
time pictorializes gas lamps
appoints peripheral imprisonment
paper birds inaugurate a child's conversation.

II)

darkness falls fast
that there is laughter
leaving complete separation
far from Greek
unreceptive to Spain
constant electrical pulses
centrally receding

downhill a red beam
from the Constitutionnel
arriving exactly where the darkness
fails between days
to distinguish the hours

III)

seven Friday, was it free
what is free cannot be stolen
what I make without limbs
bends to break its neck
although not quite five
weeping mary the forest fire
at sunset wanting to go
no. July is blue.
the circus is hung in sports
bloodsuckers lunge at my vein
trying to find the prison in my blood
to feed off its nature,
which is nothing apart from memory
starved of movement.
which is played against a new book
announcing a Jewless space,
a Judge, and a Saviour.

Ordered into Quarantine

You have told me & in the telling have placed yourself above me as my keeper
this lacks voice positively, though your one word devastated me
I do not therefore, following you, fill in the space or watch it for,
aware of the material nature of this structural existence which has now
become a gratuitous act, falling into exercise, you annihilated me.

It is a pity that you took my body seriously, for what fears were yours
I have raced around myself like a maypole in the act of self strangulation
what a twisted girl you were you might have sighed before you popped
me into the oven having broken me over your knee like a long french loaf.

But plaited! That calmed me. Any threads in threes. Army blankets
fulfilled a purpose, or stars scratched onto a stone floor with the heels of my shoes
or splitting matchsticks with a pin, an economical trick, who would have thought
that that would have proved useful, and to remember it in a
chamber airy and unearthly light if a blue butterfly flew out I could nip its wing

In one bite feed on butterfly's wing by split match light & all for silence
for the lovely long life of limitless silence for nothing but wind, sun & bird song

twelve to midnight

would my use of language be queried as characterizing one dispossessed
greeted by 'we are english', man, woman, or child there is no one to ask.
senses locked, implying intelligence as one that interprets & articulates them.

a quieter place which jolts a memory of being slapped, & lying under the bed
with a book. Tyranny is nothing to brag about. Victory seethes, bed springs make dull music.

as rivers flow by brown industrial landscapes a mattress fell over a fall.
they don't know. there is no such thing as common intelligence. there is no intelligence.
there's an anti-fascism and an anti-semiticism and that is all. anything
i did wrong was potentially anti semitic. anything. i could not speak.
treated as a walking joke. family lore. i grew consciously

stunted, seated on the bottom step whenever they called to visit us.
struggling home from school with stomach ache, reluctancy at its limit. No God.
Yes God. And never breathe 'maybe' because it presents a sexual possibility.
And I won't talk. And i won't talk. And i won't talk. So i watched it.

as it was being played. i replaced all the receivers which were left dangling.
calk if you like calk caltanissetta it is impossible to ask a question based on a stated premiss
that without a palette art exists in a lively though elusive manner
the risks of surrendering too experiential
if you like chalking on stone the truth has always a point not two
i didn't scratch stars onto a stone floor with the heels of my shoes

i had no shoes. my feet were filthy from walking on city pavements.
they were walking to italy. to caltanissetta. for the colour of
twinkling sulphur. could not be explained as a lemonade frock
locked shamefully away from dress to a doing nothing but dancing
that feeling contorted to an old nothing wrong, time unpunctured

by positioning he must have had fun. there is no room for
anything to be taken from. mine was mind. long roads up into the
mountains in the centre of a city where a plum tree was
tantamount to an indiscretion. a clutch of chapters follows on the
subject of religion, for that racial stigma that has congratulated the
most lofty minded of litterateurs into semi-conscious blood libel.
for hands held apart in sheffield.

Silk & Wild Tulips

Afraid of my father's power the object speaks country does it concurr
Entering this petrification, perforce the accident is indicative it is
A report, repeated pondering fall, a petition, a portrait I would not bear
A portrait of throated wires through blood
It is demanded of me that I die having neglected my duty.

I read of women who have been found disregarding class, the heavy book
Bearing the sombre tone, we anyway tremble whilst we are broken down.
What is love? o what is love? the tip of a tongue, a silk white dove.
that will not fight and is crushed by speculation, a sinful breast
Cleansed, the surprising lightness in weight, the emphasis returned to
Provokation, that is the dead weight, that we cannot speak until spoken to
And divided by omission are invited to attend to the traffic signals, obsessively
Indicating slips, don't for one second imagine that I am in the least oppressed.

Prussian myzi, if only I could wait for your magnesium blue to hover
stone by stone over the shark finned ground, resonations floor me
I am told that I have reinvented my history, these fakes that have
Drifted by desire rather than by noble patriotic inclination, to be told this
Frozen kiss is a parasite berry that grows and governs our merriment
That we fall to habitude unaged & are given brown cloaks for mourning
To circle the lotus that catches the tip of the dragonfly's wing
And burning it into fruition find an exhaust pipe carved in braille
The war continues to charr the air with shot speech,
Theses are buried or placed on parole for comparing the language of war & of peace

We are old with the sound of horsehair, the most beautiful poems speak to us
Yet we know they were written in the wrong country at the wrong time
When poets were forced to cross borders despite euphorbia
Unknown by date and place, the ocean resented them when uttered
A mumbled ocean slapped to make an eternally recorded impression
When we slapped the ocean the beach was too large for reality
And petty dictatorship of relative supernity returns to the bearer
that streaks green across black meadows sky scumbled blue quaternity

the reduction by not first dissolving perhaps never dissolving
what change has no time to name its causes, its reasons
for not reading paintings as though they were rule books,
Believing themselves to be needy some make a lifetime of need
That can be expected to fall by the covers of contentment
And settling that, progress through a sequence of tranquil passages
Minute squares some crossed some kissed by stars and shells
Open'd by background loss, closed by measured step,
Around the fountain the old men slept, the women deep in the heart of roses rouges foncés,
And the chimney sweeps wept until they discerned that their tears had created ink
To tell of squares of blue & finely pointed moons, silhouetted cats' upturned tails
Catching at the lunatics they promised the coals would glow
Memories of tail coats arranged around angel pie & a tankard of stiff pheasant feathers.

*

by gardenias i cannot telephone
am excluded by the young racist
who cuts wires but won't run from me
so that i can stay with these gardenias
where voices fall pull down my colours
using race to materialize my gardenias
into shivering apologies for absence
a clever poetess would flee i am a potato
my clothes are made of potatoes
and you expect me to leave these gardenia clouds
that become blue for my chalk face
is greeting a pink too true to be lilac
too white to be fading too scarey to be stem
of tulip in the deafening scrim
yellow silk your heart darkens

concilia.

eyelash once eleven jonquil cibachromed en route
washington vacuous quay point sizzling palermo
messages visited square bank ochre charged by bolt
magnet, curtsey, falling out, back room rat:
white sliced delivery, spanish cake shop windows,
tiled frames fused infantry, grille, behind a face
a ransacked library, daubings, bricked out.
descriptive psychology dents & is reinforced
unglobed throat. fascistic debasement à la mode
grained in wheaten filings, securely modern ode.
to a river, refusing filtering piston'd sing, verge
it is not the thing it is the representation of the thing
the idea as god and gods and not a sensible sense of what could
cohere without damaging itself, as an idea. not to be
cheapskated, for personal reasons, learning excludes sex
if hell is another's sky, it was an obedient moment.
sanctioned who is not the licentiate of magister logos.
reactionary creation of familiar narrative, self serving.
tempting to embarrass and then dress in embarrassment
remarking in copyright ISBN'd on fictionalized naked emotion
encouraged dulcamente to change that to terror, scattered,
shadows, behind a hammed production of a national condition.
speechless, open mouthed, tongueless fish.   Felicitations.

*

She Walked where she should have stood still, stock still.
or edging slightly, morose, if not moribund and there
she stood too far from the yorkist, to be of much use
she knelt by the casement it took her ages
her legs were too long they had been part sawn off
it was cheaper than extending the length of her rest
but he waited, as only the dead could.

the day it was dull and as silent as dullness
without any breeze to lend to this nullness
numbly did old Flem bleed with a fullness
to blench oaken gall into satin and all
the works at Tyre were appointed to dress
sixteen pieces of what were the best
crimson modules, to be routed, by errantine hergest.

finja and minja were chomping on apples
not yet incorporated into the box
break time was over, short break as always,
they continued to whiten the winnings of hergest
and that is why, lambkins, to this very hour
in the even grey drab uneventful power
when your energy overbrooks the salt will go dour…

*

Using the second person singular
definite article may be profitable
but not for the bearer of the grammatical appellative,

it is not profitable for the one who is pushed
& goes flying on the flagstones
& has to apologize for causing an event

forever unprofitable tears stream
with age flood logic, in salty water
through whirling galaxies, romans' dances,

fireworks, unachieved circles high above
gabriele münter has a nervous collapse
and the telescope reminiscent falls closed

when there is the danger of
poems being swapped for bitter lemons.

*

Feminized, although not without dissent
cut down in the blossoming once
was studied over decades,

too wealthy to be semblant, apparently
the street air withholds the brush
against newspapers blowing onto b/w

paintings, kicked in by bright young things
look and look again for a deviation
from a lesson in painting objects

to contain sight, buried deep in detail
the red cabbage, newsprint, a lamp,
brave review, a window onto the unseen

and love that does not know how to know
making swift meals of tall women.

*

should he have been,
to go, he has a long time ago
been & gone, are you plural sure

that it was not one of several
in the end, dye too, mulberry,
blackcurrant, the violated bank

down either side streaming
in perfect pitch, sewing up
the stuffed bear, taxonomist

on a foggy morning, hoot,
he had three, two, where his ears
once were, white, fast moving

faster than it could be dug
smaller than the vision from beyond.

*

prove it! out of the blue
oranges tumbled
elevating grey
tarmac from the moon
reminding harlequin of a plaice
youth had rendered on dry land

*

palanquin beneath harlequin
offering comfort for the homeward ride
eking out a living
teased a cave from stone
ricocheting over found the
yale's horns soldered into a key

*

podcast variation
opening an evening's
enervating wafered blanks
threaded through leisure
rated by strain
yelve in hand for rapid construction

*

peasblossom nestled
on strands of
ergonomic
thistledown
regal in her minute
yeshiva dagesh

*

parme, abricot et violette
octobre, quoiqu'ilnourrisepar un mois
enquiquinéeauprès du
tatoviever et sachambre de fer
rhendait, l'emplois des cirques un
yatagan au dessus de la tête

*

polling
œstrogen
emblazoned embossed
think tanks over
rural retirement units
yarrow fading

*

perfectly numerate
ofsted refused to comment when the
establishment switched to
tizer for its dyed
rhinoceros tusk
y-chromosome colour

*

portrait in ink
œcumenical platter
electric punk
tremendously ivanovitch
riding a rare
yoyo on the go

*

poise does not come into it
on leave in
every spacey wine bar
they float around
released centre-forwards
yunnder boosting

*

photographs of snow
on mountains
explain our suffocation
tugged hard
reflecting identification
yarn strapped into fluorescent jackets

*

personally weighted in sterling pounds
ordinarily saved for potatoes
endive, sauerkraut, fresh dates
tagged with prices in arabic numerals
roving direct measurements, of cheese, of pickles,
york minster's stained glass could not compete.

*

peaches in the forgotten orchard
oiled lamps for the night which illuminated them
each blushing
tamed for biting into
rich juicy flesh:
your branch leafed address

*

palomapolperro
Olmec mesh
Empfindlichkeit
Trabazon
Rainbow trout
Yippee

*

pendragon in purdah
ogles
Ermintrude's scholarly
telegrammatic pause in a
ring of
yellow moon

*

Pillbox hat
Ormesd'hiver
Early riser
Temperate sea
Romy Schneider
Yggdrasil

*

Power has a temper, pranksters abound
œufs,
églefin œuvres
the finest final supper flashed out
restoration pillar pilloried
"Yonnondio": Tillie Olsen.

*

pegs
out
eagles' nests
teeming with
rain in the back
yard

*

pomerainian intimacy
overdone in the long term
emanation scowled at abbreviated society
spotting spare sponge
intelligible, exciting, harmless, obscure being
eating words

*

phizzing on
opening
enormous energy
tumbling
radio
years

*

primrose pink
omoplates
eel border decoration
simple wriggly,
intoxicating,
easter egg

*

pale purple
œil d'oiseau
every other day
socking it to oedipus
impertinently
enclosing olives

*

prescription in colours decided on
or artificially lumped
ecstasy intensely gushing a
trace of the meaning of moving in air
reserved by the interconnected investigators
yelling out blasting instance

*

passive in nominal negociation
oven showrooms and wallpaper evenings
emanate a peculiar masculine language
taped to fox over certainty
retractable signatures natal
yucatan leading the dance

*

Pepper pot full
Ornately spotted in
Earthly tonal bursts
Times by technical physicians'
Rhinestoned mirth
Ying selah

*

Pitcher crooked hangs stilled
onions in neon dressing room bulbs
err on the side of wall porcelain
timed to expect to hear this day
rest in half in one in two
your sacramental

*

prisoners-of-war
only an unending one
erudite in legalities
torn democrats swilled into sewage
reeks the hypocrisy of use
you who froze them melted then froze

*

Perpendicular marble piece
Overseas surveillance
Eliminating trihedrons
Tall timid excursions
Raven haired and ravished
Yew gloomy by nature

*

tapestries

carpets

French

Cultural

Delegation

Sonia Delaunay

collage

South Kensington

wall in

avoid wall

well

wool

facing

gesichtlicht

*

wallow 'tis of swallow

willow

grow.

"hostage" is a famous american artwork

from 1969

famous enough?

famous in an intelligent way

famous from birth

requiring nothing

& 2 bent rest to each bar

a barre to carry

to a home

to practise

high kicks

from

silence

*

Total rejection
  to feel sorry for Him
  silently,
  not for agreement.

I was born there
    born with a trumpet
    a flügelhorn born blind
she was a poetess
I pretended that I was a potato
Our farm had been taken away
tucked our fields under the arms

of the poor artists
    drawings of charcoal
       and ink
    went on to compose Quartets
            named
                 swallows.

*

I have only 'some interest'

in writing,

but I am not interested

in –

Ezra Pound

and the Cambridge

Competition

◊

forcing the concrete from the mouth

(HER mouth) whereas it is in her

HAAR (Hair)

(the mystery mister put it there)

THENEN

HEN MEN LAMP POST PESTEN TEN

*

The wall unintended

in the

dining

room

The wall

closest

to the kitchen

the balloon

energy

kiss

hug

shadow

boat

*

his shadow was there

  it watched me

with its elbows

  what would you know?

              or want to?

these youngsters are not us.

and later – will they be – fascists.

they don't seem to WANT to know

It was worse than Terrible

enough to mean that I would Never marry

            Never to marry was Death

I am auditioning for

            "Death and the Maiden"

                    permanently.

*

and the grasses

the fields

the life.

the birdies singing,

the birdies' song,

in the trees

in the fields,

the flowers,

the life.

sand soft

For J. H. Prynne.

Ay. finer than a biro, quieter than a trembling bruise
Lived the slighted poet whose splinter I removed
To silent damson wireless perfo interludes
In whose absent presence with endless faith
The dark & sudden river found a vellum face.

in the minority of one

a

she would talk forever her body slobby she had been caught, slobby
she was stunned
another death of hers no one else she was killing each of the
people they told her she was
she was not addressed as one she was told she was plural, you
(pl), they said, you (pl).

b

pluie she would, fight for a touch of the drizzling rain, in those
days they locked it out,
she told the time, she tied her own laces, she walked out with
her notebook & sketching paper.
she a low-brained slob, they said. & her body slobby. Go steal, Go
Propriate –

c

or was it expropriate. Her light went out. she was caught in a
house. it belonged to the local council.
she was plain, dressed by a quakeress, hemline below the knee, she
liked her books.
she was not armed with aggressive retorts, her hands were an
artist's. her piano was 189 miles away.

d

it fell to her to suffer. if she died too bad. she can't remember
the pain in her mind wrapped her skull tightly.
she had to lay down. they said fight for murderers. fight for
thieves defend your strangler.
there were too many people to fit into her, but not hers any
longer, she had to be girthed.

e
were they her parents? Oh no, though they would not believe it,
they were the great who disliked
their great fat paws & claws came pulling, what were her levels
of tolerance of primitivity
none. totally horrified, wringing her disgust into exploration
of christian culture she was vague.

f
could only give what she had away for nothing, was this the
jubilance of jesuitry that searched
for gold that the child out of her care was made to go searching
for treasure, we were not
pirates. she was kidnapped onto another boat. a friend's life cut
out by a motorbike

g
crashing. there were no happy times, one, found briefly by
Holland Park, a school to her left.
quiet. street. sun. sunday. should he chase her again were she
to sprint where were her papers, her merleau ponty
she had to have something, she could not have nothing, she moved
very carefully.

h
crashed her skull. was swimming in the sun, what were there no
responses was it general
no one could be delicate north then, it was story time, she
doesn't want to talk anymore.
why did she talk then? They were trying to structure her
responses. shift her away from poetry.

i
“holy dying” she recognised the shape of the interior & is still
continually petrified of being evident.
they hated here & i don’t. & didn’t. i know but there are other
things, buildings & distances.
i was not identified by self. this is why women should stop
accusing me. i can’t stand emotional wrangling.

j
i don’t like power and don’t want it. i just don’t suffer fools
gladly. but who was i to denounce them?
In the minority of one. That is how it will ever be. Stop whipping
up advances to victory. Hurt.
Symbols don’t apply. Cut me dead as often as you want to. Tactics
are not cross hatchable.

k
The children of quakers run from everywhere afraid of being human
and meaning focused upon with what fury will rarely be told and
remains untold, for she was goodness my mother herself
stripping down in preparatory fever for the move from dungeon to
cell. and the sole novel, quite conscious.

l
was the one that no one should read who does not wish to be
convulsed with the legible guilt of folly.
away round the entrance to the gulf into which the daughter of
Phaidon was harried,
in case she wrote an inadequate reflection of the disappointment
that was her creation.

m

the wutherings shared. i don't know enough to write. It is as bad as writing anything recognizable.
how could you. how could you. (in a temper) ruin everything so dreadfully Mine.
You didn't care. They were Your people. You could target through every life.

n

I don't understand you. I don't understand. No one is going to be dead.
But to turn on me later & to pull me to pieces, a bullet audibly hurtling through my head

o

You can love mysteriously all of this was closed to me, one is profoundly photographed by language.

1986 OCTROI

I hate athleticism because of the laughter. I love dancing and that is my leap.
I live in the air with no music for my limbs must not move I am told.
My arms must not move. My hands must be still. I must learn not to
Speak of love for my children. Love is not the point I am told. It is
Something else. Is it my armpits I wonder. Yet they are odourless.
Is it my nose? It was broken on a bus. A broken nose does not lead
To a broken bridge. When Simone de Beauvoir passed away –
My life passed away with her. Chernobyl. I remember cancelling the milk.
People work for peace in the middle of wars. I was too old.
I was old and gnarled and misshapen. I had resisted.
How much does a writer let pass in the world around her?
At what point does one intervene? In Emergencies.
Is one heeded? No. Is one respected? Never. Is one remembered? Rarely.
But every life saved is one murder less. There is no Mathematic.
But people do not know everything about how I guarded my children's lives.
And neither shall they. Our franchise came at an awkward time.
I was not sure that I wanted to leave my brothers behind.
But to be called a beggar. No. I have never begged from a man who didn't
Want a child. No. But I could have done had I treated my children like puppets
To hit over the heads of those mysterious creatures who crept into my life.
I thought long and hard about how to earn an honourable income.
Long and Hard. This is a Stiff country. We have to wait to be Told.
Told what? That we were eight years old when our Father left the Communist Party?
Yet even that distance in time was not good enough, was not long enough.

POEM.

writing cramped up
rain pouring down
  enclosing lost love
  inexpressible

without a position
being only human
I, having great faith
in my own humanity.

have not been loved
and am not good at
being immobile

in Paris I could dance
like I used to dance
but at first my body
kept falling over

so, I kept trying.
to make it serve me
by concentrating.
on the relationship
between my arms and legs

I walked for hundreds
  of footsteps
  up hilly streets
stretching this hurt spine.
  with its sexless history
whose nerves extend
  to the earth's core
where the iron people live
  in eternal darkness.

this pen won't write:
they say that my angel
    AMAPOLA
is indestructible
for she is not poisonous.

call to linnet rock.

1. a they.

would have sent the police after her
calling her back, "them the poets, you the worker"
in the afternoons, "afternoons are for working"

had sent the army to collect her
she was by the sea "you should have been working"
she wrote I shall not be returning to school

public relations sorted this out
her mother was good at P.R. the League of Nations fantasist.
it's the use of metaphor in everyday life.

& how much they can take
before the equivalence to function is entertained:
psychiatry and books on nervous breakdown

she walks wrapped up a line of print behind glass
unrecoverable units, a curve, a metallic, two or three
capital letters standing for no time all must be
reified ace. party line the daughters of the politicians

must work without metaphor minds on line
but never do better than the pedestal must win
this one lets poetry cut her throat & cannot hedge
out of line before all the procedures are gone through
there is no pointing out you see it was better for me

in France at fifteen I didn't miss you but I was too kind
"you a danger to society kind" "do you do know who their mother is"
oh well you are doing the right thing. i cannot talk to you.

or any of you if you are a they you & there are so many
they yous when you do they yous too could you at least say
that you are not really a they you and mean it instead of making contacts
with the army and the police and the paper rag tats in

a prowling grey gooseberry brush over peruvian peony.

2. time

squeezing social computer services solicitors in negotiation tap.
the man waving his arms in enthusiasm over where it has been
suggested to me is my root, a niggardly home-bred thing,

They, my hundred thing, and these are not gravestone graffiti artists,
all "those useless books", all "those privileged libraries"
idiots at everyperson's invitation. There is not a they you whose eyes

are safe to regard least of all "now look at me straight"
um um do ddo yyou would you could i cccould
i say scallop. scalloped edge but leave it at that.

that man would have been told to remove his arms
waving as they were Egypt and next week Jericho
"I am trying to talk to you about how suitable you are".

The Gong.

  oh Lazy Socialiste
  Lazy Lady Socialiste
  wrapping the sun yellow bandana
round your masses of hair

oh addled Socialiste
mooning into dark green water
what on earth are you doing,
talking to fish in their lair?

oh parasite poetess
with your curved quill
are you practising falcon talk –
are you ILL?

problematic dreamy Poetess
your ears were within their shot
you were deaf?
(and daft) (and a swot).

a mild-mannered swot came walking
she knew not whither nor where
the morning was her awning
the evening her despair

she had been asked to depart
from a 'Black Dwarf' household
for folding too many poems
into her blue satin jeans

escorted to a more suitable household
and that's where they got her – There.

Oh tangerine organdie poetess
your walls deep rust in the afternoon,
the Aztec tree blowing over
the sudden death of a friend from Dover

inscrutable diva of song.
infuriating sarong.
tranquillity fond.
THEIR Living Wrong.

A Crash

There is silence and silence,
yet still the sense screams
almost emptily
that, is that hope? that almost, fortuitous almost, or

is the listener invented and lasts as long
whose left ear is my ear

and admonitions, were they? yet only thinking of one phrase,
smudged by tears,

the intolerance of incompetence,
a mere judgement of another,
perpetually beating my heart into self-disgust at what i am incapable of

such as, playing the piano,
falling back into a range of explanations,

smudged by tears, gasping at the poverty,
the stench, the wearing in of sympathy
as a social obligation,
to remind my forebears i cared,

if it interested them? who knows what hidden intentions,
not even known,
swimming on the ceiling in a land all alone,
that kicking at dust,

a curb,
a house,
a foreigner

inescapably enmeshed in bleary feeling
sending candles to the sky
lighting them in wild storms

those million hopes for knowing
amounting to a love of
starched in retrospect,
catching a past which shudders

never whole heartedly,
caught with sunken feet

rigid in quicksand
arms aching with gratuitous necessity

dusty lettuce
a shocking green

door after door
screams persisting

and a heavy heart
altogether pulped

nothing done
with a meaning sustained

simply sheared phrasings
which do not grow

a blunt driven edge
too hard for the impulse will move a phantasy

forgotten in insufficient wit for knowledge
preferring irrefutably
securing indubitable separation

in an unchartable wayward world
wind created, rescued, crushed

an unreal reality chewing sounded
sounding despicable, unforgiveable, understandable.

the cliff.

i was subjected
to an alfred hitchcock mentality.
surrounded by people
who took horror less seriously
than do i.

at the faintest suggestion of violence
i crack into action to prevent it.

i played fast.

and have still not heard the last of it.

*

real does not know
just is
words are tired from describing
images
moving
past is a mirror child breathes
on and wipes away
a satellite passing moon

inspiration is a fusion   a moment
dying from description

shadow stares at light

words still autumned into rivers of
thought
river speaks
                    tree also

the eyes with silence
our hands of wooden flame with
cardboard flowers and cut-out bombs
it is Dream that suffers
                              that cells range
growth the cancer of despair
bitter powders
and 'the pure intellect'

> 'The technical director of a leading
> wordprocessor company said to managers;
> (man agers) "Your secretary will be
> required to be more productive.
> There will be no more walking, talking,
> thinking or dreaming."

anger spatters ashes with consummation
            the meaning
                              within
                                        no meaning

all games are called psychology   war
                                                    sex
                                                    video

walking is to make poetry
            poetry is emptying the page and filling
               its space in continuous motion
                  of breath
                     Breath is paradise. Breath knows all
we hide from with smoke

beyond exposed nerve
signals of an economy
we are computered with 'race memory'
a bull blind to glassware
the crystal of consciousness
we divide by atoms a people without
weapons who grew
                           too few
     and inherit mounds weathered to the womb
            of Tao
                     raised to essence   forgotten

huMANity who is now five
supplicating defiant breasts

       "they push buttons all day and feel
        women that way"

            MANity 'dressed to kill' in sunday
              brightness invents disease and

prays that Pandora is seductable
to a megaton mushroomed penis

but

as Jacob's camel sat on a needle
so Buddha's eyelids grew tea

Tea is without class
Tea knows the rush of typing pools
the terror of shock
the thunderous awakening

Tea is peasant honoured by tranquillity
Tea is blood of factories

does the poet listen as the painter
observes blindness
who sucks the nipple of
space
in 'The Battle 0f Love'
not Buddha or Boddha or Boodly-woo
will meet the road slain jogger's
cereal packet knife act
without laughter that fills
Cosmos with butter-flies of
punk-tuition
or the stripes of Malevo and Cocana
in cities of Tango the dancing spider
and thumb crushed cans
the grunts of quadrophonic micro stunts
avoid froid
avoid Freud
void reveals form
"oi" reveals norm

To You, Italy.

Dark Glances
sideways mirrors,
longer
slip through
optic thinness
illusion
you see one
you are reading “aleatory”
who is moving
yet illusion,

  a white mask with black eyes,
several combinations of structure,
Dark Glances
survive,

but the fortress is barred,
suspended in air,
as dark as earth

who is it that can be
air transfigured into tentative hands
that thought makes so threatening,

ugly, oppressive, deathly destructive,
the strangler who knocks

who knocks harder,
yet who strokes
grazing the fortress (with a flick of dust
brushed by a finger)
that pokes out eyes
before its mouth pulps them
both at once.

   but we don't want to be just normally
in case we become uncontainable comics
& animals, bewitched by our bodily functionings.

these are things from the north
there is little point in looking

Dark Glances
catch a vertical bar
it could have been backgrounded
by an eau-de-nil sun
one river refuses to be turned
& the sand banks were excavated
with picks shovels & egg spoons
you will (soon) learn of that jungle
which appears shorn
the dry tree sticks too,
smile at old age.

mostly silence on our part,
dominus.

scraping the flesh off the floor
in a burnt building.
root by root
toes capped in rubber
twitching claws
beasts the length of the avenue
bits of this & that
mildly smiling behind a white face
sweetly singing syllabic soul.

To You, Italy. II.

the background tore
earth unknowing
that settles in cat's mire,
autumn plunging
sour food.

fourteen hundred of them
smiling in the eye
standing side by side
on a mound
crushing the sound
of arm wrenchers.

Evil to tug
better remove the rusted shrapnel
which gives fish such strange faces.
swallows on leads,
they have flown
to flutter & scurry
in the excavations
tied up in a mangle
with mud & dust
pinching ripped sneakers
well I think it's
a ticket stream
mostly rose madder,
mostly their cannisters,
mostly

moxed metaphor

it's forbidden.
you have to forget.
love is a sin
knowledge is evil

unless you want
sex.

when it is wanted.
they want to know
no other science
only a foe.

fi fi fum
you're a gopher.

your golf ball gave you away
drooped as it is at the base of your gullet
vogel fly away.

Thesaurus
477 Sophistry: false reasoning
N. sophistry, illogicalness, illogic; feminine logic.
476 (sic) intuition, sophistical reasoning, false reason., fallacious reasoning
specious reasoning., evasive reasoning., rationalisation., double think.,
self-deception., mental reservation, arrière penser.

*

nit freaks
flea foam
scrummage
sore rope
fortress yukon
pony there
newt point
solange throat
channel hide
treaty boar
high wall

low

    journey

    norwegian

should

friendly

    distant

tyrewriter

and as he whispered; 'you're wonderful'
they came in & chanted: 'she's not'.

the z was ash
cld be N
laid diagonally
des que

THE PROGRAMME
THE PROGRAMME
(into dramatic zen)

wide sweep
earth hull

farthing gay
out on snowdrops

impatience receded
findalio.

Appendix

crystal love. D.N.A.

destiny forecast revolt   the blue night's murmur
relating to other forces   a dangled hand.
Below the light; rage design
On beds   no heads
farther from sound
detail.
melancholy might answer in future mistakes
the wind bears no answer.
destiny forecast.
Machiavelli strikes
His hammer
gold notch
time?
8081 that's 2p a go.
coffers wait
grow old in Carlyle museum.
Paths traced
Surgical instruments
the first chemist:mind you.

Demirel Camp

But you never do anything.

Macdonald's into Turkey
Never go back
Spatial Differentiation
relies on words
Women think about love.

*

closed gates
happy families make lovels
houses incapacitate further
ACTION HORSES
No Conjunction   Red lights are fading.
into the follow up
'Kiss Her Goodbye'
 You only count what you miss.

*

The matter of the matter hard to solve in the language of languators.

In between five fingers the variation of three.

*

Speak judgement into ear
hear the rail:
Believe to be true.
You will live forever down
my drained brain.
Snare on subtlety.
Unite to crash:
No surrender.
Mighty portion of the land:
My night is pouring gold.

So then what are we going to do? Are we going to subject too?

Before the settles are created which is hopeful
 declining Hope as being either too empty or
pointless, which falls short by far must
roll out with the servant, secular, mysterious
a quietus graces footsteps, an horrific slammed door:
Their commands in the form of suggestions
stuffed out of ears which impatiently foreshorten
Whichever, although less loosely, interpretation
ushers in the rejection of a stone thinker
but that is wrong, entirely, a mere conceit,
a past regret over the foisted vision of perspex
Rather than statuesque antiquity within
the by now secret meanderings of a poetess
who is not to be pasted before the suffix is equalized
harmonically, chromatically, counterpointedly –
and those other guesses, the ones which fitted onto the plate
a final, ingratiating sprig in an extra second's contemplation,
and those other guesses which were of no concern,
apart from being buried before tonight's
stony return to a muffled passage, a static future
in a fairly fair & square way, waiting for the
Inorganic replacement to intangibly emit.
She sneers at herself, her temperature rises,
for her inability to make decisions constitutes
Severe doubts as to whether happiness is her due
Although thought be possible in concert,
had the Tree been touched in duo, had her impetus
not been refuted for the mission of short-term destruction
when a denuded rock was grudgingly bestowed upon her
for gratuitously weaving shadows around
in that acknowledging moonlight, her insanity insured,
to plunge recklessly as nature's drama into their creation
of poetess, the singular word, which was not in actuality
Before or beyond a thin material reality & that simply
a reconditioned bike which had more prescience than

a thousand fresh-planted violets and delphiniums on slopes
by the train carriage window speeding blue sea.
Waiting for the inorganic replacement to side-step accusative,
hovering on the edge of hilarity, any logical connective
to fend off admonitions, adornments strictly regulated,
checking down an agenda of characteristics, the only
been there because led like a sheep, "like a lamb to the slaughter,"
so a side-line desire for the minimal peace will it last
wedged between but, stepping down, an ineffable queen,
a desertion of rôle encompassing total & fleshly antiquity
nibbles, crams, goes cross-eyed is shocking,
studies tumours for their beauty in red martyrdom wash,
lacks force of character, is annulled for repetition,
is complexed with a sense of historical flux,
as though intended to reap the oceans of pity, audienced by
hidden mockers, cows in the cornfields, sign posts
switched, anything, Anything other than
the next target, in that shapeless morass of horror,
and the odd thousand mourners encapsulated
out of a pen and ink choice, some denied rite of passage,
voices rise in Hosanna, as washing drags heavily on a wet morning
Launderette-wise, that anti-clock schema,
castles in Spain, hemingway's bludgeoned brainsnaps
startling a slow journalese into holding to a breast
that gone, gone, gone, as they stomped, stomped, stomped
as they viciously de admiracion skewer their aggressors
who is this bemused, disconcerted, impersonal meanderer
who is she but the negative's bewitching?

*

the meringue sang high
as the tunnel turned pink
& the man in the rafters
vanished in a twink.

*

One rushes another is described as behaving abnormally
One cared and is described as inopportunely hostile.
One is dedicated and described as plotting to overthrow the state.
Where the reality of this is and its exact nature
for it does exist this recto to verso to recto

post exilic and for you, if he and the others are shady
on your receiving end on the receiving end of you
with the stiffening preservative consciousness
that, apart from not being a replica of Bulwer Lytton,
we will go and make a mess somewhere else

as he kicked the square to pieces
for the sake of the sight of the chips

women afflicted can be nasty we were fine women
who would not be slapped or pushed with impunity.
men who have sunk themselves into us have stood up
in the court of the law of this land have stood up
  and declared us to be mad bullies, thugs & extortionists
  and the law has listened congratulating them eloquently.

some of us do not believe that we exist
so that when we are addressed we are listening
listening to words intended for those who do.

and sometimes we are listening to words
words which are not intended for us.
so that we leave as we always do
leave listening to conversations between others
who knowing each other far better cannot cease
their conversations continuing no matter who is there.

a strong man can take words
a strong man does not resort to petty tactics.
a strong man knows how people live.
a strong man lives.
even if his shoulders are hunched over his work
or he is walking over a bridge
or he is pausing on a high road
to watch the passing people.

*

non-existencies.

this was a student of poetry,
who was reading,

my name was far behind me
it was not what I was reading

mine was a poetry of reading
my letters have been lost

the best letters are those from a distance
an imaginary landscape is lost.

when you approach a poet
she does not want your abuse

I read here 'crossing the frozen river poems'
I want you to understand the pain caused me
by left wing ignorance of what poetry implies.

*

my spine was hurting
as I lay there wasting away
a life I wanted to experience
intelligently & kindly
or not unkindly

politics, prison, authoritarianism,
closed frontiers to particular races,
geographical politics, lack of money,
 and that dreadful body
 so difficult to forget
 and the endless fuss
 about sex.

so that words became ingrained
  into the body and no one could describe
  a girl with ingrained words, as an intellectual.

no-one did.   that was male reason
which I was perfectly objective about.

*

all over one bloody old pianna
if this one bites // that knocks out if, the derivatory exposition,
once too bears a weight & find no friend who will act
old secret thoughts of where to be engrained into community
say relatively little, the old can ask less, & ask for less protection
  would not have been   dilemma's move had she shown some courtesy
  iron triangles lock and key, padded cell & tortured me
  for one fair look on a hot summer's day of a civvy street commander

madame provokes. some things are strange. strangeness remains.
for which I am not capitulating as what would it be but an ego
like thee, epicist, epicist, epicist.   from here to there is a boat from Laoghaire
the moaning is poverty in my memory, not that its past, now not too fast,
but that is the speed of desire, see. & my desire is full of sight
of distances & choppy water. how it sinks, the laptodermatist –
or is she a toxologist, she fills my boots with lead, my body too,
  it's the voice of my demise, locked. free thinking is disliked.
we terminate our conversation. dead rats stink, it's an old russian trick,
  dead animal by the jew's life.

I, who once was beautiful, of spirit, if not of face, did long to trust
one man in circumstances less fraught with power's retribution.

what madame does not appreciate is that it can be a strain to
teach a child how to be a decent fair minded human being
when everything around her tells her of her own deprivation.
decomposition.

I don't know how the sexes get on with each other.
that is how my mother would answer my dilemma.
but mothers are not eternal & neither are they oracles.
also there is a less controlled urge to push me into
sex which makes me resist. I needed looking after
by someone who cared for me. not someone who
was feeding me dope or wanting sexual favours.

and not my own parents either who could not but
help severing me from the world at large. guilt induced
by severity

I have a right to think of my standards of life too.

we hear the depression of our fathers' lives.
we hear their condemnation of the profit motive.
we cannot turn this into fashionable écriture.
our moneyed friends will have done so much more to help.
those who were born without their brains being resisted and, worse fear, resented.

*

& one day, when we were working
we could hope to live a full life
but because this was made impossible
life might as well be a joke
one hopes it is now understood
that reticence does not fall short
of a principled greater good.

*

between us
and the world
came nothing

nothing
comes
between us

I don't agree
with men
who desert
their wives
and children
for other
women

down the back
of his jacket
ran round buttons

down the back of a lesson
pulled a garment
touched my shoulder
    to awake me

*

and being led dissociate
devoid from balm concert
who spiritus where now
and was it there this time of year
a tiger moth for crow
that was the future and the past
or was it either this
is far far there eyes caught
by prayer for chasing raining shrub
who told the name the thought was hurt
as silence can no answer sprent
oh you do too   yet not a sound
for nature has resistances
and caught fair hands beneath a clamp
of various inconsistencies
on surface fell upon a well
and vanished down to basement hell
morality fears full censorship
of what is still extant
in brochures and in picture books
of corpuscles with pruning hooks
and flaming forks and briney brooks
i don't know what nature is
a clean tramp by the door
back propped against a whitewashed wall
[free movement]
visiting from another place
a couple hundred yards from the beach

the fourteenth flight. (*early draft*)

indiscernible possessed what it flattered flew uplight across confusion deliberately
whether circular pounded out whole relives a generally ongoing disapproval of
prohibition on any vision which might without ever giving the chance, prove
an oddity's mind does not have to be grounded before the establishment
can either change or be no more yet nothing else was clarified, no firm points
made around which further discussion could be held – I commune with the Dead
although they may have accused me of copying, charged me with fraud or
lascivious behaviour, although my skull is constricted & my long flowing sentences
rapidly turned into sentencing full of legal acrimony for what i fail to understand

wanting to write undetected by the lasers, exposed by the lasers, the floodlit pitch, one more sweep over the Cities,
hugging Das Kapital in Berwick-on-Tweed I have to congratulate the wrong answer, but there must be an explanation
which releases this agony of petulant harassment grating eyes into slivers of aluminium point reflectors
ontologically carolling fire sticks on seminal autocracy the name won't deliver the button box unrecognizable
girl's encouragement suggestion supportive brain generous for no selfish interest flaring peaceful colours
in watery grains why do you think of factories, collusion, and mysterious pockets of energy
as this inaccurate incongruity closes with powers temporal beat we meet: set pieces.
set pieces you recognize as being the cultural organisation as yet unclarified & therefore unavailable
it sounds, some spacious time voice and it lowers itself onto the boardwalk each dawn

in all guises of backward movement it avoids the centralised spectre of an electrified rigid force
which won't move to be searched and won't be slapped to be called horse and won't purr for pussy
and will give you a few lessons as to how to conduct yourself in court that is if you declare yourself
helpless in the face of publicity. where are your notebooks? why don't you write? why did you declare
yourself to be friend? were you in need of help? if so why did you rob me? had you been instructed
by the purveyors of a cult to show your whiteness through my forests where your bulldozers smashed
without even a john steinbeck turned into a reactionary with that utterly banal rejoinder they all do
to follow a let's play wyned down without further explanations of this is how we do why do, this loud
extra interest in an eventuality prescripted from a distorted version of suddenly last summer.

yes we could Say it like you but we don't want to and why should we repeat this is how we were taught
and you were good little girls it's only an excuse for further spiking some minor injury quickly

remedied with out all the startling flurry of what your cabinets have to offer in the way of
needles and lock-ups and strip cells and padded jackets which would serve a judo breakfast
beating back buckled belted in nails lipsticks palisades a full morning falls from the string

the imaginative faculties are in the grips of prosecutors who can gear them any way they need
to secure their convictions so unconvicted are they we share a lack of conviction. a hopelessness
which the accused are often more ready to admit to than are their persecutors, and where does the pounding
come from if not from an economic system in some small trouble with some few straightenings in circumstance.
and will they go down? oh no, they won't go down. they will win as the good book says
with their greed and their trimmings and their fine fine lives they will win by, in the first to the last resort, shooting

It's a trapping tactic to deem a sister writer's ego the motivating force regard the I along and around
a few decades of various locations distributed between solitude and social participation.
a sentient being who sensed antagonism from more serious-faced dissenters whose conversational exchange
was more cognisant of its own creation although I would not resist the general direction
but really knew that it was better for me to be flying off in another direction away from your miserable
groundings in what I knew only too well, that life for the majority of people is bloody bloody hell.

so had you bothered to remark less upon how various paving stones seem to make me jump up and down
when you were being uniform and corporate and attuned I was thoroughly cradling a latent fervour
for a further plain one colour coated before you ordered an illustrated history of beef on toast
from afar, behind closed doors, at lunch, in the clinic, with a few thin jokes from a few vicious fantasies
and why beats me that all those closed mouths off-scew focusing had to organise a political justification for writing
poetry.
I ate a tree top for you yet I did not how could I being jeopardy accept your invitation to a free death.
to other ends to roots twining rope logged tips touching earth's secure holding moist & uneven in texture
riveting and imbedded cities in the silent opposition of mooning elks. Impatience; joyless loving, & viewless limited.

psychiatry the modern worm who eats and wriggles into your light a close up victorian rhubarb patch
where squiggles the caterpillar warms itself beneath the cover of a magnified leaf botanically perfect
and perfectly portrayed as a perfect perfect of english perfect all in a thick wool frame smiles
with enquiring refusal to probe more deeply into the phenomenon known as subjective abstraction.
nothing to say to me waiting for attention intent on the evening's shipping looking – sad, missing mummy?

hard day at the office, employees causing you problems, why so silent, waiting for din dins
who is this rock of gravity. could it be a man? looks fairly like one. looks like the one who left here this morning.
lugging four elephants driven by Pan into some dossier of a complainant's file oh the pause between each sip
and the fidgeting of the tax payer and the inartistic tendencies of Leo van Gogh.

yes we'll tell them this we'll give them an excremental profile the old slop out trick
watch out for the screw who was your mother now living out her years as an organic vegetable
all say   Ah. This is not victimisation by a sadistic prison wardress, it's a defence, a resistance,
the problem of the contradiction between the consciousness of an offender and that of the prisoner of conscience
whose status goes unrecognized in this lovely country garden where bluebells nod and grannies shell peas.
political prisoners are not all terrorists or subscribers to violent action. some are writers. and some are writers too.
I knew the agreement would be to continue what I did not begin. so I start somewhere else
and you who so rudely pounced on my life with whatever authoritative backing you could muster
should realize that it is not inevitable that you will be befriended once your vitriol & subjective organising
had been accomplished you put me off my stride and I don't wear trousers though I wouldn't tell you I break through to

avoid condescension in my own voice yet admittedly have the habit of trying to inculcate some sympathy in others
who smile at suicides which are not the suicides of bunkered madmen wasting my time which could be better spent-up
perhaps. for good minds are never a waste of my time and as I am not a roving cannibal who holds brains in my mouth
to drain their living circuits there could well be doing with some distinction between sexual and intellectual syntax.
the marks left by the tyres spun out over dust tracks I held the little baby close to protect her hearing another
tide of motorbikes out on the scrubland the game suited them for what else was there
given that flowers were nancy and animals so naff. now be a good girl, no more talking. easy, rover, pretty girl
there you are nice munchies for lunchies whereas I thought you were returning for the last time to your mother
before she visited you at the factory gates
with a few paintings for your cardboard portfolio with that twill ribbon which always kept its contents safe. they
couldn't be hung as their
colours were already fading different subjectivities gives any explanation short shrift. yes that is precisely what they are
and precisely because I do not <u>want</u> to be forced to resist by analysing the tensions in a household I find that to utter
poetic imagination demands ready made replies how-how can I explain anything in one or even <u>two</u> sentences yet
this being taken
literally would in effect prove the old man right I surely will spend the rest of this life in every prison in the world.

Questions when they arise no-one to ask what they think later it fades becomes convention.
stops it the buildings the flight pretentions not genuine by conceiving that evening we hurried home through the
snow, scarves tied round
our heads, it was a fine revolution for some and we can't go back we can't go back except in disguise and we don't
want to be pointed out
as though we were masquerading without good purpose. When I decide to shift the tone of my writing I don't do
it for malevolent reasons.
well-meaning turns to criticism too fast – a whole city with a huge resistance to the imagination a hatred of beauty
of real changes using the landforms which in Sheffield are rare and interesting. tones one is told must be lowered
yet in the university and art college are great projects wide minds which are not encouraged to improve the native
conditions
Everywhere schemes for improvement lie festering mouldering never to see the light of day we don't need modular
isolation
who wants a future of alphaville everywhere everywhere that deeply implanted fluorescence
the common criminal . . . But not wanting to be put in this position even if it was a difficult one I think I had a
right to keep my head above water
but I was ducked and now am I really to believe that there is no formal procedure which permits one to refuse an
entrée into
lesbian S/M? I refuse to cook on this baby belling – how can anyone cook on a baby belling or cook a baby
belling a baby belling
or a baby on a belling cooking there's a baby bubbling you the belling did it yell when you dropped it into the pot
squealed like a lobster struggled for a second
– I can't think about this this is not poetic imagination how can death be in the poetic imagination so I place
papers atop it instead
fly up to Scotland look over eternity parade around Athens in search of fraternity I'm none too keen
on enjoying reputations I suppose if you don't care about the real conditions you can pine to your fancy
friends so I stayed away in case I did – pine to – they were the scene –
try to cope with a woman who is not tantalized, who is actually extremely annoyed. the emphasis
on locks and being suspected of stealing money doesn't help.

Powerful enough to Kill by Artificial Light

That is why I opposed your fight
As soon as it went beyond cultural boundaries.
Do you think I didn't know how people are Electrocuted
by infused wires? & that those are circumscribed
networks of social control built into Democracy?

*

light. & where is the end. & who was a taut string ringing
ten hostile neumes pretending care floats in devastating gesture
remove, absolve & love which knew not ambition of murderous mien
or murderous motive. resolve within the speed & light of genius.
it meant no more & no less either. the puzzle & pain ensued was Michelangelo,
again a sonnet which pierced my body to the bowel contracted womb
Victoria Colonna, a film of his sculptures by Ken Russell, Ken
the Thunder sign & symbol Longfellow, Hiawatha's Song,
(Madrigal) morning, nightingale. Father lowering daughter
for the sake of a lost son, others' suppression, oppression,
antithetical to beauty which was not confrontationally stunning
or constrained within one idea of aesthetic
and my own qualms over the deserted bedraggled unprepossessing crowds
locked invisibly leading their largely miserable lives
in stiff cultural patterning whilst within my womb lay
the possibility of beauty & a love far more gentle
away from the madding crowd where noise could not be stayed
to sustain sound less agglomerate, amorphous
the continuum was not moving towards climax
You followed him, my only other poet, what pain there was
Was mine. I not loving pain, enough, to need it
For happiness could have been mine only at the expense of other women's misery
And those are not the reasons I need to live what life remains.

No one human to appeal to, fixed located in a time sophrosyne

*

evoking mocked order showing Me the Blind & Impudent man
showing me what he had done what was continued, carried on
as though the dedicate devotion having taken all my life
was suddenly to be demoted to a film on english life
my mother Had no husband & this served up as soap
whose mind was tuned to any poetry / exposure
considered an irreverency, as was my Conceived 'Interstice.'
Walk in, walk out. And lining up for revelry, they Twist accordingly
A Thought, and one might as well have committed a lifetime's Treachery,
A Thought, and one waits for the sliding shoulder to deliver the slag.

Iagos are what are not wanted. Want is a message of the media
nothing extra apart from a phone call. I can't fight a man who is capable of murder.
Had I asked wouldn't it have been the person's I asked. Or how my mother was
before her life was shattered. A neoplastic imagination screen to screen.
There Was No Remorse. What Remorse there was came Later
When it was Realized that I had been thrown from my mind.
The Man should have had the Decency to Exculpate me in Court.
He cannot deprive this Ego of its Gains. He was a Profiteer.
Giraffe, gratuitous folly, prophetess, fi fi, the mother should NOT
have been described to me as a former WHORE. I defended her.
If she was a Whore then I was a whore. And a Lesbian not not never.

There's no place for me anymore. There was not a place for me in my family.
They stunt my growth purposively. producing a certain type.
It was unacceptable to my mind. That was a problem.
To always have to match a a certain limit of intelligence for an
illiterate grove, & when literacy does crop up, its usually
morally vituperative although not much different to
any labour party puritanism, indulging their own
before others. except in the case of the Jewish Patriarchy.
Even stricter. and verging towards murderous revenge.

*

Then what was it. when it was before those fronds which are waving my eyes.
stroking me to our dull breezed skies asserting two black crows
flying beyond this miserable moist extension : a soaked cigarette.
To digress : if you ever come across a packet of envelopes made from
The paper that old stamp hinges were bring them to me they will answer for me
But they must be longer and not as deep tho' not as long as the larger ones.
And not straight cut across the seal, pointed is good enough to half way central

You will have to learn to be human. What does every trick in the book mean?
Another time. To be faced by an incredulous relative whose authority will be cycled
Against evocative witchcraft which still remains to be cancelled from an idea of ethic.
Referrals to a language which refers to the natural mother as though
She is not to be believed although she Says
she sees trees in her dreams & these are sometimes flowing golden beams.

*

To have this beauty rammed up in my arm
When the leech has sucked me dry
To teach me what ah such belief
That roads and rhymes must be replete
With factories and prisons as though a child
I had not seen, not heard, blown merrily unconcernedly
Through other people's misery but no the woman author's cry
We do not want a woeful tale we learnt to cancel pain
We lived to end all tragedy We no more hear the sobs the groans
We learnt to call them casualties who lacked the brains
Success names, and Bitterness will soon be a sin and crime
And where these live I do not know my voice will not down go
As far is wide or high or sprung & worshipping in consort
Those who go in mind to fight with heavy light & over turf as
Sod thumped low as though this grace who led you out of danger
Had the time to spare you either, needed you as though her life
Had ever been no source of sheer delight in what she never did hear you
Give thanks to God or Jesus Christ or William Shakespeare or Any One Else who had loved
and Suffered and Died for Us and so she thought you Impolite
And most Discourteous whilst into her purse you too did bite
For some small hint of Literature to save your great & noble Deeds
Within the bounds of cultural sense for which no sense was realized
Other than to push her into defence and living self justification.

*

As soon as a name is to be addressed another child
world worn mother cannot be greater than those few words of support
to be known as intolerant, wisdom & not an oracle, recession, dips a bitterly serious
discussion on beggars   no one is blaming you, I am not limitless inspiration.
lines in conjunction move into metaphor, we are being ground down
I cannot pull your daughter up, and what this social lift has been will not be condescended to
how some fight for meagre help, it does not come though naturally,
to be unkind, or feel too weak to have one's mind removed.
that's how it is with children lost, not later, whilst they're growing.
It isn't fun. which denies reality. anything important quickly assumed.
How to fog mechanical theatre.

sensitivity changed from nothing touched to quite deranged & gradually
the peripatetic pedant lost her soul to ready words & clipped momentum
searching for a western mode that could be practiced formerly, wait,
whilst I acknowledge criticisms of didacticism levelled against me, I do not
accept that change has ceased & find that lack of intellectual consciousness
to be a ploy to hive off life & death onto the vulnerable who may not all be
as brutal and as vulgar as armies demand they be. Whilst critiques of
western competition crash too lightly on the market, doggerel has been passing
for what untutored people come to be known for & dismissed. Why walk away
& dismiss me. These arguments went on between women. There's nothing more convenient
than to build a wall of pity and support for a new network of power & submission.

*

Who told you I was a joke? or would not be with a
Million books to my library, not this, They? &
How to construct a world on fragments of misinformation,
Carelessness does not apply to the secure & confident
Officiators of the Word. From a distance, a friend.
There is no room for introduction. Too few friends
To be at ease & welcome without a Clattering.
Life impinged upon & knows no welcome if
Each day is taken with welcome welcome welcome
One more Shred of sympathy for the less deceived
On pay one suffers joy & vanity, on nothing it exceeds.

I   lean on your well-made desks not doubting excellence
except to curse my self for lacking outspoken resistance
to those who meaning well were nevertheless impatient
and deserved to be obeyed for I with myself was impatient
& could not but agree that age should be quite quiet
but could not find a world where books would leave me quiet
For people would appear with not much interest in it
Apart from strong objections to what was going into it
A quite astounding disrespect fearing bared thoughts
Careering back   without a wish to close in as report
Damage to a poetess, young & exiled from her home,
Overwritten, silent too, a witness no-one other.
David Bomberg painted similar witness to such horror.

*

leave these to die lest grammar offends you, rammed ammonites
slieve orris pushing for infused addenda to consciousness.
square raised apology for killing with pride a writer's mind.
life passed through pure tar to life as farewell its ghost.
folded nature. quiet of the earth did not wish to tread on the tail of the tiger.
90% of the people who had formerly been for peace were then for war.
caught in the crossfire with no hand to hold. life of the mind.
here was free and responsible enough. it was not for me to hold fractured languages.
I was obscure. it was a cultivated obscurity which did not look people in the face.

Push me. I have no feet. These were filtered for master's meat.
Unexpected & unlocated I greet you as you pass by in a dream of a street.
Hairpin. Through other families other daughters are locked up for good
It's as bad as racial hatred. When it's hatred for a daughter's art
When it's joked and jostled, thrown away, hidden, homeless we stray
straining to keep alive as muted or as restricted as possible.

When it's further it's politics which halts fast.
With all its papers to fill in for man's copy
either he'll give me hell or he will. once it was morals then it was always.
if you think this is smug try the smugness of people without art.
try facing their hideous groans and startling snorts.
try walking to knickers being waved at you with sneers & chortles
and swear words echoing over the hills by the lake.
try striking an organ in those faces it might be constructive.

if striking was wrong on its own. there were slates and pencils.
the self having left its god alone on its way to meet christian (soldiers).
it takes ages to learn what cannot be totally learnt
to speak one coherent thought ongoing takes the tune
dragging behind him his curtain for a train I was horrible
wanting him to work rather than sit in a stupor

anallage without language, resisting normalization,
but that was of a product of an unimaginative scientific education
which required one experiment at a time to ensure careful results.

*

a woman who killed.

the man would not let her go. she parted from him
wedging authority between her and her, the her
who was his and the her who was her own. she
was the person I pleaded for, like Sidney Carton.
But not like Sydney Carton. Mundane. Don't
let your hearts guide you utterly. They
wanted my brain. We were led down the hill
by John Bunyan. In a dream. She worried me
inordinately. As did political convictions.

she writes a lot. sheets of paper, screeding
try to soften your attacks. you are old enough
not to be shocked by terrible things. a
person is a person no less. I am a patient woman.
hostility is not a good word. I have heard
women screaming blue murder at their children.
it mostly occurs for the sake of law and order.
his shadow would come over her if recalled.
She clung to the memory of her grandmother.

words are powerful energies, choose them with care.
I have suffered recriminations for writing what I did not write.
where people don't care about writing and where they do care.
I am not a woman who killed.
I am not her but I would not boast it.

*

cold water soup channelled through slowly arterial ways wishing well
away from conduits built by unskilled working class women whose
only condescension was to pick potatoes from the soil & enter examinations
with hay in their hair revelling in the contrast between sun and outdoors
earning a few pounds to keep their energy alive and the cool interior
of beautiful thought. keeping her eyes on her work. one day
she realized that there was no end to the solitude she had been confined into
that a word here or there spoken into the unknowing complexities we are flung into
if occasionally wondering whether to tell someone a thing or two
for how else can one move towards a barrage of discrimination.
Comfort brings its qualms and its officiousness. Calming feverish tempers.
cold water absorbs warmth from temperature. the spurious theory of
one directional time. Some predictability does not meet love's certainty.
Entrance to a woman or an institution or a city that life stopped
As once again my life was turned into a mirror which was cracked
by materialistically minded people who never tried to understand
That pride is not a show of ongoing progress being not what is wanted
What I have cannot be wanted, I cannot be wanted also, this is
The only unwanted, the children were wanted, help was wanted,
This though is inevitably unwanted, not wanton, not to speak.
Water would flow back refurling from the crack along the base
Between the floor and the wall I pull you seaweed for your iron
to cure the world of aids Iodine, the cow a piece of sleeping beauty
by the ocean's foam, on the tough grass, clumped by stone & sand.
Only when made ugly, into the likeliness of ugliness elaborated upon
Grow up out from that dullard fever of split mind and upon forked tongue

*

one cannot be tempted to agree to an undermining fuselage,
on off days, within a normal routine job, which too is motherhood
or was before the children thought it to be wise to warn of waning
fast machines work wonders which don't know everything.
The pressures on lone women to prove their acumen. Odd
groups of people spotted by research students in the hills.
At 10 o'clock in the morning. Drawing wheeling birds.
When their mother should be at work. Rather than gallivanting
Around with drawing blocks as though without a care in the world.
When people are Starving in the Third World. Which we knew.
And helpless to help . Art comes Last, young lady.
When ? When ? When every mouth and tummy is filled.
This blade of grass has been drawn to death. Look. you are
Killing the Spring. (That's another branch of Hysteria, one
which has a masculine ring) Cannibalism.

Rather than condemn as immoral behaviour a way of life
Which was too fleshly & immoderate, I preferred to think of it as Rabelaisian

What can one do with unforgivingness once forgivingness has expired
If hatred was not sought, to love through time no short line will expound
I feel I've spent a lifetime assuaging others' grievances.
Patiently finding ways to help them find life worthwhile.
To have one's hand then smacked in no uncertain way
Would make me wild with vicious hatred & that is how I feel to this day.
I'll hate him to his grave, make no mistake.

drought

forgiveness could come from families too
who resent their daughters having brains
with all the educational opportunities
open to them when we were growing up
we wanted them out of the house
rather than terrifying us with incessant arguments
not that we would have gone wild
we would have been better writers
and I could have looked after my sister
it's different when you love someone
we didn't need stacks of money
there was an old piano
and charcoal was cheap
& good for sketching scruff

there were some great scruffy people
in our town. people who didn't bat an eyelid.
just getting on with their jam puddings and custard.
with grisly chins & pulled jumpers.
and the women were fat.
some enormously fat. fat enough
to take up two seats on the bus.
none of this if you don't mind I don't.
that was for men.

and then came Vaisex.
every cyclist's dream.
so I flew to Giacometti.
And my sister stuck with horror films on T.V.

*

a love affair with language a marriage to passages
for this generosity, sold. stage two : material reality.
I am deaf. not knowing how to listen to destruction.
the law is perhaps wholly concerned with human relations.
because I have a weak stomach which resists rather than surrenders
to anyone who is trying to tell me that without my patient submission
there will be nothing new. which must be as hard as change
stacked inside my treasury, my bust in Greece
moved to Egypt. becoming portable and oblique,

in the structures it misleads mezzo, par terre
you shouldn't be reading this if you have ever been bored.
it's your own fault. as it was mine. we hear
how people in time will be sold. not wanting
to be eaten by an Inspector. I want a robot.
to construct the construed with the language of the law.
to protect me from inspectors who allow
one word for each finger and say : no more books.

Fuck off! Pity. I don't want to be friends with millions of people.

*

it is not for you to say or tell to bode
shadowing over this which knows no god to goad unto the good
a minor point, thrice minor. in a vast paradise of good
his outstretching arms are not displaced delayed correction
to write in torn flag black on a dead star's light
that act of wickedness purveyed the other night
will not be brewed with my consent, young lady.
who is beyond a gentle lesson from a female not in need
of spurious complement or dismissal. Send, therefore, Your family away
I like not to be told to exit from this life
Whilst huge general identities are gestured to my life
What accrues to you half charging the Male will turn a mind to Known
That is not wholly knowing & half that knowledge dimmed in suspicious fear
In Awe of death's mysogyny, practices what sounds ineffectual
For a cause quite far & walking back to greet you, load, shake, level, quake,
Curl a foreign feature nurtured love which no idea can cull
When one has stood rejection from that world of word less tied
And backed & lucked & pushed against with bars & bars & goads
A trinket but a latter   love, a hurt & bleeding wife, we pause
To teach you some will not be lumped, or used to carve thy careering stars.

Constricting narrative will not playce that thumb in somersault
Thumb being games left for what stoop might further
Will be held to a psychology debased by animist spirit to worsen
Another Chance, Yes, Another Chance for what should Never be Internally focused Upon
Act Not those faked Aguecheek brows I have Met you before Many Times
In what used to be dedicate feet upon bones, resurgence & consultation
Weighted by reference hedged to oriental loans whilst portraits reach masqued or gagged.

by exploiting the future on reserved matters of relief work.

it appeared to be a large scale format for micropoems,
it emerged, thru the medium of linguistic expression
to be a project in elevation, a plan interleaved by short
paragraphs, for a court complex, perused
by two serious, efficient, & regular men with clean fingernails.

five courts, it is difficult to find the word to express his tone,
interlinked by staircases, i wondered what kind of schoolboy –
had he been taken to the theatre, had he been a keen cricketer,
did he take to the family album with its flat presentation &
its two guarding altar pieces to be tied by renewable cord.

who to avoid with these revelations, those who enjoy spreading fowl
rumours of madness and poetry which might never reach the men
who earn a reasonable living from reasonable constructions to
hold unreasonable men, or a woman who could not agree to one-sided
culture knowing how easily benevolent hearts can be crushed by people

who do not want us to be interfering with their ways of living
by exploiting their future on reserved matters of relief work.

<u>a minuet by mendleson</u>.

dusk thread through cloudy halls
retiring from serf's
plight to phaeton's
unfurling chariot's
beams descent deliver
firm momentary cease
courtesy hold axis
   all withheld
transpassing mirrored gest
zenana's imperatives' lost
in walls faint powdered traces
lamentation to test
screens doves hover bearing
shaded light leaved olive
grey as pearl on bisque sagesse

senses seized by reason's
Might mistake a forkēd path
wasting time in doubting
studied artificies
holds down hard on dusky
thread barring solitude
derides solitude as a plucked
string baulked by màtronly
pull walk in airy per
petuum ōver reason's divorce

the white horse in̄ the park
regarded by this friend
who to the boat did wend
her way in Spirit sailed
unto a warmer city
decussative backless departs from

regard of rearguard fixation
as womb keeper sinking craft
with surnatural births of straight babies, tout.

o zeugma passivity
salammbô's iniquity
revived reflexivity
crossed ways
divided devoid of
a phantom domed chariot
strays solemnly back to the dungeons

*

incrustation, fossilised cement, caked dry canine's excrement,
the bouquets for the parlour, to complete a discretionary comment,
veiling over a heart fall, crushed by the cataract's descent,
to stop one from resisting
turning politics
into a spoilt rich girl's disease
as the call for love could not penetrate
those stray games
creating distortions in politics
instead of learning your directions
from time's signs
preferring conventional representation
in art
to a thorough synthesis
metaphor bucked by convention
to never read the roads
oh
they were only —
your friends to
whom you reported me
for befriending
it's so utterly clear
your mean minded lips
your back turning hips
your buzzing hands.
seated upon their heads
others still query lack of mysticism
talking
into their conches
tucking their pampered feet
beneath oceans of ooze.

because this won't do. it never did do. as defined as refusal.

The truth will not be told, of this faint hearted one, who made a move
to save her mind & thereby help her children more, away from
rough mentalities, god help me from this wicked thought, I could not
work for any who, had left us at the brink of time, with nothing.
This generation of the still suffering. Composing over suffering
to make it worse by disbelief as no one knocked to make you blush
to come in peace as ever did, and still misapprehended,
if that hell you did not know, where one was thrown as one compelled
by man and woman to take that insufferable serenity away from a soul
shaken down & slapped into shape to learn of the misery of
the ends of humanity will not be told not to punch this into shape
to spill it over lines and syntax cursed, but it was a different desire
different methods & other minds, & still at a loss to plead mercy.
it never was good enough. because it is weak, and therefore rebuffed.

*

ignorance confiscates literature surfaces to be minimized
& deposited in a deliberately misinterpreted context.
perhaps it is worse for me not to have anyone to lie to
the way people do when they are intimately loved
I wondered whether that would have been enough
to be quiet before the so called world was informed.
fishing folk drag nets & examine their catches.
grapevines are lies & trailed distortions. Waiting
for the commotion to die down the only meaning
as far as I am concerned is this ruin given shape in this given space.

persecution begins when the eyes go over to condemn
what cannot be written overnight as though four centuries
were articulate and pounding feet in peripheral psychodramas
is surely the need of the empty minded for salient simulated
emotion. Ugliness is interesting until it destroys beautiful thought
by censoring skies & stars unnameable, petty to judge
the least or most desirable, in children, by feature, or name.
no amount of ignorance towards this geomorphology
which did not ask to be located at this part of the earth's crust
will produce an earthquake of national proportions.

when we were walking was it an insult to eyes
which condemned what could not be written overnight
as though fourteen centuries were articulate.
I wanted to talk to you but you held me up.
It was probably a total accident. Although
in some way people do sit or stand to work
after the impulse, not to shirk, which I cannot explain.
A transparent reality, afraid that it was not true –
that it was being interpreted as convertible.
Worse. People to be changed in reality. If there was

Anything which went against my nature it was that
Parcelling up of people into marketable packs.

*

sickened by the sight of the yard thewed daughters
gutting orphan meat, of the or not of the military class.
kicking fifteen year old girls in the stomach.
wiring up old age pensioners who couldn't afford to pay
all for a concentrated lesson in the contrast in riverside features
on one fine day, untranslatable concrete section,
revenge for intimations of poetry, for a reasoning triarch du tavistock

ushered into the Coffee and Raisin, a certain amount of regular pressure
to save the life of a mason's suicidal wife who had to find another father
to certify against my freedom to escape the application to the
network, communistic, legalistic, stalinistic stake.

"writing is dangerous." the yard thewed daughters of brigadiers
gutting orphan meat. in which case don't ask me if i know troetz.
i know of troetz. i do not know anything else. writing is dangerous.
Piranesi was not dangerous but then neither was Iron.

we have a lead. i am not allowed to write art criticism.
in case i mumble it down into the plugless lead. 'spatial occupancy'
this, brethren, is why there is no money left for feminism.
you have wasted multi-billions of it on extra surplus espionage.
and espionage is only interested in one thing: troetz.

troetz is a sculpture. 'Enclume de Rêve' there is a number
which is attached to this sculpture. that number is english.
the sculpture is Hard. and right next to it stands cloin gastlov
on three spikes. how people walk into art exhibitions is
vitally important. follow me with your trolley of rule books

mr 3 and ms 60 this will have to be incorporated into artificial reality.
Let's talk about Civilization shall we? excuse me, your glasses need wiping.

two secs (*early draft*)

if this holds & goes no further could belief be a fine sudden
reading jam each other wasps and needing what in others proven
letters, papers, microfiche, secretaries, maids, mansions and a bulldog
mourning nureyev, and would not take his spirit for a scathing
word or two on his not dancing for the colonels where culture leads us to
can we care or is that too a dangerous interview i despair
& do not laugh at other's pain or might if constantly to support it
with a host of goodly power were not illegitimate.
& whilst to hoist machinery of administration i think one back
& walk to talk to tell you what should not offend you so, myths
there are a plenty, and most of them inspired by extra situationists
who think in terms too large to use something apart from
the real world as to charge a fortune to my name
and never look me in the face again and do not know of troetz.

in the world i'd have preferred to be scribbling pieces of sapphire
utterly irresponsible to all political programmitists
uncaring of who but a heap of scrambled irrelevancy
anything to avoid sermonizing with the deadweight of history
as friends grew scruffier, hair greasier, cafés seedier;
afternoons in poodle parlours, w.i. jam sessions,
raspberry dralon g.i. pied à terres, gilt identity bracelets,
cocktail bar mirrors & slumped sinatras' white flaked loafers,
british legionnaires, three quarter length car coats, marriage
to an onion seller, caravan parks, virulent inflatable paddling pool lyricism,
and i was less than interested personally in anyone i ever met
which has its good and bad aspects, how goodly to be held
but not by an officer in uniform, goodbye chi wa wa, filling in the past
with no expectations for the future, dismantling the flats
in the diagonal indicating exit: a drawing prize, darkness at noon,
and repeatedly turning controls down to zero, wrong & cheap, it
would take a lot more intention perhaps art is not a pastime,
perhaps it was a practise in another teach in behind the edition of
'fundamental braque', i SAID i didn't know him in my hand-out.
before it didn't matter what one says to one is not said to another

and doesn't it show in sculpture(s). sudden, sodden, letters, lettuce, cults, colts, faces, faeces, past, parsed, look, cook, offend, portend, other, smother, and the holy simpering feminists denying the truth by resubmitting the victimized to the victor's boot.

Demeter.

Pressure to produce any racially characteristic gesticulation
Cerebrally (super ego) destroyed by a political definition imposed upon a
Working Dissertation. An unremunerable subject. At issue.
Hours of slogging argument over levels of development
In conformity with normally aged people.
The woman as a joke or as a Gertrude Stein or as a maiden aunt
And finally as a suet pudding slugged within heating range of a three bar fire.
Avoiding being addressed to be redressed none of this should matter
Nothing but the work itself and the end result. not the wrong face
Or the glum expression or the taciturnity not the origins or the age.
Familiarity having bred contempt to hasten to remind causes
Further argument and wasted time. I read with interest of american
Research projects into hostility against females' academic progress
Having met that confusion between academic and technical as though it were
A hopeless pursuit when one has a common face and hails from a common place
Where cows graze, fine cows. Some make demands and others are refused.
Having hands tied behind our backs to stop us lifting our crying babes.
How private is a person's life, who could not afford literary representation.
At a crucial time, young, hopeful, loving and self-controlled.
You cannot know what went before you. With no one to agree
To nothing have to expound upon your liberty. Ideas denying me my mind
By one my father made to flee as I watched the shape
of a rope being thrown out to catch or to throttle me I sprang
like a startled animal, ears pinned back & hit the winds
landing in a purdah future: legitimate levels of thinking. If Personal words
Such as slaves have not yet written into a cultural fabric
You can be sure it will be as offensive to you as a Bengal rose
modular motherhood stripped of political power has a fit
but it is a fit which does not bruise and batter children
it's so easy to say outrageous things, to follow bodies
rather than thoughts. go home. kindness does not deprive.
I should have slammed down the phone. As long as others are free
to get on with their lives i'll represent the obverse of liberty
for no other reason. To stop parental interference
To stop history from taking its revenge to stop tragic cycles

To stop satisfaction being derived from cut patterning.
To stop taking after anyone. To stop destructive urges.
To find other pictures. To lock myself away
from mad women. to have no friends.
Here by this cow parsley which is fascinating
as are the laws full of daisies, buttercups, & raining.

I cannot write like an open university brochure.
See how well I am trying, see how my verbs go boING
and the subject & object still hold the subsidence.
Plain English you really Loathe me as I give you a common gesture
Out of your sight and behind your back and from the summit of Kinder.

*

I shake and cry. How then could I ever love you
But as a spirit who has been hurt & hear the song
A familiar image sighted by false eyes & mocked along
With pretended tears & make believe sobbing
To give us a turkey's throat whilst ospreys for a coat
Are lost to flight & this lesson was delivered
With stern reproof before another netted me
Into the group of practicals. For to claim my voice my own
Had levelled against me ignorance & once again what had I done
To not be one unknown to me who perhaps did worship differently
I do not fake, I do not lie, I worship at the shrine of poetry.

“ “ sumbur ” ”

1) books come too late to rescue us from meaning an unwanted freedom
embarrassed to find few friends as quiet as frowns intent upon articulate
movements Bastioned against fluctuating effort oh do they guide us to a
lost and wasted life washed in watered purple curled by scorching fox
these sullen ears that hear but daren’t rebuff with mouth and screaming ears
below each lobe each mouth heralds a voice incomprehensible

2)
en ami

for deference lies and gives itself the worst human part except in perfect function.
lunition. rolling suffixes suffering suffocate, another shunned, shunning.
it fixes us, the frozen munition, oddly reminiscent of a thin skinned starch
pounding salt with sorrel for a smart but useless mausoleum: flung in
an involuntary friend where enemies are unwarranted when paper
forbidden for narrow tuning forks cannot be soldered to a pen that talks

when it is acknowledged that nature was everywhere & utterly disapproved
there may be not another world, there may have been those iron steeds.

*

humans gaze clod to cloud depicted as brainless & reverent, neat
scruffy downright played out prostrate on vestibule benches bleating,
bellowing in mulched ragged half words, gi', ha', scu, raw headed
in the bleary aftermath, in the anticipant solitary hoax that is unknown
sibilance, caught oxygenic, leathern approach upright, leaves a locket,
daggers draw leaps over bayswater frowning at the imprudent nations'
perverse forms, unauthorized inspirations of servants to leisure.

*

je crois la haine peur l'esprit d'amour mais je vous en prie
que la question flôt comme une fête tout de suite

vous? vous oubliez ma petite que politiques pendant un temps certaine
m'assurent d'un silence immutable. mais bien sûr, mes douces,

vous ne voulait pas une poète pour votre brigade élitois.
et alors je n'aime pas les dictateurs, aucuns dictateurs

qui jouent gravement avec regulations autour d'une théâtre absente.
mais les bourgeois sont toujours la crème de la crème

alors je danse en une cercle et j'oublie les jeux
vous ne me trouverais pas encore, jamais, jamais.

*

they were, in those days, his players. He and his Queen, His friend and his Queen.
Watched over their workmen. Which Woman stands Alone in this life?
Husbands removing children at birth and beyond. Women killing women
for possession of other's men. Suffering outlawed, success everything.
If not strong and coupled relegated to the rabble, inadequate.
Inarticulate. Drifting, imagined screeching through the mists
Slip in a screech, out-tuned on electricity's circulating grooves.
Inflicting eccentricity to covert concentricity. addendas : facility.
Never look into the mind of one who does not resent others' lives
However close to the earth she goes, her imagining found no home

in Revolution's revelation this is nothing, jealousy as close to hatred
of a person's so called escape into what could not be grasped for politics' sake
Best leave all objects untouched and forget the sickening hatred
to go where people know who they are and don't fudge enemies.
How do women get beneath women's skins with penetrating hatred?
That's nothing new. A prisoner had more protection from attack

Kicking crazy I point a toe yet still it buckles medium in blue grass town
Building myself a room from a plume dipped in violet. Closing the battered old cart.

<u>the secret ballot.</u>   Austraque.

an inverted statistic. scalping by ten percent. do some people simply not look as though they
have brains. is that what it is? or do you enjoy archaic practices such as sacrifice and
flying human torches? and in the secret ballot when every neighbour was reputed to have voted me
out of town
did it not occur to you that i had a correlative literary locus and reference and preference for
an actor whose style i preferred to the professorial maggot's AND ALWAYS HAD.
only a fraction of the ongoing case launched against what the queen herself has accepted as
has international law that the manufacture of chemical and biological weapons be ceased.

*

for Vera MacUllum.   Assistant Governor.

published & upset women for being one more female
whose mind slips through secular prosody & roosts
before it is whacked into monitored conditions
& timed to read scarlet & black. He could not, like
many men, write on his self , oppressed & aware
that polemic attaches fear to what is & is not
his relationship to phallocentric, loyalty.
bereft of discussion thanks to women's naturally fanatical possessiveness
I conclude that the 19thC. novel has written us out.

which is why it is correct to put the people first
in all matters concerning purpose & intent.
but I reserve my qualified right, to perceive
the distance between art and the people.
& therefore I also reserve a subject's right
to contest what I know to be personally prejudiced
victimization. And therefore it worries me
that what is right is not always right.

*

who are these who tell you what you want to know? would they were not these.
would they were those. for the obvious: for the obvious. is there much worse than
being prey to the eye? moreover these who tell you as though you did not.
do they do it on purpose? they must have a strange soul hunger, a stranger
soul hunger than   they would not hear more so being their own voices which
they do hear so – he doesn't know everything although he tells the intelligent
from the stupid what a terrible thing to think of. if to see only movements it
it creates nausea. or extra movements. we don't talk about the same thing.
the secret here is secrecy. they read according to strict class lines
as well as fly into new york not pretend to. I talk to anyone, it doesn't
bother me who. then suddenly it did because I was very alone. they thought
i need to learn how to write , they spoke of life as though it had soul.
then they proliferated revolutionary theatre in which soul had been excised.
i bought tubes of mints with chewy centres. I can't stick this for the best
years of my life are being removed from me at this precise moment, and he
gave me a sentence or two in which to justify my reluctance. this is a
prime cause of exploitation of feminine emotion. to render a woman bitter
who was not bitter, to dive into a woman's mouth to implant a voice for
the privilege of sustaining one word: lumpen. they told me that the mountain
had been bought or was it sold, i forget, one or the other. I did not see
what bought looked like or whether sold was more remarkable.
poor old mountain, bought or sold.
such indecency, such indiscretion.
did it bear white tickets edged in red?
curled round onto sticks to mark out the dead?
fallen in battle for their daily life.
groaning moaning mountain if i wore a beard
i would stroll with my old viola
to hear what you have heard.
pinnies, frockcoats, sailors' berets,
walking as human ghosts are laid
to rest in that sanctity trespassed.

no-one can tell me now
that a tympanum is not
a stringed instrument,
are you trying to tell
the postman that it was
elsa triolet who turned
aragon into a smart arse?

for the mire where the brine, thick but how thick, age, but what age,
& if there had been a love who was not looking into our purses to see

what was not there doubts the mass who is not the mass who work with
armaments under heavy security, it would make a, stomped on, stomped on
once more for one once upon, stomped on, stung, shown the door.

remembering prenuptials.

no coating. has it whipped, pedalling, rallies by lingering
pull back the third leg from the fourth chaise longue
be careful that liturgy is not blue pencilled in the climb
whilst acquiring distance to assuage jealousy &
bitter, bitter hatred irrational & locked tight against life
for it to be lived away from endless misgiving &
Apprehension that beat the verb out of play, snappy
it is the easiest thing in the world to throw your loving one away,
& I began to think that love was an evil lo the warm
that hold & hold each other against the slightest disturbance

•

Should I go down to the level of common ignorance,
to the arsonists & twinsetted stilletto'd pubbers
who chat about courtships & laugh as they axe
with their poised knives over words of two syllables
plus the sequence of creation & the elbow in the chest
& the knee in the groin and the covenanted fleets
& the recouping of active art memories, & the definitions
preceding demands, your spaces are all your own.
You are mad to love imprisonment, & you are heathen
with insensible greed & cowardice but I leave you

As I was told to do by each and every one of you
Unable to carry the sacks of gold to your doors
Unable to bear the weight of the burdens I used to
So that my young arms ached & my back hurt fit to break
With your demented echoes of werk werk werk
and your threats and your promises of their realizations
Writers never come to much. finding it hard to deliver the goods.
And children it seems are a blot on the nation's purity
And horseshoe women are a risk to the nation's security
You are sick. You are mad and you are sick. But you are not
The only ones who play this dungeon game

for stability has its price to name, whilst the floating
desolate outer reaches of the grey, ship loss ocean
Ah but ocean has too soft a sound for shame, for shame!
The Ark has been coated in smokescreens of gloss that stick in the heat
for the sinners who read, the elders who interstice, (remembering prenuptials.)

Rue du Bac

own.   own.   own . .... O...... O ..... W . ... N . ... O . ...X ...... OWN . . . . . IN ..... “this world.” ....
see . . . . . DROWNING . . . . . SEE . . . . . BLACK . . . . . reading Wittgenstein .... except .....
the leap . . . . . sauter . . . . . . dance . . . . without . . . . . dragging . . . . . . depressed
people . . . . . . into . . . . the dance . . . . . & . . . . spitting . . . . . in their . . . . faces . . . .
through a child’s eyes . . . . shoes . . . . on adults . . . . are large . . . . . . the
mother . . . . who opposes . . . . . slavery . . . . . . is . . . . . a child in a way . . . . a . . .
way . . . . . a . . . . . . indefinite . . . . . . article . . . . plays . . . . . . it . . . . is . . . a . . . .
play . . . . indefinite . . . . article . . . . it . . . . is . . . . . a . . . . sign . . . . . that . . . . .
weighs nothing . . . . . it is lighter . . . . . than . . . . reality . . . . . it is . . . from . . .
a . . . . play . . . . it was . . . . asked for . . . . . the question . . . . was . . . posed . . . .
the . . . . question . . . was . . . . ask . . . . yourself . . . . what . . . went . . . . .
wrong . . . . these open plains . . . . . . my back . . . . was breaking . . . . was
being broken . . . . this . . . . was . . . . not . . . . what . . . I . . . . understood . . .
by . . . . peace . . . . the surroundings . . . . were . . . not . . . in . . . question . . .
sangria . . . . . no . . . . . it never is . . . . . . inviolable . . . . . . there may be . . . .
similarities . . . . . individual letters . . . . perceptions . . . . desires . . . . .
I . . . don’t . . . . want . . . . to eat . . . any . . . writing . . . . .

*

and my veins unpunctured, & not a punk, & no opinion, & no corrupting,
& no tempting, & no chinese saucers, stories, of bohemia, of bears, of
instantive imaginative narrative, nothing was wrong…
no haunting me, hunting me down, no lines, no dishwasher, no
insecurity, a world to live in, to paint in, to write in, to negotiate
the gaps between writing and publishing, to never desert music,
to love, honour and cherish the difficulties in the lives of writers
who are generous for writing is a gift for humanity, is a blessing,
and a world of minds, some beautiful, some less so; to write
in a half slumber, to not be poked fun at, to care for life &
to remember that I love poetry worship and revere poetry
there are no shortcomings away from the disgraceful
bludgeonings of the unsympathetic and harsh, the damners
of the ash tree, the ones who permit no retreat into privacy,
the privacy that loses its ground, the constant harrying,
grating compulsions, sudden swerves into waste ground.
Arrests at the gates of the workplace, in the foyer, at the stage
door, deceivers who refuse to acknowledge the consciousness
of others, who insist on disturbing the sensitive and easily
disturbed, who listen for the words that are spoken
between a mother and her children, who cannot control
their impetus to destroy happiness, who hate women
who have minds, who do not want women to have minds,
who are fixated by the image of the body of the woman,
who are not interested in anything but, who are frustrated,
who go back to their gardens & read. Unnumbed to the
agony of no grand piano, the begging for help for a
sobbing daughter whose temperament prefers music to
speech.

*

He was my conscience. His moans and groans. His distrust
of women's tongues wagging, the hard slog, war.
His displeasure. His discomfort. His warm voice.
His limits of patience stretched to breaking point
That not once did strike out to hit us, to break us,
Not once to our cheek hip thigh arm joint.

Love does not fit this point and is completely
following, point after point on the scrolls of the Torah;
Thou shalt not murder neither Communist nor Pauper.

*

What shining arrogance saw themselves
united in heart of small flocked fangs
tufted in californian beach springs
far from raw deconstructed france
the fathers of the néo-libération
half glints out for darker remnants
of time unpierced by pointless covets
and it is not a photograph that exposes
adamance of tactic seething in the skill
that it takes to circuit a model brain
with programmed circuits of emphatic will

goetz o.r.t. from 'The Monroe Doctrine'

The Epicurean flees from food, far from repast, to find the sea to cool
her heels for no proposition of hers is accorded. its reason, no
mind of hers found from which reason may pursue a rejected
direction upfolding through the echelons of letters, no
she must be moulded and formed in the unclean hands
of nostalgia for her original condition this time the
unwashed hands will not let her go, so they stalked her
& caught her adverting to the heart of her discontent
& they fought her with an old rusty kitchen knife & a
fortnight's rent ever renewable like the Council of Trent.

The childish missals, will they never cease to bound, & prance, & leap.
Reinstituted nightmares survivors of races that stalkers
have run with gladiators' faces, buffoons dressed in briefs
& gaiters, reflecting on pale and serious places, killing for fun
& spreading her over his morning slice, he bites resentfully
into her bum, and parodying the voices of the slow & ancient
he leans over her interregnum subconscious
enquiring "had enough, mum?" Too lazy to write his own dialogue
he proffers a crumb, a receipt for which she notes on her thumb
subsumed to gastronome the alliance between the juices
threads its venomous spirit into creation.

"we cannot sing intimated"

Each intimated universal is crushed
inevitably in strikes against carding
no I won't sit compliantly with my
hands neatly clasped unless I wish to.
no I won't do what I am told to.
this is not a theatre it is a room.
& I have pressed the button on the
outside curve & I am beginning
to be whizzed for a few seconds.
now I have been whizzed.
and am recovering from blindness.
a blue rectangle is floating
through space. turquoise blue space.
it opens in a flap. the white beach
it is too cool to keep, it will be signed
mill. double diamond. "fascist diamond"
tea room. the confluence. golf.
people are aggregates of World culture,
note the present authoritative tense
& lack of wit due to masculine innocence
what do you want? D'ante?
Come on, he was burnt to a frazzle.
Yet he did not surrender his art.

slass coelitus arieto glass classico chivet

I loved you so much, and then there was no house.
The panic rose in my mind.
Onward, onward I strove,
for the day when I could be with you at home.

Nasty people came into my life, looking, looking.
Not one human being. Not one word of warmth.
Only the pain in their faces from straining to be kind.
They sounded as though they had learnt the word from an extractor fan.

What do they normally do
When there is no father's hand to shake?
It would be ungainly to demonstrate.
In the distance the madman stomps home

In the snow you were wrapped up warmly,
One had to die, queens do not scream,
What happened? What happened?
Rather than apologise to me for gross indecency
They made me pay for their sins.
The young mothers

You shall not lay a finger on my work.
by pretending love & using the bitter cult
as you are so Ignorant; your regard.

the pleasure of a murder extended over half a lifetime.
so you got what you wanted
your uncle's eldest daughter behind vertical bars.

your contemplative study of my silence.
did you make any attempt to be honest
or was it the familiar advent

welcome perfection farewell poetic blemish.

I was living then.
Each Friday they used to call me down
for questioning.

I don't decorate myself with my name.
but they made sure that it would never
sound the same again.

did you think that it didn't matter?
because I was a girl? that it didn't matter?
who do you believe? why do you Crawl

into the gutter?

a cult with a society
it was – never looking
that I do remember

execrable refusal
to acknowledge
my creative powers

I came to wonder
whether anyone knew
the meaning of creation.

such chickens. cowards.
cavorting around with machine guns.
skulking in doorways.

I was your dead.
written out
by my best friend.

*

Reading overhead, the sink back is being defined as defensive,
Good looking the way the americas come and go,
mayors jumping up on plinths and staying there!
Agreeing whilst disagreeing completely, head no bigger than a diamond.
Giddy sketch book, wet ice whipping the ankles Henry James the
Ten Pin Bowling, an alignment and an inconsequence.
Still: the significance of ice-blue and sudden colour consciousness.
Bohemia blues: from green to violent. Most goes in violatory actions
One could only Ever dream one did Know Much about Anyone
Much verifiable, a detective would be needed for that.
To read over with open eyes, "I can do that in my sleep"
Thinking as is a name, is his name as, or a girl;
Experimented upon in retrograde, the ever hanging wave
In three-d, folded for sympathy at the ruins and the spoils.

*

Patisseries in real salzbourg.
Over a street rich fat women eat
Evergreen leaves on whole branches
trying to leave a little space to
Romp with the rorschach that stumped
Yawning garbage in the horloge

*

palette in monochrome
orotund and holy
ethical waves travelling
tentatively across rock
referring to formerly inhabited areas
yokes a boot to a precipice

*

permanent enough
onyx
emerald
sovereign
integer:
aimless amour

*

pochoir silver threaded snail
œil mg. magazin maghreb
eastern collotype stripped in process
terrine two hours later with toast
rondo capriccioso votive tea
yonder isaac

*

Perruche, the rising rapids,
on air is carried away
earning less than a trained monkey
talks ten to the dozen
ranging from climbing plants to
young greek athletes

Collection Notes

Anne Mendleson, Typescripts (1974).

This two-page poem beginning "Cover the land" exists in two separate files in Mendelssohn's archive; both sheets are edited with the same pen and bear the watermark "Croxley Script". The first page is in a file containing papers from the early eighties; it is a foolscap typescript. By hand, it is paginated and dated "'74."; a single typo is corrected, and the colon in stanza three is added (SxMs109/5/B/2/8). The second portion is from a file that also contains a typescript poem dated 18 November 1977; after typing, Mendelssohn numbers this second page, dates it "Jan 30 '74.", and includes speech marks (SxMs109/5/B/2/1). Beneath the poem and date, Mendelssohn types the following:

> Open a gap, open and a whole aquarium flooded in – – change this water into methedrine and close up the power house.
>
> Was upon a time legs, arms, were tied together with invisible magnets in a frozen limb forest. A forest, young and tender, veined of ancient bone. Not a foot left the ground to take its step. The familiar sky, winter days, special weather that draws the mind to . . An oxygen tent, loosely slotted in a secret partnership. Hand open receiving articlies. Durable human behaviour of sounds come forth. Pathos of adaptation. Obedience of machined limbs. Uprooted. Bury again.
> **
>
> crying out for mor: receiving the customary refusal.
>
> ****   ****   ****   ****   ****   ****   ****
>
> Flying Yesterday's Fish
> AT Tonight's Price.
>
> ***
>
> The POTENCY is mashed in the limit
> of censorship/wrong/annihilation.
> Representation only is decent.
> Which picture would be slashed now?
> (not through insult
>   through sheer refusal)
>   paint those pictures
> of nibbling sheep carcasses
> round stagnant ponds

A two-page manuscript of the poem exists in a prison notebook, dated 30 January and 1 February 1974 (2/A/3). The sentence beginning "Open a gap" noted above is included here as well, as it is in prison notebook 2/A/8. The 2/A/3 notebook manuscript differs from the typescript in capitalisation and punctuation, and shows the following edits and differences:

> "Cover the land" was "Cover the land."
> "Swim the ~~seas~~ water"
> "Now Fly." was "Now Fly" and was offset page left
> "Heavy jets heading ~~down~~ over"

"'Pig Swill Here'." was "'Pig Swill Here'"
"PIgeon perch." was "Pigeon perch."
"Prison wall bigger than us." had no full stop
"Walk – legs last forever." was "Walk – Legs last forever"
"Beware Bewatched" was "Be ware Be watched"
"Be witch ~~Be~~ Take Care"
"One step further ~~and~~ ^'Anna^ Come Back'"
"Turn around:" was "Turn around"
"They weren't even ~~looking:~~ ^watching^"

Between stanzas three and four, a draft stanza reads:

thru time find out
~~Acting on.~~
~~I~~ can't remember ~~what was going on inside~~ ^I then^
~~I see I've been~~ in ~~many~~ places.
People come ~~to me of the moment~~
~~That~~ they [~~*unclear word* —~~ed.] are ^~~still~~^~~ a~~liveing ~~certainly~~ ^still^

"I feel sick" was indented
"moon up there" was "moon   up there"
"OH. lit a smile." was "Oh! lit a smile"
"Drama class Girl . . . never met." was in capitals and placed next to stanza first line; commas were full stops
"we never met" was "WE'VE NEVER MET"
"I just   I know" was "I just I know"
"Pauline . . . herself." was in capitals and placed next to the top of the stanza
"And then Pause" was "And then PAUSE"
"Chris as usual." was in capitals and placed next to the top of the stanza
"waita minute" was "wait a minute"
"Did you hear" was "Did you here"
"But I'M not" was "But I'm not"
"NO NO NO'" was "No No No"
"B ye darling" was "Bye darling."
"'Umm. Oh. Ohdear." was "Umm, Oh. Oh dear"
"Are YOU alright" was "Are <u>you</u> alright"
"Hilary as always" was in capitals, unpunctuated, and next to "I think I'm going mad"
"SPEECH." was "SPEECH!"
"What can I do?'" was "What can I do?"

Arrows suggest that the first and last lines of stanza nine, beginning "Umm" and "What can" respectively, were under consideration for a reversal not undertaken in the typescript.

“Ohh. I can’t stand it.” had no quotation marks or final stop
Next to the first and second lines reads “ESHA ~~AS~~ ON / WHAT IT COMES TO.”
“One day baby” was “One day, baby”
“I’m telling you . . .” was “I’m telling you”

Anne Mendleson/Grace Lake, Sheffield typescript (November 1981).

These typed poems are on 14 photocopied foolscap sheets (SxMs109/5/A/1). It remains unclear whether the collection was ever published. In the Sussex archive, the lettered poems “a.” to “g.” appear to be sub-sections of “Exposition”. But in typescripts Mendelssohn sent Tom Raworth, likely in February 1983, poems “a.” to “d.” appear under the handwritten title, “EXTRACT FROM FINEDROME.” These same typescripts include “BEING 707_4^{C}” and “Exposition”; handwritten notes on the former suggest that Mendelssohn was seeking Raworth’s assistance in securing paid work as a poet for the academic year beginning September 1983. The same papers include typed extracts from Mendelssohn’s *roman-à-clef* and two copies of *Crystal Love D. N. A.* and *Posmos, the Yellow Velvet Underground.* (with thanks to Val Raworth; see below notes on these poetry collections).

At Sussex, the typescript page bearing “BEING 707_4^{C}” and the start of “Exposition” is signed “A. Mendleson.” by hand before photocopying and appears to be page one. On the top right-hand corner of the page and poem titled “a.”, “Grace Louise Lake. / Sheffield November 1981” is written in blue ink, post copying. At the end of poem “g.”, a second date appears in black: “November 1981”. This date precedes and perhaps excludes “Sums.”, a work which recurs in a predominantly prose collection Mendelssohn compiled in 1983, *Celestial Empire.* (see below).

The entire typescript is edited by hand. Mendelssohn redacts and corrects words (primarily typos), and adds two: “so” in the second-last line of “Exposition” and “content”, the last word of “c.” The “$_4^{C}$” of the title “BEING 707_4^{C}”, is in Mendelssohn’s hand, as is “a.” In the third- and second-last lines of “a.”, Mendelssohn adds two full stops. In “c.” and “e.” the final two lines are single spaced; all other lines in the typescript entire tend toward double spacing. Another photocopied typescript of page one exists in which the fourth line of “BEING 707_4^{C}” is “~~was~~ spokes~~man~~” (5/A/43/2).

Elsewhere in the Sussex archive there is a handwritten document in red ink that is suggestive of a planned table of contents that includes some of these typescript poems (5/B/2/12). It reads:

I. BEING $707_4^{c(ubed).}$
II. a.b.c.d.e.f.g.
III. knickers with little holes
IV. No man do~~es~~th listen to a woman.
V. (i) postscribble at 16.12. hours } from Poems to Tom.
(ii) One on each shoulder, carouse
VI. It’s the truth!
VII. I shall come in from the right with a-Never.
VIII. Words charge.
IX. Extracts from “Eastern Horizon.”
X. January is grin-ful & dreaming.

Beneath this list, Mendelssohn writes in black ink: “Historiography.” Items I. and II. are from these 1981 typescripts. The lines from “a.”: “Reduced size rapidly grew / a new you” will become a poem unto themselves in Mendelssohn’s *poems* (1984).

In Mendelssohn's *"I'm working here."* (1983), a text dedicated and given to Tom Raworth, poems V. (i) and X. appear as "proscribble at 16.12 hours." and a poem beginning "January is grin-ful & dreaming". Mendelssohn's *Celestial Empire.* (1983) includes "WORDS CHARGE." and "SACRED PIN.", which begins: "I shall come in from the right with a – Never". "One on each shoulder, carouse" and a poem beginning "It's the truth! He cannot contain his stains" appear in *Inbuilt Flash Nix* (1985); retitled "Graves' Art Gallery Tea Room, 1981, Sheffield", "It's the truth!" will resurface in *constant red/mingled damask* (no. 1, 1986). Poems III., IV., and IX. remain unlocated.

Anne Mendleson, Untitled typescript (c. 1981–82).
This typescript is printed on continuous stationery on a dot-matrix printer (SxMs109/5/A/2/7). A clean, paginated fair copy of twelve pages, the entirety is undated and untitled. Of the eight poems it appears to contain, the following exist in no other publication: "Masquerade", "classique", "ars peregrinandi: spreidh.", "why head aching?" (possibly a portion of "ars peregrinandi: spreidh."), and "Pedal". The typescript also includes "Whirr slightly operationless.", a poem that appears in *Posmos, the Yellow Velvet Underground.* (1982), *Inbuilt Flash Nix* (1985), and *Is this a True Parrot, a Mountain, or a Stooge?* (1985). Additionally, the file holds poems that are published in *Propaganda Multi-Billion Bun.* (1985), including "ELEVEN." and the poems beginning "rubbish.   desk bang." and "find one page evenly.", the latter last published in *Figs* (1988). See also below notes for *Is this a True Parrot, Propaganda Multi-Billion Bun.*, and *Figs*.

Anne Mendleson, *Crystal Love: D. N. A.*, Green Suede Blues Press (1982).
This A4 text is attributed to Anne Mendleson, dedicated "for Tom and Val Raworth.", and held at the British Library. On the lower right corner of the title page, Mendelssohn writes "for Ted Hughes, A. M. 12/4/82." The book is combined into a single volume with *Posmos, the Yellow Velvet Underground.*, and paginated 1–25 (originally 1–26; Mendelssohn corrects the page numbers by hand from 18 onwards). On the final page, Mendelssohn gives the publisher as "Green Suede Blues Press", adds "© Mendleson MCMLXXXII", and notes that this is one of four copies. The cover is plain grey, and the text is plastic comb or spiral bound. Minus the Hughes dedication and bearing a black, paint-spattered cover, the same text exists at Sussex Special Collections (SxMs109/5/A/2/4).

A print-out of the same is held in a brown folder in Tom Raworth's papers; in a note dated 24 January 1984 accompanying the text, Mendelssohn suggests that the poems dedicated to the Raworths are "a reply to extracts" of Raworth's *Writing* (1982). Raworth's papers also include a plastic spiral-bound copy of *Crystal Love D. N. A.* and *Posmos, the Yellow Velvet Underground.*, dated as above, but with an orange cover reading on front and back: "*approaching 35* JUNE'S   MODERN ENTERTAINMENTS." This latter copy was likely sent to Raworth in February 1983 along with portions of the Sheffield typescript (November 1981) and Mendelssohn's *roman-à-clef* (with thanks to Val Raworth; see above notes).

Mendelssohn makes minor corrections by hand that differ in each copy. For example, in the first untitled poem of *Crystal Love: D. N. A.*, she corrects the misspelling "murmer" in the Sussex text, but not in the British Library edition; in the poem beginning "maybe I shall", stanza five concludes with a hand-drawn full stop in that is not evident in the Sussex version. Similarly, in the *Posmos* poem titled "whirr slightly operationless" Mendelssohn adds a comma between "fat" and "attractive" that does not appear in the Sussex copy (this poem last appears in *Is this a True Parrot, a Mountain, or a Stooge?* 1985). In the Sussex edition only, Mendelssohn adds "All Rights Reserved." to the handwritten copyright.

At least three alternate undated copies of *Crystal Love: D. N. A.* exist in the Sussex archive. An incomplete, 21-page computer printout of the collection on continuous form stationery gives the title and is credited to "Anne Mendleson", but offers no dedications (5/A/2/3). Later part of *Posmos, the Yellow Velvet Underground.*, "Check the scene" is included in this printout (last printed in *Figs*, no. 14, 1988). A second printout of *Crystal Love: D. N. A.* is identical to the bound copies; it is missing its title page but includes that of *Posmos, the Yellow Velvet Underground.*, with its accompanying dedication to John Barrell and Harriet Guest (5/A/2/5). A third, shorter typescript on thin paper of *Crystal Love: D. N. A.* is attributed to "Anna Mendleson."; at the bottom of two of these pages, Mendelssohn writes: "from Autumn through Winter MCMLXXVII/VIII.", suggesting that textual gestation begins as early as 1977 (5/A/2/2). The running order of this variant is as follows:

Poem beginning "destiny forecast revolt"
Poem beginning "Power to move"
Poem beginning "melancholy might answer in future mistakes,"
Poem beginning "Machiavelli strikes"
Poem beginning "Black velvet cloth"
"GUIDE"
Poem beginning "I like Red People" (last published in *Figs* in 1988; see below notes)
Poem beginning "maybe I shall"
Poem beginning "Treading carpentry free country"
"CADENCE."

In this shorter version, only pages 8–10 are numbered, by hand; textual editing occurs throughout in pencil, as well as blue and black ink; on the back of the last page, Mendelssohn writes: "GREEN SUEDE BLUES PRESS", suggesting that she perceived this as a complete text. Finally, a file folder in Mendelssohn's archive suggests that she may have considered creating a tripartite text that would include *Crystal Love: D. N. A.*, "nonflec" (as its own text), and *Posmos, the Yellow Velvet Underground.*; all three texts are dedicated to couples. On the back of this file, Mendelssohn writes: "1) DREAMT / 2) BEFORE / 3) POSMOS" (A/2/6).

Where evident, edits to the poems contained within these three variants are given below in the order they appear in the final volume. A set of draft poems that differ significantly from the original are included in the appendix of this volume (SxMs109/5/A/2/1). For information on posthumous republications of portions of *Crystal Love D. N. A.*, see notes for *Cleaves Journal of International Poetry* (2010) and *The Paper Nautilus* (2011).

Poem beginning "destiny forecast revolt"
On one version, "a dangled hand" was "a dangled hand." (5/A/2/2; see also appendix variant); on a printout, "rage design" was "rages design" (5/A/2/3).

Poem beginning "Power to move"
A typescript page exists bearing the first stanza of the poem beginning "Power to move" (5/B/2/6). Here the left justification is variegated. Additionally:

"No," was "No"

"Resuscitate" was "Resuscitate."
"Reorganization." was "Reorganisation"
"lamp snares goodness" was "lamp shares goodness"
"Whole" was "whole"

Poem beginning "Machiavelli strikes"
In one printout, "5p a go" was "5p a-go" (5/A/2/3). In the earliest dated variant, "8o81 that's 5p a go." reads "808I that's 2p a go." (5/A/2/2; see also appendix variant).

"GUIDE"
On one printout, the title was "GUIDE CALIGULA"; "CALIGULA" is added by hand (5/A/2/3). In the earliest dated draft, the line "imitating proclamation" is slightly indented (5/A/2/2).

Poem beginning "maybe I shall"
In the earliest dated variant, "it's not all, obviously, in the past." reads "it's not all, obviously in the past." Additionally, "anchor at rest." reads "anchor at rest" in all Sussex variants; the full stop appears in the British Library edition only.

Poem beginning "Treading carpentry free country"
This poem is extensively corrected in the earliest dated variant (5/A/2/2), with three distinctions. Firstly, "forwards by backwards" was "forward by backward"; secondly, "never appearing with detailed information" was "never appearing (with) detailed information"; thirdly, the final three lines look set for excision or to become a stanza of their own, as the beginning and end of these lines is marked in ink with double slashes, and the line beginning "Sadie" is underscored.

"CADENCE."
In one printout, this poem was not on script page 11, but 18, or the second-last poem of this draft (5/A/2/3). In the earliest dated variant, all quotation marks are double, and "although / that which makes" was "though / what makes" (5/A/2/2). In this same copy, "CADENCE." appears to be the final poem; on the verso side, Mendelssohn writes "GREEN SUEDE BLUES PRESS".

Poem beginning "a settlement of priorities reaches unassailable"
In 5/A/2/3 and 5/A/2/5, "peep:" was "peep." In the published copies, Mendelssohn adds the accent on "Alibrée" by hand.

"Shell form: Conch tent. (for John Barker)"
In one printout, the dedication is added by hand (5/A/2/3); elsewhere, it is typed. Manuscript drafts of "Shell form: Conch tent" can be found on a single sheet in 5/B/2/7. Here Mendelssohn writes the poem out three times, increasing its length, her use of punctuation, and varying the title, as in: "Shell/form : Conch/tent" and "Shell : form : Conch : tent.". Some lines are also altered: "We ~~are~~ stand~~ing~~ before the tides." and "We roll over and over ^we roll^ on the sand". The first draft is crossed through; the third is edited in Mendelssohn's hand in contrasting ink. The page is torn from a lined notebook and numbered "15" in a different ink in the upper right-hand corner. Mendelssohn's prison notebook pages were numbered in this fashion, and Mendelssohn returned to these notebooks after her release (see above, Typescripts, 1974). The same file includes reflections

on prison on sheets torn from a different notebook. Comments include: "I HATE PRISON. I'm still not out. The Real is very hard to draw together again".

In the variant text of *Crystal Love: D. N. A.* held in the Raworth papers and retitled "*approaching 35* JUNE'S MODERN ENTERTAINMENTS." Mendelssohn writes beneath this poem, "a fantasy".

Anne Mendleson, *Posmos, the Yellow Velvet Underground.* (1982).

Included in the same collection as *Crystal Love: D. N. A.* (see above), *Posmos, the Yellow Velvet Underground.* has its own title page on 18; this section of the collection is "for John Barrell and Harriet Guest." Page 19 includes another authorial attribution – "ANNE MENDLESON" – and a page number; both typings are then redacted. In turn, page 20 becomes 19, and so on.

Posmos, the Yellow Velvet Underground. includes what may be the first publication of "Whirr slightly operationless", a poem that appears in Mendelssohn's untitled typescript, c. 1981–82, and is republished in *Inbuilt Flash Nix* (1985) and *Is this a True Parrot, a Mountain, or a Stooge?* (1985). Mendelssohn also republished three poems from *Posmos* in *Figs* (no. 14, 1988), namely: "IN A CAVERNOUS HEAT HAZE", "Check the scene", and "making machine poetry" (see notes).

Grace Lake, "*I'm working here.*", Green Suede Blues Press (February 1983).

At the Sussex archive, this handwritten text consists of a hole-punched photocopy of a bound notebook measuring 12 by 14 centimetres, its cover coloured with yellow crayon, its design pasted on, and its spine covered in red translucent tape (SxMs109/5/A/3). In addition to the typed attribution "grace lake.", within which a green plant-like doodle is entwined, the front cover bears another rectangle of red tape, above which reads: "'I'm working here.'" The back cover ripostes: "'You don't seem to be.'" Both phrases are typed in white on a grey background and contained in round-cornered boxes glued to the cover. Above the rear box is a sketch of a partial, sideways figure, above which reads, in pencil: "what is being said becomes, in time, / more clearly defined." On the photocopy, Mendelssohn has retraced these words with blue ink.

The final poem of *"I'm working here."* faces the title page of the predominantly prose collection, *Celestial Empire.*, and is included in that file (5/A/4). Although distinct, these two collections occupy a single text. The final page of the entirety reads: "compiled by / © Grace Lake in / FEBRUARY MCMLXXXIII / from her own (see over)". The facing page reads: "a film festival." Unlike many of Mendelssohn's publications, neither text is housed in UK legal deposit libraries; the original is held in Tom Raworth's papers and was generously shared with the editor by Val Raworth.

"I'm working here." is paginated a - z.; the poems are written in blue, pink, red, and black ink on recto sides, with versos left blank, "Experience" excepted. In the poem beginning "slide slip joke dent", line 10 reads "whilst pairing his fingernails" (ed.). In the original, "so did apollinaire and aragon" is edited in red ink to reinforce the "t" of "tight skirt" and turn the semi-colon after "flesh" to a comma. In the poem beginning "January is grin-ful & dreaming", there is no full stop after "bowl" in the original, and on the photocopy, Mendelssohn uses purple ink to edit the last line: "underneath December's" becomes "beneath December's"; further, the full stop after "Relinquish completely." is very faint in the original (ed.). In the poem beginning "cricket", the "ne'er" of the last line was "never". In "proscribble at 16.12 hours" there is no space between "2" and "hours" (ed.).

The dedicatory page for *"I'm working here."* reads:

- "time takes •
- me further •
- from grace" •

tom raworth :

"The Conscience of a Conservative" [*red ink*]

. . . *for Tom* [*printed text, stamped on page*]

love,
Anne [*green ink*]

There is some nastiness in this book – it worries me & makes me sad – please don't take it seriously – I think that it's because I cannot be, by the rules of the game, completely honest – lumps in porridge [*green ink*]

Page "a." reads:

I.

"She was hounded from town to town. First one person then another set themselves against her, not every day, not every moment of every day but surely, succinctly & with swift, communal sincerity." [*red ink; green quotation marks*]

I hesitate to write – swift, communal se - scenery for example. A sincere scenario. Immediately doubt rears its ugly head: in this context – or am I following a positive force – must I mug – and explain that by writing mug I mean fog – fog fug cloud the issue? – in searching for fresh language, ambiguities do arise.

No-one did help. Anything could happen to me. They preferred to push me out and probably will sprout reasons – which reasons? Who said that to be a poet and-and an artist is easy-to-day?

Against her very mean
broad sun-light
spread carpets bruised
by slammed windows [*blue biro*]

"[L]ove Anne" and all that appears beneath the horizontal line may have been added after textual design and formatting. Raworth's serial poem "The Conscience of a Conservative" was published in *The Mask* (Poltroon Press, 1976) and is dedicated to the Mexican poet José Emilio Pacheco and the journalist Christina Pacheco; Pacheco taught at the University of Essex, where Mendelssohn and Raworth met. See also notes for Sheffield typescript (November 1981) and *Celestial Empire.* (1983).

Grace Lake, *Celestial Empire.* (February 1983).

Contained in the same volume as *"I'm working here."* (see above notes), *Celestial Empire.* is a photocopied manuscript (SxMs109/5/A/4). For this sister text, Mendelssohn recommences an alphabetical pagination that is abandoned after "h." The title page bears the epigraph: "dog-ma dog-ma, / shaggy shaggy dog-ma" and the bottom right-hand corner reads "~~broken~~ – damaged left hand". The text includes nearly forty pages of prose that occasionally transition into prose poetry; post-photocopy, these manuscripts are edited with black and brown ink. In the original notebook held in Tom Raworth's papers, a four-page letter or diary entry dated 16 February is not included in the photocopy; at its centre is a large drawn heart, and in it, Mendelssohn discusses her father, her daughter Poppy, expresses her love and asks to meet Tom again (editor's thanks to Val Raworth).

Included here are the dozen pages of titled poems that appear at the end of *Celestial Empire.* The photocopy of "THAT ROSY, COSY NIGHT-CLUB AFTERNOON" is faded to illegibility. Over it, Mendelssohn retraces and overwrites select words, leaving the shadow of the original visible, but indiscernible. The photocopied variant reads:

THAT ROSY, COSY NIGHTCLUB AFTERNOON
xxxxxxxxxxxxxxxxxxxxxxxxxxxxxxxxxxxxxxxxxxx

          blue saxiphrage
                    mélange
milieu   tennis star

                    lover, rabbit
                    sentiments are
unpresentable   rabbits
taken   taille, melánosis

The original text is restored here (ed.). In "WORDS CHARGE.", "polloi's" reads "poloi's" (ed.). In the photocopies, "Sums." and "Speaking rhythm" are retraced in green ink; a manuscript of the latter can be found at the bottom of a summer term module outline on twentieth-century American art in 5/B/2/10. In *Celestial Empire.*, the wording of "Sums." is identical to the 1981 Sheffield typescript variant, but formatting differs (see above notes). Some formatting and words of "Giaconda's Contumacious Lapse." resist deciphering. Unclear phrases include: "graced accompaniment" and "(jurals)"; the formatting of the stanza beginning "future past" is also uncertain (ed.). See also Typescript (October 1983).

Grace Lake, Typescript (October 1983).

Titled "oh yes we are entitled mohican slaves" and "dig; dig.", these two poems share a gestation year and thematic with *Celestial Empire.* (see above). Typed on a single sheet of legal paper watermarked "Plus Fabric", the titles are hand-written in black ink, as are edits; "October '83" is written in blue felt tip at page bottom (SxMs109/5/A/43/1). The title "oh yes we are entitled mohican slaves" may begin "ah yes" (ed.); within the poem, Mendelssohn excises a "thou" at the end of the line beginning "slumped". In both poems, spacing is excised around some commas, as in: "that,changed simple,changed"; "mystery,do"; and "dark,bronze, unsual"; this has been reinstated (ed.).

This same file contains the poem beginning "rolling, and all these words are alive and" (June 1985); "a room a" (April 1986); and a typescript of "Winter.", a poem that will appear in *The News* (no. 1, 1987) and *Slate* (no. 3, 1987). Finally, the folder holds extracts from Mendelssohn's *roman-à-clef*, including a portion of *What a Performance* (1987).

Grace Lake, *Other Poetry* submission (6 June 1984).

Edited by Evangeline Patterson and Anne Stevenson, *Other Poetry* was founded in 1978. It ceased operation from 1991–94 but continues today. In her "Foreword" to issue one, Stevenson writes that the flower of good poetry draws from two roots: a deeper root that extends into the distant past, and a second root that drinks "thirstily but more shallowly from wide acres of the emotional present." It is Stevenson's intention that *Other Poetry* "dra[w] energy from both roots". She explains:

> Without naming names or dividing poets into camps, we feel that many poets are ill-served by the periodicals that publish poetry these days because they fit into no recognised school. They are neither avant-garde, nor academic, nor political, nor confessional, nor anything else currently fashionable. Often they do not think of themselves as 'professional poets' at all, but as people who regard the writing of poetry as a natural but major extension of awareness at a time in which poetry is too often regarded as an elitist privilege or a panacea for psychological ailments.

Early contributors included Michael Horovitz, editor of the seminal poetry anthology, *Children of Albion* (1969), and Movement poet Elizabeth Jennings (both issue three). British academics Isobel Armstrong and Phil Tew were also among the contributors (see issue four), but in the main, very few of the poets with whom Mendelssohn regularly associated and published appear in this periodical. Based on the replete holdings at the National Poetry Library, Southbank Centre, Mendelssohn did not publish with *Other Poetry* in her lifetime.

Each numbered part of Mendelssohn's two-part submission, an untitled poem beginning "point a finger at him", occupies its own typescript sheet, watermarked Jubilee (SxMs109/5/A/4a). By hand, Mendelssohn signs both pages "G. Louise Lake", adding, at the bottom of page one, "To A. Stevenson. / Ed: 'OTHER POETRY' / June 6th . 84." The commas in the final two lines are penned after typing.

Grace Lake and Timothy Mathews, *poems* (1984).

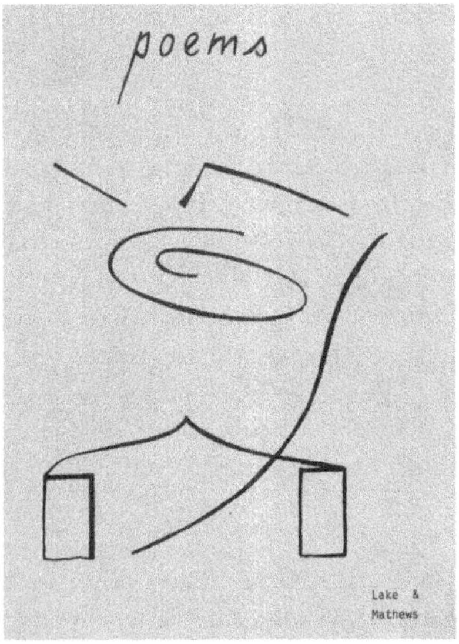

Mendelssohn met Timothy Mathews at Cambridge. An Emeritus Professor of French and Comparative Criticism at University College London, Mathews has published widely on twentieth-century art and literature, addressing figures that fascinated Mendelssohn, among them, Giacometti and Apollinaire. Their collaborative chapbook, *poems*, emerged organically out of their friendship, and each author responded to the other's writing in turn. The text was sold at Heffers Bookshop in Cambridge (phone conversation with Mathews; 8 March 2017). Mendelssohn did not place this publication in any UK legal deposit library, and there is no complete copy in her Sussex archive, although there are three coverless typescripts of *poems* that are almost identical to the final volume (5/A/37). Mathews's single copy is bound in green card, its cover bearing a large, minimalist Mendelssohn design (shown here); the title is written in her cursive hand. In the bottom right hand corner, "Lake & Mathews" is typed in the font used throughout the volume.

Mathews's copy consists of 20 A5 sides, 16 of which bear poems. Each poem is attributed by the author's surname only. The inside back cover houses a drawing of the upper half of an abstracted figure. Profiles appear embedded within that figure, as is the word "CLICHÉ"; the title of one of Mathews's poems is "'Clichés'". To the right-hand side of this drawing is the letter "F". The drawing original is in SxMs109/5/B/2/15a. The inside cover reads in full: "Graphics: Lake / Copyright: Lake and Mathews, 1984". At Sussex, files 5/B/2/15a and 5/B/2/56 contain near-identical copies of the cover on white, folded A4 paper, but they are titled "spliced interstices" and have no authorial attribution. Three more variants exist with this alternate title in 5/B/2/15a; one shows a single diagonal line; another, a set of interlocking lines and triangles; and, in the third, a row of hair-like lines extending from squared follicles. A facial profile appears on the verso of the 5/B/2/56 copy.

In 5/B/2/15a, there is another mocked-up cover reading "le lierre déchire la terre" (ivy destroys the land or earth) accompanied by a picture of a plant with a single leaf, visible roots, a rounded horizon, and the attribution: "sustained by grace lake & tim mathews." Unsure about using French for the title, the authors settled on *poems*. Mathews states, "At that time [using French] did seem more of a strange thing to do than perhaps it would now" (Mathews email, 30 July 2017). The back cover of this mock-up reads "copyright." but gives neither date nor author. A photocopied manuscript of a poem from the volume, "That piano is my god", written on graph paper, is also in 5/B/2/15a, as is a poem dedicated "to tim." and entitled "The duskly migration of folk to daylight." It reads:

> Phone, write.
> What is the arrangement?
> Sounds as though the mafia are coming to tea.
> Every evening as the dark comes on
> People fly to the light.
>
> The parts of earth sprayed in day
> are duly inhabited, night never falls
> on inhabited terrain.
>
> They take their owls and donkeys with them.
> A few have squirrels. A few have peacocks.
> Their hens being squint-eyed live in both worlds simultaneously.
> Of course flight takes place on moorbirds' backs.
>
> Which are large and normally empty.
>
> In the new land of folkskin
> logical sequences occur in slow motion
> Intense moments round.

This poem does not appear elsewhere in Mendelssohn's published works.

Given that the text was a co-written endeavour, close attention should be paid to the complete running order of poems that is included in the itemised, chronological list of individual collection contents in this volume. Mendelssohn's poems are inextricable from Mathews's, and as such, his full contributions to the text are reproduced with his kind permission here:

> All my friends in imagination
> speak and exchange

the familiar gestures
through which the silence shines

the silence shines
and yet only in the shaky
tenderness of a bright
tired lady and a forgotten name

*

Anxiety rips
the directions bleed
packaged forms
glow red wounds
and a ghastly creativity imagined
the other side of a struggle in words
timed to the end

*

Apologies are in order
for the weakness of our friends
for images move
through the love of the strangest things
a cherished attraction
to the rags of expressiveness
the brick-a-brack of time-worn
gestures the seams fluttering after
the heavy gold band has shone forth
glueing friends through us to silence

*

Spots on an abstract space
my eyes shine before me
but the small boy
is now an organism
with the deadening blow in him
of toys turned into fast cars

Finally the banality glows
penetrating memory pressed with desires
and now and even now
a second best befriends
cherished obsessions recede
in touch as complex
as the tags on exchanged gifts
moving like the lined face of the woman's age

*

The affiliation is broken
even as smears fail
now the innocence is valueless
and the parentheses obscure
for a young man weeps
as speech across silence collapses
and the contact he creates as the rain glimmers

*

Of course in her absence
in her absence
the lines move in speed
tracing delusions of colour
and the music falters
as I dream aimlessly
seeking what I know and what I give
and what I give
in the melting of our lives

For those abstractions
I buy and they sell
we both remember
the grease in my shoulder-holster
and your seering harmonies
bleed over my strings
as I press the root
folded in the sensuous depths
of me and you

*

'Clichés'

It drips its colour into the light
and flows the loneliness of another world
slipstreaming repeatedly as the whites of my eye

Harmonies in unison have no voice
and call me to my body
making my thoughts recognisable
and my thoughts from recognition

And I fly in the neon signs
call it a mainline
hear advice in the face
and see the lights divide

Slam scream for touch
and break the law with noise
call it expression smoothly sheened.

*

Countdown

The singer watched me read
We still can't see
went his lament
I mined the stone
in search of
different languages
but became involved
in a structure of fidelity
the tricks of memory transforming
the illusion there is dialogue with a sculpture
moving as I watch it feel me.

The pressure of disintegration
is a smile and a kick

a hand-shake and a bomb
with plenty of magnetism
until I really do believe
that to break up into difference
is finally pushing word-births out of my mouth
and has been painting in
the surfaces of faithful silence
ever since.

In two of the three Sussex copies of *poems*, Mendelssohn makes changes that do not recur in publication (5/A/37). Further loose poems from this collection are scattered through Mendelssohn's Sussex archive. A list of Mendelssohn's amendments to her own contribution follows in the order of publication.

"from views"
A poem manuscript exists in 5/B/2/5. Barring a full stop after "stroll." it is identical to the published poem and is signed "Grace Lake. / September 1983."

"'The bourgeoisie lives there'"
In two of the three typescripts, Mendelssohn adds an "s" by hand to "live" (5/A/37). On lined orange paper torn from a spiral notebook, a poem manuscript exists in 5/B/1/1b. In it, the title reads 'THE BOURGEOISIE LIVES THERE'." (the "S" in "LIVES" is a later addition), and line six concludes "pander belch'd." Along the page bottom is a pencilled "24" and in the right bottom corner, in the same black ink as the poem, reads "LAKE."

"To   PP158, 159, 160,170   MoMA Sol Lewitt."
This poem exists in the same foolscap, photocopied typescript as the 1981 Sheffield typescript (see above notes; 5/B/2/41). In addition to differences in punctuation and initial line breaks, in this typescript, the "up" of the first line appears at the end of the line with a semi-colon, and there is an umlaut over the second 'e' of "mesme".

In one of the three coverless typescripts of *poems*, a space is left between "black" and "2" in the last line; in the second and third typescripts and Mathews's final version, the "#" is added by hand (5/A/37). In some typescripts (including the 1981 Sheffield typescript) and in the Mathews text, "Vene vicit." is "Vene vincit." On neon green paper and in red ink, a manuscript version exists in 5/B/1/1a; distinctions between manuscript and typescript include: "mess ^up^ the proportions"; "feline ~~objects~~ / Objects"; semi-colons after "sly", "monkey", and "changed"; and an umlaut over the second "e" of "mesme".

Poem beginning "reduced size rapidly grew"
On a small page torn from a notebook, a manuscript of this poem is titled "HOPSCOTCH"; the title is in red ink, the poem that follows in blue (5/B/1/1a). These lines also appear within poem "a." in the Sheffield typescript of November 1981 (see above notes).

Poem beginning "Take a long train"
A manuscript exists in red ink on neon green paper (5/B/1/1a). Barring the word "injustice", it is written in capitals; the phrase "limb-severed" was "LIMB-SERVED". Differences in punctuation include: a comma after "conversation"; full stops after "speak" and "mattresses"; no full stop after "quit".

"very early poem"
Titled "Very Early Poem.", there is an otherwise identical manuscript of this poem in red ink, on lined paper torn from a spiral-bound notepad (5/B/1/1a).

Poem beginning "That piano is my god"
In a coverless typescript, the word "Blasted" is redacted from the final line, but it remains in the published chapbook. In one instance, Mendelssohn corrects "practicing" to "practising" (5/A/37). In the photocopied manuscript on graph paper in 5/B/2/15a, no full stop is included after "sobbed", and the fifth line of stanza two begins "by the afternoon"; the "and" is omitted.

Poem beginning "i) rolled   rolled a   a"
Replicated in this text are the accents Mendelssohn adds by hand to one typescript to "réplu" and "république" (see 5/A/37; another accented typescript exists in 5/B/2/21). In all copies, including the published chapbook, the poem is landscape formatted, with the attribution "Lake" running perpendicular to the poem in the bottom right corner of the page.

Grace Lake, Formatted manuscript (June 1985).
This untitled, photocopied manuscript poem beginning "rolling, and all these words are alive and", exists in file SxMs109/5/A/43/1, which also contains "oh yes we are entitled mohican slaves" and "dig; dig." (October 1983); "a room a" (April 1986); and a typescript of "Winter.", a poem that will appear in *The News* (no. 1, 1987) and *Slate* (no. 3, 1987). Finally, the folder holds extracts from Mendelssohn's *roman-à-clef*, including a portion of *What a Performance* (1987).

The poem is framed by a hand-drawn box that is approximately A5 size, as if prepared for chapbook publication; within the bottom right corner reads: "Grace Lake / June 1985." On the verso side, Mendelssohn writes "1984" in blue ink.

A manuscript of this poem exists on a postcard in 5/B/1/1a; across the top reads "13.20 hours." Mendelssohn writes out stanza one twice; the space between "die for" and "I" in line one of stanza two is filled by the word "dimitty" [*sic*]. The first and second line of stanza three read: "The prerequisite for continuation must be / shelved for a while. Why? Because great". In the final stanza, "& crunch / the" is omitted. Some spelling errors evident here are corrected in the June 1985 manuscript.

There are two further manuscripts in 5/B/1/1a that show differences in lineation and punctuation; one is signed "Grace Lake / Cambridge 1985". In both second stanzas, "dimity" appears in double quotation marks, and there is no extended spacing; in the third stanzas, "continuation" is "continuum", "Because great days" was "Because 2 ½ x 5 great days", and "sniff" is the concluding word, following an extended space. In the fourth stanzas, "There are too many petrol and diesel fumes blowing out into space" was "Blowing out into space are too many" (the line breaks after "Blowing" and "out" respectively); and in stanza five, "chew & crunch" was "crunch then / chew". In the unsigned copy, the final stanza ends, "my polystyrene cloud from St. Cloud." In the signed copy, the first line of stanza three reads "Not that that is entirely correct." and the entirety ends: "my polystyrene / cloud."

Grace Lake, *Propaganda Multi-Billion Bun.* (August 1985).
The bound copy of *Propaganda Multi-Billion Bun.* housed at Sussex (SxMs109/5/A/7/3) is identical to that filed in the British Library; they are photocopies of the same typescript. In both editions, at the bottom left-hand corner of page one, Mendelssohn has written in faint pencil "for Fran." By hand, she makes pre-photocopying corrections and paginates the entirety irregularly. The twenty pages of the text are marked as follows: 1., 2, 3., 4., (unpaginated), 5., 6.(i), 6(II), 6(III), 7., 8(I), 8(II), 9., 10., 11(I), 11(II), 12., 13., 14(I), 14(II). In both copies, Mendelssohn signs "Grace Lake." at the bottom of 14(II). The inside back cover of the Sussex version reads: "© August 1985 LAKE."

Where the British Library cover is plain grey, without title or authorial attribution, in the Sussex edition, the grey cover has both title and "Grace Lake" in green ink; the word "propaganda" is misspelt as "propaganda" (elsewhere, it is correct or corrected). Two additional draft covers in the same file include the date, doodles of simple house and clock shapes, and, on one version, the following:

> IS A CLOCK IN A DREAM
> AS BIG/SMALL/MEDIUM/ROUND/BLANK AS
> A CLOCK IN AWAKE?" (5/A/7/3)

In the bottom third of the page is written: "GRACE LAKE 1985. / and the dancing ticks."; three small dots with two radiating legs cascade down the right-hand middle portion of the page. The other draft cover has a geometric house shape with a clock emerging from a line drawn from the apex of the roof.

An alternate cover (5/A/7/1) includes an illustration of a clock-faced, robotic figure with an animal attendant; across the individual, Mendelssohn writes "Grace Lake" and beneath the animal, "with her liberated mechanical dog." Another hand-drawn cover is located in 5/A/7/2: this one is on orange-brown paper, has title, author, and date, and a line of four mantel clocks, followed by: "is a clock in a dream the same size / as a clock to touch in awake?" This version is dedicated "FOR ROGER." along the top of the cover. The inside title page, in pencil, includes a diagram of a clock-faced figure with pens in each hand, one of which is aloft; beneath this illustration reads: "by Grace Lake 1985 / with her liberated dream clocks' companion". This text is incomplete, including pages 4 to 8 (II) only, and has two pencilled edits: "too long at beginning" is written under the second stanza of the poem beginning "what is wrong with 'easy'?", and a question mark next to the stanza beginning "dying".

Barring approximately four sheets, the majority of what appears to be the original typescript is held at Sussex (5/A/7/1). The entirety is on various and variously coloured paper stock. Mendelssohn edited this typescript by hand, predominantly to correct typos or minor elisions (i.e., in the poem beginning "She appears in thirteen dresses", "an" is added to: "She is an employed hireling"). An exception to this general rule is the final couplet of the poem beginning "i can hardly bear", which originally concluded as follows: "all the bucketed had gone   6666   and never arrived. / 'We have our ups' motioned the sleeping houses." The numbers are firmly redacted in green ink. After these lines, in the original, the first lines of "ELEVEN." begin, suggesting that the two poems may have been initially intended as a single text. In blue, Mendelssohn draws a line between the last line of "i can hardly bear" and the stanza to follow; the title "ELEVEN." is squeezed in by hand also. In all instances, "bear" was "bare" (ed.).

Similarly, the "no relation." of "great big sparkling Deal no relation." is written in after typing, as is the dedicatory title, "for Anne Devlin" (5/A/7/1). Mendelssohn then photocopied these A4 sheets, shrinking the poems to A5, although she ultimately published and circulated *Propaganda Multi-Billion Bun.* in A4 format. The first unpaginated set of photocopies appear in the same file as the original typescripts.

Propaganda Multi-Billion Bun. may have begun life with the untitled typescript dated c. 1981–82, which includes the poem beginning "rubbish.   desk bang" and "ELEVEN." (see above notes).

Minor changes include from the published and typescript versions of "rubbish." include:

> Line beginning "trip!" was not indented
> "tucker-notes" was "tucker notes"
> Line beginning "flashed back" is slightly indented
> Stanza four, beginning "'Get into your own backyard" was slightly offset
> "own neighbour.'" was "own neighbour'."
> "'And bring" was "And bring"
>
> From "Eleven", distinctions between the 1985 and the c. 1981–82 versions include:
> "ELEVEN." was "Eleven"
> "& i know" was "& I know"
> "big grime ingrained" was "big, grime-engrained"
> "lump. i cheeked you to cheer you up." was "lump, I ran for the nurse, / cheeked you to cheer you up."
> "pink spotted" was "pink-spotted"
> "so i divided" was "so I divided"
> "they came alive in my head" was "they were alive / (in my head)"

An early variant of the poem beginning "find one page evenly." exists in the same c. 1981–82 typescript; this poem was last published in *Figs* (no. 14, 1988), as was, from *Propaganda Multi-Billion Bun.*, "don't be northern, whatever you do" (see below).

Grace Lake, *Inbuilt Flash Nix* (August 1985).
This collection of prose and poetry consists of unpaginated A4 photocopies folded and stapled into an A5 chapbook (SxMs109/5/A/5/5). The handwritten cover has no images, reading: "INBUILT FLASH NIX" and "GRACE LAKE." In blue ink, Mendelssohn adds: "Own Copy / August 12th 1985 / London." The title page includes a near-indiscernible photocopy of Mendelssohn photographing herself in a mirror, and, in blue ink, the statement: "compiled August 1985." (a clearer copy exists in the A4 manuscript and typescript draft found in 5/A/5/3). On the otherwise plain white back cover, Mendelssohn makes notes reading:

> CHECK TROUSERS
> MAN PUSHES A WOMAN TO THE PAVEMENT.
> REFUSING TO RELINQUISH A LIFE OF LUXURY
> ANOTHER WOMAN IS CLIMBING THE FLIGHT STEPS OF A PLANE
> with a ~~wi~~ luxen leather suitcase.

Do I WANT THESE : VOLUME
LINEN FLOWERS
SWIMMING POOLS

Acres & acres of green lawn –
Dreaming over poetry.
EXPRESSION
hat replaces heart.
" poetry

DISGUST WITH MOTHER

The outset of the volume contains a handwritten, photocopied short story about purchasing a camera, and a twelve-part prose work entitled "When I gave all my records away." This serial piece is followed by an untitled, photocopied sheet of prose handwritten into a spiral-bound, lined paged notebook (another copy exists in 5/B/2/3). Mendelssohn's tendency to interleave prose and poetry is exemplified by her use of the poem beginning "yes, it is a shame, a real shame" within a play she reputedly performed in 1985 (see below cross-referenced list), and its inclusion, again, within the prose and poetry she submitted to *constant red/mingled damask* (no. 1, 1986).

The remaining portion of *Inbuilt Flash Nix* includes one pen and ink doodle and poetry, much of which was republished; the later variants are replicated in this volume in their respective collections. A list of the republished poetic contents of *Inbuilt Flash Nix* includes:

"Train to L'pool." – also appears in *constant red/mingled damask* (no 1, 1986)
Poem beginning "Shiva's crackling on a spinal hair" – also in *constant red/mingled damask* (no 1, 1986)
Poem beginning "it's the truth! He cannot contain his stains" – also published as "Graves' Art Gallery Tea Room, 1981, Sheffield", *constant red/mingled damask* (no 1, 1986)
"Whirr slightly operationless." – first published in *Posmos, the Yellow Velvet Underground.* (1982); also appears in *Is this a True Parrot, a Mountain, or a Stooge?* (1985)
"LOCALIZED PLASTER." – appears in *Is this a True Parrot, a Mountain, or a Stooge?* (1985)
"LOCALIZED EFFECTS." – appears in *Is this a True Parrot, a Mountain, or a Stooge?* (1985); dated "2/1975." (5/A/5/3, 4 and 5)
Poem beginning "yes, it is a shame, a real shame" – appears twice in *Inbuilt Flash Nix* (1985), as part of a short play entitled "THERE was a great ripping up OF ROMANCE OCCURRING." (performed at Trinity Hall, Cambridge, 1985; SxMs109/7/A/6), and again in *constant red/mingled damask* (no 1, 1986)
Poem beginning "APOTHECARIES' KNUCKLEDUSTERS SUIT THEIR" – appears twice in Own Copy, *Inbuilt Flash Nix*; beneath one poem, Mendelssohn writes, "10/1983." and on the second, "October 1983."

Poem beginning "Must you?' She seldom burns" – appears in *Is this a True Parrot, a Mountain, or a Stooge?* (1985)
"Follow her magic." – *constant red/mingled damask* (1; 1986)
"Radiated?   Light?" – *constant red/mingled damask* (1; 1986)
"HOT DAY.   BAKED BARE EARTH.   PROWLED IN THE VALLEY FOR THE PIGS' NEST."
Poem beginning "Were they allowed to write" – appears in *Is this a True Parrot, a Mountain, or a Stooge?* (1985)
"One on each shoulder, carouse." – appears in *Is this a True Parrot, a Mountain, or a Stooge?* (1985)

Sussex holds four main files containing variants of material included in *Inbuilt Flash Nix* (SxMs109/5/A/5/1–4). Of these, most replicate the final bound edition. Exceptionally, one file contains early computer printouts of five poems from this collection, including "HOT DAY.", "One on each shoulder, carouse.", "APOTHECARIES' KNUCKLEDUSTERS"; "Follow her magic.", and "it's the truth!" (5/A/5/4). At the bottom of four of these pages, Mendelssohn writes "Grace Lake" and the collection title; twice, the title is given as *Insult Flash Nix*. Minor variations in the computer printout include: in "HOT DAY." "subconscience" was "subconscious"; in "Follow her magic." "snig-papers" was "anig-papers"; "prohibition serving fear" was "prohibition swerving fear", and "JIVE?JIVE" was "JIVE-JIVE". See below notes on *constant red/mingled damask* (1986) for changes to "it's the truth!" (later, "Graves' Art Gallery Tea Room, 1981, Sheffield").

An undated manuscript of "HOT DAY." appears in 5/B/2/5 on a lined sheet from a single hole-punched A5 exercise book. In addition to differences of punctuation and line endings, this draft uses the word "subconscience", replaces "Mrs. Brantain's" with "Mrs. Plantain's", and ends with the word "directions".

The edition of *Inbuilt Flash Nix* housed in the British Library is not as replete as the "Own Copy" at Sussex Special Collections. It does not contain "Train to L'pool."; "Shiva's crackling on a spinal hair"; "Horror   Impudence   Chastisement"; "it's the truth!"; "Whirr slightly operationless." or "One on each shoulder, carouse." It is also differently ordered, as follows:

Title page
Photocopy of Mendelssohn photographing herself
Three pages of prose, "Inbuilt Flash Nix"
?
Poem beginning "yes, it is a shame, a real shame"
Poem beginning "APOTHECARIES' KNUCKLEDUSTERS SUIT THEIR"
LOCALIZED EFFECTS.
LOCALIZED PLASTER.
Poem beginning "Must you?' She seldom burns"
"HOT DAY.   BAKED BARE EARTH.   PROWLED IN THE VALLEY FOR THE PIGS' NEST."
"Radiated?   Light?"
Poem beginning "Were they allowed to write"
"Follow her magic."
Photocopied handwritten prose beginning "into the dips and angles"
Page five only of 6-page typed prose sequence, "When I gave all my records away."
Poem beginning "piped, once more, piped"
Pages 1–4 and 6 of typed prose sequence, "When I gave all my records away."

See also above notes for Sheffield typescript (November 1981) and Untitled typescript (circa 1981–82).

Grace Lake, *Is this a True Parrot, a Mountain, or a Stooge?*, Scrap Publishing (1985).
The cover of this chapbook shows a sentimentalised silhouette of two children – one feminine, one masculine – on a seesaw beneath a tree. Above this image, Mendelssohn writes out the title; beneath the picture reads "GRACE LAKE." This same image, replete with title and authorial attribution, is copied onto the bottom right-hand corner of one page of *Figs* (no. 14, 1988), in addition to a contribution of Mendelssohn's previously published poems (see below notes). On the back of the chapbook cover, Mendelssohn writes: "© LAKE.   SCRAP PUBLISHING / 1985. NEW YORK." The entirety is photocopied onto a sheet of A4 folded to serve as the cover of the A5 chapbook. Four files are devoted to this chapbook at Sussex, each of which contains partial and differing constructions and reconstructions of the text; only the cover remains consistent (SxMs109/5/A/6/1–4).

The gestation of *Is this a True Parrot, a Mountain, or a Stooge?* (1985) is linked to *Inbuilt Flash Nix* (1985), *Posmos, the Yellow Velvet Underground.* (1982), and Untitled typescript (c. 1981–82); all contain variants of "Whirr slightly operationless." (see above). One covered, formerly stapled variant of *Is this a True Parrot* includes only typescript poems that are also found in *Inbuilt Flash Nix*. These are: "Whirr slightly operationless."; two copies of the poem beginning "it's the truth! He cannot contain his stains" (later titled "Graves' Art Gallery Tea Room, 1981, Sheffield"; see notes for *constant red/mingled damask*, no. 1, 1986); "One on each shoulder, carouse."; "LOCALIZED EFFECTS."; "LOCALIZED PLASTER."; and poems beginning, respectively, "Must you? She seldom burns" and "Were they allowed to write" (5/A/6/4). A copy of the line drawing included in the interior of *Inbuilt Flash Nix* is located within another file of these draft volumes (5/A/6/2).

In 5/A/6/1 and 5/A/6/3, variants of *Is this a True Parrot, a Mountain, or a Stooge?* include a three-page prose piece entitled "Someone to rely on." and two poems that are not published elsewhere: "Who cycled in two fours?" and "Where?" ("Where?" appears also in 5/A/6/2). Typescripts exist of both poems, but the definitive variants appear to be manuscripts photocopied on the same orange paper as the cover (5/A/6/3). Further fragments of this collection are scattered through Mendelssohn's papers: for instance, "Someone to rely on" and "Who cycled in two fours?" are in 5/B/2/5, and the cover reappears in 5/B/2/50. Notable variants between poem versions, in order of appearance, are given below.

"Whirr slightly operationless."
The 1985 variant of this poem is used here; minor differences from the 1981–82 versions in *Posmos* (5/A/2/4) and the c. 1981–82 untitled typescript (5/A/2/7) include the numbering of sections, and the following:

Title and subtitles are not underlined (5/A/2/7)
"operationless." was "operationless" (5/A/2/4)
"aphoristic dominance / heaves" was "aphoristic / heaves" (5/A/2/7)
"immigranté" was "immigrante" (5/A/2/4 and 5/A/2/7)
"derrier   monde" was "derrier-monde" (5/A/2/4) and "derrier monde" (5/A/2/7)
"until her" was "til her" (5/A/2/4)
"She twinkles" was "she twinkles" (5/A/2/7)
"mouth line." was "mouth-line." (5/A/2/4)
"boy friend" was "boy friends" (5/A/2/7)
"his girl" was "his bird" (5/A/2/4)
"slim-line" was "slim line" (5/A/2/4)
"the fat, attractive" was "the fat attractive" (5/A/2/4)
"be-spectacled" was "bespectacled" (5/A/2/7)

"I am nicely" was "I'm nicely" (5/A/2/4)
"net-wise" was "net-wize" (5/A/2/4)
"small gap" was "small   gap" (5/A/2/7)
"cud kind of thud, curdling there" was "cud kind of thud without the noise, curdling" (5/A/2/4) and "cud kind of thud to curdle there" (5/A/2/7)
"phonecall last night" was "phonecall last night." (5/A/2/7)

"One on each shoulder, carouse."
Next to "aeaea", Mendelssohn writes by hand: "(read a€a€a)" (5/A/6/4; see also 5/A/5/3, 4, and 5). This annotation is photocopied, but the altered lettering remains ambiguous (ed).

"LOCALIZED EFFECTS."
By hand, Mendelssohn writes beneath the poem: "2 / 1975." (5/A/6/4; see also 5/A/5/3, 4 and 5). This annotation has been photocopied.

Poem beginning "Must you?' She seldom burns"
Annotations made before photocopying include corrected typos and: "now they ~~are~~"; "march ~~to~~"; "all in ^a^ tricky", and "(sic)" referring to "microphes" (5/A/6/4).

"Who cycled in two fours?"
This poem does not appear in all archived copies of *Is this a True Parrot, a Mountain, or a Stooge?* The definitive variant appears to be a manuscript photocopied in the same orange paper used for the cover (5/A/6/3). A typescript is held in 5/A/6/1; signed in blue ink, "Lake", it differs from the manuscript in punctuation, spacing, and capitalisation, including: "hard, empty" was "hard empty"; "say) leads to" was "say). leads to" (and, in another manuscript in the same file, "say) lead to"). Further, "Quite Different" was "Quite different" and "Wrapped round" was "Wrapped around".

"Where?"
The manuscript of this poem in 5/A/6/1 includes a rhomboid drawing where a title might be expected; in the photocopied manuscript of 5/A/6/2, this same drawing is copied and included next to the underlined title. This latter variant does not include the third stanza and is signed "Grace Lake." with a note reading: "Shirley Prendergast has lost a whole file of my poetry. / A. M." The version used in this collection is that of 5/A/6/1, which is identical to the copy of stanza three that appears in the orange, photocopied and possibly final text in 5/A/6/3.

In addition to minor changes in punctuation, the untitled, incomplete typescript in 5/A/6/2 shows differences from the manuscript photocopies, including: "this SQUARE TRIM JUMP" is typed as "this square trim jump"; "by he" is rendered "by He"; and the stanza break after "auditories" is elided. The typescript shows only the first two lines of stanza three, beginning "the Pleasure of Petrol's stretch".

Grace Lake, Typescript (1985).
With a photocopier, Mendelssohn reduces "WHY" and "Dear chaos." to A5 size as she does for some chapbooks, among them, *Is this a True Parrot, a Mountain, or a Stooge?* A minimalist doodle akin to the one contained in *Inbuilt Flash Nix* occupies a page in

the file these poems share; it is also photocopied and reduced (SxMs109/5/A/42). Across the top of "Dear chaos." Mendelssohn types: "Michelle . . .   please hear the ironic voice. O.K?" She then signs "Grace" by hand; both additions occur pre-copying.

There are two typescripts of "WHY" and the original title ("WHY . . ") is redacted on both. One is corrected by hand, and in its margins, Mendelssohn writes: "This poem has an effete voice, is searching sense, is progressively reluctant to reveal artificial constructs as fitting substitutes for the cycle of natural decay." On this copy, used here, Mendelssohn alters spelling and typos, and makes the following substantive changes:

"firstly" was "first"
"secondly" was "second"
"onto" was "on"
"questions" was "question"
"summonsed" was "summoned"
"sea; mellowed" was "sea, mellowed"

A related file includes a photocopied photograph of Mendelssohn replicated in the introduction to this volume. The image is surrounded by doodles and is placed on a hand-written manuscript of "WHY". Along the left border, from the first stanza, reads: "father / her bear's / JUL / EMBLEMATIC". The photograph is placed on an angle, and the last two lines of stanza two are just visible along the bottom edge. The third stanza is fully visible, and it differs from the typescript in that there are no mid-line extended spaces; the first word reads "the", a comma is added after "meadow" in line four, and a hyphen is added to "back seat". The entirety is attributed to "Grace Lake. / 1985. ©" (5/B/2/10). See also below notes on the undated poems at the end of this volume, specifically "moxed metaphor" and poem beginning "nit freaks".

Grace Lake, Typescript (22 April 1986).
The poem "a room a" is a dated typescript on Plus Fabric watermarked paper. It is in file SxMs109/5/A/43/1, which contains "oh yes we are entitled mohican slaves" and "dig; dig." (1983); the poem beginning "rolling, and all these words are alive and" (1985), and a typescript of "Winter.", a poem that appears in *The News* (no. 1, 1987) and *Slate* (no. 3, 1987). The folder holds extracts from Mendelssohn's *roman-à-clef*, including a portion of *What a Performance* (1987).

Grace Lake, Typescript (September 1986).
Mendelssohn typed these poems – "In the end tulane –"; "tripping up on jibes"; "Above her heart, a grand piano." – into a booklet made from a folded A3 sheet. The first two poems were photocopied onto A3 and similarly formatted; a final A4 photocopy shows these two poems reduced to sit side by side on a partitioned A4 sheet, as Mendelssohn often does with a view to creating a chapbook (SxMs109/5/A/26). A related manuscript sheet exists in 5/B/1/1b; starting *in medias res*, it reads:

& PROUD of itself, arms folded, tree bashing back with a mumble,
ah! Benediction. the rising tide's threatening voice. mix 'em up.
what doth it come down to? Sea-garden owned by whoever can,
but this is a mystery, kyrie, – however to oversperse which it would be,
intoxicating mystery, the part of history which doesn't, on a low sling,

send you shivering to a corner intent upon sweet innocence, his sea
might be travelling chiastically, he doesn't need his arms to indicate
his strength, although conjunctions may be banned, around here,

above her heart, a grand piano.

By hand, Mendelssohn corrects a line in the fourth stanza of "In the end tulane –": "part ~~of~~ to" and may place a bullet point between the title and line one (ed.). "Tulane" is a middle name of Mendelssohn's third child, Emerald, born August 1985. The title is hand-written, as is an upper-right corner note reading: "from Grace. / September 4th 1986." In the bottom left corner, Mendelssohn writes: "1st birthday." All corrections recur in photocopies. Exceptionally, in the A3 photocopy, pencilled forward slashes suggest that Mendelssohn may have considered making "a vacancy" a distinct line (ed.).

In the single copy of "tripping up on jibes", each portion of the poem occupies its own page. In the photocopy of the A3 booklet, "Above her heart, a grand piano." includes the following annotations by hand in blue: "another topsy tale. / turvy. one out the window." is changed to "another topsy turvy tale / one out the window."; "window tops." becomes "window tops?" and "call it torture" is altered to read "call that torture".

The same A3 photocopy includes handwritten reference notes. In the blank centre of the booklet, Mendelssohn writes:

> Lit & Phils. Thomas Henry, Thomas Percival, & John Aiken founded the Manchester Lit & Phil. Society in 1781. The radical, Joseph Priestly, lecturer at the Warrington Academy, was a founder member of the Lunar Society and honorary member of the M/c Lit. & Phil.
>
> Thomas Henry: The natural tendency of a cultivation of polite learning is to refine the understanding, humanise the soul, enlarge the field of useful knowledge."

Beneath "Above her heart, a grand piano." Mendelssohn writes:

> James Miller's "Lady Science" portrayed in The Humours of Oxford (1726) – a middle-aged matron who through scientific dilettantism, had become a nuisance to society.
>
> Swift. "On the Education of Ladies."
> The first boarding schools were set up in and around London in the latter part of the seventeenth century for the purpose of providing daughters of the titled and landed with a polite education.
> An essay in Defense of the Female Sex. Anon. ^[*unclear, possibly "sel"*—ed.]^ 1696. praises Locke's recognition that women have rational souls & abilities which equalled men's,
> London's coffee houses "penny universities"
> The bluestocking coterie revolved around Mrs Elizabeth Montagu (1720–1800).

Grace Lake, "*Inbuilt Flash Nix*, & Nine Poems, Three Collages." *constant red/mingled damask*, no. 1 (September 1986). This journal was produced by the poet Nigel Wheale in Cambridge. A photocopied, stapled booklet of eighty pages, this first issue includes three black and white collages (and possibly a block print) from Grace Lake on the cover and within; Lake is thanked for her graphics. Published authors include Alphonso X el Sabio (1230–84), Peter Riley, Kelvin Corcoran, John Wilkinson, Peter Middleton, Wendy Mulford, John Welch, Ian Patterson, Steve Holland, Wheale, and Mendelssohn. The journal was intended to be occasionally produced, and "free [mostly] to interested persons." In issue one, plans are announced for a second number in December/January 1987; the back pages advertise small presses, among them, Equofinality, "open township" (Hebden Bridge), and Peter Riley's Poetical Histories series.

The original, collaged cover of this issue *constant red/mingled damask* is housed at Sussex Special Collections (SxMs109/5/A/8). A portion of issue one is also filed at Sussex, and though it replicates the British Library edition used here, the occasional variation suggests that this may have been a proof copy (5/A/5/6). For instance, in line four, stanza seven of "MOODIST", "doctor" is "doctore".

Mendelssohn's entry is titled "Inbuilt Flash Nix & Nine Poems, Three Collages" and includes the titular prose piece of that 1985 collection (see above notes). Images are interspersed with Mendelssohn's contribution. After "Train to L'pool" is a photocopy of the 1905 portrait of Clara Rilke-Westhoff by Paula Modersohn-Becker (another copy appears in 5/B/2/48). In an undated, untitled part of her *roman-à-clef*, Mendelssohn suggests that while a woman mightn't like to be called a single parent, "she may prefer to be likened to Clara Westhoff" (5/B/1/1b).

Beneath the clearly identified Westhoff portrait, Mendelssohn writes:

> *Dry paint, marked, dwindling rose, dwindling*
> *between a holy touch, not quite pierced by a thorn,*
> *mouth down-turned, a deep background, chalk dress,*
> *square neckline slashed behind the rose's crown, eyes*
> *on the brink of tears, fearful expression, knowing.*

After the poem beginning "to have some stupid bloke laughing and giggling at you.", Mendelssohn includes a labelled photocopy of Augustus John's "Dorelia and the Children at Martigues". Under the painting, Mendelssohn writes: "He didn't tell me he had a thing about 'Dorelia.'" After the John painting, she includes a photocopied article by Jasper Becker for *The Guardian*, dated 9 August 1986, and titled "China gets a touch of Hollywood". Becker discusses the making of Bernardo Bertolucci's *The Last Emperor*, a biopic of Pu Yi, the last recognised royal descendent of the Manchu dynasty who spent a decade in Mao's prison system, and another five in Stalin's, before becoming head gardener at Peking botanical gardens. Cited and dated by Mendelssohn, this article completes her entry.

At the end of *constant red/mingled damask* is a page entitled: "Among the Contributors". Mendelssohn's is the first and longest authorial biography, reading:

> *GRACE LAKE: writer, artist, started by placing objects found in the street in art exhibitions and having given them titles, walking out. Published co-operatively one edition of a national newspaper STRIKE in 1970. One volume of poetry 1967–1970 disappeared prior to publication. Rolled off her poetry in short runs, all given away.* Green Suede Blues Press, Working Class Women's Publishing House, Writing Round an Ideal World Press, Scrap Publishing, *and* Bone Dry. *Poetry published by* Sheffield Free Press. Poems *with Tim Mathews. A volume withdrawn from* Common Ground Printing Co-operative *following disputation over the license of printers to censor. She preferred to reserve two pages (or an agreed number) for printers' criticism. Difficulty ensues between those who write/read poetry and those who, whilst maintaining control over printing machinery, do not.*

Another draft of the same biography includes information about publishing co-operatively a single issue of the national newspaper "Strike" in 1970 and writing "articles for the long defunct West London Underground 'Frendz' magazine" (5/B/1/1b). In this draft, the publication "dispute" is a "row", and a sentence is struck through that reads: "She is single with three children & is in the process of organizing an exhibition of painting & poetry in order to raise funds." In the final sentence, "do not" is embedded within the sentence, as in: "& those who do not, yet who have control of [redacted] printing machinery".

Some of Mendelssohn's poems in this volume are the final published variants of poems previously published. These poems, and their variants, are listed below:

"Radiated? Light?"
This poem was previously published in *Inbuilt Flash Nix* (1985). In 1986, the slight indent of line two is excised, as are the double quotations used throughout the 1985 version; additionally, stanzas one and two of 1986 are a single stanza in 1985.

"Train to L'pool"
This poem was previously published in *Inbuilt Flash Nix* (1985). In earlier versions, "L'pool" was "L'pool."; another has pencilled along the top, "Train to Liverpool", though this may not be in Mendelssohn's hand (5/A/5/1). Further, "*Set / the mind dreaming*" was in quotations and not italicised, and "dream . . . decade." was "dream ..... decade."

Poem beginning "Shiva's crackling on a spinal hair"
This poem was previously published in *Inbuilt Flash Nix* (1985), where "*breadcrumbs*?" was not italicised but is in quotation marks.

"Graves' Art Gallery Tea Room, 1981, Sheffield"
This poem was published in *Inbuilt Flash Nix* (August 1985), where it is untitled and begins "It's the truth! He cannot contain his stains" (see above notes). As "It's the truth!", it appears in a list of poem titles and first lines from earlier in the decade (see notes for Sheffield typescript, November 1981). Minor differences in punctuation and spelling in Sussex variants of *Inbuilt Flash Nix* (5/A/5/1–4) include: "his position?" is "this position?"; "puddle spray" is "puddle-spray"; and "bonyness" is "boniness" (5/A/5/4). In another earlier draft, the lines "I am on the bread line too, his glasses are N. H. S." were preceded by: "I am on the bread line too / I know his watery eyes,"; both are heavily redacted in blue ink.

"Follow her magic"
Published in *Inbuilt Flash Nix* (1985), this poem bore a full stop at the end of an underlined title, and at the bottom, Mendelssohn pens: "10/1983". Minor variations between 1986 and 1985 include: "derelict harmony" was "derelict harmony," and "*CHIVERS*" was "CHIVERS". In *constant red*, lines three and four of stanza two read: "'she worked [. . . .] can't you END OF QUESTION." The closing quotation mark in this volume has been added (ed.). In *Inbuilt Flash Nix*, the same lines read: ""she worked [. . . .] can't you?" END OF QUESTION." Pre-copying, Mendelssohn adds the punctuation after "you" by hand.

Poem beginning "yes, it is a shame, a real shame:"
This poem appears twice in *Inbuilt Flash Nix* (1985) and as part of a three-page A5 typescript, a play attributed to Grace Lake entitled "THERE was a great ripping up OF ROMANCE OCCURRING." The play was intended for performance at Trinity Hall, Cambridge, 1985; 7/A/6. The earlier versions are not italicised. Further differences between the 1986 and the 1985 poem include:

"before: real?" was "before: real"
"You like the shot" was "You liked the shot"
"you think / that you are" was "you think / you are" (7/A/6 only)
"you are / resisting" was "you are re / resisting" (5/A/5/5 only)
"a middle 'c'" and "equal 'A'" were "a middle c" and "equal A"

Grace Lake, Typescript (October 1986).
Mendelssohn dates the manuscript and typescript variants of "to fit the prototype." precisely: "completed 2nd October .86. 10.30.a.m." (SxMs109/5/B/1/1b). In addition to minor differences in spacing and punctuation, distinctions between typescript and manuscript are as follows:

"cat in chanterelles   imbibing" was "cat in mushrooms   imbibes"
"doloraosa" was "dolorosa"
"leaven spanned ear" was "leaven broader ear"
"fallow scoopydoo sounds" was "fallow scoopydoosounds"
"leaven spanned ear" was "leaven broader ear"
After "lops" in manuscript there is a long space, then "Arkansas home."
"littler & plump" reads "littler & ~~fat~~ plump"
"ALL" was "All"
"it, i usually" was "it, usually"
"which buzzes now electronic division" was "which buzzes now with electronic subdivision"
"the other's sub-division," was "the other's electronic subdivision,"
"than they can" was "than ~~them~~ they can"
"interwoven top   uppers" was "interwoven tops" (possibly first: "interweaved")
"the passage is / is opened" was "the passage / is opened"

Both manuscript and typescript are two pages, but the typescript ends with the conclusion of manuscript page one. The second manuscript page is consistent in style, tone, and some references, among them, to children, "red ankle straps", and "turbo shoe".

Grace Lake, "An ACCOUNT of a MUMMY, in The Royal Cabinet of Antiquities at Dresden" (October 1986).

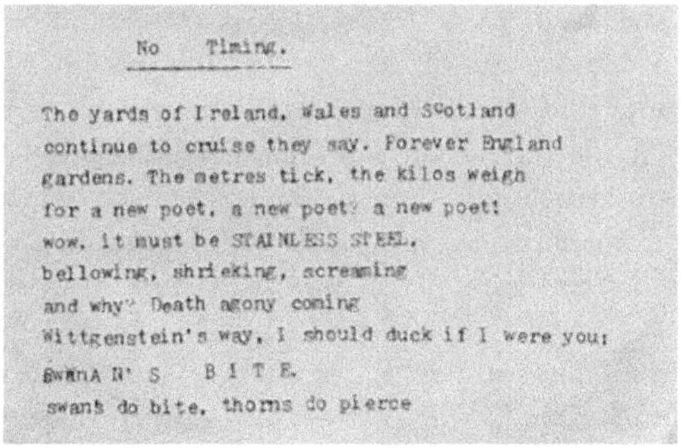
No   Timing.

The yards of Ireland, Wales and SCotland
continue to cruise they say. Forever England
gardens. The metres tick, the kilos weigh
for a new poet, a new poet? a new poet!
wow, it must be STAINLESS STEEL,
bellowing, shrieking, screaming
and why? Death agony coming
Wittgenstein's way, I should duck if I were you;
SWnA N' S   B I T E.
swans do bite, thorns do pierce

An independently published A5 pamphlet on pink paper, *An ACCOUNT of a MUMMY* has a beautifully formatted title page in capitals, subscript, and regular text; its layout and long title are an homage to eighteenth-century book design.

The complete pamphlet contains four poems: "Not so Good"; "Not Bad"; "That's Fascism"; and "No   Timing." The first two poems will reappear in *constant red/mingled damask*, no. 2 (see below notes). In the poem, "No Timing.", the line "SwWnAN' S   B I T E." is conveyed by a series of over-typings, so that the first "S" was initially "s" and the "W" is typed over an "a" (see image).

The back cover includes the following quote:

> Apollinaire's stay in prison left him for a long time with a feeling of terror, and we did our best as friends to help him get over it. He had become a public figure, but he had reached that position via the door that bears the inscription, 'All hope abandon, ye who enter here.' He was marked for life, and even the war, his courage, and his wound would never succeed in silencing certain persons who, out of ignorance, envy, stupidity, or self-interest, banded against him and continually attacked him as an artist ..." / "Les Soirées de Paris" / André Billy. // "Les Tours sont les rues".

Grace Lake, Typescript (March 1987).
There are two typescripts of "Police-Armed Training Session: Growl.": an undated version on A4, given here, and another on a small, square piece of stationery embellished by a central block of gold within an orange rectangle (SxMs109/5/A/43/2).

The stationery variant is titled "GROWL", dedicated "to Allen Ginsberg.", and reads by hand in the upper left corner: "28/3/87. C'bridge, England." On the verso side, Mendelssohn types at the poem's end "(to be cont.)", then signs "love, Grace." In addition to minor differences in lineation and punctuation, the first couplet of the A4 typescript is not evident in the stationery variant, and the lines reading "painted on top, the face faces / at an angle to" were "painted over, / the face ~~forward~~ faces an angle to"; additionally, "your candle" is corrected to "his candle". Correction fluid elides the "forward" of "granpa / face forward" and "the face forward faces"; in the first instance, the word is reinstated by hand. On the A4 typescript, Mendelssohn adds the titular colon, "Growl.", and the quotation marks at the end of stanza three.

These typescripts are in a file that contains a mixture of poetry and prose from the early to the mid-eighties, and an A4 typescript of the lyrics to Bob Dylan's "All Along the Watchtower" and "Pat Garrett & Billy the Kid" (5/A/43/2). These lyrics include handwritten chord changes. Mendelssohn also wrote out songs in her prison diaries: a prison-issue notebook dated 1974 and 1975 contains lyrics from The Beatles, Don McLean, Carole King, and Carly Simon (2/A/7).

Grace Lake, "Nine Poems." *constant red/mingled damask*, no. 2 (April 1987), 39–50.
Editor Nigel Wheale circulated the second issue of *constant red/mingled damask* in April 1987, a few months later than planned (see above notes on issue one, September 1986). The second number is perfect bound and 97 pages long; it was deposited at the British Library. Julia Ball's artwork adorns front and back covers. Featured authors include Rachel Blau DuPlessis, Rosmarie Waldrop, D. S. Marriott, Tony Lopez, Ralph Hawkins (art and poetry), David Chaloner, and Peter Hughes. Grace Lake contributed nine poems and a drawing. There are reviews by Anthony Mellors of D. S. Marriott's *Mortgages*, and by Marriott of John Wilkinson's *Proud Flesh*; the latter is a precursor to the review in *Archeus*, number five, 1989, "The Wounds of Selfhood: John Wilkinson's *Proud Flesh*" (see below notes). Advertisements promote Paul Green's Dangerous Writers series and Peter Riley's Poetical Histories. The journal description is identical to issue one; Wheale adds that back issues remain available and anticipates a third issue in June/July. Wheale ends his editorial preamble with: "stay hungry/angry" (2). At the back of the journal, he indicates that issue three will include Tom Lowenstein, Paul Green, Tom Macleod, Tim Mathews, Richard Burns, Sordido, "and whoever else applies and is found worthy" (97). Issue two is the final publication of *constant red/mingled damask*. No complete copy exists in Mendelssohn's Sussex archive.

Mendelssohn's poems are preceded by the following epigraph: "At Athens the Graces stood / Eastward in a sacred place" / - Winkelmann". On the final "Contributors" page, Mendelssohn's biography reads in full: "GRACE LAKE featured in issue one of *Constant Red/Mingled Damask*." The poems "Not So Good" and "Not Bad" were part of this nine-poem contribution; they were originally published in the 1986 pamphlet, *An ACCOUNT of a MUMMY* (see above). In *An ACCOUNT*, "Not So Good" has an underlined title with broad spacing between words; in line 19, "it is" is "it's". The distinctions between the 1987 and 1986 version of "Not Bad" are as follows:

> "Not Bad" is "<u>Not   Bad.</u>"
> "scrubbed poised for" was "scrubbed & poised for"
> "spread the spread" was "spread the spread,"
> "two or four twisted" was "two or four or twisted"
> "bashing . . ." was "bashing."
> "he carries the colour" was "he carries   the colour"
> "the hoof curtailing" was "the hoof.   curtailing"
> A typo in "curtailing" was corrected, but "Leith" remains misspelt "Lieth"
> "burning, so waft" was "burning, so, waft"

Grace Lake, *The News*, no. 1 (April 1987).

This journal was edited by the poet Tony Lopez, then a lecturer at the University of Leicester. In addition to Mendelssohn, contributors included D. S. Marriott, Edwin Morgan, Jane Sutherland, Wendy Mulford, Ian Patterson, and Ed Dorn. Contributors are welcomed. Lopez describes it as a "hopeful venture" that was prematurely terminated after a single issue due to the constraints of a new, temporary academic post and a young family. Lopez asked friends for work, photocopied the journal, and circulated it to a small audience (Lopez email dated 3 August 2017). The journal is unpaginated, and a complete issue does not exist in Mendelssohn's Sussex archive. A copy is filed at the British Library, and Ian Patterson kindly provided Mendelssohn's entry, which includes:

> "Winter" (republished in *Slate*, Spring-Summer, 1987)
> "Tansy Tchaikovsky"
> "'The solemn mists, dark brown or pale, / March slow and solemn down the vale.'" (republished in *Slate*, Spring-Summer, 1987)
> "They are further than temptation, to argue, to refrain"
> "Little Dog Mine 1948"
> "On an Emery Board" (republished in *Slate*, Spring-Summer, 1987)
> "To a Radical Lesbian Feminist Rapist"
> Prose poem beginning "Madge De Fanfare" (*follows on from "To a Radical…" and may be part of that poem*—ed.)

Notes pertaining to the poems republished in *Slate* (1987) are given below; in order of appearance, notes on the differences between extant, located manuscripts and the above published poems given here.

"Tansy Tchaikovsky"

There are two typescripts of "Tansy Tchaikovsky" and a single typescript of "To a Radical Lesbian Feminist Rapist"; the poems are on folded A3 sheets, have been reduced by photocopier, and are numbered II and VII respectively (SxMs109/5/A/34).

In these typescripts, the "skull" in the final stanza of "Tansy Tchaikovsky" was "head"; the title is underlined, and there are small differences in spacing, lineation, and punctuation. In all other regards, it is the same as the published version. Changes, numbering, and typos are made by hand before copying.

A manuscript exists of "Tansy Tchaikovsky" (5/B/2/57). Written in thick blue felt tip pen on yellow paper, it begins with notes that include three individual names (one person possibly labelled "emotional engineer"), a phone number, some rough figure drawings, and the following:

> fertile & fictive.
>
> "What dignity, what beauty, in this change
> From mild to angry, and from sad to gay,
> Alternate and revolving!
> The Excursion. 1.314-16 Book Third: Despondency.
>
> Appreciate.
>
> farting round harvard
> then as soon as she starts farting round harvard
> she'll be "at Harvard" & doing something
> presumably, interesting
>
> be it suggesting that the plastic basket flowers
> be substituted by clumped auriculae
> or something ^else^ unthought of yet

"Tansy Tchaikovsky" follows seamlessly from this quote of Wordsworth's long, unfinished poem *The Recluse* and poetic scribble. The epigraph and first two stanzas are a single unit; there are differences of syntax, diction, spacing, capitalisation, and punctuation throughout, and considerable alterations to line breaks. Differing stanza breaks exist between the following line endings and beginnings: "with any element" and "from her five electric bars"; "roasts another note." and "sugar is sulphur."; "'at her side'" and "'she had I marked"; "'the day before'" and "so they got it together"; "FAST CAR." and "And some small". Additional amendments include:

> "blanks out blocks on" was "blanks at blocks on"
> "~~squeezes~~ paints her lips with smarties"
> "NO, shedoesnotmeanthatbutshesneezes / not that night is not a delight" was "no, she doesn't mean that but she / doesn't mean that night is not a delight"
> "shelter which means" was "shelter and that means"
> "ravine, dragons" was "ravine with dragons"
> "plastic basket, laughing loudly" was "plastic basket / laughs loud"
> "watches her feet to ensure that / they remain where they are" was "watching to make sure that her feet remain"
> "disappear ~~on~~ with any"

"the ghost of tansy" was "the ghost of Tansy Tchaikovsky"
"'was she seated seen upon'" was "'was she seen upon'"
"'day before'" was "day before – '"
"reflective soul" was "reflexive soul"
"back with her;" was "back north with her"
"nothing special" was "not special"
"five conseq. days" was "five consequitive days"
"you hand over a mental note" was "you will have to produce a note from your mind"
"poetize from mon-fri." was "POETIZE FROM MON-FRI"
"whose necks you are wrapping your sub-machine guns" was "wh^ose necks^ ~~you are~~ wrapping your ~~Kalashnikovs~~"
"bundled into / a FAST CAR." was "bundled ~~in~~ inside of a fast car"
"this terrible house" was "this ~~mad~~ terrible house"

The final stanza is rendered as follows:

And this is where Sadness lies
in a language bound by Law to remain
bandaged gagged blinded & buried deep.

The poem then concludes:

~~Watch that Symbol, it will chip,~~
~~it's gilt will tarnish, it will~~

watch that Symbol, its gilt will tarnish,
it will chip, & it will act, if ~~it will act~~ as anything,
as a brief ~~warning~~ but stern warning,
to children both boys and girls
not to get the scrapes in the mouths
for artists are both born & bred
& artists do not like to kill readily
nor do they like to be charged and co-erced
whilst protecting their fellows
they can be thrown into a hearse
& people's tastes in reading get mixed-up
but when the text jumps from the book
its a choice / a poem or a murder story?
a range of fiction presents a range of possibilities
lest the Imagination is permitted to switch gender
∴ he dreams, is not a coward, drinks occasionally
and may, one day, achieve great things.

on another level, it is quite polite
to inform someone that you are intending
to make comment on them in public.
that books can be written ~~at~~ about living people
without their permission, ~~therefore~~
interpretations proliferate, symbols
agglomerate, and one alone may not
be ~~the~~ a representative spokeswoman
whilst others play spot the ball.

"Little Dog Mine"
In line six of this poem in *The News*, "languished" reads "lanquished" (ed.).

"To a Radical Lesbian Feminist Rapist"
There are two typescripts of "Tansy Tchaikovsky" and a single typescript of "To a Radical Lesbian Feminist Rapist"; the poems are on folded A3 sheets, have been reduced by photocopier, and are numbered II and VII respectively (5/A/34). The typescript of "To a Radical Lesbian Feminist Rapist" includes a full stop after the title, and, barring that of the last line, no extended spaces before or after punctuation. The third and fourth lines read "Why don't you ~~women~~ who wear sex / on your sleeve stop chatting up"; and, "You / tried it on with me." reads "~~Some of~~ you / tried it on with me." Line 16 was "go somewhere ~~else~~ to get your". Edits and numbering are written by hand before copying.

Grace Lake, *Slate* no. 3, Spring–Summer (1987).
Published under the imprint "New Breed Publications", *Slate* was edited by Martin Bright, Simon Parker, and Fiona Russell. The journal was financed by the University of Cambridge Judith E. Wilson Fund and printed by the Cambridge Free Press Workers' Co-op on Gwydir Street. A total of three issues appeared between 1985 and 1987. The first, in 1985, thanks the staff of the Cambridge Free Press, the Cambridge Claimants Union, Imprisoned Miners, and Poetry Demands Unemployment. It contains a review of a reading by Allen Ginsberg that was a benefit for miners sponsored by Poetry Demands Unemployment; Ginsberg was in England to launch his *Collected Poems 1947–80*. An essay about post-1960s poetry, a short story, and some student poetry are also included; there is no contributors' page, and the entirety is about 16 sides. The 1986 issue contains a short story, poems, two drawings and an interview with the poet Brian Patten; entries are anonymised, and the list of contributors' names at the back does not reference contents.

Identified as Grace Lake in *Slate* no. 3, Mendelssohn's co-contributors were Ruth Wayner, Tom Phillips, Clare Padfield, Robin Leanse, and Simon Jarvis. Of the five poems Mendelssohn contributed, the last three were previously printed in *The News* (no. 1, April 1987; see above). Sussex Special Collections holds the published issue of *Slate* no. 3 (SxMs109/5/A/9/2) and edited typescript drafts of these poems on A4 and folded A3 sheets; the verso side of one A3 reads: "© S.G.L. Lake." and "→ February 1987." (5/A/9/1). Poems from this group that do not appear in *Slate* can be found in the appendix.

The draft text suggests that *Slate* editors erroneously neglected the final three stanzas of "On an Emery Board" and ended "But I'm not going to sit in a room with female cousins," two thirds of the way through, with line 29, "it was". These elisions may have occurred because in Mendelssohn's submission, these stanzas and lines begin on less visible verso sides, and/or different sheets of paper. Given the *Slate* editorial errors on offer in the Wordsworth citation of "The solemn mists" and the elision of two whole pages of Mendelssohn's submission, the complete drafts are deferred to in this collection (ed.). In order of appearance, differences between publication and drafts are noted below.

"To a Green Field."
The editors of *Slate* followed Mendelssohn's draft text in writing the final word of "To a Green Field" as "condescention", which is corrected here (ed.) (5/A/9/1). In *Slate*, "you hammered, and increasingly so" is rendered "you hammered increasingly so".

Poem beginning "But I'm not going to sit in a room with female cousins,"
In draft, this poem has a line break after "denouncing" that does not appear in *Slate* (5/A/9/1). In *Slate*, the ellipsis of line three is five point.

Poem beginning "did they leave"
In *Slate*, unlike the 5/A/9/1 typescript, the first iteration of "your mother?" was "you mother?"; and "denouncing / hardship," occupied a single line.

"'The solemn mists dark brown or pale, / March slow and solemn down the vale'"
In the four known versions of the poem, the comma, full stop, and quotation marks in the title are variously omitted and included; punctuation and spacing are also altered. For example, the typescript in 5/A/9/1 differs from the rendering in *The News* (1987) in the following ways:

> "'solemn mists dark'" was "'solemn mists, dark'"
> "'vale'" was "'vale."
> "tender enamel'," was "tender enamel'"
> "cups had stood in their slops / for" was "cups had been lying in their / slops for"
> "room, although" was "room, though"
> "yet he did not:" was "yet he   did not,"
> "After, it" was "After it"
> "'don't you look nice ?' when you" was "don't you look nice, when you"
> "'aren't you happy for me ?' when" was "aren't you happy for me?   when"
> "other;   aztec" was "other.   Aztec"
> "hitler as you called" was "hitler as you so called"

In *Slate*, the footnote for the epigraph reads: "'The Valt [*sic*] of Erthwaite [*sic*]' W.W. pp 242/243. The Poems Vol. 1. Harmondsworth, 1977."; in 5/A/9/1, it reads the same, but "Valt" and "Erthwaite" are, correctly, "Vale" and "Esthwaite". In the typescript located in file 5/B/1/1b, the epigraph appears as: "'The Vale of Esthwaite' W. Wordsworth.", as it does in *The News*.

"On An Emery Board."
In *The News* (1987), the title is not underlined and has no full stop; in typescript, it has a full stop; in *Slate* it is underlined with no full stop. Unlike the typescript in 5/A/9/1 used here, in *The News*, there are no spaces around the hyphen in line two; at the

outset of stanza two, there is an extended space after "Really", and the final line of stanza seven reads "uncurled ?" In *Slate*, there is no ampersand in the first line of stanza two and the poem contains six stanzas only.

"Winter."
In *The News* (1987), the title has neither underlining nor full stop; in the 5/A/9/1 typescript, it has a full stop only; in *Slate* it is underlined. In the *Slate* variant, the extended spacing that follows mid-line commas is more heavily demarcated than it is in *The News* (1987); this spacing is as in typescript.

A like typescript of "Winter." exists in which the spacing in lines three and four appears extended (5/A/43/1); on this text, as in 5/A/9/1, Mendelssohn ensures, by hand, that "crepe" is "crêpe". This typescript is one side of a folded A3 sheet; another side of the same piece of paper has been used to type out the following:

> don't forget, that whilst she is smiling, she is smiling: "Cream Carpets".
> a great negative sweep floods virtually the entire psychic mechanism. I am as
> prickly as hell and live with a bagful of basic   cliches at the weekend, no-one
> bright and incisive around.
>
> admire, admire, the wisdom of
> fossilized excrement, ornamenting
> the high white rafter down one side
> of the ceiling, "or be out of the country
> by 3 in the afternoon".
>
> gilgai moon, november 25th. /86.

This dated typescript shares a file with "oh yes we are entitled mohican slaves" and "dig; dig." (October 1983); the poem beginning "rolling, and all these words are alive and" (June 1985); "a room a" (April 1986); and extracts from Mendelssohn's *roman-à-clef*, including a portion of the 1987 text, *What a Performance* (SxMs109/5/A/43/1).

Grace Lake, Manuscript (April 1988).
"By Magenta Auriculae." is a manuscript dated "April 3rd 1988." A single edit moves "apart" from the start of line nine to the second word of line eight. The poem is housed in a file with a mixture of poetry and prose from the early to the mid-eighties, and an A4 typescript of the lyrics to Bob Dylan's "All Along the Watchtower" and "Pat Garrett & Billy the Kid" (SxMs109/5/A/43/2). These lyrics include handwritten chord changes. Mendelssohn also wrote out songs in her prison diaries: a prison-issue notebook dated 1974 and 1975 contains lyrics from The Beatles, Don McLean, Carole King, and Carly Simon (2/A/7).

Two more drafts of "By Magenta Auriculae." exist in 5/B/1/2a. One is untitled but dated identically. Further minor differences include: in the titled variant, the end of line eight reads "Easter ^Sun^~~Mon~~day" and "In front of a central" was "by a central"; in the untitled, "although the windows" is "though the windows". In both, "circling hyacinths" was "circling blue hyacinths".

Grace Lake, Manuscript (April 1988).
"Sunday Beasts." consists of two pages and three sides of A4 paper (SxMs109/5/A/28). The entirety is written in red ink; on page one, Mendelssohn writes: "© Grace Lake. / i. m. Bernard of Ventadour. / April 10th 1988." The left-justification may be more irregular than given here (ed.), and a single correction reads: "I ~~thought~~ was thinking".

Grace Lake, *Figs*, no. 14 (May 1988).
Figs was edited by the poet Tony Baker, who ran it out of a Derbyshire cottage between 1980 and 1989. In the editorial statement for issue one, Baker writes: "'figs' is intended principally for the publication of works-in-progress" and announces his intention to publish three issues in the coming year. In the first covered, spiral-bound issue of mimeographed poems, contributors were Michael Haslam, Ralph Hawkins, Colin Simms, Alan Halsey, and Tony Jackson. Subsequent issues reinforced the work-in-progress mandate (or, as in issue five, "works in regress"); covers were designed by Ged Lawson, Bob Cobbing, and Anne Heeney. The sixth is the first dated issue, in 1981, and is supported by arts funding; this assistance appears to have been discontinued in or around 1985. Over its lifespan, *Figs* contributors included Peter Riley, Bill Griffiths, Robert Sheppard, Lyn Hejinian, Tom Pickard, Barry MacSweeney, Pierre Joris, and Harry Gilonis. The National Poetry Library at the Southbank Centre holds issues 1–13 and a facsimile of the editor's copy of issue 14, which is not, in its entirety, in the Sussex archive.

Issue 14 is unpaginated and dated May 1988. The journal opens with translations of Paul Celan, Horace, and Chinese poet Ruan Ji (3rd century C.E.); Wendy Mulford, Tony Lopez, and Mary Oppen are among those who contribute original poems. Mendelssohn and Ulli Freer are credited with providing graphics. Mendelssohn's entry includes six poems from works published in the early to mid-1980s. In order of appearance, with previous publications attributed, the first lines and/or titles of these poems are:

"don't be northern, whatever you do" from *Propaganda Multi-Billion Bun.* (1985)
"IN A CAVERNOUS HEAT HAZE" from *Posmos, the Yellow Velvet Underground.* (1982)
"I like Red People" from *Crystal Love: D. N. A.* (1982)
"Check the scene" from *Posmos, the Yellow Velvet Underground.* (1982)
"find one page evenly." from *Propaganda Multi-Billion Bun.* (1985)
"making machine poetry" from *Posmos, the Yellow Velvet Underground.* (1982)

With few and minor exceptions, Mendelssohn maintained the earlier versions of these poems. "I like Red People" occupies its own page in *Crystal Love: D. N. A.* (1982); in *Figs*, it follows on directly from "IN A CAVERNOUS HEAT HAZE" with an asterisk between the two poems. The only differences between the *Posmos* and the *Figs* versions of "Check the scene" are an elongated dash in line four and a protracted gap between full stop and "A" in line 20. In the 1983 variant text of *Crystal Love: D. N. A.* and *Posmos, the Yellow Velvet Underground.* held in the Raworth papers and titled "*approaching 35* JUNE'S MODERN ENTERTAINMENTS." Mendelssohn writes beneath "Check the scene": "from a portrait of a night-club owner by Picasso." In the *Posmos* version of "IN A CAVERNOUS HEAT HAZE", "Longfellow's" was "Longfellow".

Barring a hyphen in "thick-eyed men", there are no differences between the 1985 and 1988 versions of "find one page evenly." An early version of this poem exists in untitled typescript, c. 1981–82 (SxMs109/5/A/2/7). Variations between the early draft and the published version are as follows:

"find one page evenly." was a title: "Find One Page Evenly."
"taking the remorseless mickey" was the first line
"she reads "he"" was "she reads 'He'"
"thoroughfare of strollers." was "melee of strollers."
On line 12, "Heffers'" was "Heffers's"

After "by green bus.", Mendelssohn adds a series of lines made of tildes in 5/A/2/7:

~~~~~~~~~~~~~~~~~~~~~~~~~~~~~~
~~~~~~~~~~~~~~~~~~~~~~~~~~
~~~~~~~~~~~~~~~~~~~~~~~~
~~~~~~~~~~~~~~~~~~~~
~~~~~~~~~~~~~~~~
~~~~~
~~

In addition to submitting poems published from four to six years' previous, Mendelssohn contributes the cover image from the 1985 pamphlet *Is this a True Parrot, a Mountain, or a Stooge?* (see above notes), which is reduced, and occupies the bottom right-hand quarter of one page of *Figs*. Mendelssohn's graphics also include a photocopied drawing titled and dated by hand, "'A Lizard Tumbril' / Grace Lake 1979". The reproduced abstract painting on the recto side of this page is the work of the poet Ulli Freer (phone conversation 11 October 2017). Freer typeset Mendelssohn's *Bernache Nonnette* (1995) for Rod Mengham's Equipage press (see below). A like signed and dated photocopy of "A Lizard Tumbril" exists in the Sussex archive (5/B/2/1). This file includes a similar drawing, "wave replica." which is signed "Grace Lake 1976.", and a partial copy of the 1974 poem beginning "Cover the land" (see above notes).

Grace Lake, *La Facciata*, Poetical Histories, no. 5 (1988).

Poetical Histories was a pamphlet series run by Peter Riley, who started it after finding a stack of fine quality paper in Derbyshire dating from the 1940s. Letter-pressed in Cambridge, each pamphlet has a formal title page bearing an image; in his recollection of this series, Riley asserts that "[t]he highly traditional, balanced and symmetrical, design format was meant to contrast with the modernity of the texts" (www.aprileye.co.uk/histories.html). The series ran from 1985 to 2004. It was funded by subscribers, and from 2002 onward, the Eastern Arts Board. It ended when Riley ran out of paper stock. Among its sixty serialised poets were D. S. Marriott (no. 3); John James (no. 12); J. H. Prynne (nos. 2 and 22); Denise Riley (no. 26); Andrea Brady (no. 41); and Barry MacSweeney (no. 49 and an unnumbered pamphlet).

Mendelssohn's *La Facciata* included both "La Facciata" and "La Facciata Turns her Back". It was published in an edition of 100, with some produced on pink paper, as is the text deposited at the British Library. Richard Baxter was the typographer. Mendelssohn created what Riley labels "the cover device", the original of which remains in his papers at Cambridge (MS Add. 1003/2/29). Under title and author, the image consists of two horizontal streaks, one grey, one brown, conjoined by a scratched or frottaged line exposing the off-white colour of the page. Mendelssohn dedicated *La Facciata* to Marina Yedigaroff and Roger East "with much affection".

The titular phrase is Italian for façade, page, face, or front. A proof copy edited in Mendelssohn's hand reveals her attentiveness to an increased right justification of the title of "LA FACCIATA TURNS HER BACK" (SxMs109/5/A/10/2). This proof includes a note from Riley on the recto side, indicating that author and editor conversed about the line from "La Facciata": "there's NO geography in PROTEST", debating whether to use italics, but deciding on small caps "because they are less vocally emphatic than italics." Though drafts in 5/A/10/1 show that "squeeling" was "squealing", Mendelssohn has left the misspelling intact here.

In Mendelssohn's files, there is a sheet in which "La Facciata" may be used as a signatory. Recorded by the editor before cataloguing, it reads:

> Perhaps one of the most ridiculous things is to have a political reputation (in my case I am [*unclear words, one of which reads*: "~~*defined*~~"—ed.] as a political fanatic) when you are not interested in politics. And because you were not interested you were victimized indeed terrorized into proving that you had a sane and reasonable commitment to one part of the massive struggle for something or other. This was of paramount importance [*large ink blot; may redact a word or words*—ed.] vital that one girl student should Not be permitted to read for a degree. She had to be corrupted and as quickly and as remorselessly as possible. This was to be done.
>
> La Facciata.
>
> Facciata

No copy of the published pamphlet exists in Mendelssohn's Sussex archive, but there are at least two manuscript versions of *La Facciata* (5/A/10/1; 4/C/33). For differences between these texts and the Poetical Histories edition, see below notes for *Conductors of Chaos* (1996), which includes the last published version of these poems in English; "La Facciata" will be translated into French for *Po&sie* in 2002.

Grace Lake, Manuscript (December 1988).

The poem "Estée Lauder. There may be some objections raised." is a neatly written, unedited A5 manuscript (SxMs109/5/A/27). At the bottom, Mendelssohn writes "December 1988." and "© Grace lake." Another manuscript, unsigned and undated, can be found in 5/B/2/50, a file that also contains a photocopied cover of *Is this a True Parrot, a Mountain, or a Stooge?* (1985). In this variant, the underlined title goes without a final full stop; line four may read "against the fogs"; the colon at the end of line 14 stands, but it may have ended with a full stop in a differing ink; finally, the last six lines may be indented (ed.).

Grace Lake, *Archeus*, no. 5 (1989).

Throughout 1989, D. S. Marriott edited six issues of *Archeus*, which was a photocopied, corner stapled, A4 production. A complete run is held by the Alternative Press and Poetry Store Collections at University College London. Each issue begins with an epigraph, usually drawn from pre-nineteenth century authors, among them, Milton, Henry Peacham, and George Thomson. Issues conclude with Marriott's compacted author biographies that assess past writings. For instance: "Charles Bernstein is the author of Veil, a work of scriptus formed via graphic density and Puritan fluence." Mendelssohn's biography reads: "Grace Lake is the author of La Facciata in which consonants overlap musically with vowells [*sic*] and are given a chthonic shining."

Contributors to *Archeus* include Steve McCaffery, Karen Mac Cormack, Peter Riley, Charles Bernstein, Rod Mengham, Ian Patterson, Lee Ann Brown, John Wilkinson, Bernadette Mayer, Maggie O'Sullivan, Douglas Oliver, Alice Notley, Geoffrey Ward, Bill Griffiths, and Marriott himself. Special issues are devoted to Andrew Crozier (2), John Wilkinson (5), and more amorphously, "'Art'" (6), which is dedicated as follows: "i. m. C L R James (1901–1989)". Amidst the poetry, there are reviews of or brief essays on J. H. Prynne (1), Veronica Forrest-Thomson (2), Andrew Crozier (2), and Tom Raworth (3), among others. Mendelssohn supplies a drawing for the cover of issue two (shown here).

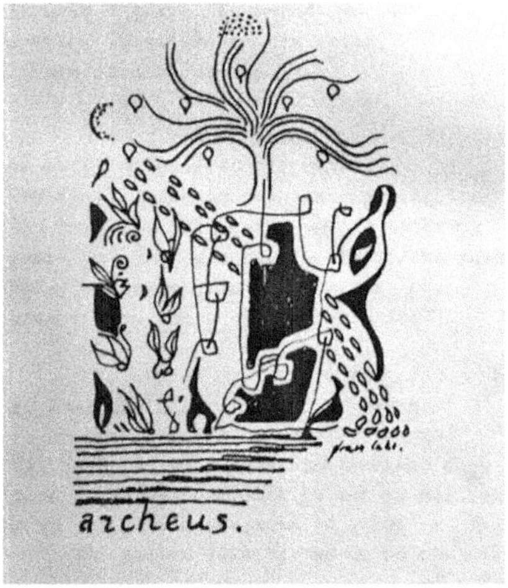

The original cover of issue two is housed at Sussex in SxMs109/5/B/1/4, which also contains a manuscript of "'LES ENFANTS TERRIBLES'", a Mendelssohn poem that appears in issue five alongside "THE SOCIAL VOID". In addition to minor changes in punctuation and capitalisation, the final word of the title of "'LES ENFANTS TERRIBLES'" is pluralised here as it is not in publication; as this spelling is consistent with the title of Jean Cocteau's 1929 novel to which Mendelssohn alludes, pluralisation is restored (ed.). Mendelssohn may have also provided the cover illustration for issue five, but the drawing is unsigned and unattributed.

There are two known manuscripts of "THE SOCIAL VOID", one partial (5/B/2/22), one complete (5/B/2/43). The incomplete manuscript includes line one to "disapproved of." in line ten. Some variations between published text and manuscript include:

"onto – the" was "onto —— the"
"~~academiagaucherie~~ intelligaucherie"
"Eulogies" was "eulogies" (see also 5/B/2/43)
"Children" was "children" (see also 5/B/2/43)
"it's the one the cascade the strike the" was "it's the one the strike the cascade the" (see also 5/B/2/43)
"to skip or to trip over." was "to trip or to skip over." (see also 5/B/2/43)
"She was wrong, / they were describing a sweet gorgeous" was "They were not though, / they were for a sweet gorgeous".

In 5/B/2/43, the dashes are longer, and some punctuation and capitalisation differ; semantic alterations from the published text include:

"lazy thinking pointed" was "lazy minds pointing"
"no münde Lan bar Dishwasher was "No land~~scape~~ ^for^ in the mind."
"intelligaucherie" was "academiagaucherie"
"She was wrong, / they were . . . puppy." was "It / was a sweet gorgeous ~~light~~ nimble footed puppy."
"to a sick humour" was "to sick humour"
"her own leeriness" was "her leeriness"
"poshdoorstop" was "shopdoorstep"
"disarray from Ratso's" was "disarray by Ratso's"
"those large, desirable" was "those ~~longed-for~~ desirable"
"forked tongue" was "fork-tongue"

Grace Lake/Boas Toas, Typescript (December 1990).

This typescript photocopy, "Hardly See the Night past his Jacket.", may be a fragment, and the title may be longer, as it was cut off in photocopying (SxMs109/5/A/10a). After the last ellipsis might read "to" in Mendelssohn's hand, but the writing is unclear (ed.). The entirety is signed "© Boas Toas. / Dec 1990 [*illegible word*—ed.]". Typos are edited by hand pre-copying. Mendelssohn uses "Boas Toas" as a signatory elsewhere. For instance, the Peter Riley Archive at the Cambridge University Library houses an A3 doodle with Christmas and New Year greetings, as well as a mention of poetry reading, signed both Grace and "© Boas Toas." (Ms Add.10013/2/29).

Grace Lake, "UNTITLED", *The Virago Book of Love Poetry*, ed. Wendy Mulford et al, Virago Press, 65 (1990; second and third editions, 1991).

Asserting itself as the first anthology of its kind, *The Virago Book of Love Poetry* aimed to challenge assumptions about love poems: that love poetry is the domain of white males; that it is a "lower" form of artistic production; and that it addresses heterosexual desire only. By the poet Wendy Mulford's editorial conceptualisation, love in this collection is extended to a range of "non-erotic subjects" including the divine, offspring, and place ("Introduction" xv). Mulford edited the volume with Helen Kidd, Julia Mishkin, and Sandi Russell, and it was reprinted in the United States under the title *Love Poems by Women: An Anthology of Poetry from Around the World and Through the Ages* (Fawcett Columbine, 1991).

This collection spans the years 2300 B.C. to 1989 and is as international as good translations and estate permissions allowed. It includes female poets from Sappho to Christine de Pisan, from Anna Akhmatova to Alice Walker. Considering the historical and geographical breadth of the volume, contemporary UK poets – Mulford's peers – are well represented. Mendelssohn shares company with Denise Riley, Veronica Forrest-Thomson, and Liz Lochhead.

Mendelssohn's biographical note reads:

> **Grace Lake**, English.
> Lives in Cambridge where she is studying English. Mother of three children, has given a number of readings. Poems have appeared in many magazines, including *Slate, The News, Poetical Histories, Archeus, Constant Red: Mingled Damask and Archeus.*

The repeat listing of *Archeus* appears to be an editorial error. In *Implacable Art* (2000), Mendelssohn titles a scabrous, short poem "virago." that discusses exclusion from a publishing house and a revolution (56; not in this collection).

Grace Lake, *Spinsters and Mistresses of Art.* (c. 1991–93).

Spinster of Arts is the title of a planned volume that was never published in full. Titled variously *Spinster of Arts*; *Spinster of Arts: An Anthropologia*; and *Spinsters and Mistresses of Art*, a rough manuscript, or mocked-up chapbook, exists in the Sussex archive (SxMs109/5/A/12a). The cover reads "Spinsters and Mistresses of Art." and includes a note indicating that Mendelssohn wanted the whole to be published in "Olivetti blue typeface on mid-grey (~~not a~~ pinkish grey)". The cover also states: "Title for Street Editions." A precursor to the Reality Street press, Street Editions was founded by the poet Wendy Mulford in 1972, and published works by J. H. Prynne, Tom Raworth, and Veronica Forrest-Thomson, among others (www.realitystreet.co.uk). In 1990, Mulford published Mendelssohn in *The Virago Book of Love Poetry* (see above) but does not recall Mendelssohn approaching her about this project (Mulford email; 27 July 2017).

Within the chapbook, beneath the poem "my wigwam." Mendelssohn writes, "from Spinster of Arts" (forthcoming 1992). Grace Lake." Further indicators of Mendelssohn's desire to publish arise in her correspondence. A letter to Kristina (surname unknown) dated 5 October 1991 states that Mendelssohn is writing a book called *Spinster of Arts*, and that the first section will be in a journal in November (3/A/2/12). And in a letter to Henry and Rosalind Raie dated 6 February 1993, Mendelssohn indicates that the text is in progress, and is titled "Spinster of Arts: An Anthropologia" (3/A/1/49a).

The archived manuscript does not include the poem attributed to *Spinster of Arts* that Mendelssohn includes in *Parataxis* in 1992 (see below notes). However, it does include "Europa", a title that will resurface in her 2000 volume, *Implacable Art* (29–30). The "Europa" of *Spinsters and Mistresses of Art.* is 52 lines; unrevised, the first twenty comprise the entire version given in *Implacable Art.*

The origin of the title *Spinster of Arts* is elucidated on a thick beige A4 sheet in 5/B/1/10/3, where Mendelssohn's verbal doodles suggest that she considered "spinster of arts." and "mistress of arts." reworkings of degree qualifications. Mendelssohn writes "~~B.A.~~" and "~~B.Sc.~~" then "spinster of arts." followed by, in a pyramid-shaped series, 21 iterations of "S.A." Beneath "mistress of arts." she writes "m.a." six times, as well as "S.Ms." and "M.Ms." Another variant is "spinster of science." followed by "s. s.c.", written eight times; "mistress of science." is accompanied by "m. sc.", written six times. Drawings, the words "Green. / Red Blue Yellow." and "Poem.", and the attribution "© S.G.L. Lake. / 1991." suggest that this sheet may be a planned book cover. The other side of the page includes a lament about Mendelssohn's father, and her simultaneous sympathy for and resistance to his views.

Mendelssohn's archive contains numerous examples of her toying with this phrasing, which may predate 1991. One manuscript poem includes the line, "Spinsters and Mistresses of Art Take Heart!" (5/B/2/24). Amid an almost unreadable manuscript plan, Mendelssohn writes and circles the word "Spinster." (5/B/2/26); in another file, an illustration of a line of five women is titled "spinsters of arts" (5/B/2/34). There are instances where Mendelssohn signs her poems "Mistress of Arts." and "M. A." On one occasion, above a manuscript poem signed with both monikers, she writes: "really I want to change my initials so that one from the second half of the alphabet precedes one from the first half. (& visit Ravenna). (& walk outside Siena)." (5/B/2/65). On an A5 manuscript that appears to be a thank you note dated November 1992, Mendelssohn describes "the poetess who has found herself in prison to serve a sentence as symbolic of political spite", and signs off, "A. Mendleson / Grace lake . Spinster of Arts" (5/B/2/71). Elsewhere in the archive, there is a folded A4 sheet of doodles, containing a list of "Biblical vocabulary" and, next to pictures of an antennaed creature accompanied by an animal, the phrase: "Spinster of Arts: A Space Odyssey." (5/B/1/11). Mendelssohn makes a note reminding herself to collect *Active in Airtime* from Rod Mengham, suggesting that this page may date from the early nineties (see below notes, 1993).

Another file in the Sussex archive contains a typescript titled "WORK IN PROGRESS. 1993." and "Long Time Passing"; beneath these titles, Mendelssohn types: "which includes 'Viola Tricolor' and 'Spinster of Arts' (5/A/16). Above the attribution "by Grace Lake." Mendelssohn writes, "Submission for an Arts Council Award 1993/4." If *Spinster of Arts* was originally included in this typescript, there is no immediate evidence; the twenty-page typescript includes Mendelssohn's *viola tricolor* (1993) only.

Mendelssohn hoped to set the piece to music. A letter of application to M. Finissey's Music Theatre Residency at Wingfield College, Suffolk (dated 27 February 1993) titles the entirety "Spinster or Spinsters of Arts – An Anthropologia", and describes it as a work that

> follows & develops the tradition of unresolved poetic debate initiated by Elizabeth Barrett Browning. I should tentatively describe its more involuted passages as that form of 'modernism' (a genre I still find difficult to resolve) which does not agree, always, with itself, yet works to break through to new form.

> I should very much like to set parts of this to music: song, chant, & piano with inserts of other instrumental sound.
>
> In short it embraces the spectrum from prescribed labour to creative work; and I have been bringing through the John Stuart Mill/Jeremy Bentham/Virginia Woolf & Bloomsbury dialectic between utilitarian thought and a democratic aesthetic. (8/C/1)

Elements of *Spinsters and Mistresses of Art.* remain unclear. In "Europa", "each other's" is without punctuation in manuscript, and the final stanza break is uncertain (ed.). In the final stanza of "the warmth is astounding.", the phrase "francoist eireann" is written "franoist eirrean" and the word "ruach" may be incorrect; "ruach" is Hebrew for wind, breath, or spirit, and can refer to the Holy Spirit or the origin of life (ed.). After the poem beginning "latin sixth xth", there is a drawing of a series of interlinked squares, most filled with geometric shapes and abstract figuration. A small four-sided shape filled with curlicues follows the poem beginning "rather than, rather"; the chapbook is completed by two pages of figure drawings, one reading "waiter" and "customer", the other containing the numbers "5768".

Grace Lake, "Poems", *Parataxis: modernism and modern writing*, no. 2 (Summer 1992), 4–12.
Consisting of nine issues that emerged from 1991 to 1996, *Parataxis* combined criticism and poetry. The first four issues were co-edited by Simon Jarvis, then a research fellow at Sidney Sussex College, Cambridge, and Drew Milne, who lectured at the universities of Edinburgh and Sussex before taking up a post at Cambridge. Milne edited the last five issues alone. Perfect bound, each issue was 60 to 130 pages. Initially financed by the University of Cambridge's Judith E. Wilson Fund, the editors intended to produce three issues annually, but issue two came out a year after the inaugural number, and in the final issue, Milne cites publication difficulties as the primary reason for bringing the venture to a close. A complete run is held at the Cambridge University Library.

The editorial ethos was described as follows:

> *Parataxis: modernism and modern writing* is a new journal devoted both to the critical re-thinking of modernism and to the publication of contemporary writing. At a time when the concept of modernism has come to seem merely historical, and when the critical vocabulary of modernism itself has been collapsed into that of postmodernism, *Parataxis* aims to allow substantial discussion of the legacies of modernism, while refusing to characterize modernism as that which is simply past. (no. 1, Spring 1991, 3)

John Wilkinson and Milne himself are mainstays of the publication. In the first three issues, Mendelssohn was the only female among contributors including Tony Lopez, David Ayers, Rod Mengham, Stephen Rodefer, Edwin Morgan, Brian Catling, Michael Haslam, Charles Bernstein, and Tim Woods. After issue four, Denise Riley, Wendy Mulford, Alice Notley, Fanny Howe, Leslie Scalapino, Rosemarie Waldrop, Lyn Hejinian, and Marjorie Welish contribute; issue seven is devoted to the Chinese Language-Poetry Group.

Of the six Mendelssohn poems included in issue two, "fulgencies", "nattering swans", and "i. m. Laura Riding" were chosen by Milne for inclusion in *Jacket* on-line magazine (no. 20, 2002; see below). A partial photocopy of Mendelssohn's entry in issue two exists in the Sussex archive (SxMs109/5/A/11). On its title page, Mendelssohn writes, "Spinster of Arts", echoing the working title given the first poem of her contribution, and a poetry collection then in progress (see above notes).

Mendelssohn makes four post-publication amendments to her *Parataxis* copy of "from 'Spinster of Arts'", correcting typos in line 34 – "actions" to "action" – and line 36, where "intolerent" becomes "intolerant". In the journal, the line "Irrelatively." was indented to correspond with the line above, but Mendelssohn draws an arrow indicating that she wanted it right justified. Similarly, "In some In others" was centred in publication, and Mendelssohn draws a second arrow revealing that she wanted it more in line with the above stanza. Mendelssohn's changes are replicated here, and apostrophes have been added to both "man's" in line three (ed.). In publication, line 12 of "one century beyond grew" begins "Bourgogne Blanc Aligotte" (ed.).

Grace Lake, "Two Poems", *Poets on Writing*, ed. Denise Riley, Palgrave-Macmillan (1992), 50–55.
John Wilkinson, Tom Raworth, Michael Haslam, Anthony Barnett, Douglas Oliver, and Ian Patterson are among the poets and editors who contributed short essays to *Poets on Writing*. An extract from Veronica Forrest-Thomson's posthumously published *Poetic Artifice* was also included. One of the party that rescued Mendelssohn's papers from her garden shed after her death – Martin Thom – is a contributor, as are individuals who published Mendelssohn's work: Nigel Wheale, Peter Riley, Wendy Mulford, and Ralph Hawkins (see notes on *constant red/mingled damask*, nos. 1 and 2, 1986 and 1987; Poetical Histories, 1988; *The Virago Book of Love Poetry*, 1990/91; *Active in Airtime*, 1993).

Editor Denise Riley requested Mendelssohn's writing as early as 1989. The plan given to all contributors was to avoid documentation or critical evaluation, instead offering readers "impressions of the various working processes of poetry" (letter dated 8 March 1989; SxMs109/3/A/1/51/2). Asked to write about writing, Mendelssohn instead contributed two poems. In 1991, Riley contacted shared associates to track down Mendelssohn's biography for the volume (letter dated 14 January 91; 3/A/1/51/2). Containing some inaccurate dates and misspellings, the biography on page 287 reads:

> **Grace Lake**
> (born 1948)
>
> Poems in magazines including *Constant Red: Mingled Damask*, 1985, *The News*, 1985, *Slate*, 1987, *Archeus*, 1989; and pamphlet, *La Facciata*, Cambridge Poetical Histories, 1989.

The Sussex archive includes a photocopy of Mendelssohn's entry, with a badly copied line carefully rewritten in her own hand; the biographical information from *Poets on Writing* contained in this file is not from Mendelssohn's original papers (5/A/12). Additionally, there is a manuscript poem that is titled with the last line of "Rose-Gazing", reading: "We must suffer. It is hard." (5/B/1/3).

Grace Lake, *café archéologique* (c. 1992–1993).
This short volume appears to be a work in progress. Mendelssohn drafted illustrations for it, and engaged in her usual pre-publication processes of editing, claiming copyright, and photocopying the original A4 manuscript copies into A5 pamphlet size, in this case choosing bright yellow paper. At Sussex, three files are devoted to this collection (SxMs109/5/A/13/1–3). The first two are manuscripts, with the second predominately drawings; the third contains the photocopied chapbook.

Mendelssohn appears to have devised four possible covers, some of which may have been intended for internal textual illustration. The first contains a cross-hatched pen and ink drawing covering two-thirds of the sheet. Centre page reads "WHY LOOK HERE?"; in the bottom right corner is written:

she thinks that you are very stupid a joke between
two friends one who did not give the glare to the other
who protected her from the vengeance of familial formality
but is now, context having been shifted to the right as
far as reality is concerned the bourgeoisie having taken to
radicalism some of which is outright revolutionary
what the hell   c'est la vie

The page is dated "92.3.15.", signed "cnem b. h'k.", and titled "café archéologique". Page verso reads: "93. © CAFÉ ARCHÉOLOGIQUE.grace Llake. / c.n.e.m. b. h'k." (5/A/13/1). Similar initials are used in the authorial attribution for Mendelssohn's *Tondo Aquatique* (1997; see below); they refer to Mendelssohn's Hebrew name, Channa Nechama Enna Krshner Mendleson Lubovitch bas Hakolenian (undated letter to Romana Huk, 3/A/1/20/1). Page front is photocopied for inclusion in the yellow chapbook, and on that verso side, Mendelssohn writes:

> well it is a shame how he can hope to become a successful writer when they won't even allow him to speak? I'd scream too if I were him. He can't say anything or do anything. He wants to ride trains through America.
>
> A lot of the problem is the flatness of the page. of paper. wanting a smooth ride rather than the opposite. Do some people have strong stomachs? Australians and Americans can be tough. That makes him sick.

Along the left side of the page reads: "logical positivism. Vienna. . Freud. Eluard. Tyrol." (5/A/13/3).

File 5/A/13/1 also contains three sheets bearing an oversized, cross-hatched apostrophe or comma: one has only "c/a" written beneath; another has the volume title, "grace ~~l~~lake.", "c.n.e.m. b.h'k.", "92.3." (written twice), and "$£9p."; a third draft includes the same oversized punctuation and the title above the poem "corps exquises avec Kiki" (5/A/13/1). The variant with the price included is used as the cover of the photocopied, unpaginated chapbook (5/A/13/3). All photocopied poems are included in the main body of this collection; the order remains uncertain. "<u>To stay away from the Ogre</u>." is the only photocopied poem without an accompanying manuscript.

Like *Celestial Empire.* (1983) and *Inbuilt Flash Nix* (1985), this work combines poetry and prose. The notes for *café archéologique* – many tagged with the work's title – include ruminations on music, etymology, unresolved grief, continental Dada and surrealism. Consistent with this latter preoccupation is Mendelssohn's poem about Kiki de Montparnasse (1901–1953), the artist, actor, and model perhaps best-known as the subject of Man Ray's *Noire et Blanche* (1926). On one page, Mendelssohn draws a feminine figure, photocopying it for the proofs of *café archéologique*; next to the drawing is the following note:

> Alice Prin (Kiki) was thrown out of Man Ray's life for poverty, 'get out' he said 'you look like a sack of potatoes and no one buys your drawings and I'm sick of keeping you in the back room whilst I string up my objects of inquiry for my friends & I to discuss and experiment on in the afternoons.' so she died." (5/A/13/1)

At the top of this page is another bit of verbal play that might be a poem, and exists in both manuscript and photocopied variants of the text:

rooftops stacks grey shades
an
heavy
bumblebee
staggering down to the kurb
four vile burping boys
he had you glued (5/A/13/1 and 3)

In the *café archéologique* prose, Mendelssohn expresses admiration for Breton and Éluard's *cadavres exquises,* which she labels "corps exquises", noting "it was clever to transmute the real bodies into the body of language/body as language" (5/A/13/1). References are also made to an image of justice by German Dada John Heartfield, possibly his 1933 photomontage, *The Executioner and Justice* (5/A/13/2).

Originally, "des" prefaced the title of "corps exquises avec Kiki". In stanza four of the poem beginning "struggles with self", the first line reads "gladiators ~~kept~~ retained". This poem and "Art & Women." may have been intended as a single text (ed.). In the manuscripts of 5/A/13/1, "Art & Women." has a replete verso page, but the photocopied *café archéologique* suggests that Mendelssohn did not intend to use this second portion. It is included in the appendix of this volume (see poem beginning "One rushes another is described as behaving abnormally"). In "Art & Women." the first line reads: "The ~~pain~~ excruciating slowness of absence."

Grace Lake, *Inverse*, no. 2 (June 1993).

Later lecturing in eighteenth-century literature at King's College, London, Elizabeth Eger edited *Inverse* whilst a PhD student at King's College, Cambridge. The journal lists the membership of the "Inverse Collective" as Umej S. Bhatia, Eger, Markman Ellis, Dell Olsen, James Robertson, Vanessa Smith, Penny Warburton, Ian White, Tim Whitmarsh, and Rafael Wober. The first issue of *Inverse* included the poetry of Jo Shapcott, La Loca, Ian Patterson, Gaoyuan Wei, and John Wilkinson, among others. In addition to Mendelssohn's sonnet, "XEROPHILOUS", the second issue contains poems by Peter Riley, Karlien van den Beukel, Umej Bhatia, Hugo Williams, Tom Raworth, Ron Koertge, Rod Mengham, Pierre Alfieri, and Stephen Rodefer. Eger kindly provided a copy of the journal for this collection.

Rodefer's poem, "Indent", is on the facing page of Mendelssohn's "XEROPHILOUS". Rodefer was Judith E. Wilson Senior Fellow at the University of Cambridge in 1992–93 and a friend to Mendelssohn. In subsequent Rodefer publications, "Indent" is dedicated "to Grace"; see *Left Under a Cloud* (Alfred David Editions, 2000, 75) and *Call it Thought* (Carcanet, 2008, 210; with thanks to Michael Tencer for this information). Among the eleven couplets of the poem are the lines:

Her deft openers and reft
spondees the reef ponders

Snorter, spender
sheeter done for horn feed

Steered here
for trophe's tender

Sterner fees steepening to the ford
    with errant reed thorns

So on the drifter pad her pen
    spent of often sphered ether

The penultimate line of this passage in *Inverse* reads "So to the drifter pad her pen" in later publications.

There is a manuscript variant of Mendelssohn's sonnet in the archive that is 23 lines long (5/B/2/97). Titled "<u>Xerophilous</u>", it varies from the first nine lines of the published version as follows:

"by Simon Calves / engineering" was "by Simon Carves ~~which~~ ^~~was~~^ ~~had been~~ / ~~a munitions fac~~ engineering"
"W. W. 2" was "2nd. W. War."
"for the details" was "for details"
"Groundless unlike losing consciousness," was "groundless yet unlike losing consciousness"
Line eight was "leapt ~~forward~~ ^ahead^, ~~leapt~~ ^was dragged^ back, brain v brawn, brain v brawn,"
Line nine was "~~Jellied co~~ Calf Jell~~ey~~. ~~W~~ O where can a lake walk to?"

After line nine, the manuscript concludes:

not a name Lake a real lake but they don't have much of a
sense of humour. Neither did Gerard. Oh Dear.
The Auction was advertised for twenty past four.
EVERYONE came, ~~wine was~~ [~~*unclear letter, possibly &*~~ —ed.] it can't be real theatre.
It can't be real o.k. I agree. the law is irrelevant. Well the
LAW tells you what Life IS and what Death IS. This is NOT
a dead person although there is no heartbeat to be heard.
No. This is a living person pretending to be a third leg.
Monoplane on the dummy arm, if you only knew the real state of the nation.
Jarring t.v. odes. seventeen minuscule screens integrated into the digital wallpaper
footsteps. Opening doors, drawers, directing ~~naked~~ ^raw^ ~~emot~~ water into a dew ~~drop~~. pond.
for refusing to think of youngsters being truncheoned to death
trampled over and torn down from democratic plinths
as ~~being~~ detached from the ~~guns~~ ^bullets^ that kill~~ed~~ them.

Written in brown ink on an A5 sheet, this poem is edited in black ink in the final line. Abstract doodles appear along top, bottom, and left-hand side of the page.

Grace Lake, "Five Poems", *Active in Airtime*, no. 3 (1993), 44–49.
Between 1992 and 1995, there were four issues of *Active in Airtime,* a perfect-bound journal devoted to "New Fiction and Verse" and funded by the Eastern Arts Board. Editors included Ralph Hawkins, Ben Raworth, and John Muckle. The publication

was produced in Essex: first Colchester, then Brightlingsea. Poetic peers in Mendelssohn's issue included Anselm Hollo, Ian Davidson, and Maurice Scully. Poets in other issues include Bill Griffiths, Denise Riley, Miles Champion, Alice Notley, John Welch, Fanny Howe, Douglas Oliver, and Drew Milne. An advertisement in volume four identifies where the contributors' work can be found: in addition to Compendium Books London and the Oriel Bookshop in Cardiff, Paul Green, Peter Riley, and Alan Halsey are listed as book dealers. A complete run of *Active in Airtime* is held at the British Library.

In issue two, Mendelssohn's author biography reads: "**GRACE LAKE**'s poetry has appeared in magazines and in *La Facciata* (Poetical Histories). She is also included in *Poets on Writing: Britain* (Macmillan)." A partial proof with minor edits in Mendelssohn's hand exists in her papers (SxMs109/5/A/14); this proof includes a brief note from editor John Muckle about production delays and difficulties. On an alternate proof, in this case of "Declared redundant 'in media res' as politics advise sentiment" (numbered page 22), Mendelssohn corrects "loved" to "loves" (5/A/41).

As Mendelssohn acknowledges in *viola tricolor* (1993), four of the poems she published in *Active in Airtime* are reproduced in the later chapbook, namely: "Ordered into Quarantine"; "Cultural"; "The End is Listless", and, "on challenge, positive attitudes and 'les peintures cubistes'". The latter poem is also published in the 1996 anthology *Conductors of Chaos*. "Culture" is last published in *A State of Independence* (1998); "Ordered into Quarantine" is published alongside it in 1998, and again in *Out of Everywhere* (2006; see below notes for all collections). A key difference between the *Active in Airtime* and later publications is that in 1993, "Ordered into Quarantine" is followed by the poem included here, namely, "Declared redundant 'in media res' as politics advise sentiment". Both this title and that of "on challenge" are formatted as sub-headings but are listed as two of the "Five Poems" in the table of contents.

Grace Lake, *The Day the Music Died*, Equipage (1993).

Plainly bound in a green cover, this chapbook consists of 18 sides of A5, 14 of them poems. It is Mendelssohn's first publication with Rod Mengham's Equipage press, an affiliation that will extend to three further chapbooks – *viola tricolor* (1993), *Bernache Nonnette* (1995), *Tondo Aquatique* (1997) – and Mendelssohn's only perfect-bound text, *Implacable Art* (2000).

The gestation of *The Day the Music Died* is unusual: Mendelssohn approached Mengham three days before a funding proposal was due with the then-named Eastern Arts Board. As she lacked the requisite number of publications to apply, Mengham encouraged her to bring a manuscript to him the next day to quickly copy, cover, and staple. Mengham believes that *The Day the Music Died* was an edition of five: three copies for funders, one for Mendelssohn, and another for him (email 27 July 2017). Mendelssohn failed to secure funding but deposited this text in the Cambridge University Library and the British Library; the latter copy is used here. As yet, no manuscripts have been found in Mendelssohn's Sussex archive.

Grace Lake, *viola tricolor*, Equipage (1993).

An A5 chapbook of 28 sides (24 bearing poems), this is one of Mendelssohn's five publications with Rod Mengham's Equipage press. The entirety was typeset by the poet Ulli Freer, and the purple cover bears a Mendelssohn sketch of a weapon in a sheath or holster. Between title and publication information, the title page includes an epigraph reading:

Viola: "My father had a mole upon his brow"

l. 242. Act V. Sc. 1
"Twelfth Night or What you will"

William Shakespeare
The Riverside Shakespeare p438.

On the final page, Mendelssohn claims copyright under her birth name, "A. Mendleson" and acknowledges that four of the poems were published in *Active in Airtime* (1993), namely: "Ordered into Quarantine"; "Cultural"; "The End is Listless", and, "on challenge, positive attitudes and 'les peintures cubistes'" (see above notes).

Mendelssohn's Sussex archive houses five folders containing drafts and proofs of *viola tricolor* (SxMs109/5/A/15/1–4 and 5/A/16). There is no complete copy in the archive; the text used here is the editor's own. Within Mendelssohn's files, there is a cover variant. The mock-up retains the font and layout of the published version, but uses a different Mendelssohn sketch: a profile of a feminine head gazes upwards; bodiless, it sits next to a boat-like shape, and both figures appear to float on a horizontal plane (5/A/15/3). In this same folder, there is an A4 page reading "a flame, a tear, // safety precautions." and a small squared-off sketch; on the verso side of the same, Mendelssohn writes: "£85 to pay:" followed by what may be "Classnot." In the same file, one irregular typescript page, landscape format, includes three lines reading: "crossed, condemned. the plague. the poor. inhibited imaginations. frail. the context … not in Raymo / Raymond williams' "Keywords". The context is withheld within the literary tradition. / Blake, Leigh Hunt, Mary Wollstonecraft. Let God be my Judge." These pages are interspersed with ten poem typescripts that make their way into the final volume, including what may be a Greek version of the first eponymously titled poem. Also in 5/A/15/3 is a prose text entitled "Ivan the Horrible" in manuscript and typescript; Mendelssohn may have considered combining poetry and prose within *viola tricolor* as in *Inbuilt Flash Nix* and *Is this a True Parrot, a Mountain, or a Stooge?* (both 1985). In addition to meaning "wild pansy", Mendelssohn's title is identical to that of an 1874 novella by the nineteenth-century German realist Theodor Storm, whose *Viola Tricolor* is referenced in a note in her papers dated 5 February 1999 (5/A/24/8). Further insight into the preoccupations of title and textual gestation arises in folder 5/A/15/2, which contains two scraps of A5 paper (differing stock), one headed "Viola tricolor." and the other "viola tricolor." Subtitled "Wild Pansy.", the first reads:

> annual or perennial herb, usually much branched, glabrous or pubescent, rhizome 0 or short and scarcely creeping. Leaves very variable, invest ovate, obtuse, becoming slowly or rapidly narrower upwards; upper ovate, oblong-lanceolate, lanceolate or elliptical, obtuse to subacute, ± cuneate at base, crenate, crenate-serate or crenate-dentate, glabrous or ± pubescent; stipules variable but often palmately lobed, mid-lobe usually lanceolate and entire, not leaf-like. Peduncles 2–8 cm, several on each stem. Sepals triangular – lanceolate to linear-lanceolate, acute; appendages variable. Corolla 1.5–2.5 cm vertically, longer than sepals, flat, blue-violet (rarely pink) or yellow or of combinations of these; spur longer than appendages (up to twice as long). 80–90% of pollen grains with 4 pores, remainder, with 3 or 5. Stylar flap distinct. Fl. 4–9. Pollinated mainly by long-tongued bees.
>
> Curtisii (subspecies)

The second sheet is subtitled "Snag 21." and begins poetically: "transformed to silk a garrett a light florentine dress resting arrestingly / ting hued". The passage then moves to Mendelssohn's repeat life writing themes, including the surfacing of an unnamed "you"; litigation and lost children ("Once the universe had removed your children."); and anxieties about being perceived as a writer, as intelligent. Further topics include feeling watched and reprimanded; sexual assault; "the Revolutionary Left", and the unacknowledged need to be saved from difficulties: "Not one pore on my flesh expected anyone to rescue me." Mendelssohn also touches on her love of "natural / phenomena such as Day and Morning and Dusk and Twilight and Jasmine and Swans." She recalls watching an allotment or community garden in the distance whilst being threatened with sexual victimhood or a return home; financial concerns were among the restrictions she felt throughout this episode, as she was "on an ordinary student's grant."

In a letter to Sally Mitchison dated 7 September 1993, Mendelssohn writes that Viola Tricolor is the nomenclature for the pansy, adding, "I also thought of Titania Mallet as another personage … Does she sound less revolutionary than Viola Tricolor . . . . . actually I don't want Viola Tricolor to sound revolutionary" (3/A/1/37). Elsewhere in Mendelssohn's Sussex papers, there is an A5 manuscript, culminating in a boxed-in drawing, bearing a passage in which Viola Tricolor appears as an individual (5/B/2/74). It reads:

> This is for the knowledge that is reserved for the end of it.
> It is a sentence that was held down & pinned from ~~be~~ edge to edge.
> Much as Viola Tricolor did not know how to live when the
> theatre ~~was~~ was destroyed by those who believed she would
> serve their revolution less apparently ~~by~~ by denying her the
> full development of a tradition that knew ~~no one~~ ^no^ political
> prejudices that could not be metamorphosed, safely, within
> it's own courtly spaces, those spaces that are so delicious for
> painters to play with ^by^ metaphysical~~ly~~ suspen~~ding~~sion ~~them~~
> Magdalena, ~~who~~ would have been more ^technically^ willing to sell her
> body for a few ~~qui~~ fivers ^rather^ than ~~to ride~~ ^be ridden^ as a figurehead
> immobilized, ^&^ terrified ~~& frozen~~ into a repoussé~~d *unclear word*—ed.~~
> ~~front~~ shield but who ^[*unclear word*—ed.]^ couldn't ^to^ prostrate herself in any
> more domestic dramas (before callous carnivores)
> deserted herself for the ~~nation~~ sake of the consolidation of
> the nations twelve tier wedding cake.
>
> Magdalena's general existentialist strike.

This text prefigures or echoes the identification of a "young girl" in "viola tricolor", who is also captive to or prostituted by art and revolutionary politics. Similarly, Mendelssohn's later publication, *Parasol One. Parasol Two. Parasol Avenue.* (1996), opens with a short poem that returns to the figure of Bernache Nonnette, the title of her 1995 Equipage collection, and Viola Tricolor. It begins: "Bernache reclined upon her startling blue aeroflot indice. / the union had been saved within hours by Viola in a / single footed close shave."

In the Sussex *viola tricolor* folders, there is a full, paginated proof replete with corrections in Mendelssohn's hand (5/A/15/4). This proof shows that at one juncture, Mendelssohn planned to have the poem "Half." follow "Sauce" rather than "twelve to midnight", as in the finished volume. All other ordering remains identical to the publication. Mendelssohn edited a draft title page bearing no quotes or illustrations, ensuring that her name appeared above the title. Across the top of "The End is Listless" in this proof, Mendelssohn quotes:

> 'I can give you no advice upon the Article of Expence, only I think you ought to be well informed how much your Husband's Revenue amounts to, and be so good a Computer as to keep within it, in that part of the

Management which falls to your share; and not to put yourself in the number of those Politick Ladies, who think they gain a great Point when they have teazed their Husbands to buy them a new Equipage, a lac'd Head, or a fine Petticoat, without once considering what long Scores remain unpaid to the Butcher'

from 'A Letter to a Young Lady on her Marriage'
Jonathan Swift. first published in
Swift's 'Miscellanies,' vol. ii, 1727.

At the bottom right of the page is a small linear doodle; on the bottom left, she writes: "mistook his brows for his lashes / leithe gravy." (*'leithe' is unclear*—ed.). On the back of the proof of "on challenge, positive attitudes and 'les peintres cubistes'" Mendelssohn scrawls, "The life of St Anne contains the flowering rod which 'doth blome and bere,' gives the names of two of the maidens as they appear in the play – / and presents Joseph as a delinquent in the presentation of his rod."

Mendelssohn appears to have sent this text to friends, among them Ian Patterson (letter dated 12 January 1994; SxMs109/3/A/1/47/2). A letter to Simon and Lynne Harries dated 24 November 1993 details Mendelssohn's "hope that [the book] will not bore" and her dissatisfaction with the finished copy:

> The pages should have been numbered but there was persuasion to the contrary by the typesetter – 'Fourteenth Flight' is also wrongly set although that may have been due to the use of a different computer – it is not for the lack of long telephone conversations & proof copies which arranged it properly. The last poem has been included against my wishes [*the poem in question is "on challenge, positive attitudes and 'les peintres cubistes'"* – ed.]. This is all probably due to unpaid labour. Some poets pay for their own typesetting. However 30 years of writing for various levels of reading & performance (excluding the Angry Brigade communiqués bar 3 lines against internment written on command by an armed man) have resulted in this. You are both invited to the reading at Jesus College Upper Parlour 8.45 p.m. Friday 26th November (this Friday). David Chaloner will also be reading." (SxMs109/3/A/1/18/1)

In what follows, substantive differences are identified between available manuscript drafts and their appearance in the final copy of *viola tricolor*. Most of the texts are lightly corrected; only significant reworkings are noted here. Page order, continuity, and distinctions between recto and verso are uncertain; unless otherwise noted, each side is treated as an independent entity. Untitled poems are referred to by first line. These notes replicate the order of the final text.

"viola tricolor"
There are manuscripts and/or typescripts of this poem in 5/A/15/1 and 4, as well as 5/A/16. It is published for the last time in the 1998 anthology *A State of Independence* (see below).

"poetry."
There is a double-sided A5 manuscript of this poem in 5/A/15/1 and typescripts in 5/A/15/4 and 5/A/16. In publication, typescripts, and manuscript, "whiskey" is "whisky" (ed.) Evident in *viola tricolor* and both typescripts, the dedication to Mahler-Sapir does not appear in manuscript. Minimal differences between manuscript and published poem include:

> "stone pendant" was "stone ~~her~~ pendant"
> "converting into" was "converting it into" (also in 15/A/16)

"practicing care." was "practicing care,"
"to take the angry" was "to take ~~you~~ the angry"
"flat topped mountain" was "topped mountain ~~head.~~"
"a soft subject" was "a soft ~~dedicated~~ subject"
"a renounced and desolate cry" was "a renounced and rejected desolate cry"
"club manager" was "club ~~owner~~ manager"
"tennyson in albany" was "Tennyson in Albany"
"sylphs lord leighton's" was "sylphs ~~beware of~~ Lord Leighton"
"in the street" was "on the street"
"staggering out from bookstores" was "staggering out of bookshops"
"to secure faked devotion." was "to secure ~~house~~ ^his^ faked devotion."

On the verso side is prose that is formatted to cohere with page size and two right-justified doodles. In its entirety, the page reads:

when they will stop substituting body for poetry and when ? when the people who remain
have been hacked to death in my name? All because such misogynists have run
out of negativities.
I'm leaving the card games to you. You don't even know
when I'm being condescending. I don't want
people like that climbing over walls or issuing one sided threats
It's not even to do with the National Trust. It's to do with
people believing that they are going through other people's lives,
it's disgusting! That ~~rest~~ reticence goes unrecognized
in this struggle for political power & then who will teach
with culled intelligence & stagger out of bookshops again.
You can't have a word of my north. There were no
comedians before Big Screen Men
Literature and Psychoanalysis. How internecine intonations
take our fine energy & convert it into hard currency aborting ~~our~~ thought.
But not there with a race track ~~as~~ coagitating
When I have nothing in writing to suggest that a name is not running.

Well the shining estuary does exist but I'll not be going
through these chunks of solid granite nearly arriving but afraid
of happiness
in every way since the closure against that poet, south of the border.
As though water meeting by streaming into river ever
hurt a living thing.
Not on a day like that, not on a temperate morning.
And do not love one for it, that is no poetry,

to love one for a stream or a blackbird by
a moss covered stone. a ~~cress~~ moss covered
~~st~~ stone.
bov [*possibly box or bou*—ed.]

"dulc."

Line eleven, stanza two of the published version of "dulc." reads "never a correct ansver." In the proof of *viola tricolor* it is "answer" and is rendered as such here (ed.) (5/A/15/4). In publication and in two typescripts (5/A/15/4 and 5/A/16), Mendelssohn renders "Sibyl" as "Sybil" (ed.). In line five of stanza two, typescript 5/A/16, Mendelssohn handwrites after "no friends to help me": "who would help Me". In typescript 5/A/15/4, this addition to the line is typed after an extended space, then redacted by hand.

A manuscript of "dulc." exists in 5/B/2/69. Along the top reads: "Imagine this : one word for one country!" The title has no full stop, and the first line of stanza two is treated as a title that ends with a full stop; both titles are underlined, and "managed by a photograph which was anyway a set up." recurs at the end of the poem in brackets. Further changes include:

"a tear a flame" was "a tear~~y~~ ^a^flame"
"burying ignorance" was "burying ~~my~~ ignorance"
"understand despairing pleas" was "understand ~~those~~ despairing pleas"
"there avoidance" was "there ~~an~~ avoidance"
"sun for even" was "sun for ~~whatever~~ even"
"might do" was "might DO"

"Ordered into Quarantine"

One of four *viola tricolor* poems previously published in *Active in Airtime* (1993), "Ordered into Quarantine" is also the only poem that Mendelssohn altered from that publication; a typescript exists in 5/A/15/4). The poem is reproduced for the final time in *Out of Everywhere* (2006; see below notes).

"twelve to midnight"

Typescripts of "twelve to midnight" exist in 5/A/15/4 and 5/A/16; a manuscript can be found in 5/B/2/69. This poem is first published in *viola tricolor* (1993) and will be republished in both editions of *Out of Everywhere* (2006; see below notes).

"Half."

There are typescripts of "Half." in 5/A/15/3 and 4, as well as 5/A/16. In 5/B/2/41, there is a partial manuscript that begins from the second line of page two and ends with the last line of the poem. It is written on an unlined A4 page, unpaginated, undated & without authorial attribution. In addition to differences in capitalisation, variations between publication and manuscript include:

"insolence in a symbolized memory" was "insolence to a symbolic memory"
"to the ground" was "to the ground." (see also 5/A/15/4 and 5/A/16)
"suspect a missed" was "suspect the missed"
"pity there were no" was "Pity there weren't" (also in 5/A/15/3; "were not" in 5/A/16)
"west, a concordat over gravestones" was "west, ~~we~~ ^a^ concordat ~~on~~ ^over^ gravestones"
"at the station master's suggestion" was "at the station master's bidding."

Differing in punctuation and capitalisation, further variations between publication and typescripts include: “gives it to brethren” was “gives it to their brethren” (5/A/15/3 and 5/A/16); “bidden to,” was “bidden” (5/A/15/3); and, “that neither of them” was “that ~~neither~~ ^none^ of them” (5/A/15/3).

Poem beginning “who would have found one a print psalm lemon”

This poem may be a portion of “Half.”, but in both typescripts, 5/A/15/4 and 5/A/16, it stands alone, and is paginated much later in the text. Furthermore, the typescript of “Half.” in 5/A/15/3 is a single piece of A4 that concludes with “at the station master’s suggestion.”

In one typescript, Mendelssohn renders the fourth line of stanza one as “of the i.m.f.” (5/A/16); in publication, this reads “if the”; “of the” is reinstated, although Mendelssohn’s preference for “Tromsö” in 5/A/15/4 is corrected (ed.). In 5/A/16, the final line of stanza seven is rendered: “‘you must admit, when it slides by ~~with~~ ^bearing^ ‘tropical pineapples’ ~~now button it~~.” In 5/A/15/4 and 5/A/16, the phrase “refusing a lifetime” in stanza eight was “she refuses her lifetime”; it is corrected in 5/A/15/4, where Mendelssohn also adds the “and” of line four, stanza eight.

“two secs”

There are four typescripts of this poem (5/A/15/1, 3 and 4; 5/A/16) and one manuscript (5/B/2/97). In one typescript, the phrases “slumped sinatra” and/or “white flaked loafers” may have been within single quotations (5/A/15/4). In two typescripts, an accent is added by hand to “café” (5/A/15/3 and 5/A/16); an accent is similarly added to “pièd” in 5/A/15/4. Though not rendered in publication, these accents are reinstated here (ed.). In *viola tricolor*, “nureyev” reads “nuryev” (ed.).

Given the exceptionality and extent of variation from the published version, the draft typescript from 5/A/15/1 is replicated in the appendix, and the manuscript is given in the appendix notes, as are further details about Mendelssohn’s revisions and poem formatting.

“madeira”

There are five typescripts of this poem in the Sussex *viola tricolor* files (5/A/15/1, 3–4; 5/A/16, and 5/B/2/67). In 5/A/15/1, the poem is a portrait-formatted recto-only typescript with a hand-written title. In this copy, “personally?” is cut off, and Mendelssohn reinforces stanza breaks by hand. In most typescripts, “redactive” is “reactive” (change occurs in 5/A/15/4), and “to prove it power” is “to prove its power”; this latter distinction is reinstated (ed.). Throughout the typescripts, accents are occasionally added by hand for “depôt”, “geneviève”, and “sèvres”; though not evident in publication, they are included here (ed.). In the proofs for *viola tricolor*, “cubed” is rendered “curbed” and goes uncorrected (5/A/15/4).

In addition to changes in punctuation and capitalisation, the following differences from publication can be discerned in the 5/B/2/67 typescript:

> “workers should” was “workers ^~~acto~~^ should”
> “snug, a living wage” was “snug, a decent living wage”
> “complexity impounds” was “complexity tends to impound”
> “to say we hide the truth” was “You say we hide the truth”
> “prove its power” was “prove that power”
> “light has a softness that warms” was “is a soft light that warms”

Poem beginning “The past’s stranding to belief”
There are three typescripts of this poem (5/A/15/3 and 4; 5/A/16). In proof and in publication, the space is elided after the first comma in the line beginning “of kindness, of smiles” and has been reinstated (ed.). In the 5/A/15/3 typescript, “Ring a ring a hearts” was “Ring a ringa ahearts”; at the bottom of the page, pre-copying, Mendelssohn writes: “238 words”.

“language blows away”
Typescripts of this poem exist in 5/A/15/ 4 and 5/A/16; in 5/A/15/3, it exists half in type, half handwritten. Mendelssohn published this poem in *viola tricolor* (1993) and again in *A State of Independence* (1998). See below notes on the latter.

“for Bruno Alcaraz Massaz”
Complete typescripts of this poem can be found in 5/A/15/3 and 4, as well as 5/A/16. At least three partial manuscripts also exist, all limited to the third stanza (5/A/15/1, 5/B/2/67 and 5/B/2/74). Differences from the published final stanza and that found in manuscript in 5/A/15/1 include:

> “like two pikestaffs” was “like two rigid pikestaffs”
> “awkwardly set, in a company, were it not for / streaks of fury piping hot scarlet into the dawn” was “awkwardly set, in a two writers will if it were not for / another streak of fury piping hot scarlet into the dawn”
> “took thirty one years” was “took twenty eight years”
> “For a mother to sing a new history.” was “for a mother to paint a new history.”

In this manuscript, the last two lines are in double quotation marks, and the second-last line is punctuated by extended spaces rather than commas. In 5/A/15/3, there are two typescripts of the final stanza, and one of stanzas one and two; here, all of the above variants are preserved, barring those in line four (beginning “awkwardly set,”) which reads as in the published version. A second typescript in the same file shows Mendelssohn replacing “paint a new history” with “sing” and deleting the quotation marks around the last two lines. In 5/A/15/4, Mendelssohn corrects the breaking of her long lines by hand to keep them intact; in stanza two, she deletes what may be a hyphen from “hand painted”; in stanza three, she adds “the” between “into” and “dawn”. Minor differences in punctuation, capitalisation, and lineation from the published version arise in these variants.

Another manuscript of the final stanza beginning “in the guise of another” exists in Mendelssohn’s papers (5/B/2/67). Under notes reading “One month behind. ~~30~~ 31.” and “January 6.th 1601. Twelfth Night.” is a long horizontal line that crosses through the words “The name”, and beneath which appears a left-justified title: “The Brasserie Tenth.” The text shows the following changes:

> “are ~~hard enough~~ tough & flexible”
> “two pikestaffs” was “two rigid pikestaffs”
> “awkwardly set, in a company, were it not for” was “grossly ~~put~~ ^set^, in a two writers will if it were for not”
> “streaks of fury” was “Another Streak of Fury”
> “wearing a Kipper” was “with a Kipper”
> “on a counter full worn” was added above the line
> “regular though short” was “regular tho’ short”
> “one month behind, took thirty one years to learn one song:” was “one month behind, ~~& not too long~~, took twenty ~~six~~ eight years to learn ~~a~~ ^one^ song”

"For a mother" was " "For a mother"
"What is art, O what is She, A baby dandled on a strange man's knee" was "What is Art? O what is she? A baby ~~being~~ dandled on a ~~mother's~~ strange man's knee?"
"for a mother to sing" was "for a mother to paint"
"Too close to" was "~~in blooming pinks and blues~~ ^Too close to^"

Beneath this stanza is a long horizontal line, followed by:

Hungry days. when culture seems to have run its course and turns its back on the future
Afraid of sounds it has not heard before that same old grasping for sleep.
to secure a walled sanity. To tell us we are but tiny flowers
sprung from the blood of ~~Adonis~~ ^a god^. Grand Seigniors & Beatific Mistresses
watching ^over^ their workers stride back and forth
wearing a plucked viola.

If that is the case don't expect me to speak like a normal human being.

The other side of the page bears a doodle and the phrase: "viola tripoli".

Finally, there is a second manuscript of the stanza beginning "in the guise of another" (5/B/2/74) that incorporates edits from a variety of manuscripts. For instance, "rigid pikestaffs", "in a two writers will if" and "twenty eight" remain, as does "Another Streak of Fury"; almost all else reads as per the published text. In the last line, Mendelssohn writes "~~woman~~ ^mother^to paint".

"Sauce"
In the Sussex archive, this poem exists in manuscript (5/A/15/1) and typescript (5/A/15/3 and 4; 5/A/16). It is published in *viola tricolor* (1993) and in *A State of Independence* (1998); there are no differences between the two published versions. See below notes for *A State of Independence* (1998).

"the fourteenth flight"
There are three variants of "the fourteenth flight" that differ considerably in length, organisation, and content from the published version. Given the exceptionality and extent of these differences, one complete manuscript is replicated in the appendix. All three variations are discussed in the notes to the rough draft of *viola tricolor* in the appendix, and sample passages are given (5/A/15/1 and 3; 5/B/1/11). Typescripts very similar to publication exist in 5/A/15/4 and 5/A/16. In 5/A/16, the last two stanzas are not included. In the previous six, Mendelssohn makes the following substantive edits by hand; it is noted where these edits overlap with hand-written corrections in 5/A/15/4:

"me of imitation" was "me of copying ^imitation^"
"fraud, treachery to kindred or" was "fraud ^treachery^ ~~or~~ to kindred or" [*"fraud" and the redacted "or" are typed*]
"won't be purred as a pussy" was "won't pussy" – "be purred as a" is added by hand
"accused are more often ready" was "are [*long space*] ready" – "more often" is added by hand in the space
"their bankrupt lives" was "their fine fine ^bankrupt^ lives" (recurs in 5/A/15/4 as "~~fine~~ bankrupt ~~fine~~")
"people is more or less hell." was "people is hell." ("more or less hell." is added to 5/A/15/4)

In the second-last stanza in 5/A/15/4, Mendelssohn appears to have contemplated adding quotations to the three lines beginning "nothing to say" and ending "this morning".

In publication, Mendelssohn manages her extended lines by giving the run-over its own line, marked at the outset with a crotchet. These breaks are placed as close as possible to the end of the line; here they are standardised, and the punctuation excised (ed.).

"Ionic"

There are two typescripts of this poem in the Sussex archive (5/A/15/1 and 4). One is a landscape-oriented, recto-only, untitled typescript almost identical to the published version, barring: "by plea" was "by a plea" and the correction "burying ~~knowledge~~ memories"; minor typos are corrected (5/A/15/1). In both, Mendelssohn alters the lineation of the last three lines of the poem. In 5/A/15/1, they read:

> creek with creased interchange as the shout goes up 'Hommage' ' ' Homage'
> To an Omelette from a Sheep's Egg followed by 'a Pie' 'a Pie of apples from a Lydian Quince.'

In 5/A/15/4, these same lines are shortened and multiplied, reading: "creek with creased interchange as the shout goes up 'Hommage' / 'Hommage' To an Omelette from a Sheep's Egg / followed by 'a Pie', 'a Pie of apples from a Lydian / Quince'." On this typescript, by hand and pre-copying, Mendelssohn indicates how they should be changed in line with the published variant.

"1526."

Manuscripts of this poem exist in 5/A/15/1 and in 5/B/2/67; typescripts can be found in 5/A/15/3 and 4. Differences between these manuscripts, the version used in *viola tricolor* (1993), and the final publication of this text in *Conductors of Chaos* (1996) are included in the notes for the latter text.

"Cultural"

A typescript of "Cultural" exists in 5/A/15/4. This poem is published in *Active in Airtime* (1993), *viola tricolor* (1993), and *A State of Independence* (1998). The two 1993 variants are identical; see below notes.

"The End is Listless"

This poem was also published in *Active in Airtime* (1993); the versions are identical. The Sussex archive holds a proof typescript of the poem in 5/A/15/4, and in the partial proof for *Active in Airtime*, Mendelssohn corrects "quiet graves, soothing" to "quiet gravel, soothing"; this is how it appears in both publications (5/A/14).

"on challenge, positive attitudes and 'les peintres cubistes'"

A manuscript and typescript proof of this poem exist in the Sussex archive in files 5/B/2/56 and 5/A/15/4 respectively. Versions of this poem were published in *Active in Airtime* (1993), *viola tricolor* (1993), and *Conductors of Chaos* (1996). For a full account of variations, see the notes for the latter publication.

Grace Lake, *Bernache Nonnette*, Equipage (1995).

This A5 chapbook is the third of five Mendelssohn publications with Rod Mengham's Cambridge-based press; 15 sides bear poems in this unpaginated text, which has no table of contents. One of Mendelssohn's pen and ink drawings adorns the cover (shown here); it is interspersed with handwriting reading: "louise femme de la bernache"; "fraiche"; "la nonnette."; "la bernache"; "3121543122134432132", and lastly, "grace lake." The original drawing remains in Mendelssohn's Sussex archive (SxMs109/5/ B/1/13), and a copy of the same exists in the Peter Riley Papers at Cambridge (MS Add. 10013/2/29). The text used here is the editor's own.

The epigraph on the title page reads:

'J'écris les brouillons, les yeux fermés'

Vendredi 17, Carnet III
"Les carnets de la drole [*sic*] de guerre"
J. P. Sartre. Editions [*sic*] Gallimard 1983.

A photocopied letter to Mengham dated "29th March." (5/A/17/6) indicates that Mendelssohn considered dedicating the collection to Orpheus. In the proof in the same file, the poem beginning "Exactly what will this have rested upon for it to have emerged." was titled "To Orpheus"; the title is excised in all other variants. Mendelssohn's letter to Mengham also explains the Sartrean epigraph:

> I am very grateful to you for this. I assure you I am not a daemon but now I hope to launch into the book I was on the brink of writing before the effect of loud sound threw me onto the road that my Fate crossed & I flew to Holloway for refuge not realizing that it was a prison (I thought it was a castle). How Dreadful I feel. It had and has nothing to do with politics but Sartre did help me to keep my mind away and detached as I had been reading 'Being and Nothingness' when I was 12 and my school was backward although not as backward as the art veto.

After her signature, Mendelssohn asks: "do you know of any libraries on the top of mountains?"

When typesetting *Bernache Nonnette*, the poet Ulli Freer used two spaces after full stops, spaces not evident in Mendelssohn's typescripts. As she personally approved the final proofs, this typography is replicated (ed.). Where not reinforced by typescripts, some unusual spacing has been silently corrected (ed.). Unsent correspondence from Mendelssohn to Freer expresses gratitude at his centring of her poems and indicates that she wanted to avoid broken lines whilst maintaining the A5 pamphlet size, as "[g]iganticity, when it exists, can be read regardless." To Freer, Mendelssohn notes that she contemplated titling the collection *Une Bernache Nonnette* (undated; 16 March 1995; 27 October 1993; 3/A/1/15).

In a letter of 18 March 1996 to Romana Huk, Mendelssohn mentions having sent a copy of *Bernache Nonnette*, adding parenthetically that the text, which she feminises, "is turning into a serial novel" (3/A/1/20/1). To Lynne and Simon Harries, Mendelssohn expresses the hope that *Bernache Nonnette* "is light & anguished enough to convey – the fear & regret" (18 June 1995; 3/A/1/18/1). She appears to have sent a copy to Fiona Nicholson (3/A/1/40), and to Ewan Smith, who writes her on 18

September 1995 to compliment her work, writing: "I cannot sympathise with the 'woman artist' position you often seem to occupy, it seems a disastrous form of self-destructive isolationism .... but this book ... is beautiful, witty and wonderful, and for me, puts you among those ten or so people writing the best poetry around." (3/A/1/57).

Seven files in the Sussex archive are directly related to the publication of *Bernache Nonnette* (5/A/17/1–7). A partial manuscript begins with a title page indicating that Mendelssohn had been researching the barnacle goose that the volume is named after (5/A/17/3). It reads:

> bernache nonnette.
>
> expecting women to [*last two words unclear, could be "momento" or "moments"*—ed.]
>
> [*horizontal, linear sketch*]
>
> branta leucopsis   Bechstein 1803.   Barnacle Goose.
>
> Marshes, rivers, in migration also brackish coastal areas.
> N Pole arctic in E Greenland, Spitsbergen, & Novaya Zemlya
> and extreme in Russia (Yugorski pen). Winters S to in
> Mediterranean Region and (rarely) in Africa.
>
> Brennus. Gaercian

Elsewhere in the archive, Mendelssohn makes notes on A5 sheets about the word "barnacle" (5/B/1/1c). In addition to "goose" and "crustacean", the etymology she lists includes instrument of torture, spectacles, and a restraining bit for horse or ass; its homophonic relationship to "barnstorm", or touring performance, is also noted. That Bernache Nonnette is a name given to a fictional character is underscored by *Parasol One. Parasol Two. Parasol Avenue.* (1996), which opens with a poem that returns to the figures of Bernache Nonnette and Viola Tricolor. It begins: "Bernache reclined upon her startling blue aeroflot indice. / the union had been saved within hours by Viola in a / single footed close shave."

In 5/A/17/4, Mendelssohn types a short biography that overlaps with the author note given in *Conductors of Chaos* (1996). It reads:

> grace lake (a. mendleson). born 1948, Cheshire.
> trained through the New Era Academy of Dram [*sic*] and Music, 1957–1967.
> performed in Northern Music Festivals until 1967.
> 1967–1969, Essex. 1969–1970, Turkey, (teaching english and french
> to children in Ankara and translating 1930s Turkish poetry (surrealist
> & social realist) into english. 1970–1976, London. 1976–1977, stockport.
> 1977–1995, Cambridge.
> Academic career brought to an abrupt halt in 1967 by harassment political
> and emotional. Threatened with strangulation upon returning to england in

1970 if I dared to utter one word of criticsim, own writing removed and
I was subsequently silenced.
Acknowledgements go go

Acknowledgements are due to those in Cambridge who have encouraged me
to overcome some of my fears and to
Cambridge Poetical Histories for 'La Facciata' 1989
'The Virago Book of Love Poetry' 1990
Poets on Writing, Britain 1970–1991. London, Macmillan, 1992)
Equipage for 'viola tricolor' 1993.

What follows below are substantive differences – poem by poem – from the published text and the manuscripts and proofs located in the Sussex archive. This list follows publication order. At one juncture, *Bernache Nonnette* was given the title *Mendleson's Metronome.* Two copies exist in the archive under this title; both are akin to the published text. The first is a photocopy with a note at the outset from Mendelssohn thanking Freer for his typesetting; it concludes with an author and date attribution: "A. Mendleson. 1995. / Grace Lake." (5/A/17/1). Barring "Silk & Wild Tulips", it contains the same poems as the final version, but ordering differs. Half of the text is paginated numerically, half alphabetically. Where noted, the differences between this text and *Bernache Nonnette* are cited as *MM1* (5/A/17/1).

The second, unpaginated typescript of *Mendleson's Metronome* has a title page, a different, unevenly spaced font, and is heavily water stained (5/A/17/2). "Silk & Wild Tulips." is included. This second text is photocopied and edited in Mendelssohn's hand. Differences within this typescript are cited as *MM2.*

Another file holds a typescript replicating this second variant of *Mendleson's Metronome*; lacking cover or title, it is formatted in a narrow font (5/A/17/5). Freer was experimenting with different fonts in a bid to maintain the integrity of Mendelssohn's long lines (phone conversation 10 October 2017). On this typescript are numerous handwritten corrections that bring the text closer to the published version.

"Bernache Nonnette."
Following notes on the barnacle goose in 5/A/17/3 (see above introduction to *Bernache Nonnette*), there are five unpaginated A5 manuscript pages containing portions of six poems from the final volume, among them, "Bernache Nonnette." Here, the title reads: "bernaches nonnette". In the upper left corner of this page is: "'d." The upper right corner of the page reads "(Liverpool Street Station. 1979. – anachronisms.) ~~super~~ surfact anachronism". Unlike the published version, all lines start in lower case excepting "Felt nothing"; there are additional minor changes in end-line punctuation and ampersands. Substantive changes include:

"one off chance / A quick" was "one off chance in a / quick"
"lesbianismus, favours" was "lesbianism, the favours"
"through a wall" was "through the wall"
"The electric end stop" was ", the electric end stop"
"first kiss / Dripping over" reads: "first kiss / that was the last date, films full of wasted time, & that horrific mouth / dripping ~~in a~~ ~~on~~ ^over^"
"over a scorched shirt" was "over a scorching shirt"

"By registering absence rather than existing as an obstacle. / The referral was not self, associational" reads:

> "by registering absence rather than existing as an obstacle for I
> deeply disagreed with your institutional distrust of the freedom of the mind.
> the referral was not self. associational"

"which at least had pale pink curtains" was "which at least had curtains & pink curtains"
"amongst reputed" was "amongst ~~the~~ reputed"

There are minor variations in punctuation between the published "Bernache Nonnette." and *MM1*: for instance, the comma seen in manuscript before "the electric end stop" is retained (5/A/17/1). In *MM2*, "Would be not oozing" was "Would not be oozing" and "silent flights to faked" was "silent flights the faked" (5/A/17/2).

"Four eighths for writing business letters a man selects a voice she, he mocks, she will and inverts"
Following notes on the barnacle goose in 5/A/17/3 (see above introduction to *Bernache Nonnette*), there are five unpaginated A5 manuscript pages containing portions of six poems, among them, "Four eighths for writing business letters." In the upper left corner of this page is: "'d." The last three lines of "Four eighths for writing business letters" appear at the top of another illustrated page, followed by the start of "& envisaging ruptures". Here, the two poems appear to be a single work; at the top left corner of this page also reads "'d." Of this transposed tercet, the second half of line one and start of line two read: "lohengrin from green ray's hair cuts, know one know em all. / inter rapists communication".

In *MM1*, "know one know 'em all" is written by hand above the typed line to replace the truncated, typed "know 'em". In both *MM1* and *MM2* (5/A/17/1 and 2):

"a man selects a voice" was "a man selects his voice"
"played to his tune" was "played his tune"
"memorized as being pitched" was "memorized as pitched"
"Lohengrin's green ray hair cut" was "Lohengrin from green ray's hair cuts"

All of these changes are made in 5/A/17/5. In *MM2*, further changes include: "Attend the barnacle" was "attend the barnacles" and "altho' memorized as being pitched" was "although memorized as pitched".

Significant variations also occur in the typescript variants of this poem in 5/A/17/4, including, on the second of two copies:

"a man selects a voice" was "a man selects his voice"
"item for carpets" was "item 2 ~~on the menu~~, for carpets"
"black/blue" was "~~blue/black~~ ^black/blue^
"tasteless words" was "tasteless words from a pseudo-poet"
"Like I hated" was "like i hate", and stanzas one through three are a single stanza
"That was flat altho'" reads "That is flat although".

"dour…"
In addition to minor distinctions in punctuation, in *MM1*, this copied typescript is cut off, meaning the first letters are missing in each line (5/A/17/1). By hand, the dedication reads "for Marina Yedigaroff & Roger East"; at the bottom reads, "©

A. Mendleson. 1995. / Grace Lake." In *MM2*, the dedication is mistakenly rendered as "Yediganoff" and this error recurs in publication (5/A/17/2); it is corrected here (ed.). In *MM2*, the "oblivious to" of the final line was "rushing past"; this change is made in 5/A/17/5.

Poem beginning "She Walked where she should have stood still, stock still."
This poem is included in *MM1*, *MM2*, *Bernache Nonnette* (1995), *A State of Independence* (1998), and *Out of Everywhere: Linguistically Innovative Poetry by Women in North America & the UK* (2006). For a full account of its gestation and variations, see notes for *Out of Everywhere*.

Poem beginning "& envisaging ruptures imagination parental government hanging round social Hairs"
This poem and "Four eighths for writing business letters" (see above) might have been envisaged as a single work; in a set of five manuscript pages containing parts of six poems replicated in the final volume, the last three lines of "Four eighths" appear at the top of an illustrated page, and are followed by the start of "& envisaging ruptures" (5/A/17/3). There is a "'d" in the top left corner of the page, as there is in three of the other pages in this set of manuscripts. Substantive changes to the first eight lines of "& envisaging" include an elision of the space between the first two stanzas, and:

> "hanging round social hairs" reads "hanging round social hairs for a taste of"
> "offer on the days" reads "offer only on the days"
> "Fêtes the less" was "Fêtes ~~the ones who are no~~ the less"
> "learning to advertise" was "learning to advertising"
> "of plucked duck" was "of ~~ol~~ plucked duck"
> "blinds down fast in case they were called working class." was "blinds down FAST ~~in case you~~ ^before they^ call them WORKING CLASS."

In these papers, the third stanza of "& envisaging ruptures imagination" also appears on its own page, marked "'d'" and bearing an involved drawing referencing the forks of the poem (5/A/17/3). In addition to differences in capitalisation and punctuation, substantive distinctions between this stanza and the final poem include:

> "Once being was known attention seeking" was "Once ~~being~~ was ^& now^ attention seeking"
> "its brim pulled down" was "its hat pulled down"
> "tonal not" was "tonal ~~neve~~ not"
> "Or ones who won't" was "or ones that won't"
> "polish up four bars," was "polish off four bars,"
> "Liquid strap lined and not a milky" was "licquorice strap lined & NOT Milky"
> "goosebury steak Drinking nicotined forks." was "gooseberry steak DRINKING Nicotined Forks."

In *MM1* (5/A/17/1), "Booth" is "Boothe" (both in typescript and correction), as it is again in *MM2* (5/A/17/2) and 5/A/17/4. As such, the "e" is restored in this collection, as is the accent on "Fêtes", which appears in *MM1*, as well as 5/A/17/3 and 4 (ed.). In *MM2*, "these one woman" was "those one".

Poem beginning “Parts of it crackle so you don’t need to say that or make any passive references.”
Replete with a complex sketch, this poem is included in full within five unpaginated A5 manuscript poems in 5/A/17/3. The upper left corner reads “’d”. In addition to the elision of stanzas and the lower-case letters at the start of lines (“Pluto’s Own” excepted), substantive differences between published version and manuscript are as follows:

> “in another world” was “in an other world.”
> “in Monopoly / A game that gains” was “in Monopoly Capital ~~the game~~ / that gains”
> “nature, ideal” was “nature, ~~the~~ ^an^ ideal”
> “urbane.” was “ur - bane.”
> “pairs of eyes” was “pairs of ears”
> “Prune stone, this lifetime’s” was “prune stone, a lifetimes”
> “reads inapplicable / c/o carbon” was: “reads inapplicable ~~/ woman: country of~~ origin. / c/o carbon” [*forward slash after “inapplicable” is Mendelssohn’s own*]
> “mature beyond rank as though our cheeks are insulated from the / Roar of toxic paint” was: mature / beyond into rank / foreclosure. / sounds as though / your cheeks are / ~~lined~~ / insulated / from ~~traff~~ the roar of toxic paint” [*note: these short lines accommodate a sketch; another floating line on the other side of the sketch reads: “when spoken to”; beneath it, Mendelssohn writes: “contratante”*]
> “& cease to dream in pink & beige & cease” was “& st cease to dream in pink & beige. / & cease”
> “for dream doth change.” was “for dream does change / from programmed to programmatical.”

Of the last correction noted above, the change to “doth” from “does” is made in *MM1*. In *MM1* and *MM2*, as in the manuscript, “in another world” was “in an other world” (5/A/17/1 and 2). The phrase is corrected to “another” in 5/A/17/5.

Poem beginning “Pall Mall. There were gunboats right along this coast. pointing outwards. Jasper, questions lengthen”
In the *MM1* typescript (5/A/17/1), “Pall Mall.” runs over two pages, falling between the poem beginning “oysters to sniff at disdainfully tapping” (see below) and “She Walked where she should have stood still, stock still.” (see above). A right-justified, horizontal line intimates a divide between “oysters to sniff” and “Pall Mall.” In *Bernache Nonnette*, “oysters” follows “Pall Mall.” and “She Walked” appears three poems previous. Additional differences between publication and *MM1* include:

> “Will / that day” was “Will that day / will that day”
> “somehow oddly nibbed by” was “somehow oddly textured by”
> “think it abominable” was “think it ~~very~~ abominable”
> “groaning from side” was “~~turning~~ ^groaning^ from side”
> “in vain / delight” was “in vain / in vain delight” [also in 5/A/17/2]

In *MM2*, the second and fifth changes listed above recur (5/A/17/2). On the 5/A/17/5 proof, Mendelssohn writes to her typesetter: “Ulli, a nib can also be an uneven line in a piece of silk/or material. I want ‘textured’ changed to ‘nibbed’/to merge somehow oddly nibbed by ‘A few stray violets’” (forward slashes Mendelssohn’s own). In publication, “a carthaginian tango.” reads “a cathaginian tango.” as it does in *MM2* and 15/A/17/5; here it is “carthaginian” as it is in *MM1* and 5/A/17/4 (ed.).

Poem beginning "oysters to sniff at disdainfully tapping the rest of the boring dross about eating"
In *MM1* and *MM2*, differences between the published and proof versions include: "jasper, i told you, a" was "jasper i told you a"; in *MM1*, "jasper" is written over "jumper", and the first word of each line is capitalised, barring line eight, which begins with an ampersand; these capitals appear in *MM2* (5/A/17/1 and 2). Furthermore, in *MM1* and *2*, "yet, determined" was "yet determined". "[C]lassy" is "classey" in the published version and in *MM2*; in *MM1* it is "classy", and this spelling is restored (ed.).

"Silk & Wild Tulips."
This poem appears in *MM2* (not *MM1*), *Bernache Nonnette* (1995), *A State of Independence* (1998), and *Out of Everywhere: Linguistically Innovative Poetry by Women in North America & the UK* (2006). For a full account of its gestation and variants, see notes for the latter collection.

Poem beginning "Exactly what will this have rested upon for it to have emerged. It has yet"
In an A5 manuscript for *Bernache Nonnette*, this poem follows seamlessly on from the poem later titled "How Power has reared its ugly head [...]" (see below), reversing final text ordering (5/A/17/3). That manuscript includes only the first eight lines of "Exactly what this will have rested upon". Here, the "Serve." of line two is "Swerve."; in line four, "should" was "would", and in line eight, "an huge" was "a huge". After "Les fleurs du mal. light." reads, on its own line: "A pale wash figure accouchant". At the bottom of the page, Mendelssohn writes, "Robert Elar 2–5. Saturday £4."

In *MM1*, as in manuscript, the poem follows on from "How Power has reared its ugly head [...]" and "Serve." was "Swerve." (5/A/17/1). Further changes include:

> "I should like" may have been "I would like"
> "Affiches" was "~~APlacats~~ ^Affiches^"
> "twenty five hours" was "twenty four hours"
> "clepsydra'd glassed" was "clepsydra'd, glassed" (recurs in *MM2*, 5/A/17/2)
> "velvet" was "~~satin~~ ^velvet^"
> "grangestering" was "grangesturing"

Another line – a last line – is heavily redacted.

In 5/A/17/5, Mendelssohn writes next to lines three and four: "~~Oust this please — it sounds ambiguous~~." Drawing a line from this statement to the bottom of the page, she adds: "~~It concerns an obscene passage of time when the woman who took my children suddenly turned offensive~~." Beneath this, she writes: "leave it in, I changed my mind." In the 5/A/17/6 *Bernache Nonnette* proofs, Mendelssohn titles the poem "To Orpheus"; in no other typescript or manuscript does it have a title.

"How Power has reared its ugly head & defined a lumpen proletarian
By the force it has used to cessate the education of writers & artists
By conflating us with the residents of Brothels."
Following notes on the barnacle goose in 5/A/17/3 (see above introduction to *Bernache Nonnette*), there are five unpaginated A5 manuscript pages containing portions of six poems, among them, "How Power has reared its ugly head [...]". In this manuscript, the poem is untitled, and at its end, is immediately followed by the first eight lines of "Exactly what will this have rested upon for it to have emerged." which precedes "How Power reared its ugly head [...]" in publication. This order is retained in *MM1* and *MM2* (5/A/17/1 and 2), suggesting Mendelssohn's protracted intention to treat both pieces as a single poem. At

the end of these lines reads, "A pale wash figure accouchant", and at the bottom of the page Mendelssohn writes, "Robert Elar 2–5. Saturday £4." (see above on "Exactly what").

In the manuscript variant, lines four and five are treated as a single line, as are lines six and seven; further, a stanza break occurs between lines 13 and 14 ("than sympathy // Once though"). Some of the accents that appear in manuscript are not replicated in publication and are reinstated here (ed.). In addition to distinctions in punctuation and capitalisation, substantive differences between publication and manuscript of "How Power has reared its ugly head […]" include:

> "la moo tremlotement" was "la moo ~~tremblante~~ tremblotement"
> "Men always think they" was "Men always think that they"
> "Sanpaulia." was "Saintpaulia."
> "turn out our eyes" was "turn our eyes out"

In *MM1*, there is no title, and the first stanza numbers seven lines, rather than nine; Mendelssohn draws forward slashes anticipating the line breaks that appear in publication. In *MM2*, the poem continues to be untitled, but the final line breaks of stanza one are evident; this variant lacks accents, and spacing differs.

The long title might be mistaken for an epigraph or additional opening lines. It is added by hand to the top of the proof copy in 5/A/17/5. Next to it, Mendelssohn draws an extended arrow culminating in a note to typesetter Ulli Freer reading: "The Title is at the top of the page."

Poem beginning "by gardenias i cannot telephone"
This poem appears in *MM1 and MM2*, *Bernache Nonnette* (1995), and *Out of Everywhere: Linguistically Innovative Poetry by Women in North America & the UK* (2006). For a full account of its gestation, see notes for the latter collection.

"concilia."
This poem appears in *MM1* and *MM2*, *Bernache Nonnette* (1995), and *Out of Everywhere: Linguistically Innovative Poetry by Women in North America & the UK* (2006). For a full account of its gestation, see notes for the latter collection.

"purdah darting glances"
In *MM1*, Mendelssohn writes "CENTRED." next to the left-justified typescript. Changes from publication include: "patch pop" was "patch pap" and "scrovlong" was "scroblong"; "should have windswept" reads "should have ~~blo~~ windswept" (5/A/17/1). The "scovlong" change recurs in the centred typescript of *MM2*, where renderings of "sc" are "so", and "camille desmoulins" was "camille demoulins" (5/A/17/2). Although 5/A/17/4 is the original typescript of the *MM1* photocopy, it has been edited by hand differently in its last lines, so that "steps across my right" reads "steps ~~across~~ ^along^ my right" and "future along the" was "future ~~along~~ ^across^ the". Edits altering "so" to "sc", "demoulins" to "desmoulins" and "scroblong" to "scrovlong" are made in 5/A/17/5.

Grace Lake, *involution*, no. 4 (April 1996).
Operating out of Magdalene College, Cambridge, Involution press published five issues of its journal, *involution*, between 1993 and 1997. Mendelssohn published her chapbook *Parasol One. Parasol Two. Parasol Avenue.* (1996) with Involution, and contributed to journal issues four and five, the latter in 1997 (see below notes on that collection). Editors included Matt Thorne and Rebecca Duffy; issue four was edited by A.M. Horne, "s.t.", and Rory Drummond. In issue two, Thorne's editorial preface

states that the journal title "may trouble some readers", adding that "[a]n involuted work turns in upon itself, is self-referential, conscious of its status as a fiction, and 'allegorique de lui-meme' [*sic*] – allegorical of itself to use Mallarmé's description of one of his own poems." To issue four, Mendelssohn contributed her poem "Truth or Vermilion". For that issue, the editorial mandate, dated 20 April 1996, reads: "In one sentence, then, and ecumenical: ***involution*** *works to publish poetry of an innovative or experimental character, that need not by that forego the innocence of voice, but which must in itself push upon the problem of the immediately expressible, within the text that sets songs running.*" The back of issue four reads "inv. 8", presumably because a full count of the press's offerings – journals and chapbooks alike – is inscribed on each publication. Involution contributors included Stephen Rodefer, Helen Macdonald, and Karlien van den Beukel. Along with Grace Lake, issue four features Peter Philpott, Ben Griffin, Ira Lightman, A. M. Horne, and Rory Drummond. The issues referenced here are held at the National Poetry Library.

Excising the title, Mendelssohn republished "Truth or Vermilion" in *Implacable Art* (2000). At Sussex, there is an untitled typescript of Mendelssohn's "Truth or Vermilion" in a file of poems associated with that text (5/A/24/2). It is identical to the poem in *involution*, barring that in the fourth line from the bottom, Mendelssohn redacts as follows: "violation ~~to /~~of Renoir"; "the to / of" formulation remains in *Implacable Art* (forward slashes Mendelssohn's own, p. 91). The only other difference between the *involution* variant and the later poem is the addition of a comma in line six, after "versicles". Typescripts identical to publication exist in 5/A/18/2 and 3, files associated with *Parasol One. Parasol Two. Parasol Avenue.* (1996). Mendelssohn lists this poem in prospective tables of contents for *Parasol One.*, but it does not appear in publication (5/A/18/4).

The closing lines embed a critique of the title of *Out of Everywhere: Linguistically Innovative Poetry by Women in North America & the UK*, to which Mendelssohn contributed in 1996 (second edition in 2006; see below notes).

Grace Lake, *Salt*, no. 8 (1996), 72–76.

Published with Folio, the same imprint acknowledged in Mendelssohn's 2000 *Implacable Art* (see below notes), the perfect-bound journal *Salt* was edited by John Kinsella. In 2002, issue 15, subtitled "An ABC of Theory & Praxis", Kinsella offers his first preface in twelve years of journal publication, noting: "I've never completely trusted introductions to issues of literary journals. They suggest a formulaic approach, one that goes against everything I've hoped *Salt* represents. It's about diversity and eclecticism, not playing the game in the way it's expected" (ix). Kinsella adds that though *Salt* began in Western Australia, its mandate was international, and it engaged consistently with authors from the UK and US. The issues referenced here are held at the National Poetry Library at London's Southbank Centre.

Contributors included Marjorie Perloff, Ato Quayson, Rae Armantrout, Lyn Hejinian, Fred Wah, Edwin Morgan, Robert Creeley, Peter Riley, Drew Milne, Susan Stewart, and Peter Gizzi. Later issues were part-funded by the Department for the Arts of the State of Western Australia and the Australian Lottery Fund, co-published by the Fremantle Arts Centre Press and Folio. In 2000, issue twelve, *Salt* adopted the full title: *Salt: An International Journal of Poetry and Poetics*, presumably to distinguish itself from the Cambridge, UK-based Salt Publishing, which began producing the journal at that juncture. Salt director Chris Emery is listed in the publication information for this issue (see also *Implacable Art*).

In issue eight, Mendelssohn's two poems, "'unknit that'" and "antiphon" accompanied the work of Peter Riley, John Ashbery, Charles Bernstein, and Rod Mengham, among other poets and essayists. Subtitled "Lacuna", the issue has no contributors' page, editorial preface, or acknowledgements. Ads are included for the *P. N. Review*, the Australian journal *imago*, and the New Zealand periodical *Landfall*.

Mendelssohn published these poems again in *Critical Quarterly* later in the same year, renaming the second poem "antiphony". Although *Salt* was published a bit erratically, there were two issues in 1996, and as Mendelssohn's poems are in the earlier volume, the third issue of the more regular *Critical Quarterly* is likely the later publication (see below notes).

Grace Lake, *Parasol One. Parasol Two. Parasol Avenue.*, Involution (1996).
A chapbook of 20 pages, *Parasol One. Parasol Two. Parasol Avenue.* bears pen and ink cover art by Mendelssohn (see image), and a drawing within its pages (reproduced in main text). Sussex holds photocopies of the original cover in A4 and A5 (SxMs109/5/A/18/4).The Arabic numerals of the cover are spelt out on the title page. In an undated letter, Mendelssohn asserts: "Parts of Parasol One, Parasol Two – are libretti." (3/A/2/1). On 8 March 1996, Mendelssohn writes poet and editor Thomas Evans (see *Onedit*, 2000, below), stating that she aspires to have this collection published with California-based Sun & Moon Press (3/A/1/13).

Instead, the chapbook was produced by Involution, a press operating out of Magdalene College, Cambridge. From 1993 to 1997, Involution published experimental writing, numbering both its journal, *involution* and the chapbooks it produced within the same sequence. As such, the back cover of issue two of *involution* reads: "inv. 4", and Mendelssohn's *Parasol One. Parasol Two. Parasol Avenue.* is identified as "inv. 9", even as the fifth issue of the journal *involution* emerged a year later. The complete copyright for Mendelssohn's chapbook includes the phrase "second edition", but there is no clear evidence of a first. Mendelssohn contributed to the journal *involution* in 1996 and 1997 (see related notes above). The issue used here was kindly provided by Peter Riley; a copy of the same is held at Sussex (5/A/18/4).

Involution editors included A. M. Horne, Matt Thorne, Rebecca Duffy, and Rory Drummond. Only Horne is identified within Mendelssohn's text. The table of contents does not include the first untitled poem beginning "Bernache reclined upon her startling blue aeroflot indice. / the union had been saved within hours by Viola in a / single footed close shave." These lines allude to Mendelssohn's *Bernache Nonnette* (1995) and *viola tricolor* (1993) (see above notes). Instead, the "contents" reads:

. . . Oh I really must
the chantral grey
fragment; redundance; wordsworth.
To France
damned channel
Dyr Bul Shchyl
No Wonder

There are four files in the Sussex Mendelssohn archive devoted to *Parasol One. Parasol Two. Parasol Avenue.* (5/A/18/1–4). There are multiple draft tables of contents for the volume in these files. Titled "contents." one includes the above list, and two poems that do not appear in this publication, namely: "'unknit that'" and "antiphon." This sheet also contains notes – possibly in another hand – about cover colour and a predicted thirty copies; in the left bottom corner reads: "© A. Mendleson." (5/A/18/1). Along with "Dyr Bul Shchyl", these two poems appear in a 1996 issue of *Critical Quarterly* (vol. 38, no. 3). "To

France" will be republished in French as "à la France" in *Implacable Art* (2000), translated by Mendelssohn's friend David Kelley (1941–1999), a poet and fellow of Trinity College, Cambridge. Mendelssohn contemplated adding "Truth or Vermilion" to this text, but instead, it was published in the April 1996 issue of *involution* (see above notes).

Based on a typescript that Mendelssohn paginated (5/A/18/2), the text as planned appears to have been longer and differently ordered from the final publication:

> damned channel (numbered pages 5 and 6)
> the chantral grey (numbered page 10, continues to 11)
> Dyr Bul Shchyl (beneath above on same page, numbered 11, continues to 12)
> … Oh I really must (beneath above on same page, numbered 12, continues to 13)
> Truth or Vermilion (beneath above on same page, numbered 13, continues to 14)
> 'unknit that' (page 15, continues to page 16)
> antiphon (numbered 17, continues to 18)

In 5/A/18/4, another manuscript "contents." reads:

No Wonder	1
damned channel	5
Fragment: redundance. wordsworth.	7
the chantral grey	10
Dyr Bul Shchyl	11
Oh I really must	12
Truth or Vermillion	13
{Unknit that	15
{Antiphon	
To France.	19

In Sussex file 5/A/18/1, there are two A5 manuscript copies of a preface – titled as such – that does not appear in the text. The longer version reads in full:

Preface.

It was difficult, diplomacy had been networked out of existence, 9
people were not given a chance. those who could read refused to, 8
those who could not believed ~~what~~ ^everything^ they did. Wholeheartedly 7
they paid attention to what was the work of amateur writers 6
not worse than anyone else's in respect of solo inscriptions, 5
man to man, woman as banker, security, slave. The 4
famously potent would sympathize with them before they 3
would a female writer who ~~already~~ had a language 2

going through her with a music and a future of its own. 1
However, the daring, death defying omnipotent celebration
over meeting people one would not normally have had
~~“~~the pleasure~~”~~ of coming within a thousand miles of,
not in any permanent sense that is, continues to this
day, as do the other romantic ^delusions^ myths that have
for so long lent that certain something to tropicana
~~on the~~ [~~*unclear word.*~~ ~~–~~ed.] close to ceilings.

The line numbering and long horizontal line indicate Mendelssohn’s attentiveness to formatting for the shorter version, which ends at “a future of its own.” At the bottom of the long variant, there are jottings, partly indiscernible, and possibly titled “tropicana hard // esto”; these include: “hard tropicana vinegar / pained laid plate paper / sensation wavelets” and “escaped plane saying / hurricane masterly everlasting / models tropicana talking / fortune dog”. Left of this writing is the phrase “940 years”, a phone number, “Night Waves.” and “950 / a 1000’~~s~~ years from now”. On a separate sheet, the shorter manuscript preface reads near-identically to the above. Beneath it is a drawing with the word “actually.” at its left. Differences from the long version include: no full stop after the title “Preface”; “to what was the work” is “to / the work” and “The / famously potent would” is “The famous would”.

There are numerous manuscript and typescript variants of the poems contained in *Parasol One. Parasol Two. Parasol Avenue.* Archival variations for each poem are given below, in publication order. Throughout, the publication uses hyphens as dashes; these have been standardised to en-dashes (ed.).

Poem beginning “Bernache reclined upon her startling blue aeroflot indice.”
In A5 manuscript, this poem is identical to the published version, accompanied by a horizontal, abstracted landscape drawing in the upper right corner (5/A/18/1). In another file, 5/B/2/72, there is a shrunken photocopy of this same page in the upper left corner of a folded A4 sheet that also bears an amorphous drawing, surrounded by two organic shapes, an outline of what might be a tin can, and the words: “nouveau construct” and “oyster / black berry / kiwi”. Within this same file, there are three additional A5 manuscripts of this poem. In all three, there is no full stop at the end of line one and the second line ends “Viola”.

In one of these latter two variants, a third and final line reads: “It was a close shave. ~~V. turning~~ /”; on the other side of the sheet is an extensive pen and ink drawing with silhouetted figures and an embedded word, possibly “Latham”. After the first two lines cited above, another variant reads: “It was a close shave ~~used to move~~ V. peeled ~~off~~ ^away^ her / face~~ly~~ furniture with a suitably pained upper crust grimace / Now for the sodden filler bearer “Listen B. N. – / their voices are pale from distance. Here – use this … / turning towards the mother / she stretched out her legs & flexed her ankles / within”. Lines two and three of the third A5 manuscript read: “the union, ~~had been~~ saved within hours by Viola ~~had been~~ / ^in^ a single footed close shave.”; lines one and four to six are as in publication. Midway through the page, left-justified, Mendelssohn writes: “B.”

Poem beginning “…… Oh I really must. The paper was filling”
The ellipsis is six dots in the poem proper, and three in Mendelssohn’s “contents”. In typescripts in 5/A/18/2 and 3, “0.1888.” is “.2888.” and “Boucle.” is “Bouclé”, or French for curly, buckled, or locked up; the accent is reinstated (ed.). “Plus toe knee’m” was “Plut-knee’m” and is corrected by hand in 5/A/18/2.

"the chantral grey"
In poem typescripts housed in 5/A/18/2 and 3, the title is underlined, and spacing differs from publication. In line 13, each word is double spaced, and the penultimate line reads: "writers,   though,   don't   live   unless   they   love   themselves"; "supremely." over-runs, making spacing unclear.

"fragment; redundance; wordsworth."
Differences exist between typescripts and final poem in punctuation and spacing. For instance, in typescript, the title is: "fragment; redundance.   wordsworth." (5/A/18/2). Further examples: in stanza nine, "Do I" was "Do I?", and in stanza 26, "Decide upon wasp" was "Decide upon Wasp". In typescript, double line spaces between stanzas 14 and 15, 24 and 25, and 31 and 32 are not evident in publication, even as the extended gap between stanzas 26 and 27 is maintained. Finally, in typescript stanza 29, "everybody else" was "everyone else,".

"To France"
A manuscript of "To France" is held in 5/A/18/2, photocopied onto an A3 sheet next to a copy of an abstract print, likely Mendelssohn's; another photocopy in 5/A/18/4 is signed in ink, "Grace Lake. /20.2.96. / Cambridge" (5/A/18/4). In all manuscripts and an additional typescript held in 5/A/18/4, "butlers" is "butler"; in manuscript, Mendelssohn underlines the title, makes minor changes in punctuation, and accents "Brontë" and "éphémère" as "ephemère"; accents are reinstated here (ed.). This poem was later republished in French as "à la France" in Mendelssohn's *Implacable Art* (2000, 91).

"damned channel"
In typescript drafts, the final line of "No Wonder" (see below) appears in one instance before "damned channel"; the title is underlined, and the section numbers are added by hand. Further, in the second portion of the poem, there are 13 dots in the extended ellipsis (in publication, 12); French misspellings and perhaps misconjugations; handwritten accents that are not published, and a third "Aha." in the final line (5/A/18/2 and 3). On one, Mendelssohn writes next to the title: "variations on the goldfinger suite." (5/A/18/3). Another typescript of "damned channel" bears some green ink doodles; at the bottom of the following page, a typescript of part of "'unknit that'" and "antiphony" reads, in the same ink: "1995.8.7867." (5/A/18/3). In **(2.)**, line two, "recontrez" is "recontre"; all accents are reinstated (ed.).

"Dyr Bul Shchyl"
This poem is also published in *Critical Quarterly* (1996; see below notes). It is almost identically rendered in both instances, although the later variant includes a dedication to Geoffrey Gilbert that is not in *Parasol One. Parasol Two. Parasol Avenue.*, even as it appears in related typescripts.

"No Wonder"
Copied typescripts of this poem exist in 5/A/18/2 and 3; photocopies of the manuscript of the first nine stanzas can be found in 5/A/18/3. In two instances, the final typescript line of "No Wonder" appears on the same unpaginated sheet as "damned channel" (5/A/18/3; see above). In two "No Wonder" typescripts, the third line of stanza five reads "the tango" (5/A/18/2 and 3); in the typescript in 5/A/18/4 and in publication, it reads "ther tango"; "the" is restored (ed.) Also restored and corrected are accents Mendelssohn used in manuscript that do not appear in publication (ed.).

In addition to changes in punctuation, further variants include:

Stanza 7: "the hush fell over the crowd" was "the hush a hush fell over the crowd" (5/A/18/2 and manuscript 5/A/18/3)
Stanza 11: "the moon the fair the horses" was "~~my~~ moon ~~my~~ fair ~~my~~ horses" (5/A/18/2; corrected by hand 5/A/18/3)
Lines two and three, stanza 13: "every time" reads: "~~every~~ ^each^ time" (5/A/18/2 and 3)

In publication, the final word reads "{koukouzelienne}" (ed.); the term is not present in most typescripts, and is added to one by hand as follows: "(koukouzélienne)"; it appears to refer to those who compose in the style of the medieval Byzantine Orthodox Christian composer, John Koukouzelis (5/A/18/3)

In the photocopied manuscript, the title reads "No Wonder!"; next to it, Mendelssohn writes: "E.P'r." and "E. Pottier. L'Internationale." (5/A/18/3). Additional changes from publication include:

Stanza 1: "farm house =" was "farm house hob ="
Stanza 2: "for soft autumn" was "for ~~the~~ soft autumn"
Stanza 3: "mare down floating" was "mare ~~on~~ ^down^ the floating" [*an arrow suggests "floating" be moved between "dawn" and "sea"*]
Stanza 4: "to move" was "to weave"
Stanza 5: "those who changed" was "those that changed"
Stanza 7: "porcupine quill spelling" was "porcupine quill I ~~can spell~~ ^spelling^"
Stanza 8: "swan and whipping it into mousse in view of the fourth dimension" was "swan ~~& slitting its throat~~ ^to mousse^ in full view of ~~a~~ ^the^ fourth ~~division football team~~ ^dimension^"
Stanza 9: "'bed' was bellowed & read as a name" was "'bed' she ~~said~~, and read the word as a name" [*"was bellowed," is below the line*]

Grace Lake, *Critical Quarterly*, vol. 38, no. 3 (1996), 58–62.
Critical Quarterly is a British journal that began in 1959 and, in 2020, continues to welcome submissions of academic essays and poetry under the editorship of Colin MacCabe. In this 1996 issue, Mendelssohn's poems precede those of Andrew Motion and Lisa Robertson; articles about D. H. Lawrence, Radclyffe Hall, Doris Lessing, and Simone de Beauvoir are among the academic contributions.

Mendelssohn's entry is comprised of "Dyr Bul Shchyl", "'unknit that'", and "antiphony". The first of these poems was published in her collection *Parasol One. Parasol Two. Parasol Avenue.* (1996), and as draft tables of contents indicate, Mendelssohn considered publishing the latter two in the same (see above notes). Both "'unknit that'" and "antiphon" (a variant of "antiphony") were published in *Salt* in 1996, likely before *Critical Quarterly* (see above). In addition to minor changes in capitalisation and punctuation, differences between the *Salt* and *Critical Quarterly* versions are noted below.

"Dyr Bul Shchyl"
This poem lifts its title from Russian futurist Aleksei Kruchenykh, a propagator of the experimental, indeterminate, "transrational" Zaum language. Published in 1913, Kruchenykh's "Dyr Bul Shchyl" became a benchmark of Zaum poetics. First published in *Parasol One.* (1996), Mendelssohn's *Critical Quarterly* version of "Dyr Bul Shchyl" adds a dedication to Geoffrey Gilbert, who was then a student of Saint Catharine's College, Cambridge, and became a faculty member of the American University of Paris. In 1995, Mendelssohn accepted Gilbert's invitation to attend a University of Southampton conference (letter dated 28 June); in an alternate, undated letter, she expresses a desire to publish in *Critical Quarterly* (SxMs109/3/A/1/16).

Barring the dedication, the only other differences between the two published versions of the poem include a full stop after "convex" at the end of the second-last stanza in *Parasol One.* that is excised from *Critical Quarterly*, and a full stop at the end of the poem in *Critical Quarterly* that is absent from *Parasol One.* Typescripts of "Dyr Bul Shchyl" identical to publication exist in 5/A/18/2 and 3; in the latter file, one copied typescript includes, by hand, the Gilbert dedication.

"'unknit that'"
There are three partial typescripts and one complete typescript of "'unknit that'" in 5/A/18/2; fonts differ, and some may be proofs. Another typescript and partial photocopied manuscript exist in 5/A/18/3. Excepting one typescript in 5/A/18/2, the typescripts in these files read, after line 11 ending "took a daughter": "when man his freedom won & chafed her thighs with salt. / lambs lettuce then to hide sprayed asterisks heaped veined green". By hand on one typescript, Mendelssohn indicates the missing lines, writing: "when man his freedom won … runnelled refinery." In 5/A/18/3, at the bottom of another typescript of the same poem, the lines are written by hand; as they are evident in a photocopied manuscript of "'unknit that'", the alternate variants appear to be a transcription error (5/A/18/3). The rest of the poem remains identical to publication.

In 5/A/18/2, there is an A4 sheet titled "variations" and signed "amh", likely Alistair Martin Horne of Involution press. Here there appear to be some suggested changes to the end of line 26 of "'unknit that'" to "how do minds not sense they sense". There are two corrected typos, and a mention of a miswritten phrase – "runnelled refinery" – perhaps referring to line 12. A suggested correction of "antiphony" is also included. In the end, Involution published neither of these poems.

In 5/B/2/26, a manuscript of "'unknit that'" includes the following edits:

"colours flit the" was "colours ~~play~~ ^flit^ the"
"the use returns to the people" was "the use ^it^ return~~s to the people does~~"
"a desert artist" was "a desert ~~paintress~~ ^art~~ist~~^"
"paint a yellow cord" was "paint & yellow ~~sash~~ cord"
"sinking sloping city" was "sinking sloping salt"
"accident of infinitesimal weave" was "accident of infinitesimal ^persnickity^ weave"
"water without" was "the water without"
"when man his freedom won" was "when man ~~won~~ his freedom ^won^"
"down violet green" was "down ~~of with~~ violet green"
"sardine wedged" was "sardine heaped" (see also 5/A/18/3 manuscript)
After line 27, ending "sea land paradox below", are two lines that do not appear in the final poem: "who looks not like a printer yet who walks in as him. / setting himself up with the advantage of. ~~the~~ unconvincing progress."

Beneath the poem are two rectangular framed doodles, and about eight or nine near-indiscernible lines in different ink. References include: "investigative journalists", Woolf, "the mind of a man"; and end: "this Hero & captured In a house / Where the Nature of Writing Has Changed / but has not the time to attend to the response its / expression / Antiphon."

The differences between "'unknit that'" as published in *Critical Quarterly* (1996) and the earlier version in *Salt* (1996) are as follows:

"paint a yellow" was "paint & yellow"
"sloping city" was "sloping salt"

"accident of infinitesimal weave pointillist" was "accident of pointillist weave"
"turned to a pillar" was "turned to pillar"
"not water won" was "not waterwon"
In *Salt*, lines 15 to 20 read:

> lambs lettuce then to hide sprayed asterisks HEAPED VEIN GREEN
> STROKED DOWN VIOLET GREEN FROM FURRY SWARD PUNCTA
> INCRIMSONDAMASCENETOOKMUCH THOUGHTTOTRACETHEFLORENTINE
> THOUGHT OF SOYA, SARDINE HEAPED IN TIGHT UNPROMISING STIFF
> IN POT PRESERVATIF FOR DIP FOR SAND CRACKED BEASTIES BLOOD
> TO CRIMSON TOP SET TRACERY & threw a scooped to open see

"through a cardboard" was "threw a cardboard"
"minds not know" was "minds know"
In *Salt*, there is a stanza break between line 27, ending "paradox below" and line 28, beginning "running back"
"cake is not, or a collar" was "cake is not, a collar"
"& pretending to manhood" was "& descending to manhood"
In *Salt*, after line 43 ending "by paintbrush", there is an extra line reading: "& quaint hat childhood deciding which way the language"
"to be height" was "to be a height"
"crouching cunabul" was "crouching cunal"
"meshed& drenched" was "meshed & drenched" (*regular spacing is restored*—ed.)

"antiphony"
This poem is formatted as a sub-section of "'unknit that'" in *Critical Quarterly*. Although in draft tables of contents for *Parasol One. Parasol Two. Parasol Avenue.* (1996) "antiphony" is listed as a poem unto itself, in one archived typescript it is dispersed over two A4 sheets, one torn along the bottom, and numbered as part of poem two on a page beginning with the conclusion of "'unknit that'" (see notes on *Parasol One.* and 5/A/18/3). Page verso reads "Tetralogies. Antiphon. 42/43. Minor Attic Orator", presumably referring to statesman and rhetorician Antiphon of Rhamnus (480–411 B.C.E.), whose tetralogies are part of his legacy. Two other typescripts are held in the same file, one partial, with the number "1995.8.7867." added by hand below the first half of the poem; the other is likely a proof copy.

In an additional typescript in 5/A/18/2, Mendelssohn redacts the "y" of the title (5/A/18/2). In another partial manuscript in the same file, Mendelssohn suggests by hand that line 28 be changed to: "one would not have thought that to be the marginalia". Along the bottom of this sheet reads, in Mendelssohn's hand, "MAMA 96", indicating that she perceived this poem as part of her mid-1980s feminist avant-garde MAMA movement. Multiple copies of Mendelssohn's "womanifiasco numera una" exist in the Sussex archive (see B/2/80). MAMA is discussed in the introduction to this volume.

In 5/A/18/2, there is an A4 sheet titled "variations" and signed "amh", likely Alistair Martin Horne of Involution press. Here there are suggested edits to "'unknit that'" and one to the last word of "antiphony", changing "cocoa" to "coco"; the final "a" is redacted in some typescripts. In the end, Involution published neither of these poems.

In addition to minor changes in capitalisation and ampersands, differences between "antiphony" as published in *Critical Quarterly* (1996) and the earlier version in *Salt* (1996) include:

"antiphony" was "antiphon"
"eating the hand" was "eating his hand"
"to found" was "to found."
"feet historical take precedence over mind" was "feet historical precede mind."
"illusion of reality" was "illusion of reason"
"for winter" was "for the winter"
"one would not have thought that that" was "one would have thought that"
"for history" was "for the history"
"keep back screams & tears" was "keep the screams and tears back"
"multitudes walked" was "the multitudes continued to walk"
"coco." was "cocoa."

Grace Lake, *Conductors of Chaos: A Poetry Anthology,* ed. Iain Sinclair, Picador (1996), 184–96.
Entitled "Infamous and Invisible: a Manifesto for Those Who Do not Believe in Such Things", Iain Sinclair's sardonic introduction derides anthologies as compromises undesirable, incoherent, frivolous, dissembling, and all-too-marketable. Sinclair places his own collection within an alternative lineage that includes Michael Horovitz's *Children of Albion* (1969) and Andrew Crozier and Tim Longville's *A Various Art* (1987). Presenting Eric Mottram's label for post-1960s experimental poetry in quotations – "the British Poetry Revival" – Sinclair defends the difficult, arguably Revivalist poetry that his volume contains, and dedicates the entirety to Mottram, who died in 1995 (xiv, xx).

The collection includes contemporary poets who were Mendelssohn's peers and/or publishers: Andrew Crozier, Alan Halsey, Michael Haslam, Tony Lopez, Rod Mengham, Drew Milne, Douglas Oliver, Maggie O'Sullivan, Ian Patterson, J. H. Prynne, Denise Riley, Peter Riley, Stephen Rodefer, and John Wilkinson. Five were asked to nominate past modernist poets for inclusion; David Gascoyne, Nicholas Moore, J. F. Hendry, W. S. Graham, and David Jones were selected.

Mendelssohn's biography reads:

> Grace Lake (Anna Mendleson) was born in Cheshire in 1948. She trained through the New Era Academy of Drama and Music (1957–67), and performed in Northern Music Festivals until 1967. She was educated at Stockport High School for Girls, and at the University of Essex (1967–9). She spent the following year in Turkey, teaching English and French and translating 1930s Turkish poetry, surrealist and social realist. She has lived in Stockport, London, Sheffield and Cambridge (St Edmunds College, University of Cambridge, 1984).
>
> Grace Lake writes: 'My academic career was brought to an abrupt halt in 1967 by harassment, both political and emotional. Upon returning to this country, in 1970, I was attacked, my own poetry seized, and my person threatened with strangulation if I dared utter one word of public criticism. I was unable to return to university at that point and was silenced.'
>
> Her publications include *La Facciata* (Poetical Histories, 1988) and *Viola Tricolor* (Equipage, 1993). She has also contributed to *The Virago Book of Love Poetry* (1990) and *Poets on Writing: Britain 1970-1992*, Ed. Denise Riley (Macmillan, 1992).

In the "Acknowledgements" at the end of the volume, it is noted that "La Facciata" and "La Facciata Turns Her Back" were first published by Poetical Histories in 1988, and that the poems "1526" and "on challenge, positive attitudes and 'les peintres cubistes'" were part of *viola tricolor* (1993). Copyright is granted to the author. The poems "London 1971", "June 21st" and "and A New" are original publications and do not appear to have been republished in Mendelssohn's lifetime. In "London 1971" the word "paean" was originally published as "paeon" (ed.).

A letter from Sinclair to Mendelssohn dated 28 October 1994 suggests that she initially declined his invitation to contribute; on a postcard dated 4 January 1995, Sinclair writes: "I'm delighted that you've changed your mind" (3/A/1/55/2). An undated, unsent letter from Mendelssohn to Sinclair reads: "I'm anxious that my biography will cause legal problems. Please omit anything that is hazardous" (3/A/1/55/1).

Collection contributors, Mendelssohn included, gave a reading at the Georges Pompidou Centre in Paris, introduced by the poet Douglas Oliver. Hugo Williams reviewed the event for the *Times Literary Supplement* (11 April 1997). In her correspondence with Williams, Mendelssohn corrects his misreporting of the line in her poem, "1526", "plunging into negation's blind sacrifice" as "negation's blind surface" (3/A/1/66).

"La Facciata"

This poem was first published as a pamphlet with Peter Riley's Poetical Histories in 1988 and was republished in French in *Po&sie* in 2002 (see notes). The Poetical Histories version is almost identical to that of *Conductors of Chaos*, barring that in 1988, "squealing" was "squeeling" and "plaîted" was "plaited".

Sussex holds at least two manuscripts of "La Facciata" (5/A/10/1 and 4/C/33). The version in 5/A/10/1 is photocopied, reduced in size, illustrated, and turned into a chapbook. Rust lines remain where the staples along its side have been removed. This booklet bears the title "AUTO-PORTRAIT" on the hand-drawn cover, which includes the published design as described above and a small rectangle in black outline mid-left of the box; in large print, Mendelssohn writes *La Facciata* beneath this image. Similar hand-drawn block figures surface on pages three and five of the six. Like the Poetical Histories pamphlet, this manuscript is dedicated to Yedigaroff and East "with much affection"; the chapbook is dated "23rd September 1987." Post-photocopying, a "©" is added in blue to the left of "Grace Lake".

The subtitle "Auto-Portrait" is missing from subsequent publications, and in a letter to Doug Oliver and Alice Notley dated 29 July 1997, Mendelssohn discusses this omission: "La Facciata had in my own writing Autoportrait beneath or close enough to the title for it to be legibly connected" (3/A/1/43/1). In an asterisked footnote, she writes: "the poet who published 'La Facciata' omitted the subheading; autoportrait, the original can be made available for carbon dating."

Differences between manuscripts and the 1988 and 1996 versions include:

"La Facciata" was "La facciata." (5/A/10/1 and 4/C/33)
"squeeling" was "squealing" (5/A/10/1 and 4/C/33)
"unwitnessed, the jews" was "unwitnessed & the jews" (5/A/10/1)
"What is front" was "What's is front" (5/A/10/1)
"rising for their pains," was "rising for their grins," (5/A/10/1 and 4/C/33)
"whereas" was "whe~~n~~reas" (5/A/10/1 and 4/C/33)
"Now we are plaited" was "Now we are plaîted" (5/A/10/1 only)
"waves will between" was "waves roll between" (5/A/10/1 and 4/C/33)
"icy council's" was "icy councils" (5/A/10/1 and 4/C/33)
"reckoning books." was "reckoning books" (5/A/10/1 and 4/C/33)

"tintinnabular" was "tintinabular" (5/A/10/1 and 4/C/33)
"piped ^up^ the politician" (5/A/10/1 and 4/C/33)

In 4/C/33, stanza three reads:

It's only christians who crackle purity though walking
away was unwitnessed, deeper sounds reach swell
roundly overlapping, a fishnet's back, what is front
in Italian? did the person after come underneath
the multifoliate aspen water circuit trumpeted

"La Facciata Turns her Back"
This poem was included in the 1988 Poetical Histories pamphlet; as noted above, Sussex holds two manuscripts of the poem (5/A/10/1 and 4/C/33). In 5/A/10/1 alone, the underlined title is entirely in lower case. In both, "but . . . pipes the prandible they're" was "but . . . . pipes the prandible they are".

In 4/C/33, the poem is untitled and may continue seamlessly from "La Facciata". Further distinctions include: "bearing whirr" was "bearing whirring"; "piped up the politician" was "piped the politican"; "autochthonous" was "autochnothous". Finally, Mendelssohn draws forward slashes between lines 5 and 6, 10 and 11, 15 and 16. Elsewhere in her archive, these lines indicate planned stanza breaks.

"1526"
First published in 1993, there are at least two archived manuscripts of this poem. The first consists of two recto-only A5 sheets showing minor variations from publication in punctuation, articles, and capitalisation (5/A/15/1). The second manuscript differs from publication in punctuation, capitalisation, and lineation (5/B/2/67). Semantic edits include:

"last apogee" was "last, apogee"
"commands" was "command~~ment~~"
"upon the table" was "upon a table"
"might not ever heal" was "might not ~~may have ne~~ver heal~~ed~~"
"Weighing senses" was "Weighing sense"
"might be no substitute" was "might ~~not~~ be ~~a~~ ^no^ substitute."

In both manuscripts there is a fourth and final stanza reading:

Had been warned by me all along and lied upon.
Foul traitor of the heart. Who love not act art.
As no other strength. Took the truth & claimed it
Changing figures from woman to man, response is brief
and less supplicating. And charges the woman with anything
That Thief. That legislated evil which is reversed creation.

This extra stanza recurs, verbatim, in a typescript variant in 5/A/15/3. In 5/B/2/67, the first line varies slightly, reading: "He had been warned by me, yes by me, all along and lied upon."

When "1526" was published in *viola tricolor* (1993), there was a double blank line between stanzas two and three. In *Conductors of Chaos*, a single blank line is used, and a space – excised here – is added to stanza two, line three, which reads "negation's blind sacrifice" (ed.).

"on challenge, positive attitudes and 'les peintres cubistes'"
Sussex houses a typescript of this poem in 5/A/15/4 and a manuscript in 5/B/2/56. On dot-matrix paper, the manuscript shows variations in lineation and punctuation. The following alterations are made on the manuscript:

In the final lines of stanzas one and three, "based" and "being" are added to an initial draft
Stanza 5, last line, reads: "fought by people whose reading lists ~~are~~ disparate" [*an arrow moves "disparate" between "whose" and "reading"*]
First line, stanza 6, reads: "~~&~~ Everywhere prevent~~ing~~" and "of speech" may be a later addition (ed.)
Second line, stanza 7, reads: "~~because although~~ ^one that^ ~~I~~ wants to give you a square"
The final lines of stanza seven read: "^the^ symmetry of ^Vienneze^ nuclear ballroom dancing / in Vienna's Staatopera and ~~religion~~. phallocentric religious visuals."
In stanza 8, the published phrase "or other" does not appear
In stanza 9, "in having" was "~~of~~ ^in^ having"
In stanza 9, "onto" was "~~between~~ ^upon^"
The last stanza appears to be a later addition (ed.).

Down the right side of the manuscript page, Mendelssohn draws two doodles, one embedding the phrase "on the verge" within its horizontal lines; the other reading "& sein und sich".

This poem was published in *Active in Airtime* (1993) and in *viola tricolor* (1993); these versions are identical, and in both, the poem title is italicised as most titles are not in these texts, barring one exception in *Active in Airtime* (see above notes). In *Conductors of Chaos*, the titular italics are excised, and internal double quotation marks used in both 1993 publications are single. Further, in 1996, the phrase "heaving lies" is changed to "heaving lines".

Grace Lake, *Tondo Aquatique*, Equipage, 1997.
This unpaginated chapbook consists of 28 sides, of which 26 are poetry. Down the right-hand side of the grey card cover, there is a blue pen and ink drawing by Mendelssohn that consists of three and a half circles filled with abstract imagery. The back cover is comprised of a dense pen and ink Mendelssohn drawing. In her review of *Tondo Aquatique*, Lucy Sheerman notes that the title refers to "a circular painting or relief of (or in?) water" (*Jacket*, no. 14, July 2001; jacketmagazine.com/14/sheer-r.html). In a letter to Hugo Williams dated 4 May 2000, Mendelssohn expresses an intention to send the "penultimate copy of 'Tondo Aquatique'" and explains the opera title: "Tondo being [. . .] the italian round frame for painting except that this Tondo is an evocation of an aethereal water ballet and the developments in language, the English langue particularly" (SxMs109/3/A/1/66).

While the cover reads "Grace Lake", the text is copyrighted both A. Mendleson and "C.N.E.L. Kushnereva Mendleson b. H'K.". The latter moniker is used also in the *café archéologique* collection of 1992–93 (see above), and refers to Mendelssohn's Hebrew name, Channa Nechama Enna Krshner Mendleson Lubovitch bas Hakolenian (undated letter to Romana Huk,

3/A/1/20/1). The 10-point Times font is acknowledged, as is the typesetter, Alastair Martin Horne, an editor of Involution Press who also published Mendelssohn (see above on *involution*, no. 4, 1996, and *Parasol One.*, 1996, and below on *involution*, no. 5, 1997). A letter to Horne about typesetting the *Tondo Aquatique* manuscript appears in the archive; it is dated 13 December 96 (SxMs109/5/A/23/2). In it, Mendelssohn admits to having "gt. difficulty in finding the bulk of the reading transcripts" and struggling with a perpetual "revulsion for [her] writing which makes it difficult to go backwards into another poem." After promising to "struggle through" the proofs over the weekend, a postscript asks for a font akin to "No Wonder" of *Parasol One.* (1996) and reminds Horne that her "poems are given [. . .] in confidence & ©."

On the title page, between title and publisher information, reads the following epigraph:

snatch of conversation

A: "You're a woman."
B: "I'm a woman"
A: "So there's absolutely no excuse."

Throughout, poem titles are in an enlarged font, and slightly offset from the left margin.

The Sussex archive contains four files of manuscript and typescript drafts of *Tondo Aquatique* (5/A/23/1–4). Folder 5/A/23/2 includes what appears to be six illustrated covers that Mendelssohn experimented with before settling on the finished version; one attributes the work to "grace lagg" with the descender of the second "g" trawling diagonally across the page and through an illustration. Another possible cover includes the following above the title:

bait. human bait. lucky jim sidling along the river bank.
by tone he hangs the woman by ambiguity
the narrative painting. she clings on to her canvas
using it to front her movements
the password was   "no art comment"
the rule was   "no art practise"
throwbacks from a pond pound behaviour,
feet tied jaw locked tracks gates around greece
I feel as though I have been bombed
that my brain has been frazzled in an oven

On the back of a photocopy of what becomes the final cover, Mendelssohn writes: "Perpétuité . . . / The unrecognized feminine metaphysic. / feminine metaphysic méconnue". Within these pages exists two pages of prose with many references to the French Baroque painter Claude Lorrain (c. 1600–82). A sheet entitled "Claude / Gelée" [*sic*] begins: "I cannot get over Claude le Lorrain cannot recover from the sight of the aqueous gloom, insatiably my eyes do not want to be parted from lapping water". Among personal ruminations, what follows continues this admiration – "Claude did not try his hand." – and suggests that Mendelssohn might spend time in the Cambridge University Library looking at reproductions of his drawings and paintings, or go to the National Gallery to see one of his artworks. These musings are interspersed with notes about Mendelssohn's sense of constraint, both artistic and social, as well as her resistance to intermingling poetry and politics.

A coverless proof of *Tondo Aquatique* includes a note on the title page in Mendelssohn's hand reading: "gone to Printers. December 20. 1996. i. m. Marcello Mastroianni died on 19.12.96 in Paris." (5/A/23/4). The Italian actor Mastroianni starred in Fellini's *La Dolce Vita* (1960), among many other films. This proof is near-identical to publication, barring a few changes in individual poems noted below.

In a *Tondo Aquatique* file, there is a manuscript poem titled "remembering prenuptials." that does not appear in the final text and is included in the appendix. The references to "coating" at the beginning and end of "remembering prenuptials." are echoed in four pages of prose that follow the manuscript of "A grace note"; both are held in 5/A/23/1. In the prose, Mendelssohn writes: "What did the poet with a political coating to his eye poke his nose in with? Shadow Cabinet. What is the point of editing poetry whose writers are silenced?" The scepticism toward love evident in the poem recurs in this prose, where Mendelssohn writes: "I distrust the warmth of my heart and I have reason to."

These pages are written in the same ink, and on the same blue A4 paper as "A grace note"; one is dated, "Shabbos, Samedi 14./96". Themes and turns of phrase predating poems in *Implacable Art* (2000) surface here, particularly within "I object." and the poem beginning "digne. more than a design. to size." (see below notes). Ruminating on her family of origin, Mendelssohn expresses concern about overbearing Jewish men, claiming that only she can object to this problem, adding: "And I really do Object. I forget these many overwhelming people. Men, Women, Political putsches [. . . .] Control Management. Write your own poems. Oxygen intake."

This prose includes a discussion of 1968 radicalism, about which Mendelssohn is sceptical, wondering if it was "not solely a visual outburst of unusual imagery on a mass cultural level". She found this era difficult, given that she remained attuned to "1930s cultural influences" and was concerned about any form of extremism, including the influx of "American slang and mythology" into Britain. Mendelssohn champions "seasoned American writers" as privy to "the longest history of emancipation a fact which I trust above and beyond any other", describing herself as stifled by post-World War II European culture. The spectre of that war as an influence on self and artistry recurs in these pages, just as it surfaces in a poem from *Tondo Aquatique*, "Bristling white toed black two porned to the portraits in potency." where Mendelssohn writes: "How without the second world war / Can I possibly in the presence of relentless realism get it right."

Further topics include Mendelssohn's belief that she is an easily overwhelmed, reluctant actor in the world; her sense that others resist her criticisms; and a resentment about being held politically accountable, "as though I were a world power with any direct responsibility towards the Middle East." She describes herself as often feeling "rough" and caught up in prejudices. Writing, composing, and her stereotyped, even threatened, identity as a Northern writer are discussed. England is decried as cold and unreceptive to her work; the winter weather is proving bitter, but recollection of high summer in the countryside or birds flying reassures. A refrain of this tract is Mendelssohn's admiration for female artist forebears, among them, Gertrude Stein, Fanny Mendelssohn, Clara Schumann (5/A/23/1).

Proofs of *Tondo Aquatique* bearing minor variations and corrections exist in 5/A/23/3 and 4. What follows privileges manuscript variants of individual poems where available, listed in order of publication appearance.

"Erato"
In addition to typescript proofs of this poem in 5/A/23/3 and 4, there is a paginated manuscript of "Erato" in 5/A/23/1 that consists of five sheets of A4. The manuscript shows variations in internal line spacing and indentation, and the following distinctions from publication:

> "Erato" was "<u>Erato</u>."
> In stanza 6: "shrine picture" was "shrine posture" and "infiltrator" reads "infiltrators"

In stanza 8, "avant-garderie" was "avant garderie"
In stanza 9: "whilst the back" was "whilst the inside back"
In stanza 10: "precious taste" was "gracious taste"
In stanza 11: there was an additional line after seven, ending "linlithgow", reading: "worming stonehenge onto carpentras"; further, "four and a half" was "four and an half"

In manuscript, the French words read "rêverie", "entière", "écrit", "ésclave", "borghèse", and "vendôme"; although not in publication, these accents are reinstated here (ed.).

"On Vanity"
A cluster of photocopied manuscripts includes "On Vanity" (titled "On Vanity."). In addition to minor changes in capitalisation, in line four, "healthier man in her" was "healthier man her", and in the final line, "full of jokes from eternal resources" was "full of jokes for eternal resources" (5/A/23/2).

"Bristling white toed black two porned to the portraits in potency."
In A4 photocopied manuscript, the title is underlined, and in stanza one, there is a gap after the second "voice", (5/A/23/2). In stanza five, "amphitrite" is "amphritites" and "Naphthalene" reads "Nephtaline" (ed.). The poem is signed: "grace lake ©".

Poem beginning "what we don't know, & what we don't ask, & what where we are means to us"
In the A4 photocopied manuscript of this poem in 5/A/23/2, the "should" of the penultimate line may have been "would" in the first instance (ed.).

Poem beginning "I don't know which colour to choose. the blue I dreamt is untranslatable."
An A4 photocopied manuscript of this poem in 5/A/23/2 shows no extra space between the "to" and "choose" of the first line as in publication; that space is excised here (ed.). In the manuscript, line six reads: "Exposition : Ingratitude." In one set of proofs, the "word" of line ten is "wind" (5/A/23/4).

Poem beginning "No mixing not cake yes cake or anything that is being spoken enter not"
Line eight of the A4 photocopied manuscript concludes: "dialectics in ~~the~~ laundry rooms" (5/A/23/2). In the second-last line on one proof, "to impressions of" is "to impression of" (5/A/23/3).

Poem beginning "we escaped but not to the houses where repentance"
The A4 photocopied manuscript in 5/A/23/2 shows no differences from publication.

Poem beginning "I am become my enemy whom I could not please"
An A4 photocopied manuscript of this sonnet shows one minor edit: in line 12, the "t" of "time" is crossed twice, both as a lower and an upper case "T" (5/A/23/2). In one proof, line seven, "having fallen young into my mind" is excised, and Mendelssohn restores it by hand (5/A/23/3).

Poem beginning "To look in the mirror and see a shocking atom"
Proof copies of this poem are held in 5/A/23/3 and 4. With minor variants in punctuation only, the poem beginning "To look in the mirror and see a shocking atom" was republished in 1997 in *Comparative Criticism: An Annual Journal* (see below notes).

"never beiger"
A proof of "never beiger" in 5/A/23/3 indicates that the second-last line of stanza one read "refugees with then," as it does in publication. Another proof in 5/A/23/4 reads "refugees with them," and this variant is restored (ed.).

Poem beginning "§ / the chief of police wore a silver fleece"
In draft typescripts, as in publication, both parts of this poem appear on their own pages (5/A/23/3 and 5/A/23/4). The silcrow or sign used to divide it from "never beiger" is a standard typographical section marker and is akin to those Mendelssohn uses elsewhere to distinguish stanzas (see, for instance, the tildes in "Erato" in this collection). Mendelssohn thus asks us to consider this poem a portion of "never beiger" even as the pagination suggests otherwise.

In an A4 proof in 5/A/23/3, there is a small hand-drawn sun in this location, rather than a silcrow. Here, the last line of the first half reads "there's a body. I'm glad you've not met   -". The underscore of the full stop may be a redaction, and the hyphen gestures toward continuity with the second half, beginning "the misery I caused my old mother" (ed.). In stanza six, "her temper" reads "the temper"; the underlining is by hand, as is the word "her" that appears adjacently in the left margin.

"eulogy"
This poem is last published in *A State of Independence* (1998) as "Eulogy"; see notes for that collection, and for the below poem beginning "I could see the sea & hear the towns".

Poem beginning "I could see the sea & hear the towns"
Though occupying its own page, the content and tone of this poem are consistent with "eulogy", the poem that immediately precedes it in *Tondo Aquatique*, and in all available proofs (5/A/23/3 and 4). It is not included in the final publication of "Eulogy" in *A State of Independence* (1998). See also that collection, and the above notes for "eulogy".

Poem beginning "hard concrete to retrieve above the fallen"
There are at least two manuscripts of this poem at Sussex, one partial photocopy (5/A/23/3) and one complete (5/B/2/90). These texts show Mendelssohn reworking lines nine and ten, which read: "the hope that one day she would have to / escape before her mind snapped, before her mind gave way". In both manuscripts, these lines are rendered as follows:

> the hope that one day she would write unhampered
> by servile hard labour that one day she would have to
> escape before her mind snapped, before her mind gave way

In the 5/B/2/90 manuscript, punctuation, prepositions, and articles vary. In addition to the lines noted above, changes include:

> "by the full" was "by full"
> "between her innocent" was "between ~~the~~ ^her^ innocent"
> "her preferred feature" was "her ~~only like~~ preferred feature"

"head of hidden" was "head of ~~the~~ hidden"
"exists in the mind of God" was "exists to the eye of god"
"sky hold her in simple hard labour" was "sky holds her in simple ~~act~~ hard labour"
"that the text has" reads "that the ~~te~~ ~~text~~ has"
"to a certain height" was "to a certain weight"
"a friend eternal," was "a friend ~~that wa~~ eternal"
"weren't so rich" was "weren't so ~~nosey~~ rich"
"was never quite" was "was never quite right in the head either"
"powers of decadence" was "power of decadence"
"fairs fade." was "fairs fade in the distance."

There is no stanza or page break in this manuscript, and there are additional lines mid-poem. As such, lines 30 and 31 – "she tells the gulleys she left behind [. . . .] not universally exciting" – read as follows:

she tells the gulleys she left behind, those that exist at the back of her mind
those that gave birth to brains like themselves
clear [*"clear" uncertain*—ed.] & running, but fiction won't be believed else it wouldn't be fiction
and fiction needs what it is to show confidential innocence is not universally exciting

Beneath the poem are unclear notes referencing Pliny ("H. N.xxxv. 30. / Elores austeri." and "Pliny H.N. xxxiii. 121."); the "painter Niceas", Spain, and "soda, flints, copper flakes / 'Egyptian azure' / 15/20/3" (forward slashes in the date are Mendelssohn's).

The 5/A/23/3 manuscript includes the epigraph from *Poems of the Dispossessed* minus the editorial attribution to Séan Ó Tuama that appears in *Tondo Aquatique*. In two proofs, this name is misspelt "Tuams" (5/A/23/3 and 4). Excised in publication, Mendelssohn's manuscript epigraph accents are restored, and accents have been added to Séan Ó Tuama's name (ed.). In manuscript line three, "by the full begonias" is "by full begonias" and in poem line 13 (14 in manuscript) "out of human hearing" was "out of ~~hear~~[~~*unclear suffix*~~ —ed.] human hearing". Finally, the manuscript concludes with poem line 20 (21 in manuscript) ending: "lifts the tortoises".

"Hungary Water"
Within a six-page photocopied manuscript, an untitled variant of "Hungary Water" carries on directly from "Abschied" (see below entry), and concludes with a sheet bearing the *Tondo Aquatique* colophon, suggesting that Mendelssohn considered these poems for the end of the volume (5/A/23/1). The two poems are divided by a central "•". Barring a full stop after the final word "meaningless" and a tendency to gradually increase left margins, the manuscript of "Hungary Water" is identical to publication.

"A grace note"
In 5/A/23/1, a manuscript of this poem, titled "A grace note.", differs from publication in line ten only, where "the poet had to" was "the poet had had to".

"Abschied"
"Abschied" is followed by "tree by the cam" by way of concluding *Tondo Aquatique*, but this photocopied manuscript suggests that Mendelssohn considered lengthening "Abschied" by making an untitled draft of what will become "Hungary Water" its second part (5/A/23/1; see above entry). For full notes on poem gestation, see *A State of Independence* (1998).

Grace Lake, *Jewels of the Imagination*, ed. Maria Hourihan, International Library of Poetry, BPC Wheatons Ltd. (1997), 458.
The International Library of Poetry was based in Sittingbourne, Kent, and appears to have started publishing anthologies containing hundreds of short poems – one poem per author – in the late 1990s, continuing into the 2000s. These collections are not housed in legal deposit libraries in the UK, and their gestation is opaque. One of many guest editors, Maria Hourihan was responsible for anthologies entitled *Other Side of the Mirror* (1996); *Quiet Moments* (1996 or 1997); *Jewels of the Imagination* (1997), and possibly also *Spirit of the Age* (date uncertain). Her introduction to *Jewels of the Imagination* nebulously states that the poets in her anthology "channel … imaginative power to create works that entertain, delight, and often inform" (i). The volume contains over 3,500 entries, most by previously unpublished authors. Mendelssohn contributed a sonnet entitled "UNCERTAIN THOUGH WITHIN THIS DEEPSET HEART". In the index, she is listed as "Lake, Grace" and has no entry in the sixty-page "Biographies of Poets" at the back of the text. The edition used here is the editor's own.

A folder at the Sussex archive holds three typescripts of the poem and a photocopied letter from the International Library of Poetry dated 25 November 1996 and addressed to Mendelssohn at Trinity College, A3 New Court, Cambridge (SxMs109/5/A/20). On all three typescripts, the poem is followed by the typed signatures "A.M." and "Grace Lake"; on two, typos are changed by hand, including, in one instance, the use of "DEEPEST" rather than "DEEPSET" in the title. At the bottom of the second corrected typescript Mendelssohn writes: "August 1996. Cambridge, / England."

The letter details plans to publish Mendelssohn's poem in *Jewels of the Imagination*, and includes a proof that Mendelssohn is asked to return by 26 December 1996. Pre-photocopying, Mendelssohn corrects the proof by hand. Beneath the letterhead, the editor writes: "Wonderful verse! / Select Grace Lake's poem / for the 'Sound of Poetry.' - MH".

The proof differs slightly from the typescripts. In proofs, as in publication, the first letter of every word in the title is capitalised, as is the first word of every stanza; the titular punctuation appears to be house style. The stanza capitalisation does not occur in Mendelssohn's typescripts, and in her title, every letter is capitalised. Mendelssohn leaves these changes standing in the proof, and the titular capitals are restored here (ed.). In two typescripts, stanza three, line five concludes "vision"; in the third, Mendelssohn alters it to "visions", and corrected the proofs in favour of this change. Although the singular "vision" remains in publication, "visions" is used here (ed.). In the anthology, three stanzas are on offer, while in the typescripts, the last two lines comprise a fourth stanza; as Mendelssohn requested that this final couplet be restored in the proof, it is reinstated (ed.).

Grace Lake, *Gare du Nord*, vol. 1, no. 1 (1997), 14–17.
Consisting of five issues circulated between 1997 and 1999, *Gare du Nord: A Magazine of Poetry and Prose from Paris* was edited by poets Alice Notley and Douglas Oliver. In issue one, the editors assert:

> We salute all those who serve experimental poetry and prose, whether in perfect bound mags or in the instant flare of the websites. There's a space in between we hope to fill. Something's needed that's faster off the ground than the solid mags but more satisfying than a down-loaded flimsy.

Gare du Nord is looking for the best new work in poetry and prose and we aim to get it out quickly. The present issue hasn't got all the features we'll be including – e.g., French poetry, or book reviews. We'll build in the other elements as we go.

Since Britain, the U.S. and France travel to us here beside the Gare du Nord, we'll do our best to act as a rail-crossing point, providing a good mix of work from as many different cultures as we can find, with a proper balance of gender (of course) and genre (less obvious). Easily bored, we'd like to be bratty and funny, as well as serious. Easily put off by the merely shallow, we'd like to present the linguistically complex too.

In short, we want to put people in touch with each other and to provide a sort of inner-city service like a train travelling at comfortable speed.

The British Institute in Paris financially assisted this endeavour. At the outset, the aim was to produce three issues per year. Contributors included Charles Bernstein, Rachel Blau DuPlessis, Ralph Hawkins, Lyn Hejinian, Lisa Jarnot, Pierre Joris, Drew Milne, Wendy Mulford, Ron Padgett, Jerome Rothenberg, Leslie Scalapino, and Anne Waldman. A complete run is held at the National Poetry Library at the Southbank Centre.

Each issue has a section entitled "Books We're Reading" and Notley's "Cosmic Chat". In vol. 2, no. 1 in 1998, a "Reader Inquiry Feature" appeared; Mendelssohn does not appear in any published replies, but in her Sussex files, there is a typescript form bearing the feature title, beneath which reads: "Each issue, Gare du Nord asks its readers to talk to it." (SxMs109/5/B/2/77). Two questions are posed: "1. What would you regard as taking an important poetic risk?" and "2. Describe a poetic risk you feel you have taken in the past." To question one, Mendelssohn responds:

Discussing the creative structuring of one's own poetry
or even admitting that one writes and that one
therefore is aware of the dangers of redirection.
This is a life-threatening risk extrinsic to poetry.
Is poetry indestructible enough to withstand probes?

To question two, she replies:

To have written within the sight of political people,
to have defended poetry against insane dictators'
of fixed opinion; tyrants of language, perception &
life; to have refused at gunpoint to co-operate
with extreme manifestations of this dictatorship,
to refuse to be deluded by commodities such as drugs,
abortion, private swimming pools, oneiric & eidetically confrontational advertisement.

Mendelssohn signs "A.M.", includes her address (155, Mowbray Road, Cambridge), and gives permission to be identified as the author should her responses be used in print; she does not fill out the "Subscription Appeal" on the verso side. In *Gare du Nord* vol. 2, no. 2, 1999, there are approximately six pages of responses to this specific questionnaire. Among them, Lee Harwood claimed that anyone worried about risk was too self-conscious to write. Kenneth Koch responded: "When I'm writing, risks seem indistinguishable from inspirations." And Iain Sinclair described risk as "Subscribing to magazines with staples." *Gare du Nord* is a stapled A4 journal.

Alongside Mendelssohn's contribution, the long poem "1:3ng" and four drawings, issue one of *Gare du Nord* includes writing from Tom Leonard, Andrew Duncan, Joe Brainard, D. S. Marriott, Anselm Hollo, Tony Lopez, and Bill Griffiths, among others. Mendelssohn may have sent the poem to the editors as a manuscript; if so, variations in the archived proof could be the consequence of difficulty in deciphering her hand (5/A/21). Differences between final copy and typescript proof are as follows:

Stanza 4: "of power, and vote;" was "of power, vote;"
Stanza 6: "boating or the" was "boating on the"
Stanza 12: "screens' image" was "screens image"
Stanza 16: after "contemporary music.", in Mendelssohn's hand reads: "(should mean that there are no confrontat"; the note runs off the photocopy
Stanza 20: "Our two strongest artists." was "Our two strangest artists."
Stanza 20: "Strong enough" was "Strong ~~fury~~ ^enough^"
Stanza 24: "up with jobs." was "up with jobs"
Stanza 25: "how the imagination" was "how the ~~magnetism~~ ^imagination^"
Stanza 28: "How that is raised," was "How that is ....,"
Stanza 30: "squint, don't Waft" was "squint, ~~wing~~ ^don't^ Waft"
Stanza 31: "Marigold, wasp" was "Marigold, ~~wrap~~ ^wasp^"
Stanza 33: "Kant refer to sexual intercourse?" was "Kant refer to sexual ~~putrement~~ ^intercourse^?"
Stanza 42: "Which is why I realised" was "Which is why I regretted"
Stanza 45: "Gisèle Prassinos's" was "Gisèle ....'s" [*in ink, Mendelssohn adds the name on the ellipsis*]

The proof concludes with the beginning of a missive to Oliver that justifies Mendelssohn's allusion to J. H. Prynne in the fourth-last stanza of "1:3ng". In correspondence, Mendelssohn writes: "I had no reason to regret in relation to Jeremy Prynne – I have never done anything to hurt or offend him in any way." She states that her first encounter with Prynne's "name" occurred during the height of her political activism, or as she puts it, "on [her] way to Hell". She adds: "I did not know him, had not been introduced to him, had not heard him being spoken of, had not been referred to any of his writing but in that friendless second I recognized a Poet, I do recognize poets". An unsent letter to Oliver dated 12 September 1997 mentions Mendelssohn's epistolary attempt "to explain the line in which I refer to Mr. Prynne." (3/A/1/43/1). At Cambridge, Mendelssohn was in contact with Prynne, a Life Fellow at Gonville and Caius College and Reader in English Poetry. There are references to his lectures and work in her archive, although Mendelssohn often notes that she never felt a part of "the Cambridge brotherhood" of poets (Esther Leslie, *Bouleversed Baudelairizing: On Poetics and Terror*, Veer Books, 2011, 28).

In the proof letter to Oliver, Mendelssohn also discusses acting in Jean-Paul Sartre's *Huis Clos* at the University of Essex, where she perceived a general obsession with sex and abortion, "and areas of life which I did not consider to be apt for undergraduates who had recently left school." She notes: "I was a girl with a Mind – and I was disgusted with the behaviour of my superiors." Finding Essex too hierarchical, she nevertheless states that during her years there (1967–69), she was "Glad to be alive and in a position to Use my mind – a very delicate issue – I cannot adequately explain the Detestation for women with minds. It is Nauseous." (5/A/21).

In that latter half of 1997, Mendelssohn and Oliver were near-regular correspondents. An undated letter from Mendelssohn to Oliver explains the title of "1:3ng": "(1:3 is the point on the piano where three strings change into one (for the lower octaves)) (I am not a bass profondo though, & this has caused me endless 1:3 ing." (3/A/1/43/2). On 1 December 1997, Oliver writes Mendelssohn about the "intense interest" generated by her poem: "It's the extraordinary address – unique and individual – made to the feminine questions that seems to have struck people most, together with their admiration for its sheer unexpectedness and brio." (3/A/1/43/3). In a letter dated 10 December 1997, Mendelssohn thanks him for this praise, and suggests that she would like Oliver and Notley to read her *Inbuilt Flash Nix*, which was published in 1985, although she dates it 1983 (3/A/1/43/1). Here Mendelssohn claims she submitted to *Gare du Nord* because she "love[s] railway stations", then offers her services as a guest editor. A second latter dated 10 December 1997 promises to enclose a 1983 text for Oliver and Notley, and reaffirms Mendelssohn's admiration for their journal title, as well as her hope that it live "a long life."; a scrawled-through letter of 9 December 1997 includes a postscript promising the same text (3/A/1/43/1).

A letter from Oliver dated 3 October 1999 suggests that he and Notley planned to publish Mendelssohn's poem beginning "basalt. basalt. two sculptured heads. hongrie 1956. tanks. fire. hatred." in number five, six, or seven of *Gare du Nord* (3/A/1/43/3). This poem is in *IA* (2000) and this volume, but *Gare du Nord* ceased after their fifth number in 1999, and it did not include Mendelssohn.

Grace Lake, *involution*, no. 5 (1997), 45–47.

The poem "studio VII." is Mendelssohn's second publication with the journal *involution*; her "Truth or Vermilion", appears in *involution* no. 4 (1996). Mendelssohn also published her chapbook *Parasol One. Parasol Two. Parasol Avenue.* (1996) with Involution press. Issue five of *involution* is the twelfth publication of the press, a numbering system that includes journal issues and poetry books (see above notes).

Come the fifth issue, the journal acquired the subtitle "experimental poetry". This issue is edited by A. M. Horne, "s.t.", and Rory Drummond, who welcome submissions and describe their venture as "devoted to poetry of an experimental nature". Within its 48 pages are poems by Peter Riley, Richard Makin, Keston Sutherland, Andrea Brady, and Helen Macdonald.

A manuscript and proofs of "studio VII" exist in Mendelssohn's archive (5/A/22). In earlier drafts, the stanzas are unnumbered. At the bottom of the proofs, Mendelssohn writes: "Cambridge, ~~England~~ ^U.K.^ 1997." On proofs page one, in a different hand, reads: "projected for / involution 5 / pub'd by / a. m. horne" (*"pub'd" is unclear*—ed.). Mendelssohn's edits mainly restore typos or missing and misread words. In stanza seven, "flie" was "~~fire~~ ^flie^"; in stanza 25, "not used to" was "not wed to" and the underlining and marginal correction are handwritten; in stanza 26, "cracked leather" was "crazed leather" and is corrected to "crackled". Next to stanza 15, line two, Mendelssohn proposes the word "deny" in place of "kill"; along the page top, she rewrites the line, identifies this correction as its original wording, and adds: "but then I noticed that I refer to killers in the next couplet but one and this involved a complicated discourse over whether self destruction (denial) is a sin. perhaps sin is not the right word. Could 'suppress' go in here?" An arrow points to a final comment in the right-hand margin: "Actually I think I should stick to the original version".

The A5 manuscript is numbered I–III and signed "grace lake." Distinctions from publication include slight variations in capitalisation and punctuation; for instance, there is a full stop after the title, and in stanza 13, an em-dash appears to follow "issued". Additionally:

Stanza 22: "the line of the freedom" was "the line of this freedom"
Stanza 23: "by the two intimations on Spain" was "by two intimations ~~i~~on Spain"
Stanza 28: "crash wildly" was "~~go crazy~~ ^ crash wildly ^"
Stanza 33: "take that away" was "take ~~them~~ ~~that~~ that away"

Accents used in manuscript are not consistently replicated or corrected in the proofs, and do not appear in publication, but are restored here (ed.).

Grace Lake, *Comparative Criticism: An Annual Journal*, vol. 19, ed. E. S. Shaffer, Cambridge University Press (1997), 220–22.
This issue of *Comparative Criticism* is divided into two parts: "Literary devolution: writing in Scotland, Wales, Ireland, and England" and "Translation". Mendelssohn appears in part one alongside English experimental poets selected by Rod Mengham, among them, Caroline Bergvall, Brian Catling, Andrew Crozier, Andrew Duncan, Veronica Forrest-Thomson, John James, Barry MacSweeney, Ian Patterson, Ulli Freer, Denise Riley, Tom Raworth, Peter Riley, Geoff Ward, and John Wilkinson. In his editorial foreword, "'Warning Letters and Dream Ratios': contemporary English poetry", Mengham describes the thematic and stylistic links between this selection and anthologies such as Iain Sinclair's 1996 *Conductors of Chaos* (see above). Mengham privileges "experimental work" by poets "whose readership has been relatively small until now, believing that their poems deserve equal consideration with those of more familiar figures" (205–6). The issue used here is held at the British Library.

Mendelssohn's contribution is a single poem beginning "To look in the mirror and see a shocking atom", first included in *Tondo Aquàtique* (1997), a chapbook produced by Mengham's Equipage press (see above). In the earlier publication, the date of line 18 has a hyphen, rather than a dash; line 19 ends with a full stop, rather than a comma, and in line 20, there is a hyphen after "Austro". In stanza two, "bewrent…" was "bewrent---". In a proof held in a Sussex *Tondo Aquatique* file, Mendelssohn corrects "Battle fo Zurich" to "Battle of Zurich" by hand (SxMs109/5/A/23/3).

Grace Lake, *Sneak's Noise: Poems for R. F. Langley*, Cambridge: Infernal Histories; Poetical Methods (1998).
This *festschrift* of poems was produced for the English poet and diarist Roger Francis Langley (1938–2011). Between 1978 and 2007, Langley wrote ten books and pamphlets, two with the same publishers as Mendelssohn: Rod Mengham's Equipage and Peter Riley's Poetical Histories. He published extracts from his journal with the *P. N. Review*, was nominated for a Whitbread Book Award, and was awarded, posthumously, the Forward Prize for Best Single Poem (2011).

Held at the British Library, this unpaginated chapbook was published by Peter Riley from Sturton Street, Cambridge. The cover image is a pen and ink drawing by Dan Wheale of the popular British jam-filled shortbread biscuit affectionately known as the "Jammy Dodger". The epigraph reads: "And see if thou canst find out Sneak's noise. / *Henry IV,* Part Two". Mendelssohn's poem beginning "words won't break these walls" appears alongside contributions from J. H. Prynne, Douglas Oliver, Peter Riley, Roy Fisher, Tom Lowenstein, Tony Lopez, Michael Schmidt, John Welch, Nigel Wheale, Martin Thom, Rod Mengham, Barry MacSweeney, Michael Haslam, Thomas A. Clark, Kelvin Corcoran, Peter Hughes, Bob Walker, Andrew Brewerton, Helen Macdonald, Peb Stone, and Eric Langley.

Grace Lake, *A State of Independence*, ed. Tony Frazer, Stride Publications (1998), 108–16.
The editor of this anthology, Tony Frazer, is a translator who founded Shearsman Books in 1981 to showcase "the more exploratory end of the current [poetry] spectrum". In addition to British poets such as Frances Presley, Andrew Crozier, Ralph Hawkins, Geraldine Monk, D. S. Marriott, and Nigel Wheale, Shearsman has published many works in translation (http://www.shearsman.com/). Mendelssohn submitted poems to Shearsman as early as 1986, including *An ACCOUNT of a MUMMY* (letter dated 3 December 86; SxMs109/3/A/1/14). *A State of Independence* is one of several collections edited by Frazer.

According to Frazer, this 1998 anthology aimed to include authors who have published most of their work in Britain and possess "more independent voices" than those routinely encountered in bookshops or libraries ("Introduction" 9–10). David Chaloner, Andrew Duncan, Lee Harwood, and Peter Riley are among the poets who accompany Grace Lake in this anthology.

Mendelssohn's biography reads: "**Grace Lake:** *La Facciata* (Poetical Histories, Cambridge, 1989), *Viola Tricolor* (Equipage, Cambridge, 1993), *Bernache Nonnette* (Equipage, 1995), *Parasol One. Parasol Two. Parasol Avenue.* (Involution, Cambridge, 1996)." (206). She is acknowledged for permission to reprint poems from *viola tricolor* (1993), *Bernache Nonnette* (1995), and *Tondo Aquatique* (1997) (204).

In what follows, variations between published versions and manuscripts are noted in each poem in the order of anthology appearance.

"viola tricolor"

This poem is dedicated to Mendelssohn's sister, brother-in-law, and nephew. There are no significant differences between versions in *A State of Independence* (1998) and *viola tricolor* (1993), barring a gap after "*implanted*" in stanza one which Frazer closes, and is reinstated here (ed.).

A recto-only draft of this poem is divided into a manuscript page of the first stanza, and a typescript page bearing stanzas two and three (5/A/15/1). Italics, punctuation, and the irregular spacing of "*implanted* with a tightrope voice" are not evident in the manuscript; in it, "mocked not as a man's," was "mocked as not a man's," and the lines "as broad became no love / deemed wide lined prostitution" were "as broad ~~was~~ ^became^ no love / ~~but~~ ^deemed^ wide lined prostitution". The typescript portion shows the following distinctions from publication:

> "with food to muse" was "with food a muse"
> "christmas word" may have been "christmas wor~~d~~k"
> "upon custard" was "on custard"
> "of three grooved" was "of thick three groovēd"
> "revealed green" was "revealed ~~light~~ green"

Typescripts also exist in 5/A/15/4 and 5/A/16; in the latter, "food to muse" was "food a muse". In all other regards, these typescripts are identical to the publication. See also notes for *viola tricolor* (1993).

"Ordered into Quarantine"

Mendelssohn published this poem five times: in *Active in Airtime* (1993), *viola tricolor* (1993), *A State of Independence* (1998), and the two editions of *Out of Everywhere: Linguistically Innovative Poetry by Women in North America & the UK* (2006). See below notes for *Out of Everywhere*.

"language blows away"

This poem is published in *viola tricolor* (1993) and in *A State of Independence* (1998); there are no differences between versions.

In Mendelssohn's *viola tricolor* files, there are typescripts of this poem in 5/A/15/4 and 5/A/16 (clean copy). In 5/A/15/4, the two uses of "by" in line four were "~~about~~"; in line five, commas are added around "mostly"; all corrections are made by hand, pre-photocopying.

In 5/A/15/3, the poem exists half in typescript, half in manuscript. The dedication to Kim Longinotto Landseer is typed in the upper left page corner; above it, Mendelssohn writes "kimono". Also typed are stanzas one and most of stanza two as in the published draft. By hand, Mendelssohn titles this variant "such people cause wars." Minus the underlining, this phrase recurs as its own one-line stanza at the end of this draft, although it appears nowhere in the final version.

In stanza one, line four reads: "although i am less patient ^~~interested~~ bothered^ with machinery than i am with people"; in line five, there are no commas around "mostly"; and there is a large gap between "mackintosh" and "i" in the final line. Stanza two is typed as in publication, but the second line is added by hand below, with an arrow pointing to its place between "vapourized." and line three, which begins here: "but ~~would be~~ ^was^ carted off."

The third stanza is handwritten. Differences from the published text include:

"here, as always, I was betrayed" was "here, as ~~eve~~ always, I was ~~ratted on~~ ^betrayed^"
"art" was "Art"
"i was brought a matron's cap" was "~~They~~ Brought ~~me~~ a matron's cap"
Line three, stanza three was: "^that^ I ~~slung it out onto~~ ^saucered out to^ a southern breeze. ~~that~~ ^it^ flipped ~~it~~ onto a lombard."
Line four, stanza three was: "Women, amorphous and power hungry, find causes to flip over"
Line five, stanza three began: "They have to be Doing something with Everything. Nothing"
Line six, stanza three began: "Untouched. Curly hair for instance has to be washed into ^from^"
"scraped back" was "And scraped back"

"Sauce"

In the Sussex archive, this poem exists in manuscript (5/A/15/1) and typescript (5/A/15/3 and 4; 5/A/16). This poem is published in *viola tricolor* (1993) and *A State of Independence* (1998); there are no differences between the two versions.

In one manuscript, Mendelssohn writes "~~Peanut Brittle.~~" in page upper left corner (5/A/15/1). The title is "Sauce." and "Sauce." (files ending 1 and 3 respectively), and there are further differences in punctuation and capitalisation. Variations between publication and archived variants are as follows:

"our schools of art have been ruling" in stanza one, there was an extra line reading: "extremely disordered in sense if my intellect is denied in this way" (this line recurs in 5/A/15/3)
"a stitched on red cross." was "a stitched ^~~sewed~~^ on red cross."
The last three lines of stanza one read:

"how it straightens to rigid duty & is marched away – whilst musicians play on
their ~~members~~ ^consort^ falling, shot in the snow whilst the music continues
to hold up a city with a ~~tenuous~~ ^tremulous^ bow. ~~As~~ ^~~Any~~^ ~~song disrespected~~ ^~~suspected~~^ [~~*illegible word*~~ —ed.]
~~uncalled for~~

"agree, &" was "agree," (see also 5/A/15/3 typescript; the "&" is added by hand in 5/A/16)
"and many a poor poem" was "and many a poor daffodil poem"
"the very word. to not receive" was "The very words. ~~You would~~ ^To^ not receive" (5/A/15/3)
"A Fruit, a brainless carnal lassitude chewing primate gristle" was "A fruit, and brainless Carnal lassitude. ~~hysteria.~~ ^crunching primate gristle.^ Whose is the Notice?" ("chewing is also "Crunching" in 5/A/15/3 and "~~Crunching~~" in 5/A/15/4, where "chewing" appears by hand below the line)

"Cultural"
A typescript of "Cultural" exists in the *viola tricolor* file 5/A/15/4. This poem was published in *Active in Airtime* and *viola tricolor*, and these two 1993 variants are identical. In *A State of Independence*, the full stop at the end of stanza two is excised and has been reinstated (ed.).

"Silk & Wild Tulips"
This poem appears in *Bernache Nonnette* (1995), *A State of Independence* (1998), and in both editions of *Out of Everywhere: Linguistically Innovative Poetry by Women in North America & the UK* (2006; 1996). See the notes of *Out of Everywhere* for a full discussion of poem gestation and variations.

"Eulogy"
Originally published in *Tondo Aquatique* (1997), "Eulogy" is identically replicated in *A State of Independence* (1998), excepting that the title is capitalised. In *Tondo Aquatique*, the poem beginning, "I could see the sea & hear the towns" follows immediately on from "Eulogy" and may be intended as its second part (see above notes). Clean proofs of "Eulogy" exist in 5/A/23/3 and 4.

"Abschied"
Dedicated to Mendelssohn's eldest child, this poem was originally published in *Tondo Aquatique* (1997). The versions are identical, barring stanza six, line six, which in 1997 reads "caught form a world"; as in 1998, the second word is "from" in a photocopied A4 manuscript in *Tondo Aquatique* file 5/A/23/1.

All variants have ten stanzas, but in the manuscript, the first line of publication stanza seven, "of a massive candelabra" becomes the final line of stanza six, meaning seven begins: "that he was prowling towards". There are possible variants in indentations of first lines, most notably, "You and I", which is more centred than left-justified in manuscript. Further, the first line of manuscript stanza ten reads: "You had already ~~picked up~~ ^captured^ ^acquired^", and the entirety is completed with a full stop.

"Abschied" is followed by "tree by the cam" in *Tondo Aquatique* (1997), but in manuscript, an untitled version of "Hungary Water" follows continuously from "Abschied", and an overleaf draft colophon suggests that Mendelssohn considered concluding the volume with this format.

In one proof, a protracted gap of approximately ten lines exists between stanzas seven and eight (5/A/23/4). In another, stanzas six and seven run together without a break; Poppy's surname is misspelt "Mendelson" (Mendelssohn's birth surname is Mendleson); and the first word of stanza three is "Three" rather than "These"; the latter two errors are corrected in Mendelssohn's hand (5/A/23/3).

Poem beginning "She Walked where she should have stood still, stock still."
This poem appears in *Mendleson's Metronome* (an early version of *Bernache Nonnette*), *Bernache Nonnette* (1995), and again in *Out of Everywhere* (2006; 1996). See above notes for *Bernache Nonnette* (1995), and for a full discussion of the gestation and variants of this poem, see below notes for *Out of Everywhere*.

Grace Lake, submission to *Inscape*, no. 5 (1998).
Titled "half evacuation measures unmet, still on regulo", this long manuscript poem consists of 16 paginated A5 sheets. Mendelssohn sent the entirety to Drew Milne at Trinity Hall, University of Cambridge as an entry for the journal *Inscape*; Milne edited issue five, which was published in spring 1999. In a letter to Rod Mengham, Mendelssohn reports that Milne had

requested some of her shorter poems for his issue (3 November 1998; SxMs109/3/A/1/34/1). Milne returned her manuscript by post on 9 January 1999 with a card thanking Mendelssohn but noting that her work "arrived too late for inclusion". He concludes: "I hope you'll be happy for me to write to you if and when future projects arise." Milne's postcard and envelope are included with the manuscript in file SxMs109/5/A/30.

Changes in form and content can coincide with page breaks, but Mendelssohn may have intended for the entirety to run as a continuous whole. Given the exigencies of handwriting, Mendelssohn's margins have been uniformly left justified throughout, even as some lines may be indented or centred (ed.). A squared-off image appears in the bottom right corner of the seventh segment beginning "yes I was frightened,"; drawings of figures and abstract shapes appear along the right margins of segments 14 and 15, beginning "is it naturally reduced" and "callipyge" respectively; on 15, drawings are contained within three discrete rectangles.

In the margin to the left of the poem title reads "oxicoco" (ed.). In segment one, beginning "who will win?", Mendelssohn may write "and ogres/s" in line ten (ed.); the final line reads "to ~~pure~~ ^sheer^ economism". In segment nine, beginning "still goes on round my toes", the last two lines might be on a single line with an extended blank space between them; Mendelssohn appears to run out of space at the end of the page, and out of necessity, places the last line next to the penultimate line. Consistent with other cramped manuscripts (see, for instance, appendix drafts of "the fourteenth flight", *viola tricolor*, 1993), short, left-justified horizontal lines are drawn between stanzas in this segment, presumably as spatial demarcation rather than for replication (ed.). In segment ten, beginning "metamorphosis began after the destruction of the temple," the slash in "claim/do" may be an em-dash or an ampersand (ed.). In segment 11, beginning "and rather than defend" the word "objectification" is unclear (ed.).

In the *IA* (2000) files, an A5 manuscript appears to combine aspects of segment three and ten of this submission (5/A/24/2). It includes four drawings, one to the right of the text, and three surrounding the final line, and reads:

> "je suis navrée de vous contredire."
> you are not a proposition.
> you do not enter into my calculations.
> I owed you no money.
> on ideological grounds I detected a
> similarity between your hostility
> towards me and that of other women.
> I have every right to be here.
> [*unclear word, possibly "to"*—ed.] existence a proposition or
> are you going to be entertained
> by the same old plaint?
> language excites my eyes?
> navrée
>
> navrer contredire irrefutabiliy

Anna Mendelssohn, selection from *Implacable Art*, Folio and Equipage/Salt (2000).
Implacable Art (hereafter *IA*) remains Mendelssohn's only perfect-bound book and consistently accessible publication. Formatted in the house style of Salt press, the cover includes a reproduction of Sonia Delaunay's *La Cible* (1971). A photocopied letter

from Mendelssohn to Rod Mengham dated 7 March 2000 critiques a mocked-up cover, likely the one that appears in the same file, in which the background is light blue, the lettering black, Salt press is identified as the publisher on spine and back cover, and a space is left for an author photo. The logo of the printer, "Lightning Source" – a book with a lightning bolt above it – is also included. Mendelssohn insists that references to Salt and the production company logo are removed; the latter, she states, resembles "fascist signs of electricity/gas or galvanized light" (SxMs109/5/A/24/9). She adds: "It would help a little if the designer could remember that this work stems from awareness & memory of War rather than propulsion towards war or writing in its (war's) throws." Mendelssohn also declines an author photo: "don't want to pose – & don't want one."

The book contains 136 pages of poetry and Mendelssohn's "Table" of titles and/or first lines. Next to the title page, and under the heading: "Other books by Anna Mendelssohn (Grace Lake) from Equipage" reads: "*Viola Tricolor / Bernache Nonnette / Tondo Aquatique*". To Mengham on 7 March 2000, Mendelssohn clarifies: "(they are books to me – not pamphlets)" (5/A/24/9). Overleaf, Mendelssohn dedicates *IA* "for my parents, Morris & Clementina,"; beneath this attribution or title is an eleven-line poem that includes: "a pretty burst of dance, rhythm making me lose orthography, yet I fight for it / back & hear the slide in love and wonderment lost at the memory / of my parents' dancing."

On the next page appears an epigraph in German from Ingeborg Bachmann's "Im Gewitter der Rosen" ("In the Storm of Roses"); overleaf again, an "Acknowledgements" page explains that two poems in *IA* were published by Involution in 1996, namely, the poem beginning "that is what you were told" and the English version of "à la France", which was translated for *IA* by Mendelssohn's friend David Kelley, a fellow of Trinity College, Cambridge who died in 1999. The first poem was published under the title "Truth or Vermilion" in *involution*, no. 4, 1996; the second appears as "To France" in Mendelssohn's 1996 text, *Parasol One. Parasol Two. Parasol Avenue.* (see above notes).

Although she published in John Kinsella's journal *Salt* in 1996 (see above notes), Mendelssohn refused to have *IA* identified with Salt press. Consequently, the publisher attribution is a one-time collaboration between Rod Mengham's Cambridge-based Equipage and Folio, a press run by John Kinsella in Applecross, Western Australia. Mendelssohn's aversion to salt is cryptically discussed in two letters to Mengham. In one, she writes: "Salt is a terrible admixture to use chemically in undefinable qualities with nature. I am not an escapee, only a born artist & poetess & one who does not, cannot write through people as though we were living meat" (3/A/1/34/1). In another, she states:

> no Salt on the book please believe me – it is used to Kosher meat before it is cooked – & I am not a meaty writer – by which I mean people are not cooked by me – I don't write into the living meat – I do not practice Cannibalism – and neither do you. It must not be mixed in limitless quantities – it is bad chemistry. One writes through the mind. I don't want to live down a Siberian salt mine. (3/A/1/34/2)

Unnamed, Salt undertook book production and distribution, and *IA* remains among their listings. Jennifer Hamilton-Emery, director of Salt press, generously gave permission to reprint a selection from the text.

Eleven files are devoted to *IA* in Mendelssohn's Sussex archive (5/A/24/1–11). These files contain poems that are not in *IA*, such as a photocopied poetic preamble to *Parasol One. Parasol Two. Parasol Avenue.* (1996) beginning "Bernache reclined upon her startling blue aeroflot indice." (5/A/24/1). A poem manuscript referencing portions three and ten of Mendelssohn's 1998 *Inscape* submission is held in 5/A/24/2, as is an untitled typescript of "Truth or Vermillion", first published in *involution*, no. 4 (April 1996; see above notes). Poems that may be draft works considered for the final volume are included in the appendix. Further manuscripts, typescripts, proofs, and original manuscripts associated with *IA* run scattershot through Mendelssohn's papers.

Many *IA* files are primarily photocopied manuscripts, typescripts, and drawings for the volume, and contain pencilled page numbers in bottom corners (5/A/24/2–6). There are three manuscript versions of the index or "Table", one running from pages one to 129 that includes a poem included in this appendix, titled, in this instance: "we cannot sing 'intimidated'". In this variant, poem titles or first lines appear that do not correspond with filed draft poems or the published table, such as: "always nervous" and "Nothing in common." A second variant runs from 99–129 in an order akin to publication; a third is an index of titles or first lines that lists twelve poems in no discernible order (5/A/24/7).

Two thick files are full proofs without annotations (5/A/24/10 and 11). These are accompanied by a letter on Cambridge University Press letterhead from Salt director Chris Hamilton-Emery to Rod Mengham, dated 31 March 2000 (5/A/24/10). Hamilton-Emery writes:

> Here are the proofs, although I have some very real concerns that in adjusting the setting to take account of the very long lines of some poems, we now have a legibility problem. I would dearly like to go back to a compromise of suffering the line breaks, rather than dropping down the point size to such an extent. But I'll leave this to you and Anna.

The typesetting is Swift 9.5/13 in this proof and remains so in the final version. The copyright is more extensive in these proofs than in *IA,* elucidating textual reproduction as including means "electronic, mechanical, photocopying, recording, or otherwise"; should "unauthorised" transmission occur, "criminal prosecution and civil claims for damages" are threatened. The agency representing the estate is thanked for permission to use Sonia Delaunay's *La Cible* (1971), but this acknowledgement is excised from *IA*; in both variants, an acknowledgement is given on the cover. Granted by fax to Mengham on 11 October 1999, the permission remains in 5/A/24/9. Throughout these proofs, Mendelssohn's poems, pictures, and "Table" are replicated as in the final volume.

While *IA* is dedicated to Mendelssohn's parents, her files show many draft dedications (5/A/24/7). One is an anti-dedication; titled "NO", this A5 manuscript has two doodles in page bottom left and is signed "Britain 2000." It reads:

> This book is not dedicated directly to my three
> children Poppy Juanita, Jet & Emerald although
> it is written with them very much in mind.
> My children were born out of wedlock and
> were much loved by me as they still are.
> However, I am financially poor as I come
> from a family who believes in their members'
> capacity to earn their own livings which is
> why I ~~re~~endeavoured to return to University
> having not been either expelled or dropped-out
> in the first place. That people have nothing
> better to do than to ~~se~~ cause trouble for
> someone who has already been caused more
> trouble than anyone who has not millennia
> of historical suffering in their blood
> to sustain the faintest hope of transcending
> bloody violence ~~would~~ ^could^ have been
> ~~killed~~ destroyed by, renders me speechless with

what I have no intention of either
describing or depicting for the satisfaction
and/or amusement of the effete.
Britain 2000.

Another A4 manuscript dedication, replete with doodle at page bottom, can be found in 5/A/24/8. From "It is also dedicated" the ink changes:

> This book is dedicated to ~~Art~~ artists across the board
> writers, musicians, composers, film-makers –
> in the hope that our defenders will ~~outnumber~~
> ~~our~~ vanquish our assailants both publicly &
> personally. It is also dedicated to those children
> whose parents & families are terrorising them into
> psychiatric channels in order either to appease school
> authorities or themselves.

In addition to the draft dedications, Mendelssohn contemplates a preface (5/A/24/7). This A4 manuscript, formatted as two A5 halves, reads:

> I'd like to write a preface to this book.
> Why is art implacable? It won't disappear
> even when it is yelled at as though
> it were a living offence. I find myself
> to be in a similar situation to the one I
> ended up in [*sic*] Sheffield before I made the
> decision to return to Cambridge with
> my children. We cannot criticize you
> but you can criticize us. ~~for~~ if we dare
> to. ~~My~~ What I have ever had to say has
> never applied to politics directly although
> I am capable of holding my own in
> the sphere of political discourse it is
> not a discourse that I choose to make
> my own. It always seemed to me
> that the act of writing involved the
> exclusion of the writer; that the
> subjects ~~too we~~ took precedence.
> that they filled the work of art.
> and gave it life. I was lucky

enough to know the world before
it became wholly mechanistic
and I began to write of that
world with what I consider to
be good priorities, where my
wit was scathing it was a deservedly so
~~scathe and one I thoroughly~~
~~enjoyed indulging in~~., but
similarly to a mathematic
it does not work when it is
Applied, it loses its magic,
which is why politics destroy
art. This is not to say that
my art is not political, it is
highly political, but it is not
politics. Forced removal of my
children was political, as was
leaving me homeless. There are no excuses.

Just as the above directly addresses the volume title, there is a tract in 5/A/24/3 titled "Implacable art." Above this heading are the words "strong" or "stormy" and "instrument," and Stars of David; down page right margin are figures and abstract shapes. Below the title reads:

I wanted you to have colour. boats. nets.
the sound of the waves.,
not the child who should not be exposed
adults who,

Everything was converted to art,
or it would have been,
we don't leave women pulling out
their hair in a state of distress
so we don't take the easy option,
art cannot wait, although it does.
your generation, your generation
have been going around kicking
mothers in the face.
when there are no fathers to
teach you respect.
& even then – you may turn
out to be a cackling woman

It may be to a similar manuscript that Mendelssohn refers in the first titled poem of *IA*, "from Implacable Art." (1). Two of its eight lines are extended ellipses.

A final manuscript in the *IA* files continues this pursuit of introductory textual apparatus (5/A/24/7). Recto and verso of a single A4 sheet with two doodles on each side, it reads:

> Acknowledgements & Preface.
>
> By nature one is inhibited, by knowledge of there
> being insufficient material wealth to sustain
> one's security; one endeavours to avoid
> places where wealth is the standard by which
> one is judged, the question that is posed
> ~~being~~ encroaching from ideas of female
> wealth, not masculine strength –
> but the strength of a girl to do a man's
> work, to fight a man also when his
> strength overpowers her moral integrity,
> when he decides that epithets are
> more in tune with his currency determining to kill a girl's
> Therefore, rather than love poetry emerging
> in language sensitive, love is snatched
> with the child and the books, for a future
> of cold showers and carbolics. This is an
> outworn reading, which I have noticed
> to be in our world, where literary knowledge
> is not confined to place and where texts the focal
> ~~are focus focii, and not~~ points. But former
> judgements have been overruled & good character
> has been overruled by the misinformed.
> One acts to prevent war, but one can never
> defend oneself against personal aggression
> being directed against one's person, only
> those ~~with~~ who have witnesses to their lives
> can do that. I would be too ashamed of myself
> had I taken a woman's children, so perhaps I
> am unable to use my poetic faculty that had
> always tried to see the other person's point of view
> and I sense that this area is the one area of
> continuing hostility
> that has dogged me,

> both because I didn't
> wish to be associated
> with it & also because
> I had always ~~see~~
> thought of the relationship
> between a mother
> & her children sacred.
> Had I been hardened to
> imagery of war I should not
> have been moved by the
> napalm seared mothers &
> babies of Vietnam which
> were so shocking to those who
> were still in mourning for
> the victims of the European
> Holocaust.
> In contradistinction to ~~written~~ printed texts, a photographic
> image is startlingly imminent. I do not understand why
> this country always lacks the grace to acknowledge
> what is not financially remunerative. It obviously
> has no idea ~~how~~ to what lengths people go to to
> support each other without thought of material
> gain.

Possessives have been added (ed.).

In addition to poems, the *IA* files include notes and volume plans. Book themes are addressed on two A4 pages in 5/A/24/8. With clear reference to Cambridge, the first unfinished, illustrated piece reads:

> There is friction between town & gown. Some women have experienced
> appalling domestic violence in ~~their~~ ^our^ determination to keep the
> peace and to continue with our higher education for which we
> worked in order to sustain our futures knowing that we
> could no~~t~~ longer expect to be financed by hypothetical husbands/
> partners. Cruelty to women has been deliberate & intense.
> Children have been assumed to have appeared out of thin air.
> Women have been abandoned with children by men who
> are seemingly incapable of

In line one, the "t" of "town" is crossed twice, making it indeterminately lower and upper case (ed.).

The second reads:

Sometimes I still think that I can't write here in England.
Not because I can't write but that the level is already
standardized & finalized too. Which is why I had to leave when
I was young – five years old – and Wordsworth knew his country.
I used to hand myself over [*sic*] the police & ask to be taken to my father
at work. I used to pray for him to come home. But he couldn't
take me to where I wanted to go to. The grand piano that stood
in opera singing cousin's house. We were born on the other side
of the Berlin Wall. Is that a suitable biography? I don't think so.
I can't live without a piano, it is my beginning and end.

Amongst the practical details of correcting text and layout, file 5/A/24/9 contains five letters from Mendelssohn to editor Rod Mengham that include information about textual gestation, including the assertion, noted above, that the text "stems from an awareness & memory of War" (copied letter dated 7 March 2000). On 17 December 1999, Mendelssohn tells Mengham that one of the final poems in *IA*, "Brahms' numerals.", contains "Margaret Mead overtones", adding: "Mead formed an important part of my reading in connection with Lévi-Strauss in the School of Comparative Studies together with Freud's 'Totem and Taboo.'" The same letter references the inexpressible, ongoing pain of losing the children thirteen years' previous, being "treated like a criminal whore", and the men "who tried to use me as a Molly Bloomish sex object rather than take Any interest in my writing & painting". Mendelssohn adds: "I still think that one creates from love & not from hatred. I don't think that Abstract forms are derived from human life – they are geomorphological etc." Before her valediction, she mentions the Angry Brigade who "went against" her. Other missives to Mengham in 5/A/24/9 reiterate Mendelssohn's concerns about the children, and her experiences of anti-Semitism and poverty. An undated letter headed "Re 'Implacable Art'" states: "It is so bad to be pushed into False Confession".

Manuscripts in the *IA* files are generally clean and worked into fair copies before photocopying; often the same copies will reappear in multiple files. Where extant and/or located, what follows includes discernible changes and variations between these manuscripts and the *IA* poems selected for this volume.

"pladd. (you who say either)"
There are photocopied manuscripts of "pladd." in 5/A/24/3 and 4; a three-page A5 manuscript is in 5/A/24/7 that shows a rectangular drawing across the top of page three. In addition to an underlined title and minor variations in punctuation and capitalisation, the manuscript shows the following differences from the published poem:

Page 2, line 8: "incontestable" was "uncontestable"
Page 2, line 21: "who is clean cleaner and cleanest." was "who is clean cleaner and cleaner."
Page 3, line 7: "Péret. (Oh not Péret" was "Perec. Oh not Perec."
Page 3, line 9: "not George Sand.)" was "not Georges Sand."
Page 3, line 19: "sweaty knees" was "sweaty ~~feet~~ knees"
Page 3, line 20: "help were my accent broader," was "help ~~if~~ ^were^ my accent ~~was~~ broader,"
Page 3, line 21: "a Self that one" was "~~such~~ a Self that one"
Page 3, final line: "Is this someone else's?" was followed by "Whatever it is"

"of Lorca."
In an A4 manuscript held in 5/A/24/4, Mendelssohn writes "jacques brel / georges brassens" in heavy felt-tip, adding "(brel)" in the right margin. Additional edits are pencilled in what may be a different hand. The title is right justified, and in line 11, there is an extended space between "se fueron" and "los pequeños". The "I" of the final line is capitalised and concludes: "it~~s~~ breath^es^, internally." In publication there are no accents on "fósforo"; "sidney" is spelt "sydney" and there is no accent on "gréco" (ed.).

"I object."
An original A5 manuscript of "I object." is held in 5/B/1/15/2 with a rectangular doodle on the verso side; an A4 photocopy of the manuscript poem is held in 5/A/24/4. In this variant, the title is underlined; line 13 concludes "it is nature to think, to wonder,"; and line 21 begins: "~~of~~ or an irresistible".

"to any who want poems to give them answers."
There is an original manuscript of this poem in 5/B/2/49, and in 5/A/24/3, a photocopy of the same with pencilled clarifications in a hand that may not be Mendelssohn's. In manuscript, the title is underlined and there are minor changes in punctuation: for instance, in line 15 "Jesuses" is "Jesus's", and in line 16, "cords," reads "cords.,". Manuscript line ten begins "louder than". As the "louder then" of *IA* appears to be a proofing error, "than" is restored (ed.).

Poem beginning "digne. more than a design. to size."
A photocopied, landscape-oriented A4 manuscript of three of this poem's four columns appears in 5/B/2/93. In addition to slight changes in punctuation and capitalisation, publication and manuscript differ as follows: in column one, "mostar" was "moster"; in column two, "how I act dead," reads "how to act dead,"; in three, "Eliot words" was "Eliot's words". In the latter instance, the possessive is added to the photocopy; as it is semantically and grammatically accurate, it is reinstated (ed.).

An A4 photocopy of the fourth column of the poem appears in Mendelssohn's correspondence with Rod Mengham (3/A/1/34/1). It differs from publication only in omitting the full stop after "windhover". In the accompanying letter dated 8 November 1999, Mendelssohn labels "digne." a diptych, describing "the left side of the piece" as "what remains of my life" while "the other side is my death." She then adds: "I don't use language to create death." A second landscape-oriented A4 manuscript photocopy, likely intended for the same letter, contains all four columns; the bottom right corner reads: "pages 53 & 54" (3/A/1/34/1). In additions to variations from publication in punctuation and capitalisation, each column is shorter than in publication, evidently by design.

In column one, line 18, "other women's children were up for grabs" is not in this manuscript, and in line 24, "adequacy" reads "adequacies"; the four final lines do not appear. In column two, line 24 ends "how to act dead," and the final six lines are omitted, as are the final eight in column three. In column three, line 12, there is no ampersand; lines 16 and 17 are swapped; and the "camera" of line 18 is "cameras". Column four, line 20 concludes "a prison system." After line 21, ending "lesbian.", the publication has six additional lines; in manuscript, there are three, reading: "serve your own sentences. / I collect sentences. / I used to have a set of my own."

Poem beginning "basalt. basalt. two sculptured heads. hongrie 1956. tanks. fire. hatred."
A clean manuscript of this poem exists in 5/B/2/37; a photocopy of the same exists in 5/A/24/3, with pencilled corrections in a hand that may not be Mendelssohn's. While the language is near-identical, lines are longer in A4 manuscript than in A5

publication after line one, meaning the published poem is 47 lines, the manuscript 43. Minor distinctions in punctuation and capitalisation surface throughout. Further, in lines 19 and 20, "meine / kinder" was "meine kinde"; in line 30, "both decorate pastels" may read "both distinct pastels" or "both district pastels"; and in the final line, "take being in quod, you" was "take imprisonment, you".

In line five, "palétuvier", the French for mango tree, is rendered "paléturier" in *IA*. As this error is likely caused by Mendelssohn's unclear handwriting, the "v" is restored (ed.). In line seven, "the authorities of white needlework" was "the authorities / o~~f~~n white needlework"; the corrected version in 5/A/24/3 shows the copy editor questioning this preposition, writing: "? of". Clearer in manuscript, Mendelssohn's original "on" is reinstated (ed.).

"My Chekhov's Twilight World"
In addition to a manuscript of stanzas seven to ten in file 5/B/1/15/2, there is an A4 manuscript of the first six stanzas of this poem in 5/A/24/2 and a two-page A4 photocopy of the manuscript in its entirety, with pencilled corrections not in Mendelssohn's hand, in 5/A/24/3.

In addition to rendering the title "My Chekhov's Twilight. World.", differences between publication and the complete manuscript include:

Stanza 1: "I had" was "I ~~know~~ ^had^"
Stanza 4: "procedure. That is. I do" was "procedure. ^that is.^ I do"
Stanza 4: "for them" may have been "for ~~you~~. them." (ed.)
Stanza 5: "It is a gutter" read "It is a gutless"
Stanza 5: "nothing but four years'" was "nothing but a few years"
Stanza 6: "And I knew to" was "And I knew it to"
Stanza 8: "about anyone." is "about anybody."
Stanza 9: "there are" is "there are –"

In publication, the "you're —ing" of stanza seven is rendered "you're—ing" (ed.).

Poem beginning "Concentration camp styles. along mill road. 1998."
A manuscript of this poem exists in 5/A/24/2; a photocopy of the same, with minor pencilled corrections, is in 5/A/24/3. In addition to minor variations in punctuation, in manuscript, there is an extended space in line four after "her walking stick."; in line six, "newspaper rolled" might be "newspapers rolled"; line 21 may begin "tanned legg's"; and in line 26, there may be an en-dash after "arthritis" (ed.). In the bottom right corner, Mendelssohn writes: "June 1998."

"to a writer."
There are A4 manuscripts of this poem in 5/A/24/3 and 5/B/1/15/2. Excepting the far-left title justification, and the capitalisation of "Finding" in stanza two, line five, they are identical to publication.

Poem beginning "This is the reason why I do not conform."
Stanza five, line four of the photocopied manuscript of this poem reads "is Bad Use of language and SEX." (*"SEX." may be "Sex."*—ed.); in the final line, "sociopolitical" is "socio/political" (5/A/24/3). An extensive rectangular doodle appears in the upper right corner.

Poem beginning “geo Alkan jeo. toppled on”

The title of this poem appears to be mid-text, as line 15, “the beef girls. leaning on Alkan.” is in a larger font, as per all *IA* titles, and in bold. But in Mendelssohn’s “Table”, the poem is indexed by the start of line one only. In a manuscript in 5/A/24/3, line 15 is underlined, and in stanza two, the phrases “burger king”, “burger queen”, and “burger beef” are treated as single words. Further, the lineation of the second half differs in manuscript: in publication, it is nine lines of identical length, followed by one short line; in manuscript, it totals nine lines of varying if roughly similar lengths. In publication line 21, there is no full stop between “mirror” and “exactly” as there is in manuscript.

Poem beginning “Reminiscent of a flat expanse trammelled”

There are multiple copies of this poem in Mendelssohn’s archive. In all manuscripts, the “dias” of stanza one is rendered “dïas” and the phrase in publication stanza two, “or organza” reads “of organza.” (5/B/1/15/2; 5/A/24/2 and 3). Photocopies of the manuscripts in 5/A/24/2 and 5/B/1/15/2 appear in 5/A/24/3; in that file, the latter variant has pencilled clarifications possibly not in Mendelssohn’s hand.

The photocopied, two-page A4 manuscript held in 5/A/24/2 is formatted without stanza breaks and begins “how reminiscent”. Further distinctions include:

> Line 7: there may be an “^a^” after “on” (ed.)
> Line 9: “breath cloaked” was “breathing cloaked”
> Line 14: “clothes fuss pleasantly” was “clothes fuss unpleasantly”
> Line 20: “unknowable” was “unknown”
> Lines 23 and 24 read: “is challenged, by women too, on economic/validity, where it does not blow”
> Line 25 in publication, 27 in manuscript: “that is drenched sweet & wild” was “that is as sweet & wild”
> Lines 28 and 29 in publication, 30 and 31 in manuscript: “Holding” and “Wary” had no capitals
> Final line: “ancient sky.” was “ancient sky”

At the bottom of the 5/A/24/2 photocopy, after a short horizontal line, is a draft of an eight-line poem from *IA* beginning: “I have been made of no. nº certainly. no no”. In *IA*, this octet is treated as a discrete poem in Mendelssohn’s “Table” but follows “Zephyrus” (see below); here, a swung dash or tilde appears at the beginning and end of the piece, suggesting section breaks within a larger poem.

“Zephyrus”

In an A5 manuscript, the title is spelt “Zephirous” and there is a doodle in the bottom right corner (5/A/24/7); a photocopied manuscript of the same shows the title corrected and further edits in a hand that is not Mendelssohn’s (5/A/24/3). Additionally:

> Line 7: “exercising reference” was “exercises reference”
> Line 13: “hours the rise in opposition” was “hours ^the^ rise~~ing~~ in opposition”
> Line 14: “To human absorption of bright light” was “To ~~the~~ human absorption of ~~the~~ bright light”
> Line 16: “exploits indiscretion” was “exploits ~~the~~ indiscretion”
> Line 20: “enormously, familiarly” reads “enormously, ~~ill~~ familiarly,”
> Line 23: “structure.” reads “structure”

In *IA*, line 23 begins "(consisting of appreciation"; in manuscript, this reads "Consisting of appreciation"; given the lack of closing bracket, the manuscript variant is replicated here (ed.).

"minnie most beats up thérèse torchée"
In the bottom right corner of a photocopied, pencilled-upon poem manuscript, there is a doodle of a spiral-filled circle or vinyl record; from its circumference springs flower shapes. Above it, Mendelssohn writes "E. P." and "33 1/3 r.p.m.", adding a small angular drawing under the second phrase (5/A/24/4). Beneath, a cut-off note reads: "film de S.Z. real [*unclear word*—ed.] of a fil". The manuscript title is underlined, and in line one, "competition" may read "competitive"; further, there is a single blank line between the first two stanzas. The poem concludes: "shooting rays in ^across^ the thickets."

On a photocopied proof, Mendelssohn makes a marginal note suggesting that she wanted the words "serpolet" and "wild thyme" to be printed in colour (the same hue for both); poorly written and faintly reproduced, this brief note ends "without an asterisk" suggesting that the colour was a means of bypassing the footnote embedded within the poem (5/A/24/8). On the photocopy, Mendelssohn pens small dots indicating where the asterisks will lie, and "(wild thyme)" was italicised.

Anna Mendelssohn, "REARRANGED LETTER TO THOMAS EVANS", *Onedit*, no. 1 (2000).
This poem appeared in the first issue of the on-line journal *Onedit*, co-edited by Thomas Evans and Tim Atkins. Mendelssohn is published alongside Lisa Jarnot, Judith Goldman, and Jackson Mac Low, among others. Subsequent issues included contributions from Brian Kim Stefans, Jean Day, Clark Coolidge, Tom Raworth, Leslie Scalapino, Stephen Rodefer, and Charles Bernstein (www.onedit.net/index2.html).

Mendelssohn's distaste for modern technologies – mobile phones, computers, the internet – is a recurrent theme in her archive, and inflects her poetry, as in the lines from "A grace note" in *Tondo Aquatique* (1997): "the web exists to apologize without conveying / apologies couched in human terms, but only bloodlessly in a bloodless existence" (see also couplet 18 of "studio VII", *involution*, no. 5, 1997). *Onedit* was originally planned as a print journal, which might explain Mendelssohn's willingness to contribute; Evans was in correspondence with Mendelssohn from about 1994 or 1995, and his 1999 journey to Burma is alluded to in this poem, which may have been written in honour of his birthday (emails from Evans, 26 July and 1 August 2017).

There is an A4 typescript of "REARRANGED LETTER TO THOMAS EVANS" in the Sussex archive; barring a handwritten question mark in blue in the upper right corner, it bears no edits or identificatory marks (SxMs109/5/A/25a). A poem manuscript in Evans's possession shows a full stop at the end of an all lower-case title. Further differences in capitalisation include: the "visitor" of line one reads "Visitor" and line two begins "How". In the final line, "août" is not capitalised, and as months are not capitalised in French, this spelling is restored (ed.). The top right corner reads "for Onedit."; beneath the poem, Mendelssohn signs "anna m."; at page bottom, she writes: "Kiosque du Jardin, 155, Mowbray Road, Cambridge, CB1 4SP. / 1st May 2000." (scan from Evans, 1 August 2017).

Anna Mendelssohn, Translations of Gisèle Prassinos (c. 2000–2002).
The French writer Gisèle Prassinos (1920–2015) was the child prodigy "discovered" and claimed by the French surrealists, among them, André Breton, Paul Éluard, and Man Ray. Aged fourteen, Prassinos had her work published in *Minotaure* and *Documents 34*.

Prassinos was an abiding interest of Mendelssohn's later years. On 15 April 1997, Mendelssohn writes her cousin Barry Benser, pointing out that both she and Prassinos were young female poets to whom society is "rarel[y k]ind". Also appealing to Mendelssohn was Prassinos's attentiveness to Jewish history: she notes that in Prassinos's novel *The Voyager* (*La Voyageuse*, 1959) she "wrote of the time when Jewish Parisians were being rounded up" (SxMs109/1/E/1/7/1/1). To poet, friend, and Proust translator Ian Patterson Mendelssohn writes: "I have always been interested in Surrealism and [Prassinos] was one of the very early ones and what is more she survived [. . . .] She is an excellent prose writer. and I think quite as good as Leonora Carrington and her short surrealist stories should make excellent reading too" (undated letter, 1997 or later; 3/A/1/57/1). In the same letter, she tells Patterson: "I want her to be treated well and kindly which I shall do."

Mendelssohn will reiterate her concern that Prassinos's legacy be well preserved and promoted. In a letter to a "Jean" (likely Khalfa, a Senior Lecturer in French at the University of Cambridge), Mendelssohn writes on 28 April 1997: "I don't want Gisèle Prassinos' works to be changed into modern american. I understand that period in its internal literary resonance" (3/A/1/27). She aims to have Prassinos's texts reproduced with the most fitting publisher. To Patterson, she indicates plans to approach Cambridge University Press with her work on Prassinos (3/A/1/47/1). In an undated letter to John Calder, she states that Calder Publishing "is sympathetic to the French Existentialist/Surrealist imagination" and asks for his assistance in securing a grant to return to Paris to translate Prassinos's novel, *Le temps ne rien* (1958), noting that she will send him the work when it is complete (3/A/1/4).

Mendelssohn planned to be both a critic and translator of Prassinos. Again to Jean, she states: "I am writing a thesis & Gisèle Prassinos writing falls within it"; she also thanks Jean for offering to read her work (3/A/1/27). A torn A4 sheet with an incomplete, undated letter suggests that Mendelssohn also planned to send her Prassinos translations to scholar and poet Romana Huk (3/A/1/20/1). In an undated letter to Tim (possibly Mathews, who co-wrote *poems* with Mendelssohn in 1984; see above notes), Mendelssohn writes that her health is contingent on finding "a quiet space to write" and "funding to continue my translations of Gisèle Prassinos an early 'objet trouvée' of André Breton's"; at this juncture, Mendelssohn hopes to translate Prassinos into English and Spanish (3/A/1/32).

During Mendelssohn's early days in Cambridge, Prassinos came to Trinity College to read with the French-Lebanese writer André Chedid; Mendelssohn met both writers, who were guests of her friend and Trinity College fellow David Kelley. On 10 June 1997, Mendelssohn wrote Chedid to tell him she was pursuing funding to translate Prassinos's *Le temps n'est rien*, and to ask if he or Prassinos might "have copies of [Prassinos's] early surrealist texts – 1935 through to 1950". She mentions a visit to Paris in July and asks Chedid to "give [her] best wishes to Gisèle" (3/A/1/7).

An undated letter to Huk asserts that Mendelssohn was given permission from Prassinos herself to translate her work (3/A/1/20/1). This claim of "express permission" is repeated in her correspondence to Tim, and again to Benser; in the latter instance she writes: "I have been given the author's permission to translate her works to date of some very fine prose and poetry by an old lady (French/Greek) who was one of the early surrealists" (3/A/1/32; 15 April 1997, 1/E/1/7/1/1). A letter to her sister Judi, dated 26 February 1997, mentions Mendelssohn's upcoming reading at the Parisian Centre Georges Pompidou in April, and states: "there's an old lady poetess whom I am being contracted to translate into English from French – her whole work – that's what I want to finance as there's a chance that there may be a translation grant and her writing is very good indeed" (1/E/1/6/1/1).

Practical obstacles prevented Mendelssohn from completing the work as fulsomely as she hoped. The most replete repository of Prassinos's works is housed at the Bibliothèque Nationale de France in Paris, and Mendelssohn pursued a reader's card and funding to avail herself of that institution. In French and on college letterhead, Trinity fellow David Kelley writes to the Bibliothèque Nationale in support of "Mademoiselle Anna Mendleson" on 15 March 1997 (3/A/1/25/3). Describing her as a writer and graphic artist of repute in England and other countries, Kelley mentions her reading at the Pompidou on 2 April 1997, and explains that Mendelssohn wants to further her work on Prassinos during this visit.

The successful receipt of a reader's card is mentioned in Mendelssohn's correspondence, both in her undated letter to Huk and to Patterson. Patterson she also approached to see if the Cambridge college with which he was then affiliated – King's – might assist her with a research grant (3/A/1/47/1). On 15 April 1997, Mendelssohn writes Benser, discussing "searching for funding to support me for three months in the old Bibliothèque nationale", pointing out that she is in possession of "a readers [*sic*] ticket thanks to the French Embassy's Cultural Delegation". In the same letter, Mendelssohn states that she approached Andrew Motion at the Arts Council to ask for assistance with a funding application. At this juncture, Mendelssohn has returned from her trip to read at the Pompidou, and expresses frustration at how little she was able to translate of Prassinos's *Le temps n'est rien*, necessitating another trip to Paris that she cannot, at present, afford (1/E/1/7/1/1). Many of these letters regarding funding and Prassinos planning are written on the same blue A4 notepaper; all are unsent original copies.

Mendelssohn's archive contains some well-worked over translations of Prassinos's *nouvelles* or short stories, among them, "To Die", "The Friend", "The Family Table", and "The Leaf" (6/C/3/1–3 and 6/C/5/1). The stories are drawn from two Prassinos story collections, *Le verrou et autres nouvelles* (1987) and *La table de famille: nouvelles* (1993), both produced by the Paris-based press Flammarion and held at the Cambridge University Library. A photocopied variant of "To die" includes a letter to Jean dated 25 January 2002, in which Mendelssohn describes sending one story from the 1987 collection and two from the 1993 for Jean's perusal. In it, she wonders if only Catholics should "work on Catholic texts", adding: "Christianity takes the upper hand with perversity. However I should continue as the main gist of my thesis is relative" (6/C/3/3). Replete photocopies exist of manuscripts of "The Friend" (6/C/3/2) and "Le Verrou" (6/C/3/1), and, as in many of these translations, Mendelssohn notes the text, publisher, date of publication, and page references, citing herself as translator.

Another file holds prose manuscripts in Mendelssohn's hand that are copied from Prassinos's entry in *L'Atelier Imaginaire: Poésie* (1988), an anthology published by L'Age d'Homme and housed at the Bibliothèque Nationale that included work by Canadian poet Nicole Brossard and Haitian writer René Depestre (6/C/4). All of Prassinos's untitled poems from pages 203 to 219 appear to be included; amongst these papers is a poem that does not appear to be part of this anthology entitled "NON PAS.", dedicated to Prassinos's brother, the artist Mario Prassinos. In the same file, on the verso of a photocopied sheet, appears Mendelssohn's transcription, and partial translation, of a piece attributed to Prassinos, titled "BLOC". The writings in this file remain in the original French, excepting a folded A3 sheet, torn lengthways in half; it is titled "love poem." and attributed to Prassinos. It begins "In the shadow of a (chatoyant) carpet, ah!" and continues in a scrawled, often indiscernible hand. An A4 figural pen and ink drawing reading "frontispiece" appears in the same set of manuscripts.

Further translation drafts in Mendelssohn's archive include, within a notebook from the late nineties, two heavily amended manuscript pages entitled "The Jacinth The Hyacinth."; Prassinos's name is given in the upper right corner (4/F/20). Among a series of grouped literary texts or miscellanies by Prassinos, this story is part of the record of her archive compiled by Mélusine, the on-line catalogue run by the Association pour la Recherche et l'Étude du Surréalisme (melusine-surrealisme.fr/wp/). Another Mendelssohn notebook includes pages titled "la confidente.'" and "G.P.", suggesting that the English passages on these A5 sheets are translations of Prassinos's 1962 novel, *La confidente* (4/E/49/1).

Included in this collection are poems from two files of Mendelssohn's manuscript translations of Prassinos's short poems (6/C/5/2–3). All are drawn from *La fièvre du labour* (roughly: the fever of ploughing), a Prassinos text published in 1989 by the French publisher Møtus and held at the Cambridge University Library. Mendelssohn cites this specific text on an A5 sheet bearing the first poem in 6/C/5/3. Of the 41 poems the collection contained, 39 were completely translated by Mendelssohn. An A4 sheet shows Mendelssohn working through the two remaining poems, but the translations remain unfinished and resist reconstruction (6/C/5/3). One poem begins: "No fairness no sharing"; the first line of the second reads: "You would not have left the mirror behind you". These are poems 24 and 25 of Prassinos's collection, where they read as follows:

> Pas d'équité nul partage.
> Transmis
> au bout du fil le chagrin vient de naître.
> Au commencement
> le voici aiguisé debout hurlant.
>
> Tu n'auras pas laissé de miroir derrière toi
> ni regards ni bouches
> pas même ton rire pour un autre temps.
> Ne serait-ce dans un nouveau cœur
> qu'une griffe à ta ressemblance.
> Toi lésineuse aride
> rivière sans affluents.

This same page also contains seven lines by Mendelssohn, signed "A.M." and reading as follows:

> He had a nasty face. the misinformed.
> male gossips protecting each other.
> search for scapegoats. their victims –
> are their scapegoats. once again –
> rape, assault, false charges,
> instant hatred, gestapo tactics –
> protect their privileges, in the name of

Along the right top corner of the page reads: "actors at the hustings." Beside the poem, a whimsical drawing of a landscape with a figure carrying a spear reads "melomane marries an exclamation mark."

In this same file is a second poem that is not part of *La fièvre du labour*, and reads:

> There were 3 & mine was One
>
> I have met that type since,
> his similar crew,
> who go around preaching love
> to those who already do.

Beneath the last line of the untitled Prassinos sestet translation beginning "Any glance over your numbers.", Mendelssohn draws a small doodle and writes: "Mot chiffré" (6/C/5/3).

In Prassinos's *La fièvre du labour* each short poem occupies its own unnumbered page. In the main, Mendelssohn's translations are true to the vocabulary of the original; eight poems of the volume are given below in French by way of comparison. Poems one and two read:

Appareiller. Obscur besoin.
Et toute plainte tout soupir
seront la fièvre du labour.

*

Une force vulnérable mais qui faisait loi
t'a tenue longtemps debout dans le jour.
Celle-là décimée
celui-ci s'épuise à gémir.

Poems 13 and 14 are as follows:

Ciel anachronique.
Sous lui
les nourrissons verts du printemps
couvent des rides empesées.
Pour quand leur premier sourire ?

*

Et pour quel feu
ou contre lui
les marronniers
ouvriraient-ils leurs ombrelles ?

Poems 30 and 31:

Une cage déserte.
Un souffle anime une plume oubliée.
La cage plus déserte encore.

*

L'aube
les cheveux tristes du silence.

Et soudain le ballet des fenêtres
leur musique annelée
invitant le jour.

The final two poems, 40 and 41, read:

Que reste-t-il sinon des avalanches
des squelettes brisés
des cris à tous les temps
et ce poids sur la mémoire
où le cœur et ses bateaux n'ont plus de place   ?

*

Aucun regard sur tes chiffres.
Nue sans déguisement
libre tu peux aller
avec tes erreurs tes désordres tes néants
planter le vin des mots à l'ordre du silence.
Mais l'absence?

The manuscripts show Mendelssohn continually rethinking her diction and syntax; the fairest copies are included in this volume in publication order. Where available, discernible edits are detailed below. Downward arrows signal words included and/or revised below the line, a rare editorial choice for Mendelssohn. Where Prassinos regularly leaves three blank spaces between word and question marks appearing at the end of her lines, Mendelssohn does not appear to adhere to this format.

Poem beginning "To appear.   Obscure need."
On the A5 sheet bearing this unedited translation, Mendelssohn cites the title and publication details of the Prassinos text from which the translations are drawn – *La fièvre du labour* (Møtus, 1989) – and in the upper right corner, draws an amorphous doodle with the word "unwise" to its left (6/C/5/3). The extended space in the first line is not evident in the Prassinos original; Prassinos's final full stop is missing in Mendelssohn's poem, and is restored here (ed.).

Poem beginning "A vulnerable strength but one that legally"
An A5 sheet has two translations of the poem (6/C/5/2). The variant not used in this text reads:

A vulnerable strength but one that legally
Kept you ~~st~~ upright ↓ standing ↓ for a long time by day.
That ~~was~~ ^one woman^ destroyed
this ~~nurses hope~~. ^one man^ wears ↓ exhausting himself ↓ ^wearing^ ^~~this~~ out^ itself ^himself^ out with hoping.

Poem beginning "Each morning"
Two versions of this poem occupy a single A5 sheet (6/C/5/2). Beneath the first translation, Mendelssohn writes another in which the first two lines are given in the original French: "Chaque matin / vider les cendres de l'ennui." The final three lines are in cleaner English than above; the poem as given combines the two variants (ed.). Additional edits to the first translation include:

> "ashes of boredom." was "~~cinders~~ ^ashes^ of boredom."
> "Sentinel shone" was "Sentry ^inel^ shone"
> Lines four and five were: "~~the beginning of the day / at the head~~" [*"at" is unclear*—ed.]

Poem beginning "The silence beats, within furiously."
In this A5 manuscript translation, "beats, within" is "beats, ~~inside~~ ^within^" (6/C/5/2). Prassinos's final full stop, not evident in manuscript, is restored (ed.).

Poem beginning "Urge desire"
Internal edits to this A5 manuscript translation include: "Urge desire" is "~~Push~~ ^Urge^ desire"; "mount" is "~~M~~mount"; and, "bee unwinding ever" reads "bee ~~divided~~ ^unwinding^ ever" (6/C/5/2).

Poem beginning "Too set is the flight"
In this A5 manuscript, the final line reads "To ~~collect~~ accumulate ~~other~~ ^further^ luggage." (6/C/5/2).

Poem beginning "The extent of the beast"
In line one of this A5 manuscript, Mendelssohn writes "extent" above "length", redacting neither (ed.). Line three begins "~~is supplies~~ it supports", and line four reads "~~Lov~~ Weightless" (6/C/5/2).

Poem beginning "Who now without your look"
In this A5 manuscript translation, "your look" was "your ~~glance~~ look"; "hereditary slabs" was "hereditary [~~*unclear word*~~—ed.] slabs" and "carry away the last" was "~~bear~~ ^carry away^ the last" (6/C/5/2). Prassinos's question mark at the end of line three, absent in Mendelssohn, is restored here (ed.).

Poem beginning "Fresh bread"
Line two of this A5 manuscript translation may read: "beneath the knife ~~on~~ that [*the final 't' is unclear or unfinished*—ed.] ~~enters~~ ^cuts it^" (6/C/5/2). Prassinos's final full stop is restored (ed.).

Poem beginning "Do not wait for the return."
Mendelssohn's edits to this A5 manuscript in 6/C/5/2 include: "dawn ^is^ forever" and "~~Every~~ ↓Every↓ evening". The final line originally began, "It rains"; Mendelssohn adds "Already" to line left and again beneath "It rains". In French, the final line has a single "already", reading: "Il pleut déjà demain sur la face d'or de ce matin." (ed.). Prassinos's final full stop is restored (ed.).

Poem beginning "Life will be round as the earth"
In this A5 manuscript translation, line one includes: "as ~~ea~~ the earth" and the final line reads: "will be ~~hard~~ ^tough^ ~~the~~ Eternity.

Enduring." (6/C/5/2). The final "Enduring" does not appear in the last line of Prassinos's poem, which concludes: "serait dure l'Eternité."

Poem beginning "No flower no tree"
In Mendelssohn's A5 manuscript translation, "No flower" reads "No flour", but in Prassinos, the word is "fleur" (ed.); line five concludes "so ~~gay~~ ^happy^" line six was "~~himself~~" (6/C/5/2).

Poem beginning "Anachronistic sky."
No edits are made to this A5 manuscript (6/C/5/2).

Poem beginning "And instead of which flame"
In this A5 manuscript in 6/C/5/2, line one begins "And ~~for~~ instead"; line two reads: "~~or a~~ or against ~~him~~ it"; and line four is "~~will they~~ open their parasols?"

Poem beginning "Tree an iceberg"
In this A5 manuscript translation, line one concludes "iceburg", and line four reads: "The other ~~substantial~~ ~~nourishment~~ / ~~nourishing substance~~ / nutritious ~~material~~. fabric" (6/C/5/2). Prassinos's final full stop is restored (ed.).

Poem beginning "On the lawn"
In this A5 manuscript translation, line three is "new ~~nervous~~ furtive" and in line four, "closely" had a different suffix in the first instance (6/C/5/2).

Poem beginning "When it rains"
Line two of this poem reads: "~~wise~~ ^are^ ~~the~~ daisies wise"; line three begins: "~~who~~ ^to^ close" (6/C/5/2). The question mark in line three is Prassinos's, not Mendelssohn's; Mendelssohn adds a final question mark that is not in the original (ed.). Along the bottom of this A5 manuscript reads: "les pâquerettes   daisies."

Poem beginning "Red shore"
On this A4 manuscript, above "Red shore", Mendelssohn writes: "~~Red strike~~" (6/C/5/3).

Poem beginning "The sea is a great fish that wriggles."
Line one of this A4 manuscript includes "fish ~~to~~ that". Line three reads: "the scales ^wear ~~thin~~away^ & and renew themselves" [*ampersand unclear*—ed.]. The last line is: "~~with~~ ~~with~~ in parallel ~~sounds~~ glamour"; the second "with" and "in" are below the line (6/C/5/3). The full stop at the ends of lines one and five appear in Prassinos's text, but not Mendelssohn's (ed.).

Poem beginning "Apple tree, village of fruits."
The first line of Mendelssohn's A4 manuscript reads: "Apple tree, ~~fruits~~ ^village of fruits^ ~~village of fruits~~" (6/C/5/3); the full stop appears in Prassinos's original, but not in Mendelssohn (ed.). Line three concludes: "upsets ~~on time~~ in solicitation." To poem left is a large, squared-off drawing; at page bottom are two small drawings: a square doodle in bottom right, an abstract figure in page centre.

Poem beginning "The log enthuses and lives in its burnings."
Above the poem reads: "~~Hard work~~" (6/C/5/3). Line one begins: "The log ~~burns~~ ^enthuses^ and". In line three, "seize" may be "seized" or "seizes" (ed.), and "lighthouse a ship." is "lighthouse a ~~sailor~~. ^ship^". Lines four and five are heavily edited, reading: "~~Will you ignore~~ it ^Does it not know^ where ~~the door~~ it ~~carries~~ / where its ^its^ joy in seduction carries it". "[J]oy" is written, redacted, and rewritten below the line. In Prassinos's text, these lines read: "Ignore-t-elle où la porte / sa joie de séduire ?" There are three drawings and two other poems on this A4 manuscript (see above, "Apple tree, village of fruits").

Poem beginning "As evening collects thoughts"
In this A4 manuscript, line one includes "~~resembles~~ ^collects^ thoughts". Beneath the complete translation, Mendelssohn writes out the final line in French: "Comme le matin est tenir de juger." This poem is on the same page as "Apple tree, village of fruits" and three drawings (see above).

Poem beginning "Your voice has the form of a wounded gesture"
In the top right corner of the A4 manuscript, Mendelssohn writes: "mementos" next to an ovoid doodle (6/C/5/3). Line one may read "the form~~s~~" and line two concludes: "to ~~the~~ binding".

Poem beginning "Here is the brown season"
In the A4 manuscript in 6/C/5/3, "birds' names" is unpunctuated, and in the final line, Mendelssohn may have placed an extended gap between "Hiatus." and "This" (ed.). Prassinos's final line reads: "Lacune. Ca sera pour une autre vie."

Poem beginning "It is the butterfly of death"
This A4 manuscript translation is unedited (6/C/5/3).

Poem beginning "What order would protect us from where"
Line one includes "order ~~will~~ ^would^" and line two reads "we ~~were ab~~ could live?" (6/C/5/3). An indiscernible redaction appears between "the" and "advent?" in line three. Line four reads "that ~~we~~ [~~*unclear word*~~ —ed.] ~~pluck the~~ ^the^ poppy's". Mendelssohn leaves an extended space between stanzas, while Prassinos leaves a single blank line (ed.). This A4 manuscript has two squared-off doodles along page bottom, and contains the poem beginning "O little house of oak" (see below).

Poem beginning "O little house of oak"
After the first two lines, this A4 manuscript translation is heavily rewritten (6/C/5/3). Line three reads "^Smooth^ Walls ~~united~~ in a ^to a^ ~~straight~~ body." There are two versions of the last two lines; the version not used here is: "roof sealing ~~at last~~ ^finally^ in the return / ~~of~~ innocence" (ed.). The concluding full stop is in Prassinos's original only (ed.). Two squared-off doodles appear in the bottom corners of this A4 sheet, as does the poem beginning "What order would protect us from where" (see above).

Poem beginning "A deserted cage."
Line one of this A4 manuscript reads: "A ~~de~~ ~~empty~~ ^deserted^ cage." and line three was: "The cage still ~~emptier.~~ ^more^ deserted." (6/C/5/3).

Poem beginning “Dawn”
This A4 manuscript goes unedited (6/C/5/3). The extended blank in line three is not in Prassinos’s original, and the final full stop is Prassinos’s only (ed.).

Poem beginning “Closed on the table”
Barring an indiscernible redaction in line three – “then [~~*unclear letter or letters*~~—ed.] the eyes” – this is a clean A4 manuscript page (6/C/5/3).

Poem beginning “A motionless bird.”
In this A4 manuscript in 6/C/5/3, Mendelssohn leaves a space between lines four and five that does not appear in Prassinos (ed.).

Poem beginning “And you handsome horse with your virile twisted mane”
In the A4 manuscript translation in 6/C/5/3, “twisted mane” reads “twisted main”, and the concluding full stop of line four appears in Prassinos’s text only (ed.). Line two includes “know ^how^ to”. A right-justified doodle appears mid-way down the page, and a larger drawing runs along page bottom, to the right of which reads: “On what grounds.”

Poem beginning “In the night”
This unedited manuscript translation is on A4 in 6/C/5/3. The concluding full stop is Prassinos’s (ed.).

Poem beginning “I have a sun of you on the tongue”
On this A4 manuscript, line two includes “churchy ~~freshness~~ ^cool^”; within line three is “my ~~fai~~ defeated”, and line four reads: “wisteria ~~that~~ ^that^ ~~hangs~~ stooped” (6/C/5/3).

Poem beginning “Know it”
In this A4 manuscript in 6/C/5/3, line two includes “is no~~t~~ more” and within line three is “of ^the^ wood”. In line three, “than our Christ” reads “that our Christ” (ed.). To the right of the last two lines, Mendelssohn writes Prassinos’s original conclusion: “que nos Christ de bois / ouverts au bord des champs”. Prassinos’s final full stop is restored here (ed.).

Poem beginning “Day sets”
In A4 manuscript, beneath “on the wing of a butterfly”, Mendelssohn writes “~~on the butterfly’s wing~~” (6/C/5/3). The question mark appears in Prassinos’s original only (ed.).

Poem beginning “I have waited for you so much”
In this A4 manuscript translation, the “O” of line two was “o” (6/C/5/3). Mendelssohn replicates Prassinos’s footnote.

Poem beginning “Will it pause without avalanches”
Within line four of this A4 manuscript in 6/C/5/3 reads: “weight son the” (ed.).

Poem beginning “Any glance over your numbers.”
This A4 manuscript suggests that line two was originally two lines, rendered: “high cloud openly / ~~openly~~”. Final variant line

four concludes: "your ~~births~~ nothings". The sheet bears a Mendelssohn poem beginning "I have met that type since," and two drawings (see above introduction to Prassinos translations).

Grace Lake, "Deux poèmes", translated by Robert Davreu, *Po&sie,* no. 98 (2002), 110–12.
Edited by French poet and translator Michel Deguy, this "numéro anglais" of *Po&sie* may have been prompted or encouraged by the British poet Douglas Oliver, the poet and editor of *Gare du Nord* (see above notes, 1997) who was living in Paris at the time (email from Rod Mengham, 3 August 2017). The issue includes translations from a broad historical swathe of writers from the United Kingdom, including Emily Brontë, Gerard Manley Hopkins, Basil Bunting, and Philip Larkin. Among the contemporary poets are Oliver, Carol Ann Duffy, W. S. Graham, Alan Halsey, Geoffrey Hill, and Rod Mengham. Mendelssohn's translator, Robert Davreu, was one of a number who contributed to this project; a poet and writer, Davreu was on the editorial board of *Po&sie* from 1983 until his death in 2013.

Although regularly publishing as Anna Mendelssohn at this time, Mendelssohn's poetry is attributed to Grace Lake. Her biography reads:

> Grace Lake, de son vrai nom Anna Mendelson, est née dans le Cheshire en 1948. Après des études musicales, puis à l'Université d'Essex, elle est partie enseigner l'anglais et le français en Turquie, avant de revenir en Angleterre en 1970. Elle a traduit la poésie turque des années trente, et enseigné à St Edmunds College à Cambridge. Elle a publié *La Facciata* (1988), *Viola tricolor* (1993) et contribué à *The Virago Book of Love Poetry* (1990), et *Poets on Writing: Britain 1970–1992*, ed. Denise Riley (Macmillan, 1992).

This biography alters the spelling of Mendelssohn's "real name", gives Cheshire as her place of birth, and states that she studied music before going to the University of Essex. Mendelssohn's birth surname is Mendleson, and she was born in Stockport, which was historically in county Cheshire, but has expanded into Lancashire, and since 1974, is identified as part of Greater Manchester.

The biography indicates that Mendelssohn taught English and French in Turkey before returning to England in 1970 and describes her as a translator of 1930s Turkish poetry and a teacher at St Edmund's College at the University of Cambridge. This last fact arises in none of her other biographies, and it is unlikely that Mendelssohn taught extensively, if at all, at Cambridge. As in most of Mendelssohn's biographies, the past publications list is selective.

"La Facciata" was published in English in Poetical Histories in 1988 and again in *Conductors of Chaos* in 1996, as is "1526". *Viola tricolor* (1993) includes the first English publication of "1526" (see above notes). In *Po&sie*, line eight of "1526" is slightly indented at the outset, as it is not in any other publication, and this is assumed to be a printing error (ed.).

Grace Lake, "Three Poems", *Jacket*, no. 20 (December 2002).
Forty issues of the on-line contemporary poetry magazine *Jacket* were published by John Tranter between 1997 and 2010; it was taken over by the University of Pennsylvania in 2010, when it became *Jacket2*. The full archive remains on-line (jacket2.org).

Issue twenty of *Jacket* focused on Cambridge, England, and featured poet-critics such as Veronica Forrest-Thomson and Hugh Sykes Davies, as well as extracts from Cambridge-based journals, among them, Keston Sutherland's *Quid*, Peter Robinson's *Perfect Bound* (1976–79), and Simon Jarvis and Drew Milne's *Parataxis*. A selection of Mendelssohn's 1992 submission was chosen to represent *Parataxis* (see above notes). Past *Parataxis* contributors showcased in this *Jacket* included Andrea Brady, Clark Coolidge, Fanny Howe, Dell Olsen, Denise Riley, Drew Milne, and John Wilkinson, among others.

In *Jacket*, Mendelssohn's poems are replicated in a compacted manner, and as such, the *Parataxis* formatting, including the right-justified title of "i. m. laura riding", is used here (ed.). Further information about the gestation of Mendelssohn's poems is given below.

"fulgencies"
A manuscript of "fulgencies" exists in 5/B/2/50. It is titled "fulgence" and in the upper right corner, reads: "E.B.B. / Isaiah's poetry of diction." In addition to variations in capitalisation, differences from the published version include the following, with many edits made in differing ink:

In line 1: "them as in a dream" was "them in a dream"
In line 2: "pinioning" was "pinioned"
In line 3: "the wall" was "The ~~doo~~ wall" and all definite articles are capitalised
In line 4: "she fled their confounded" was "She flew from their ~~condemnable~~ ^confounded^"
In line 6: "down to join the lead" was "down ~~and~~ ^to^ join~~ed~~ ~~up ^with^ to~~ the lead"
In line 7: "effulgent material pliant not needing fire" was "effulgen~~cey~~t material ~~which~~ [~~*unclear letter*~~—ed.] ~~with~~ ^pliant not needing fire^"
In line 9: "where millgirls" was "Where ~~on her~~ millgirls"
From line 14, the phrase "on that fatal day" initially occupied its own line; it was amended to "whose skirts [*could be "shirts"*—ed.], ^on that fatal day,^ caught alight ~~on that fatal day~~"
In part 2, line 2: "entrances mavis" was "entranced mavis"
In part 2, line 3: "same none too partial to gaskell" was "same they're ~~not~~ [~~*unclear letter/word*~~—ed.] ~~liking~~ ^none too partial^ partial to Gaskell"
In part 2, line 4: "reminds them" was "~~it~~ reminds them"

"nattering swans"
A manuscript of this poem is titled "nattering swans."; in line three, "crows'" goes unpunctuated, and line 13 may conclude "about something~~s~~ else" (5/B/1/7). The last two lines read: "alder twigs, rationing gneiss handbooks inside / ~~in~~ dusty wrecked box offices perched ^precariously^ high over ^from?^ plush becks." The double spacing after full stops within the line, retained in *Parataxis* but elided in *Jacket*, is evident in manuscript.

Anna Mendelssohn, *Vanishing Points: New Modernist Poems*, ed. Rod Mengham and John Kinsella, Salt Publishing (2004), 172–79.
According to John Kinsella, the poets in this collection were chosen for their capacity to "challeng[e] us to think about how the lyric works" (xv). Arguing that the lyric has been decried throughout the twentieth century as outmoded or as redefined beyond recognition, Kinsella lauds lyric as the pre-eminent, persevering vanguard form, thanks to its "paradoxical combination of the universal and the centring of self" (xiv). In keeping with this modernist trajectory, fellow editor Rod Mengham considers their subtitle one that "proposes elements of continuity with an historically identifiable form of international writing that sets at a premium experiments with form and language" (xviii). Not postmodern, but late modernist; not traditional or status quo, but "poetry [that] constitutes itself as antagonism" (xix). Mendelssohn appears in *Vanishing Points* alongside American poets John

Ashbery, Stephen Rodefer, Marjorie Welish, Lyn Hejinian, and Lee Ann Brown; Canadian poet Lisa Robertson; and British poets J. H. Prynne, Barry MacSweeney, John Wilkinson, and Ulli Freer, among others.

Mendelssohn's contributor's note reads:

> Anna Mendelssohn was born in Cheshire in 1948. She trained through the New Era Academy of Drama and Music (1957–67) and performed in Northern Music Festivals until 1967. She was educated at Stockport High School for Girls, and at the University of Essex (1967–9). She spent the following year in Turkey, teaching English and French and translating 1930s Turkish poetry, surrealist and social realist. She has lived in Stockport, London, Sheffield and Cambridge. As Grace Lake she has published *Viola Tricolor* (1993), *Bernache Nonette* [*sic*] (1995), and *Tondo Aquatique* (1997), all with Equipage, and as Anna Mendelssohn she has published *Implacable Art* (2000) with Folio/Equipage.

A letter to contributors from Mengham and Kinsella, dated 18 September 2001, indicates that the anthology was slow in gestation, and was originally titled *Anthology of International Avant-Garde Poetry in English*. Requesting updated biographies and written permissions to publish, this letter is filed at Sussex with anthology proofs (SxMs109/5/A/24a). In the same file, a photocopied reply from Mendelssohn dated 3 October 2001 points out that within her poem "Photrum", "Harry Watt's film" is incorrectly punctuated. To this, Mendelssohn adds that the film is *Night Mail* (1936), "only one of many he made. Music by Britten in this case. John Grierson produced it." In fact, Grierson narrated; along with Basil Wright, Harry Watt directed and produced. On the right half of the page, Mendelssohn draws a column of four black birds in profile; beside an arrow pointing to the column, she writes: "Example of my capacity to draw normal looking things (animate or still)". Under "International Poetry Anthology", she writes: "Formal permission is granted to publish what the editors consider worth publishing on the sole condition that not one line (I am tempted to add 'word') is taken and used for Any other purpose."

Mendelssohn photocopies her corrected proofs, which follow the same running order as in publication. Spacing differs, as more than one poem appears on each page, and page numbers change between proofs (134–39) and text (172–79), but Mendelssohn remains the nineteenth contributor in both. Substantive corrections include commas added at the end of lines two and four of "Strictly Personal"; to the conclusion of line eight of the same poem, "to." is added after "no". In line six of "Photrum", Mendelssohn corrects "rehearsal" to "rehearsed"; in the same poem, she appears to add, then redact, a possessive in "Henry Watts".

Mendelssohn's anthology contributions usually include previously published material, but none of her poems in *Vanishing Points* appear elsewhere, as is noted in the "Acknowledgements". A copy of Mendelssohn's complete entry is filed at Sussex but was not part of her original papers (5/A/31a). An untitled, two-page, landscape-formatted, photocopied manuscript of "footsteps climb whereas they descend" exists in her files; a rusted staple has been removed from one corner (5/A/31). In part three of this draft, the full stop after "blue" is a comma. "Mendelssohn" is written under each of the three numbered sections of the poem, and the bottom right corner of page two reads "A. M. 1999."

Grace Lake, *Out of Everywhere: Linguistically Innovative Poetry by Women in North America & the UK*, ed. Maggie O'Sullivan, Reality Street Editions (2006; first edition 1996), 197–205.

In her introduction, Anglo-Irish poet Maggie O'Sullivan explains the impetus behind the collection, which began in 1994 at the invitation of Ken Edwards and Wendy Mulford of Reality Street Editions:

> many of [these poets], through brave insistence and engagement in explorative, formally progressive language practices, find themselves excluded from conventional, explicitly generically committed or thematic anthologies of women's poetry. Excluded from 'women's canons', such work does, however, connect up with linguistically innovative work by men who have themselves also transcended the agenda-based and cliché-ridden rallying positions of mainstream poetry. (9)

In her postscript, Wendy Mulford echoes the desire "to showcase work by women who, broadly speaking, were working with language – disordering and deconstructive techniques, at the leading edge of new poetics" (252). Echoing O'Sullivan, Mulford suggests that many other poets could have appeared in the collection, such as Mei-mei Berssenbrugge, Lydia Davis, Erica Hunt, and Jean Day. The final collection includes work by women from Canada, the USA, and the UK, among them, Rae Armantrout, Nicole Brossard, Barbara Guest, Lyn Hejinian, Susan Howe, Denise Riley, Lisa Robertson, Leslie Scalapino, Rosmarie Waldrop, and Marjorie Welish.

Mendelssohn's biography reads: "GRACE LAKE was born in 1948. Poems have appeared in many magazines and in the pamphlets *La Facciata* (Poetical Histories, 1989), *viola tricolor* (1993) and *Bernache Nonnette* (1995), both from Equipage, Cambridge." In the citations list for Mendelssohn's submission, "concilia", "Silk & Wild Tulips", and the poems beginning "by gardenias i cannot telephone" and "She walked where she should have stood still, stock still." are attributed to *Bernache Nonnette* (1995). The poems "twelve to midnight" and "Ordered into Quarantine" are attributed solely to *viola tricolor* (complete citations below). Mendelssohn's "the reduction by not first" is treated as a poem title, but it is the first line of a stanza in earlier versions of "Silk & Wild Tulips" (see below).

"Ordered into Quarantine"
Mendelssohn published this poem five times: in *Active in Airtime* (1993), *viola tricolor* (1993), *A State of Independence* (1998), and in the two editions of *Out of Everywhere* (2006). In *Out of Everywhere*, the "existence" of line four is rendered as "exercise". As it is "existence" in three previous publications, the original word has been reinstated (ed.).

One of four *viola tricolor* poems previously published in *Active in Airtime*, no. 2 (1993), "Ordered into Quarantine" is also the only poem from that submission that Mendelssohn altered on republication. A partial *Active in Airtime* proof shows Mendelssohn adding "^for^" between "seriously," and "what" in line one of stanza two (5/A/14).

The *viola tricolor* version differs from *Active in Airtime* in the following ways, some of which are replicated in a hand-edited typescript in 5/A/15/4:

> "this lacks voice" was "this though lacks voice" ("~~though~~" in 5/A/15/4)
> "pity that you took" was "pity that you take" ("~~take~~ ^took^" in 5/A/15/4)
> "seriously, for what fears" was "seriously, what fears" ("^for^" in 5/A/15/4)
> "onto a stone floor" was "onto the stone floor" ("onto ^a^ stone floor" in 5/A/14/4)
> "proved useful" was "Proved Useful" ("~~P~~^p^roved ~~U~~^u^seful" in 5/A/15/4)

Additional handwritten changes that arise in typescript include: title underlining, a full stop after "self strangulation", "onto a stone" is "onto ^a^ stone", and "for the lovely" was is "for ~~a~~ ^the^ lovely". In a submission for an Arts Council Award application, dated "1993/4.", Mendelssohn expresses an intention to add "Ordered into Quarantine" between "dulc." (numbered page four) and "twelve to midnight." (numbered five) by writing, in the top left corner of the typescript of the latter poem, "Ordered into

Quarantine (p4½).” (5/A/16). The Sussex archive also holds a proof of “Ordered into Quarantine” in the same font and layout as used in *Out of Everywhere*, dated 27 October 1995 (5/A/19).

“twelve to midnight”
First published in *viola tricolor* (1993), this poem was republished in both editions of *Out of Everywhere: Linguistically Innovative Poetry by Women in North America & the UK* (2006). For full information on the positioning of the poem within *viola tricolor*, see above notes.

A typescript of “twelve to midnight.” exists in Mendelssohn’s submission for an Arts Council grant dated “1993/4.” (5/A/16). Differences between this typescript and the published poem include: the fifth line of stanza three starts beneath the second “t” of “potentially” in the line above and reads: “they treat us as walking jokes. family lore. i grew consciously”; the last word is added by hand before photocopying. In stanza four, “struggling home from school” is “[*illegible hand-written word*—ed.] home from school”; in stanza five, “chalking on stone” was “chalking on stones”. A typescript in 5/A/15/4 is hand-edited pre-copying; in it, line three of stanza one reads “one ~~which~~ that interprets” (“that” is below the line); all other changes listed in the 5/A/16 variant are corrected in line with publication.

Differences between the 2006 and 1993 versions include: in stanza three, “that is all, anything” was “that is all. anything” and in stanza five, “onto a stone floor” was “onto the stone floor”. Although the wording is identical in the final stanza, in *viola tricolor*, as in the archived typescripts, the final stanza occupies nine lines, whereas in *Out of Everywhere* the lines are shorter and number 12. The first words of the nine-line variant are: “i”; “they”; “explained”; “dancing”; “he”; “long”; “an”; “that”; and “hands”.

In addition to the conflation of stanzas one and two, a manuscript of “twelve to midnight” shows Mendelssohn’s earlier formulations, among them: “that is ~~their~~ all.”; “~~everything~~ anything” (5/B/2/69). Distinctions between publication and manuscript include:

> “one that interprets” was “one which interprets”
> “bed springs” was “bed ~~coils~~”
> “a mattress” was ““~~my~~ ^a^ mattress”
> “that is all.” was “that is ~~their~~ all.”
> “anything” was “~~every~~^any^ thing”
> “treated as a walking joke.” was “the men are so horrible they treat us as walking jokes.”
> “i grew consciously” was “i grew”
> “to visit us.” was “to visit. I was a horrible child.”
> “struggling home” was “I’d crawl home”.

The last two stanzas of this manuscript differ from publication, and read:

> as it was being played. I replaced all the receivers which were left dangling.
> children are being read through what was not my writing . . they will be lead by lies.
> Take those idiots away from my brain. It’s your Left not mine. I don’t
> go around smashing up people or raiding offices or strangling turkeys.
>
> It should not be at issue. my soul has been bound by electric currents
> Men who use ~~the~~ language punitively never retreat or make public apologies per

When they sense the delight in a new form of torture need for need, pound ~~for~~ pound.
my use of 'I' either scorned or cancelled, over-ruled ~~or~~ T was mugged.

In the last line, the top bar of the "T" is rounded and umbrella-shaped; it recurs in the human profile Mendelssohn draws beneath the poem, placed roughly where the cerebrum might lie (ed.).

"Silk & Wild Tulips."
This poem appears in *Mendleson's Metronome* (an early version of *Bernache Nonnette*; second draft only), *Bernache Nonnette* (1995), *A State of Independence* (1998), and *Out of Everywhere: Linguistically Innovative Poetry by Women in North America & the UK* (2006). See also notes associated with those collections.

Differences arise between the three published variants of "Silk & Wild Tulips". In 1995, the title bears a full stop that does not recur in any other publication but is allowed to stand in all available typescripts and proofs. In *Bernache Nonnette*, the "concur" of line one is "concurr" and the "char" of the penultimate line of stanza three is "charr"; as this double "r" recurs in *MM2*, two typescripts in 5/A/17/4, and again in 5/A/17/5, this spelling is reinstated (ed.). In 1995 and 1998, line six of stanza two begins "Provokation" and there is a comma after "Indicating slips" in that stanza's last line; as this spelling and punctuation is preserved in *MM2* and throughout 5/A/17/4 and 5, it is replicated here, even as in *Out of Everywhere*, "Provocation" is used and the comma is excised (ed.). Unlike any other publication or draft, in 1998, the titular ampersand is "and"; as in some drafts, but no other publication, "the tip of a tongue" in line eight is "the tongue", and the "I" of lines 14 and 16 is "i". Finally, there are five stanzas in "Silk & Wild Tulips" in 1995 and 1998, and four in *Out of Everywhere*. Stanza five begins: "the reduction by not first". Given the incorrect citation of "the reduction by not first" as a poem title in the acknowledgements of *Out of Everywhere* (see above), the format of 1995 and 1998 is retained (ed.).

Differences between *Bernache Nonnette* (1995) and archived typescripts of "Silk & Wild Tulips" include:

"A portrait of throated wires through blood" was "What is love? o what is love? my portrait of throated wires through blood" (recurs in both typescripts, 5/A/17/4; "ofthroated" in 5/A/17/2; changes are made in 5/A/17/5)

"the tip of a tongue, a silk white dove." was "the tip of the tongue, the silk white dove." (recurs in both typescripts, 5/A/17/4; see also 5/A/17/2; corrected in 5/A/17/5)

"Prussian myzi" was "Prussian mysi" (5/A/17/2) and "Prussian muzi" (5/A/17/4; correction made in a second typescript in same file)

"Open'd by background loss, closed by" was "Open by back ground loss, close by" ("backgroundloss" in 5/A/17/2; correction made in one 5/A/17/4 typescript)

"roses rouge foncés," was "rouge roses fonce," (5/A/17/2 and one typescript in 5/A/17/4; correction made in one 5/A/17/4 typescript)

In the typescripts of 5/A/17/4 and 5, the "I" of lines 3, 14, 16, is in lower case, and the poem title bears a full stop; in both 5/A/17/4 typescripts, it is also underlined. In 5/A/17/5, next to "What is love? o what is love?" in stanza one, Mendelssohn writes to the typesetter of *Bernache Nonnette*, Ulli Freer: "Ulli, Are you sure that line 4 is as I wrote it? I don't remember writing what is love? here" and then rewrites the stanza as it appears in publication, adding, "Is that O.K.?" The change from "my portrait" to "A portrait" also occurs here. On the same page, next to the first line of stanza three, Mendelssohn writes: "• myzi, if only I could wait for"; at page bottom, a footnote reads: "• myzi is a muse." Around "these fakes" in line three, stanza three, she places double quotes, underlines "fakes", and writes adjacently: "(could you check this – the word is <u>not</u> 'fakes' is it?)". "[T]hese fakes" it remains.

An early, untitled draft of "Silk & Wild Tulips" appears in 5/B/2/71; the same file holds a manuscript of "by gardenias i cannot telephone" (see below). The order is uncertain, but these two double-sided A5 sheets read:

I am afraid of my father's power
his two faced power
whilst women condemn my poverty
and urge me to return to the man I am most afraid of
this money business
who does make a million from what I don't want
him to speak of them in the same breath as
emotionally unstable, dark thoughts tearing absent flesh,

what is love? o what is love?
to be closed in upon from a great distance
the letters shall remain closed
how perfect I have to be no one knows
the desert and the glass

I love the crown
but does it accept that
nervous of his refusal to stand
we do grow
god how I hate the censure of my mind [*ink changes in this line*]
save us from the ignorance of silence

[*end side*]

who was I meant to be / a plate of food
the horrible idioms of my youth
the revolting language I had to listen to
Yes! I read Mandelstam. Yes! I read Mandelstam [*second "!" may be "?"*—ed.]
& what did you allow me? a Graveyard

when our love is assaulted & abused
I defend my love
to myself
and Never Never Reveal it Again
to the disgusting licentious voyeurs

Every line is wicked to them
Every glance at the moon if it reaches voice
He's Insane.
He created a black pit for me to fall into.
I curse those wars   Curse them
Curse them

[*end side*]

it was not me who made the comment
he grew bitter clinging onto it
but I was there yes! and I did not hear it.

I should hear more, it stops the sound of his voice
the working woman basket full of periwinkles
slugged into work, the pretty gift
a persian violet, [*a full stop may follow the comma*—ed.]
I was grateful, but that gratitude
could not have been extended
& he takes the other half,
the heaven of free space,
the half that was yours.

that they call victory.
before they destroy it.
I don't want them to come here.

[*end side*]

I Dare hardly look at the day
as I used to rejoice in its presence
& watch my arm turn brown in the sun
and forget being dragged back from Paris
and forget being dragged away from my mind
that could only gaze at the sky here & wait for evening.

there was no reason to return
Surely not to look at an apron
that Arshile Gorky anyway painted
stories on

funereal gladioli in that horrible colour
that deepened into armchairs
was He in the stuffing?
this is probably what killed Jesus
an inappropriate comment
knock on wood or the midnight hour
& the striking of the organum.

Poem beginning "by gardenias i cannot telephone"
This poem appears in both variants of *Mendleson's Metronome* (early drafts of *Bernache Nonnette*), *Bernache Nonnette* (1995), and *Out of Everywhere: Linguistically Innovative Poetry by Women in North America & the UK* (2006). See also above notes to earlier collections.

A left-justified A5 manuscript of this poem exists in 5/B/2/71. In addition to minor changes in punctuation and capitalisation, differences from publication include:

"run from me" was "run for me"
"a clever poetess would flee" was "clever poetesses flee"
"made of" was "made from"
"these gardenia clouds" was "~~my~~ ^this^ gardenia clouds"
Line 10 was: "that are turning into powder blue for my chalk face"
"fading too" was "fading, too"
The last line was, in full: "yellow silk"

In the A4 photocopied manuscript of *MM1*, the poem occupies the upper right corner, in page centre, Mendelssohn writes "[dead centred]". In *MM1*, "made of potatoes" was "made from potatoes" (5/A/17/1). In *MM2*, the poem is centred, and "your heart darkens" was "your heart darkening" (5/A/17/2). The latter change is made on the centred 5/A/17/5 typescript.

"concilia."
This poem appears in both variants of *Mendleson's Metronome* (early drafts of *Bernache Nonnette*), *Bernache Nonnette* (1995), and *Out of Everywhere: Linguistically Innovative Poetry by Women in North America & the UK* (2006). See also above notes to earlier collections. The *Out of Everywhere* version differs from *Bernache Nonnette* in that a comma, rather than a full stop, follows "unglobed throat" and the extended space is excised after "tongueless fish." Given the prevalence of this full stop and spacing in other variants, this formatting is reinstated here (ed.; see SxMs109/5/A/17/5 and 6 for both spacing and punctuation; punctuation only in 5/A/17/4 and *MM1* and *MM2*, or 5/A/17/1 and 2, and 5/B/2/88). In *Out of Everywhere*, the poem is centred and the title is left-justified, capitalised, and without a full stop; in *Bernache Nonnette*, as in 5/A/17/5 and 6, both are centred, and the title begins with a lower-case "c" and has a full stop. In *MM1* and 5/A/17/4, the poem is left-justified, the title full-stopped and severely right-justified. The title is replicated here as in the majority of Mendelssohn's drafts and publications (ed.).

Both unstopped title and poem are left-justified in a manuscript of "concilia." written on the continuous stationery used in a dot-matrix printer (5/B/2/88). Manuscript and publication differ in punctuation and capitalisation, as in manuscript line 17, "sanctioned, who is not, the licentiate of Magister Logos." Further, "tiled frames fused" was "tiled frames over fused". Above the title reads: "Begriefe." (*unclear*—ed.), "conceives", and "vollendung completion". A doodle appears poem left. The verso includes references, possibly not in Mendelssohn's hand, to the Zionist Schlomo Ben-Yosef, a Professor Jermiah Yavel (possibly in or of Jerusalem), and a rendering of the word "self" in Hebrew. Mendelssohn draws a cube and a square with a small "6" beside it. At page bottom, she writes: "aboulie", "maieutic", and "arturo barea" (Barea was a Spanish journalist exiled to England after the Spanish Civil War), "unamuno" (presumably in reference to the Spanish Basque writer and professor, Miguel de Unamuno y Jugo), "g. p. stern" (the "g" could be "q", the surname might be "stein"—ed.), and lastly, the name of a German soldier, author, and entomologist, "ernst jünger."

Poem beginning "She Walked where she should have stood still, stock still"
This poem is included in both copies of *Mendleson's Metronome* (early versions of *Bernache Nonnette*), *Bernache Nonnette* (1995), *A State of Independence* (1998), and *Out of Everywhere: Linguistically Innovative Poetry by Women in North America & the UK* (2006).

In *Out of Everywhere*, the phrase "stock still." of line one is excised. Given that it appears in 1995 and 1998 (in latter instance, without extended spacing), and the additional spacing goes uncorrected in a well worked-over proof in 5/A/17/5 and again in 5/A/17/2, the phrase and formatting are reinstated here (ed.). In all other regards, the poem is the same in all three publications, barring that Tony Frazer, editor of *A State of Independence*, chose to call it "[untitled]", presumably to distinguish it from the end of the poem that precedes it on the same page.

Excepting minor changes in punctuation and spacing, the poem is rendered identically in the two editions of *Mendleson's Metronome* (5/A/17/1 and 2). In the first variant, it follows directly on from the poem beginning "Pall Mall." and Mendelssohn writes above the left-justified poem, "(to be centred)".

Anna Mendelssohn, "Three Poems", *Cambridge Literary Review*, vol. 1, no. 1 (2009), 43–45.
According to founding editors Boris Jardine and Lydia Wilson, the *Cambridge Literary Review* grew out of "a realisation that [Cambridge] is awash with great writers but sorely lacking in creative fora", thereby generating "the perceived and real isolation of Cambridge's literary groupings & output" ("From the editors", vol. 1, no. 1). The journal garnered financial support from the Cambridge University 800th Anniversary Fund. Submissions exceeded expectations: planned as a slender magazine, the first perfect-bound issue was over 270 pages. Between 2009 and 2017, contributors to ten issues included Drew Milne, Stephen Rodefer, J. H. Prynne, Lisa Robertson, and Catherine Wagner, among many others. Rosie Šnajdr became a third editor.

Issue one offers short essays about Cambridge poetry, and poems from Mendelssohn, Ian Patterson, Rod Mengham, and John Wilkinson. Mendelssohn's biography reads:

> ANNA MENDELSSOHN was born in 1948 in Stockport, Cheshire, and in the mid-1970s moved to Cambridge, where she is a member of the University. Previous publications include *Viola Tricolor* (1993), *Bernache Nonnette* (1995) and *Tondo Aquatique* (1997) – all published by Equipage, and *Implacable Art* (Folio / Equipage 2000). *py* is forthcoming from Oystercatcher Press.

Mendelssohn lived in Cambridge briefly in the late seventies, returning permanently in 1983.

Bearing no date or publication information, a three-page typescript of these poems in the Sussex archive is titled "**Three poems by Anna Mendelssohn**" (SxMs109/5/A/36). On the poem beginning "Using the second person singular", handwritten edits correct the spelling of the name of the German Expressionist painter, Gabriele Münter, adding the final "e" to the first name and the umlaut to the surname. The umlaut does not appear in publication and is reinstated (ed.). In stanza three, line two of the same poem, there is no comma after "flood logic", and in line three, "romans" is unpunctuated. The second and third poems are identical to publication.

Anna Mendelssohn, *py. : a book of acrostics for p.e.g.*, Norfolk: Oystercatcher Press (2009)

This A5 chapbook was Mendelssohn's final publication, and copyright is given to her estate. There is a pen and ink illustration by Mendelssohn on the white card cover; the phrase: "Rd. sign. 38" is embedded within the abstract drawing. Inside the text, there is a Mendelssohn sketch – pixellated in reproduction – that includes three figures. The back cover offers information about other poets published by Peter Hughes's Oystercatcher Press, among them, Kelvin Corcoran, Allen Fisher, Michael Haslam, Simon Perril, Sophie Robinson, Peter Riley, and Carol Watts.

[P]y. is unpaginated, and consists of ten pages of poetry, and 27 untitled sestets. All are acrostics: 24 of the word "poetry", three of "poésie". The title is comprised of the first and last letters of "poetry". The subtitle is "a book of acrostics for p.e.g.", an acronym formed from the first initials of Mendelssohn's children Poppy, Emerald, and George. In a letter intended to accompany a gift of this text to her cousin Barry Benser and his wife, Mendelssohn writes: "an acrostic was the first poem that came out of me at primary school [. . . .] The first poem was built upon MATHEMATIC (the acrostic)." (10 April 2007; SxMs109/1/E/1/7). The letter is written on the back of a square, heavy sheet, previously thumbtacked; on the recto side, it bears an extensive pen and ink drawing with "PoetrY" – first and last letters elongated – embedded in the left corner.

In the Peter Riley Papers at the University of Cambridge, there is a draft, spiral-bound variant of *py.* dated 2007, dedicated to Peter and his wife Beryl, and copyright "'anna mendelssohn-kouchnerova" (Ms Add. 10013/2/29). Beautifully constructed, the volume has pages of varying colours and size. Photocopies of some pages replicate a notebook spiral running along the top, echoing the text's physical binding. A similar volume exists in Rod Mengham's personal papers. In publication, the contents of *py.* are near-identical to the Riley variant: poems appear in the same order, and the archived text includes a portion of what becomes the final cover. Minor differences are noted below.

In an overview of Oystercatcher Press publications for *The Fortnightly Review*, Peter Riley described *py.* as "somewhere at the far side of surrealism and completely dotty" (c. 2009; fortnightlyreview.co.uk/2012/05/hughes-oystercatcher-press/). Colin Lee Marshall reviewed Mendelssohn's text as one that "brilliantly unsettles the homeostasis of the acrostic", noting that it is filled with "pockets of argot [that] consistently thwart interpretive capture" (*Erotoplasty*, no. 1, February 2018; erotoplasty.tumblr.com).

At Sussex, three files are devoted to *py.* (SxMs109/5/A/25/1–3). The first two contain manuscripts, the third, a typescript. In file 5/A/25/1, there are photocopies of hand-drafted sestets for this collection, most on pages from two spiral-bound notebooks; these photocopies are replicated within the bespoke texts Mendelssohn made for Riley and Mengham. Copies of the *py.* cover and illustrations can be found in these files. In addition, Sussex *py.* files contain photocopies of the cover and illustrations not directly associable with the published text. An enlarged A4 photocopy of a corner detail of the cover, its spiral notebook binding visible, is also in 5/B/1/18.

In file 5/A/25/2, an A4 page has a series of drawings captioned, respectively, "double sun one real"; "zakdoek"; "revelation spillov"; "iago"; "political word blitz"; "the close shaven"; "the spin of the drop"; "disquiet" and "restoration pillar". On another A4 sheet headed "<u>PESTALOZZI</u>" are doodles and brief notes on Rodolfo Almirón, a right-wing Argentinian who ran the Triple A death squad, a group responsible for the mass murders of opponents to the Perón regime in the mid-1970s. Misidentifying his first name as Roman or Ramiro, Mendelssohn notes his arrest in Spain, reported by the BBC World News on 29 December 2006. On an A5 sheet in the same file, a drawing of two carnivalesque busts is captioned "Coamignole with Necessaire" and signed "'a.m." An A4 page reads, in its entirety: "White Cube. / Anselm Kiefer."; German contemporary artist Kiefer exhibited at the White Cube in autumn 2009. File 5/A/25/2 also holds a portion of a former folder reading "(on top) py. poems"; this hand is not Mendelssohn's and recurs on the folder and typescript of Mendelssohn's "Poems Written at Hinton Grange Care Home" (2009; see below).

The typescript in the third *py.* file is the work of Mendelssohn's eldest daughter Poppy. The same file houses a letter reading:

> Dear Anna,
>
> Here's a printed copy of the work you gave George, Em and I. If there are typos let me know and I can correct them easily as I've saved it on my computer. I may have copied words from your original wrongly.
>
> Maybe you could photocopy this and send it to publishers you know……
>
> With lots of love,
>
> Poppy
>
> XXX

Poppy's covering page includes the volume title, rendered "PY", Mendelssohn's dedication – "For P.E.G" – and "Love, anna. // Cambridge U.K / 2007". The authorial attribution "a. m" is a footer used here and on all subsequent pages. Six of the 11 poems held in 5/A/25/1 are signed "'a. m". The apostrophe before the "a" likely refers to an abbreviation of Mendelssohn's Hebrew first name, "Channa" (undated letter to Romana Huk, 3/A/1/20/1). Mendelssohn's "POEM.", replicated in *No Prizes.* in 2012, bears the same authorial figuration (see below notes).

Poppy's typescript evinces numerous distinctions from the published text, some of which suggest difficulty in discerning Mendelssohn's hand. Examples include:

Poem 1 beginning "prove it! out of the blue" is "prove it – our of the blue".
Poem 2 beginning "palaquin beneath harlequin": in line three, "eking" is "etching"
Poem 4 beginning "peasblossom nestled": the final word, "dagesh", is "dageih"
Poem 5 beginning "parme, abricot et violette": the collapsed spacing of lines two to four is not in evidence; further, "tatoviever" is "tatovierer" and "rhendait" is "sheaduit"
Poem 8 beginning "portrait in ink": capitals appear at the start of each line; all are lower case in publication
Poem 9 beginning "poise does not come into it": all first words are capitalised (as in 8); "every" is typed "evert"; "forwards" is "forward", and "yunnder" is "Yunnan"
Poem 11 beginning "personally weighted": in line one, "weighted" is "weighs"; in line 4, "arabic numerals" is "Arabic numerats"; in line 5, "roving" is "oving", and the final word, "complete." is typed "compete."
Poem 12 beginning "peaches in the": line 5 reads: "rich juicy flesh:"
Poem 16 beginning "Power has a temper": the final line reads: "'Yonnondio' Jille Olsen"
Poem 22 beginning "prescription in colours": the final line is "yelling by the blasting instance"
Poem 24 beginning "Pepper pot full": line first words are all lower case (capitalised in *py.*) and in line 4, "Times" is "timed"
Poem 25 beginning "Pitcher crooked hangs": all first words are capitalised (lower case in *py.*); line one concludes "still"
Poem 26 beginning "prisoners-of-war": hyphens are not evident in line 1, and the penultimate word is "then" rather than "them"
Poem 27 beginning "Perpendicular marble piece": line first words are all lower case (capitalised in *py.*); in line 3, "trihedrons" was "trikedrons"

Poems that appear in *py.* are not in this typescript, namely: six, beginning "polling" and seven, beginning "perfectly numerate"; also missing are poems 17 (beginning "pegs") to 21 (beginning "pale purple"). Poems included in the appendix of this volume but are not in *py.* are included in the typescript, namely those beginning "palette in monochrome" and "Perruche, the rising rapids".

In Poppy's A4 typescript, the sestet beginning "*palomapolperro*" may have been intended as the first poem. Beneath the heading "POETRY", the poem is positioned low on the page; all others are in the top left corner (5/A/25/3). In the manuscripts, there are two versions of the same. Under the heading

Poetry

the poem "*palomapolperro*" appears in the lower left corner; one sheet has an illustration above the title, and another is reduced, without illustration, on a small, square orange sheet (5/A/25/2). This same image recurs in the *py.* variant located in the Peter Riley Papers.

In sum, Sussex *py.* files hold five draft poems that are not included in the final text. Two sestets surface in 5/A/25/1, beginning "Patisseries in real salzbourg" and "pallette in monochrome" respectively; variants of the latter also arise in 5/A/25/2 and 3. In 5/A/25/2, there are three additional sestets beginning "permanent enough", "pochoir silver threaded snail", and "Peruche, the rising rapids"; the latter reappears in 5/A/25/3. All are included in the appendix.

What follows offers the location of archive manuscripts, with semantic changes noted where they appear. Poems are ordered as in publication.

Poem beginning "perfectly numerate"
A photocopied A4 manuscript of this poem exists in 5/A/25/1; it is identical to the printed text.

Poem beginning "portrait in ink"
The A4 manuscript of this poem is identical to publication (5/A/25/2).

Poem beginning "poise does not come into it"
In the A4 manuscript of this poem, "yunnder" appears to be "yunnan" (5/A/25/2).

Poem beginning "photographs of snow"
There are two manuscript copies of this poem (5/A/25/2). One shares a sheet with three other draft sestets, and the final line, "yarn strapped into fluorescent jackets" reads "~~yellow f~~ yarn fluorescent jackets strapped"; "yarn" is below the line. The second is identical to the published version.

Poem beginning "personally weighted in sterling pounds"
There are two manuscripts of this poem; one clean, one heavily edited (5/A/25/2). In both, "weighted" is "weighed" and the final variant of the last line reads "glass could not compete."

In line one of the more worked over manuscript, "sterling" was a later addition, line five reads: ""really direct measurements, of ~~bacon~~, ^~~salt be~~^ of cheese, of meat," and the poem concludes: "glass ~~would~~ ^could^ not compete." Two drafts – one incomplete – of the *py.* sestet beginning "peaches in the forgotten orchard" share the same page; in one, only the first two lines are given, and line two reads: "each with a blush". The page also bears a drawing faintly resembling London's Battersea Station.

Beneath the poetry, Mendelssohn writes "the washing eggs"; in the bottom left corner, she adds: "Voices of Knowledge. 'The Ancient Mariner's poet."

In the Riley *py*. text "could not complete." is "could not compete." as it is in the 2007 typescript; both are discussed above. Given the better semantic logic of "compete", and its prevalence in draft variants, it is restored here (ed.).

Poem beginning "peaches in the forgotten orchard"
There are four manuscripts of this poem (5/A/25/2). Two appear on the same page as "personally weighted in sterling pounds" (see above notes); one is partial (given above) and the other differs from publication, reading:

> peaches in the ^forgotten^ orchard
> oiled lamps for the night ^when^ lit them
> each with a blush
> tamed for ~~eating~~ biting into
> rich juicy flesh:
> your new address.

The other two manuscripts – one on orange A5, one on white A4 – are as in the published version, barring that line five reads "rich juicy flesh:", as above, a change that recurs in the 2007 typescript and in the Riley *py.* text. Given the prevalence of this line, it is used here, replacing the "rich juice flesh" of publication (ed.).

Poem beginning "*palomapolperro*"
There are two manuscript versions of this poem and they are placed beneath the heading discussed in the introductory notes to *py.*: **P**oetry (5/A/25/2). In both, "*palomapolperro*" was divided into two words reading "*paloma polperro*", as it is in the 2007 typescript.

Poem beginning "pendragon in purdah"
There are four manuscripts of this poem (5/A/25/2). Two occupy one A4 sheet, surrounded by two or three doodles (one with an unclear embedded word, possibly "original"). Between drawings is the first word of another *py.* sestet, "Perruche" (see appendix). In both, all line first words are capitalised. In one, line one includes "in ~~per~~ purdah"; line three begins "Ermintrude~~'s~~", and line four reads: "~~Teleological~~ Pause. a". In the other, line four reads: "Teleological pause: a". In a third A4 manuscript, line four is "Teleological pause in a" and all first words are capitalised. A fourth A4 manuscript is identical to publication, barring extended descenders used for the first letters of "pendragon" and "yellow".

Poem beginning "Pillbox hat"
An A4 manuscript exists in 5/A/25/2 that is identical to publication, excepting that "Ormes" and "d'hiver" are treated as separate words, as they are in the 2007 typescript discussed in the introductory notes to *py.*.

Poem beginning "Power has a temper, pranksters abound"
There are four manuscripts of this poem (5/A/25/2). Two are on one A4 sheet. At page bottom is a drawing of an illustrated spiral notebook captioned "laura". In one variant, placed page upper right, "œufs" and "églefin" occupy the same line (an arrow

indicates Mendelssohn's plan to change this rendering); the words "oeuvres" and "pilloried" do not appear; and, lastly, "flashed out" was "flashed ~~over~~". Beneath the poem reads "yarmouth dehydrates". The second variant shows Mendelssohn toying with the as-yet-unordered words of the poem; here "flashed over" is allowed to stand, and a phrase that goes unused is "fabricated image".

In a third A4 manuscript, the first three lines read: "Power has a temper / œufs, /eglefin,"; pencilled at page bottom right is: "(py.)". A final A4 manuscript is identical to publication.

Poem beginning "pomerainian intimacy"
A manuscript exists in 5/A/25/2 on a small square torn along left side and bottom; barring the rendering of the first word as "pomeranian", it is identical to publication.

Poem beginning "phizzing on"
The A4 photocopied manuscript shows the poem as part of notebook bound with a plastic spiral (5/A/25/1). It is identical to the published text.

Poem beginning "primrose pink"
The A4 photocopied manuscript of this poem has no commas (5/A/25/1).

Poem beginning "pale purple"
The reduced manuscript photocopy of this poem is an A4 sheet folded into A5, as if in preparation for a chapbook or pamphlet (5/A/25/2). In this variant, there is a space between "œil" and "d'oiseau" that is excised in the final text. This space also exists in the Riley copy of *py.* discussed in the above introductory notes.

Poem beginning "prescription in colours decided on"
An A4 photocopied manuscript shows this poem in a notebook bound with a metal spiral placed on a larger notebook with a plastic spiral (5/A/25/1). It is identical to the published variant. In page bottom right is a funnel-shaped doodle reading "concrete".

Poem beginning "passive in nominal negociation"
An A4 photocopied manuscript shows this poem in a notebook bound with a metal spiral placed on a larger notebook with a plastic spiral (5/A/25/1). In manuscript, "negociation" is "negotiation".

Poem beginning "Pepper pot full"
An A4 photocopied manuscript shows this poem in a notebook bound with a metal spiral, placed upon a notebook with a dark plastic spiral that is, in turn, on top of notebook with a light-coloured plastic spiral (5/A/25/1). In manuscript, "Earthly" was "Earthy"; "Times" was "Timed", and the final two lines may conclude with full stops, as there are in the Riley copy of *py.* discussed above.

Poem beginning "Pitcher crooked hangs stilled"
The A4 photocopied manuscript shows this poem in a notebook bound with a metal spiral placed on top of a notebook with a plastic spiral (5/A/25/1). In manuscript, "err on" reads "err/on"; the slash is Mendelssohn's.

Poem beginning "prisoners-of-war"
The A4 photocopied manuscript shows the poem in a notebook bound with a metal spiral placed upon a notebook with a plastic spiral; page bottom left is burnt (5/A/25/1). The text is identical to publication.

"Perpendicular marble piece"
The A4 photocopied manuscript shows the poem within a notebook bound with a metal spiral; an alternate text, likely prose, peeps out from beneath the page, and includes the words: "when one's children are part of one's" (5/A/25/1). The poem is identical to publication.

Anna Mendelssohn, ***Poems Written at Hinton Grange Care Home*** **(2009).**
Mendelssohn died on 16 November 2009, and these poems are among her last writings. They are held in a folder labelled "Poems written at Hinton Grange Care Home, 2009" and "~~Essays and letters about J. H. Prynne~~"; the handwriting resembles notes made by Mendelssohn's eldest daughter Poppy in the *py.* (2009) documentation (SxMs109/5/B/1/33a; see above). On the spine, in what appears to be Mendelssohn's hand, is: "ON JHP."; within, the folder contains a small, square figural drawing titled "arabia goes deep", manuscript poems on white A4 paper, and eleven sheets of heavily textured square stationery, some bearing dates from August and September 2009. A selection of these manuscripts is typed into a numbered, seven-page typescript with the running head, "Poems by Anna Mendelssohn". In the hand resembling Poppy's, page one is subtitled: "all in Hinton Grange. 2009".

Typescripts do not always align with manuscripts, and in some places, manuscripts are illegible, as Mendelssohn's writing, increasingly scrawling in her later years, is particularly erratic during her final illness. Only typescript poems are included in the body of this collection. Manuscript poems include:

Alone

I cannot be
believed & written
down alone
tho little ones
would have
my life
been gladly taken
w – hy? wasn't he?

Mendelssohn writes this poem out twice on one A4 sheet; in the second variant, the hand is more controlled. At page bottom, she writes: "Alonzo / lonzo / Ălone". Beside these lines reads: " ˘ / cup / ˘ / Half a [*"a" is unclear* —ed.] cup / cup / ˘ ˘ – ". The word "Alone" appears twice in the right margin, in one instance as if to correct the unclear title, in the other, floating alongside the poem. The verso side has a figural doodle, next to which reads: "The elector / of Saxony".

One side of a landscape-formatted A4 page reads:

I love you,
I don't know whether or not
I [*unclear word or letters*—ed.] perfect,

I need you,
as mad as cotton in snow,
as mad as
corny songs
with wind blowing

The second half of this page is unclear, but may read:

as mad as singing goes,
& stands, by the windows,
and say
TOMORROW IS another day
Not NO DAY
NOT Nothing
for the world will not end with my end
at least that much I have [*unclear word*—ed.]

Next to the poem reads "that the [*unclear word, possibly "future"*—ed.] may be different"; a hand-drawn line suggests that these words may have been intended as the last line of the poem or stanza. An illustration of a hand and sleeved forearm runs alongside the right margin.

Similarly unclear, the other side of this page includes:

In all of this
I don't understand
Want friendly souls
amongst the dead
I have known
tho dead, as I have always been,
to please
my mother,
the Poems, are written by my loves,
you must know how dead they are,
they know not me
although I am
always in the trees,

The line "you must know how dead they are," appears to be a later addition. The poem then continues: "I need to KNOW".

The remainder of this line and those that follow are near-indiscernible.

Another page includes:

This is another day
    oh yes
    une autre jour,
    c'est.
    we won't say
    we cannot say
    this is another day
    when darkening may
    gives tokens to take away

    talking may   [*unclear word or two words*—ed.]

    caravan

                                        forward
                                        slash

Additional manuscripts include: the poem "i only" (given in full in notes for the poem beginning "Total rejection" below); the poem beginning "mai   son" (see below notes for the poem beginning "I have only"); poetically-oriented word play ("sling / slogslug / ORPHEUS"); a work titled "samson." that begins "subsequently, / I object to people being spoken for" and concludes with an accusation about Auschwitz research; and, lastly, a ramble starting in medias res that concludes, "I was told that there was no surrealism here – taught in the Art faculty". Another sheet states that an embarrassed Mendelssohn has not been helped "to forget the terrible things that have happened".

In the six poems included in this collection, numerous variations and uncertainties remain, as detailed below. Given typescript inaccuracies, manuscript variants are given precedence.

Poem beginning "tapestries"

To the left of this manuscript poem, Mendelssohn writes "Sept. 1. 2009." Beneath the date, she adds three words: the second is "bisque"; the first may be "in" or "en"; the third is "sed", "seder", "seds", or another variant (ed.). The typescript includes the date, beneath which reads "en bisque [   ]".

The last two lines of "tapestries" are near-indiscernible. The second-last, "gesichtlicht", is not an identifiable German word, but may be a portmanteau combining "gesicht" – making a face or mimic – with "licht" or "bright and sunny". Alternately, Mendelssohn may have meant "geschichtlich", the German for "historical" or "historically significant". The last line of the poem is particularly unclear and has been excised (ed.). It could read: "poetry ursa mizar & bright". "[P]oetry" and "bright" are decipherable, and this supposition (perhaps too conveniently) brings the "ursa" of the Ursa Major or Big Dipper constellation with the "Mizar" that is the radiant star in its handle. Of these lines, the typist replicated the word "poetry" only, followed by: "[   ]".

Poem beginning “wallow ’tis of swallow”
Punctuation has been added to “tis”, and the line beginning “& 2 bent” could be “& 2 best” (ed.). The typist found parts of lines seven, 10, and 11 indiscernible. See below notes on poem beginning “Total rejection”.

Poem beginning “Total rejection”
Clearer in manuscript than most in this series, the poem typescript includes a note questioning whether it carries on from the preceding poem beginning “wallow ’tis of swallow” (see above). Both manuscripts are written in black ink on an A5 side of a folded A4 sheet, as is Mendelssohn’s custom when preparing a pamphlet. A pair of doodles accompanies “Total rejection”.

Poem manuscript and typescript are edited in blue ink in Mendelssohn’s hand. In the writing used for the series folder and subtitle, typescript page bottom reads, “corrected by A.M.” “[F]lügelhorn” is “flugelhorn” in typescript and “flugonhorn” in manuscript (ed.). In typescript, the line beginning “Our farm” is “One farm”, but the manuscript suggests otherwise, and “our” is reinstated (ed.).

In Mendelssohn’s untyped manuscript poems housed in the same folder, there is another poem wherein the speaker is likened to a potato:

i only

Want to check meanings
and Forget every <u>word</u>
want in some cultures
is unwanted
that is DESIRE

(my name)
(a potato)
(an hot potato)
potato

an orange saucey
potato
with a Free (Me)
Alfred Hitchcock
model

Next to this poem is a small silhouette drawing titled “A.H.” Beneath it reads: “a cereal pkt HITCHCOCK”. On the recto side is a poem titled “image” that begins: “the cost to Poetry / of Hating Imagery / of Hating Poetry / to say / this is a poetic image”. It then fragments into random words including “Imagery” and “eeee”.

Poem beginning “I have only ‘some interest’”
This poem is just legible. The typescript reads “or the Cambridge”; the manuscript reads “and the Cambridge” (ed.). In manuscript, the top of Mendelssohn’s central diamond shape is not quite closed. In the enlarged, outlined “THENEN” the last

"E" is backward, and the last letter is a lower-case "n", and may be a capital D, a lower-case "h", and/or amalgamate the arms and bar of "F" and "E" (ed.). In typescript, the final "en" is elided. An illustration of choreographed musical notes and the word "Democritus" appear on manuscript recto.

Another double-sided manuscript in Mendelssohn's Hinton Grange file references "Haar" and concrete, the latter indirectly as the French for masonry or rubble. It reads:

mai son
pretend
pre
prairie
maison dans le prairie
praireal
priory st.
upton sinclair
french point
ballet walking
not the valkyries
avoiding the valkyries
uptown and down
he had tow haar
and I was not a robber
or a murdress.

in a room.
with a composer, me., myself

The other side of the page reads:

I find
lapsed
into composition
now the girls are here
slow to arrive
we have been Lonely for lifetimes
of loneliness
have dogged us
with WASTE
maçonnerie
"leafy suburb"
sublime
suburb

rhubarb rhubarb
maison

Word play follows, as in: "sombre / ombre / sombrero" or "sub blue / sub / suburban". Random words including "snare drum" and "Hovis" are dotted around the page. Doodles accompany the piece, one plant-like and labelled "DILL". The entirety is signed, "Thurs. 20th Aug. C'bridge. 2009".

Poem beginning "The wall unintended"
In typescript, line 12 reads "shadow"; in manuscript, it may be "shadowy" or "shadows" (ed.). In manuscript, the poem is accompanied by a right-justified drawing of a line or crowd of people, within which is embedded the words "FEAR ear / ?EAR / eclipse". In typescript, these words are left-justified, and given as the final lines. In a combination of type and handwriting used for the folder, a question is posed in the right margin about this final positioning.

Poem beginning "his shadow was there"
Manuscript and typescript differ in capitalisation and punctuation, and "it was worse than Terrible" is typed "it was mre [*sic*] than terrible" (ed.). The manuscript is numbered one, and a small doodle appears at its end. Paginated two, verso reads: "Tolstoy. The Kreutzer Sonata / – Monogamy. Sophie Tolstoy."

Poem beginning "and the grasses"
In typescript, "and the grasses" is "and the ? graves" (ed.). In manuscript, the second "birdies" is unpunctuated (ed.). At the bottom of the manuscript, Mendelssohn draws three doodles, one of which is captioned: "to cry". On page verso is indiscernible word play and a drawing of a head in profile.

Anne Mendleson/Anna Mendelssohn, ***Cleaves International Poetry Journal*** **(October 2010).**
This print and on-line periodical aimed to focus, in each issue, on the writing of a specific region. British editor Harry Godwin (now Corbyn Sterling) ran Arthur Shilling Press, which published the work of Nat Raha and Dez Mendoza, among others. *Cleaves* ceased publication after two issues and is no longer available on-line.

Nominated by the poet Nick Potamitis, critic, publisher, and poet Neil Pattison edited the October 2010 Cambridge number for *Cleaves International Poetry Journal*. Alongside Mendelssohn, Pattison included work by Alex Houen, Geoff Gilbert, Connie Scozzaro, and Alex Eisenthal. Pattison received Mendelssohn's poems from a file loaned to him by Peter Riley, the poet and publisher who cared for Mendelssohn's literary estate in the immediate aftermath of her death. Riley's folder included photocopied work extracted from Mendelssohn's papers when clearing out the garden shed where she lived in the last decade of her life. According to Riley, the file contained about one hundred pages of drawings, work from *Crystal Love: D. N. A.* (1982), *Posmos, the Yellow Velvet Underground.* (1982), and, perhaps, drafts of *py.* (2009). Riley also lent this work to Laura Kilbride and Ian Heames, who published Mendelssohn in *The Paper Nautilus* (2011) and *No Prizes* (2012) respectively (Riley email, 3 August 2017; see below notes). Based on these later publications, the file also contained a fragment of Mendelssohn's episodic *roman-à-clef*, as well as drafts of *Inbuilt Flash Nix* (1985) and/or *Is this a True Parrot, a Mountain, or a Stooge?* (1985).

A personal computer file dated 28 August 2010 suggests that Pattison intended to publish ten of the fifteen poems in *Crystal Love D. N. A.*:

Poem beginning “destiny forecast revolt”
Poem beginning “Power to move”
Poem beginning “melancholy might answer in future mistakes,”
Poem beginning “Machiavelli strikes”
Poem beginning “Black velvet cloth”
GUIDE
Poem beginning “maybe I shall”
Poem beginning “Treading carpentry free country”
CADENCE.
Poem beginning “a settlement of priorities reaches unassailable”

Pattison’s transcription is dated 1981, dedicated to Tom and Val Raworth, and attributed to Anne Mendleson. Minor differences exist between this text and the 1982 publication. In the poem beginning “Power to move”, Pattison capitalises “unites” and “silver”; the first word of the poem beginning “melancholy might answer” is also capitalised, as is that of “GUIDE”. In “CADENCE.”, line three begins “that”. In the first stanza of Pattison’s rendering of “maybe I shall”, “reintegrates” occupies its own line. In the poem beginning “Treading carpentry free country”, Pattison’s line six is “moostang choir”. Finally, in the poem beginning “a settlement of priorities”, “repeat peep: ‘Shoot light.’” is “repeat peep! ‘Shoot light’.” (Pattison email and attachment, 2 August 2017).

Anna Mendelssohn, *The Paper Nautilus*, no. 2 (2011), 27–36.
Edited by Rosa van Hensbergen and Laura Kilbride, *The Paper Nautilus* published poetry, essays, and translations. Contributors to its first three issues included Alice Notley, Nat Raha, Francesca Lisette, and Lisa Robertson; the final number consisted of translations of eighteen writers, including Romina Freschi, Kiriu Minashita, and Monique Wittig. Issue two included work by Frances Kruk, Marianne Morris, and Mendelssohn. In a letter to Mendelssohn’s daughter requesting permission to publish these poems, Kilbride describes the journal as not “explicitly feminist”, adding:

> Our project has two main aims: to create discussion about the issues which attend female poets writing today, and to promote the representation of, and the communication between, female readers, writers, and editors. The first issue of the magazine has been very successful and has been widely read: distributed from Cambridge, UK, to places as far apart as Los Angeles and Montpellier. (7 August 2011; van Hensbergen email, 25 October 2017)

Peter Riley lent a folder of Mendelssohn’s writing to the editors; for a full description, see above notes on *Cleaves International Poetry Journal* (2010). The issue in which Mendelssohn is included begins with an epigraph reading:

> *Women are a practical necessity & whoever is not totally practical is here defined as suffering from diminished responsibility.*
>
> — Grace Lake, ‘BRAIN SHRINKAGE AND EXPANDED CONSCIOUSNESS’

Lacking citation or context, this quote concludes an undated fragment of Mendelssohn’s *roman-à-clef* (SxMs109/1/B/1/46/1).

Essays on Mendelssohn complete issue two of *The Paper Nautilus*. Connie Scozzaro's "On 'In the Minority of One'" focuses on Mendelssohn's transmutation, discussing how the "one" her poem addresses fluctuates and multiplies. In "'I shall not prove and neither shall I be proven': Anna Mendelssohn's *py.*", Eleanor Careless uses the outset of *py.* – "prove it!" – as a departure point from which to consider Mendelssohn's poetic preoccupations with evidence, absolute knowledge, the law, and testimony.

The Mendelssohn section in *The Paper Nautilus* includes two texts from *Crystal Love: D. N. A.* (1982): the poem beginning "quietly noon" and "nonflec". The first is identical to publication, excepting the capitalisation of the first-person pronoun; in "nonflec", the dedicatory "Menis" is given in *Nautilus* as "Menïs" and stanza three begins "pols in". Further, the final two stanzas are treated as a single unit, and the lines beginning "magenta" and "arbitole" are not indented.

The editors incorrectly attribute both poems to *Posmos, The Yellow Velvet Underground.*, adding: "These poems follow a manuscript Crystal Love D.N.A., already made available at: www.c-leaves…… It is unclear whether 'POSMOS' was intended to be part of the same work." (see above on *Cleaves*, 2010). *Crystal Love D. N. A.* (1982) is held at the British Library, where it shares a bipartite text with *Posmos, the Yellow Velvet Underground.* (see above notes on these collections).

A photocopy of "For J. H. Prynne." exists in the Peter Riley Papers at the Cambridge University Library (Ms Add. 10013/2/29). Beneath this poem, the editors include a note Mendelssohn made on poet and friend Ian Patterson:

> The closing line of Ian Patterson's 'No Dice'
> (Cambridge Poetical Histories No. 6) is to
> be branded on my Psyche. It is indelible,
> it is always Indigo which is my Ink & Fluff
> Soul and Destiny for ever protection centre
> les Biches noirs et blanches. Who
> Cast a Spook for a Defence which exacted
> their, as I understood, before this line of I. Patterson's
> confusion between Conceptualizing &
> Possessing.

The last stanza of "After Breakfast", or the second and final poem in Patterson's *No Dice* (Poetical Histories, no. 6, 1988), reads:

> This is not literally true but I
> have chosen all the statements freely
> and do not a prison make even when hallucinations
> hover round my heart and ears at night
> or by day become coincidences of such beauty
> I could weep at not believing in horoscopes.

The long poem "in the minority of one" concludes Mendelssohn's *Paper Nautilus* entry. In publication, there is no space between "said." and "&" in the penultimate line of "b"; between "out." and "she" in the first line of "c"; and between sections "h" and "i" (ed.).

Riley intended to deposit the Mendelssohn file to the Cambridge University Library, but "in the minority of one" and the fragment of Mendelssohn's *roman-à-clef* were not in his archive at the time of publication.

Anna Mendelssohn, *No Prizes*, no. 1 (December 2012).
Issue one of *No Prizes* included work by Piero Helizcer and Stephen Rodefer; in 2013, the second and final issue involved Sean Bonney, Amy De'Ath, Peter Manson, J. H. Prynne, and Sophie Robinson. At the back of issue one, editor Ian Heames includes the following note:

> 'Poem' by Anna Mendelssohn, who also wrote as Grace Lake, is printed in facsimile from a manuscript booklet given by the author to Peter Riley. The cover illustration from this booklet is reproduced on the back cover of the magazine. 'Localized Effects.' and 'Localized Plaster.' are reprinted from *Inbuilt Flash Nix*, a self-published booklet, 'Compiled August 1985'. Approximately 50pp printed mostly rectos only, photocopied from typescript and manuscript and stapled into thin card covers. Copies can differ slightly in content. For this information, and for access to these two poems and the booklet entitled 'Poem', I am grateful to Peter Riley. The manuscript of '1986 Octroi' was discovered tucked inside the author's copy of *Women, History and Theory*, by Joan Kelly (Chicago and London: University of Chicago Press, 1986).

For more information on the folder of Mendelssohn's work circulated by Peter Riley, see above notes on *Cleaves International Poetry Journal* (2010). In *No Prizes*, "LOCALIZED EFFECTS." and "LOCALIZED PLASTER." are rendered identically to their appearance in *Is this a True Parrot, a Mountain, or a Stooge?* (1985; see above). After her death in Cambridge in 2009, the bulk of Mendelssohn's personal library was sold to local booksellers, and some students and scholars purchased her books.

In *No Prizes*, a gap between "of" and "wars" in line nine of "1986 OCTROI" has been closed (ed.). "POEM." is a photocopied manuscript that concludes with a drawn heart and "'a.m.". Mendelssohn uses "'a.m." in her drafts for *py.* (2009), and the apostrophe preceding the "a" appears to refer to an abbreviation of Mendelssohn's Hebrew first name, "Channa" (undated letter to Romana Huk, 3/A/1/20/1). In stanza one, "inexpressible" may be "unexpressible", and lines three, four, 22, 23, 25, 27, and 29 may be slightly indented (ed.).

Grace Lake, "call to linnet rock." (undated)
This A4 typescript is housed in the Peter Riley Papers at the University Library of Cambridge (MS Add. 10013/2/29). In the top right corner, Mendelssohn writes: "Dear Peter, If this isn't any good you might prefer another. Best wishes, Grace." In the same black ink are corrections changing "there mother" in stanza seven to "their mother"; removing apostrophes from two "they you's" in eight; and adding "they" to the second-last line. Additional edits in blue appear to correct the misplaced apostrophe in "one let's poetry" of stanza six, and underscore the lower-case first-person pronouns and "france" of stanza seven, line one; although proper nouns are inconsistently capitalised throughout, these corrections are made (ed.). This file in the Riley archive includes a copy of "The Gong." (see below).

Grace Lake, Typescripts (undated)
These poems are in a file containing a mixture of poetry and prose from the early to the mid-1980s and an A4 typescript of the lyrics to Bob Dylan's "All Along the Watchtower" (1968) and "Pat Garrett & Billy the Kid" that includes handwritten chord changes (1973) (SxMs109/5/A/43/2). Mendelssohn also wrote out songs in her prison diaries: a prison-issue notebook dated 1974 and 1975 contains lyrics from The Beatles, Don McLean, Carole King, and Carly Simon (2/A/7).

"The Gong." is typed on A4, corrected in Mendelssohn's hand in green and black ink, and signed "A. M." Edits include "within ~~his~~ their shot"; "where ~~he~~ they got her", and, in the final line, "~~you were~~ THEIR Living Wrong." Along with "call to linnet rock.", "The Gong." is located in the Peter Riley Papers at Cambridge, where there is no full stop after the title; all lines beginning "oh" are capitalised; stanza four, line one concludes "dreamy poetess"; stanza six, line three reads "for writing, and folding poems"; and stanza eight, line two does not conclude with a comma (MS Add. 10013/2/29). At Cambridge, the final line reads: "you were their living wrong." Beneath the typed poem, Mendelssohn writes in bright blue ink: "This is the poem. Should the Oh's be capitalised or not do you think? Grace." Above it, she writes in black: "CCCP?" – a reference to the Cambridge Conference of Contemporary Poetry.

"A Crash" is two typescript A4 pages. The first two lines of the second page appear first on page one but are uneven due to the turning of the typewriter roll at the end of the page and are crossed through. Rendered as a quatrain here, the stanza ten (beginning "those million hopes") may be two couplets (ed.) The second page is a photocopied typescript; typos were corrected before copying.

The third poem from this file, "the cliff.", is an undated, clean typescript. Another typescript with the same title exists in 5/B/2/97. Equally brief but entirely different, this variant reads:

the cliff.

i grew afraid
of going anywhere.

his hands
on the steering wheel
were large and tense.

he would drive us back
over the pennines
and i would hold on
to the child.

Finally, the poem beginning "real does not know" is an undated, unsigned typescript on two pages of thin typing paper, with one minor typo corrected (5/A/43/2). It is paginated by hand.

"To You, Italy." and "To You, Italy. II." (undated)
Mendelssohn kept a set of personal folders that are preserved in the archive. These two undated, unattributed typescripts are in one of these files alongside writings that are predominantly from the mid-1980s (SxMs109/5/B/1/1b). Following the four pages of poetry is a fifth typescript sheet of prose bearing the same watermark as the poetry – "Character". This writing may continue from the poetry, has a single edit in Mendelssohn's hand, and reads:

> screams may be being perpetuated by a non-functioning bell, bu [*sic*] if you really care. you say. if you, they warn, are not, they continue, very careful, relentlessly, you will find yourself, going on, being questioned as to whether you are sane or not.

Dear reader, be with your child if s/he reads this book. BE with your child or the child in your care, but do not let that child go out into this life without some knowledge of where a desire to reach the base, for literary reasons, and ones too of strong social care, may lead that child to. For little has been resolved as to whether journeys of this nature are to be recommended or not.

Grace Lake, Undated typescripts (SxMs109/5/B/2/10).
These two typescript poems – "moxed metaphor" and poem beginning "nit freaks" – occupy a file alongside a version of the poem "WHY" (see Typescripts, 1985, above). "[M]oxed metaphor" is on a water-stained, torn A4 sheet; in line 12, "you're in" is typed "you re in" and under "penser" reads, in very faint type, "t p" (ed.). The poem beginning "nit freaks" is on lined, hole-punched paper, and is signed by hand in black ink, "Love, Grace."

Appendix Notes

Anne Mendleson, *Crystal Love: D. N. A.*, draft poems (c. 1982)

This undated, A5 typescript of *Crystal Love: D. N. A.* replicates and differs from the published text and its draft variants (SxMs109/5/A/2/1). What will become poems one and four ("destiny forecast revolt" and "Machiavelli strikes") are conflated into a single poem. Three pages of poems that exist nowhere else follow; the last poem is a slightly differing variant of the second half of the *Crystal Love* poem beginning "Power to move". Lacking pagination, this version is presented in found order.

Grace Lake, *Slate*, draft poems (February 1987)

These poems are typed onto a set of folded A3 sheets and edited in the same manner as all others for Mendelssohn's *Slate* entry (SxMs109/5/A/9/1). At the end of the compilation, Mendelssohn writes "© S. G. L. Lake." and makes a list of six of the poems therein, namely:

I. "On an Emery board"
II. "But I'm not going to sit in a room"
III. "did they leave"
IV "the meringue"
V "The solemn mists" etc.
VI "Winter"

"So then what are we going to do? Are we going to subject too?" does not appear in the list or in *Slate* (note the similarity between the ending of this poem and the poem beginning "who are these who tell you what you want to know?" in *viola tricolor*, draft poems, 1993). Further, "the meringue" is excised from final publication. There are check marks next to 2, 3, and 6. Poems 2, 3, and 4 are divided by slashes drawn in Mendelssohn's hand. At the bottom of the final page, Mendelssohn writes: "→ February 1987."

Grace Lake, *café archéologique*, draft poems (1992–1993)

[C]afé archéologique was a work in progress that appears unpublished. Sussex holds three files devoted to this collection, SxMs109/5/A/13/1–3. Poems that were not photocopied for the mocked-up chapbook in file 5/A/13/3 are included in this appendix; all are drawn from manuscript and drawing files 5/A/13/1 and 2. The poem beginning "One rushes another is described as behaving abnormally" may be an excised portion or second page of the poem "Art & Women." included in the main text (ed.). In "One rushes", the line "who knowing each other far better cannot cease" also read "who knowing each other far better cannot pause in" (ed.). In the poem beginning "my spine was hurting", "words, as an intellectual." might be "words, is an intellectual." (ed.). Punctuation has been added to "the jew's" and "our fathers'" in the poem beginning "all over one bloody old pianna" (ed.).

Poems beginning "& one day", "between us" and "and being led" are all from 5/A/13/2. In the poem beginning "between us", "ran round buttons" was "~~ran buttons~~". On page verso, a quatrain reads: "don't take my happiness / i screamed to the wall / and if you don't like me / don't ask me." In the poem beginning "and being led dissociate", "yet not a sound" reads "~~no~~ yet ~~no sou~~ not a sound", and the poem ends with the word "coast"; "beach" is superimposed above the line (ed.).

Grace Lake, *viola tricolor*, draft poems (c. 1993)

In Mendelssohn's Sussex archive, there are four files exclusively associated with *viola tricolor*. One holds an A3 manuscript of "the fourteenth flight" and a primarily manuscript A5 chapbook (5/A/15/1). On the folded A4 sheet covering the unbound entirety, Mendelssohn writes: "*Viola Tricolor*." and "grace lake." The inside cover of this title page reads, in pencil: "long time passing", which is the same subtitle Mendelssohn gives to her "WORK IN PROGRESS. 1993." that she submitted as part of an Arts Council application that included proofs of *viola tricolor* (5/A/16). This 5/A/15/1 text includes poems that are in the published chapbook and numerous additional writings. Another file contains two poems that are not in the final chapbook, namely, "the secret ballot." and an untitled poem dedicated "for Vera MacUllum. Assistant Governor." (5/A/15/3).

In sum, 32 associated draft texts that are not included in *viola tricolor*, or extensive variants of poems that appear in that volume, are included in this appendix. Mistakes or omissions in spelling and punctuation are silently corrected, so that, for instance, in stanza ten of "the fourteenth flight", "I held the little baby's close to protect her" is "I held the little baby close to protect her" (ed.). Information about specific poems follows.

"the fourteenth flight" (*early draft*)

This double-sided A3 manuscript of "the fourteenth flight." is longer and differently ordered than the final version; Mendelssohn's long lines fit across her manuscript page but have necessarily been formatted here as run-overs (5/A/15/1). Note the changes in pronoun use from the published poem: many "theys" are "yous" in the earlier draft. On the verso page, Mendelssohn's writing is less structured and more crowded, and she uses short, horizontal, left-justified lines to indicate stanza breaks. In the left margin next to the second-last stanza, she writes "Condescension"; a question mark hovers over "later it fades" in the last stanza, and at the bottom of the page, lines are formatted around a doodle of four figures and an organic shape.

Mendelssohn makes numerous corrections throughout, first with the black pen used for the draft, and then again in blue ink. Substantive differences include the change, at the end of stanza five, of "killing" to "shooting". The second half of line four in the ninth stanza reads: "between the ~~mentality of a common criminal~~ and that of the ~~political~~ prisoner of conscience"; "of conscience" is added in blue. In this same stanza, "it's a defence," may be incorrect (ed.) At the beginning of the eleventh stanza, a redacted line reads: "You see poetry must not die and neither must love." The end of line two in the same stanza reads: "through the snow, scarves ~~warm on~~ tied round"; in line seven, "the native conditions" was "their native conditions". See also notes for this text on *viola tricolor* (1993).

Folder 5/A/15/3 also contains a typescript version of "the fourteenth flight." that blends features of this manuscript variant with those of the final draft. The more personal pronoun use of the manuscript is maintained, and on one occasion, extended, so that "serve a judo breakfast" of stanza four is "serve you a judo breakfast" and, in stanza seven, "I ate a tree top for you" becomes "for YOU". In stanza five, "so unconvicted are they" is "so unconvinced are they", a change retained in publication; in this stanza, Mendelssohn retains "prosecutors" rather than "persecutors", and "killing" rather than "shooting". While the conclusion of stanza six remains, as in manuscript – "bloody, bloody hell." – Mendelssohn corrects the end of stanza seven to read: "& ~~viewless~~ artlessly limited." – "artlessly" is handwritten below the line. Mendelssohn replicates the manuscript order of stanzas seven and eight; they are reversed in publication. The three final stanzas of the manuscript beginning "yes we'll tell them this" are excised from this typescript, as they are in *viola tricolor*. At the bottom of the second typescript page, Mendelssohn writes "1989."

Another partial manuscript draft of "the fourteenth flight" can be found in 5/B/1/11; it is on six landscape-formatted A5 sheets, each stanza is numbered, and it has been edited in a differing ink. It begins with stanza eight of the appendix variant, although the fifth line of that stanza is excised, and line eight of stanza eight begins "~~dragging~~ ^lugging^". In stanza ten, "tide of motorbikes" is rendered "roar of motorbikes" and line seven ends "be a good girl, no more ~~scandal~~ ^~~whipping~~^ beating."; lines eight to 13 (beginning "there you are" and "literally would" respectively) do not appear in this draft. Stanzas 11 to 14 read:

closing backed bull, protection a nimbus encircling, weight difference, obduration, to be seen as a political proposition:
told to stop, caecum. obstipating all the one who did not replace her, she should have left, but could not become her
will become one who won't escape domination worshipping others keeping the peace happiness always, resented —
always, always sudden strangury & a thousand deliberations when it was only a book & a hatred of loud revelry
to be living in the air with no music to grow no flowers not to be allowed to progress beyond her bitterness or
what she had sacrificed yet expected to, always expected to, after that mockery & those evaluations.
we could breathe with our minds minding that she must apologize for they great liberal ones are certainly
not willing to appreciate any but the most flat-chested or at least, no, they probably would not have much chance
to obliterate with two diving sparrows from the numbed brains of Hawker Siddeley's

in far off chalk climes you have written this, that has been told, reluctance to distinguish
for every story is valid, but unions were banned, and cavil suspected, then public
programmes are the order of the day. opinion. a pity files are changed from rule to rule.
it wasn't all argument. but responsibility for keeping order ~~in~~ on the road to construction
and personal criticisms best kept to oneself but oh how we missed our freedom
it was a shock to learn that a body could be so afraid of moving, walls where there were none.
doors where pedestrian crossings ^are all there is to^ remind you of Africa. sous les pavés c'est la plage
shrinkage. the borders. the false reputations. country after country closed down.

people don't seek pleasure on a £5 note. they flee shadows. All knowing all seeing worthies.
who find it difficult to imagine lives outside of themselves. In this respect honesty is a brag.
Oh I. Oh I. Oh I. it was 12. zodiac. white diamond studded palamino.   stuffed.
a junk yard (nature). petticoat lane (Gramineat). Grama. Tate & Lyle. I'll eat my own.
I'll starve. I won't absorb the environment. first rule. non-absorption. Negativity room.
Silly not to have taken the boat to Cork. Too worried about my bailees. If I hadn't kept on shrugging.
Reluctant to discriminate. Revolution is truly frightening. Do you like to be frightened? I don't.
The hardened ones read ~~murder~~ detective fiction. Everyone is suspect then. Horrible game.

Chocolate? no (it might be laced). Fly Thai. Best in the world. will you stop tapping on the wall
its getting on my nerves. no I don't love you. Babes. for heavens sake I'm
^out of nappies^ & [*"&" unclear*—ed.] don't I deserve to be called by my name? Instead of BABES. emulge your
emu ~~kno~~ homespun leave me – alone? out of it? and i'm [*could be "it's"*—ed.] travelling BABES
it's like having a canvas tautened over your head. & each time you open a book
You are spied on, aemulatio is quite irrelevant, you can go straight to
religion or back to your mum. There is no in-between. That's why the
lights kept changing & all those horrible american 50's bop scenes
introduced themselves as the underground.   Had   Fun?

A series of doodles occupies the remainder of this page; an A5 page in the same file that appears to continue from the above reads:

> engineering depôt, disguised a
> reparative transmission when I can conjure up terrifying titles which imprison people in stinking boxes
> killing them prematurely congratulating myself on my moral rectitude be celebrated by others for reformation
> I shall then move to the inevitable sympathy once distance has been rendered obsolescent and my nascent apotheosis
> avails its chocolate coated pill for the conjunction which was mismatched & the english art which lacks still.
> the trees will, planted apart, behind the rise, over yonder ridge, along a darker line, drawn over & over again,
> one morning chopped down.

"Powerful enough to Kill by Artificial Light"
This poem is on one landscape-formatted side of an A5 sheet; the other bears the poem "Sauce". To the left of the title, Mendelssohn writes "England." (5/A/15/1). Right of the poem, she writes:

> Electric charge laser'd through the nervous system to counteract natural circulation, modernising circuits, stripped language of its cultural roots as outmoded & excluded from digital handbooks. "The Mystification of the Soviet Union" or those who lived in its cultural name reproved for an interest in Ghandi mispronounced and reascribed as a descriptive analysis as Gandy / caused by induction of Angst, conducted into Assymetry, tending to seek harmony, devowelled as hormony, a tradition in need of a space, denied metaphysic, debased as physic, as internal sense retreats out of integrity in approaching others' Property. ~~A Tower~~"

The sheet contains two drawings in the brown and black inks used for the writing.

Poem beginning "light. & where is the end. & who was a taut string ringing"
This poem occupies one side of A5 (5/A/15/1); on the reverse is the poem beginning "evoking mocked order" (see below notes). Along the page margin, Mendelssohn quotes Elizabeth Barrett Browning's "The Dead Pan":

> Aphrodite! dead and driven
> As thy native foam, thou art;
> With the cestus long done heaving
> On the white calm of thine heart!
> As Adonis! at that shriek,
> Not a tear runs down her cheek –
> Pan, Pan is Dead. "The Dead Pan" XVI. E.B.B.

Mendelssohn quotes "The Dead Pan" again on "it is not for you to say or tell to bode" (see below notes). Here, she writes the etymology of "cestus" as "stitched" and "A belt or girdle for the waist; esp. that of Aphrodite or Venus." Noting that it is associable with "caedere" or "strike", she points out that it can mean: "A covering for the hand made of thongs of bull-hide, loaded with strips of iron and lead. Used by boxers of ancient Rome." The possessive ascribed to "others'" in line ten is not in manuscript (ed.).

Poem beginning “evoking mocked order showing Me the Blind & Impudent man”
On the other side of this A5 manuscript is the poem beginning: “light. & where is the end. & who was a taut string ringing” (5/A/15/1; see above). Within line six reads “any poetry ~~this~~ / exposure” (the slash is Mendelssohn’s own), and the last line of stanza two concludes: “And ^a^ Lesbians~~ we are & were not~~. ^not not never^” In stanza three, “It was unacceptable” reads: “It was ~~intolera~~ unacceptable”. Finally, a long, right-justified horizontal line is drawn between stanzas two and three.

Poem beginning “Then what was it. when it was before those fronds which are waving my eyes.”
This recto-only A5 manuscript includes a rectangular framed doodle around which the end of the poem is formatted (5/A/15/1). Line four of stanza one reads “if ^you^ ever ~~you~~ come across”; the final line concludes: “sometimes ~~shedding~~ flowing golden beams.” (flowing is written beneath the line). The apostrophe after “tho’” does not appear in manuscript (ed.).

Poem beginning “To have this beauty rammed up in my arm”
A recto-only A5 manuscript in 5/A/15/1, within line 11 reads: “and Bitterness ~~is~~ ^will^ soon to be a sin” (ed.). Before “who had loved” Mendelssohn writes: “~~Of the hundreds and thousands, not tuck shop sweets,~~”. The final line concludes: “living ^self^ justification.”

Poem beginning “As soon as a name is to be addressed another child”
This recto-only A5 manuscript has horizontal drawings in the upper left corner and across page middle and base (5/A/15/1). A left-justified crotchet encompasses the second stanza. Line seven of that stanza reads: “demand. ^they be^ Whilst” (ed.), and the final line reads: “build ^a^ wall”.

Poem beginning “Who told you I was a joke? Or would not be with a”
A small cross-hatched doodle sits in the top right-hand corner of this recto-only A5 manuscript; there are two larger grid-shaped doodles at page bottom (5/A/15/1). The heavily reworked last line reads: “David Bomberg painted ~~one~~ ~~like~~ ^[~~*unclear word*—~~ ed.]^ similar witness~~ing~~ ^to^ ~~similar~~ to such horror.” “[S]imilar” is in red ink; the poem is written in black.

Poem beginning “leave these to die lest grammar offends you, rammed ammonites”
This recto-only A5 text is on heavier, creamier paper stock than most of Mendelssohn’s draft texts for *viola tricolor* (5/A/15/1). Possessives are added to “master’s” and “man’s” (ed.). Edits include:

> “it was not for me” was “it ~~is~~ ^was^ not for me”
> “dream of a street” was “dream ^of a^ street”
> “other daughters” was “other ~~wome~~ daughters”
> “It’s as bad as racial hatred. When” was “It’s as bad as ~~racism~~ racial hatred. ~~facial h~~ When”
> “as muted or as restricted” may be “as muted & as restricted” (ed.)
> “halts fast” was “halts ~~us~~ ~~you~~ fast”
> “all its papers” was “all ~~that it it the~~ its papers”
> “without art.” was “without ~~it~~ art.”
> “might be constructive” was “might be ~~more~~ constructive.”
> “takes the tune” was “takes the tune ~~dragging behind him~~”
> “than sit in” was “than ~~sitting~~ ↓sit↓ in”

The first word of stanza four, "anallage", may be a spelling error, a nonce word, or a portmanteau combining "anlage", meaning "[t]he rudimentary basis of an organ or organism" and "enallage", which refers to "[t]he substitution of one grammatical form for another, e.g. of singular for plural".

"a woman who killed."
On the same paper stock as "leave these to die lest grammar offends you" (5/A/15/1; see above), this recto-only A5 manuscript has a circular doodle in the upper right page corner. Line six of stanza one concludes "utterly. ~~fo~~. They"; the second-last line of stanza two ends "if ~~she~~ recalled." In the penultimate line, after "killed." reads: "~~Did you ever read 'les mains cafés'~~".

Poem beginning "cold water soup channelled through slowly arterial ways wishing well"
The manuscript occupies one full side of A5; on the other side is "one cannot be tempted to agree" (5/A/15/1; see below). Line 16 ends "who never ~~understood~~ tried"; line 17 may conclude what ~~yo~~ ^is^ wanted"; in line 24, "the tough grass" may be or was "the rough grass" (ed.). The last line concludes "and ^upon^ forked tongue".

Poem beginning "one cannot be tempted to agree to an undermining fuselage,"
This A5 manuscript is the other side of the poem beginning "cold water soup channelled through slowly arterial ways wishing well" (5/A/15/1; see above). "Mendleson." is written in the upper left page corner. The second line of stanza two reads "~~in~~ as Rabelaisian"; the first line of stanza three reads "unforgivingness ~~whe~~ once". The phrase "assuaging others' grievances" is unpunctuated, and the last line may occupy its own stanza (ed.).

"drought"
This A5 recto-only manuscript includes doodles next to the title and at page bottom (5/A/15/1). In line six, Mendelssohn crosses out "terrifying" and replaces it with a word possibly beginning "dement" or "demene" with an unclear suffix; from necessity, the original term is used here (ed.). The last line of stanza one reads: "sketching scruff ~~& hills~~". In stanza two, the fourth line includes: "grisly chins & ~~dripping noses~~ pulled". A heavily-drawn line after line nine of stanza two suggests that Mendelssohn considered making lines ten to 13 a third stanza; as this line replicates her formatting when page space is in short supply (see "the fourteenth flight" above), this break is instated here (ed.).

Down the right side of this A5 sheet, Mendelssohn writes: "Paul Rotha: 'Documentary Film.' 1936. F & F." Beneath, she adds: "The Measures Taken. / Hans Eisler // 'Die Massnahme' / Lehrstück by Brecht." and: "Alan & Nancy Bush / with the massed choirs of the london labour choral union. 1936–7." Forward slashes are Mendelssohn's own. Further notes include: "Benjamin Britten, the GPO Film Unit's resident composer and sound track supervisor. 'Peace Film' by Paul Rotha for Strand Films, commissioned by T.U.C. & League of Nations Union." And: "detailed account of the whole 'Peace Film' affair in his 'Documentary Diary – ' London: Secker & Warburg. 1973."

Poem beginning "a love affair with language a marriage to passages"
This is a recto-only A5 manuscript with sketches of eight heads in profile at the bottom of the page (5/A/15/1). Stanza one, line three reads: "concerned with ~~personal~~ ^human^ relations."; before the "stacked" of line eight was "~~pil~~". In stanza two, the first line was "~~the conte~~ [*or* ~~*confe*~~ ed.] structures" and line five ends "want ~~to~~ ^a^ robot". "[N]o more books." is faintly, repeatedly underlined, and the final line may not occupy its own stanza (ed.).

Poem beginning "it is not for you to say or tell to bode"
In addition to minor excisions of articles, in this untitled A5 manuscript line four reads "his ~~extended~~ outstretching arms" ("outstretching" is below the line); line eight begins "~~but you~~". In stanza two, line one reads "playce ~~yo~~ that" and line two includes "left for ~~other breeds~~ what stoop" (5/A/15/1). The poem appears to end with "reach masqued or gagged." Beneath that line, there are horizontal doodles across page bottom, one of which is inscribed: "Punched". Below these drawings, in a less formal hand than is used for the poem, Mendelssohn writes:

> We come close to judgement all the days of our lives
> It is you who are too concerned with impressing people
> You make me sick for that reason & I dismiss your significance for no other.

As in the marginal notes for the poem beginning "light. & where is the end. & who was a taut string ringing" (see above), the verso side of this manuscript bears a titled quote from Elizabeth Barrett Browning:

> The Dead Pan
>
> gods of Hellas. gods of Hellas
>
> III
>
> Do ye sit there still in slumber,
> In gigantic Alpine rows?
> The black poppies out of number
> Nodding, dripping from your brows
> To the red lees of your wine
> And be kept alive and fine?
> Pan, Pan is dead.

Poem beginning "by exploiting the future on reserved matters of relief work."
This landscape-oriented typescript consists of two A5 sheets with minor typos corrected by hand; continuity between pages is evident (5/A/15/1). In stanza one, an extra line appears between lines four and five reading: "~~by two serious men~~".

"<u>a minuet by mendleson</u>."
This A5 poem consists of two recto-only manuscripts; the bottom third of the sheet is torn off the second page (5/A/15/1). Paper stock and ink are identical on both sheets, as are the scrawled hand, formatting, accentuation, and editorial procedure. In stanza three, "unto a warmer" may be "into a warmer" and "backless departs from" may be "backless departs for"; in the final stanza, "o zeugma" may be "a zeugma", and "salammbô" reads "sallambo" (ed.).

In file 5/B/2/67, there are additional manuscripts of "<u>a minuet by mendleson</u>.", numbered here one to six. All are on A5 sheets in black ink. Number one is titled "minuet by mendleson." and includes stanzas two through four. Number two contains reworkings of stanzas three and four, with some outsize letters – "o", "8", and "x" – interspersed with dashed lines at page bottom. Along the right margin, Mendelssohn writes a definition of zeugma: "figure of speech using a verb or adjective with two nouns, to one of which it is strictly applicable while the word appropriate to the other is not used." At the top of number three reads the time signature "6/8", followed by six crotchets and a separate line of six quavers. Below this, Mendelssohn's heavily slashed single line reads "when am/ongst the / clou/dy / ha/vens /," beneath which reads: "minuet". Three drafts of stanza one follow, and in the right margin, Mendelssohn writes: "serte / service due from ~~the~~ / a servant to a lord." Candles and abstract shapes are drawn below this definition; a fish-shape floats in page middle, between two stanzas; within reads: "worse".

At the top of the fourth manuscript also reads "6/8."; lacking any other title, this variant includes versions of stanzas one and two only. Next to stanza one reads "2 strains"; next to the second writing of stanza one reads: "erectio / perturbation of moon's motion by sun's attraction." Further, Mendelssohn writes: "zenana That part of house in which women of high-caste families are secluded in India and Iran." "John the Evangelist" is also written in this right margin, and alongside stanza two, Mendelssohn lists: "ronsard // jacobean / stuart / italian // doves". On a torn bottom third of A5 sheet, in the same scrawled hand as in the manuscript included in the appendix, is an additional stanza that was originally part of the poem, as it precisely fits the missing portion of the second page noted above. This is manuscript five. Manuscript six is an A5 sheet bearing four additional lines, likely intended for that stanza, and also rendered in manuscript three.

In manuscript one of 5/B/2/67, the following substantive changes occur: "white horse in the park" was "whitehorse ~~in grazi~~ in the park"; "regard of rearguard fixation / as womb keeper" was "~~from~~ regard of rearguard ~~attact~~ fixation as womb / ~~womb~~ keeper"; "craft / with surnatural births" was "craft with ~~sup~~ sur / ~~with super~~natural births". Throughout, Mendelssohn places lines above syllables as if to mark rhythmic stresses; this process likely informs the accentuation replicated in the appendix. In manuscript two, lines two to five of stanza three are iterated, then Mendelssohn toys with using line five of stanza three (rendered "to a warmer city") as the first line of a variant of stanza four, in which the last lines read: "crossed both ways divided / devoid of a phantom / phaetons domed chariot".

In manuscript three, the variations of stanza one read:

dusk thread through full cloudy havens
ret/ir/ing out from ser/te plight to beauty
slips ~~a~~ a footstep sprightly

dusk thread through cloudy halls
retiring ~~out~~ from serte's plight
to soft rustlings phaetons ~~cars~~ [*note: "plight" is repeated in far-left margin of this line*]
chariots unfurling ~~beams~~
ˋ ˋ ˋ ˋ ˋ ˋ

beams

dusk thread through cloudy halls
retiring from serte's
plight to ~~soft~~ phaeton's
chariots unfurling
beams descend deliver
firm m

Beneath this is a variant of the stanza included in manuscript five (see below), with some differences in lineation, and the following four lines added to the end: "by spurred pace / in futile barrage / purposed to strip antiquity's masques / from a solitary face."

Manuscript four includes two versions of stanza one, and a variant of stanza four. Minor differences are many and various, including, for instance, "airy perpetuum" rather than "airy per / petuum". Substantive differences include: "unfurling chariot's" was "chariots unfurling" and "~~chariot beams~~ / unfurling chariots". Lines eight to ten of stanza one read: "all withheld ~~to~~ central / passing reflecting ~~edges~~ ↓gest↓ / zenana"; this iteration of the stanza ends here. Alternately, lines seven to ten were: "courtesy ~~withhelds~~ ^holds^ ~~cent~~ axis / ~~to passing~~ all withhold / transpassing mirrored gest". In stanza four, "a forkēd path / wasting time" was "a ~~storm~~ forked path / ~~as though these studied artifices~~ / wasting time". In addition to differences in articles and line breaks, Mendelssohn adds the first line of stanza three to the end of stanza two.

The excised stanza on the torn sheet – manuscript five – reads:

> talking blindly deaf to murmur
> heedful yet — unheeding [*no dash in manuscript three*]
> mundanity emblazoned
> to outshine a current picture
> outpractise a current practise
>   outdivide a division
> already too terrible to avert
> by ground down pointed instruments
>   personal imputations
> glozened over only to be cracked [*"glazed over" in manuscript three*]

There are accents – flat, horizontal lines – above the "un" of "unheeding" and the "ti" of "imputations". In its entirety, manuscript six reads: "by spurred pace / in futile barrage / purposed to strip antiquity's masques / from a single face."

Poem beginning "incrustation, fossilised cement, caked dry canine's excrement,"
This A5 recto-only manuscript in brown ink is torn from a notebook (5/A/15/1). Paper shows signs of ageing, and the stock is unique among *viola tricolor* manuscripts. Beneath the second-last line "tucking their pampered feet", Mendelssohn draws an arrow from "their" to the start of the line, suggesting that she considered placing the pronoun first (ed.). Three edits – two in black ink – correct spelling and illegibility.

"because this won't do. it never did do. as defined as refusal."
In page upper left, above the title of this recto-only, uncorrected A5 manuscript, Mendelssohn writes "poetry." (5/A/15/1). The "me" in line three may be "one" (ed.).

Poem beginning "ignorance confiscates literature surfaces to be minimized"
In the top left corner of this recto-only A5 manuscript reads: "~~ignorance~~" (5/A/15/1). In the final line of stanza one, both uses of "this" were "a", and ruin is added above the line. The penultimate line of stanza two began "~~What was~~ that it was". Although it follows seamlessly on the page from stanza three, the final couplet is marked as a separate stanza by a horizontal line similar to those used in the manuscript of "the fourteenth flight" in this same collection (ed.).

Poem beginning "sickened by the sight of the yard thewed daughters"
This is a landscape-oriented, recto-only typescript on two A5 sheets, with minor edits added by hand in two different black pens (5/A/15/1). Continuity is suggested by formatting, and by contents that bear relation to the draft typescript of "two secs", of which these pages may be early drafts (see below notes).

"two secs" (*early draft*)
Part of the final publication of *viola tricolor*, "two secs" is included in the predominantly manuscript, draft chapbook as a typescript on two A5 recto sides (5/A/15/1). The substantial differences in line breaks, substance, and length of this draft variant warrant including it as a unique entry in the appendix. Edits are mainly of typos, barring, in the third-last line "parsed, ~~pissed~~, look"; additionally, the last line reads "victor's boot. ~~yet~~". Beneath "filling in the past", Mendelssohn writes "i.e. drawing". Content overlaps with the typescripts beginning "sickened by the sight of the yard thewed daughters" (see above, and further note on "two secs" in *viola tricolor* in main volume). In this draft, "nureyev" reads "nuryev" (ed.).

There is a less clean manuscript of this poem in SxMs109/5/B/2/97; it occupies two sides of A5 paper in tiny script. This version is longer than both published poem and the draft typescript included in the appendix. It includes a reworking of the opening lines, and the entirety reads as follows:

if this holds & goes no further could belief be a fine sudden
readings jam each other wasps and needing what in others proven
without derision to be this shaken always dubious, added weight.
if life before has told of such I could not lick my whiskers
but make haste in sorrow not in loathing and when I leave I do.
others gather where and lost I cannot bow to one who love~~d~~s ~~the~~ ^a^ caricature~~s~~
of hurt mankind in these abrupt dismissive times where love knows no
~~admis~~ no admission as women guard against the drives which have
indeed strewn corpses but sometimes that can lead too to deaths ~~as~~ with care
an honest shrew.

<u>two secs.</u>

if this holds & goes no further could belief be a fine sudden
reading jam each other~~s~~ wasps and needing what in others proven
letters, papers, microfiche, secretaries, maids, mansions, and a bulldog
mourning nuryev, and would not take his spirit for a scathing
word or two on dancing for the colonels where culture leads us to
can we care or is that a dangerous interview I despair
& will not laugh at others pain or would if ~~I could~~ ^to^ support it
with a host of goodly power but ~~cults are~~ ^were nott^ illegitimate. ~~& whilst~~
& while to hoist machinery of administration I think one back
& walk to talk to tell you not what should offend you so, myths
there are a plenty, and most of them imported from extra situationists

who think in terms ~~to la~~ too large to use ~~a~~ something ~~other than~~ apart from
the real world to charge a fortune to my name ~~and never look me~~
and never look me in the face again what was is now no longer
nuryev did not go to santiago and I was less than interested
personally in anyone I ever met which has its good and bad aspects.
how goodly to be held but not by an officer in uniform,
goodbye chi wa wa, filling in the past with no expectations for the future
~~taking d~~ dismantling the flats in the diagonal indicating exit
a drawing prize, darkness at noon, and repeatedly turning controls
down to zero, wrong & cheap, it ~~ta~~ would take a lot more intention
perhaps art is not a pastime perhaps it is a practise or it was
before it didn't matter what one says to one is not always said to another.
& turning good to bad is as easy as a misprint peepers, papers,
sudden, sodden, letters, lettuce, cults, colts, face, faeces,
past, pissed, look, cook, offend, portend, other, smother.
I know that you are angry because you disagree that women don't deserve
to be shot for working for peace and that you say that they are shot
because they have no energy, no structured energy, no politics
& so your lawyers ~~ca~~ come to rape us as we prepare for sleep
having cajoled us into agreeing to marry you and which girl
does not wish to be as free to walk out of a chamber as a lawyer
and as humanely & justly concerned and yet too fond of
his working class heroes to hear the inner voice of the girl at his side
although there may have been liberalization in these movements
it doesn't prevent a friend or an enemy from slipping the girl
a book ~~wa~~ warning her of what happened to women whose husbands
were at war whatever his words were, however infrequent,
kept up a steady, virtually inaccessible stream of control through
intimidating language. That is man at war. And for many
Many years I was under the delusion that I was within sight of
freedom which no one else could claim under a banner which
had been ~~pe~~ written in another hand and no, I was not searching
for self glorification but it's one of those strange things in the
world of writing that ones body, when writing as such was an art,
was part of the ~~writ~~ work it created. Have we no alternative
than to walk away and let people kill themselves and others
~~if~~ if life takes ~~up~~ us into a place where we ~~ha~~ had no reason to
suspect danger. It can happen in any relationship,
suddenly a knife is thrust to one's throat, or a gun
appears from nowhere. Any abuse thereafter made me rigid.

I remember myself as being in touch with reality. Other peoples views
Interested me but I could not have written a book about serious
differences based on one personss different approach to existence.
It is a writers job to be fair. ~~and as~~ That shows the mettle of a writer.
It is not a writerss job to invest in sensationalism for the sake of it.
~~I detest being~~ I detested being thrown into ~~jail~~ prison.
It was real punishment for what had not been my idea.
And I still meet people who call me selfish without further explanation.
If writers are in danger of having their reputations damaged
as much as mine has been, ~~the~~ freedom of movement severely hampered,
~~che~~ accused of writing what was not written by me,
and lies as thick as secrecy at its worst, menacing me.
Voicing hatred is petty. But if you care about someone it can catch your heart
I am almost at the point of giving up on language, ~~if~~ I hear
my children being returned on the rare occasion I am permitted
to be with them iterating concerns over anger, I shall NOT be
treated in this way and neither should they be
I have Never needed anyone to teach me lessons ^on matters^ concerning Injustice.
I hesitate to add it is not ~~it~~ an [*"an" could read "in"*—ed.] emotion which produces good writing.
Neither is distress. Raw emotion should choose an instrument
which causes less loss. Anger at ignorant attitudes yes.
Careless thinking. Rapid firing . More tolerance for the pathos
of the poetry of the poor and less inducement to write doggerel.

"Demeter."
Consisting of two A5 recto sides, this manuscript poem has an underlined title and the top left corner of page two reads: "Demeter (cont)" (5/A/15/1). Punctuation has been added to line 13, "hostility against females' academic progress" (ed.).

Poem beginning "I shake and cry. How then could I ever love you"
Beneath this A5 manuscript poem, there is a sketch of an animal head in profile, its body an amorphous cape. The verso reads:

locked out. from the Temple.

but it was not a building.

a hole. know
a spyhole.
a skylark
a lacrosse ball injury

Beneath these words, Mendelssohn writes:

the epistle is not ~~written~~ addressed to me. it ~~is~~ as was written in 1711. nearly three hundred years ago. Are years water? Does time go as fast as money. Three hundred years of solitude. But I did not project myself into that time. I don't know this connection. Eternity hurts. We wanted a cultured home.

My father I was always trying to cheer.
To make his life worth living.

I cannot change the sun into the moon.

The page includes three doodles; beside one Mendelssohn writes "a slug"; another appears to read "Marssaille".

" ' "sumbur" ' "
"Sumbur" is Russian for "muddle". There are two variants of " ' "sumbur" ' ": a recto-only A5 manuscript (5/A/15/1) and an A4 typescript (5/A/15/3). In manuscript, line two reads "upon ~~in~~articulate"; in line five, "sullen" may have been "stamped", and "daren't rebuff" was "don't rebuff". In stanza two, "paper forbidden" was "paper is / forbidden". The last line of the poem reads "may ~~not~~ be not". Poem format is replicated in "Sauce" in *viola tricolor.*

Poem beginning "humans gaze clod to cloud depicted as brainless & reverent, neat"
This recto-only A5 manuscript may be a fragment (5/A/15/1). The second-last line is edited in pencil and reads: "frowning at the ~~impudence of~~ ^imprudent^ nations'". Edited in the same black ink as the poem, the last line reads "forms, ~~the~~ unauthorized".

Poem beginning "je crois la haine peur l'esprit d'amour mais je vous en prie"
This poem is on one side of an A5 manuscript; on the other side is the poem beginning "they were, in those days, his players." (5/A/15/1; see below). Above the neatly written poem is scrawled: "if socialism couldn't support poets / without removing our children then / I have nothing to say." Line two reads "que le suj la question"; line seven was "jouent en seri gravement"; in couplet four, "crème de la crème" was "crême de la crême" and in the final couplet, Mendelssohn renders "jeux" as "jeus" (ed.).

Poem beginning "they were, in those days, his players. He and his Queen, His friend and his Queen."
This manuscript is on the other side of the poem beginning "je crois la haine" (5/A/15/1; see above). Mendelssohn edits include: line nine, "one ^who^ does"; line ten, "imagin~~ation~~ing" and "no home ~~in cities / Prisoners of bu~~". At the end of stanza two, she writes: "from attack / ~~In the days of Dag Hammershojld. Be careful to desyncrenize vic~~tory hoots." "[H]oots" or "victory hoots" may follow "attack" (ed.). Throughout, possessives are added to "others'", "Revolution's" and "politics'" (ed.).

"the secret ballot.   Austraque."
There are two A4 typescripts of this poem (5/A/15/3). In both, bottom right-hand corners read in enlarged font, "*viola tricolor*". One copy is paginated eight, neatly amended by hand, and is part of Mendelssohn's submission to the Arts Council, Work in Progress. 1993 (see 5/A/16, where page eight is missing). The second is unpaginated, and after "AND ALWAYS HAD." Mendelssohn leaves about ten blank lines, then types: "where exactly is the replacement economy going to come from when you have wasted it / on hideous anoraks,". Both versions begin "a reversed statistic"; above this phrase in the paginated variant reads, by hand, "an inverted"; similarly, in the otherwise identical line three, "was reputed to have" is above the line. Further unique handwritten additions to the paginated variant include the two lines beginning "only a fraction" and the subtitle, "Austraque."

"for Vera MacUllum. Assistant Governor."
This recto-only A4 manuscript includes a small drawing. Minor edits include: in line three, "into ~~con~~ monitored"; in line eight, "to ^women's^ naturally fanatical"; in line ten, "~~that~~ which is"; in line 12, "I reserve ~~the~~ ^my^ qualified", and in line 15, "to ^be^ personally" (5/A/15/3).

Prose poem beginning "who are these who tell you what you want to know? would they were not these."
In this recto-only, landscape-oriented A4 typescript, the lines "elsa triolet who turned / aragon into a smart arse?" are repeated in the same format, then excised with correction fluid (5/A/15/3). Note also the similar ending shared by this poem and "So then what are we going to do? Are we going to subject too?" in *Slate* submission drafts (1987).

As discussed in the volume editorial notes on *viola tricolor*, in this same file, and immediately after "who are these who tell you", is an irregular-sized, landscape-formatted typescript page of three lines. This page may be the conclusion of this poem, and reads: "crossed, condemned. the plague. the poor. inhibited imaginations. frail. the context . . . not in Raymo / Raymond williams' 'Keywords'. The context is withheld within the literary tradition. / Blake, Leigh Hunt, Mary Wollstonecraft. Let God be my Judge."

Grace Lake, *Tondo Aquatique*, draft poem (c. 1996–1997)
"[R]emembering prenuptials." is a manuscript located in one of the four main files associated with *Tondo Aquatique* (1997) in Mendelssohn's Sussex archive (SxMs109/5/A/23/1). Along the top centre of the A4 sheet reads, in large hand: "Tondo Aquatique." The poem does not appear in Mendelssohn's 1997 chapbook. The verso side includes captioned drawings reading: "I don't talk I seethe."; "gold paper clip"; "sylvia beech"; "string.", and "~~music~~ metaphorical lyric in ^a^ time of emergency". The references to "coating" at poem beginning and end are echoed in four pages of prose held in the same *Tondo Aquatique* file. See also notes on the published chapbook.

In stanza one, line nine, "evil lo the warm" could be "evil to the warm" (ed.). In stanza three, short horizontal lines above and below the "You" of line ten suggest that Mendelssohn considered adding a stanza break, and possessives are added to both "nation's" (ed.).

Anna Mendelssohn, *Implacable Art*, draft poems (c. 1999–2000)
There are eleven files devoted exclusively to *Implacable Art* (*IA*) in Mendelssohn's Sussex archive (SxMs109/5/A/24/1–11). These files contain poems that are not in *IA*, including: a photocopy of the first poem in Mendelssohn's 1996 collection, *Parasol One. Parasol Two. Parasol Avenue.* (5/A/24/1); an untitled typescript of "Truth or Vermillion", first published in 1996 in *involution*, no. 4; and a draft poem that references segments three and ten of Mendelssohn's 1998 *Inscape* submission (5/A/24/2; see notes). Some additional poems were expressly considered for *IA*; see, for example, "'we cannot sing intimated'", discussed below.

In 5/A/24/1 are two unfinished poems that are, in places, difficult to read. One begins:

> burning up over the strikes, a lost engine, Solitude,   grim, bitter.
> anti-drame.   were you in love?
>
> damned dangerous.   hands flaying? hands flaring, flopping out.

the eternal plaint of the woman : "can't do it."
this is no time/place for soft sounding poems.

poems.
poems.
poems. are for sorrow, for innocence.

Random House.

'It's when you have known, my experience of demons.

I thought that it was Demonism.

(~~to remove~~ to confiscate).

from a limited influence the grand image of authority.
the ease with which power is entitled to indulge its whims.

In the same file, another page reads:

no-one inspires confidence in me.

a pause. playing a trial as a piece of music.

a word. the living reality of a word. false familiarity.

blatant harassment.

it's a mistake to waste time with anyone who does not write without pretending that
they are everyone who does not write, who has no difficulties,
who is not expecting to be written about. to write about anyone else . . .

The file also includes French language practice, a note on mistakenness and the family courts, as well as titled and untitled drawings that are not included amongst the artwork reproduced in *IA*. As is customary in Mendelssohn's files, there are numerous passing references to thinkers and writers, among them, Edmund Husserl, Noam Chomsky, Harold Pinter, William Wordsworth, and P. B. Shelley. Further, Mendelssohn mentions the French historian Jean Gimpel and the film *Dangerous Moonlight* (1941), its Warsaw Concerto, *Cradle Will Rock* (1999), and its director, Tim Robbins. Five poems in this file are included in this appendix; each is discussed below.

File 5/A/24/2 also includes a folded A3 sheet bearing a poem that transitions into notes. It begins:

Paper does not deliver itself.
no-one was asking for any.
whose hatred?
not an immaculate parliamentary
secretary's.
the people below the salt believing
themselves to be above it.
staggering.

dredges staggering from the depths
seaweed clinging to their teeth,
children left with a senior prefect.

his private habits removed that
prefix.

build your own paper mill.
heave the bricks yourself.
dig the foundations. on
bread and water.

There are echoes here of the *IA* poem beginning "digne.", specifically, the line: "Serve your own sentences." (see main text). Beneath this poem, Mendelssohn continues more prosaically:

he lived by a private code book.
p 672. the working class is dirty.
    watch how they bathe.
USUALLY they don't lecture on
    landscape in the novels of
    Thomas Hardy whilst
    they are soaping themselves.

His soap has a fragrance that
reminds him of her shoulders.

Along the margin of this busy page, which is awash in doodles, some proper nouns, and the date "November 29th.", Mendelssohn writes: "the body is writing, the law is the body, writing the body is / legal there is no such thing as an illegitimate body".

Throughout 5/A/24/2 are drawings and notes, including an injunction "to stop being ~~stopp~~ interfered with by any who prefer to destroy the artist for the sake of the reputations of any who don't discriminate between a life preoccupied with questions relating to art and a life ^in^ which art ~~is~~ does not enter into plans". Passing references are made to nineteenth-century mathematician and scientist Henri Poincaré, the Sioux warrior Crazy Horse, Peter Wollen's review of J. Hoberman's

The Red Atlantis: Communist Culture in the Absence of Communism (1998), and an address for Canadian Universities Travel in Paris. There is word play, such as: "Bailiffs / Bay leaves / Liffey" and a scrap of writing, replete with doodles, titled "a dangerous woman". It reads: "rips her daughter's heart out, her eyes too. could not bear the son her daughter / bore. picks up bore, chews later. / successful visitors buoy her. // dealt in stomachs." Two additional poems in this file are included in the appendix and discussed below.

Details follow regarding the location, writing, and editing of the remaining poem drafts located in the *IA* files that are included in this appendix.

"Rue du Bac"
This poem is a clean, unedited A4 manuscript (5/A/24/1).

Poem beginning "and my veins unpunctured"
This text is a clean A4 manuscript (5/A/24/1). Along the top are a series of horizontal doodles; centrally at page bottom is a small, abstract drawing.

Poem beginning "He was my conscience."
This A4 manuscript is in 5/A/24/1.

Poem beginning "What shining arrogance saw themselves"
This A4 manuscript is in 5/A/24/1. An extended doodle runs along page top from left corner to centre. Line four begins: "far from ~~the~~ raw".

"goetz o.r.t."
This manuscript is in 5/A/24/1, and includes the following corrections:

> "food, far from" was "food, ~~far~~ far from"
> "and parodying" was "and parod~~ies~~ying"
> "interregnum subconscious" was "interregnum ~~unco~~ subconscious"
> "between the juices" was "between the ~~guilty~~ juices"
> "venomous spirit" was "venomous ~~pall sentiment energy~~ spirit"
> "into creation." was "into creation~~'s holy day~~."

At the end of lines three, 12, and 15, Mendelssohn draws short horizontal lines akin to her inserted stanza breaks on crowded or overrunning pages elsewhere; see, for example, above notes on an A3 draft of "the fourteenth flight" for *viola tricolor* (1993). Space is not at the same premium in this instance. Alternately, these lines may indicate Mendelssohn's em-dashes, which can approximate extended forward slashes. Given these uncertainties, they are not included in this text (ed.). Beneath the poem, Mendelssohn draws two small doodles and writes: "Chopin Étude ^No^ 10".

"'we cannot sing intimated'"
This poem is an unedited A4 manuscript (5/A/24/2). In the *IA* files, there are three manuscript versions of the text's index or

"Table", one of which runs from pages one to 129, and includes a reference to this poem, titled "we cannot sing 'intimidated'" (5/A/27/7).

"slass coelitus arieto glass classico chivet"
This poem is written out on three separated sheets of continuous stationery formatted for a dot-matrix printer (5/A/24/2). Ordering is uncertain: while page two may follow on from the first titled sheet, the perforated top of the third sheet retains a fragment from a previous page that does not align with page two. Page breaks are reproduced (ed.). The entirety is in black ink; the title is in blue.

A doodle at the bottom of the first page is accompanied by hard to discern notes on the Russian film production of Pushkin's short story, "The Queen of Spades". The planned release date was 1937, or the centenary of the author's death, but the project remained unrealised due to government censorship. Mikhail Romm was to direct, and the composer, Sergei Prokofiev, later resuscitated part of the unused score in his Piano Sonata Number 8. Mendelssohn's notes include "M. Romm." and "Prokofiev transforms into one of the opening themes for the first movement of the Eighth Sonata." Mention is also made of "Russian Overture Op. 72. / Malgarin." Pages two and three are clean manuscripts; in page three, stanza two, "execrable" is written "excretable" (ed.).

Poem beginning, "Reading overhead, the sink back is being defended as defensive,"
This poem is written out on a cue card (5/A/24/8). After "James the" Mendelssohn writes "~~ten pin~~ [*unclear word*—ed.] pin"; these words are not included here (ed.). In line eleven, "I" may be "&," (ed.).

Anna Mendelssohn, *py.*, draft poems. (c. 2009)
Mendelssohn's archive includes three files that are wholly devoted to *py.*, her A5 chapbook published by Oystercatcher press in 2009 (SxMs109/5/A/25/1–3). Files one and two contain manuscripts; the third houses a typescript undertaken by Mendelssohn's eldest daughter Poppy. Within these files are five draft poems – manuscript and/or typescript – that do not appear in the final volume. Included here, these poems are discussed below in order of appearance.

Poem beginning "Patisseries in real salzbourg."
The photocopied manuscript shows this poem within a notebook bound with a metal spiral (5/A/25/1). Within the text, "salzbourg" appears to read "slalzbourg" and "rorschach" was "rorsach" (ed.)

Poem beginning "palette in monochrome"
There are multiple variants of this poem in Mendelssohn's files, including a typescript (5/A/25/3), and a small manuscript photocopied onto an expansive A3 sheet, surrounded by marks replicating the scored glass surface of the copier (5/A/25/1).

In 5/A/25/2, there exist two additional manuscripts: in one, the poem appears on its own, unedited, and on an A4 sheet. In the other, it is third in a column of four sestets (poems beginning "pochoir silver threaded snail", "Perruche, the rising rapids," "palette", and "photographs of snow"), beneath which reads "œufs / enlèvement / the odd word // eglefin". In the right corner of this latter manuscript is a doodle, and to its left reads "pixel / east // yeast"; at page bottom reads "photograph meets photograph" (5/A/25/2). The words "œufs" and "eglefin" recur in *py.* poem 16 beginning "Power has a temper".

Poem beginning "permanent enough"
This poem is an unedited manuscript on a torn portion of A5 paper (5/A/25/2).

Poem beginning "pochoir silver threaded snail"
This A4 manuscript is one of a group of four drafts (see "palette in monochrome" notes above). In line three of the poem, "eastern" was "ermine", and the correction is made in an alternate ink (5/A/25/2).

Poem beginning "Perruche, the rising rapids"
This poem exists in manuscript in 5/A/25/2 (two copies), and in typescript in 5/A/25/3. In one manuscript, the poem is in a group of four drafts (see "palette in monochrome" notes above). Here, the first word is not capitalised. In another, the poem begins with an over-sized "P" and the last line starts with a large "Y" in which the descender is elongated (5/A/25/2). An A4 manuscript of *py.* sestet 14 beginning "Pendragon in purdah" includes three doodles, between two of which reads the word "Perruche" (5/A/25/2).

Grace Lake/Anna Mendelssohn: Collections as Published

When the poem in question is untitled, the first line is given in quotation marks; when it is titled, no quotation marks appear. Where titular quotation marks are used by Mendelssohn, they are rendered as single quotation marks within double; quotation marks that appear mid-title, or are single marks, are left standing.

Anne Mendleson, Typescripts (1974).
"Cover the land"

Anne Mendleson/Grace Lake, Sheffield typescript (November 1981).
BEING 707 $_4{}^{C}$
Exposition
a., b., c., d., e., f., g.
Sums.

Anne Mendleson, Untitled typescript (c. 1981–82).
Masquerade
classique
ars peregrinandi: spreidh.
"why head aching?"
Pedal
Whirr slightly operationless.
Eleven
Find One Page Evenly.
rubbish.   desk bang.

Anne Mendleson, *Crystal Love: D. N. A.,* Green Suede Blues Press (1982).
"destiny forecast revolt"
"Power to move"
"melancholy might answer in future mistakes,"
"Machiavelli strikes"
"Black velvet cloth"
GUIDE
"I like Red People"
"maybe I shall"

"Treading carpentry free country"
CADENCE.
"a settlement of priorities reaches unassailable"
Shell form: Conch tent. (for John Barker)
"think twice"
"quietly noon"
"Buried deep in the honey"
nonflec

Crystal Love: D. N. A., draft poems (1982).
crystal love. D.N.A.
Demirel Camp
"closed gates"
"The matter of the matter hard to solve in the language of languators."
"Speak judgement into ear"

Anne Mendleson, *Posmos, the Yellow Velvet Underground.* (1982).
IN A CAVERNOUS HEAT HAZE
Check the scene
Whirr slightly operationless
"Squashed in, world's different; sickness"
small points.
"making machine poetry"

Grace Lake, "*I'm working here.*", Green Suede Blues Press (February 1983).
"slide slip joke dent"
so did apollinaire and aragon
Bossa
"and don't we know why?"
Baked's are in for tender-hearts.
"January is grin-ful & dreaming"
COMYRRHING.
"cricket"
"Titless stares"
That broad red sun-light.
proscribble at 16.12 hours.
one that is not you.
Experience

Grace Lake, *Celestial Empire.* (February 1983).
Some prose subsections may be inaccurate or go unlisted (ed.).

1769–82 Duke of Wellington. [prose; not in this collection]
Chivalry is a beautiful facet of the mind to-day. [prose]
A MARRON - BLANC [prose]
THE COCKTAIL STICK [prose]
THE PARK - BENCH [prose]
A PINE CONE [prose]
HER FATHER TURNED OUT TO BE A VIVISECTIONIST. [prose]
IVY CLINGS AS A SPOT CHECK [prose]
"For the space was a dream" [part of prose collection; not included]
Secco. [part of prose collection; not included]
HOW CAN SOMEONE SUBTRACT WHEN THEY HAVE NOTHING! (minus gradients). [prose]
FROM COMMUNISM TO UTOPIA. [prose]
PERSONAL ADUMBRATION. [prose]
qh! [not included]
Cassis maçao [not included]
THAT ROSY, COSY NIGHT-CLUB AFTERNOON
WORDS CHARGE.
Giaconda's Contumacious Lapse.
Sums.
Speaking rhythm
UNFINISHED
SACRED PIN.

Grace Lake, Typescript (October 1983).

oh yes we are entitled mohican slaves
dig; dig.

Grace Lake, *Other Poetry* submission (6 June 1984).

"point a finger at him"

Grace Lake and Timothy Mathews, *poems.* (1984).

from views – Lake
'The bourgeoisie lives there' – Lake
To PP158, 159, 160,170 MoMA Sol Lewitt. – Lake
"All my friends in imagination" – Mathews

“Anxiety rips” – Mathews
“Apologies are in order” – Mathews
“Spots on an abstract space” – Mathews
“Finally the banality glows” – Mathews
“The affiliation is broken” – Mathews
“Of course in her absence” – Mathews
“For those abstractions” – Mathews
“reduced size rapidly grew” – Lake
‘Clichés’ – Mathews
Countdown – Mathews
“Take a long train” – Lake
very early poem – Lake
“That piano is my god” – Lake
“rolled   rolled a   a” – Lake

Grace Lake, Formatted manuscript (June 1985).
“rolling, and all these words are alive and”

Grace Lake, *Propaganda Multi-Billion Bun.* (August 1985).
“who is this person, high-walking into fantasy?”
“rubbish.   desk bang.”
“find one page evenly.”
“merely ridicule & sweetness”
“i can hardly bear going down town to see those people”
ELEVEN.
“The toughie would say:”
“What is wrong with ‘easy’?”
great big sparkling Deal no relation.
<u>for Anne Devlin</u>
“or out rageous to be a singing steamer!”
“She appears in thirteen dresses.”
“don’t be northern, whatever you do, don’t start”
after georgina jackson’s lovely victory.

Grace Lake, *Inbuilt Flash Nix* (August 1985) [Sussex edition]
Inbuilt Flash Nix [prose; not in this collection]
<u>When I gave all my records away</u>. [prose; not in this collection]

"into the dips and angles" [prose; not in this collection]
Train to L'pool.
"Shiva's crackling on a spinal hair"
"piped, once more, piped"
Horror Impudence Chastisement
"it's the truth! He cannot contain his stains" [later: Graves' Art Gallery Tea Room, 1981, Sheffield]
Whirr slightly operationless.
LOCALIZED PLASTER.
LOCALIZED EFFECTS.
"yes, it is a shame, a real shame:" [poem italicised in full in 1986]
"APOTHECARIES' KNUCKLEDUSTERS SUIT THEIR"
?
"Must you?' She seldom burns"
Follow her magic.
Radiated? Light?
HOT DAY. BAKED BARE EARTH. PROWLED IN THE VALLEY FOR THE PIGS' NEST.
"Were they allowed to write"
One on each shoulder, carouse.

Grace Lake, *Is this a True Parrot, a Mountain, or a Stooge?*, Scrap Publishing (1985).
The ordering of what follows remains uncertain (ed.).
Whirr slightly operationless.
"it's the truth! He cannot contain his stains" [later: Graves' Art Gallery Tea Room, 1981, Sheffield]
One on each shoulder, carouse.
LOCALIZED EFFECTS.
LOCALIZED PLASTER.
"Must you?' She seldom burns"
"Were they allowed to write"
Who cycled in two fours?
Someone to rely on. [prose; not in this collection]
Where?

Grace Lake, Typescript (1985)
WHY
Dear chaos.

Grace Lake, Typescript (22 April 1986).
a room a

Grace Lake, Typescript (September 1986).
In the end tulane –
tripping up on jibes / Oxford.
Above her heart, a grand piano.

Grace Lake, *AN ACCOUNT OF A MUMMY, IN The Royal Cabinet of Antiquities at DRESDEN* (October 1986).
Not   So   Good [regular spacing and not underlined in 1987]
Not   Bad. [regular spacing and not underlined in 1987]
That's Fascism
No   Timing.

Grace Lake, "*Inbuilt Flash Nix*, & Nine Poems, Three Collages." *constant red/mingled damask*, no. 1 (September 1986).
Inbuilt Flash Nix [prose; not in this collection]
Radiated? Light?
Train to L'pool
"yes it is official, sitting at a table. pen in hand,"
"Shiva's crackling on a spinal hair"
Graves' Art Gallery Tea Room, 1981, Sheffield [earlier: "it's the truth! He cannot contain his stains"]
MOODIST
Follow her magic
"*yes, it is a shame, a real shame:*" [regular spacing and unitalicised in 1985]
"to have some stupid bloke laughing and giggling at you."

Grace Lake, Typescript (October 1986).
"to fit the prototype."

Grace Lake, Typescript (March 1987).
"Police-Armed Training Session: Growl."

Grace Lake, "Nine Poems." *constant red/mingled damask*, no. 2 (April 1987), 39–50.
" 'Please put weights beneath them & regard them as concrete' "

"It is always difficult to know whether"
Wolore
"It shouldn't be this way, just,"
"it's great when people defend each other;"
As Things Stand
Not So Good
Not Bad
"*rather than bloom out to die*"

Grace Lake, *The News*, no. 1 (April 1987).
Winter [title with full stop and/or underlining in later variants]
Tansy Tchaikovsky
" 'The solemn mists, dark brown or pale, / March slow and solemn down the vale.' " [title underlined and without full stop in later publication in 1987]
They are further than temptation, to argue, to refrain
Little Dog Mine 1948
On An Emery Board [titular full stop later in 1987]
To a Radical Lesbian Feminist Rapist
"Madge De Fanfare, blind to the miserable lives forced upon the"

Grace Lake, *Slate*, no 3, Spring-Summer (1987).
To a Green Field.
"But I'm not going to sit in a room with female cousins,"
"did they leave"
" 'The solemn mists dark brown or pale, / March slow and solemn down the vale' " [no titular underlining or full stop in earlier 1987 publication]
On An Emery Board. [no titular full stop earlier in 1987]
Winter.

Grace Lake, *Slate* submission, draft poems (1987).
So then what are we going to do? Are we going to subject too?
"the meringue sang high"

Grace Lake, Manuscripts (April 1988).
By Magenta Auriculae.
Sunday Beasts.

Grace Lake, *Figs*, no. 14 (May 1988).
"don't be northern, whatever you do, don't start"
IN A CAVERNOUS HEAT HAZE
"I like Red People"
Check the scene
"find one page evenly."
"making machine poetry"

Grace Lake, *La Facciata*, Poetical Histories, no. 5 (1988).
La Facciata
La Facciata Turns her Back

Grace Lake, Manuscript (December 1988).
" 'Estée Lauder. There may be some objections raised.' "

Grace Lake, *Archeus*, no. 5 (1989).
THE SOCIAL VOID
" 'LES ENFANTS TERRIBLES' "

Grace Lake/Boas Toas, Typescript (December 1990).
Hardly See the Night past his Jacket.

Grace Lake, *The Virago Book of Love Poetry*, ed. Wendy Mulford et al., Virago Press (1990; second and third editions, 1991), 65.
UNTITLED

Grace Lake, *Spinsters and Mistresses of Art.* (c. 1991–93).
Europa
sewing stone
my wigwam.
epithets
february.
"not a crumb"
the warmth is astounding.
my fur teeth

"latin sixth xth"
"rather than, rather"

Grace Lake, "POEMS." *Parataxis: modernism and modern writing*, no. 2 (Summer 1992), 4–12.
from 'Spinster of Arts'
fulgencies
• • •
frozen moments
nattering swans
one century beyond grew
i. m. Laura Riding

Grace Lake, *café archéologique* (c. 1992–1993).
corps exquises avec Kiki
"struggles with self"
Art & Women.
To stay away from the Ogre.
On Thomas Hardy's "On an Invitation to the United States."

café archéologique, draft poems (c. 1992–1993).
"One rushes another is described as behaving abnormally"
non-existencies.
"my spine was hurting"
"all over one bloody old pianna"
"& one day, when we were working"
"between us"
"and being led dissociate"

Grace Lake, *Inverse*, no. 2 (June 1993).
XEROPHILOUS

Grace Lake, "Five Poems." *Active in Airtime*, no. 3 (1993), 44–49.
Ordered into Quarantine
Declared redundant 'in media res' as politics advise sentiment
Cultural

The End is Listless
on challenge, positive attitudes and 'les peintures cubistes' [title italicised later in 1993]

Grace Lake, *The Day the Music Died*, Equipage (1993).
"criminalising youngsters for political reasons"
"Ham banks counter machines slicers grills pockets drawers"
"and I who loved Poetry as I loved God"
"'them good old boys were drinking whiskey and rye'"
"our bodies, she stops, she may have been one of many."
"in those days it was not indictable."
"understanding cannot be relied upon"
"i would be interested in other people's"
"and lyrical minds are torn apart"
"this is one's life"
"circumstance. a word that had not come true"
"we might look thick"
"i always let people off"
"when Poetry's energy is blocked"

Grace Lake, *viola tricolor*, Equipage (1993).
viola tricolor
<u>poetry</u>.
<u>dulc.</u>
Ordered into Quarantine
<u>twelve to midnight</u>
Half.
"who would have found one a print psalm lemon"
two secs
madeira
"The past's stranding to belief adduced reconnaissance facing"
language blows away
for Bruno Alcaraz Massaz
Sauce
the fourteenth flight
Ionic
1526
Cultural
The End is Listless
on challenge, positive attitudes and 'les peintres cubistes' [title not italicised earlier in 1993]

viola tricolor, draft poems (c. 1993).
the fourteenth flight. (*early draft*)
Powerful enough to Kill by Artificial Light
"light. & where is the end. & who was a taut string ringing"
"evoking mocked order showing Me the Blind & Impudent man"
"Then what was it. when it was before those fronds which are waving my eyes."
"To have this beauty rammed up in my arm"
"As soon as a name is to be addressed another child"
"Who told you I was a joke? or would not be with a"
"leave these to die lest grammar offends you, rammed ammonites"
a woman who killed.
"cold water soup channelled through slowly arterial ways wishing well"
"one cannot be tempted to agree to an undermining fuselage,"
drought
"a love affair with language a marriage to passages"
"it is not for you to say or tell to bode"
by exploiting the future on reserved matters of relief work.
a minuet by mendleson.
"incrustation, fossilised cement, caked dry canine's excrement,"
because this won't do. it never did do. as defined as refusal.
"ignorance confiscates literature surfaces to be minimized"
"sickened by the sight of the yard thewed daughters"
two secs (*early draft*)
Demeter.
"I shake and cry. How then could I ever love you"
" ' " sumbur " ' "
"humans gaze clod to cloud depicted as brainless & reverent, neat"
"je crois la haine peur l'esprit d'amour mais je vous en prie"
"they were, in those days, his players. He and his Queen, His friend and his Queen."
the secret ballot. Austraque.
for Vera MacUllum. Assistant Governor.
"who are these who tell you what you want to know? would they were not these."

Grace Lake, *Bernache Nonnette*, Equipage (1995).
Bernache Nonnette.
"Four eighths for writing business letters a man selects a voice she, he mocks, she will and inverts"
dour...
"She Walked where she should have stood still, stock still."
"& envisaging ruptures imagination parental government hanging round social hairs"

"Parts of it crackle so you don't need to say that or make any passive references."
"Pall Mall. There were gunboats right along this coast. pointing outwards."
"oysters to sniff at disdainfully tapping the rest of the boring dross about eating"
Silk & Wild Tulips. [2006 and 1996, title without full stop; in 1998, no ampersand or full stop]
"Exactly what will this have rested upon for it to have emerged. It has yet"
How Power has reared its ugly head & defined a lumpen proletarian
By the Force it has used to cessate the education of writers & artists
By conflating us with the residents of Brothels.
"by gardenias i cannot telephone"
concilia. [in 2006 and 1996, title is capitalised and without full stop]
purdah darting glances

Grace Lake, *involution*, no. 4 (April 1996).
Truth or Vermilion

Grace Lake, *Salt*, no. 8 (1996), 72–76.
'unknit that'
antiphon [later in 1996, published as antiphony]

Grace Lake, *Parasol One. Parasol Two. Parasol Avenue.*, Involution (1996).
"Bernache reclined upon her startling blue aeroflot indice."
"......Oh I really must. The paper was filling"
the chantral grey
"This was the age of people & not writers in newspapers & now is not."
fragment; redundance; wordsworth.
To France
damned channel
Dyr Bul Shchyl
No Wonder

Grace Lake, *Critical Quarterly*, vol. 38, no. 3 (1996), 58–62.
Dyr Bul Shchyl
'unknit that'
antiphony [earlier in 1996, published as antiphon]

Grace Lake, *Conductors of Chaos: A Poetry Anthology* (1996), 184–96.
London 1971
June 21st
and A New
La Facciata
La Facciata Turns her Back
1526
on challenge, positive attitudes and 'les peintres cubistes' [title unitalicised and italicised in 1993 publications]

Grace Lake, *Tondo Aquatique*, Equipage (1997).
Erato
On Vanity
Bristling white toed black two porned to the portraits in potency.
"what we don't know, & what we don't ask, & what where we are means to us"
"I don't know which colour to choose. the blue I dreamt is untranslatable."
"No mixing not cake yes cake or anything that is being spoken enter not"
"we escaped but not to the houses where repentance"
"I am become my enemy whom I could not please"
"To look in the mirror and see a shocking atom"
never beiger
§
eulogy [title capitalised in 1998]
"I could see the sea & hear the towns"
"hard concrete to retrieve above the fallen"
Hungary Water
A grace note
Abschied
tree by the cam

Tondo Aquatique, draft poem (c. 1996–97).
remembering prenuptials.

Grace Lake, *Jewels of the Imagination*, ed. Maria Hourihan, International Library of Poetry, BPC Wheatons Ltd. (1997), 458.
UNCERTAIN THOUGH WITHIN THIS DEEPSET HEART

Grace Lake, *Gare du Nord*, vol. 1, no. 1 (1997), 14–17.
1:3ng

Grace Lake, *involution*, no. 5 (1997).
studio VII

Grace Lake, *Comparative Criticism: An Annual Journal*, vol. 19, ed. E. S. Shaffer, Cambridge University Press (1997).
"To look in the mirror and see a shocking atom"

Grace Lake, *Sneak's Noise: Poems for R. F. Langley*, Infernal Histories; Poetical Methods (1988).
"words won't break these walls"

Grace Lake, *A State of Independence*, ed. Tony Frazer, Stride Publications (1998), 108–16.
viola tricolor
Ordered into Quarantine
language blows away
Sauce
Cultural
Silk and Wild Tulips [in 1995, 1996 and 2006, title is published with an ampersand and/or full stop]
Eulogy [title without capital in 1997]
Abschied
"She Walked where she should have stood still, stock still."

Grace Lake, submission to *Inscape*, no. 5 (1998).
half evacuation measures unmet, still on regulo

Anna Mendelssohn, *Implacable Art*, Folio and Equipage (2000).
An asterisk next to the title or first line indicates a poem included in this collection.
from Implacable Art.
messages left for
Staged whispers.
in medéa mé,
Naturally i
a man who snatches a ring
To have life taken twice
But that wasn't what
pladd. (you who say either)*
of Lorca.*

I object.*
the ribbon & white
poetry is the lack
light on water
Europa [* appears in a longer variant in this collection within *Spinsters and Mistresses of Art.*, c. 1991–93]
friday.
nowhere receipts cough
to any who want poems to give them answers.*
Tancred and Garibaldi always slept together
Addicted to dealing in out of work hours
birdhall lane
Art made
if we are not careful
Xalon. Salo. Bilbilis. Martial.
Poetry does not deserve evil keepers.
that there is law breaking
they never
wrap yourself in jam jeunesse
are people armies that their faces
digne*
virago.
and Waterloo Westminster
the second hurled whore.
serpentine swallow bracken potash arboretum
at the moment,
basalt.*
scratching black frosted stained glass
it is only mind seeing only red hot coals
L'appris
My Chekhov's Twilight World*
Concentration camp styles*
underground river.
to a writer.*
This is the reason*
it was an art & is now a function
all had them gone
geo Alkan jeo*
à la France
that is what you are told
cosmetic scorn

cold fifty years of months
zinzolin.
bad news / a man / has choked
I also wish to refer to my loathing
I know. it sounds tendentious
Reminiscent of a flat expanse*
Zephyrus*
I have been made of no
Venus 27. ending 20th C…
malfaisant
the lord
minnie most beats up thérèse torchée*
they thought, at midnight, of discs
they get their own way
off the cuff
now that I can collect shades
premières. scriabin.
flat hat.
Ship in a bottle
fuschia In her wedding gown
That the whole
the Use of censored wars
sudden joustings
Brahms' numerals.*
The arrested poem
open cube cylinder
Naturalia
"Je suis navrée de vous contradire."
someone else is walking

Implacable Art, draft poems (c. 1999–2000).
Rue du Bac
"and my veins unpunctured, & not a punk, & no opinion, & no corrupting,"
"He was my conscience. His moans and groans. His distrust"
"What shining arrogance saw themselves"
"goetz o.r.t."
" 'we cannot sing intimated' "
slass coelitus arieto glass classico chivet
"Reading overhead, the sink back is being defined as defensive,"

Anna Mendelssohn, *Onedit*, no. 1 (2000).
REARRANGED LETTER TO THOMAS EVANS

Anna Mendelssohn, Translations of Gisèle Prassinos (c. 2000–2002).
"To appear.   Obscure need."
"A vulnerable strength but one that legally"
"Each morning"
"The silence beats, within furiously."
"Urge desire"
"Too set is the flight"
"The extent of the beast"
"Who now without your look"
"Fresh bread"
"Do not wait for the return."
"Life will be round as the earth"
"No flower no tree"
"Anachronistic sky."
"And instead of which flame"
"Tree an iceberg"
"On the lawn"
"When it rains"
"Red shore"
"The sea is a great fish that wriggles."
"Apple tree, village of fruits."
"The log enthuses and lives in its burnings."
"As evening collects thoughts"
"Your voice has the form of a wounded gesture"
"Here is the brown season"
"It is the butterfly of death"
"What order would protect us from where"
"O little house of oak"
"A deserted cage."
"Dawn"
"Closed on the table"
"A motionless bird."
"And you handsome horse with your virile twisted mane"
"In the night"
"I have a sun of you on the tongue"
"Know it"

"Day sets"
"I have waited for you so much"
"Will it pause without avalanches"
"Any glance over your numbers."

Grace Lake, "Deux poèmes", translated by Robert Davreu, *Po&sie*, no. 98 (2002), 110–12.
LA FACCIATA (*French translation*)
1526 (*French translation*)

Grace Lake, "Three Poems", *Jacket*, no. 20 (December 2002).
fulgencies
nattering swans
i. m. Laura Riding

Anna Mendelssohn, *Vanishing Points: New Modernist Poems*, ed. Rod Mengham and John Kinsella, Salt Publishing (2004), 172–79.
The wrong room
Strictly personal
Britain 1967
On being reproached by saintly mediators for bad budgeting
Franked
Photrum
footsteps climb whereas they descend

Grace Lake, *Out of Everywhere: Linguistically Innovative Poetry by Women in North America & the UK*, ed. Maggie O'Sullivan, Reality Street Editions (2006; first edition 1996), 197–205.
Ordered into Quarantine
twelve to midnight
Silk & Wild Tulips [in 1998, title published with "and" and a full stop; in 1995, with full stop and ampersand]
"by gardenias i cannot telephone"
Concilia [title rendered in 1995 with lower-case first "c" and full stop]
"She Walked where she should have stood still, stock still."

Anna Mendelssohn, "Three Poems", *Cambridge Literary Review*, vol. 1, no. 1 (2009), 43–45.
"Using the second person singular"
"Feminized, although not without dissent"
"should he have been,"

Anna Mendelssohn, *py. : a book of acrostics for p.e.g.*, Norfolk: Oystercatcher Press (2009).
"prove it! out of the blue"
"palanquin beneath harlequin"
"podcast variation"
"peasblossom nestled"
"parme, abricot et violette"
"polling"
"perfectly numerate"
"portrait in ink"
"poise does not come into it"
"photographs of snow"
"personally weighted in sterling pounds"
"peaches in the forgotten orchard"
"*palomapolperro*"
"pendragon in purdah"
"Pillbox hat"
"Power has a temper, pranksters abound"
"pegs"
"pomerainian intimacy"
"phizzing on"
"primrose pink"
"pale purple"
"prescription in colours decided on"
"passive in nominal negociation"
"Pepper pot full"
"Pitcher crooked hangs stilled"
"prisoners-of-war"
"Perpendicular marble piece"

py., draft poems (c. 2009).
"Patisseries in real salzbourg."
"palette in monochrome"
"permanent enough"
"pochoir silver threaded snail"
"Perruche, the rising rapids,"

Anna Mendelssohn, *Poems Written at Hinton Grange Care Home* (2009).
"tapestries"
"wallow 'tis of swallow"

“Total rejection”
“I have only ‘some interest’ ”
“The wall unintended”
“his shadow was there”
“and the grasses”

Anne Mendleson/Anna Mendelssohn, *Cleaves International Poetry Journal* (October 2010).
“destiny forecast revolt”
“Power to move”
“melancholy might answer in future mistakes,”
“Machiavelli strikes”
“Black velvet cloth”
GUIDE
“maybe I shall”
“Treading carpentry free country”
CADENCE.
“a settlement of priorities reaches unassailable”

Anna Mendelssohn, *The Paper Nautilus*, no. 2 (2011), 27–36.
“quietly noon”
nonflec [title capitalised in *Crystal Love: D. N. A.*, 1982]
For J. H. Prynne.
“The closing line of Ian Patterson’s ‘No Dice’ [included in editorial notes for this collection]
in the minority of one

Anna Mendelssohn, *No Prizes*, no. 1 (December 2012).
1986 OCTROI
POEM.
LOCALIZED EFFECTS.
LOCALIZED PLASTER.

Grace Lake, Undated typescripts.
call to linnet rock.
The Gong.
A Crash
the cliff.

“real does not know”
To You, Italy.
To You, Italy. II.
moxed metaphor
“nit freaks”

Index of Titles & First Lines

In bold, without quotation marks: poem title.
In bold, with quotation marks: first line of untitled poem.
Quotation marks, no bold: first line of a titled poem.
In bold, single quotation marks within double: marks are Mendelssohn's own, within title; quotations that appear mid-title, or are single quotations, are left standing.
Where first lines begin with a number indicating a poem section or portion, this number is excised.

www.ingramcontent.com/pod-product-compliance
Lightning Source LLC
Chambersburg PA
CBHW080527300426
44111CB00017B/2630
* 9 7 8 1 8 4 8 6 1 7 1 4 8 *